Saving Your Brain

Saving Your Brain

The Revolutionary Plan
to Boost Brain Power,
Improve Memory, and
Protect Yourself Against
Aging and Alzheimer's

JEFF VICTOROFF, M.D.

BANTAM BOOKS

New York   Toronto   London   Sydney   Auckland

SAVING YOUR BRAIN: THE REVOLUTIONARY PLAN TO BOOST BRAIN POWER,
IMPROVE MEMORY, AND PROTECT YOURSELF AGAINST
AGING AND ALZHEIMER'S

A Bantam Book / July 2002

"HOWL" FROM COLLECTED POEMS 1947–1980 by ALLEN GINSBERG
Copyright © 1955 by Allen Ginsberg.
Reprinted by permission of HarperCollins Publishers Inc.

Book design by Rachel Reiss

Library of Congress Cataloging-in-Publication Data
Victoroff, Jeffrey Ivan.
Saving your brain : the revolutionary plan to boost brain power, improve memory, and
protect yourself against aging and Alzheimer's / Jeff Victoroff.
p.   cm.
Includes bibliographical references and index.
ISBN 0-553-10944-8 (hbk.)
1. Brain—Aging.   2. Alzheimer's disease—Prevention.   3. Memory.   4. Memory
disorders—Prevention.   I. Title.
QP376.V52 2002
612.8'2—dc21   2001056732

Published simultaneously in the United States and Canada

PRINTED IN THE UNITED STATES OF AMERICA

BVG   10 9 8 7 6 5 4 3 2 1

This book is dedicated to D. Frank Benson, M.D. (1928–1996), late Douglas S. Rose Professor of Neurology at UCLA School of Medicine, mentor to many young behavioral neurologists and model for the ideal of the scholar-teacher-physician. He was fearless in exploring new paradigms, warm in his personal manner, always generous to his students, and ever compassionate to his patients. We miss you, Frank.

Acknowledgments

I have many people to thank for the things they have taught me, and for the support they have given me in the course of writing this book. Norman Geschwind at Harvard, Marsel Mesulam at Northwestern University, Jeffrey Cummings at UCLA, Robert B. Daroft of Case Western Reserve University, John Morris at Washington University, Caleb Finch at the University of Southern California, Steve Massaquoi at MIT, Robert Sapolsky at Stanford, and innumerable others have been teachers, friends, and inspirations.

I thank the John Douglas French Foundation for Alzheimer's Research for their early faith in me, and the Alzheimer's Association for their generous support of my research and their tireless work on behalf of all those touched by this heartbreaking condition.

And finally, I thank my wonderful wife, Alla, for her support and love during the countless days and nights that have turned this book into a reality.

Contents

Preface

This is a book of good news. It offers people powerful ways to protect their brains from aging-related decline. As a clinician and researcher who has long been roused by the wonders of the brain and behavior, I'm increasingly impressed by how much we know about ways to control brain aging—and how little we've taken advantage of that knowledge. It's high time we put our discoveries to work for the sake of our brains.

Much of the good news I'll be offering in this book is based on the recent explosive growth of brain science. It would be exciting enough to say, "We finally have practical ways to save the brain." But recent discoveries take us further. We are beginning to be able to *strengthen* the brain, to *enhance* the function of that vital organ that is the home of our minds. If you take advantage of everything we know, and put into action a few carefully selected measures, you can almost certainly optimize your brain function and significantly lengthen your mentally active years.

Of course, I offer no miracles, no magic end-runs around the facts of life. The brain is part of the human body, and the human body is designed for a maximum life span of about 120 years. While that life span limit will be bypassed by genetic engineering incredibly soon (for better or for worse), those of us who are currently adults should not expect our bodies, or the brains that reside within them, to exceed that natural limit by much, no matter how good our fortunes or how clever our medicines. Still, within that 120-year limit, the life span varies enormously—and probably only about *one-third* of that variation is determined by our genes. That's a terrific discovery. It means the *other* two-thirds of our life span is determined by environment and lifestyle, which in turn means that we potentially have a great deal of control over how long we live—and how well. Similarly, the rate of brain aging is only partially controlled by our genes. So even though our brains are bound to deteriorate somewhat as we get older, *we can do a lot to protect them*. This new paradigm is overturning many antiquated ideas about the brain. Contrary to the old way of thinking, the lifestyle decisions we make day by day can profoundly influence how long our brains will work at their peak potential. It's time to break this news. That is the reason for this book.

As a neurologist, I have learned some astonishing things from working with my patients, and as a neuroscientist, I have made a handful of discoveries. But the discoveries I describe in this book go far beyond my own contributions. They are the offspring of thousands of scientists in hundreds of universities who have devoted their lives to studying the amazing human brain. Paraphrasing Newton, I have only climbed onto the shoulders of these giants and tried to see as best I can.

The view from there is awesome. Frankly, the vista of neuroscientific discovery is expanding so rapidly that it's almost beyond our ability to appreciate it in all its lush detail. For that reason, this popular account of the never-finished business of science must be a "Good Parts" version; it offers the highlights—the dramatic peaks—in a way that will hopefully do justice to the wondrous new landscape before us.

Even as I report on the latest discoveries about how to protect your brain, however, I must balance excitement with prudence. Some discoveries we can be *very* sure about, and some are quite likely to be true, but others are just our best guesses. So it's my job to explain when I'm discussing a well-proven fact, when I'm using facts to estimate a likelihood, and when I'm speculating. The red-hot popularizing of science, the expanded availability of research data on the Internet, and the increasing influence of science on public policy have created a volatile atmosphere in which it's important to make these distinctions in order to help people identify the take-home truth in matters of personal health.

I must also strongly urge you to talk with a trusted personal physician before making any major health care decisions. As we will see in Part II, each of us may benefit from slightly different ways of optimizing our brain function. Surprisingly, even a decision as simple as whether to take an aspirin a day may have profound and highly individual consequences. That's why I encourage you, especially if you have health problems, to recruit your own doctor as a partner in the adventure of neuroprotection. Doctors are imperfect, but American medical training is the best in the world; your doctor can be, literally, a lifesaver.

Saving Your Brain

PART I

What's Happening to Us?

INTRODUCTION

Why Brains Change

Facts which at first seem improbable will, even on scant explanation, drop the cloak which has hidden them and stand forth in naked and simple beauty.

GALILEO GALILEI, 1638

It was a brisk clear night in Bethesda. I was visiting the National Institutes of Health and staying with Steve Massaquoi, a good friend ever since the days of our neurology residency together. Both of us were eager to continue our decade-long dialogue about the mysteries of the mind and brain, as we did whenever we got the chance. When we headed out for dinner, however, we ran into Steve's neighbor, Michelle, a vital twenty-three-year-old—a diplomat's daughter, free-spirited and brimming with intellectual fire. So our party became a threesome.

Steve had been planning to tell me about his exciting new research on the way the brain controls movement, but instead, over sushi and cold beer, our talk turned to the nightmare that was then unfolding in Bosnia. Michelle was furious about reported Serbian atrocities. She seethed about Sniper Alley in Sarajevo, a mass grave discovered outside Vukovar, the rape camp at Omarska. She cited dates, locations, and estimated numbers of victims. She was encouraged that Serbian leader Slobodan Milosevic had announced his concern about the brutality, and she expressed fervent hope that the impending United Nations intervention would end the crisis. But for all her mastery of up-to-the-minute news, Michelle was surprised when Steve told her that this region had been the exact flashpoint of World War I, and that many Serbs harbored bloody animosity against their Croat and Bosnian neighbors because of their collaboration with the Nazis during World War II. Steve had less detailed knowledge of the most recent outrages, and he asked Michelle to bring him up to date. He was equally incensed and sighed at the centuries of to-and-fro violence in the region. He drew analogies to other seemingly interminable ethnic conflicts, admitted to having doubts that UN intervention would put a lasting cap on the violence, and, most of all, expressed concern about whether Milosevic could really be trusted to rein in the atrocities.

Michelle and Steve were both animated, insightful, and bursting with facts, bantering as lively equals. No one at that table would have noticed any difference in the vigor of their brains. If there was any subtle difference in what they knew or how they thought, one would put it down to personality, or education, or different interests. We hardly ever consider the possibility that adults think differently at different ages because of natural changes in the brain. But they do.

Later that night, when Steve and I had dropped off Michelle and the two of us returned to his apartment, he said wistfully, "These kids."

I thought he meant Michelle. He did, in a way. But the afterglow of her bright company had actually reminded him of a deeper truth. In every moment of his spare time, Steve was working on a Ph.D. up in Boston at the Massachusetts Institute of Technology (where he's now a professor). One might think the schoolwork would have been a cinch for such a brilliant fellow, already a highly accomplished medical researcher. But it wasn't. Steve was working his brain out. He described what it was like to sit in lectures next to eager classmates a decade and a half younger.

"They come in to class and absorb it all like sponges. They party and throw Frisbees and never think twice about what their brains are doing. It's automatic. Effortless. 'Okay, Maxwell's electromagnetic equations—whatever.' " He mimed the shrug of adolescent omniscience. "For them, it's like running laps in the park. For me, it's like climbing Everest!"

Here was my friend Steve, educated at Harvard College and Harvard Medical School, creative and indefatigable in the application of reason to ideas, one of the brightest guys I know, complaining about the limits of his brain. In his thirties. And therein hangs a tale.

The brain changes.

That single fact lies at the heart of this book. Steve was making an astute observation: he sensed, as many of us do, that as we grow up and grow older, our brains and minds work differently. Michelle—and Steve's fellow students—simply thought differently with their fresh twenty-something brains than he did with his ripe thirty-something brain. For all our brains' wondrous activities, they are like any other physical object, vulnerable to change over time, and susceptible to the slings and arrows of daily existence. To be sure, our minds and the physical brains that underlie them have a certain continuity that gives us our lasting sense of personal identity. But the basic fact is clear: our minds change during our lifetimes because our brains mature and because, like it or not, they age. Given this fact, it would be terrific if we could increase the odds that our brains and minds would change—as much as possible—for the better.

Before going further, it might be useful to distinguish between *brain* and *mind*. The definition of *brain* is easy: it's just a three-pound mass of tissue, the part of the central nervous system that's located inside the skull. It's harder to define *mind*. From the Greek *vous* to the Latin *mens* to the French *esprit,* thinkers have long grappled with its meaning and found it as elusive as a handful of fog. For the purposes of this book, let us simply say that the mind is a person's nonphysical identity or sense of self, conscious and unconscious. Yet our nonphysical mind is absolutely rooted in our physical brain. As the saying goes in neurology, there may be mindless brains, but there are no brainless minds. As a result, if our brains change with age or with illness, so do our minds.

And change they do.

The human brain changes in somewhat predictable ways: childhood, youth, and adulthood all have their characteristic sorts of thinking. This is the second fact at the heart of this book: the brain changes, in part, according to a natural plan. The maturation of brain and mind is as much a part of human development as the timing of a girl's first menstruation and a boy's first facial hair. Our brains and minds have their seasons, with different strengths at different periods of life. Some activities, such as learning languages, may be effortless at age three but become tough after age fifteen and extremely hard after forty. Some academic fields, such as certain branches of mathematics, are best learned by people in their late teens and early twenties; and (quite contrary to the assumptions of the tenure system) novel contributions to these fields are rarely made by anyone over thirty. Some fields, like literature and art, find people of age twenty and seventy-five on an equal footing in terms of creative force, though creativity morphs in interesting ways over the years. And some fields, like social philosophy and jurisprudence, are almost exclusively the bailiwick of mature minds. Steve and Michelle can both talk about world affairs over sushi and beer with the authority of adulthood, but Michelle's brain is peaking in some abilities that are already declining in Steve's, while Steve has acquired some mental skills that Michelle has yet to develop. Michelle is more agile with newly learned facts, but Steve is better at constructing the long view—putting recent events into the context of the broader perspective granted by his extra fifteen years of life on earth. There is a division of labor, a kind of natural provisioning of the brains of younger and older people in human communities for their special and somewhat different tasks. "Young men are fitter to invent than to judge, fitter for execution than for counsel, and fitter for new projects than for settled business," said Bacon. Throughout our lives, there's a continuous ripening of mind. This is based on the ripening of the brain.

The brain changes not just with age but with experience. Were it not for experience, our eyes would never learn to see, our hands to reach, our thoughts to find voice in language. That's the third fact we want to keep in mind. "Let us now consider the various types of human character," wrote Aristotle more than two thousand years ago, "in relation to the emotions and moral qualities, showing how they correspond to our various ages and fortunes." In this single phrase, *ages and fortunes,* Aristotle captured an essential truth of brain science: part of the way our minds work depends on our age, but another part depends on our individual fortunes, the storms and tides of our personal experience on earth. It's not enough to say that our minds and brains blossom and evolve according to a biological plan. Our humanness, our intriguing difference from other species—even from other apes—is rooted in our nervous system's extraordinary ability to respond to life's experiences. Our brain is never a *fixed* mass of tissue. It is a hardy, resilient, and ever-changing part of us, continually adapting and learning.

On the one hand, this is a wonderful fact of life. The maturing of the brain makes possible types of thinking that younger people simply cannot manage. On the other hand, change can be disconcerting. As we gain some properties, we lose others; that's why, like my friend Steve, we may come to realize that youth confers certain unmatchable advantages in mental skills. That was certainly the way it felt to him, taking high-level math tests in his thirties next to youthful MIT scholars whose major health challenges were acne and raging hormones. For some of us, this change can be problematic to the point that the drawbacks outweigh any advantages. We enter rooms and forget why we've done so. We hesitate as we speak, trying to find a familiar word. We look too long for our keys, our glasses, our cars in parking lots. We may even worry that we're starting to lose it. And indeed, some of us eventually will experience change so extreme as to be called *dementia,* which literally means "decline in mind." The most common cause of dementia is called Alzheimer's disease, but as we will see, this so-called "disease" actually overlaps greatly with typical, natural, aging-related brain change. So, for whatever reason, some of us will undergo a degree of brain change that is bothersome or even tragically disabling, while others won't.

And this is the fourth cornerstone of this book: there is clearly *variation* in how the human brain ages. Some people experience more troublesome cognitive loss as they get older, and others experience less. So, is there anything you can do to boost your chances of being among those whose brains work best? How can you protect your brain and optimize the function of your mind? This is a thrilling and urgent quest for modern medicine—and it is the subject of this book.

Deep Impact

There's a collision coming. Neuroscientists know it. People working in the trenches of public health and health policy know it. But most of us don't. We go about our daily lives unaware; we shrug or whistle or look the other way. *Not me,* we think. *That thing's not going to land on me.* It is. The comet of brain degeneration is coming fast.

Today there are four million Americans with Alzheimer's. Alzheimer's and other aging-related brain degenerations are now the fourth most common cause of adult death, after heart disease, cancer, and stroke. You may already know a few neighbors, friends, or relatives who suffer from memory loss, but things are about to get much worse. Aging-related neurodegeneration (which we can abbreviate ARN) is the most rapidly growing cause of death in the United States. Unless we do something about it, and right away, it is certain to have a deep and painful impact—like a collision with an errant comet—on life throughout the modern world.

Why is ARN worsening at this moment in history? Why us? The reason is somewhat ironic: we've learned how to live *long,* and forgotten how to live *well.* On the one hand, for the first time in history, people here (as in many countries) are surviving health problems that once would have killed them in their fifties and sixties. That means they are finally living long enough to be vulnerable to ARN. On the other hand, as we will show in this book, modern lifestyles are almost perfectly designed to boost the risk of Alzheimer's. As a result, ARN is overtaking the other major causes of death like a freight train passing a donkey cart. It is the paradox of progress.

A child born in the United States in 1900 had an expected life span of forty-seven years. Forty-seven! Many died earlier from childhood diseases, and some lived much longer, but this was the average. An American child born in the year 2000 can expect to live to *seventy*-seven, fully thirty years longer. But the most head-turning figures are those that describe what is happening right now in the upper age brackets of the U.S. population. In 1900 there were 3.1 million Americans aged sixty-five or over. In 1995, however, 33.5 million people, *eleven times as many as in 1900,* were in this age bracket; and the number in the eighty-five-and-older group is *twenty-nine times* what it was in 1900. What is becoming of us? We are aging. Hide this discovery as we might behind the mask of youth that is our popular culture, we are aging, and we must face it boldly if we intend to do something about it.

First, there is the good news. Doctors have studied the heart and discovered fifty genes that influence its health, as well as several hundred drugs that optimize its function. Heart attacks are yielding to these discoveries: deaths from heart disease are falling at the rate of 2.5 percent per year. We've studied strokes (damage to brain cells caused by blockage of blood flow or rupture of blood vessels in the brain) and because of the simple act of controlling blood pressure, we've seen a two-decades-long decline in the frequency of strokes. Doctors have also studied cancer, and advances in early detection and treatment have led to cures for some patients and big gains in survival for many others. Between 1990 and 2000, cancer death rates fell almost 5 percent—the first measured decline in human history. We've won all these health benefits due to better health care, nutrition, sanitation, education—and to the women's movement, which has influenced everything from breast cancer research to osteoporosis prevention to the realization that gender differences are important in the diagnosis and treatment of disease. Of course, not all the news is good. The threat of drug-resistant infections such as tuberculosis and malaria is growing worldwide, and HIV is cutting a terrible swath through populations that cannot afford the new drugs. But to a startling degree, we are living in good times with expanding horizons of longevity. For all these reasons, as we reap the mixed blessings of our extraordinary science, you and I will very likely live to a ripe old age.

We should restrain our cheers, however. As the World Health Organization said in its *World Health Report 1997*, "Longer life can be a penalty as well as a prize. A large part of the price to be paid is in the currency of chronic disease." Many of these chronic diseases can be traced straight to some of modern civilization's very unhealthy trends. We are drowning in an ocean of plenty. Advances in food production have given people in the first world ready access to seductively delicious foods and multiplied the proportion of the population slowly dying from the effects of diabetes, heart disease, and obesity. Advances in technology have "rescued" us from physical labor, leaving us nearly paralyzed with inactivity. Advances in entertainment have turned us into passive consumers of a blitz of digitized circuses, encouraging our hasty retreat from the life of outdoor action for which our bodies so beautifully evolved. And the accelerating pace of modern life, combined with new threats to the stability of the family, whips us toward the psychological brink. Furthermore, we've done *far* less than we should to overcome the health risks that we already know about. The result has been a huge jump in diabetes, in high blood pressure, in fat-clogged arteries, in mental stagnation, depression, and stress. So we are living longer, but we are living far from optimal lives. In fact, it is important to point out that our current lifestyles are quite unnatural, very different from the short but physically vigorous lives for which we evolved. As far as the brain is concerned, the progress of Western civilization can be described in a nutshell: we live long enough that our brains are at risk, but we often choose lifestyles that boost our risk of cognitive decline! Alzheimer's disease in particular has multiple causes, but to an extent that we are just beginning to admit, *Alzheimer's is a disease of civilization.*

The largest group of people in history to live to see their sixty-fifth birthdays is the baby boomers, those born between 1946 and 1964. This baby boomer cohort is a demographic bump, moving like a pig through a python. Between 2011 and 2029, all the surviving baby boomers will reach age sixty-five. As they age, they will revel in their longevity and wealth: all their sacrifices to stay in school, to climb the ladder, to test their souls working long hours at sometimes less-than-gratifying jobs, and to save for the future will indeed pay off in added years of prosperous life on earth.

To what end? So that they can see their memories decline? Aging-related brain change is the most democratic of events: sad to say, it will hit *all* of us, should we live long enough. We are at high risk of becoming a nation of isolated souls blessed with plentiful food, treatable cancers, really good artificial hips—and failing minds. Who would have thought it? The most educated, affluent Americans in history stand to lose the very selves they've worked so hard to fulfill.

Bravely Facing the Facts of Life

Years ago, when only a small and especially healthy part of the population lived into their seventies or eighties, dementia was rare. "Senility" or "hardening of the arteries" was an anomaly that affected only a very few of our elderly friends and neighbors. "Alzheimer's disease" was almost unknown and was not feared as it is today. Uncommon as senility was, it fit neatly the conventional notion of a disease: a clear deviation from the usual course of life. Consequently, we came to view "Alzheimer's" as something very different from "normal aging." This ancient approach of dividing "health" from "disease" has served us well in many areas of medicine, and when applied to mental decline, it offers a certain comfort. It implies that only *some* of us will suffer from intellectual decline. But we can no longer assume that, just because a person is losing his memory, he is suffering from a "disease." With the huge increase in the number of

people enjoying greater longevity than ever before, we have made a crucial (if somewhat disconcerting) conceptual leap: *aging-related brain
change is a fact of life*. It is *not* a minority problem. It's a 100-percent-
guaranteed feature of being human.

As the subtle difference between Michelle's and Steve's mental styles illustrates, some cognitive capacities are probably already slipping away
from us in our twenties and thirties. In fact, neurodegeneration may begin as early as the *teen* years. In this regard, the brain is very much like
the heart: change is inevitable. Not everyone will have a heart attack, but
everyone's coronary blood vessels will become somewhat stiffer and narrower with age. That's part of humankind's natural destiny. In the same
way, not everyone will exhibit the full-fledged clinical picture popularly
known as Alzheimer's, but *every* brain will decline somewhat with age—
which means that *everyone* may be able to benefit from preventive measures.

The bottom line is that, because of the inescapable demographics of
our maturing world, aging-related neurodegeneration is already beginning to affect a *huge* proportion of its people. Put simply, unless we act
soon and definitively, the aging of the population will create an epidemic
like none the world has ever seen—an epidemic of stumbling minds. And
the risk group for this decline is the biggest one of all: the human race.
Unlike so many other epidemics that have fallen on humanity, unlike
other comets that have hurtled toward us, we can see this one coming
with crystal clarity.

What can we do about it?

Fight back!

Fighting Back

The readers of this book are among the first people in history who are
likely to survive to an age when they will experience memory loss. But
fortunately, they are also the first people in history who will be able to use
scientifically based strategies to defend their brains against memory loss.
Since the beginning of the 1990s, our knowledge of nervous system aging
has seen extraordinary advances. A successful defense is finally possible.
For the first time ever, we are actually able to discuss reasonable steps to
save our brains.

Attention to brain health is long overdue. Decades have passed since
the fitness movement evolved from a fringe behavior on Santa Monica's
Muscle Beach to a widely valued way of life throughout the modern
world. But it has taken us much longer to turn our attention to protecting our brains, the very essence of our identities. We're swimming in

an ocean of promising discoveries. It's time to put what scientists have learned into action. It's time for our brains to join the fitness movement.

To make this big leap forward, we've got to start on solid ground. Much of what we can do for our brains is in the way of an educated bet. The better we're educated, the better the bet. To serve that goal, Part I of this book will provide a brief tour of the human brain. It will show you how this marvelous web of pulsing cells, circuits, and messengers evolved for survival and love and memory, why evolution itself has given us brains with a heartbreaking tendency to deteriorate, and why the idea of "Alzheimer's disease" oversimplifies the amazing story of human aging. Then, Part II will show you how to fight the demons of aging-related brain degeneration one by one and, insofar as nature allows, optimize the function of your brain.

Please feel completely free to leap ahead to get the answers in Part II. But I promise that the answers will make more sense after reading Part I— the entrancing story of memory loss.

Okay, let's save some brains.

CHAPTER 1

Adam's and Eve's Brains

> My theory would give zest to recent & Fossil Comparative
> Anatomy: it would lead to a study of instincts, heredity, &
> mind heredity . . .
>   CHARLES DARWIN; PERSONAL NOTEBOOK, 1837;
>   HIS FIRST INKLING THAT EVOLUTION HELPS EXPLAIN
>   THE MIND AND BRAIN

Why did brains evolve? What are they for? It may not be immediately obvious how these questions relate to saving our brains, but they do, for one
important reason: *evolution explains aging-related brain changes.* The
very word *evolution* conjures images of misty pasts and private events, the
astonishing tales of trillions of creatures over billions of years, meeting,
embracing, stirring a new life into being and with it a DNA dynasty. At
some point in that incredible story, a human Adam and Eve appeared, the
first of their kind, with brains exactly like ours. Of course, the lucky mutations that led to humanity may have occurred several times before human beings really took hold as the world's dominant hominids; it's even
possible that humans arose independently in several places and that our
mental image of one Adam and Eve is a fine romance rather than a biological fact. But most likely, at some point between 100,000 and 200,000
years ago, the first few babies who had truly human brains were born.
They were the founders of the world's human population—our genetic
Adams and Eves.

Evolution is responsible for how human brains came to be, why they
flourished, and why they are vulnerable to change with age. Indeed, the
evolution of the brain—its genes, its neurons, the dazzling expansion of

its cortex, the niche we evolved to fill at the edge of some long-ago forest, and even the way we have strayed from the lifestyle for which evolution prepared us—is the real explanation for why our brains are likely to get into trouble as we grow older. That story began in the molecular Garden of Eden.

Fruits from the Garden

Life at its most basic level is an organism's ability to make copies of itself, using the magnificent DNA molecule as a sort of biological copy machine. We've all seen pictures of DNA shown as a double helix that looks like a long, twisted ladder. Our *genes* are strung out along the DNA ladder, one after another, in a carefully determined sequence. Though scientists assumed for decades that there were more than 100,000 human genes, one of the most humbling findings of the recently completed Human Genome Project has been that it probably takes only about 40,000 genes to make a human, not many more than it takes to make a worm. Yet these genes on human chromosomes carry the basic instructions that make us us— and that make every one of us different from everyone else.

But life is not just a matter of genes. As impressive as the Human Genome Project has been, it only lets us peek at the blueprints of life. In order for these gene blueprints to make anything useful in the body, they must first be translated into proteins. *Proteins* are molecules that are manufactured based upon the precise blueprint instructions from our genes. But even after a protein is manufactured, it's *still* not ready for work; it must first be folded into an amazingly complex shape if it's ever going to do its job. A misfolded protein works about as well as a crumpled paper airplane—it falls quickly with a disappointing thud. It can even act as a poison. As we will see very soon, misfolded proteins are probably the secret of many aging-related problems in the brain, including Alzheimer's.

Contrary to the popular vision of DNA as the fixed and stable essence of life, genes are changing all the time. Such changes are called *mutations;* they can affect everything from eye color to height, brain size to behavior, and they occur spontaneously, randomly, sheerly by chance. Mutations are one of the clever ways that nature changes our DNA in a busy and continuous trial-and-error form of genetic engineering. Only a few mutations turn out to be beneficial; most don't. Those rare changes in DNA that help the organism survive and reproduce tend to be carried on, because they increase the chances that the organism will make copies of itself. This is the essence of *natural selection.*

But organisms pay a price for DNA's changeability: mortality. No matter how many useful mutations have arisen over the course of the last four billion years, one thing has remained inescapable: *every molecule of DNA is destined to break down*. This is a crucial point in understanding why we and our brains cannot live forever.

Fortunately, the breakdown of DNA does not mean the end of life on earth, because there is reproduction.

Thanks to reproduction, our DNA has a shot at immortality, even if we as individuals do not. At first, reproduction took place in just one simple way: an organism split in half. But about 900 million years ago, nature developed a new strategy: two organisms encounter one another, mix their genes, and create offspring. This is what we call *sexual reproduction*, or sex. Like mutation, sex is a great way to make new combinations of genes.

Sex also favored one more step in evolution: the advent of multicellular beings. Now, multicellular beings obviously need some way for their cells to communicate with one another. Throughout nature, they communicate by chemical signals. One way to do this is by *hormones,* or chemicals that pass through the bloodstream to stimulate cell activity. But hormonal signals are pretty slow. So another step in evolution was the development of *neurons,* the fast-signaling cells of the body. Neurons work best if they are close enough together to coordinate their actions. So eventually nature evolved neurons in clusters—in other words, *the brain*.

To put the whole story in its purest biological terms: since DNA is destined to break down, evolution produced an amazing array of beings that serve as DNA copiers. A central nervous system is a great way to keep all the parts of the body in touch with one another, which helps an animal survive and reproduce. Brains—in the final analysis—are clusters of signaling cells that make animals good vessels for the immortality of DNA.

Hopeful Monsters

Brains have been a feature of earth life for 600 million years, and they all do pretty much the same thing: help a creature to survive. But they do this job using two very different strategies, the small-brain strategy or the big-brain strategy.

Ants, for instance, are born with tiny, highly efficient nervous systems. Such tiny-brained creatures devote most of their energy to running their muscles; their nervous systems require little power, since they provide nearly automatic programs for living and breeding. At the other end of the spectrum, evolution has produced some species that have huge brains; these are the toothed whales, including the dolphins, and the great apes, including us humans. But it's not just size that matters; animals with big brains are also unusual because their brains tend to burn a disproportionate amount of energy. As big as it is, the human brain constitutes only 2 percent of our body weight, but it uses nearly *20 percent* of our energy—a heck of a lot for only a few pounds of tissue. Our huge, energy-guzzling central nervous system might be considered the Chevy Suburban of animal brains.

Of course, we shouldn't assume that big brains are "better" than small brains. Evolution is not striving to reach some pinnacle of cerebral perfection; it's just experimenting, trying different strategies to see what helps the reproduction of DNA. (At a picnic, it's sobering to think that the small, energy-efficient-brained ants coming to join us might be considered the real evolutionary winners: insects make up 90 percent of the earth's land-based biomass!) Nonetheless, as natural selection worked on the big-brain theme, it came up with a particularly remarkable group of animals, the *hominoids* (the superfamily that includes gorillas, chimpanzees, humans, and their ancestors) who together represent a true brain revolution.

The extraordinary thing about hominoid brain evolution is that so much happened so fast. Over the last six million years—a tiny fragment of evolutionary time—the hominid brain grew from just 400 cc, the size of a small orange, to 1350 cc, the size of the modern human brain. Why did the brain grow so fast? Probably because any new ape that has both a good memory and the ability to make clever associations has an astonishing capacity to learn about his world. The result was a positive feedback loop in which a fast-learning ape with a slightly bigger brain could manage more sophisticated social behavior, and sophisticated social behavior—as one might imagine—favored reproductive success.

What happened next was a snowball effect: new genetic flukes brought about further brain changes that supported incredibly sophisticated behaviors such as self-awareness and abstract thinking. Natural selection kept one old brain feature, the *limbic system,* a deep and ancient brain part that still works beautifully to support learning and emotion. But evolution kept piling on more and more *neocortex* (new cortex), the outer shell of the brain, where memories are stored and blended to make an incredibly adaptable self. The result was a brain that ballooned in size from 850 cc to 1280 cc in a remarkably short evolutionary time, until—in an event lost in the mists of prehistory—the first children were born with brains significantly better than any before. Those children would come to be called *Homo erectus* (erect man). And this explosive expansion in the size of the brain implied more than just cleverness and insight; it also had remarkable implications for the way earth's newest apes related to one another.

This was the problem a million years ago: evolving big brains had major advantages, but the revolutionary new apes could not be born with their brains fully formed—their heads would simply be too big to fit down the birth canal. One possible solution would be to expand the birth canal, but this would interfere with the female's hips to the point of jeopardizing her ability to walk and run. The other solution was for the baby to be born with only a *partly developed brain.* That's exactly what happened. The brains of Homo erectus were born halfway built— a plan that has been passed down to us. And that's why a human newborn's brain continues to grow at a fantastic pace right through the first twelve months of postnatal life. So, in a sense, we are all born a year premature! Our brains need the nine months of pregnancy plus the twelve months after birth just to reach the maturity we'd expect in a newborn chimp.

The fact that earth's new apes were born with such immature brains, and were therefore highly dependent and in need of prolonged early life care, had profound implications for human behavior. It meant that the mother had to provide an extraordinary amount of time and energy to nurture and educate her helpless child. It decreased the number of offspring she could effectively rear in her lifetime. It made her more vulnerable to predators. And for all these reasons, it probably made her somewhat more dependent on a stable bond with a provision-carrying mate. As a result, males and females and babies would *all* benefit from a key feature of emerging human behavior—the capacity for devotion, which assures the infant of nurturing, the mother of support, and the father that his investment of provisioning energy is for the sake of his own children, which requires faith in the mother's fidelity. All of these changes favored a brain in which thoughtful planning was beautifully integrated with tender feelings. With the arrival of Homo erectus, the countless love stories of humankind began.

The snowball continued to roll down the hill of evolution. Better and better brains came into being through lucky mutations, until two new apes leaped onto the world's stage, crowned by a beautifully dome-shaped head and a brain size of 1350 cc: the *Neanderthals,* our close rivals, and *Homo sapiens,* the people we could call our genetic Adams and Eves. By luck or skill, Homo sapiens soon bested the Neanderthals to become earth's dominant ape. Something old—the limbic system—and something new—the neocortex—had evolved to make an unbeatable combination. This was the brain revolution. We are the result. Because it's risky to leap so far and fast in evolution, animals that undergo such a leap are sometimes called "hopeful monsters." Thus, the revolutionary apes, starting with Homo erectus and including both Neanderthals and Homo sapiens, could be deemed the hopeful monsters of the hominid world.

That rapid leap to a highly plastic brain—a brain that can readily change and adapt—came with a cost. Indeed, the brain revolution is probably deeply linked to our current need to save our brains. The reason: a brain that's brilliant enough to support complex social structures and cooperative hunting in Africa, farming in the Fertile Crescent, writing among the Egyptians, and the medicine of Hippocrates is a brain that can overcome many threats to mortality, making our life expectancy grow longer and longer. *But the human brain was not built to last as long as we are now asking it to.* As DNA-based matter, it is vulnerable to deterioration if we manage to outlive its natural limits. This may be the ultimate evolutionary irony: a brain that has thought its way into a life span beyond evolution's design. Aging-related neurodegeneration may be the price of human genius. We, at the cusp of a new millennium, are the first who will really pay this price, as modern medicine lets us live to an age at which virtually all of us will notice some of those effects on our thinking, and some of us will be devastated by them. So we—the first victims of this price of genius—had better use some of that genius to save our brains.

New research has given us remarkable insights into how we remember, why we forget, and what factors are most likely to protect our memories. To appreciate these discoveries, it will be helpful to take a quick look at the amazing modern human brain.

Brains for Behavior

Figure 1 shows the modern human brain. The *neocortex,* sometimes called the *cortex* for short, is the upper and outermost surface of the brain. It looks as wrinkled and parboiled as an overdried prune. Its wrinkliness is due to the fact that its surface is literally too big to fit into the skull unless it bends and folds over on itself during development. Fully developed, the brain takes on its familiar oblong shape, with the neocortex wrapped around the central parts of the brain like a thick convoluted shell.

When I was a child, the kids in my neighborhood really liked Tootsie

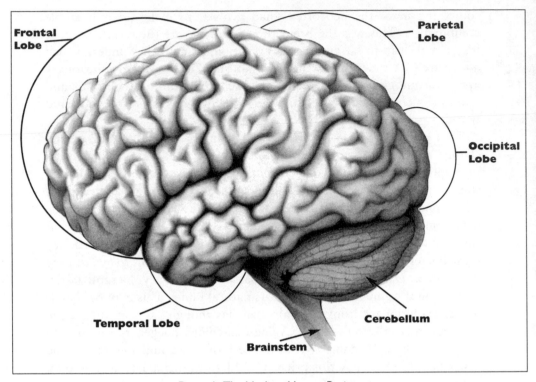

Figure 1: The Modern Human Brain

Roll Pops. These lollipops have a hard candy shell surrounding a chewy chocolate center. I've used this lollipop in lectures because it's a fairly good representation of the structure of the human brain. We have a candy shell of neurons on the outside—the neocortex and all its connections. Deeper within is the chocolate center—the deep neurons of the brain, including the limbic system. Both the candy shell and the chocolate center are perched on the plain white stick—the brainstem and spinal cord.

Let's look at these three levels of the brain, one at a time:

THE CANDY SHELL

The *neocortex*—the outermost part of the candy shell—is involved in many aspects of thinking. It contains billions and billions of *neurons,* arranged in layers on the brain's outer surface. Many of these neurons give off *axons*—long wirelike processes that connect different parts of the brain. (These bundles make up the brain's *white matter,* which sits just beneath the shell of the neocortex.) The neocortex has two halves, right and left, and each half has four lobes: the *frontal, temporal, parietal,* and *oc-*

cipital lobes. Each of the four lobes has a special function: the parietal cortex is for feeling physical sensations, the occipital cortex is for vision, the temporal cortex is for hearing, and the frontal cortex is for activating our muscles. But in humans, these simple functions actually take up only a small part of each lobe. The rest is for weaving associations across the grand tapestry of experiences and ideas—what might be called *thinking*. For this reason, the big association areas of the cortex might justifiably be called the brain's "thinking cap"—the place where we consciously consider what's happening, weigh our options, and decide on the best thing to do.

For example, let's say you see a golden-brown object with an uneven surface rushing toward you and emitting loud sounds. All this primary sensory information is woven together in your association cortex, where your brain concludes either "Ah, that's my golden retriever!" or "Gosh, that's a hungry mountain lion!"—a very useful distinction. Of course, even a kitten has enough association cortex to make this kind of distinction; at the more advanced human level, the association cortex might help us figure out how to navigate the desert by the stars, how to build a pyramid, or how to use an herb as a medicine.

Perhaps the most emblematic evidence of our humanness is the massive expansion of the *association cortex of the frontal lobes.* Our immense frontal cortex gives us mental capacities that have terrific survival value, such as judgment and self-monitoring. Without them, we're in trouble. As certain people get older, for example, they develop a condition called frontotemporal lobar dementia (FTLD). This type of brain degeneration leaves a person with a relatively good memory but an alarming loss of good sense. (One of my patients with this condition could still do a crossword puzzle without trouble, even though, bright and early each morning, he urinated on his neighbor's roses.)

The exquisitely plastic, massively networked association cells of the neocortex give humans many astonishing abilities. But we may well pay a price late in life for this magnificent plasticity. A neuron that can change is a neuron that can age: the neurons in the frontal association cortex *are among those most exquisitely vulnerable to Alzheimer's.*

THE CHOCOLATE CENTER

Beneath the shell of the neocortex and white matter lie some of the most interesting parts of the nervous system: the chocolate center, or the *deep neurons* of the brain. Two clusters of deep neurons are especially important. The first is the *basal ganglia,* which helps to smooth out the

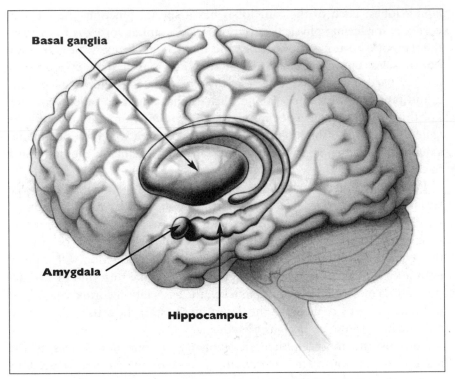

Figure 2: A See-Through Picture of the Brain, Showing the Deep Neuron Clusters

movements of our arms and legs. The second important cluster is the *limbic system,* which, as we've already mentioned, supports learning and emotion. Two vital parts of the limbic system are the *amygdala,* which is crucial for emotion, and the *hippocampus,* the most crucial part of the entire brain for memory. (*Hippocampus* is Greek for "sea horse," because that's what this prized piece of the brain looks like from certain angles.) In Figure 2, you can see the amygdala and hippocampus sitting deep inside the temporal lobe.

Finally, you can see the *brainstem* at the bottom of the brain (like the stick that supports the Tootsie Roll Pop). The brainstem is involved in basic functions such as controlling breathing and heart rate and sending commands and sensations back and forth between the body and the brain.

Figure 3 shows a typical nerve cell or *neuron.* We have about 100 billion of these, an astounding number—although in fact neurons make up only about one-tenth of the total cells in the brain. (The other nine-tenths of our brain cells are called *glia,* the supporting cells of the nervous system.) Each neuron has a *cell body,* where its genes are stored in the nu-

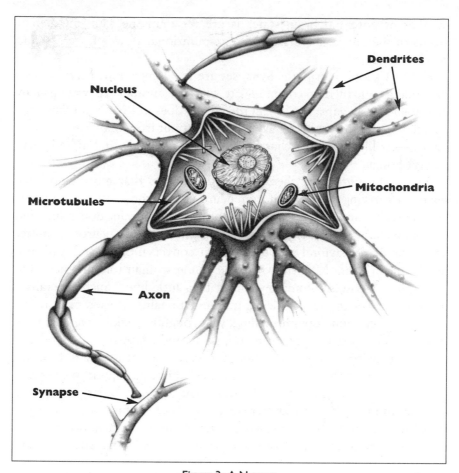

Figure 3: A Neuron

cleus; a long extension called an *axon,* which is used for sending messages; and a number of branching extensions called *dendrites,* which act
like antennae for receiving messages. Neurons also have *microtubules,*
tiny tubes that function like subway tracks to guide molecules as they
move around the cell.

It is important to realize that a neuron is not just a switch that passes
a yes or no signal down the line. A neuron may have 10,000 connections with other neurons, called its *synapses.* The neuron acts as an
amazing computer, integrating all the different signals that might come
through these 10,000 synapses to decide exactly what kind of final signal to pass on. Based on the estimates of 100 billion neurons, each with
10,000 synapses, each of which may be transmitting signals at at least
ten different levels of intensity, it has been calculated that the total

number of potential brain states is greater than the total number of atoms in the entire universe! This computational power boggles—and is—the mind.

Figure 4 shows a *synapse*. Synapses are the connections between neurons that enable them to communicate with one another. They are usually described as tiny gaps; but to call them gaps does not really do them justice; they are really sophisticated connectors built from many special molecules—less like an empty chasm between two neurons and more like an elegant bridge.

Neurotransmitters are the chemical messengers that move across the synapses, carrying information from neuron to neuron. Neurotransmitters include such popularly discussed chemicals as serotonin, dopamine, and acetylcholine. It's extremely tempting to claim that each neurotransmitter has a specific behavioral purpose, as in a conversation I overheard in a movie line in Santa Monica, when one young woman told another, "I'm feeling down—my serotonin level must be a little low." Such generalizations underestimate the wonderful multifunctionality of each neurotransmitter. That caution notwithstanding, very roughly speaking we might say that *serotonin* is important for mood, sleep, and aggression; *dopamine* is important for physical coordination, for feelings of pleasure, and for addiction; and *acetylcholine* activates muscles and helps support memory.

But *glutamate* (which we rarely hear about in the popular press) is the single most important transmitter we'll talk about in this book, because it is paradoxically both the main neurotransmitter for memory and the main neurotransmitter that causes neurons to die. Under certain condi-

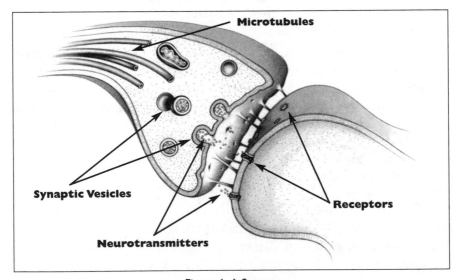

Figure 4: A Synapse

tions, the sending neuron releases *way* too much glutamate; this literally overexcites the receiving neuron to the point of death. Fittingly, we call this process *excitotoxicity*. Excitotoxicity is one of the main dealers of sudden neuronal death in Alzheimer's, head trauma, and strokes.

Still, the remarkable variety of signals in the brain is not just due to how many neurotransmitters we have; it's also due to our *receptors*. A receptor is the target on a neuron's membrane where a neurotransmitter is received. The moment a neurotransmitter binds to its receptor, the signal gets passed from one molecule to the next like a bag of mail passed along by the Pony Express, until it reaches the nucleus with the message "Turn on those genes!" This trigger leads to the manufacture of new proteins.

Admittedly, the cast of characters involved in brain signaling begins to read like the dramatis personae of a Russian novel, but the overall story is straightforward: neurotransmitters unleash a cascade of changes that are responsible for every behavior from movement to memory. In the next chapter, we'll show how neurons make memory possible.

Time and again during the modern era, people have attempted to describe the brain, often leaning on homely analogies to current technology. In 1800 they said, "The brain works like a hydraulic pump"; in 1850 it was "like a Swiss watch"; in 1900 "like a telephone switchboard"; in 1960 and after "like a computer." It's time we acknowledge that the brain is *not* like a watch, a switchboard, or a computer. In some ways, it is more like a deep blue sea teeming with life, with billions and billions of living information-movers interacting with one another, becoming better connected or separating over time, ever changing, adapting, communicating, and finding new ways to survive. In the end, of course, no analogy is altogether apt. The brain is wonderful, and only like itself.

The terrific thing about Adam's and Eve's brains is not that they evolved with all their abilities built in, but that they evolved with a most wonderful plasticity. This inherent plasticity raises an interesting philosophical question: if our brain is constantly changing, and it's never the same as it was the moment before, then who are we? We are, in a deep sense, our experiences. And how do we remember those experiences? Through memory.

CHAPTER 2

What and Where Is Memory?

> Experience is never limited, and is never complete; it is an immense sensibility, a kind of huge spider-web of the finest silken threads suspended in the chamber of consciousness, and catching every air-borne particle in its tissue.
>
> HENRY JAMES

Lisa and I sat on a hillside, bathed in the heat of the summer sun. Our neighborhood gang of young children had named the lush ravine below the Underground Jungle, but we had not come there for child's play—not for Army, or for Cowboys and Indians; we had slightly more mature fantasies in mind. When I stole a glance at Lisa, I could see that she was entranced by the wild view. We sat side by side, both of us acutely aware that we were almost touching. A blue jay winged through the trees. We pretended we were interested—a glad distraction from our thrilling uncertainty. We'd come to kiss.

I felt my chest filling and emptying, a sense of displacement. I leaned my face to hers—a bit uncertain of my balance—and saw the peach-soft redness of her cheek. This was closer than I'd ever been to another ten-year-old. When my lips touched her cheek, she turned her lips to mine. They grazed past quickly, like silk drawn over skin, an electric sensation. We'd kissed. It was my first. I've never forgotten.

What happened? That is, apart from the joy and shame and delirious sense of moving into a different life, what happened in that second in my brain? Certain chemical and electrical transactions took place that allow me, even to this day, to conjure up that memory as if it were last week. My conscious mind—that dynamic manifestation of three pounds of gently pulsing matter in my head—can willfully call up that childhood second in all its vivid sensory and emotional detail. We kissed, and multiple sensory signals reached my highly attentive neocortex, where stimulation of cell membranes led to an amazing cascade of molecular events culminating in the expression of neuronal DNA. This DNA orchestrated lasting changes in my neurons, which led in turn to what was essentially a new brain, a brain I did not have before that kiss, a brain that took in the information of that thrilling experience, judged it valuable, and altered its own cells in ways that allowed me to hold on to that kiss for a lifetime.

What is memory, and how does it work? The answers to these questions are extremely valuable, since knowing how we remember is the best way to understand why we forget. Let's begin at the beginning.

What Is Memory?

Two thousand years of philosophy and two hundred years of science have attempted to give us a good definition of memory. Saint Augustine compared memory to a warehouse of knowledge, and not just a passive storage shed, but "a place that is not a place," a mysteriously active archive that constantly thrusts things into our consciousness, sometimes giving us what we're looking for, sometimes surprising us with unbidden recollections. Philosopher-psychologist William James went a step further, noting that the word *memory* is something of an oversimplification, since there are many types of memory—such as short- or long-term, conscious or not. Such ideas are crucial for talking about memory, and they've taken us far. But the recent acceleration of neuroscience has created a new possibility: to actually find memory in the brain.

One of the earliest successes in this project was based on a stroke of luck: Donald Hebb, a professor at Harvard, released some of his young laboratory rats into his home as pets for his children, allowing the rats to explore at will. When these rats were returned to the lab, he noticed that they were better at problem solving than the other rats, suggesting that exposure to novelty is good for growing brains. Hebb decided to look at the rats' brains under the microscope—and thought he saw hints that their brains had actually *changed in response to experience.* And this is the real key to memory. Hebb correctly speculated that the brain change we call learning occurs at the synapses—the tiny bridges between neurons. Then in the summer of 1947, a graduate student named Mark Rosenzweig attended a lecture by Hebb. Excited by the idea that learning changes could be found in the brain, he deliberately reared some rats in isolation and others in the "enriched" environment of a social cage. He found that being reared in an enriched environment increased the weight of the brain—the first scientific proof of the re-markable fact that our brains are physically changed by life experi-ences.

But not all life experiences are equal in their impact. Most flit by in a moment, leaving no lasting trace; some stay with us for minutes, others for days, and others—like a first kiss—may last a lifetime. This is because there are different types of memory, supported by different parts of the brain. *Short-term* memory is the type we are most likely to lose. And by studying rare patients in whom one type of memory is damaged while others are preserved, researchers have discovered that short- and long-term memories depend on rather different brain systems.

The Long and Short of Memory

Consider H.M., a young man whose life was rapidly becoming devas-tated by epilepsy. By his mid-twenties, his fits would fling him to the ground so often that he could not safely leave his house. In 1954, in an effort to control H.M.'s terrible seizures, neurosurgeon William Scofield undertook the desperate measure of removing the hippocampal region from both of H.M.'s temporal lobes. The operation greatly reduced his seizures—but it also made it impossible for him to keep new experiences in mind for longer than a few minutes. That is, H.M. was frozen in the *now*.

For example, if you introduce yourself to H.M., he will shake your hand and repeat your name. But if he should turn away from you for a minute or two, you'd have to introduce yourself again, for he lives only in *now* and cannot remember you from *then*, even if *then* was only a couple of minutes ago. On the other hand, H.M. can chat volubly about events that happened years before his surgery—his family life, his school life, his romantic experiences—showing that, contrary to the Holly-wood notion of amnesia, he has held on to his long-term memories very well.

What we've learned from studying H.M. is that *immediate memory* does not depend on the hippocampus; that's why he can repeat your name. Nor does *long-term memory* depend on the hippocampus; that's why he can recall events from his childhood. But since H.M.'s brain can-not store new information for longer than a minute or two, it's clear that *we need the hippocampus to record new ideas and events in the brain.*

Subsequent studies have confirmed that the hippocampus is absolutely vital for recording new memories—but it doesn't do this work alone. Other parts of the temporal lobe, including the amygdala, help record life experiences and ideas in our private memory banks. Taken together, these structures make up the *medial temporal lobe memory system,* or MTL. Put simply, the MTL is the brain's main tape recorder.

But if H.M.'s cerebral tape recorder was surgically removed, then how can he remember a name even for a minute or two? Because he still has a different type of memory that does *not* require the hippocampus, a type of memory we use every waking moment called working memory.

Working Memory

As the river of sensations and ideas courses through our consciousness, we all need a mental scratchpad—a place where we can briefly hold on to a thought. Scientists call this our *working memory.* Working memory brings a particular idea to your attention, placing it squarely on the tip of your mind. For example, amid the thousands of sounds and sights that might grab your attention on a sunny day in the park, let's say a friend runs up to you and breathlessly announces, "I just adopted a beautiful black Labrador puppy!" A minute before, you were not thinking about Labrador retrievers; a half hour later, you may not be thinking about them. But for at least a short time, the image of a friendly, sleek-furred little black dog will appear in your mind's eye, and your friend's news will occupy the tip of your mind. But where in the brain is the tip of your mind? Neuropsychologist Sue Courtney would answer: in the frontal lobe.

Dr. Courtney and her group at the Laboratory of Brain and Cognition at the National Institutes of Health have been able to visualize the brain as it engages in working memory by putting volunteers in a magnetic resonance imaging (MRI) scanner, presenting them with some carefully chosen stimuli, and then watching the changes in the delivery of blood to different parts of their brains. This technique of brain imaging is called *functional MRI,* or fMRI. Using fMRI, Dr. Courtney found that when people are actively keeping a new idea in mind, there tends to be a strong activation in a special part of the frontal lobe. This region, known as the *dorsolateral prefrontal cortex,* may be considered the tip of the mind, the center of working memory—the cerebral home of our conscious thoughts. To get a sense of where it is, imagine holding the front of your head in your hands as you're trying hard to remember something; interestingly, the exact part of the brain you use to focus your attention on an idea or memory would lie just beneath your hands.

Working memory lets you focus on new ideas and events. But if you are going to remember this news three minutes from now, or after dinner, or next week—or if you want to remember *anything* for more than three minutes—you will also need to turn on your MTL memory recorder. So how does the brain know when to turn on the memory recorder?

How the Brain Selects What We Remember

Describe the place where you first drank a Coca-Cola. Difficult? Now describe the place where you first made love. As we examine the treasure chest of our memories, we quickly realize how very selective our brains have been. We are constantly deluged in a roaring flood of sensations and ideas, yet only a few items really have enough value to warrant being remembered. These events, ripe with meaning and emotion, important for gaining knowledge of the world, are stored like jewels. Others have less value, disappearing into *then* without a trace.

Two parts of the brain are especially helpful for making these crucial choices: the frontal lobe and the amygdala. Like the sound man who turns on the tape recorder, the frontal lobe is in charge of pushing the electro-chemical buttons that turn on our MTL memory recorder. But it needs help in judging what events are most important to record. That's where the amygdala comes in.

As we saw in Chapter 1, the amygdala is one part of the MTL memory system. But the amygdala has a unique function: perhaps more than any other part of the brain, it *regulates our emotions*. In times of high emotion, especially when we experience fear or danger, pain or punishment, stress hormones are released into the bloodstream. The amygdala has millions of stress hormone receptors. By responding to these hormones, the amygdala helps determine whether an experience is of sufficient emotional importance to become a memory.

Consider an example: a toddler tries to play with a bee and gets stung. That's quite an emotional experience. The way the bee looks and sounds and feels is very important for her to remember. So once she feels the pain, her frontal lobe pushes the button to turn on the MTL memory recorder: "You'd better remember this!" while the amygdala essentially turns up the volume to make sure that the hippocampus records the information. The basic idea is simple: excitement revs up the brain to learn.

So far we've focused on *conscious* memories, but of course there is much more to memory than that: the great universe of *unconscious* memory. Over millions of years, we've evolved beautifully efficient systems that let us respond to life's challenges with hardly a thought. Athletic skills, musical abilities, and all manner of social instincts are learned and stored and used unconsciously. While it's beyond the scope of this book to describe all the types of memory and how they work, there's one lesson worth taking home: as people grow older, some memory systems tend to decline faster than others—and the hippocampal system is the most fragile of all. As we shall soon see, this discovery has been extremely helpful in leading us toward great ways to protect the aging brain.

The Brain's Memory Bank

Suppose you have experienced an emotionally potent event, recognized its importance, and recorded it using the MTL memory system. Now where in your brain does this memory go? We have far too many memories to store in our little hippocampus; so, once a memory is recorded, it is stored very close to the same part of the brain through which it entered in the first place. That is, the bee-sting memory is stored close to the sensory cortex, the reverie of a favorite song from your teen years is stored close to your auditory cortex, and complex memories that involve multiple types of sensation—such as the special sensory-emotional experience of your first kiss—are distributed across multiple cortical areas.

Note, however, that your memory of that kiss is not situated in any single *place* in your brain. *It exists instead as a pattern of neuronal activity.* Here's an analogy: visualize a football stadium at halftime. Twenty thousand people sit across from you, each one holding a colored card. At a signal, they flip their cards into position, and the pattern spells out a message: "Go Trojans!" The idea "Go Trojans" is not written on any *one* of those 20,000 cards; it is not located at any one seat. It exists only as a pattern of activity, like the coordinated firing of 20,000 neural responses. In the same way, memories are stored in our brains not in any one *place* but as a distributed network of neurons, primed to flip their cards of synaptic activity in a coordinated way.

So memory is all the processes we've reviewed and more. A given memory does not reside in a "place" but in the strength of the connections among thousands of neurons that talk to one another across the brain. Where is your first kiss? It is in Augustine's place-that-is-not-a-place—a synaptic web whose threads form patterns that embrace the most precious and vital of human ideas.

Lisa's lips brushed mine. *I had no choice in what happened next.* The heat of the afternoon sun, the green of the grass, the thrilling pressure of her arm, the promising scent of her hair, the soft red blush of her cheek, the warm red silk of her lips—a flood of hormonal and electrochemical events inspired and focused by emotional excitement and arousal and delight poured through the gateways of my sensory systems for touch and sound and smell and sight, simmered in the cauldron of my frontal lobe,

heated up my amygdala and hippocampus, shook and startled my brain's
DNA into action to make new proteins, rebuilt my synapses, and became
a lasting part of my young mind's tapestry.

How could I forget? How could any of us?

That we will come to next.

CHAPTER 3

The Brain's Voyage of Life

At eighteen, marriage
At twenty, the pursuit [of a livelihood]
At thirty, the peak of strength
At forty, wisdom
At fifty, able to give counsel

RABBI JUDAH BEN TEMA,
ETHICS OF THE FATHERS (2ND CENTURY)

"Should I tell him the story?" Anne asked her husband, Mark.

"What story?" I perked up.

"The one about my brain." They both laughed. Mark is a child-hood friend. We were sprawled about in the dining room spending a jovial evening, and I was meeting Anne for the first time. She had asked what I studied, and I'd said something about brains and behavior.

They proceeded to tell me the story about her brain. They took turns. They made it sound hysterical. Anne is a molecular biologist who works at the National Institutes of Health. One morning Anne rode her bicycle to NIH Building 6, where her lab is located. At midday she attended a lecture over at Building 10, the famed Clinical Center; then she returned to work at Building 6. Finishing for the day, she went outside and discovered that her bike was gone. An expensive cab ride home, a tearful complaint about deteriorating American values, and a call to the insurance company followed in quick succession. Six months later Mark attended a lecture in Building 10. He was outraged: the bicycle thief had had the temerity to park Anne's old bike right there at the Clinical Center! There it was, plain as day, shoved into the jam-packed bicycle rack. The thief had even kept her old lock, except that it looked a little . . . rustier. Realization dawned. Anne had *ridden* her bike over to Building 10 for that midday lecture six months before, then *walked* back to Building 6. The bicycle was just where she'd left it. She'd forgotten. The memory had not returned to her during the police report, or the trip to buy the replacement bike, or even during all the rides on her new bike from Building 6 to Building 10. Anne was thirty-seven at the time.

What happens to the mind as we age? Was Anne's memory lapse just a matter of chance, a momentary breach in the continuity of consciousness, or was it related to her age? You might think back to comparable episodes in your own life and wonder whether there's a pattern of progression. What does it mean when we enter a room and can't recall why? Or when we forget that the teakettle is boiling, or forget where the car is parked, or hesitate a second while we're talking as we try to remember a word, then maybe swiftly shift to use another word that's easier to bring to mind? These episodes definitely plague us more often as we move through adulthood. We may chuckle or kick ourselves for our forgetfulness, but we may also sometimes wonder: Is age doing this to us? Are these, Lord help us, the first signs of Alzheimer's disease?

This is controversial. Actually, to say "controversial" is a mild understatement; the debate about what's "normal" in the older brain sometimes takes on the ferocity of a dogfight. I even have a theory about the feistiness of this debate: at some level of consciousness, the older professors in the room realize that, if they admit that cognitive decline is normal in aging, they're admitting that they're losing their minds. As we shall see, in some ways they are.

Aging and the Human Mind

Everyone would agree that certain cognitive functions are less developed in infants and become more developed as we grow up. We'd also generally agree that during their sixties and seventies, many people decline in some of these same functions, and some people begin to decline even earlier. It is further agreed that *very* old people—say, those over age eighty-five—almost always show some cognitive loss. What is debated with animation is exactly how much brain change is "normal."

One way to get a handle on this question would be to take a big group of healthy people of different ages and compare the intellectual abilities of the younger folks with those of the older folks. An elegant research project known as MicroCog did exactly this, with very interesting results. The MicroCog study (so called because it used microcomputers to test cognition) was actually *two* studies, both directed by Douglas Powell at Harvard Medical School. One study included 1,002 physicians, while the other included 581 "normals." (I won't comment on the distinction between physicians and normalcy.) Dr. Powell divided these subjects into groups according to age and gave all the subjects the same tests of mental ability. It came as no surprise that those over age sixty in both groups showed some cognitive decline. But surprisingly, Dr. Powell found that people in their late twenties consistently did better on certain tests than people in their late thirties, suggesting that human mental decline typically begins *well before age forty*.

MicroCog is just one of many studies demonstrating that mental functions decline with age. Dozens of other studies done in the United States, England, France, Germany, Scandinavia, China, and Japan all confirm the inescapable conclusion that our cognitive ability is modest in early life, improves as we grow up, and then declines as we age. Whether we can sense it or not (and whether we want to admit it or not), that decline probably begins by about age thirty.

These studies also reveal two very interesting facets of aging: first, people with higher educations tend to decline more slowly; for instance, in the MicroCog study, the doctors declined more slowly than the "normals." This suggests that education helps save the brain. (We'll revisit this intriguing question in Chapter 18.)

Second, these studies show consistently that some cognitive abilities decline *much* more than others. The functions that are most likely to be preserved are called *crystallized intelligence*. Crystallized intelligence refers to the facts and experiences that we store in memory and use over and over, such as vocabulary, practical skills, and knowledge of general information (for instance, "What does *embark* mean?" "Who was president during the Civil War?"). The mental functions most likely to decline with age are called *fluid intelligence,* the ability to handle new information or figure out novel strategies. These fluid functions, so fragile in the face of aging, include memory for lists, memory for geometric designs, spatial reasoning, the ability to come up with words quickly, and problem solving. Older people also slow down in information processing, the ability to take in new information and rapidly figure out a good response. And older people have more difficulty handling problems when their attention is divided; "multitasking" is a joy only for the young.

For the purposes of saving the human brain, it's absolutely vital to recognize that this aging-related metamorphosis in cognitive style begins remarkably early. Consider Michelle's eagerness and optimism about UN intervention in Bosnia versus Steve's tempering of hope with a long view about the doubtful chances of lasting peace in the face of ancient ethnic enmity. We've all seen it. The young are quick studies, with unfettered enthusiasm for novelty, but their conclusions may be colored by a lack of experience; older people may experience a decline in their capacity for new learning (and may even develop a suspicion of novelty), but these changes are well compensated for by maturity and judgment. Other aspects of the same metamorphosis explain why Anne forgot her bicycle: it was probably a matter of short-term memory failing during multitasking. So at the very same time in her life when she was brilliantly finding important genes, she was also losing things. Her scientific work continues to be superb because it relies on a treasure chest of *established knowledge and creativity*, a treasure that's less vulnerable to the mental burglars of adulthood.

This brings up another important point: in our concern over the cognitive losses that come with aging, we should not lose sight of the fact that there are also *gains*.

"Always it is, that the hearts in the younger men are frivolous," wrote Homer, emphasizing the superior judgment of age, "but when an elder man is among them, he looks behind him and in front." Plato warned of the downside of aging in the *Republic*: "For we must not take Solon's word for it that growing old a man is able to learn many things. He is less able to do that than to run a race. To the young belong all heavy and frequent labors." Yet Plato also credited the upside: "I enjoy talking with the very aged. For to my thinking we have to learn of them as it were from wayfarers who have preceded us on a road which we too, it may be, must sometime fare." Again and again keen observers point out this mysterious paradox: that older people are both more likely to have problems with learning and more likely to be able to offer valuable counsel. Cartoons alternate between respectful images of the white-bearded sage on the mountaintop and cruel images of the bumbling codger. We lionize the old for their sagacity and sigh at their forgetfulness. In other words, there is a fascinating tension between the good and the bad of mental aging, between the sad fact that old age brings a decline in some aspects of cognition and the happy fact that it may also bring the unique blessings of emotional stability and wisdom.

Of course, not every young person is sharp; not every old person isn't. Not every old person is wise; not every young person isn't. Yet the typical outcome of many years on earth is a decline in some functions, and the typical advantage might be summarized as a hard-won refinement in our knowledge of what works and what doesn't.

Which brings us to the heart of the matter. The waxing and waning of brain functions is far from random. It's a sequence that serves an elegant evolutionary purpose. The forces of natural selection have produced a programmed remodeling of our brains at several predictable stages during life's journey—nature's remarkable way of matching our abilities to our ever-changing roles in our families and communities. From the point of view of the brain's voyage of life, memory loss makes sense.

The Brain's Voyage of Life

In the west wing of the National Gallery of Art, mounted as an endless circle on the four embracing walls of tiny Gallery 60, are the four paintings that make up American painter Thomas Cole's evocative series *The Voyage of Life*. The first painting depicts *Childhood*, a laughing babe in a golden boat, sailing peacefully into the light of life from a rocky cavern. Cole wrote, "The dark cavern is emblematic of our earthly origin, and the mysterious Past." The next, *Youth*, shows a bold and giddy lad, leaning forward hopefully toward an impossibly glorious castle. The third, *Manhood*, depicts a frightened man sailing rudderless into a grim scene of peril. And in the fourth, *Old Age*, a toothless graybeard sits calmly, awaiting Fate. "The chains of corporeal existence are falling away," wrote Cole, "and already the mind has glimpses of Immortal Life."

Cole's 1842 paintings movingly illustrate the four familiar stages in the voyage of human life. We may quibble with his specific choice of symbols, argue for three stages or five, or fervently wish for a less dystopian depiction of adulthood (perhaps balancing the mires of disenchantment with the fires of ambition), but there's no denying that we all go through stages of experience that come to be, then pass away. And something exactly analogous to these stages occurs in the life cycle of the brain: the four stages of aging-related brain change.

STAGE I: THE BIRTH OF THE BRAIN

Stage I of brain development covers the astonishing growth period from embryo to infancy. At this point, the main event is *neurogenesis*—the process by which stem cells acquire the special functions of neurons. Early in Stage I the rate of neurogenesis is staggering; the fetal brain grows an estimated 250,000 new neurons per minute! As a result, by twenty weeks of gestation, that tiny head is stuffed with as many as 200 billion neurons. Strangely enough, this is our lifetime peak; we will never again have so many neurons. This is because the brain develops by using a very interesting strategy: it makes more neurons than it needs, chooses the best, and kills the rest. This somewhat merciless process is a major part of the life cycle of the brain. And the tool used to accomplish this microscopic mayhem is called *apoptosis*—cellular suicide.

Apoptosis is Greek for "dropping off," as in falling leaves. Harsh as it sounds, apoptosis actually plays a crucial role in life. For example, as fetuses we have webbing between our fingers, but it disappears before the day of birth because apoptosis tells the webbing cells to commit suicide. Apoptosis is also essential to building a healthy brain. Think of it this way: if the brain is to work properly, we need to make billions of "just right" connections. Not every neuron will make such connections; some will make mistaken or bizarre connections that can be devastating to behavior. So the first neurons to make successful connections survive; all the others kill themselves.

Obviously, we're in deep trouble unless apoptosis knows which neurons to kill and which to let live. Genes provide many of the "kill yourself" instructions, but *environmental* factors are also crucial. Nutrition, blood flow, infections, toxins, hormones, gravity, movements, sounds, and possibly even the mother's mood play a role in determining which brain cells will live and which will die during Stage I. This is important for saving our adult brains because, just as the environment in the womb influences brain cell suicide, *the environment of adulthood does the same*—a compelling motivation to learn everything we can about lifestyle factors that will keep our adult neurons from killing themselves.

Midway through Stage I of the brain's "voyage of life," we are born. At that point we have about 100 billion neurons, 100 trillion or so synapses, and a well-developed hippocampus, brilliantly built to learn from experiences. But as I mentioned in Chapter 1, in order to pass through the birth canal, the enormous human brain is only half finished at birth. It continues to mature at a ferocious pace right up through the first year outside the womb. Thus, we really finish Stage I of the life cycle of the brain at about age one, taking our first steps, and speaking our very first lines.

STAGE II: THE CHILDHOOD BRAIN

The Childhood Brain Stage lasts from about age one to age sixteen. During this stage, a fascinating new process comes to dominate the drama of brain growth: the process of making brand-new synapses in response to experience, or experience-dependent synaptogenesis.

Experience-dependent synaptogenesis is the essence of long-term learning—the process through which the lessons of life are able to build completely new connections into the brain. While synaptogenesis continues indefinitely throughout adulthood, it's interesting that our total number of synapses probably reaches its peak at about age sixteen. This may be one reason that teenagers (for the first and last time in their lives) truly feel like they know it all: when you have trillions of healthy synapses, when you rarely forget things, and when your hormones fill you with a lust for life, it's easy to feel as if nothing is beyond your potential. This is also the time in life when we begin to fill our storehouse of crystallized knowledge—the kind of information that gets firmly planted in long-term memory. We finish Stage II at a peak of cerebral function. We are physically agile, mentally vigorous, and bursting with hormonal enthusiasm. In many ways (though perhaps not in all) we are ready to become parents.

STAGE III: THE PARENTING BRAIN

The next stage, from age sixteen to about thirty-five, encompasses the natural stage of parenting. True, in modern societies, people tend to become parents somewhat later in life; but in prehistoric times, when the human brain was evolving, sixteen or so was truly the beginning of the parenting years. The intellectual and emotional pressures that a human mother faces are almost unique—suddenly obliged to provide twenty-four-hour-a-day care for a totally dependent baby. Young men also face new cognitive challenges as fathers. Generally speaking, the better parents are able to meet these challenges, the more likely it is their children will survive to carry on their DNA. So the brain changes that occur at the Parenting Stage give us the exact cognitive skills we need to rear our unfinished high-intensity learners.

For example, parents need to absorb much less new information than their children do; so, even as we gain the maturity required for parenting, we actually begin to decline in our capacity for rapid learning. In fact, young adulthood actually involves pruning back synapses; the emphasis shifts from making *new* synapses to selecting the *best* synapses and letting the rest die off. The good news is that this favors the adult brain connections that do us the most good—the links between neurons that support the survival, courting, and childrearing behaviors we need most if we are to keep our species going. The result is a Parenting Brain that's robust and clever and caring. The bad news is that *these same brain changes may account for the decline we see in some aspects of cognition by age thirty.* That's why you and I may never learn more than 20 percent of the functions of our word-processing programs, while our twelve-year-olds are launching websites.

Another reason for the brain changes between age sixteen and thirty-five is that aging begins to sneak up on the brain: head trauma, oxidation, stress-related damage, and the creeping accumulation of errors in the brain's DNA all begin to take their toll. As we face these risks, nature wisely shifts our molecular resources away from making new synapses and toward maintaining and repairing our most valued circuits. For all of these reasons, the Parenting Brain segues from a high-powered builder of new synapses to a rock-stable repository of information about the world.

STAGE IV: THE GRANDPARENTING BRAIN

The final stage begins at about age thirty-five. I know that sounds very young for a "final stage," but among our Stone Age ancestors, it was indeed the natural time of grandparenting. For this reason, I refer to the brain we develop in middle age as the Grandparenting Brain. This stage is, in a sense, the culmination of the brain's voyage of life. And, like aging itself, it contains a wonderfully paradoxical mix of blessings and curses. Some of the brain changes of Stage IV slow us down and trip us up. But seen from another point of view, these same brain changes may serve as valuable adaptations that perfectly suit our new role as elders of the tribe.

Before we describe the Grandparenting Brain, however, we need to dispel the main myth of the aging brain.

In 1955, neuropathologist Harold Brody announced a discovery that inspired angst around the world. He looked at the density of brain cells, calculated neuron numbers, and concluded that the brain loses neurons throughout adulthood. Other studies seemed to confirm Brody's results. You may have heard the story: some scientists concluded that we lose 10,000 brain cells each day!

Neuroscientists now know that things aren't so simple. Yes, the overall size of the brain shrinks a bit with age—but it's not because of a mass exodus of neurons. The aging brain is smaller mostly because *neurons shrink*. That is—contrary to forty years of mythology—our *neuronal supply is usually pretty well maintained*. This recent finding has come as something of a scientific surprise. It reminds us of the time Mark Twain learned that his obituary had been published in America, and he cabled back from London: "The reports of my death are greatly exaggerated." Rumors of neuronal death in the aging brain have been greatly exaggerated as well.

Another recent discovery was even more exciting. For much of the last century, the golden rule of neurobiology was that primates like us are born with all the neurons we'll ever have. But on March 16, 1998, neurobiologists Elizabeth Gould of Princeton and Bruce McEwen of Rockefeller University reported the remarkable discovery that adult marmoset monkeys grow new neurons. And not just a few; these monkeys seemed to be *making thousands of new neurons a day*. Later that same year came the real capper. In November 1998, neurologists Peter Eriksson of Sweden and Fred Gage of the Salk Institute reported the first evidence in history of adult human neurogenesis. Based on their research, Gage estimated that five hundred to a thousand new hippocampal neurons are created each day. We are just beginning to appreciate the immense implications of this momentous discovery. Our hippocampus—the brain's memory recorder—seems to be especially good at rebuilding itself with brand new neurons. Wow.

These findings have overthrown decades of dogma. We begin the twenty-first century with a revolutionary new understanding of the brain. Yes, we lose some neurons during adulthood, but we may have the ability to replace them with new ones almost as fast as they go! The implications of this amazing discovery is clear: by looking at the environmental factors that control neuron production, you can develop a lifestyle plan to keep your brain working at the highest possible level.

Changes to Expect in Stage IV

Still, many very real brain changes typically take place as we age, some less desirable than others. First are the *physical changes in the brain*. These include shrinkage of neurons, loss of the fatty insulation around the neurons, and continued loss of synapses. Instead of making new synapses, the mature brain seems to put its energy into *broadening the synapses we use the most*. Like a bridge that gets expanded as we realize that it must handle more traffic, our most-used synapses physically expand to form broader bridges. This remarkable change may even be the physical explanation for our tendency to literally get "set in our ways": at the expense of new learning, our brains cement their best connections to preserve the most useful things we've learned.

Second are the *many changes in the chemistry of the neurons.* Neurotransmitters and hundreds of other molecules work differently in the older brain.

Third, aging means more and more *mutations in our mitochondrial DNA.* As I mentioned before, mitochondria serve as our cellular power plants. They also carry their own little load of DNA; when this mitochondrial DNA gets hurt, it's like throwing a monkey wrench into our neuronal engines; they work less efficiently and make less energy. More worrisome, like creaky old engines that dump fumes out the tailpipe, misfiring mitochondria spew out excessive molecules called *free radicals.* Free radicals can rip a neuron to shreds, destroying its vital components in moments.

The fourth big change in the aging human brain is the appearance of *aging-related neurodegenerative changes.* (Scientists use that loaded word *neurodegenerative* because these changes are often associated with a downhill slide in brain function.) The two most important neurodegenerative changes are the appearance of *senile plaques* (SPs) and *neurofibrillary tangles* (NFTs). To talk of plaques and tangles as part of normal brain aging may seem surprising; the convention has been to consider them signs of disease, not of normal aging. But that's an oversimplification. We have to carefully reconsider how sensible it is to strictly divide aging brains into "normal" and "abnormal," since scientists have now discovered that, if we live long enough, *virtually all of us will develop some plaques and tangles in our brains.*

SENILE PLAQUES

Senile plaques tend to blossom right next to our neurons. Under the microscope, they look like ball-shaped flowers—tiny pink hydrangeas. And we've recently learned how plaques form in the brain: it all comes down to the fate of a big protein called the *amyloid precursor protein,* or APP.

APP is a perfectly normal protein—in fact, it's probably the most abundant protein made by our neurons. It starts out as a very long molecule, but it soon gets snipped into shorter fragments, like a roll of cookie dough sliced into segments. Depending on where the APP cookie roll gets sliced, we get either a shorter fragment called *Abeta40* (forty amino acids long) or a slightly longer, more dangerous fragment called *Abeta42* (forty-two amino acids long).

That tiny difference in length may be the key to Alzheimer's, because the length of these fragments determines what happens next. Both Abeta40 and Abeta42 can go on to produce a protein called *beta-amyloid*. If your brain slices off mostly short Abeta40 fragments, you're okay, because this shorter version is likely to produce a gentle, brain-friendly form of beta-amyloid. But if you slice off the long Abeta42 fragment, you're in trouble. The sticky longer fragment has a notorious tendency to misfold. And these misfolded fragments aren't just useless—they're poisonous. They form a corrupted version of beta-amyloid that has a tendency to knot up into nasty toxic clumps. Ultimately, these beta-amyloid clumps turn into *plaques* that sit next to neurons. Misfolded beta-amyloid hurts our neurons in a variety of ways: it lets dangerous levels of calcium leak inside; it revs up free radical attacks; it lights an unbearable inflammatory fire; and it can even switch on neuronal suicide—a sort of pink plague on the brain. In other words, we all make APP, and we all clip our APP into smaller bits, but some of us are more prone than others to produce the longer, more dangerous bits—and to suffer the consequences.

Yet the APP/beta-amyloid system is really like Dr. Jekyll and Mr. Hyde: it may have its bad side, but it also plays an important role in healthy brain function. When our brains are developing, APP helps build our axons and dendrites. In childhood and adulthood, it may even help the hippocampus form new memories. (That's quite an irony, considering that scientists once thought of APP as poisonous to memory.) What's more, many people develop beta-amyloid and APP in their brains shortly after head trauma. Thus, some scientists are considering the possibility that the APP/beta-amyloid team is meant to act as an *injury response system* that helps contain damage after a brain injury—and even aids in healing. Neuroscientists may have been far too quick to condemn the APP/beta-amyloid system as a family of molecular scoundrels. They may actually be do-gooders who turn bad only when they misfold.

Relating these findings to the four stages in the life of the brain: the APP/beta-amyloid system may help build neurons in the Birth of the Brain, help promote learning during the Childhood and Parenting Brain stages, and help rescue us from injuries as we age. The older we get, the more likely we are to suffer some form of brain injury. Until our APP/beta-amyloid system gets corrupted by unfortunate genes or environmental factors, it may actually help neu-rons—and keep our brains in fighting trim for our grandparenting years.

NEUROFIBRILLARY TANGLES

Neurofibrillary tangles grow inside neurons; they look a little like twisted rags plopped into the middle of a cell body. As young adults, we have very few tangles in our brains. But slowly and surely, well into the Grandparenting Stage for most of us, tangles begin to appear in the MTL memory system. A German husband-and-wife team of scientists, Eva and Heiko Braak, have shown that tangles seem to build up in our temporal lobes with aging, more in some people, less in others. While other aging changes have a good side, it's hard to see tangles as anything but trouble-makers.

Neuroscientists have recently learned that tangles form because of problems with microtubules. As I mentioned in Chapter 1, every neuron has microtubules—tiny tubes that function like subway tracks to guide molecules as they move around the cell. A protein called *tau* helps hold these microtubules together, just as wooden ties connect the train tracks inside a subway. As we age, this tau protein tends to become peppered with phosphorus molecules. When this happens, *the tau protein misfolds badly,* twisting and bunching up until the neuron is burdened with a tan-gled mess—a train wreck of a brain cell. That's a tangle.

Unfortunately for memory, tangles tend to cluster in the exact area of the brain that's most vital for learning. In fact, tangles could be the result of an evolutionary trade-off. That is, in order to keep learning into old age, we must maintain a population of highly plastic memory neurons, like those in the hippocampus. But the downside of keeping such plastic, adaptable cells working in an old brain—a brain with cranky mitochon-dria, out-of-control inflammation, and other troublemaking changes—may be that *changeability itself may increase the risk of tangles.* In other words, once again, a cell that can change is a cell that can age. Paradox-ically, Alzheimer's may be the price we pay for brains that can keep learning.

You may be noticing a common theme: as we get older, our brain cells are more likely to make misfolded proteins. Beta-amyloid–filled plaques be-gin to appear at about age twenty-five, tau-filled tangles at about age forty. But the great lesson of modern brain science is that *the age at which plaques and tangles appear depends greatly on our genes, our environment, and the lifestyle we choose to follow.*

Our new painting of the older adult brain shows us how aging-related brain changes fit into the grand voyage of life. Despite a decline in some functions, the brain just keeps modifying itself for life's new roles, making new neurons, strengthening the most useful connections, and pruning away the less useful ones.

One more important biological change in Stage IV has far-reaching consequences: sex hormone withdrawal. Estrogen withdrawal in women—and to a lesser extent, testosterone withdrawal in men—moves older people out of the roiling realm of reproductive rivalry. Unfortunately, menopause seems to slightly accelerate women's cognitive decline. To a lesser extent, the decline in testosterone hampers men's physical prowess and perhaps even affects some aspects of cognition. But this decline may have a hidden benefit. As Plato says in the *Republic*: "I remember hearing Sophocles the poet greeted by a fellow who asked, 'How about your service of Aphrodite, Sophocles—is your natural force still unabated?' And he replied, 'Hush, man, most gladly have I escaped this thing you talk of, as if I had run away from a raging and savage beast of a master.' " Perhaps nature actually selected an aging-related decrease in testosterone partly as a strategy to enhance men's steadiness of behavior.

Thus, during the final stage of the brain's dramatic voyage of life, we go through our final brain changes. All of these changes—the broadening of the best-used synapses, the withering of infrequently used synapses, the culling-out of damaged neurons, and sex hormone withdrawal—may contribute to the changes in thinking style that we associate with maturity. Yes, short-term memory is impaired. Yes, fluid intelligence is jeopardized. But while these features of cognition may be sacrificed, at least two others are quite likely to be enhanced: wisdom and emotional stability.

The Grandparenting Brain

Wisdom has been defined by Paul Baltes at the Max Planck Institute in Berlin as "expert knowledge in the fundamental pragmatics of life." In prehistory, the quality we call wisdom might have included such knowledge as the best ways to find food and shelter, the importance of planning ahead for the change of seasons, the way to use plants to soothe a wound, and, above all, the unique social wisdom of the elders of the tribe—how to navigate the mazy banks and shoals of human relations. Some biologists say, "Of course we lose our minds as we get older. Once we're done making babies, we've served our purpose on earth, and evolution had no reason to give us brains that would keep working." I disagree. When we think of all the wonderful contributions made by grandparents, we know why our brains keep going long after age thirty-five: the preservation of the brain after the body has passed its reproductive peak was selected for during evolution as an absolutely brilliant way to help assure the survival of our offspring, both children and grandchildren. Relatively few humans survived to old age in the rough and tumble of the Pleistocene, but those who did played a special role: they were the guardians of knowledge, arbiters of judgment, and well-springs of advice. The grandmother who advises and assists her daughter in childrearing does her own DNA great good. The frail grandfather, no longer able to walk, may yet aid his offspring in a major way while reclining on his furry pallet, telling stories about great hunts, passing on the wisdom of the tribe.

So the aging of the brain is *not* just a downhill slide; it's *not* just nature's plan to gently phase older people out of competition with their children. Rather, the brain probably ages as it does for much better reasons. Evolution has been incredibly clever about assuring that older humans keep the exact mental skills that will optimize their DNA legacy—the ability to offer younger people emotional support and good advice. As Rabbi Judah Ben Tema put it, "At fifty, able to give counsel." Today we can finally resolve the ancient paradox that the aged are both less able to learn and better able to judge. This is the natural provisioning of younger and older people for their different roles—the ripening of mind and brain. Confucius put it beautifully:

> At fifteen I set my heart upon learning,
> At thirty I established myself [in accordance with ritual],
> At forty I no longer had perplexities,
> At fifty I knew the Mandate of Heaven,
> At sixty I was at ease with whatever I heard,
> At seventy I could follow my heart's desire without transgress-
>   ing the boundaries of right.

Yet some people obviously undergo so much age-related brain change that they suffer, and their families do too. At some point, ripening creeps toward rot. We need to figure out how the neutral or helpful phenomenon of aging-related *brain change* relates to aging-related *neurodegeneration*. Clearly, the two overlap greatly. But, at some hard-to-define point, the balance of coming-to-be and passing-away of brain functions shifts so far toward loss that it harms our ability to function in daily life.

Two factors turn aging from a mixed blessing to a cognitive curse: genes and environment. By *genes,* of course, I mean the molecular guardians of 3.8 billion years of heredity. By *environment,* I mean not just the air we breathe and the water we drink, but all the lifestyle decisions we make, day after day—and their astonishing long-term effects on our hearts and brains and minds.

CHAPTER 4

What Is "Alzheimer's," and Are You Getting It?

The Strange Case of Madame Auguste D.

Madame Auguste D. became jealous of her husband. This was not, of course, in itself a reason for mental hospitalization. But her jealousy was extreme, and was accompanied by a growing confusion, and she carried things purposelessly back and forth and screamed that someone was trying to kill her, and no one knew what else to do, so in 1901, she was committed to Frankfurt's Hospital for the Mentally Ill and Epileptics. She was fifty-one years old—much, much too young for senile dementia.

Alois Alzheimer, a psychiatrist, was called to her bedside. His admission notes were rediscovered in 1996 in a slender blue folder in surprisingly good condition. These handwritten notes, penned in outdated German script, tell as moving a tale of dementia as we might ever hear. The file begins:

> *She sat on her bed with a helpless expression.*
> *"What is your name?"*
> *"Auguste."*
> *"Last name?"*
> *"Auguste."*
> *"What is your husband's name?"*
> *"Auguste, I think."*

Alzheimer went on to describe a woman struggling with cognitive problems, disabled by memory loss, tormented by hallucinations and delusions. "At times she greeted the doctor like a visitor, and excused herself for not having finished her work," he wrote; "at times she shrieked loudly that he wanted to cut her, or she repulsed him with indignation, saying that she feared from him something against her chastity." Eventually she curled into a mute fetal ball and died, four years after admission, from bed sores.

After she died, Dr. Alzheimer looked at her brain under a microscope. He recognized a loss of neurons, as well as the plaques and tangles that other scientists had already described in the brains of older adults. But Madame D. had a very large number of *both* these changes—highly unusual at such an early age. (Dr. Alzheimer also found narrowing and fatty changes in her blood vessels, a fact often glossed over in accounts of the story which may turn out to be a key factor in our understanding of Alzheimer's disease.)

As he looked through his microscope at those tiny plaques and tangles, did Dr. Alzheimer truly find a "disease" that caused that poor woman's enfeeblement of mind? Or were those plaques and tangles just nonspecific aging changes that all of us will develop if we live long enough? One thing is certain: in opening her skull, he opened a Pandora's box. To this day neuroscientists are still debating whether "Alzheimer's" is a "disease" at all, or is simply part of the natural march of human aging.

The Standard Model

As we embark on our quest to understand memory loss, it will be helpful to know the conventional wisdom—the Standard Model. The Standard Model offers a very simple and practical way to look at human aging; that's why you'll still hear it from many doctors and read about it in popular magazines. But it actually has a rather dubious past, and a myopic tendency to lead us astray.

The Standard Model puts all older people into one of three groups: *normal* (with essentially no noticeable cognitive decline), those with *mild cognitive impairment* (MCI, a middling amount of cognitive decline), or those suffering from *dementia* (severe cognitive decline). This three-part division seriously oversimplifies what we actually see around us, for there is in fact an infinitude of degrees of change within the great spectrum of human function. Furthermore, as we saw in Chapter 3, *all* of us can expect some decline in our mental status, which means (if we are truly faithful to the Latin roots of the word) that *everyone* over age thirty is "demented." But because of our natural aversion to such a troubling observation about the fragility of the human mind, and for the sake of simplicity, the Standard Model sticks to this three-part division.

Dementia has many causes, including brain tumors, vitamin deficiency, thyroid disease, infection, lead poisoning, and even deep depression. But according to the Standard Model, the two most common varieties of dementia are the *neurodegenerative dementias* and *vascular dementia*. Neurodegenerative dementias are brain disorders in which neurons gradually die off, while vascular dementia results when vascular problems such as strokes destroy the thinking parts of the brain.

The neurodegenerative dementias are further divided into several types, of which the four most common are *Alzheimer's disease, dementia with Lewy bodies* (DLB), *Frontotemporal lobar dementia* (FTLD), and *Parkinson's disease* (PD). According to the Standard Model, each of these is a *specific condition;* each is different from normal aging, from vascular dementia, and from one another.

Rethinking Alzheimer's: Genes That Get Us in Trouble

Whether or not Alzheimer's is really a "disease," it's crystal clear that some older people have much worse cognition than others, and we need to explain that somehow. So, for the moment, let's assume that Alzheimer's is a specific brain disorder. From the point of view of the Standard Model, Alzheimer's is the most common dementia of them all, accounting for more than half of all dementia cases in the United States. Like all the neurodegenerative dementias, Alzheimer's is strongly linked to age: it afflicts about 3 percent of people aged sixty-five, about 12 percent of people aged seventy-five, and as many as 50 percent of people aged eighty-five and above—the fastest-growing segment of the U.S. population.

Despite the common notion that Alzheimer's runs in certain families, only 5 percent of Alzheimer's cases are of the true *familial* type. Three genes have been discovered that can definitely mutate to produce familial Alzheimer's disease: a gene on chromosome 21, one on chromosome 14, and one on chromosome 1. (Other familial Alzheimer's genes possibly sit on chromosomes 3 and 12.) Note that only this very small group with "*familial* Alzheimer's disease" seems to have a truly distinct "disease"—a striking deviation from typical aging caused by a mutant gene. In contrast, the vast majority of people who are diagnosed with Alzheimer's actually have *non*familial Alzheimer's, which blends more ambiguously into normal aging.

Even those of us who don't have these mutant genes may still carry genes that get us into trouble—genes that somewhat increase our risk of

Alzheimer's. These are called *Alzheimer's-risk-factor genes*. The difference between a risk-factor gene and a mutated gene is that a risk-factor gene is a perfectly normal variation of a gene that everyone carries—just as we have variations in genes for hair color and eye color. The problem is that some perfectly normal genes may make us more vulnerable to brain aging.

The best example: in 1992 neuroscientist Alan Roses at Duke University made a key discovery that changed forever our understanding of genes and dementia; he found that your risk of nonfamilial Alzheimer's disease is directly related to the *apolipoprotein E (APOE)* gene. *APOE* is a normal gene that comes in three different *alleles* (the version of a gene you get from each parent)—called—*APOE-ε2*, 3, and 4. Dr. Roses discovered that your risk of Alzheimer's disease is directly related to the number of copies of the ε4 allele you carry. People with *one* ε4 have about a 50 percent chance of getting Alzheimer's by age seventy-five, and people with *two* ε4s have a 90 percent chance; that's *eight times the normal risk*.

About 20 percent of Americans carry one or more copies of ε4, so there's a huge group of people going about their lives without knowing that they are at high risk of memory loss.

This dramatic discovery immediately prompts the question: do we now have a simple blood test to predict Alzheimer's? This question is a very hot potato. Accurate prediction of Alzheimer's carries the threat of bias by employers or insurance companies; and even more importantly (given our experience with preclinical testing in the early days of AIDS), it may lead to hopelessness, depression, and conceivably even suicide among those who get a positive test result. It's crucial to point out that *APOE* testing *cannot* really predict who will get Alzheimer's or memory loss; the ε4 allele is only a *risk factor,* just as high cholesterol is a risk factor for a heart attack. For this reason, most doctors will not even check your *APOE* genotype. However, the more we know about how to prevent Alzheimer's, the more sense it will make for people to learn if they are carrying ε4 (just as they know their cholesterol levels), so that they can act early to save their brains.

All this attention to genes shouldn't cause us to overlook the fact that *environmental* factors also boost your risk of Alzheimer's. As with many medical conditions, it really involves a conspiracy between genetic and environmental factors, including lifestyle factors. Based on twin studies, which allow us to separate the effects of genes and environment, it seems that about 50 percent of your risk of Alzheimer's is genetic (including the 5 percent of familial cases), while 50 percent is due to the environment. That means that the future of your brain depends very much on factors that you may be able to control—the environment you live in and the lifestyle choices you make.

Brain and Behavior Changes in Alzheimer's

Alzheimer's usually begins with memory problems, especially difficulties with short-term memory. Common symptoms include losing your keys or glasses or misplacing your car in a large parking lot; having difficulty coming up with a particular word or a person's name; having more than usual trouble with mental arithmetic or balancing your checkbook; leaving the water running, the kettle boiling, or the keys in the door; forgetting details of recent conversations; or even walking into a room and realizing that you're not sure what you've come for. Of course, all of us experience these things from time to time; it's only human. But for some of us, problems like these are an early warning that our brains are beginning to slowly, silently degenerate.

When these symptoms are mild, again, doctors may say that the patient has so-called mild cognitive impairment—MCI. But when cognitive problems become severe enough to interfere with everyday life, and no other apparent explanation is discovered, doctors often diagnose "Alzheimer's." No matter what we call this process, and no matter how much it overlaps with other brain disorders and with normal aging, the result is a tragedy—the slow-motion death of a human mind. People with Alzheimer's die, on average, about seven years after diagnosis.

The Standard Model states that Alzheimer's produces four classic changes in the brain: plaques, tangles, neurotransmitter changes, and neuron death. As I described in Chapter 3, plaques occur when misfolded beta-amyloid knots into toxic clumps, and tangles occur when misfolded tau turns microtubules into twisted train wrecks. The brain also loses its ability to make the neurotransmitter acetylcholine. And finally, neurons die. The loss of neurons and the buildup of plaques and tangles have a disturbing way of hitting the exact parts of the brain that we need for higher-level cognition and memory: the neurons of the MTL memory system, the neurons that make acetylcholine, and the neurons of the association cortex—the region that grants us our uniquely human thinking abilities.

For decades, scientists have been debating whether it's the plaques or the tangles that do the major damage in Alzheimer's; that debate has been so intense that it's sometimes taken on a quasi-religious fervor. Those who argue that beta-amyloid (Greek letter β) is the main problem are called βaptists; those who attribute the trouble to tau are, of course, Tauists. I couldn't make this up; the Alzheimer's literature is brimming with βaptist versus Tauist debates. But recently a new discovery has brought βaptists and Tauists together, revealing what seems to be the missing link between plaques and tangles: in 2001 neuroscientists at the Mayo Clinic in Jacksonville, Florida, and at the University of Zurich showed that beta-amyloid does not just make plaques; it's also the agent provocateur in the manufacture of *tangles*!

The way this works: misfolded beta-amyloid acts like a terrorist in the brain. Even before it makes plaques or tangles, it prevents neurons from doing their jobs and causes subtle changes in behavior. Soon, it clusters into clumps, and it starts making the little bombs we call plaques. Plaques may harm neurons without necessarily killing them, like a stick of dynamite thrown at a train. But later, after making plaques for a decade or two, the beta-amyloid terror factory may start using those plaques to help make tangles, and tangles are the real high explosives of aging—like tank rounds blasted into brain cells, producing neuronal train wrecks. While beta-amyloid is just making plaques, its impact on thinking is a bearable nuisance. *But once beta-amyloid turns on tangle production, neurons begin to die, and memory begins to crash.*

This brings us to two more terrific recent discoveries—discoveries so important that they might be called the deep secrets of Alzheimer's. First, recall that beta-amyloid is made when the longer Abeta42 fragment is sliced off from the big APP "cookie roll." Now researchers have found the molecular knives that do the slicing. APP is sliced by three enzymes called *alpha-, beta-,* and *gamma-secretase.* Alpha-secretase is the "good" secretase; it slices APP to make Abeta40. Beta- and gamma-secretase, on the other hand, slice the big APP cookie roll to yield the longer, stickier, deadlier Abeta42; so beta and gamma are the "bad" secretases. Thus, if you have too much bad secretase activity, your memory is in danger.

But even if this happens, you have a way out, which brings us to the second new discovery—every neuron has a clever system to destroy misfolded proteins. Neurobiologists have just found two parts of this system—molecules that rip beta-amyloid to shreds and help to save our brains. In 2001, a team of scientists in Japan announced that an enzyme called *neprilysin* can break down beta-amyloid. And a team at Harvard Medical School found that *insulin degrading enzymes* can do the same. Clearly, if we are running low on such enzymes, we risk memory loss. As we figure out ways to boost these enzymes, we may have a completely new weapon in our war on Alzheimer's.

The big picture is now clear: beta-amyloid is a cerebral terrorist. It damages the brain by making the small bombs of plaques and the big bombs of tangles. We get Alzheimer's because we have too much of the bad secretases, or because the system rips up beta-amyloid malfunctions, *or both.*

One cannot help but be awed by the brilliance of this scientific work. We can finally say, "This is how aging-related brain change robs us of our memories." Most important of all, we finally have terrific targets for new drug discovery. With modern computerized methods, pharmaceutical companies can test up to a million compounds per week to see if they can fight these molecular terrorists and save the human brain. That work is currently under way.

Brain and Behavior Changes in Other Dementias

Let's look very briefly at the other neurodegenerative dementias.

Dementia with Lewy bodies (DLB) affects about a fourth as many people as Alzheimer's. It is very similar to Alzheimer's, although its victims are more likely to have rigid, slowed movements and hallucinations. The brains of people with DLB have plaques and tangles as well as curious round pearl-like bodies made of a misfolded protein called *alpha-synuclein*—another case of a good-protein-turned-bad.

Frontotemporal lobar dementia (FTLD) is also very similar to Alzheimer's, but FTLD patients have more trouble in their frontal lobes. As a result, they may lose their inhibitions, sometimes exhibiting surprisingly poor judgment or acting in hypersexual ways. The brain of an FTLD patient shows lots of tau protein; that's why tau-based conditions such as FTLD are called *tauopathies.*

Parkinson's disease (PD) is usually considered a movement disorder, but about half of PD patients eventually become demented. The main problem in PD is the death of neurons in a tiny region of the brainstem called the *substantia nigra,* the brain's main factory for dopamine. Like people with DLB, those with PD often have Lewy bodies in their brains. New evidence strongly suggests that PD is powerfully influenced by environment and lifestyle. This discovery makes it urgent for us to investigate potential PD risk factors such as diet, pesticides, solvents, and infections.

The other well-known cause of aging-related mental deterioration is *vascular dementia.* Most cases of vascular dementia are related to the same factors we associate with heart disease: hypertension (high blood pressure), smoking, diabetes, and a type of irregular heartbeat called atrial fibrillation. Textbooks will tell you that "vascular dementia" is distinctly different from "Alzheimer's."

Cracks in the Standard Model

The Standard Model is a tidy twentieth-century construct based on the seventeenth-century idea that we can observe the difference between health and disease by peering through a microscope. There is a lot of truth to this story, which has taken years of hard work to uncover. But cracks have appeared in the Standard Model. Neuroscientists have come to wonder about its validity, to be suspicious of the tidy definitions of some disorders, and to seek a deeper explanation for the incredible variety of human aging. An exciting new paradigm is evolving—a new way of thinking that has profound implications for the quest to save the brain. To appreciate the virtues of the new paradigm, it will be helpful to uncover the cracks in the old one.

First, the Standard Model claims that "Alzheimer's disease" is completely different from "normal aging." But, dangled above a pit of crocodiles, any neuroscientist would admit that there are no absolute rules to separate the brain changes of Alzheimer's from those of aging. Lacking a real biological definition of Alzheimer's, the Standard Model has in fact been using an *operational definition.*

An operational definition for a disease is one that's based not on true biological understanding but on arbitrary rules. For example, back in 1850, physicians were confronted by many patients with chronic coughs. They called this *phthisis* (a term for chronic pulmonary disease) and were forced to use arbitrary rules for deciding who had this problem, such as: "Anyone who coughs for a long time has phthisis." Obviously, not everyone with a long-lasting cough had the same problem. Some had tuberculosis, some had lung cancer, some had emphysema, and some had congestive heart failure, but doctors lumped them all together, because they all fit the general definition of phthisis. It gave doctors (and patients) some confidence that they knew what they were talking about. All that changed in 1882 when German bacteriologist Robert Koch discovered the little red tubercle bacillus. In one great moment, doctors finally got a scientific way to diagnose tuberculosis—a truly distinct disease. At that point, the conventional idea of phthisis began to fade away.

Obviously, doctors use operational definitions as a stopgap, a way to categorize a disorder until they really understand what it is and how it works. The Standard Model of "Alzheimer's disease" perches unsteadily atop the base of just such an operational definition. Back in 1907, when faith was strong that diseases could be diagnosed by microscopic examination, Dr. Alzheimer looked through his microscope at the brain of Madame D. and thought he had discovered a distinct disease. But now we're not so sure. Since just about everyone will have misfolded proteins and get plaques and tangles if they live long enough, at present the only way for neurologists to distinguish between "normal aging" and "Alzheimer's" is by making up an operational definition. That's exactly what we did in the mid-1980s.

Specifically, two meetings were held in 1984 and 1985, bringing together top experts on Alzheimer's. Trying to come up with a definition of "Definite" Alzheimer's, the committee ran head-on into the dilemma we just discussed. Unlike tuberculosis, in which microscopic findings lend themselves to a clear yes-or-no diagnosis, microscopic plaques occur in normal aging; the older you get, the more of them you're likely to have. So they decided that to diagnose "Definite Alzheimer's," doctors should use "age-adjusted plaque scores." In other words, if you were a certain age when you died with dementia, and the doctor finds a certain number of plaques in your brain, he'll say, "Yep, she had 'Definite Alzheimer's.' " As an example, the definition says that a seventy-six-year-old woman with dementia *definitely* had Alzheimer's if we find sixteen plaques, but she did *not* have Alzheimer's if we find fifteen. Similarly, the definition says that a sixty-five-year-old demented man with nine plaques had Alzheimer's, but a fellow who was just one year older with the same number of plaques did *not* have Alzheimer's!

The Standard Model, based on arbitrary ratings of changes in the brain, is a practical idea, to be sure. But it's not science. It's like a botanist concluding, "Any yellow fruit larger than four inches across is a grapefruit, and any fruit that's smaller isn't," or a veterinarian saying, "Animals that weigh more than fifteen pounds are dogs, animals weighing less than that are cats," or a high school teacher separating the boys from the girls by saying, "Boys are the ones over five foot seven, girls are the shorter ones." Using an arbitrary score is just not a wise way to divide up things in nature. The Standard Model gives us false confidence as we wrestle with the complexities of human brain aging. It is well intentioned but deeply flawed.

Contrary to the Standard Model, no bright lines can be drawn between normal aging, MCI, and dementia. Yes, it's easy to see extreme cases; we can all tell the difference between a fellow who occasionally misplaces his keys and a man who wanders through the streets at dawn, looking for his childhood home. But in Stage IV of the brain's voyage of life, there is an infinitude of degrees of mental ability, from sharp-as-a-tack to lost-in-a-fog, not three neat corrals of cognition. Even the definition of so-called "dementia" is no granite milestone; it's actually a fuzzy border on the amazingly variable human journey from peak brain function to utter dependence.

Another problem with the Standard Model is that aging-related brain changes occur *throughout* the brain's voyage of life; they are not just something that happens in our later years. Some declines in brain function are absolutely built into normal development, from the natural drop-off in neurogenesis that occurs before birth, to the post-teenage decline in synaptogenesis, to the selective pruning of synapses in adulthood. In fact, the brain changes that are commonly seen as proof positive of "neurodegeneration" may be cooking away silently while we go on our first date. As Professor Ohm of Germany's J. W. Goethe University says, "The deep roots of Alzheimer's-type neurofibrillary changes can be traced about fifty years back and may even extend into adolescence." So there is no neat dividing line that allows us to say with confidence, "*This* brain has normal aging, while *that* brain has a disorder." Aging means change, and the threshold for calling a change a "disease" is very hard to judge. Menopause, graying hair, and wrinkling skin may be undesirable and sometimes distressing, but they are not "abnormal" and are not a "disease." Furthermore, the more we learn about our genes, the more open we'll need to be about what constitutes "normal" aging. Is having the ε4 allele and a high risk of Alzheimer's "abnormal"? *No.* It is part of the awesome variety of life.

Another problem is that the Standard Model focuses almost all of its attention on people with symptoms such as memory loss. But proteins misfold, synapses wither, and neurons die for many years before symptoms develop and we notice that someone we love is in trouble. We should be alert to the fall, not just to the crash landing. We should leap in with neuroprotection long before that very late and very arbitrary point when the Standard Model finally gets around to saying, "Gosh, this fellow has a brain disease."

Still another problem with the Standard Model is that there is actually a *huge* overlap between the "diseases" popularly called Alzheimer's, DLB, FTLD, or PD. Rather than four neatly segregated conditions, nature presents us with an astonishing variety of cognitive changes, neurotransmitter changes, and pile-ups of misfolded proteins such as beta-amyloid, tau, and alpha-synuclein. What's more, plaques appear in the brain after strokes, after head trauma, and even in older people with excellent memories and graceful gaits, so *plaques are absolutely not a marker for a specific disease.*

To summarize, the collection of features we currently call "Alzheimer's disease" is just an operational definition—and a shaky one at that. Yes, the popular idea of Alzheimer's as a "disease" is emotionally reassuring, since it implies that it's different from the natural course of life; but there's no genuinely scientific way to draw a line between Alzheimer's and normal aging.

Rethinking "Vascular Dementia"

Even the supposedly black-and-white distinction between Alzheimer's disease and vascular dementia is an oversimplification. The real story is much more interesting. Consider the Nun Study.

Psychologist David Snowdon followed 102 members of the School Sisters of Notre Dame religious order for many years, until they died at ages ranging from seventy-six to one hundred. When their brains were examined, many of the nuns were found to have Alzheimer's-type brain changes, many had had strokes, and about a quarter had both. According to the Standard Model, the more strokes you suffer, the greater your risk of memory loss: "More strokes, more dementia." But Dr. Snowdon's team found that strokes were actually a poor predictor of memory loss—that is, unless a nun *also* had *Alzheimer's-type changes* in her brain. In other words, the biggest factor in whether strokes leave us demented may be *how much Alzheimer's-type brain change we've developed by the time the stroke strikes.*

The Nun Study essentially says, "Beware the Standard Model." While the conventional wisdom would have us believe that Alzheimer's and vascular dementia are two entirely separate problems, we now suspect that they strongly interact and overlap. They're often as interdependent as the stick-up man and the getaway driver, since strokes have a tough time robbing the memory bank without the help of Alzheimer's. This fact nicely clarifies our picture of the aging brain: acting by themselves, plaques may not devastate memory. But if your brain is filling up with plaques—and you then add *strokes,* or *tangles*, or both—your mind is in deep trouble.

The Alzheimer's-versus-vascular-dementia dichotomy is dangerously outdated. In reality, there are many subtle shadings between normal aging and Alzheimer's, between Alzheimer's and vascular dementia, and between Alzheimer's and other types of neurodegeneration. As doctors shake off the blinders of convention, we are coming to realize that the Standard Model is a black-and-white picture of a rainbow.

This is not just an academic debate—an angels on the head of a pin brouhaha. The old idea that memory loss is a late-life catastrophe, rather than a universal problem with roots going back to the teen years, has led us to concentrate billions upon untold billions of dollars on research to "cure" old brains that may be beyond the point of no return, rather than on understanding and preventing the lifestyle problems that accelerate aging-related brain change in the first place! If we keep relying on obsolete models of dementia, we may concentrate our efforts in the wrong places, like the French massing their armor along the Maginot Line.

The Relativity Theory of Aging-Related Brain Change

It's time we completely updated our thinking about memory loss. We need a new theory of aging-related brain change to talk about the deep biology—not just the final stage, but the years and years of silent change—because there are many millions more people on earth who are experiencing these brain changes, and are at a stage where much can be done to prevent decline and naturally boost brain function, than there are people who actually have symptoms. The Relativity Theory of Aging-Related Brain Change will let us better arm ourselves in the battle for our brains.

The big picture: two types of problems besiege our aging neurons, like two armies laying siege to the castle of the brain. The first is *misfolded proteins,* which lead to various types of neurodegeneration. The second is *energy deprivation,* which includes all the vascular disorders that leave our neurons gasping for oxygen, all the aging changes that make our mitochondrial engines misfire, and even diabetes, which leaves our brain cells starving for glucose. Most important, it's vital to realize that misfolded proteins and energy deprivation *almost always happen in the same brain.* The Relativity Theory appreciates that *relative* amounts of these two problems account for the infinite shades of difference between mild and severe memory loss. Let's begin with misfolded proteins.

MISFOLDED PROTEINS

In the case of so-called Alzheimer's disease, it's easy to talk about the final, awful stages. But we need a way to talk about the millions and millions of people who have misfolded proteins accumulating in their brains *before* memory loss becomes obvious. We can refer to this long-term change as *aging-related neurodegeneration of the Alzheimer's type* (ARNAT). ARNAT encompasses the whole process at any stage of life, the everyday biology that starts in young adulthood and ultimately leads to plaques and tangles, whether or not it causes memory loss. ARNAT is *far* more common than Alzheimer's, because it includes the whole progression—from the first knots of misfolded proteins to the last desperate days. Alzheimer's is a dreadful condition, to be sure. But ARNAT is the major problem facing the aging brain.

ARNAT is as common to the human voyage of life as the changes we expect in our hormones, our skin, and our vision. Some of us experience more ARNAT, some less; some earlier, some later. That's one reason to call this the Relativity Theory of Aging-Related Brain Change; *relative* amounts of ARNAT distinguish one person from another. Dozens of factors speed it up or slow it down. That means *ARNAT/Alzheimer's is not a disease with a single cause.* And since we have personal control over many of these factors, we actually have tremendous power to control the pace of our own brain aging.

While ARNAT is the most common type of brain aging, there are variations on this theme. The type of neurodegeneration that appears in your brain depends on the relative amount of different misfolded proteins. For instance, if your brain makes mostly misfolded beta-amyloid, you may get only plaques and do relatively well. But if you *also* make misfolded tau, you're likely to get both plaques and tangles and to have noticeable memory loss. If you make only misfolded tau, you may get a *tauopathy* and eventually show the uninhibited behaviors of FTLD. If your problem is mostly a matter of misfolded alpha-synuclein, you may experience the symptoms of Parkinson's. And if your own particular style of aging involves a *mix* of misfolded proteins, you may eventually develop a mixed form of neurodegeneration, such as DLB. Every one of these conditions is, to a significant and exciting degree, preventable.

ENERGY DEPRIVATION

The Relativity Theory also reconsiders the whole problem of energy deprivation.

Oxygen and glucose are the brain's essential fuels. If the delivery of these fuels becomes compromised in any way, neurons can die, like people in a besieged castle who've been cut off from their supplies of food and water. Unfortunately, aging invariably involves many changes that can affect the delivery of these fuels. For one, diabetes directs a sneak attack on the brain by robbing it of glucose (see Chapter 8). For another, aging-related damage to mitochondrial DNA can also rob our brains of energy. But the biggest energy-deprivation problem is the *failure to get enough oxygenated blood up to our neurons.* This happens whenever our cerebral blood supply gets compromised—for example, when our blood vessels become stiff, clogged, and narrowed by atherosclerosis. The brain can tolerate a little drop in its blood supply, but at some point, *even if we never have a stroke in our lives,* the brain can no longer compensate for the strangling-off of its essential fuels, and neurons begin to suffer. This is called *cerebrovascular compromise* (CVC).

CVC is a relative problem, not an all-or-none one. It can strike with the lightning speed of a stroke, but it more commonly hurts brain cells through a sneaky, insidious reduction in blood flow. Either the sudden assault of a stroke or the sneak assault may or may not get so severe as to produce so-called vascular dementia. Just as ARNAT affects far more people than Alzheimer's, CVC affects far more people than those who get the diagnosis of vascular dementia. But it's crucial to realize that CVC is laying siege to most adult brains at this very moment. That means that we shouldn't just think about treating strokes. We need to leap in much sooner and block CVC.

Finally, the Relativity Theory sets aside the old idea that Alzheimer's and cerebrovascular disease are worlds apart. They're not. Most often, CVC overlaps and conspires with ARNAT. Some researchers even urge that we should consider Alzheimer's to be, in part, a vascular disorder. Remember Madame D.? Little has been made of the fact that Dr. Alzheimer also found atherosclerosis in her brain. In fact, those vascular changes may very well have contributed to the process that plunged her into her torments.

The realization that CVC interacts with ARN gives us a big lever for neuroprotection. Vascular changes in the heart usually parallel vascular changes in the brain. Vascular changes in the brain increase the risk that aging-related brain changes will destroy our memory. Therefore, the treasure trove of data we already have on the prevention of heart disease may buy us an unexpected benefit: whatever we do to save our hearts will probably help us save our brains.

It's time to set aside the Standard Model. It's time to fight the underlying problems that threaten our society with widespread cognitive loss— probably one of the most predictable and avoidable major medical problems in human history. The new paradigm offers us a stronger, richer, and hopefully more faithful account of the rocks and shoals facing the brain during adulthood. The urgent message of our new paradigm is that *minimizing ARNAT and CVC should be a passionate endeavor for all of us, regardless of whether we have begun to sense the ultimate insult of memory loss.*

Let's see how to do it.

PART II

What Can We Do About It?

INTRODUCTION

Twain's Maxim and Pascal's Bet

"Doctor, realistically, what can I do to save my brain?"

Part II of this book will answer that question.

Brains change with time. As we've discovered, some of those changes are potentially adaptive, such as the distillation of life's million lessons into wisdom. But some are potentially maladaptive, such as the erosion of the MTL memory system. Again, two factors control the destiny of our brains: our genes and our environment. Mutant genes powerfully influence the pace and the type of ARN. But much more common genes, like those for *APOE-ε4*, ratchet up our risk of memory loss, or lower the age at which our brains begin to fail us. We call these risk-factor genes, as explained earlier.

If our brains were doomed by our genes, we would have little reason to learn the fine art of brain self-defense. But, thankfully, *genes alone are not brain destiny*. Environment—the billions of external influences we experience from the womb to the grave and the dozens of lifestyle decisions we make that increase or decrease our exposure to such influences—also has a *profound* impact on the vigor of the brain and mind. At the moment, we can't fix our genes (although we are moving so fast in that direction that it's scary), but we *can* do a lot to improve our lifestyle and environment. That's why, to a much greater extent than most people realize, the destiny of our brains is up to us.

How big a difference can lifestyle make? A study of Alzheimer's disease conducted in Japan and published in 1994 compared 60 people with Alzheimer's to 120 people without. The investigators found that five lifestyle factors significantly increased the risk of Alzheimer's: psychosocial inactivity, physical inactivity, head injury, loss of teeth, and low

education. People who had all five of these lifestyle risk factors were
934.5 *times* more likely to have Alzheimer's than people who had none
of them.

Now that's an astonishing idea to contemplate—that we can make
choices that cut our risk of dementia more than 900 times. That's 90,000
percent! Of course, one study is not scientific gospel; data-gathering errors and statistical flukes can always skew the results. And it's hard to
claim that keeping your teeth will directly save your brain, since the connection between good oral hygiene and healthy neurons is probably very
indirect. Yet study results like this are cause for critically reconsidering
the fatalism that has undermined preventive neurology for most of the
last century. It's time to get excited about what we *can* do to save our
brains.

A similar study was conducted by my cigar-chomping, motorcycle-
riding, devoted family-man friend, Web "Wild Child" Ross. Web is the
neurologist in charge of the dementia aspects of the Honolulu Heart
Project. This huge and carefully conducted study has been following
older men of Japanese ancestry since 1965. Although 88 percent of these
men were born in Hawaii, they are an excellent group in which to study
the impact of lifestyle on cognition, since—due to strong cultural constraints against intermarriage—they are genetically very similar to
Japanese men living significantly different lifestyles in Japan. Web and
his colleagues examined 3,734 of these men, aged seventy-one to ninety-
three. They found that 5.4 percent of the men fulfilled the criteria for
Alzheimer's disease. But in a parallel study conducted on the 887 residents of Hisayama, Japan, the rate of Alzheimer's was only 1.5 percent.
This means that in two large groups of people with similar genetic backgrounds, those living in Hawaii had more than *three and a half times* the
risk of developing Alzheimer's. It seems that when Japanese men move
from Japan to Hawaii, the change in lifestyle bumps up their risk to
match that of Americans with European backgrounds. We'll want to see
more studies to confirm this, but taken at face value, this is a giant clue
that your lifestyle will probably have a huge influence on the future
health of your brain.

The immense impact that ARNAT is about to have on modern society should keep us burning the midnight oil to discover all we can about
the lifestyle and environmental choices that can protect our brains. Even
if lifestyle were a factor in only 10 percent of the risk of cognitive
loss (and it is likely closer to 40 or 50 percent), that would be a powerful reason for us to take action right now. Forget the fever-dream of a
935-fold reduction in risk. Let's say we're trying to cut our risk in

half, or even just by 25 percent. Let's say that we hope to gain only that extra bit of cognitive protection to keep us mentally vigorous enough to understand our daughter's chemistry homework, launch our website, recall a great pumpkin pie recipe, or go to law school when we're forty-five; or to learn to play the piano or finish writing that long-dreamed-of novel when we're sixty-five; or to give us three extra years in our eighties during which we can still tell a Matisse from a Cézanne, teach our grandchildren Beatles songs, and play poker with our friends (and win). That's plenty of reason to take preventive action today.

How Confident Are We That We Know How to Save Our Brains?

As we look at our brain-saving options, we're faced with tens of thousands of promising pieces of scientific evidence. (In preparation for writing this book, I reviewed more than 14,000 scientific articles.) Some of these reports are more persuasive than others. For example, basic studies done in the lab—such as those showing that ginseng may boost the cellular biology of memory—sound promising, but the vast majority of basic lab studies turn out to have no real application to human health. A greater level of confidence comes from *animal experiments,* such as those showing memory enhancement in rats that exercise. This is a little more persuasive, though every animal on earth is different, and what works in rats may or may not work in humans.

Still more persuasive are *retrospective human studies.* A retrospective study—like the ones we described above from Japan and Hawaii—looks back at what happened to people in the past, then tries to figure out how this affected their health. Another example: studies showing that people who've taken in more vitamin C from fruits and vegetables have a lower risk of stroke. Almost all the evidence for saving the brain comes from such retrospective studies. Yet we must always take such studies with a grain of salt, since whatever factor we *think* led to the health benefit might just be associated with improved health by coincidence. (For instance, maybe it's another ingredient in fruits and vegetables that really saves us from stroke.) Furthermore, a big retrospective study of *all* the brain-saving measures recommended in this book would be impossible, because few people on earth have ever adopted all these measures from an early age.

A little more persuasive are *prospective clinical trials,* in which people who already have brain disease are offered experimental treatment. One big study, for example, tested whether vitamin E helps people with Alzheimer's disease. The problem with such studies is that treatments that prevent a problem—like brushing one's teeth—are often quite different from treatments that fix a problem—like a tooth extraction.

The most persuasive studies of all—as precious as diamonds and just as rare—are the *prospective primary prevention trials,* in which doctors give a therapy to *healthy* volunteers to see if it will truly prevent memory loss later in their lives. For instance, the National Center for Complementary and Alternative Medicine is now involved in a five-year trial of ginkgo biloba to prevent dementia. This is a step in the right direction. But despite the obvious need, only a handful of primary prevention trials have been done in all of human history to test ways to protect healthy folks from cognitive loss. Consider what's involved: to do such a study properly, we would follow a large group of volunteers for many years—starting even before they have the slightest hint of memory loss—and divide them into a "treatment" group that gets to use a bunch of promising brain-saving measures, and a "control" group that gets placebos instead. But there's no way on God's green earth that we'll be able to launch such a placebo-controlled primary prevention trial for saving brains. Since Alzheimer's-type brain changes may extend back into adolescence, a really good prospective clinical trial of combined brain-saving methods would have to recruit high school students as volunteers. And since memory loss only becomes obvious and commonplace in our eighties, we would not be completely sure of the benefits for about sixty-five years! Can you imagine proposing a clinical trial that long—with, for example, 5,000 people deliberately avoiding all the best bets for saving their brains and another 5,000 using all those measures from age fifteen to age eighty—while the rest of us wait to see whose brains come out on top? No way. It would not be practical, affordable, or, most important, ethical. And even if NIH decided to launch that study, we can't afford to wait that long.

For all of these reasons, we cannot yet be *absolutely* sure which strategies for saving our brains will give us the very best results. Yet we must make practical choices today—to follow the best possible path based on the current evidence. This brings us to a guiding principle called Pascal's Bet.

Pascal's Bet

You must wager. It is not optional. You are embarked.
Which will you choose then? Let us see.

PASCAL, *PENSÉES*, 233 (C. 1660)

Pascal was a Christian. In this passage, he wished to turn the beam of proto-Enlightenment rationality onto the question of belief in God. He made a simple suggestion. We cannot know for sure whether God exists, but if we wager that He doesn't exist and we wager wrong, we'll end up burning in hell forever. So Pascal suggests that we wager that God *does* exist and act accordingly during our lifetimes. This is Pascal's Bet. Indeed, it is a reasonable approach to many of those medical conundrums in which we must choose a course of action even though we aren't completely sure how it will turn out.

Such is the nature of decision making in preventive neurology today. With the help of the Framingham Heart Study, the Nun Study, the Baltimore Longitudinal Study of Aging, the Honolulu Heart Program, the Bronx Aging Study, the Physicians' Health Study, the Women's Health Initiative, and the painstaking medical record keeping of the Mayo Clinic and of fine European scholars in Germany, Sweden, and the Netherlands, we are finally collecting precious clues about the long-term impact of preventive measures on the brain. But since some aspects of ARN probably begin in our twenties, *the sooner we begin to save our brains, the better,* so we must take action before we reach absolute certainty.

When I lecture about saving the brain, I show a slide:

> Dear HMO: Enclosed is a list of the 5 million members of your health plan. Please identify those who are *not* at risk for cognitive loss. A postcard is included for your convenience.

The point is that even though our risks vary, *every* human on earth is at risk for cognitive loss. That means we need a radical new approach. Unfortunately, the whole idea of preventive neurology is brand-new. We need to grab the big HMOs by the lapels and say, "Listen! The heart is not the only organ that needs preventive medicine. It's time to pay attention to the brain!" And we have to push for a national health care agenda that values brains as much as hearts.

As Pascal said, "You must wager. It is not optional. You are embarked." So *right now* we must take the brain-saving actions that—according to all the best current research—look to be the best bets. Part II of this book will offer those best bets. Yet the bets that are best for one person may not be best for everyone. The key is *personal* choice, since each of us is a unique individual. Which brings us to the second guiding principle of this book: Twain's Maxim.

Twain's Maxim

> I have achieved my seventy years in the usual way, by sticking strictly to a scheme of life which would kill anybody else . . . I will offer here, as a sound maxim, this: That we can't reach old age by another man's road.
>
> MARK TWAIN, AT HIS SEVENTIETH
> BIRTHDAY DINNER, 1905

Oh, Twain! You capture truths in words as children capture lightning bugs in jars! Twain celebrated his birthday by lassoing a fact: humans are diverse. The range of our diversity is so immense that if we discuss "averages," we may miss an essential feature of humanity—its wonderful variety. Therefore, as we explore different methods to save the brain, we must be careful not to assume that everyone must do the exact same things to get the ideal result. This is the wisdom of Twain's Maxim: we can't reach old age by another man's road. We must individualize our efforts to save our brains.

Twain's Maxim notwithstanding, some scientists have sought "Methuselah factors," aspects of diet or lifestyle that seem to be associated with successful arrival at extreme old age. Scholars have scoured the world in search of peoples who live long (or, more often, claim to have lived long without records to support it), then interviewed them to try to figure out what they were doing that we're not. Methuselah factors have been claimed for those living in the Hunza region of Pakistan, the Vilcabamba in Ecuador, and the Abkhazian area of the Caucasus. Unfortunately, this research has led to the conclusion that (1) most of these groups do not actually have longer-than-usual life spans; and (2) there is virtually no evidence that, for the eldest members of each group, a particular food or habit has led them to live longer. However, there is some evidence from studies of centenarians in Okinawa (as I will discuss) who indeed seem to live longer lives, not by virtue of any Methuselah factor, but by virtue of the simple combination of an optimum, calorie-limited diet, regular exercise, and the strong bonds of community. But since each of us is genetically different, has grown up in different environments, and has different physical and psychological vulnerabilities, we should not slavishly imitate what has been attributed to some other culture or people. Following Twain's Maxim, we must *personalize* our own brain-saving plans, cherishing our own individual biology.

That brings us to an incredibly important fact that modern medicine is just beginning to appreciate: contrary to the headlines, *there is no human genome.* There are *billions* of them, since every single one of us (even so-called identical twins) is actually a unique person with a unique genome. So even though we are all members of the same original human family and share the vast majority of our genes, genetic differences ought to be considered when physicians recommend a medical treatment.

A case in point: aspirin helps some people avoid strokes and heart attacks more than others. The reason may be genetic. About 25 percent of whites, 15 percent of blacks, and a few percent of Asians carry at least one copy of a gene called *P1A2*, which makes the receptors that attach platelets to other molecules in the bloodstream. But *P1A2* comes in two types, one more common than the other. As Ohio State University cardiologist Pascal Goldschmidt has reported, people who have the less common version are most likely to get more benefit from aspirin because, when they take aspirin, their systems are more likely to prevent platelets from forming death-dealing blood clots in their brains. So testing for your genotype might someday predict whether aspirin can save your brain from strokes. Discoveries such as these have launched an entirely new field of medicine, pharmacogenomics—the twenty-first-century effort that studies which drugs are best suited for people with different genes.

This is just one illustration of the importance of individual genetics for medical decision making. With the recent completion of the Human Genome Project, scientists will be moving rapidly to determine which genes cause various diseases and the individual genetic differences between people. For the time being, however, *much of the medical advice doctors give out will be based on complete ignorance of genetic differences that could profoundly influence who will benefit the most.* Physicians must be humble about stating, "This treatment helps people," when what they really mean is "This treatment seems to help *some* people."

A corollary to the issue of individual genetics is the question of sex. Scientists are finally coming to appreciate the vital medical fact that what's good for the goose may *not* be good for the gander. Human biology involves many sex differences beyond the obvious ones, yet in some areas of medicine scientists have done much more research with men than with women. Normal sex differences mean that a treatment discovered to benefit men will not necessarily benefit women. *Both* sexes need to be tested before doctors can recommend one approach for everyone.

When Mark Twain said, "We can't reach old age by another man's road," scientists had yet to discover the remarkable accuracy of that wisdom (and were about a century away from realizing that women may have health roads of their own). Knowing what we do today about variability in personal biology, Twain's Maxim takes on a deep new meaning. In the next few decades, we will discover much more about how to use biological differences to custom-tailor health care for individuals. But even today we can make sensible decisions about what are likely to be the best brain-saving plans according to age, sex, family history, health, and personal preferences.

Can Alternative Medicine Save Your Brain?

> When Chi-sun Fei sent him medicine, he received it with a deep bow but said, "Since I do not recognize it, I will not put it in my mouth."
>
> CONFUCIUS, *SAYINGS* (TRANS. D. WARE)

The dean of the school of medicine began his welcoming address to the incoming students as follows:

"Half of what we're going to teach you is true, the other half isn't. The problem is, we don't know which half is which." He had won a Nobel prize. We hoped he'd know what to teach us. This didn't seem like a promising start.

But he was right: science is never finished. Whatever we teach today will soon be history, and only fragments of what we currently believe will turn out to be useful over the long haul. This has never been more true than it is now, when the pace of biological research is moving so fast that it leaves us gasping for breath. The interval between Leeuwenhoek's first view of bacteria (in 1676) to Watson and Crick's discovery of the role of DNA (in 1953) was just 277 years, a freckle on the elephant hide of history. But the time from DNA's discovery to the cloning of an adult sheep took only forty-three years! This intense acceleration of medical knowledge makes us feel swept up in a whirlwind, and the rocketing pace of discovery, combined with instantaneous communication, means that we are constantly hearing new facts and rumors about human health.

As a result, we are barraged with what seems like ever-shifting advice: avoid salt or don't, eat margarine or don't, drink wine or don't. Who should we believe? Who should we trust? The changes in health care delivery, the rise of the HMOs, the loss of the family doctor who really knows us and has time to listen to us have all eroded our confidence in traditional medicine. At the same time, our faith in our own ability to make informed decisions about our own bodies has risen, and a healthy questioning of conventional authority is widespread. These changes may help to explain why many people have turned to alternative medicine.

The phrase *alternative medicine* is used in many different ways; it seems to have no universally embraced definition. *Complementary medicine* and *integrative therapy* are newer but are not much more precise. Whatever we call it, many reasonable people today are looking for help from sources other than traditional science-based medicine. Fierce debates have erupted. Intelligent, well-meaning folks have fled into opposite corners. A damaging earthquake schism has appeared between traditional and nontraditional sources of medical advice. Physicians sometimes forget that almost every accepted treatment was once an unproved alternative approach. Proponents of alternative medicine sometimes forget that carefully testing a treatment for safety and efficacy is a humane virtue, not a vice. Some products of the alternative approach are quite promising, such as the recent discovery that the herbal preparation PC-SPES may help men with prostate cancer, and the excellent clinical research on ginkgo biloba in Alzheimer's disease. Others are deplorable, such as the wave of sudden heart attack deaths that has occurred in the United States because supplement makers put ephedra (the active ingredient of the Chinese herb ma huang) in dozens of "energy" preparations—and declined to warn consumers of the serious risk, or to submit their products for independent testing. In climbing onto the seductive alternative medicine bandwagon, some consumers are going to be badly hurt.

Saving our brains is a heady voyage, and despite our cultural differences, we are really all in the same boat. There is only *one* medicine: the earnest, heartfelt effort to discover truths that help people in need. We should not trumpet Eastern over Western medicine, or vice versa, as if good ideas needed a compass. The effort to discover helpful truths is not the monopoly of any one culture. As Hippocrates would say, "What is useful is good."

Having said that, I must be firm on one point: all *ethical* healers will enthusiastically embrace an unbiased effort to confirm the purity, safety, and efficacy of anything they recommend. Dietary supplement–makers and other alternative practitioners who live up to this ethical standard deserve our respect. Those who don't should not be in the health care business. In this book, we will seek the best methods for saving our brains based on the currently available scientific evidence: not the best from one tradition or another, not the best from a particular belief system or professional club, just the best.

A Caveat

Some aspects of the book will be controversial. In particular, some doctors adhere to the dogma that aging-related cognitive loss is a minor matter and becomes an issue only when it progresses to Alzheimer's. That's an understandable opinion. Since the difference between old people with subtle memory loss and old people with severe memory loss is so huge and obvious, at first glance it may seem outrageous to suggest that the two problems are connected. But this impression may reflect a misguided desire to deny that aging *always* affects the human brain. Consider recent findings from the Oregon Brain Aging Study: even the top 0.5 percent of the elderly—carefully screened for optimum physical and cognitive health—showed mental decline over five years of observation. As study leader Haydeh Payami put it, "Our results suggest that not even the healthiest elderly are immune to dementia, and that the key to prevention is not innate invulnerability, as we first thought, but in delaying onset." Exactly. This vital issue—"delaying onset"—has profound implications not only for optimizing human health but for the evolution of human self-understanding.

Yet even while celebrating the potential of the new science of neuroprotection, I don't want to overstate the expected benefits or the effectiveness of emerging treatments. So I must offer a firm caveat: for all the effort to distill truth from the thousands of studies reviewed for this project, and for all my wishes to offer the best bets, I expect that some of the conclusions I offer in this book may be revised by further investigations. For that reason, I'll try to be realistic about what we know definitively, what we merely suspect, and what we are still waiting to discover. Still, we must make healthy choices today, even while we are waiting for news of the final truth. The recommendations that follow are the best I know of at this point in time.

I should also mention that this book is no substitute for the individual help of a compassionate physician. Twain's Maxim holds; each of you has your own body and brain, so please consult a doctor who knows you personally before embarking on any major changes in lifestyle or health habits.

Let's turn now to the first area that's ripe for improvement: controlling stress.

CHAPTER 5

Is Stress Destroying Your Brain?

"We are, perhaps, uniquely among the earth's creatures, the worrying animal."
LEWIS THOMAS, *THE MEDUSA AND THE SNAIL* (1979)

"I've had a stressful life," she began.

I thought it best not to interrupt. An important story often follows such a pregnant introduction. Sherry was seated across from me on the examining table, her hands lying quietly in her lap.

She went on. "I was what you'd call an army brat. You know, my dad was a career army man, and we moved every three years while I was growing up, so I think I had trouble—trouble with friends and everything." She swallowed but gained determination. "And then my first marriage didn't work out. I put him through law school, and it was just crazy with working and trying to be home with the kids, and then I found out he was seeing someone he met at his school, so we got a divorce."

Sherry trailed off as we both wondered what she'd tell me next. Her tone was matter of fact. Her hands never moved. She proceeded to recount a difficult time alone, an initial thrill of second love, another marriage, another—but more amicable—divorce, her mother's recent fender bender, a daughter beginning to date in junior high school, a brief scare two years ago from a cystic breast, some financial problems, a promising new job but with long hours, nothing catastrophic, no childhood sexual abuse or domestic violence or true poverty or even recent deaths in the family. Just the hundred wicked ills of modern life—disconnection from community, losses of family stability, time pressure, overcommitment and undergratification—with moments of genuine joy and peace a hard-to-conjure memory. She was stressed, and she knew it, and she'd come to me wondering if that could explain her occasional lapses of memory.

It could, in more ways than she may have realized. There is recent evidence that, in addition to the known impact of stress on our psyches, our vulnerable hearts, and our cardiovascular systems, stress can cause permanent brain damage. In fact, it seems increasingly likely that stress plays a role in accelerating brain aging.

But *how much* does stress hurt the brain? What part of the brain is damaged? Why is one person more prone to stress-induced brain damage than another? And most important, what can we do about it? This chapter attempts to answer these questions. The answers are not simple, because stress is not simple. Despite a hundred years of research, the subject of stress retains a certain mystery.

Beginning with the question, what is stress?

The Stress Response

The word *stress* was originally used by biologists to describe the "fight or flight" response—for example, the way the sudden attack of a lion makes a baboon either fight or run for its life. Stress can also be internal; pain or blood loss can plunge the body into an identical state of stress, even if we are not fighting or fleeing. Somewhere along the line, this scientific meaning has been muddled by increasingly casual use, to the point that we've become used to hearing that "stress" is endemic in modern life. Stress is common, but it is not just unpleasant feelings, and it does not just depend on what happens to us; it is a specific type of brilliantly coordinated response of mind and body.

It's easy to see why the stress response evolved: it keeps us alive. Let's say we half-glimpse a saber-toothed tiger through a screen of leaves. Our pupils dilate, which helps us to see the big cat better; our hearing becomes more acute to the ominous crackle of twigs; our blood pressure rises, and blood flow shifts from our internal organs to our muscles to prepare us for quick action; our breathing deepens to take in more oxygen, also preparing us for explosive physical activity; and perspiration increases in anticipation of the need to cool our body. At the same time, a host of chemical changes take place: basic energy-fuels such as carbohydrates and fats pour into the bloodstream. Renin, angiotensin, norepinephrine, and nitric oxide all start to work on our blood vessels, dilating some to feed our muscles, constricting the ones in our skin to protect us from the possibility of hemorrhage from the raking strike of those terrible claws. Our platelets also increase, ready to form blood clots in case we start to bleed. This brings up a crucial point: increased blood pressure, constricted blood vessels, fats pouring into the bloodstream, and increased clotting activity may all be terrific adaptations when we see a tiger, but if we go through these bodily changes and then neither fight nor flee—that is, when we launch a stress response without any outlet for all that pent-up energy— these exact same changes may put us at grim risk for heart attacks and strokes, the dangerous downside of our originally life-saving stress response.

This gives us the big picture. But to understand how stress can hurt our brains, we need to look more carefully at the links between mind and body—and the way that stress signals start in the brain, go down to the body, then travel up again to the brain.

At first, the sight of the tiger is not stressful in itself; it's just a sensory pattern of tawny fur, glistening teeth, and deep growling sounds. By pulling together the information supplied by the cortex and comparing it with our most emotionally potent memories, the brain arrives at the sensible observation: "Hmm, looks like a tiger." At the same time, the tiger-stimulus engages our limbic system, adding the crucial emotional reaction. Once this system gets revved up, lots of events take place in the brain, a veritable primal scream of neural activation in which the emotions shoot to the frontal lobes and we finally realize, "Hey, this is a life-threatening emergency!"

What happens next is the biological equivalent of a police siren. The information "This is an emergency!" is sent from the cortex down to the *hypothalamus,* a tiny but crucial patch of tissue at the base of the brain that serves as the master controller of hormones. The hypothalamus releases two hormonal signals: corticotropin-releasing factor (CRF) and arginine vasopressin (AVP). These messengers travel a half inch farther down to the *pituitary gland,* which releases another stress-signaling hormone called adrenocorticotropic hormone (ACTH). ACTH is carried through the bloodstream all the way down to the adrenal glands, the pinkie-size digits of hormone-producing tissue that sit atop our kidneys. The adrenals respond by releasing a flood of *adrenaline* into the bloodstream. *That's* when the first wave of the stress response really takes off.

The First Wave: Stress Revs Up the Sympathetic Nervous System

In the first wave of the stress response, adrenaline acts like emotional lighter fluid, setting off a nearly explosive burst of activity in our *sympathetic nervous system.* This speeds up our heart and changes the size of our blood vessels. On the one hand, this wave of adrenaline gets us physically ready to fight or to flee the tiger—a very useful result. But it also has a very important extra job: it helps us to remember scary events.

In an interesting 1994 study by psychobiologist Larry Cahill, subjects were told two stories. One had little emotional content, but the other involved a little boy who was seriously injured, rushed to the hospital, and treated with various medical procedures. The subjects remembered the second story much better. This is exactly what we might have predicted, since (as we learned in Chapter 3) highly emotional events simultaneously turn on the hippocampus and the amygdala, a double prod to the temporal lobe memory system. Cahill then gave a new set of subjects the blood pressure drug propranolol, to block the adrenaline surge. They listened to the same stories. The result: their memory of the highly emotional story was not enhanced. This shows that the adrenaline wave is necessary for planting emotional memories solidly in the brain.

The adrenaline wave also greatly affects our heart and our arteries. There are several good ways to measure this impact: one is to look at heart rate. For example, when we are asked to do mental arithmetic (a notorious stressor for most of us), our heart rate speeds up. Type A people, who have more of a sense of time-urgency, tend to have a bigger heart-rate response to this stressor than do the easier-going type B's; this reaction is called *excessive heart-rate reactivity*. Of course, it's good for the heart to speed up if we're being chased by a tiger, but many type A people have a too-big response to relatively innocuous events, and excessive heart-rate reactivity can cause dangerous cardiac stress. Furthermore, roughly 10 to 15 percent of type A's belong to the "angry/hostile" subtype; they are often men, and they're especially prone to heart attacks. Researchers at Allegheny College have shown that angry type A's have excessive heart-rate reactivity even to their own dreams!

Another way to look at the vascular reaction to stress is to measure blood pressure. In particular, we can look at *pulse pressure,* or the difference between our systolic (the higher number) and our diastolic (the lower number) pressure. Epidemiologist Lewis Kuller did a study with more than 250 healthy postmenopausal women who were asked to give a speech defending themselves from an accusation. The women who had the biggest rise in pulse pressure also had the most severe thickening of their carotid artery walls. Since the carotids serve the brain, this may be one reason that people who are prone to high emotions may also be prone to strokes.

A too-big stress response may sometimes mean the difference between life and death. In 1999 cardiologist David Sheps reported that people whose hearts show signs of poor circulation in a stressful situation (such as public speaking) had *triple* the annual death rate compared with their calmer peers. Results like these may help to explain another fact: a study of 20 million death certificates shows that people living in New York City are more likely than those in ten other cities to die of heart attacks. And this study was done *before* the terrible attacks on the World Trade Center of September 11, 2001. It is possible that the deadly thunder of that day will reverberate for decades as stress-related illness, harming hearts and minds and brains.

Everyone gets stressed at times; so who's at risk for a too-big stress response? New research suggests that those with *high* stress symptoms in response to *low* stress loads are in the most danger. Such people spend their lives with their adrenaline switch stuck on high, and their hearts may suffer as a result. They may even have frequent episodes of silent cardiac ischemia—inadequate blood supply to the heart muscle that may lead to a heart attack with virtually no warning. For such people, stress management is literally a matter of life and death.

More pertinent to our goal of saving the brain, there's growing evidence that a too-big stress response may lead to brain damage. First, heart attacks can cause a drop in oxygen delivery to the head, resulting in dead brain cells; second, if the heart beats inadequately, total blood flow drops and a stroke can occur; third, when the heart is damaged, a blood clot may break loose and shoot up to the brain—also causing a stroke. But *even without a heart attack* and *even without a stroke*, stress-induced changes in the vascular system can do terrible things to the brain. Chronic stress, especially in those who are temperamentally vulnerable, is associated with high blood pressure. High blood pressure not only puts people at much higher risk of outright strokes but insidiously wears away at the brain, increasing the risk for excessive damage to the white matter and for Alzheimer's (as we will discuss in Chapter 10).

The Second Wave: Stress Releases Dangerous Glucocorticoids

Shortly after the adrenal gland pours adrenaline into our bloodstream, the second wave of the stress response begins. It comes from the outer shell of the adrenal gland, the *adrenal cortex,* which pumps out three powerful stress hormones: *cortisol, hydrocortisone,* and *corticosterone.* Taken together, these three are called the *glucocorticoids* (GCs). After their release,

GCs do all sorts of things that help us deal with an emergency: they boost glucose production, alter salt balance, increase cardiac output, and constrict blood vessels. At the same time, they beat a fast path up to the brain, where they regulate stress signaling. This either revs up or calms down the stress response, whichever is in our interest at the moment. Most important for understanding how the stress response can damage the brain, *GCs exert powerful actions on the temporal lobe to help us remember emotional events.*

Not all stress is an acute, emergency response. Stress can also be chronic. Consider the work of Robert Sapolsky, a brilliant, shaggy-haired Stanford professor who travels regularly to his camp in East Africa where he studies baboons. Sapolsky has shown that subordinate male baboons—those that are much put-upon by the dominant males and are often disappointed or denied when they seek to mate with females—are essentially in a constant state of stress. Their GC levels run high all the time, as with high-stress people. It's easy to visualize parallels to modern human society: being constantly put-upon, denied, or defeated can keep our GC levels way up. Childhood abuse, as an extreme example, can cause an excessive stress hormone response that lasts into adulthood; women who were sexually or physically abused as children produce up to *six times* the normal GC response to stress. Whether it's acute or chronic, stress turns on the signaling system that sends GCs shooting from the adrenal glands up to the brain.

GCs go to the brain. Now we can see why our stressed-out brain is really at risk.

The Tiger in the Brain: Glucocorticoids and Brain Damage

When glucocorticoids arrive in the brain, they go straight to the MTL memory system, especially the hippocampus and the amygdala. In effect, the GCs tell our memory system, "Look, this event has real survival value; you'd better remember it." But the influence of GCs is not always benign. Since these hormones are so powerful, stressful experiences sometimes raise GC levels beyond what our neurons can stand, resulting in damage to the memory-critical parts of the brain.

After a few days of moderately high levels of GCs, a rat's hippocampal neurons are more vulnerable to death; after a few weeks, the dense branches of the hippocampus begin to shrivel; and after a few months, brain cells begin to die. High GC levels also lead to atrophy of dendrites, loss of synapses, and finally neuronal suicide. The harsh impact of GCs on neurons becomes worse with aging. Furthermore, stress-induced hippocampal damage may be worst when the animals have no control over their situation; that is, memory cells suffer most when animals find themselves helpless, at the mercy of the fates.

Evidence is rapidly accumulating that humans too may experience lasting brain damage if we experience severe or prolonged stress. For instance, a study of eighty former Second World War and Korean prisoners of war (POWs) found that they had seriously impaired performance on measures of intellect. A study of Australian POWs compared 101 men who had been captured by the Japanese at the fall of Singapore in 1942, and held under horrific conditions for forty-two months, with other veterans who had not been POWs; it found a slight increase in dementia among the ex-POWs but a marked increase in Parkinson's symptoms. Interestingly, a different study of 4,684 ex–Far East POWs released in 1945 also showed a remarkably high rate of Parkinson's disease. This is intriguing because one of the places in the brain that's brimming with GC receptors is the basal ganglia—the exact area affected in Parkinson's. So it's possible that stress triggers different kinds of brain damage in different people, sometimes causing more problems with memory, and sometimes causing another kind of imprisonment—the Parkinsonian shackles of physical rigidity.

It's crucial to remember Twain's Maxim: people vary tremendously, including in their response to stress. Only *some* of those who go through hellacious experiences will be psychologically overwhelmed. Among them, only some will go on to suffer lasting effects. There are two main types of lasting effects after trauma: the first is depression; the second is *post-traumatic stress disorder* (PTSD), which involves recurrent, vivid, inescapable anxious thoughts about the traumatic experience. Anywhere from 5 to 25 percent of traumatized people will develop PTSD, and up to 25 million Americans are currently suffering from it—a huge group of people who spend their lives turning on a psychological spit over the fire of the stress response.

Looking at the brain scans of people with PTSD, scientists have made some startling discoveries. In one study of Vietnam combat veterans with PTSD, MRI scans showed 26 percent atrophy of the left hippocampus—an eye-popping amount of damage. Another study, this one examining women who had experienced childhood abuse and who later developed PTSD, revealed 12 percent atrophy of the left hippocampus. In both studies, the hippocampal atrophy showed up many years after the traumatic experience—more evidence that stressful life experiences sometimes lead to lasting brain damage.

The Goldilocks Effect

All this leads to one big conclusion: our stress response evolved to save our skins, but an *excessive* stress response may harm our brains. And this brings us to a biological concept called *the Goldilocks Effect.*

Remember Goldilocks, the adventurous little girl who enters the home of the three bears and finds the porridge that's "just right"? The Goldilocks Effect is a good illustration of a critical rule of human physiology. We need a "just right" amount of hormones and neurotransmitters; too little or too much, and we get sick. The Goldilocks Effect for stress hormones can be depicted with an inverted U-shaped curve (see Figure 5). At the far left end of the curve, an innocuous experience—like a brief meeting with a stranger at a party—leads to a weak stress response. The amygdala doesn't get fired up, and it doesn't boost memory for the event (which helps explain our terrible memory for names). At the far right end of the curve, a catastrophic life experience can lead to a massive stress response, which overwhelms the amygdala and may even block our memory of the event. All of the healthful benefits of the stress response, including emotional learning, work best in the *middle* of the curve, where excitement leads to a "just right" response, big enough to make us act re-

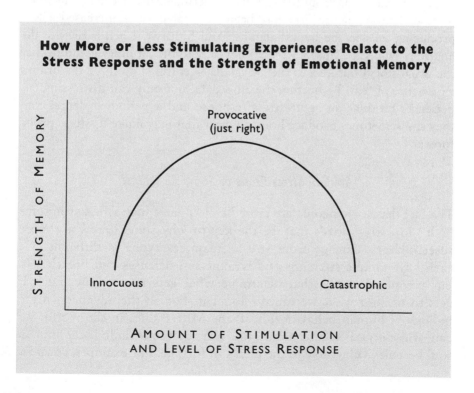

How More or Less Stimulating Experiences Relate to the Stress Response and the Strength of Emotional Memory

Provocative
(just right)

STRENGTH OF MEMORY

Innocuous

Catastrophic

AMOUNT OF STIMULATION
AND LEVEL OF STRESS RESPONSE

sourcefully and remember a threat, but not so big as to overwhelm us with terror.

Stress Can Be Acute or Chronic

There's been a great deal of research about the acute stress response, but scientists are still trying to figure out what happens with *chronic* stress, stress that persists for months or years, or that recurs again and again. Some of the most compelling research on chronic stress has been done by psychiatrist Charles Nemeroff of Emory University. He has proposed that when stress goes on and on, GCs may not be the main molecular demons. Rather, the problem may be overproduction of the hypothalamic hormone that turns on the stress response in the first place: corticotropin-releasing factor (CRF).

Nemeroff's evidence is persuasive. First, studies have revealed high levels of CRF in the spinal fluid of depressed people. Second, if baby rats are deprived of their mothers, they have lifelong increases in brain CRF levels. Third, sexually abused women, even if they're not depressed, have abnormally increased CRF responses to mild stress. If they are depressed, their CRF reactions to mild stress become astronomical, as high as those of patients suffering from the serious endocrine disorder called Cushing's disease. Fourth, depression has been associated with increased CRF-producing cells in the hypothalamus. And fifth, we'd better rewrite the anatomy books, because CRF goes not only to the pituitary gland (as per the usual story) but also to the *amygdala*—central station for the brain's experience of fear. By hurting the amygdala, not only can distressing experiences produce an acute stress response and a period of depression, they can sometimes produce brain changes that may make us stress prone forever.

Are You Stress Prone or Stress Resistant?

The fact that some people are more likely to have high stress symptoms under low stress loads may be the key to why some brains are more susceptible to damage from stress. Again, everyone is different. We each have unique strengths and weaknesses, defenses and breaches in our emotional armor that determine what gets to us, how much it gets to us, and what we can do about it. For all the advances in the biology of human behavior, for all the MRI studies in the world, we can still only speculate about the way that one individual human soul becomes vulnerable to the pricks of fortune. For example, consider the vicious cycle that ensnared—and nearly killed—a woman named Mary.

Mary's father was an alcoholic, yet she grew up to become a winner at high school track, a popular member of the band, a successful English major in college, and editor of the school newspaper. When she graduated, she snared a coveted cub reporter's job on a medium-size daily newspaper, and there found happiness in the arms of a devilishly handsome fellow reporter—until he left. She plunged into agony. She tried an affair; it made her feel worse, and she began to consider suicide. Seen in the simplest way, Mary had a stress response to the stimulus of a romantic catastrophe. But this simplification doesn't do justice to the unique mix of nature and nurture involved in her spiral into despair.

Mary's brain probably began forming its particular style of response long before she was born. She was affected by parental genes that influence temperament, perhaps by some of the same genes involved in her father's alcoholism, and by the hormonal milieu she experienced in the womb. It's even possible that the distress her mother felt about her father's drinking caused a release of excess stress hormones when she was pregnant with Mary, which modified the baby's developing limbic system in a way that made her a more sensitive child. Mary's infancy and early childhood were filled with conflicting signals, and the mixed affection and unpredictability of her father imprisoned her in a tug-of-war of the heart. This situation further influenced the growth of her brain's stress response systems before she could even read or ride a bike. Long before her first date or her first job, Mary's nervous system was primed to respond excessively to stress, as if she were suddenly forced to flee—a mental reaction that boosted stress hormones as if she were running for her life. (We might even wonder whether this predisposition to run from trouble could have played a role in her choice of high school sport.) As a result of these early influences, the loss of her boyfriend was not just any breakup. It was unassailable proof of a deep-seated dread: she was not worthy of lasting attention. This idea spun in her head like a malevolent top, tipping her off the stable platform of her life and into the mental maelstrom of major depression.

The point is that some people but not others are especially vulnerable to major depression and PTSD, and these may be the ones most likely to suffer brain damage. The slow dance toward big-time trouble has three steps. First, genes and intrauterine environment influence brain development in ways that make some people especially vulnerable to stress. Second, infants and young children may go through hardships, traumas, or possibly environmental exposures (such as to lead paint) that further affect the vulnerabilities of their brains. For example, sexually abused girls go on to become women with exceptionally high rates of depression, anxiety, and drug abuse. Third, an adult trauma provides that final push over the edge—which helps explain why Mary found herself, late one night, sitting in her car at an isolated beach with a bottle of pills and a vacuum cleaner hose taped to the exhaust, deciding which way to go.

Mary's case shows the danger of a positive feedback loop in the human psyche in which one neurobehavioral change increases the risks of another. Sleep deprivation, physical illness, pain, fatigue, and aging may act as burdens that make other stressors unbearable, tributaries joining the river of genetics and early-life events to form the final brain-threatening stress cascade. And now comes evidence of the ultimate feedback loop, a vicious cycle that makes stress and brain aging egg each other on: several recent studies have shown that Alzheimer's itself leads to a loss of control of the stress response. This potentially means that ARNAT increases our risk for a too-big stress response, which in turn accelerates the brain damage of ARNAT.

The Four Horsemen of Stress: Depression, Anxiety, Anger, and Low Self-Esteem

So who's at risk for stress-induced brain damage? Four major life-factors seem to determine whether we will face stress well defended or with our weapons hanging uselessly at our sides—that is, whether we are *stress prone* or *stress resistant*. The four horsemen of the stress apocalypse are: depression, anxiety, anger, and low self-esteem. Each has its own genetics, physiology, psychological background, and triggers. No two humans on earth are identical in the mix of these four factors, but the factors are at least somewhat predictive of who sways when a psychological earthquake happens and who gets flattened.

DEPRESSION

Everyone has periods of low mood or depression. But a *major depressive episode* is a serious psychiatric condition and one of the toughest stresses on this earth. When Mary went to the beach on that fateful night, she was deep in the black cauldron of a major depressive episode.

Major depression is not just sadness or grief or a brief downswing in the natural pendulum of mood. People suffering from a major depressive episode feel an almost indescribable pain. "I'd gladly lose a leg rather than go through that again," Mary said to me when she finally came to the clinic the year after she'd recovered. She had had all the classic signs: a very low mood for more than two weeks (in her case, seven months); a sense of being helpless to escape the pain of her life and hopeless about her future; a withdrawal from her friends and her job; the loss of pleasure in a beautiful day, in sex, in accomplishment. She spent some days nearly incapable of getting out of bed; on others she worked fitfully while trying not to cry in front of her co-workers at the newspaper. Her appetite was so poor that she often resorted to a random intake of tasteless snacks, and she lost twelve pounds in a month. She awakened at four A.M. most mornings, her head whirring with ruminations about her worthlessness and the absurdity of continuing life—until that night at the beach, when she sat in her car trying to decide how to kill herself.

Five to 12 percent of men and 10 to 20 percent of women will have a major depressive episode at some point in their lives. Of those, 15 percent will commit suicide. Psychological testing shows that depression hobbles memory, and PET scans show that it slows brain metabolism—both clues that this mood disorder is no friend to the central nervous system. Depression also takes quite a toll on the heart: a recently published study of almost 2,900 people in the Netherlands found that *minor* depression increased the risk of cardiac death by 50 to 60 percent, while *major* depression increased the risk by 200 to 300 percent!

Mary didn't kill herself. She was stopped at the brink by a fellow who happened by and thought she was having car trouble—and by some frail vestige of the will to live. Like many people who experience major depression, Mary finally began to feel an immeasurably slow, painful return toward normalcy. Yes, she "recovered." But did her brain?

About 50 percent of people undergoing major depression have high cortisol levels. If our cortisol is high enough for long enough, we probably suffer some degree of brain damage—and the first neurons to be lost are in the MTL memory center. Furthermore, by boosting GC levels, depression can make diabetes worse. In fact, recent research suggests that depression increases the risk of getting diabetes, and diabetes increases the risk for getting depressed. This diabetes-depression link is another vicious cycle by which stress can grind down neurons.

A recent study from Washington University School of Medicine in St. Louis found that people who had once been depressed, even if it was many years before, showed a 12 to 15 percent atrophy of their hippocampi—a scary sign that they'd permanently lost millions of memory cells. What's more, depression begets depression, and the first episode is rarely the last. Most patients have recurrent episodes, sometimes years apart, each one perhaps creating a risk for further brain injury. Because of this pattern, I propose that major depression be treated as a matter of medical urgency. Given the hot-off-the-presses news that stress can cause permanent brain damage, the high prevalence of major depression is a call to action. If you or someone you love has the classic signs, don't wait—get help.

Is *mild* depression also hard on the brain? Recent evidence says it is. In the renowned Nun Study, Snowdon found that nuns who had expressed more positive emotions in their youth tended to live the longest, while those who expressed more negative emotions had a higher risk of Alzheimer's. We should not leap to conclude that a simple cause-and-effect relationship exists between negativity and Alzheimer's. Nor can we assume that there's a simple solution. Physicians can't just advise people, "Don't worry, be happy—and avoid Alzheimer's." On the other hand, the evidence that low mood is bad for the brain should drive a serious re-assessment of our public health priorities. The value of mental health is not just a matter of life satisfaction; it may be a matter of neuronal survival.

ANXIETY

Another factor that contributes to our vulnerability to stress is anxiety. Again, the anxieties of everyday life—worrying about a test, a misplaced pet, an unexpectedly late menstrual period—are not the problem. The brain is most likely at risk only when anxiety climbs over a critical threshold where the stress response produces brain-toxic chemicals. Two things probably determine whether anxiety crosses this threshold: severity and duration. When anxiety is bad enough for long enough, a patient may qualify for a psychiatric diagnosis such as generalized anxiety disorder (GAD).

Felicia was the first patient I encountered who had a true case of GAD. She spent her life nearly trembling with dread. Most of the time she could pull herself together well enough to have a conversation, but her wild-eyed reaction to the sudden tick of a clock or a knock at the door gave her away. Felicia's anxiety meant that she was likely to have an excessive stress response to an event that would be manageable for most of us. In a city hit by an earthquake, she'd be the building to collapse. Fortunately, she responded to a carefully chosen medication. This kind of anxiety *might* be enough to cross that critical line toward brain injury; but given the current research, it's hard to say.

The research is much more clear about the brain-wounding potential of PTSD, which is considered a severe anxiety disorder. As already noted, brain MRI studies suggest that PTSD may be associated with a loss of hippocampal tissue. We also know that hippocampal cell loss is a hallmark of Alzheimer's disease. It's probably too simplistic to conclude, "PTSD causes Alzheimer's." A more likely scenario is that severe anxiety can damage the brain in ways that overlap with ARNAT, and increases the risk of late-life memory loss. In fact, *any* psychological condition that involves a severe stress response, especially if it skewers us on the spit of chronic or recurrent stress, may flood the brain with stress hormones and boost the risk of ARN to some degree.

Effective stress relief may pay major brain dividends down the line— one more reason to fight like hell to make sure that mental health benefits get fully funded in this era of tightfisted, half-baked managed care solutions.

ANGER

Fighting like hell brings us to the third horseman of the stress apocalypse: anger. From the evolutionary dawn of the brain, appropriate rage responses have had high survival value, but today the man who spends his life physically primed for a life-or-death struggle—as he climbs the corporate ladder, or fights his dispatcher for a better schedule, or edges ahead in rush-hour traffic—is not a survivor, he's a cardiac patient. As we have seen, the time-urgent type A person, the angry/hostile subtype in particular, is at high risk for coronary artery disease. He spends his life throwing his heart into a state of marginal function, in which it pounds hard in an entirely internal fight, a self-defeating battle that decreases cardiac output and elevates vascular resistance in a way that robs the heart of its own blood supply—a suicidal set-up for a heart attack and possibly, a stroke. The angry/hostile heart attack victim is usually a man, and he tends to be younger, heavier, and unhappier than other heart patients. And while we don't know for sure how many angry people are affected, the same fellow who spends life seething may very well also be burning up his brain.

LOW SELF-ESTEEM

The fourth horseman of stress is low self-esteem. Scientists are just beginning to study the health significance of high and low self-esteem, as well as the related issue of perceiving oneself as a success or failure. Studies show that in groups of apes, those low on the social totem pole have elevated cortisol levels and may live shorter lives. In contrast, a 2001 study of every Oscar-winning actor or actress since 1929 concluded that winning an Oscar was associated with a 3.9-year increase in life span! I don't want to leap to conclusions, but such studies offer clues that certain kinds of success, and possibly feeling good about oneself, may be beneficial to health, while feeling bad about oneself may be hard on the body. In psychological research, those with low self-esteem are often called *type D* for "distressed personality." Type D people have an increased risk for heart attacks, according to a recent study from Antwerp, Belgium. Since stress and cardiac risk factors are linked to brain cell jeopardy, it's worth considering whether people stressed by chronically low self-esteem may suffer some degree of harm to their brains.

For all the research, however, we should be wary of any categorization system that pigeonholes the infinite variety of human stress-responsiveness into a handful of personality types. Even the most stressful stimuli produce remarkable variations in response, and who knows who among us will sway and who will tumble? A cosmonaut who stayed in space for more than fourteen months was studied in depth; he experienced a great deal of stress and had brief attention problems, but once back on earth, he seemed to experience no lasting mental effects. One small but fascinating study even suggests a silver lining to trauma: psychologist Gary Capobianco asked fifteen survivors of plane crashes to complete questionnaires about their levels of distress and anxiety. Surprisingly, the survivors were *less* likely to display rash behavior or aggression than people who had never been in a crash. Thus, terrible stressors may occasionally put the rest of life in perspective—and grant survivors a sense of inner peace. Even more persuasive is the inspiring clarity of many survivors of the Holocaust. Although research clearly shows that Holocaust survivors are prone to PTSD, many *don't* have PTSD. The lesson is that we cannot presume to know how a particular stress will affect a person; some people, remarkably enough, can resist the stresses of the most nightmarish circumstances in history or imagination. For all the concern about the effects of stress on the brain, we need to balance it with the recognition that individuality is key, and *stress does not equal brain cell destiny*.

Taming the Tiger Within: Saving Your Brain from Stress

Every age from the Pleistocene to the present has confronted humankind with its own special crises, from starvation to plague to typhoons to war—and always and forever, the risk of heartbreak. What's different today, if anything, is the advent of some novel stressors. We are immersed in environments filled with challenges that we were not exactly designed for—from paperwork deadlines to rush-hour traffic—and many of us are caught up in a crazy modern time pressure that sets the hearts pounding and frays our nerves, just as the sight of a saber-toothed tiger once did. Ironically, many modern stressors demand the attention and clear-eyed judgment of our prefrontal cortex—the very part of the brain that's taken off-line by the stress response. *That's where the problem lies.* It's not that modern life is necessarily more stressful; rather, we have to respond to these stresses with a primitive arousal system that was designed for facing three-hundred-pound tigers, not four-inch-thick stacks of overdue work. In other words, cultural evolution has outpaced the evolution of the brain. By regularly revving up our GC-stress response *without allowing ourselves the explosive fight-or-flight physical relief we were built for,* our culture may be savaging our brains in new and interesting ways.

"Frayed nerves" may be more than a metaphor. Given what's at stake, we should no longer be complacent about the lunatic pace of modern life, reassuring ourselves, "Someday I'll stop to smell the roses." Our brains are running out of somedays. In addition, exciting new evidence shows that reducing stress hormones can truly save mammalian brains. Neurobiologist Heather Cameron at the NIH has shown that, if she blocks the aging-related rise in GCs, it will not only save the neurons the rat already has but restore the youthful rate of brain cell production! While we can't assume that humans get the same physiological benefits as rats, relieving stress in our personal lives may be an important factor in preserving the youthful vigor of our brains.

What, then, are we to do? Over the centuries, people have discovered a variety of ways to defend themselves from stress. The trick is to choose the stress-management technique that best suits your individual personality, coping style, and medical condition, as well as the severity of your stress.

MINDFULNESS MEDITATION AND WILLFUL RELAXATION

Mindfulness meditation is a state of detached observation and awareness of the contents of our consciousness. For some people, repeating a key phrase, or mantra, helps to maintain this state; for others, a certain body position, neutral background noise, or the smell of incense may facilitate it. Impressive research suggests that people who meditate may lower their resting blood pressure even when they're not actively meditating, may decrease their risk of heart attacks, and may be better defended against the recurrence of major depression. The evidence is so promising that, beginning in 1998, Congress gave the NIH $10 million per year to expand the network of mind-body research centers and to train health care providers in meditative techniques.

For all of the promise, however, we have to be realistic. The size of the benefit is variable, and not everyone gets it. That's the point about many mind-body therapies—big variations in individual response. Tom may get a major benefit, while Dick and Harry don't, perhaps because only a subgroup with particular genetic, physiological, and temperamental characteristics is suited to respond. Whether meditation can benefit the brains of those who have suffered severe stress is an open question. Meditation should absolutely not be the first approach for major depression, but some people under chronic stress, such as those with PTSD, may be able to use this method to good effect.

Willful relaxation is another alternative. The guru of medical relaxation therapy, Boston physician Herbert Benson, proposes that a mind-body "relaxation response" acts as the opposite of the stress response and is associated with decreased pulse, blood pressure, and anxiety. Many relaxation proponents achieve this state via progressive muscle relaxation—that is, concentrating on individual muscle groups starting from the forehead down, first tensing, then relaxing them, until they finally achieve a conscious state of overall body rest. Again, some solid scientific evidence suggests that willful relaxation can lower blood pressure in a lasting way. As with meditation, the size of the benefit varies, and who will get it is uncertain. But it's definitely worth considering.

Psychological stress-reduction methods such as meditation and relaxation therapy may well counter the effects of stress on the heart. Stress-reduction training may reduce the frequency of silent cardiac ischemia by 50 percent; in one study at Duke University, people who had cardiac ischemia during mental stress and went through stress-management training achieved a 75 percent reduction in later cardiac events such as heart attacks. Note that these methods seem to act primarily on the vascular part of the stress response—the first wave. For that reason, we can reasonably expect that they might reduce the risk of vascular brain damage. But anything that dampens the first wave might also be expected to reduce the second—the burst of GCs—so these methods may also help to protect the GC-sensitive MTL memory center.

Still, a couple of things temper my enthusiasm about these particular methods. First, stress-related brain damage is usually seen at the extremes of stress, where the brute force of physiology can outgun these gentle methods. Second, a strong element of belief is probably involved in the success of these methods. This is not to say that they won't work; they will, to some extent and for some people. But frankly, the methods may work best for a subgroup of people who are temperamentally inclined to put faith in them.

AEROBIC EXERCISE

Aerobic exercise, on the other hand, has repeatedly been proven to be a great way to reduce stress. Unlike meditation and relaxation therapy, exercise requires little belief in its effectiveness. Just do it, and the benefits will come. By channeling internal stress into external action, it actually provides the most natural possible form of stress relief. Think of it this way: humans evolved to burn off the bad effects of stress by doing exactly what the stress response prepared us to do—fling ourselves into physical activity. *That's* what our bodies and brains are crying out for when they're filled with the nervous energy of stress. All we have to do is oblige them. A 1999 British review of more than thirty scientific summaries of the subject reported that aerobic exercise enhanced mood, improved self-esteem, and reduced anxiety. Even if your stressful situation is not controllable (a mean boss is going to keep on being mean), and even if you are not going to burn off that pent-up energy in the way people evolved to (by helping the mean boss into a lake), you *can* at least take control of your own body, and taking control through exercise may be among the most potent methods of relief.

Some stressors are so severe and some people are so stress prone that stronger medicine—literally—is called for. Despite the blood-pressure-lowering effects of relaxation therapy and exercise, people who have hypertension will often need an antihypertensive medication. Type A time-urgent sorts, especially angry/hostile type A's, are in especially serious need of blood-pressure management. Actually, a combined approach may be best; a study at the University of British Columbia found that exercise *plus* stress management was more helpful than exercise alone for controlling vascular reactions to stress. To get these benefits, we need to seek out a compassionate doctor who takes an overall approach to cardiovascular health, including diet, lipid control, aerobic exercise, smoking cessation, and—if needed—carefully individualized choices of antihypertensive medications (see Chapter 10). The more stress prone we are, the more important it is that we be willing to make deliberate efforts to reduce stress in our lives.

PSYCHOTHERAPY

By "deliberate efforts" I mean serious business—beyond the quick and easy salvation we hope for from a weekend retreat, a course in yoga, transcendental meditation, or even regular exercise and blood-pressure medications. Those of us who are both stress vulnerable and heart vulnerable must be willing to undertake a major life reassessment to save our brains. We may need to change jobs. We may need to move.

We may also need to seriously examine—usually with professional help—whether a relationship is not only psychologically painful but potentially physically harmful to our heart and brain. In short, we may need to pull free of the brain-frying effects of stress with the help of psychotherapy. *Psychotherapy* is a term that gets tossed around so loosely, it's hanging on to meaning by its fingernails. (In California it could be offered by an overreaching beautician.) So I want to be clear that I'm talking about expert help by a trained professional, usually a licensed clinical psychologist or a board-certified psychiatrist, although many social workers, marriage and family counselors, rabbis, ministers, and family doctors can also make a terrific difference. Still, even among those who are well-trained, it can be hard to find the right therapist. Some people who need help may give up the search after a dissatisfying encounter with an unsuitable clinician. But just because the first mechanic you see fails to fix the brakes on your car doesn't mean you can keep driving safely. There are many expert and compassionate therapists out there, and it can be life-saving to make the right connection.

Good psychotherapy does not just boost self-esteem—it changes brains. PET scan studies clearly show improved cerebral blood flow after therapy for depression. Insight-oriented psychotherapy may literally rewire the brain, boosting the synaptic connections that are adaptive and damping the maladaptive ones. Theoretically, therefore, it seems very likely that good psychotherapy can reduce the risk of brain cell death when it helps to fight off major depression or PTSD. Counseling or therapy can also reduce the risk of vascular problems that put the brain at risk. For example, psychological counseling has been shown to prevent second heart attacks in patients with depression. And New Orleans cardiologist Carl Lavie found that adding expert counseling to rehabilitation of sixty-five hostile heart attack victims led to a 40 percent drop in the rate of hostility—not to mention bigger-than-average gains in health.

Sometimes the people who would benefit the most from psychotherapy are the last to seek it. Men may be especially reluctant to get help—perhaps because it is contrary to their evolutionary imperative to maintain a flexed-muscle facade of invulnerability. Therapists can never push reluctant people into therapy, but they can hope that the word gets out: it's not just your insight that's at stake; it's your brain.

MEDICATIONS

Finally, there are psychotropic medications. And two conditions that are very likely to benefit from carefully chosen psychotropic medications (ideally used in combination with good psychotherapy) are major depression and PTSD.

The standard medication for major depression is a selective serotonin-reuptake inhibitor, or SSRI. Medications such as fluoxetine (Prozac), sertraline (Zoloft), and paroxetine (Paxil) definitely make more serotonin available to the receiving neuron. However, recent research suggests that these drugs may also fight depression via their effects on a parade of other brain chemicals, including norepinephrine, opiates, neurosteroids, CRF, and even the pain-related protein called Substance P.

Regardless of the mechanism, these compounds work. A massive 1999 review by the Agency for Health Care Policy and Research found that 50 percent of patients improved on these drugs, compared with 32 percent on placebos. In other words, they aren't perfect and they don't work for everyone, but they do the job better than anything else we know of—and they're remarkably safe.

HERBS

For about 2000 years, it has been suspected that the little yellow flower called St. John's wort could relieve depression. In 1994 Germans consumed 66 million doses of St. John's wort looking for relief. A review of clinical studies published in the *British Medical Journal* in 1996 reported that St. John's wort was about 55 percent effective. Soon after (and with a tremendous marketing push by supplement makers), U.S. sales of this herb went through the roof. But does it actually work? Most of the studies reviewed in that much-quoted British article were too brief to draw solid conclusions; they mixed patients with very different types of depression, and none compared the herb head-to-head with any SSRI. A large study published in the *Journal of the American Medical Association* in 2001 was more careful to focus on people with moderate to severe depression—those who are most at risk from a delay in effective treatment if they used this herb rather than a proven antidepressant. After eight weeks, St. John's wort was only as effective as a placebo. Side effects such as nausea and skin rashes affect about 15 percent of those who try this herb.

We should not conclude that St. John's wort is useless. In fact, there's probably a chemical in this herb that could help some people with depressive symptoms, once we find it, identify it, and purify it. Until then, I advise the following: for major depression, don't use it. There's too much at stake, especially when we have such gratifying evidence that our modern treatments are lifesavers. For minor depressive feelings, the first step is not an herb, it's a visit to a doctor. Diabetes, anemia, sleep disorders, thyroid disease, and other ills can all manifest as depression, so people who treat themselves without a doctor's evaluation may simply be delaying getting to the root of their problem. After a doctor's evaluation, and with a doctor's supervision, some might make the personal choice to experiment with St. John's wort for mild depression.

SAMe

Another potential mood-helper is SAMe (pronounced "Sammy")—short for S-adenosylmethionine. SAMe hit the alternative medicine market like a ton of bricks in 1999, when two companies began importing large amounts to the United States to be sold as a dietary supplement. It has been touted as the best nonprescription antidepressant since St. John's wort. SAMe possibly activates the brain's serotonin system. More than 1,500 patients have been involved in controlled trials of SAMe for depression, and based on a summary of many small studies, it seems to be roughly as effective as low doses of the old tricyclic antidepressants—making this a very promising agent. But the studies have been too small, too brief, and too variable to allow confidence that SAMe is a safe and effective treatment. Give scientists a few more years to study this intriguing drug before you experiment on yourself for mild depression.

Mild depression is not likely to hurt your brain. In fact, a single episode of major depression may sometimes be followed by complete brain recovery. The real risk is from recurrent or long-standing depression—a set-up for brain cell suicide. Although I shy away from the phrase because it does not do justice to the great yin and yang of neurobiology and life experience, some people probably truly have a "chemical imbalance" that makes them prone to depression. For this subgroup, it is justifiable to con-

sider long-term—even lifelong—SSRI treatment. The goal is not to wrestle the beast of depression back into the bag every time it gets loose, but
to keep the knot tied tight.

Another nasty creature may also benefit from prescription medications:
PTSD. Recent double-blind studies have convincingly demonstrated that
SSRIs can reduce its symptoms. In the first controlled published study of
Prozac in nonmilitary patients with PTSD, 59 percent were very much improved, versus 19 percent of those who took a placebo. Based on four
large studies, in 1999 the Food and Drug Administration's psychophar-
macologic drugs advisory committee voted to make Zoloft the first drug
ever approved for the treatment of PTSD.

This news is terrifically encouraging for the 8 to 10 percent of people
suffering with PTSD and is further evidence of an essential biological
link between the most devastating forms of anxiety and depression.
It also suggests that doctors may not want to wait until PTSD is established before leaping in with help. Since perhaps 20 percent of victims
of catastrophic events will go on to develop PTSD, the medical community may want to consider mounting a rapid reaction force to stave
off the worst of the stress response. In fact, some psychiatrists have
proposed that anti–stress-response medications should be added to
the catastrophe-management programs brought in after earthquakes,
plane crashes, terrorist bombings, and personal disasters. Experimental
CRF-receptor antagonists have been developed that doctors might
give to a child after he's burnt, a soldier when he comes back mute
after a firefight, or a woman after she's been raped. The idea is not to
block the memory, but to block the vicious self-reinforcing cycle of
PTSD before it can even get started.

Overall, the health care system must adopt a completely new attitude
about severe stress. It's time to shatter the conventional myth that stress
is the province of the weak, or an unavoidable response to life's harsh
lash. We should treat major depression as a matter of medical urgency.
The health care system should act quickly to protect trauma victims from
the evolution of PTSD. It must battle depression and PTSD like the
plagues they are, fully train every physician to recognize them, provide
clear education about them as part of the public health promotion
process—and fully cover the expense of treatment. *Not* treating them
properly comes very close to cruelty.

Unfortunately, in spite of their expertise and devotion, primary care
physicians often fail to detect stress and depression in their patients.
Who can blame them? With patient-a-minute managed care, doctors

themselves are often basting in the pressure cooker of chronic stress. Health care consumers have to battle the HMOs to make the phrase *office visit* mean more than "May we photocopy your insurance card?" and "Here's your prescription." And doctors need to make depression and stress screening a routine part of primary care evaluations. This single change in the health care system might not only rescue millions of people from anguish but provide a huge dividend in the form of memory and brain-cell protection down the line.

CHAPTER 6

Is Your Job Eating Your Brain?

Perpetual devotion to what a man calls his business, is only
to be sustained by perpetual neglect of many other things.
ROBERT LOUIS STEVENSON

Stressed beyond the limits of our evolutionary design, propelled by the seductive myth that wealth ensures happiness and the fear of falling behind
in a race whose purpose we can't recall, some of us are at risk of contort-
ing ourselves into the most perverse of positions: paying for our jobs with
our minds. In fact, we are designed by the grace of a million forks in the
evolutionary road to protect ourselves and our loved ones from tigers and
famine, to have lots of sex, and to nurture the children that result. We are
not designed to face endless days of mind-numbing repetitive work, to expose our bodies to bizarre chemicals in the name of earning a living wage,
to serve a hierarchy that denies us the autonomy that befits the successful
completion of puberty, or to mask our emotions in the name of "job security" while floods of catecholamines deluge our heart and glucocorticoids
deluge our brain, without the natural relief of physical action.

Generally speaking, "going to work" is not what we evolved to do, but
can it actually harm our minds and brains? That's the question we will answer in this chapter.

We have already seen that our brains suffer when exposed to too much
stress, especially stress that is overwhelming or leads to a sense of defeat
or submission, depression, or PTSD, all of which elevate glucocorticoids.
The peak in the middle of the inverted U-shaped curve for the stress response tells us that a certain amount of stress is stimulating, and that
learning is optimized at midcurve, when stimulation is "just right." The
same is true for job-related stress and stimulation: the ideal is located at

midcurve, between too little and too much brain stimulation. *Insufficiently* demanding work—work that fails to engage the brain, work that's boring, stultifying, and numbingly empty of cognitive challenges—may actually be hard on the brain; indeed, some evidence shows that brains degenerate when denied a regular on-the-job workout. But *excessively* demanding work may also contribute to the total lifetime injury that our brains sustain. Additionally, certain jobs create special hazards by exposing us to brain-toxic substances.

Put simply, there are three ways we can optimize the health of our brains through work: (1) by seeking a mentally stimulating career; (2) by avoiding on-the-job exposure to neuron-killing substances; and (3) by following our fight-or-flight instinct when it comes to extreme job stress. The best kind of jobs are those that reward us with a sense of purpose, a feeling of mastery, and that just-right stimulation of the brain.

Mental Stimulation and Memory Loss

Certain occupations are associated with a higher risk of dementia in general and of Alzheimer's disease (the most common type of dementia) in particular. In a careful study of the risk factors for dementia in Stockholm, Sweden, epidemiologist Laura Fratiglioni compared ninety-eight Alzheimer's patients with 266 normal elderly people and found that men who did manual work had more than twice the average risk of developing Alzheimer's. This risk was independent of the men's educational level, which is known (as we'll discuss in Chapter 18) to affect the frequency of Alzheimer's. When Fratiglioni controlled for education, she showed that male manual workers were *five times* as likely to get dementia as people doing other kinds of jobs.

French researchers did a larger study: they gave memory tests to 2,720 elderly residents of Bordeaux and found that farmers, domestic workers, and blue-collar workers had two to three times the risk of poor memory in old age compared with managers and professionals. Again, this finding was *independent of education,* which suggests that spending one's life in a job lower on the socioeconomic totem pole may be bad for the brain.

In classifying jobs, some researchers refer to "high-" or "low-level" jobs, but there's no foolproof way to rate the "level" of a job. Money is obviously not the best measure; a high school physics teacher may have a life filled with intellectual stimulation, but may earn less than a truck driver. Nor does job title necessarily tell us who has a "high-level" job; two people who both have the title "manager" may have vastly different levels of on-the-job cognitive demands. People choose their jobs for many different reasons, and we can never assume that the job defines the person's intellect. Some football players have Ph.D.s. Yet for practical purposes, researchers are forced to use some kind of system to classify jobs, so they often use the "job level" categories devised for the U.S. Census Bureau. For instance, when epidemiologist Yaakov Stern at Columbia University followed 593 nondemented older people to see who would develop Alzheimer's, he divided his subjects according to the Census Bureau categories for "low-level" and "high-level" jobs. Over a four-year period, Stern found that low-level employment was associated with 2.25 times the risk of developing Alzheimer's.

A better—although still imperfect—way of comparing jobs is to estimate how cognitively demanding they are. Studies from Bordeaux, France, and East Boston, Massachusetts, suggest that more cognitively demanding occupations actually protect us against Alzheimer's. All this research supports an ancient and irresistible theory: use it or lose it. (As we will see in Chapter 18, this research on jobs and brains is just the tip of that particular iceberg; we have lots more proof that a mentally active lifestyle protects against memory loss.)

The Columbia University group dug further: they took all the folks who'd had low-level educations and divided them into those who went on to low-level jobs and those who went on to find high-level jobs. The result was that those with *low educations* who nonetheless managed to spend their lives in *high-level jobs* had only a slightly higher risk of Alzheimer's than the high-education/high-job group—suggesting that *a good job may compensate for a low-level education in terms of the brain's long-term risks*. This brings us to the *cognitive reserve hypothesis* of brain aging.

The cognitive reserve hypothesis states that some people are better protected against the brain-drain of ARNAT because they start out with more robust brains. That is, at some point before aging-related neurodegeneration begins, they develop a brain that is bigger than others, or has more neurons, or more synapses, or otherwise can stand up better to the corrosive effects of ARN. For example, babies born with larger heads appear to be less likely to get Alzheimer's. But you don't have to start out with a big head to build lots of neuronal connections; you have lots of opportunities to make new synapses, and the more connections you build during your life, the better you will likely withstand the assault of ARNAT. A well-built brain gives you a *brain reserve* that protects you against memory loss even if you lose some synapses, just as a lot of money in the bank protects you from poverty if you face a big expense. One way to build neuronal connections is by education; another is by securing an intellectually challenging job.

Other research at Columbia University used SPECT scans to study cerebral blood flow in Alzheimer's patients. A big drop in blood flow indicated relatively severe Alzheimer's. But if these low-flow patients had spent their lives working at complex jobs, they were still able to perform at a surprisingly good cognitive level—a strong hint that a high-level job may help us build brain reserves to resist the cognitive effects of ARNAT. In another fascinating study, researchers at University College London scanned the brains of London taxi drivers, who famously have a remarkable knowledge of the maze of London streets, learned during a rigorous two-year training course. The posterior hippocampus of these drivers— thought to play a central role in spatial navigation—was found to be bigger than that of nondrivers. What's more, the longer the drivers spent on the job, the bigger this brain region became. The conclusion is almost irresistible: insufficiently stimulating jobs leave us brain poor, while stimulating jobs leave us brain rich.

This discovery takes us a step beyond the theory that brains require regular activity to maintain function. Rather than "use it or lose it," we arrive at the entrancing new possibility: "Use it a lot, and make it bigger."

We have to be cautious about this conclusion, however. First, some studies from Canada, Europe, and Egypt have failed to find any link between low-level jobs and Alzheimer's. Second, we're not sure what it is about low-level jobs that may hurt the brain. It may be a lack of intellectual stimulation; it may be the stress, or the year-in-year-out feeling of being a put-upon subordinate; it may be that such jobs increase exposure to other risk factors that are really responsible for ARN (such as solvents or pesticides or lead or minor head traumas) or that the hobbies and off-duty pursuits popular with those doing low-level jobs damage brain cells. Attributing to all "manual workers" a specific kind of life is a dangerous (and perhaps biased) oversimplification. But there's probably *something* about *some* jobs (or the folks who tend to choose them) that truly increases the risk to the brain.

So let's move on to the second of the three on-the-job factors that may affect the health of our brains: environmental toxins.

Workplace Hazards and Memory Loss

Occupational health, it might be argued, was invented by Bernardino Ramazzini, an Italian doctor who in 1700 published a book called *On the Illnesses of Work*. He noted that painters, wrestlers, gravediggers, and surgeons, among others, had special health risks that were closely related to their occupations. In most cases, the health risk was obvious: painters inhale volatile fumes, wrestlers throw one another violently to the ground, gravediggers and surgeons are exposed to infection. To some extent, people doing these jobs still face the same risks today (although professional wrestling has perhaps lost in trauma what it's gained in dramaturgy). But today thousands of exotic chemicals are used in workplaces, and it has become trickier to show a cause-and-effect relationship between these workplace hazards and dangers to human health, in part because it's hard to know which ones may compromise our brains.

In the United States, as in most developed countries, a host of agencies monitor workers' on-the-job contact with potentially harmful substances. The Environmental Protection Agency (EPA), the Food and Drug Administration (FDA), the National Institute for Occupational Safety and Health (NIOSH), and the National Center for Toxicological Research (NCTR) all attempt to test virtually everything we might be exposed to at work. They test thousands of substances on tens of thousands of rodents every year. For each one they try to establish a Lethal Dose 50 (LD50), or the level of exposure to a substance that will reliably kill half the animals exposed. And they do their best to test for brain damage, putting those little rat brains under the microscope to look for strokes, brain tumors, and other signs of injury.

Three big problems prevent these watchdog agencies from successfully protecting our brains. One problem is the immense number of new compounds that move from the chemistry lab into the environment every year (more than 50,000 organophosphate insecticides alone have been synthesized), and there's no way to test all of them. The second problem is that government agencies may have been looking for the wrong indicators of trouble. An LD50 tells us what it takes to kill a rat, but the level determined to be lethal in the rat may be completely different from the level that might produce damaging effects in humans, especially subtle behavioral damage. Equally important, lab rodents live only about two to three years, making them poor models for brain damage in humans, who may experience low-level exposures to toxins over several decades.

The third big problem is that rats don't get Alzheimer's, so *none* of the thousands upon thousands of rodent experiments done by these agencies can tell us whether the substances we're exposed to at work might accelerate aging-related neurodegeneration. That will change soon: neurobiologists now have created mutant mice with some of the brain and behavior features of Alzheimer's, and they will be able to use these mice to screen chemicals for ARNAT-like effects.

In the meantime, we can look at workplace chemicals that have already been linked to human neurodegeneration, and other chemicals that may hurt our brains.

Table I

Nervous System Toxins and Toxicants

NATURALLY OCCURRING NEUROTOXINS (PARTIAL LIST)

TUBOCURARINE   Also called *curare*, a toxin from the plant *Chondodendron tomentosum*; blocks motor neurons and causes paralysis; is used as an arrow poison, and to achieve immobility in general anesthesia

BOTULINUM TOXIN   A toxin made by the microorganism *Clostridium botulinum*; found in improperly canned food; affects the nerve-muscle junction, causing severe weakness and death in most cases; is used clinically to reduce muscle spasms and even reduce facial lines

TETRODOTOXIN   A toxin absorbed via consumption of improperly prepared puffer fish, called *fugu* in Japan; blocks motor and sensory nerve impulses, causing respiratory paralysis and death in most cases

PFIESTERIA PISCIDIA   A microorganism found in fish off the East Coast; has caused memory loss among fishermen in Chesapeake Bay.

HUMAN-MADE NEUROTOXICANTS (PARTIAL LIST)

PESTICIDES   Many types; exposure is common in farming, spraying of fruit trees, houseplants, pests like ants, bees, and roaches; these agents often overexcite the cholinergic system, producing neuropathies, weakness, and mental status changes

NERVE GASES   Many types; the most common work just like pesticides, overexciting the cholinergic system, often to the point of death

SOLVENTS   Many types are used in different industries with different clinical effects, including:
ALIPHATIC HYDROCARBONS: gasoline, kerosene, propane, butane, pentane, hexane, heptane, and octane
ALIPHATIC HALOGENATED HYDROCARBONS: chloroform, carbon tetrachloride, methylene chloride, methyl chloride, trichloroethylene, tetrachlorethylene, vinyl chloride

continued on next page

ALCOHOLS: methanol, isopropyl alcohol
GLYCOLS: ethylene glycol
AROMATIC HYDROCARBONS: benzene, toluene, polycyclic aromatic hydrocarbons (PAHs)

METALS

ARSENIC	Used in copper smelting and semiconductor manufacture; found in some herbal remedies; interferes with oxidative metabolism; causes muscle spasms, seizures, agitation, memory loss
LEAD	Used in battery production, foundries; jewelry production; found in old painted surfaces; interferes with many enzymes; causes fatigue, headaches, anxiety, memory loss
MANGANESE	Used in battery production, fertilizers, gasoline additives; causes free radical damage, especially to cells in the substantia nigra and basal ganglia; causes a parkinsonian disorder
MERCURY	Used in the production of chlorine, paints, paper; also found in thermometers; inhibits many enzymes and harms membrane function; causes emotional instability, memory loss, spasticity
THALLIUM	Used in rat and ant poisoning, infrared detectors, and photocells; causes numbness, weakness, respiratory paralysis, emotional instability, and delirium
ZINC	Used in many manufacturing processes; affects excitatory transmission; causes irritability; contributes to excitatory neurotoxicity

Table 1 lists some neurotoxins and neurotoxicants. A *toxin* is a poison that occurs in the natural environment. For example, *Pfiesteria piscidia*, a microorganism found in fish off the East Coast, is associated with memory loss among some fishermen in Chesapeake Bay; it is a neurotoxin. Natural neurotoxins are listed in Table 1 partly to show that some of nature's most dangerous inventions have important clinical uses—which gives us reason to believe that scientists will eventually discover other natural substances that can help save the brain. A *toxicant,* on the other hand, is a man-made poison, a substance that may or may not have been designed for a benign purpose. As you read down the list, you may very well see a *neurotoxicant* you've been exposed to at some point in your working life.

All of these toxicants can hurt the nervous system, although it remains to be seen which are the very worst as accelerants of brain aging and memory loss. But in recent years, scientists have become suspicious that pesticides probably increase the risk of Parkinson's disease, and that solvents may increase the risk of Alzheimer's.

PESTICIDES AND PARKINSON'S: THE GENE CONNECTION

I first saw Mr. Toledo from across the intensive care unit. A big, sunburned, gentle-looking Hispanic man, he lay silently in bed, surrounded by his family, staring at the ceiling with a look of utter terror. He couldn't move. A machine had taken over for his paralyzed diaphragm. A couple days before he'd helped out a neighbor on a San Bernardino ranch, fighting the white flies in his orange trees by spraying insecticide. He did just what it said to do on the instructions: "saturate the foliage to the point of run-off." He wore no mask and no gloves, and his personal pride compelled him to do a complete job. During the night after he sprayed, he was a bit restless; he told his wife he'd had a bad nightmare. The next day she noticed that his words were slurred. Two days after he sprayed, Mr. Toledo was in a helicopter on his way to L.A.'s "Big County" hospital, where he began a two-month stay in intensive care.

That was back in 1990. At that point, I thought I knew a little about organophosphate insecticide poisoning. I knew that it was the most common type of acute pesticide poisoning; that it was chemically almost identical to nerve gas poisoning; that it blocked the breakdown of acetylcholine and pounded neurons with excess neurotransmitters to the point that they couldn't receive signals; and that even when the resulting paralysis wore off, it could leave a patient with a year of depression and memory loss. What I didn't know at the time was that exposure to pesticides may eventually cause Parkinson's disease.

Neurologists have long suspected that some environmental toxin contributes to Parkinson's. Study after study has teased us with provocative findings: higher rates of Parkinson's have been reported among farmers, among those who live in rural areas, among those who drink well water, and among welders. But these results were inconsistent. Then in 1993 epidemiologists at the Oregon Health Sciences University reported that people who were exposed to pesticides had almost *six* times the average risk of developing early-onset Parkinson's disease. Within just a few years,

IS YOUR JOB EATING YOUR BRAIN?105

studies from Kansas, Illinois, California, Germany, Spain, and Hong Kong all confirmed the link, showing that those who had been exposed to pesticides—and in some cases, herbicides—were more likely to develop Parkinson's later in life.

But we still need to know why some people who spray their fields or roaches or houseplants or fruit trees develop this terrible disorder, and others don't; and why some people with *no* exposure (that we're aware of) nonetheless develop the disease. Here neuropharmacologist J. Timothy Greenamyre at the Emory University School of Medicine made a crucial contribution by observing, first, that people with Parkinson's often have a big decrease in activity in an important part of the mitochondrial energy system called Complex I. As a result, their oxygen metabolism is off-kilter, too many free radicals are released, and neurons in the basal ganglia and brainstem are damaged by excessive oxidation, like fenders on rusty cars. We might say that parkinsonians have rusty brains. Greenamyre then observed that the common pesticide called rotenone (which is often touted as a safe, natural alternative to other pesticides and is used to kill "nuisance" fish in drinking water reservoirs) severely inhibits Complex I. Remarkably, animal studies show that rotenone hurts Complex I activity in the very same cells that die in Parkinson's. Greenamyre put these facts together and came up with this thoughtful idea: people who are unlucky enough to have *both* a genetic deficiency in Complex I *and* repeated exposure to Complex I–inhibiting pesticides may have the highest risk of Parkinson's.

Unraveling how genes and environment interact to harm the human body and brain is the medicine of the future. And Greenamyre's conclusion possibly gives us a whole new way to prevent Parkinson's. We may now have a scientific basis for finding people at risk, for developing drugs that can boost Complex I activity or defend it from environmental attack, and for revising occupational exposure laws.

In practical terms, it means that *all* of us should take steps to avoid Mr. Toledo's dilemma. Until we have a crystal-clear understanding of who's most in danger, which pesticides are riskiest, and what exposure levels we need to avoid, we should reconsider our casual use of these chemicals to protect our plants and rid our homes of bugs, and instead think of them as the nerve gases that they really are. Saving our brains from the collateral damage of suburban chemical warfare may mean avoiding contact with these toxicants as much as possible.

SOLVENTS AND ALZHEIMER'S: THE GENE CONNECTION

In the terrifying depths of World War II, when secrecy was a matter of national survival and haste was a given, Lockheed built its top-secret

Advanced Development Projects unit on a flat patch of industrial wasteland in Burbank, California, just downwind of some notoriously odoriferous chemical plants. That's why the unit came to be known as the Skunk Works. Various cutting-edge military aircraft were born on that land, including the F-117 Stealth fighter. In the course of this work, machine parts were routinely dipped into tanks of perchloroethylene; hexavalent chromium was used in painting; and various other toxic solvents, resins, and epoxies were discharged into the air and ground, leaching 130 feet through the soil to contaminate the vast drinking water reservoir deep beneath the San Fernando Valley floor.

The Skunk Works is nearly defunct. Many buildings are dark and off-limits, and the notorious supersecret research center has become a notorious Superfund toxic waste site. Its legacy lives on not only in defense advances but in the suite of billion-dollar lawsuits that have been filed by former employees and Burbank residents. The plaintiffs contend that the Skunk Works exposed them to toxins that, among other injuries, damaged their brains. But they may have underestimated the threat, since scientists have only just realized that solvents may increase the risk of Alzheimer's.

The volume of solvents produced each year in the United States is enormous, about forty-nine metric tons. These chemicals are used in many industries—in paints, in printing inks, as dry-cleaning agents, and as degreasing agents—with the result that up to 4 percent of the U.S. population, or 9.8 million people, are exposed in their workplaces every day. The crucial but still-unanswered question is whether the tens of millions of people who have had this kind of exposure at some point in their lives are more likely to develop lasting neurobehavioral problems.

Let's consider just one group of agents: the volatile organic solvent under scrutiny in the Skunk Works litigation, perchloroethylene (PER), and its chemical relatives, trichloroethylene (TCE), methylene chloride, and carbon tetrachloride. These solvents are used in many applications, but PER and carbon tetrachloride are especially common in dry cleaning. These chemicals are also found in well water (used for bathing and showering), and they may possibly leach from the vinyl lining of pipes that are used to deliver public drinking water supplies. In humans we have yet to determine exactly how much exposure is too much, but we know that these solvents can cause lethargy, mood swings, irritability, intellectual slowing, memory loss, psychosis, anxiety, and delirium. In three studies of employees of dry-cleaning shops, those exposed to PER were found to have significant deficits in reaction time, perceptual speed, and memory compared to non–dry cleaners. Based on one of these studies, researchers estimated that lifelong behavior problems might follow exposure in the air at less than 50 parts per million for just three years—*well below the currently accepted occupational exposure limits.*

Human studies have suggested that solvent exposures cause atrophy of the frontal lobes and cerebellum (seen on CT or MRI scans), changes in the white matter (visible on MRIs), and diminished cerebral blood flow (seen on SPECT scans). Dow Chemical Company has claimed that microscopic studies of rats exposed to PER show no lasting injury to the brain, but other laboratories have reported a loss of key proteins in the frontal cortex, hippocampus, and brainstem. On balance, even though we have much more to learn about the human impact of solvents, the weight of the evidence suggests that *some* solvents are bad for brains, and that *some* people who have experienced exposure suffer permanent brain damage with behavioral symptoms.

Are people exposed to solvents more likely to get Alzheimer's? The evidence is mixed: a 1991 review of three studies found no connection between solvent exposure and Alzheimer's, and a more recent study at the University of Southampton in England found no association between dementia and an occupational history of painting, printing, or dry cleaning. Unfortunately, neither the mental condition nor the solvent exposure of the subjects was accurately established in this last study. Then in 1995 epidemiologist Walter Kukull looked at almost 200 Alzheimer's patients, comparing them with healthy older people. Those who had had occupational exposures to solvents had more than twice the risk of developing Alzheimer's, and in men alone, the risk rose to *six times* normal.

So we're back in the mysterious zone of mixed results. And just as in the case of Parkinson's and pesticides, the answer may lie in the interplay between genes and environment. New research by Kukull and his colleagues suggests that solvents may hurt the brains of some people more than others because of a genetic variation in solvent-detoxifying ability. Kukull focused on one particular type of solvent called *polycyclic aromatic hydrocarbons* (PAHs), which are produced by the incomplete combustion of fuels (meaning that they're steadily coughed out of engines to waft around our cities). Kukull found that on-the-job PAH exposure by itself was associated with only a modest increase in the risk of Alzheimer's, but people who were exposed to PAHs *and* carried the gene for the inactive form of the glutathione-s-transferase enzyme had almost *three times* the risk of Alzheimer's.

Again, genes and environment seem to be working together. While the evidence for a pesticide-Parkinson's link is stronger than the evidence for a solvent-Alzheimer's link, in both cases our risk for cerebral disaster may be greatest if we have the unfortunate combination of an inadequate genetic defense and too much environmental exposure. Still, some environmental experiences may counter others: we've seen how an intellectually stimulating job possibly boosts our brain reserve. Now there's evidence from the Canadian Study of Health and Aging that people with more education may have brains that can better resist the damaging effects of glues and pesticides! Such discoveries get us closer to the intimate dance of nature and nurture that really determines the future of our brains.

MODERN-DAY MILL-REEK: LEAD AND ZINC

"There is a place in Scotland where madness is sometimes induced by the fumes of lead," wrote Benjamin Rush, America's first surgeon general and a signatory of the Declaration of Independence. "Patients who are affected with it bite their hands, and tear the flesh upon other parts of their bodies. It is called by the country people mill-reek." Almost 200 years later, heavy metal poisoning remains a major cause of behavioral disorders. Somehow, despite centuries of knowledge that lead causes mental disturbances, lead poisoning of children is still endemic in some cities, and it probably accounts for a significant proportion of developmental delays.

Early exposure can unquestionably lead to lasting cognitive problems; a British study found that people with a history of lead intoxication as children had cognitive impairments fifty years later. But it's not just the sensitive brain of the child that can suffer. In 2000, researchers at Johns Hopkins University reported a study of 535 former lead manufacturing workers; at an average age of fifty-six, these men showed excessive decline in both memory and manual dexterity. We have a pretty good idea of how this could have happened: in animal experiments lead blocks LTP, the electrical signature of learning. In humans we know that lead kills hippocampal neurons—the very neurons associated with memory loss in Alzheimer's. The bottom line is that lead and brains don't belong together.

How much lead is damaging? Elisabeth Koss and Robert Friedland at Case Western Reserve University studied 185 Alzheimer's patients with special attention to their probable lifetime on-the-job lead exposure. Overall, they found that lead exposure was associated with two and a half times the usual risk of Alzheimer's. But the group that had the highest levels of exposures had *seven* times the usual Alzheimer's risk—a remarkable increase. There's also evidence that exposure to *combinations* of lead and iron or copper boosts the risk of Parkinson's disease. We've long known that we need to save children's brains from lead. Perhaps it's time to get the word out to workers, employers, and government agencies, that saving brains from lead is not just for kids anymore.

Pesticides, solvents, and lead are just the first chapters in the Russian-novel-length tragedy of occupational exposures and brain damage. Each of the toxicants listed in Table 1 is one more furtive character in this massive drama. We instinctively shy from the noxious fumes of kerosene, turpentine, gasoline, lighter fluid, and glues reeking of toluene; this instinct helps us to protect our brains, insofar as we can escape exposure. And those of us who remember, as children, breaking open thermometers to play with that slippery, shiny stuff may now pause to consider how deadly a neurotoxicant mercury is. But there's one more character that we ought to mention, since some may not expect it to play such a dark and dangerous role: zinc.

Zinc is all around us. It's found at fairly high levels in much of the soil on the earth's surface, as well as in foods from fish to milk to nuts. One of many Jekyll-and-Hyde molecules in the brain, zinc can either help or hurt brain cells. But can too much zinc exposure on the job hurt the brain in lasting ways?

We're not sure. Dentists, welders, iron workers, and radiology technicians are all exposed to zinc, but to date there's no proof that such occupational zinc exposures cause dementia. It just hasn't been studied. On the other hand, new lab research definitely shows that elevated zinc levels kill neurons: under some conditions zinc can trigger quiet neuronal suicide (apoptosis) or explosive neuronal death (necrosis). So we have to be concerned that chronic contact with zinc may represent a previously unsuspected cerebral peril. I'd hold off on those zinc lozenges for the time being.

The solution to all of these on-the-job miasmas is in many ways beyond the control of the individual. Sure, you can try to dodge exposure to the obvious poisons. But millions of workers around the world are unwittingly exposed to hundreds of thousands of potentially brain-robbing substances each day. Knowing the safe levels is not your job; it requires a tight collaboration between science and government. Every public health problem comes down to cost versus benefit, so the question becomes just how much we should spend to discover the role of on-the-job poisons in American mental health. As NIH funding swings up and down with political fortunes, there needs to be a sensible reappraisal of the distribution of money and research effort. I predict that an objective accounting would reveal a shocking underfunding of environmental causes of dementia. If that's the scientific consensus, the next step is to shine the big searchlights of the NIH, NIOSH, EPA, the Centers for Disease Control, and the National Science Foundation on the skulking brain-poisoners of behavioral neurotoxicity.

Job Stress: Are We Working Too Hard?

In the mid-nineteenth century, German sociologist Ferdinand Tönnies was among the first to point out that the grand efficiencies of "advanced" society might have a downside. He wrote of *Gemeinschaft* versus *Gesellschaft*: the localized, community-rooted, cohesive work of pre-industrial society (the "it takes a village" philosophy) versus the competitive, soulless, striving society of industrialism, and the risk of a loss of personal identity in the modern workplace. Tönnies had a rather starry-eyed view of the preindustrial village, but his observations about modern working life still bear consideration from the point of view of stress. Why, some have asked, do Americans and others in highly competitive societies need to drug themselves up into unnaturally high gear with coffee for work, then drug themselves down with alcohol at the end of the day? Have we evolved a work ethic that is so at odds with the human nervous system that we can fulfill it only with the help of mind-altering substances? Are we working too hard or too long, or at jobs too much at odds with our natural instincts, for the good of our brains?

A study by the Institute for the Future found that workers in *Fortune* 1000 companies average twenty-four phone calls, fourteen e-mail messages, and eleven voice-mail messages a day. These facts were cited as evidence that technology, for all its labor-saving promise, is actually making our days unnecessarily stressful. The problem, in my view, is not so much that we are inundated by *technology* as that we are inundated, period.

How hard do Americans really work? We are indeed working more than we did a generation ago: in 1999, Americans worked an average of 42 hours per week, about 3.5 hours more than in 1979. The phrase "lunch hour" has become a joke; we spend an average of 29 minutes at lunch, most often at our place of work rather than going out (let alone that antique pleasure, going home). Some professionals, such as doctors in training, young associates in big law firms, and certain high-tech, political, and entertainment workers, log ridiculous numbers of hours on the job. Still, the hours themselves may not be the best measure of stress (although that's clearly a problem for some). Thirty-two hours as an intensive-care-unit nurse is perhaps much more stressful than forty-four hours as a tennis pro, and the young mother who gets credited with thirty-eight hours of weekly "work" is rarely credited in these studies for the additional fifty-two busy hours she devotes to child care. So job stress is not just the number of hours—it is part of a complex social transformation, an imposed division of life into big chunks of work and little chunks of everything else. Those work chunks may sometimes pay us psychological dividends in gratification and self-esteem, but they also impose a cost.

FIFTEEN TONS, WHAT DO YOU GET?

One recent study reported that 76 percent of American workers complained of job stress; a 1992 survey by Northwestern Mutual Life found that 40 percent of people considered their work to be "very or extremely stressful"; and a 1997 Yale University study found that 29 percent of workers feel "quite a bit or extremely stressed at work." So it's difficult to know the precise rate of real heart-thumping, brain-robbing stress, but there are surely many people with on-the-job stress so severe that it could put their brains in jeopardy.

What are the most stressful occupations? That's a tough one. One problem is the enormous number of jobs—the *Dictionary of Occupational Titles* of the U.S. Department of Health and Human Services lists more than 12,000 types of employment. Another problem is that there are so many ways to measure job stress: psychologists use the "Job Stress Survey," the "Occupational Stress Inventory," the "Maslach Burnout Inventory: Emotional Exhaustion Scale," and even the "Mutilation Questionnaire" (to assess the psychological impact on workers handling human remains after catastrophes or wars). Police work may be found to be highly stressful on the first scale, and urban school teaching highly stressful on the second, making a fair comparison of the stressfulness of teaching versus police work impossible. As a result, arguments about whose job is the most stressful get about as far as those locker room debates about which sport is tougher, marathon running or pro football.

Despite these limitations, academic studies consistently rank certain jobs as highly stressful. Table 2 lists some of these.

This list is by no means exhaustive; nor is it meant to rank stressfulness scientifically. It simply illustrates a key point: many different jobs can be stressful—white- or blue-collar, safe or dangerous, well-paid or not. Furthermore, job categories themselves don't tell the whole story. Someone doing a "high-stress" job may be happy and content, while someone in a supposedly less stressful job is completely stressed out. What makes a job either teeth-grindingly stressful or soul-satisfyingly rewarding goes beyond occupational titles.

Table 2

High-Stress Jobs

Soldier in battle

Disaster relief worker (especially those who recover bodies)

Military trainee in basic training

Public schoolteacher

Astronaut

Nurse (especially in intensive care, cancer, burn, HIV, and some pediatric wards)

Air traffic controller

Professional working with the mentally disabled, mentally ill, or victims of head trauma

Sex worker (male or female prostitute)

Short-haul bus or taxi driver

Social worker

Airline pilot

Deep-sea fisherman

Hard-hat diver

Factory worker doing a monotonous, rapid, repetitive task

Farmer on a small farm

Policeman or policewoman

Firefighter

Emergency medical technician

Attorney (especially a new associate in a law firm)

Physician (especially one in training, or transitioning to managed care)

Flight attendant (especially on long-haul routes)

DEMAND AND CONTROL

One impressive theory that gives us a better understanding of job stress is Karasek's Job Strain Model. The Karasek model essentially says that the most stressful jobs involve an imbalance in demand and control. A job that makes high psychological demands but gives the worker relatively little control or latitude to make decisions is a stressful job. *High-demand* jobs are competitive and difficult, involve deadlines, require attention to many tasks at the same time, and put us into potentially awkward personal contact with supervisors and co-workers. *Low-control* jobs involve a lack of personal choice in activities and scheduling and a lack of autonomy in decision making. High demand with low control can be a deadly combination.

Consider the two waves of the stress response (discussed in Chapter 5). In the first wave, adrenaline shakes up the heart and vascular system, boosting our risk of hypertension, heart attacks, and strokes. In the second wave, cortisol and other glucocorticoids may kill off hippocampal neurons. There's evidence that job strain whips up both waves of the stress response.

In multiple studies in which working people have been hooked up to self-triggering ambulatory blood pressure monitors, those with high-demand, low-control jobs have had the highest blood pressure. Shift work, overtime work, twelve-hour days, and noisy workplaces also boost the risk of hypertension. And job strain's impact on blood pressure does not go away at the end of the workday; people with high strain during the workday tend to have high blood pressure all night as well. What's more, the longer a person works at a stressful job, the better his or her chance of developing permanent hypertension. This fits with speculations about the genesis of hypertension: early on, we emotionally respond to stress with a temporary boost in blood pressure; after years of repeated boosts, physical changes occur in the blood vessels that make them less resilient so that hypertension becomes permanent. The cardiac consequences are predictable: in a study of working men in Sweden called the SHEP study (Stockholm Heart Epidemiology Program), the combination of high demand and low control was definitely associated with heart attacks. The Japanese have a word for it: *karoshi*—"death from overwork."

Interestingly, high demand by itself does not seem harmful to the heart. One study of job stress evaluated 102 members of the Danish parliament, and while these legislators had great job demands, they also had more control over their jobs than others. They showed no increase in risk factors for cardiovascular disease. Similarly, nurses who have more unit tenure, professional experience, and position level—essentially, more control—have lower job strain. So it's not just the high demands of a job, it's the demand/control imbalance that seems hard on us. Job strain of this type may also lead to a high intake of fatty foods by men, high body mass index in women, increased smoking, high serum cholesterol, high fibrinogen in women (raising the risk of blood clots), a fall in tissue plasminogen activator (a protective factor against strokes and heart attacks), and a narrowing of the carotid arteries.

How many of us fit this profile? Among 2,889 white-collar workers in Quebec, 20.5 percent were found to have high job strain. This means that, roughly speaking, one-fifth of workers are at risk for job-stress-induced hypertension and heart attacks. The burning heart of the matter is that *when job stress provokes hypertension, the effects on the brain are po-tentially devastating.* Hypertension is the main risk factor for strokes, and, as we've recently discovered, *hypertension also increases the risk of Alzheimer's.* An increased risk for a stroke and for memory loss is quite a price to pay for going to work.

That's just the first wave of the stress response. Then comes the second wave—the glucocorticoid surge.

GLUCOCORTICOIDS AT WORK

The boys get off the bus at U.S. Army Ranger School ready for the toughest eight weeks they've ever imagined. They're carefully selected, young, healthy, muscular—ready to wrestle sharks. Still, they don't quite realize what they're in for. That makes them perfect subjects for the stress research that the army has been conducting for years. They are plunged into tight, unfamiliar quarters with strangers and are driven far beyond exhaustion by thousands of push-ups, interminable runs, icy swims, and live-fire drills. They are insulted, berated, browbeaten, and denied normal diets, privacy, sleep, self-determination, or sympathy. Army researchers found that, during training, the recruits' cortisol-to-DHEA ratio—per-haps a better measure of stress than cortisol level alone—increases sub-stantially and doesn't recover even days after the training ends. Since glucocorticoids such as cortisol can kill neurons, the Army Ranger re-search suggests the kind of physical and mental challenges (not to men-tion constant verbal abuse) that may put the brain at risk.

Other studies have found increased cortisol levels among police offi-cers, long-distance bus drivers, air traffic controllers, men who are forced to work at a pace they can't control, and men or women who lose their jobs. Cortisol is even elevated in some people who have high levels of job satisfaction but face special stresses, such as surgeons. A change of jobs, long hours, rotating shift work, being either forced or forbidden work overtime, rapid repetitive work, workplace noise, interpersonal conflicts, lack of support from a supervisor, and a perceived risk of workplace vio-lence—all have been reported to magnify stress and may sometimes cause GCs to pour into the bloodstream, creating a state of cerebral jeopardy. And now there's evidence that job-related GCs can actually chew away at the size of the brain:

Kwangwook Cho of the University of Bristol Medical School in En-gland studied job stress among flight attendants—healthy women in their twenties who had worked for an international airline for at least five years. Their routes and schedules varied: some crossed more than seven time zones with less than five days off in between, while others had more time off. The first group, stressed by chronic jet lag, had not only higher cortisol levels than the more rested group but *smaller temporal lobes*. Women in their twenties with job-stress-related brain atrophy!

In summary, job stress can hurt neurons via both the first and the second wave of the stress response; the more control we have at work, the better we may be able to dodge this deadly hormonal duo. (Being in control at work is itself no guarantee that one's brain is safe: even a president of the United States may develop Alzheimer's.) Job stress is one of the potentially modifiable threats to the health of the brain.

Working Women and Stress

As Twain's Maxim alerts us, everyone is different, and dozens of factors determine the final impact of job stress on one's brain. Genetics, social support, stage in the life cycle, and personality may all shift us up or down the stress scale. So can gender. To a large degree, job stress is not sex-specific, but two aspects of work create special stresses for women: dual roles and sexual harassment.

DUAL ROLES

Linda Luecken and her scientific team at Duke University Medical Center studied 109 women who worked at a large company. They found that those women who had at least one child living at home excreted significantly more cortisol in their urine—evidence of severe stress—regardless of their marital status or social supports. Findings such as these make us wonder about job-stress-related brain injury among working mothers.

Thanks to the sexual revolution, a new American socioeconomic reality has surfaced. Between the 1960s and the 1990s, the United States went from a minority to a majority of women in the workforce. Society finally began breaking down the granite walls that barred women from the life-enhancing benefits of career gratification. Great new freedoms have emerged; progress has been made toward income parity between men and women; gender stereotyping of jobs is waning; glass ceilings are beginning to crack; and highly qualified women have ascended into previously sacrosanct male bastions, altering Western society probably forever. In many respects, this transformation is a long-overdue correction in the pace and direction of social evolution. From the neurobiological point of view, women may see enormous benefits: the mental stimulation and emotional satisfaction of a career may contribute to the neuronal resilience that seems to defend against aging-related neurodegeneration. And yet for many women the immediate effect is a higher level of stress—not exactly what one might have hoped for, given what we've said about job satisfaction and stress.

Why are so many women so stressed? One reason: for all of the revolutionary progress in society's discovery of the equal worth of the two sexes, women remain, on the whole, the primary child-caregivers. In 1965 only 25 percent of mothers with young children went to work, but by 1997 the figure had jumped to 65 percent. At the start of the twenty-first century, *77 percent* of college-educated mothers aged thirty to forty-four go to work. Men have caregiving instincts, tender feelings for children, and a sense of responsibility for their offspring, yet women have still been expected to be the primary child-caregivers and homemakers. Married working women do more housework than their husbands, spend more time with the children, and are more likely to pack the school lunches, attend parent-teacher conferences, and rush home when the child gets sick.

Working moms often report feeling torn apart: worried about their children when at work, and worried about their jobs when at home. But this stress seems to have a somewhat different effect on married mothers than on single mothers: a Canadian study points out that when married mothers take a job, they get a boost in self-esteem that is counterbalanced by increased job-related stress. When they lose a job, their stress levels are moderate, because the stress of job loss is counterbalanced by relief. But single working mothers pay a higher price in both situations. When they take a new job, regardless of the financial gain, their stress level remains high—as it does when they lose a job. Despite these differences, the overwhelming majority of research comes down to an important, common-sense finding: working women with children often feel stressed by their double-duty lives. And that stress has biological consequences.

Working women with job stress—especially those with children—have been shown to have higher blood pressure and increased risk for long-term hypertension over working women without job stress. They have increased production of adrenaline and cortisol. They smoke more, gain more weight, and have more preterm births, and among higher-level occupations they have an increased rate of pregnancy-related hypertension. Based upon what we know about stress, many of these vascular and hormonal changes may be precursors to cerebral injury. For a small but real minority of women, these stresses will play a significant role in accelerating aging-related brain change. From the neurobiological perspective, then, we must be concerned that some working women in every social stratum, especially working mothers and most especially single working mothers, face increased risks of job-stress-induced brain jeopardy.

Of course, the solution can't be to go back to the 1950s. Instead, we must strive to make the workplace more accommodating to working mothers, with more flexible hours, use of high technology that enables work from home, and rock-solid job security during family-related leaves. We should also find ways to support fathers in becoming more fully engaged in child care—a goal that may require not just changes in the structure of work, but a gradual, multigenerational raising of consciousness about the natural rewards men derive from childrearing. Many practical considerations and ingrained attitudes stand in the way of such social advances. But until such changes are made, women may continue to pay a high cerebral price for their dual roles.

Dual roles are not the only problem facing women. Sexual harassment continues to be the dirty secret of the working women's revolution.

THE ABUSIVE WORKPLACE AND THE HUMAN BRAIN

A shocking number of women experience unwanted propositions, repeated requests for dates, sexual insults, touching, coerced sexual activity, or even rape—sometimes by males who are their peers and sometimes by males who are in positions of authority and take advantage of their power with hints of promotions and threats of dismissal. On average, about half of all working women report unwanted sexual attention on the job. Men too are victims of harassment, although the proportion of men reporting unwanted sexual attention at work is much lower, about 15 percent.

Sexual harassment is abusive no matter who experiences it, and it is only one of a number of kinds of abuse that people may suffer in the workplace. From churlish peers to unfair superiors to sexual coercion, jobs can only too frequently become a form of torture. When epidemiologist Judith Richman studied almost 2,500 university employees, she found that 58 to 78 percent of both men and women reported abusive or demeaning behavior, entirely apart from unwanted sexual attention. The interpersonally abusive workplace can turn the daily commute into a ride to hell, as verbal aggression, physical aggression, humiliating treatment, and isolation or exclusion destroy whatever gratification might otherwise come from a job.

The health consequences of an abusive workplace are serious. Sexual harassment is associated with high levels of depression and PTSD. Harassment and abuse are associated with high blood pressure, increased drinking, drinking with escapist motives, drinking to intoxication, prescription drug use, increased smoking, and attempted suicide. At this point in our story, the effects on the brain of this kind of stress are obvious.

Sadly, the solution to the problem of the abusive workplace is not so obvious. Agencies such as the Occupational Safety and Health Administration (OSHA) and NIOSH are charged with protecting the health and safety of workers; maybe it's time for them to look beyond risks such as falling wrenches and recognize that "occupational safety and health" includes the broader need to detoxify the experience of working for the good of the human brain. Part of the responsibility lies squarely in the lap of the employers, but, for better or for worse, most of the solution to workplace abuse will continue to depend on individuals gathering the courage to act on their own behalf. Some people—either out of unconscious compulsion to self-abuse or extreme economic necessity—may feel utterly powerless to escape when they find themselves in jobs from hell. However, there are almost always escape routes. Work up that résumé and try to get out fast. Or else fight back via complaints to management or the legal system. Either response—fighting or fleeing—is better than stewing in brain-damaging hormonal juices. Remember, if you turn your anger inward and stick it out at an abusive job, you may be slowly killing your brain.

"Going to work" is an unnatural act.

If we compare the opportunistic hunter-gatherer lifestyle for which the human brain evolved with the strict, clock-based structure of work in our postindustrial age, the difference is astonishing. We have plunged so deeply into the "going to work" lifestyle that it will take a socioeconomic revolution—probably gradual, incremental, and tied to new technology—to give people of both sexes anything like the freedoms of self-scheduling work we enjoyed in the Pleistocene.

In the meantime, you might ask yourself whether your work feels natural to you. How often does your heart pound on your job—and how often is that from excitement, and how often from stress? How often do you sweat, not from heat or labor but from bitter frustration? How often do you revel in the satisfaction of your work, the sweet delight of a job well done and a mission accomplished, observed, and confirmed by your peers? How often are you tormented by frustration that you can't do it all, or by the thought that perhaps you shouldn't be doing any of it? Does your job let you pet your dog or teach your child? Does it let you stop to smell the roses? It's perhaps a new idea in the field of preventive medicine, but the way we feel at work may play an important role in the future of our brains.

As our society evolves from the industrial age to the information age, we have a chance to rethink the very basic structure of gainful employment. Indeed we must rethink it, because if we don't, we may become a nation of disgruntled souls, daydreaming of being forest rangers as we clench our jaws and hypnotize ourselves with our CPUs. While recognizing the constraints of economics, it's time to recognize the powerful workings of human biology as well. It's time for a new model of life success, a model that balances the human pleasures of love and work and play. People who feel fulfilled get more than a nice day—they may be saving their brains.

CHAPTER 7

Can Sex Hormones Keep You Smart?

In a little-noted experiment in 1952, 30 elderly women in a nursing home in Missouri volunteered for a clinical trial. Fifteen received a placebo; the other 15 received estrogen. After six months, verbal memory significantly increased in the estrogen-treated group but not in those given placebo. This discovery was essentially ignored.

Flash-forward to 1983. Victoria Luine, a young neuroscientist working at Rockefeller University, found laboratory evidence that estrogen improves the function of the exact type of neurons that deteriorate with aging and Alzheimer's. Based on this discovery, physician Howard Fillit conducted his own small clinical trial. He gave estrogen to an eighty-year-old Alzheimer's patient named Elsa. Within months Elsa not only showed improvement in her memory but was also more alert and sociable—so much so that she received a marriage proposal from her poet-boyfriend. Fillit applied for grant money to expand his clinical studies of the cognitive benefits of estrogen. He was told that his idea had "no scientific merit."

The researchers in Missouri and at Rockefeller were proposing a paradigm shift, a reconceptualization of the very idea of estrogen, and the resistance they encountered was very strong. "Estrogen is a female sex hormone," was the conventional wisdom. "It influences *sexual* behavior, not memory."

Modern biology has unveiled a much more colorful picture. Estrogen is not just for females, it's not just a hormone, and it's not just for sex. Estrogen *does* affect memory. In fact, it has an incredible ability to nourish, modify, protect, and heal brain cells. Armed with a better understanding of the biology of behavior, neurologists are now working hard to determine whether estrogen—or other closely related hormones—can save women's and men's brains from strokes, memory loss, and Alzheimer's. They are asking, put simply: can sex hormones keep you smart?

Estrogen Is a Hormone and More

It's time to reframe our understanding of estrogen. First, estrogen is not a single molecule; it's really four different molecules, although the estrogen we talk about most often is the one called E2, or *estradiol*. All four estrogens are *steroid hormones,* built on a backbone of cholesterol, so they are all incredibly similar in size and shape, even if they do wondrously different things.

Although we call estrogens "hormones," this label underestimates their amazing versatility. Generally speaking, hormones are chemicals that are squirted out by glands, then journey along the long and winding road of the bloodstream, to arrive at last at their target organ. They are the chief messengers of the endocrine system, the body's low-speed communication system (as opposed to the high-speed nervous system). While estrogens are squirted out by glands, they probably can also be made right at their place of work—for instance, by neurons in the brain. This means that they may have previously unsuspected rapid effects on behavior.

Estrogens are not just "female" hormones, and androgens (such as testosterone) are not just "male" hormones. *Both* sexes make *both* types of hormones, since every human being uses the same chemistry set. First we make cholesterol. We then convert cholesterol into *cortisol*, or *DHEA* (see Chapter 8), or *testosterone*. It's testosterone that then gets converted into estradiol, the body's main estrogen. Curiously enough, estrogens come from testosterone. The main hormonal difference throughout the body and brain is simply that women make more estrogens and less testosterone, while men make more testosterone and less estrogens.

Up until menopause, the ovaries manufacture most estrogens in women. But estrogens are also manufactured in some other parts of the body, including the fat tissue of breasts, buttocks, and thighs; the adrenal glands, those versatile pinkie-size hormone production centers perched atop our kidneys; and even within the brain itself. As menopause is about to begin (during the *perimenopausal* period), the ovaries make less estrogen, which creates a state of estrogen withdrawal. Yet even after menopause, the body continues to release estrogens from its alternative production sites. This may be evolution's way of assuring that women continue to get at least some of the benefits of estrogen—a kind of natural *estrogen replacement therapy* (ERT). Some women produce much more estrogen after menopause than others, but even those who produce the highest levels of natural, postmenopausal estrogen cannot achieve hormone levels nearly as high as those achieved by women who take estrogen replacement pills.

When estrogen arrives at its target cells, it slips through the outer cell membrane, dives down through the jelly of the cytoplasm, arrives at the nucleus, and binds to a very picky receptor that will bind *only* with estrogen and estrogenlike substances. The minute it lands on its receptor, estrogen activates genes that change the basic functions of the cell. For many years scientists spoke of "the estrogen receptor" as if there were only one. That receptor is now called the *alpha*-receptor, and it's found mostly in the uterus, breasts, and brain. In 1996 researchers at Sweden's Karolinska Institute found a new receptor by sheer luck. They were looking for a testosterone receptor in the prostate gland, an unambiguously male organ; instead they discovered a new type of estrogen receptor, now called the *beta*-receptor. We now know that the brain contains both alpha- and beta-receptors, and these brain estrogen receptors may be deeply involved in many *cognitive* as well as sexual behaviors.

So we may be selling estrogen short when we call it a sex hormone. Sure, it plays a crucial role in sexuality and reproduction, but it also has many nonreproductive effects. Which brings us to the fascinating question of estrogen's role in brain and mind.

Sex and the Single Brain

> There is no female mind. The brain is not an organ of sex. As well speak of a female liver.
>
> CHARLOTTE PERKINS GILMAN,
> WOMEN AND ECONOMICS (1898)

When Charlotte Perkins Gilman asserted that "there is no female mind," she was partly right and partly wrong. On the one hand, we should applaud her effort to debunk sexist prejudices, those sad old claims that females inevitably have weak intellects or are mentally unstable because of mood changes associated with their menstrual periods. On the other hand, we need to keep the thumb of ideology out of the eye of science. Contrary to Gilman's claim, there *is* a female mind in the sense that the average woman has brain structures, brain functions, and cognitive skills that are measurably different from those of the average man. Estrogen helps to determine these differences.

From the earliest weeks of fetal development through the last days of adulthood, estrogen is crucial mortar for the assembly of a healthy brain. In both men and women, it controls neuron birth, synapse building, and neuronal suicide. It also helps to determine *brain sexuality*, meaning all the big and little differences between male and female brains. Those differences are extremely interesting and are crucial to the survival of the species. Some behavioral differences, of course, are due partly to social programming: hidden-video studies have shown that a man will toss a baby in a blue blanket into the air like a football, and cuddle a baby in a pink blanket like a china vase, suggesting that sex-specific nurturing gets going essentially from birth. But other behavioral differences between boys and girls seem to be due to an astonishing array of sex differences in the brain, both in structure and in function. And some of these cerebral sex differences may ultimately explain one of the key mysteries of medicine: why women are more likely than men to develop Alzheimer's disease. The gross anatomical differences between male and female brains do not really explain why women are more susceptible to Alzheimer's. Instead, it's the microscopic and chemical differences that probably explain this mystery.

For instance, men probably have more neurons than women; a recent Danish study found that men had 16 percent more cortical neurons—an average of 23 billion versus 19 billion. But as Harvard neurologist Albert Galaburta put it, "What does it mean to have more neurons? It means nothing. What's important is the architecture of the circuitry." In that regard, women's brains may have *more connections per neuron*. This may be evolution's brilliant way to make the most of a smaller brain, and an explanation for the fact that, in spite of men's brain size advantage, overall intelligence in men and women is essentially identical. Still, this evolutionary trick of giving women more connections per neuron may have a drawback: any condition that causes neurons to die off—ARNAT/ Alzheimer's, for example—could potentially lead to more severe problems for women because for each neuron they lose they also lose more connections.

Sex differences also exist in neurotransmitter systems. Men may have a 50 percent higher rate of serotonin synthesis than women, and since serotonin is crucial for mood, this difference may help explain why women have a much higher lifetime rate of depression (a risk factor for memory loss).

Furthermore, estrogen controls a sex difference in the basal forebrain, which is the brain's main source for the neurotransmitter acetylcholine. Loss of cells in the basal forebrain, and the resulting loss of acetylcholine, is closely related to memory loss in Alzheimer's. Bruce McEwen at Rockefeller University has reported that taking the ovaries out of a female rat, depriving the rat of estrogen, leads to dysfunction of these very acetylcholine-making cells and a decline in memory. Restoring estrogen rescues these crucial cells and improves memory. While we must always be cautious when we leap across species to reach conclusions, studies such as this one suggest that the female brain depends on estrogen to keep up the flow of memory-crucial acetylcholine. This connection would provide a clear explanation for women's higher risk of Alzheimer's: menopause profoundly drops estrogen levels, which drops acetylcholine levels—which drops a bomb on the brain's memory circuits.

Results such as these demonstrate clearly that estrogen is very important for memory. And modern neuroscience has added a host of further exciting findings that reveal how estrogen helps the brain. It builds synapses smack dab in the middle of the hippocampal memory system. It boosts NMDA receptors, the receptors we use for learning. It improves brain blood flow. It acts as an antioxidant. Like a force-field, it protects brain cells from the free radicals unleashed by glutamate and beta-amyloid, two of the nasty toxins that cause brain cell death in Alzheimer's (see Chapter 4). It revs up brain cells to make more receptors for *nerve growth factor* (NGF), a kind of brain fertilizer needed for robust neuronal growth (see Chapter 14). Even more exciting, Dominique Toran-Allerand of Columbia University has shown that estrogen not only *assists* NGF, it may act *as* NGF. This big news means that estrogen *itself* may be an essential substance for brain cell growth and maintenance. If we combine all these effects with its probable benefits to the vascular system, estrogen is no mere "sex hormone"; it's the warrior princess of brain defense!

Estrogen replacement therapy (ERT) is actually the most prescribed medication in the United States. Clinical ERT is primarily prescription doses of conjugated equine estrogen (the horse equivalent of human estradiol), sometimes combined with progestin. The most common estrogen dose is 0.625 mg per day, although low-dose therapy of 0.3 mg per day is increasingly popular and may work just as well for many purposes. Every year about 12 million women are prescribed estrogen by itself (so-called "unopposed" conjugated estrogen), and 8.6 million are prescribed the combination of estrogen plus progesterone. Very soon the market will be crowded with synthetic estrogens—so-called SERMs, or selective estrogen-receptor modifiers. Some SERMs—including tamoxifen, raloxifene, and droloxifene—are already FDA-approved, and many more are in the pipeline, all of which will offer women more options. But since the new SERMs may have different benefits and risks from conventional ERT, and since the vast majority of research on ERT is based on studies of natural estrogen, that's what I'll focus on here.

Given the rapid increase in the world's postmenopausal population—and given the looming epidemic of dementia—it's *essential* that we answer the question: does ERT really save the brain from Alzheimer's?

Estrogen and Alzheimer's

Victor Henderson, a professor of neurology at the University of Arkansas, is Lincoln tall and Lincoln thin, with close-cropped dark brown hair and a

sense of humor dry as a desert bone. Victor and his colleague Annlia
Paganini-Hill, of the department of preventive medicine at the University of
Southern California, took a trip to Leisure World, a huge retirement community in southern California. There they studied the Leisure World Cohort,
a group of 8,877 older women who agreed to be involved in aging research.
When Victor and Annlia assessed the Leisure World Cohort, they found
something quite interesting: the longer a woman had used estrogen replacement therapy and the higher her dose, the lower her risk of Alzheimer's.

This was exciting news. The study was published in 1994. Since then a
mountain of evidence has confirmed the association. Richard Mayeux of
Columbia University found that women who used ERT were less than
half as likely to develop Alzheimer's. A study at Johns Hopkins University
that followed women for sixteen years found that ERT cut their risk of
Alzheimer's in half. The Baltimore Longitudinal Study of Aging, the Italian Longitudinal Study of Aging, and a large study conducted by the
Mayo Clinic all showed that women who used ERT had a lower risk of
dementia. In recent results from the Cardiovascular Health Study, 2,716
women were given annual tests of cognition; over six years of follow-up,
those who'd never used ERT declined almost twice as fast as those who
had. Neurologist Kristine Yaffe of the University of California performed
a meta-analysis of the research available in 1998; combining ten studies
that all included large groups of women, she found that there was *a 29
percent reduction in the risk of dementia for those taking estrogen.* In addition, entirely apart from the question of whether ERT can prevent the
dreaded problem of Alzheimer's, two large studies showed that older
women who used ERT had higher mental status scores than their peers
who didn't.

As exciting as all this evidence is, Victor Henderson cautions that we have
to hold on to our hats. The various study results are not uniform; generally
speaking, the benefit seems most consistent among younger postmenopausal
women (which possibly means that women need to begin taking ERT
quickly after menopause to get a benefit). Moreover, the lifestyle of the
women taking ERT may account for part of their cognitive advantage:
women who take ERT tend to be better educated than women who don't,
so education itself may be the major brain-saver (see Chapter 18).

Furthermore, the research contains a very curious contradiction that
might be called the Estrogen Paradox.

The Estrogen Paradox

There are two completely different sources of estrogen. *Exogenous* estrogen, like ERT, comes from outside the body, while *endogenous* estrogen

is made inside the body by the ovaries and adrenal glands. As a result, scientists have two ways to assess how postmenopausal estrogen might affect the mind. One way is to look at women who did and didn't use ERT—exogenous estrogen—to see who's "smarter." The other is to look at women who have higher and lower postmenopausal natural estrogen levels—endogenous estrogen—to see who's smarter. We've just reviewed a raft of evidence from the first kind of study: women who use exogenous estrogen definitely seem to be cognitive winners. But studies of endogenous estrogen seem to tell a different tale.

In the superb Rotterdam Study, which looks at endogenous estrogen, 3,800 women volunteered to have their hormone levels checked and were then followed for several years. Strangely, the Rotterdam women who had *higher* natural estrogen levels after menopause were *more* likely to become demented! Two other studies reported the same result: that high natural estrogen levels were associated with low memory scores. How come research on *exogenous* estrogen shows that this hormone is great for women's brains, while research on *endogenous* estrogen suggests that it hurts? That's the Estrogen Paradox.

No one knows the solution, but I can make a couple of educated guesses. First, the "high" levels of estrogen that some postmenopausal women make naturally in their bodies are not nearly as high as the levels women achieve with ERT, so it's not really fair to compare the two cases. The brain may require the larger estrogen dose provided by ERT to get a real benefit. Moreover, most estrogen, whether made by the ovaries or taken as a pill, is "bound" to big molecules and never gets into the brain; only a little bit of estrogen is not bound, and it's this "free" estrogen that does get into the brain. Kristine Yaffe conducted a clever study of natural hormone levels in postmenopausal women that specifically focused on "free," brain-friendly estrogen: she found that higher levels were definitely better for women's cognition. If her discovery is confirmed, it might resolve the Estrogen Paradox, because it would tell us that estrogen helps the postmenopausal brain regardless of whether it comes from outside or inside the body.

Some doctors have suggested that ERT might even be used to *treat* Alzheimer's. In my opinion, that's not likely to work, because, unfortunately, by the time a woman is in her seventies or eighties and meets the criteria for Alzheimer's, she's lost so many millions of neurons that a preventive treatment is like closing the barn door after the horses are already grazing in the next county. This probably explains why three recent clinical trials of estrogen for women with Alzheimer's showed no benefit. As with most diseases, what works to *treat* dementia is probably completely different from what works to *prevent* dementia. Preventing dementia is our grail.

To find out whether ERT prevents dementia, a massive, long-term, double-blind, placebo-controlled trial of ERT and memory is needed. This would require thousands of women to altruistically volunteer for a somewhat risky experiment. Impressively, two such studies are under way at the time of this writing: the first is called the Women's Health Initiative memory trial (WHIM) and involves a subgroup of volunteers in the Women's Health Initiative (WHI). Here 27,000 American women have volunteered to be randomized to receive estrogen, estrogen plus progestin, or a placebo. The results of this ten-year trial will be released after 2005. The second and even more ambitious trial is the Women's International Study of Long-Duration Oestrogen After Menopause (WISDOM), a huge study involving a ten-year trial of ERT, plus a further ten years of follow-up. Results of this bold twenty-year study will not be analyzed until after 2020.

Women today thus are confronted by Pascal's Bet. You can be cautiously optimistic that taking ERT is a good way to save your brain, but it will be decades before a truly appropriate clinical trial is executed, analyzed, and reported. In the meantime, should you take ERT to save your brain?

Each woman must answer that question based on a tough analysis of her personal benefits versus risks. Yes, a mountain of evidence says that estrogen is good for the brain, but the brain-saving benefits are not absolutely proven, and your overall health is crucial, so any decision about using ERT to save the brain depends on what we know about ERT's *other* effects on health.

ERT is a moving target. In fact, even as I wrote this book, the pendulum of medical opinion about ERT has swung past with a startling swoosh. So I can hardly guarantee that the best current information will remain the best current information. That said, we have an enormous amount of information about this popular medication; a woman can use this information—along with her individual and family health history and the help of her physician—to make her own well-informed personal choice.

Five Possible Benefits of ERT

Apart from relief of such menopausal symptoms as hot flashes and weight gain (for which the benefits are clear), what are the proposed health benefits of ERT?

One benefit is *longevity*. In the Nurses' Health Study—an ongoing study of 121,700 nurses—after twenty years of study, women taking ERT were about 40 percent less likely to have died. This striking longevity benefit is tied to the duration of treatment: if a woman stops therapy, the benefit seems to disappear after about five years.

Another benefit is protection from *osteoporosis*. When a woman enters menopause, the drop in her estrogen level provokes bone-resorbing cells called *osteoclasts* to steal calcium, which may leave her with bones so brittle that her first sign of trouble is a fracture. But retrospective studies (studies of women's past use of ERT) show that estrogen seems to decrease the frequency of hip fractures, curvature of the spine, back pain, loss of height, immobility, and need for hip or spine surgery. Again, once a woman quits ERT, the benefit disappears; in fact, her bones may catch up to the fragile state they would have been in had she never taken estrogen (a troubling thought that makes one question the final value of ERT for bones). The lack of solid *prospective* studies led the FDA to withdraw approval for ERT as a treatment for osteoporosis in 2000. Although we strongly suspect that it helps, we'll need the results of long-term studies like WHI and WISDOM to guide us regarding estrogen and bones.

A newly discovered benefit is *control of Parkinson's*. A study published in 2000 reported that low-dose ERT gave women with Parkinson's better control over their tremors and more hours of good mobility. While we need to see if other studies find the same results, this is a promising approach to improving the quality of life for women dealing with this terribly immobilizing condition.

By far the biggest purported benefit of ERT is protection from *heart disease*. Heart disease is the number-one killer of women in the United States. With the onset of menopause at an average age of about fifty-two, the prevalence of heart disease and the frequency of heart attacks among women begin to sneak upward until they reach roughly the same rate as in men. This fact has led to the completely logical idea that estrogen builds a biological barrier against heart disease, and that menopause tears it down. Maybe so, maybe not.

Many excellent studies have convincingly shown that women who have used ERT have lower rates of heart disease. But every woman is different. In the Nurses' Health Study, those who had risks for heart attacks had the greatest health benefit from estrogen, which cut the risk of premature death by 50 percent. This is five times the size of the benefit for women *without* risks of heart disease, making it almost seem that unhealthy women get the most out of ERT. Other large studies of ERT also show a 50 to 60 percent reduction in heart attacks or similar vascular problems. The explanation is that estrogen directly fights many of the big risk factors for heart disease; it lowers cholesterol, may prevent excessive blood clotting, and may heal injured blood vessels. By the 1990s, all of these facts led to a powerful collective faith that ERT saves women's hearts.

But some scientists have argued that it's unclear whether the reduction in heart attacks is really due to estrogen or to the fact that women who take ERT tend to be better educated, more likely to exercise, and less likely to drink to excess, smoke, or eat fatty diets. The only way to sort it out is a randomized trial. The early results of two of the biggest such trials in history have shaken our faith to the core.

First came the Heart and Estrogen/progestin Replacement Study (HERS). In this randomized trial of 3,000 postmenopausal women who already had coronary artery disease, those who took estrogen were *more* likely to have adverse cardiovascular events (heart attacks and strokes) during the first year of treatment than those who took placebos. But this disadvantage vanished after two years of treatment, and the net result after five years was no overall difference in heart health. Then in April 2000 came an alarming press release from the WHI, the Women's Health Initiative. Even though the actual data remain secret until the completion of the study in 2005, the overseers of WHI felt morally compelled to release the astonishing news that women taking hormones "had somewhat more cardiovascular events (heart attacks, strokes, and blood clots in the legs and lungs) than those taking placebo." The announcement was careful to specify that fewer than 1 percent of women had suffered such events, and that the difference was so small that it might be merely the result of chance. Nonetheless, tens of thousands of concerned women called their doctors within days, looking for the straight scoop: "Should I keep taking these pills or not?" By mid-2001 the American Heart Association rang in with its recommendation: if women are taking ERT for other reasons—such as reducing hot flashes or preventing osteoporosis—they can continue; but women should *not* take estrogen solely for the purpose of preventing heart disease.

In fact, it's still entirely possible that estrogen prevents heart attacks in the long run: by the fifth year of the study, women on ERT had *fewer* heart attacks than women on placebos. The fast-nearing completion of the WHI will help answer the crucial question of estrogen's potency for prevention of heart disease. WISDOM will perhaps give us even more helpful data, because it's a twenty-year-long study. But for many women and their doctors, the main rationale for taking ERT is the expected heart benefit, and unfortunately, as of 2002, that benefit remains unproven.

Since estrogen does a lot of good things for blood vessels, ERT might be expected to help prevent *strokes*. But there's a key exception: in women smokers, especially those older than thirty-five, high-dose birth control pills have been linked to an *increased* risk of strokes and blood clots. For this reason, women smokers over age thirty-five, or those with clotting problems, should not take estrogen-containing birth control pills. A parallel caution may apply to postmenopausal women smokers; they should probably not use ERT. For nonsmokers without clotting problems—the vast majority of the postmenopausal population—ERT seems to *reduce* the risk of strokes. And although all the data are not in yet, we suspect that low-dose ERT will have an even more favorable antistroke effect.

There is a deep and abiding lore to the effect that women experience *mood changes* as they go through menopause and that ERT can help. Evidence definitely supports this effect, but not all depressions that occur around the time of menopause are a direct biological effect of estrogen withdrawal on the brain. Lost reproductive capacity, the physical changes of menopause, the approach of an empty nest, or health problems in a husband may all produce depression-provoking stress. Despite this caveat, menopause probably does have a real neurobiological impact on mood. In fact, collaborators at Harvard and the University of São Paulo, Brazil, recently conducted a bold clinical trial using estradiol skin patches to treat depression in fifty perimenopausal women. It worked, perhaps because estrogen helps maintain normal serotonin activity, a key factor in smooth sailing for the limbic system. It may also account for a fascinating finding that's been observed for years but never explained: women on ERT are less likely to suffer from depression.

All of those potential benefits have led to a general agreement, especially among women college graduates, that postmenopausal ERT is a good idea. Strangely, however, *only one-fifth of the women who might take ERT get prescriptions*. And of the millions of ERT prescriptions that women have received, 30 percent go unfilled, not to mention the bottles of estrogen that sit gathering dust behind mirrors in bathroom medicine cabinets. Moreover, 70 percent of women who take ERT choose to quit after two years. Why do so few women take ERT? Surveys suggest that the gap between potential and actual treatment comes down to a single issue: fear of breast cancer. Thirty-four percent of women report that breast cancer is their greatest health concern, five times as many as those who report heart disease as their main concern, despite the fact that the risk of heart disease death is actually five times *higher* among women than the risk of breast cancer death. Even though ERT's possible life-saving benefits to the heart may outweigh the risk to the breasts, it's the threat to breasts that remains the most often-cited reason for declining to take ERT.

I recently overheard a conversation in a bustling county hospital cafeteria. One nurse asked another, "You taking estrogen?"

The second nurse smiled. "I've got two good reasons I don't want to take the risk."

We clearly need the best possible understanding of the true risks of ERT.

Four Possible Risks of ERT

Breast cancer is justly dreaded as a debilitating, potentially disfiguring, and sometimes deadly disease. But a chasm separates actual and perceived risk: on average, women overestimate their risk of getting breast cancer and underestimate their risk of recovery if they do get it. They commonly perceive that the risk is higher in their thirties and forties, when the disease is actually most common in the sixties and seventies. But even at that age, the risk is modest. Suppose Sherie is sixty and wants to make a decision about whether to use ERT. Unless she's one of the small number of women with the *BRCA1* or *BRCA2* mutation, she actually has only a one-in-thirty-four likelihood of developing breast cancer in the next ten years. For every thousand Sheries aged sixty to sixty-four, based on the Ontario Cancer Registry for 1995, only three will die of breast cancer, while *nine* will die from vascular diseases that may be reducible with ERT. So an excruciating aspect of any woman's decision about ERT is that she has to balance the instinctive horror of losing a breast against the simple fact that heart disease and strokes are by far the bigger danger. The completely unexpected news that ERT may *not* be quite the heart savior we had thought tries the soul. Doctors need to respect the deep feelings involved in women's decision making, rather than just presenting the numbers.

Nonetheless, the numbers—the statistical results from large-scale studies—do offer some anchors in the storm. In the Nurses' Health Study, estrogen actually seemed to *reduce* the risk of breast cancer during the first five years of treatment. In the Iowa Women's Health Study (a study of 37,000 women published in 1999) women who had taken ERT had no increase in the most common and deadly forms of breast cancer, invasive ductal or lobular cancer, which account for 85 to 90 percent of invasive breast cancers. Instead, the increase occurred only in the less common, more easily treatable forms—and that risk increased for women who had taken estrogen for more than five years. Similarly, in a third large study—this one conducted by the National Cancer Institute and released in 2000—women who had taken combined therapy (estrogen plus progestin) for less than four years had no increase in breast cancer risk. This study also found that, however long a woman takes ERT, the risk drops sharply once she quits; four years after stopping, her risk is the same as it would have been if she had never taken hormones.

The lining of the uterus is vulnerable to cancer throughout a woman's life. Unlike the ambiguous evidence regarding breast cancer, the evidence that ERT can somewhat increase the risk of *uterine cancer* is clear. But when ERT is combined with progesterone, an increasingly popular option, this second hormone causes the lining of the uterus to shed monthly, which seems to dramatically reduce the risk of uterine cancer.

The Cancer Prevention Study II, which has followed more than 675,000 women for fifteen years, found that women who used ERT for more than ten years had nearly double the risk of *ovarian cancer*. We do not yet know whether using progesterone at the same time will avoid this risk. But the total lifetime risk of ovarian cancer is so small (less than 2 percent) that health researchers suggest the favorable effects on other parts of the body probably outweigh any risk of ovarian cancer.

Some evidence suggests that ERT can increase the risk of *lung cancer,* but that risk is very small among nonsmoking women.

A Guide for a Very Personal Decision

We're entering a new age, discovering exciting things about estrogen that turn our old assumptions on their heads. But frankly, we still don't have a perfect way to balance the risks and benefits of ERT. Setting the brain aside, the main issues are the possible prevention of heart disease and strokes versus the possible risk of cancer. Some doctors have been saying, "Take estrogen for three to five years, then stop." That's probably a great compromise, but it may turn out that the heart benefits just *begin* to kick in at the five-year point—about the same time the cancer risk begins to creep upward.

Then we add the brain benefits to the scale. There's some evidence that the longer a woman takes ERT, even up to twenty years, the lower her risk of Alzheimer's. These days practically no doctor would recommend twenty years of conventional ERT, but it's still unclear how to balance the possibility that long-term treatment gives us the best overall brain-saving benefits against the slowly increasing risk of cancer. If a woman follows the plan that seems to make the most sense—to use ERT for a few years and then stop—will she reduce her risk of Alzheimer's over the next couple of decades of her life, truly setting back the clock, or will she just get a temporary reprieve until the day she quits estrogen, then revert to the same risk of dementia as if the clock sprang forward? No one knows. So women must make a personal choice—a choice that awakens deep instincts of fear and hope.

As Twain's Maxim promises, everyone is different, and any of a hundred personal factors could tip the balance of this choice one way or the other. That's one reason a doctor comes in handy. In helping with this de-cision, a woman's doctor will typically take into account her age at first and last menstrual periods; family history of all types of cancers, heart disease, and osteoporosis; personal history of breast cancer or benign breast disease; past use of any hormones, including oral contraceptives and infertility treatments; any genetic markers for cancer (and soon, for Alzheimer's); and personal diet, exercise, and smoking habits. With all these factors on the scale, some doctors are turning to computer programs to help make the decision!

Recognizing that any simple system is imperfect, and that new discov-eries could derail the best-laid plans at any time, I offer the following sim-plified guidelines:

First, decide if you have a higher-than-usual risk of Alzheimer's. For the sake of simplicity, that would mean high blood pressure, thyroid disease, a head injury in the past, or one or more close relatives with Alzheimer's. A woman with a higher-than-usual risk of Alzheimer's, or whose doctor suggests that she has an elevated risk of osteoporosis, should seriously consider taking ERT for three to six years. It may help to save her brain and bones, while adding a very low additional risk of cancer. A woman who has a higher-than-usual risk neither of Alzheimer's nor of osteo-porosis should also consider taking ERT for three or four years for its perimenopausal benefits; she may get a cognitive benefit as an added bonus. On the other hand, women who have a higher-than-usual risk of breast, uterine, or ovarian cancer—those who have had these cancers themselves, or whose close female relatives have had these cancers before age sixty, or who know that they carry one of the breast cancer genes—should probably forgo ERT, no matter what their risk of Alzheimer's or osteoporosis.

I recommend time-limited ERT for the two groups named above—which account for the majority of postmenopausal women—not just be-cause I've been impressed with the cognitive benefits or concerned about cancer risks with longer treatment, but because I predict that, within a few years, we will be playing in a brand-new ballfield.

For one thing, we'll have the results of the WHI and WISDOM trials. For another, ERT may very well pass into history as we increasingly turn to selective estrogen-receptor modifiers. SERMs are taking over, giving us a way to target the exact cells that need help while limiting collateral damage to bystander organs. When the switch-over to SERMs is com-plete, much of the baroque clinical calculus and personal anguish in mak-ing this decision will be obsolete. If the evidence continues to build that long-term hormonal therapy can help save your brain, we will soon be able to say with confidence—just do it.

ADAM and ART

If Wilhelm had been a ship, he'd have been an icebreaker. His jaw thrust out like a prow cutting its way into Baffin Bay in February. He had asked that his wife give him just a moment alone with "the professor." His eyes never wavered from the wall behind my head. "I am not longer able," he informed me in his moderate German accent, "to have the sex." He was fifty-five. And although he never quite brought himself to say so out loud, he was sad. He ached to the depths.

Depression, of course, can cause sexual dysfunction, but in Wilhelm's case the sadness seemed to have followed some months of disappointing nights. He didn't have diabetes (a very common cause of diminished erectile potency). He did have high blood pressure, but the antihypertensive medication he was taking was not the kind that usually interferes with erections. I asked him, among other things, how often he shaved.

"Of course, every day!" He reached for that clean-shaven icebreaker prow. But he acknowledged that maybe, for the last few years, he hadn't really *needed* to shave daily.

We ended up doing some blood tests. Wilhelm, as it turned out, was one of the millions of adult men with ADAM—androgen decline in the aging male. Sexual potency may be just one of the things at stake. ADAM may also erode men's minds.

Normal adult male testosterone levels are 300 to 1,000 nanograms per deciliter (ng/dl). Men are considered to be in hormonal trouble when their testosterone levels fall enough to produce symptoms such as loss of energy, loss of competitive drive, decreased libido, decreased muscle mass, decreased growth of facial and body hair, and difficulty achieving or maintaining a penile erection. This condition is clinically referred to as *hypogonadism*. The actual measurement of testosterone in the blood may be less important (certainly to the patient) than the symptoms of hypogonadism, but roughly speaking, levels below 200 ng/dl spell trouble. Interestingly, erectile potency may not be the best clinical indicator; even castrated males with no testicular testosterone have erections.

Due to changes in both the pituitary and the testes, testosterone declines inevitably with age. Testicles wither a bit, with a loss of the cells that make sperm. The whole picture has sometimes been called "andropause," the male equivalent of menopause. But andropause is something of a misnomer, because unlike women in menopause, men retain their reproductive potential for many years after these changes begin, and the changes are so remarkably insidious in onset that men are barely aware of what's happening until that fateful night when they admit to themselves, "Hmm, I guess I'm not nineteen anymore." The incomplete and variable nature of the condition has led to the proposal of the more accurate term *ADAM*.

Low testosterone levels are found in 20 to 30 percent of men over age sixty-five. Full-fledged clinical hypogonadism, with all the symptoms, is found in just 7 percent of men younger than sixty, but it increases to 20 percent in those older than sixty. These modest-sounding numbers create a sense that ADAM is a problem only for a minority, but that's false. In fact, for *most* men, aging causes an increase in sex hormone–binding globulin (SHBG), which basically makes testosterone less available to do its job. As a result, the testosterone levels that most doctors measure are misleading, and *almost all* men experience some symptoms of ADAM. Entirely apart from erectile dysfunction, ADAM can involve behavioral symptoms such as sleep disruption, depression, anxiety, and irritability.

What does ADAM do to the brain? Unlike the flood of data on estrogen and cognition—and unlike the flood of data relating testosterone to aggression, violence, sex drive, and all-around feistiness—there is only a relative trickle of information regarding testosterone and cognition. We know that men's memory declines with age, and that their testosterone levels decline as well, but it has yet to be conclusively shown that the first fact is related to the second. The available research falls into several batches: some studies look to see whether men with low testosterone have cognitive problems; some studies look to see whether boosting low levels up to normal improves cognition; and some studies look at whether men with supernormal testosterone levels have supernormal mental abilities.

In a classic series of studies done at the University of Hamburg in the 1980s, for example, 117 normal young men were tested for a variety of behaviors. Men with high-normal testosterone levels had more frequent sexual activity, more sexual aggressiveness, and more frequent orgasms— and they scored higher on measures of spatial skills. A treatment study was done at Oregon Health Sciences University with "normal" elderly men (which really means men with hundreds of aging-related biological changes in their brains, including lower levels of available testosterone). When the men's testosterone levels were boosted to 150 percent of normal, their spatial skills became supernormal. So at least spatial ability seems to be testosterone dependent—a new idea to think about as we search for our misplaced car in a big parking lot. Yet some very interesting evidence points to a Goldilocks Effect: higher testosterone may mean better spatial ability only up to a point, beyond which very high testosterone actually leads to subpar performance.

Other aspects of cognition also seem to depend on testosterone. For example, in a study from the University of New Orleans, hypogonadal men were shown to have lower verbal skills than normal men; treatment with testosterone restored their verbal fluency. And in one of the best studies ever done in this field, researchers at the University of Washington gave injections of either testosterone or placebo to 25 healthy men aged fifty to eighty. The results made news in 2001; after six weeks of treatment, the men who got testosterone showed definite improvements in *both* spatial and verbal memory. Studies such as these have led naturally to the suspicion that men need to maintain their sex hormone levels during aging if they wish to keep their brains in top working order.

But it may oversimplify the matter to look at testosterone alone.

The final effects of ADAM on men's brains may be due, in part, to the parallel decline in other hormones, such as estrogen, DHEA, DHEAS, or insulinlike growth factor-1 (ILGF-1). This sounds a little technical, but it could be a crucial point for planning good hormone replacement therapy for men. For example, ILGF-1 seems to save neurons from suicide; if some of the cognitive changes attributed to ADAM are really due to loss of ILGF-1, then testosterone replacement therapy by itself wouldn't fix the problem, any more than an oil change would fix a car that's out of gas. Furthermore, in both the Oregon and Washington studies I mentioned above, researchers concluded that testosterone's effect on men's cognition may also depend on *estrogen*. I'll bet the house that it's not going to come down to anything so simple as one-hormone-one-cognitive-benefit. Estrogens, androgens, other hormones and receptors, and molecules we have yet to discover are all mixed into the soup of human consciousness; aging-related changes in behavior are surely due to complex checks and balances among multiple ingredients.

Which brings us to the bottom line: it's clear that ADAM has serious health implications, perhaps including brain jeopardy. As baby boomer men experience a waning of their sexual powers, their muscular strength, and their energy, there will be enormous pressure for a more comprehensive approach than "potency" pills such as Viagra. We need to develop a scientifically strong anti-ADAM defense plan. We need to consider the benefits of *androgen replacement therapy* (ART).

There is nothing new about the dream of ART. As Stanford biopsychologist Robert Sapolsky puts it, the first experiment in all of endocrinology was doubtless the discovery—probably made after a ferocious tussle and the application of a sharp object fifty thousand years ago—that men behave differently without their testes. By the turn of the twentieth century, the value of testes for sexual vigor was unquestioned, and some of the males who ran studies of human aging further presumed that the mysterious "testicular factor" might serve as the proverbial fountain of youth. Captains of industry and heads of state lined up for injections that contained ground-up testes of bulls, dogs, or roosters. This treatment produced pain at the injection site and some horrific infections, but its widely acclaimed impact on aging and sexual performance was a big, fat placebo effect.

Even after the isolation of pure and highly effective testosterone, prior to 2000 ART meant painful testosterone injections with very brief effects, or skin patches that sometimes fell off or caused allergic skin reactions. Then in 2000 AndroGel was approved for men with low testosterone levels. AndroGel is the first easily applied topical gel form of ART. Men can rub it on their shoulders, upper arms, or abdomens once a day; the skin becomes a temporary repository that slowly releases testosterone into the bloodstream. As one businessman in the AndroGel clinical trials said, "I could sell this stuff on the street. I noticed an improvement in my strength. I wasn't as tired. I wasn't depressed. Sexually it has done wonders." The availability of this easy-to-use form of testosterone is already rocketing ART from the nether regions of academic endocrinology into the daily practice of family doctors. By one estimate, AndroGel will soon be used by five million or more men in the United States alone.

Predictably, anything that sounds this good has a downside, and indeed ART has some potentially serious side effects. Giving men extra testosterone may increase their risk of heart attacks. It can also accelerate prostate cancer in men who already have it. (It may or may not increase the prostate cancer rate in healthy men.) So the present plan is to recommend ART only to men with abnormally low testosterone levels (less than 300 ng/dl). But ever since ART became widely available over the Internet, some men are doing dangerous personal testosterone experiments, self-prescribing it in escalating doses to produce levels way beyond the normal range. They get big muscles, and they get big libidos. But they also get acne, balding pates, and aggressive mood changes—and some of them have developed serious liver damage. The risk/benefit equation has yet to be solved. "Does it improve strength and bone, but then men will die of heart attack or prostate cancer?" asks Ronald Swerdloff, the endocrinologist who headed up the AndroGel clinical trials. The answer will come only with clinical trials that follow men for ten to twenty years.

The question we're most interested in is whether ART will save men's brains. Perhaps. We don't have the impressive laboratory evidence of a brain-saving benefit for androgens that we do for estrogens, although one intriguing report from the University of Texas says that androgens can prevent tau protein from becoming hyperphosphorylated (one of the key problems in ARNAT). Again, as with estrogen, the right question is not "Can ART cure Alzheimer's?" but "Can ART help prevent cognitive loss?" And as with estrogen, the answer must come from big prospective studies of ART for healthy normal men. Such studies are now barely on the drawing board, so it may be years before we can announce with scientific certainty, "Hey, guys, it's not just for sex. ART can save your brain."

If ART can't save brains, however, then maybe estrogen can. When extra estrogen is given to men with coronary artery disease, it reportedly increases their exercise capacity while protecting their hearts. If estrogen can defend men from heart disease, it may also save their brains from strokes and conceivably offer the same amyloid-fighting benefits it does to women. These ideas have led to the jaw-dropping proposal that men take ERT. In fact, psychologist Barbara Sherwin of McGill University has found some evidence that estrogen can boost visual memory in young, healthy men. It's currently fairly far-out to predict that ERT will protect men from Alzheimer's, but if further studies confirm some of these preliminary hints, ERT-for-men might shift from the far-out to the front page.

As ever, we must consider the side effects. Estrogen grows men's breasts and decreases their sex drive, so conventional estrogen therapy will never become popular. A much better alternative is for men to take custom-designed estrogens that don't have feminizing effects. Soon they will exist. In just a few years, designer estrogens may be able to protect men's brains without lowering their libidos or raising their voices. In 1970 Edgar Berman, personal physician to former Vice President Hubert Humphrey, declared that women were unsuitable for many jobs because of their "raging hormonal imbalances." Today Dr. Berman might choke on his stethoscope to find that estrogen enhances aspects of cognition for both men and women—and that we're seriously looking at ways to give estrogen to men to improve the function of their brains.

In the meantime, I'll make the following recommendations. One, men with symptoms of ADAM should tell their doctors. Two, family doctors—the heart and soul of preventive medicine—should screen for ADAM in men over fifty at their annual physicals. Some men are quite reticent to discuss these issues, but a few simple questions usually reveal who should get sophisticated hormone tests. Three, men with clinical hypogonadism should start ART—under the supervision of a flesh-and-blood doctor, not an Internet virtual pharmacist. As the recognition of ADAM increases and the safety of novel forms of ART improves, we can expect a huge benefit for millions of men in quality of life—and perhaps in quality of thought.

The Future of Hormone Replacement Therapy

Ideally, we want to use an arrow rather than a cannon. We want sex hormone therapy that defends brains and hearts and bones but does not increase the risk of cancer in other organs. Two strategies are becoming increasingly popular to achieve this goal: one is the use of herbal estrogens; the second is the use of SERMs.

With regard to herbal estrogens, some supplement sellers claim that plant-based estrogenic therapy can provide all the benefits of ERT without the side effects. As a result, hundreds of thousands of woman have turned to licorice, dong quai, blue or black cohosh, vitex, soy isoflavones (the active component of soybeans and related plants), evening primrose, or wild yams. All of these indeed have some estrogenic activity, and soy isoflavones may truly reduce hot flashes. The problem is that any substance that has estrogenic benefits must bind to estrogen receptors; and any substance that binds to estrogen receptors has the potential to increase the risk of cancer. So depending on unknown chemical characteristics, herbal estrogens could increase or decrease your risk of cancer—and we have even *less* information about the size of that cancer risk than we do for pharmaceutical estrogen! Some scientists point to the high-soy diet in Asian countries to explain their low cancer rates, while others have shown that even low doses of soy isoflavones *increase* the cancer rates in animals. Eating some soy is fine as part of a richly varied diet, but it's premature to recommend herbal hormone replacements.

The real promise is held out by the newer SERMs. One of them, raloxifene (brand name Evista), may provide the same benefits as estrogen without increasing the risk of uterine cancer. It has been approved by the FDA for the treatment of osteoporosis. In one Harvard study, raloxifene was shown to decrease LDL ("bad" cholesterol) and to lower fibringen levels, both of which could perhaps reduce the risk of strokes. Another study investigated the effects of raloxifene on mental functioning in almost 3,500 women. While the group as a whole showed no benefit, the drug *did* make a difference for women over seventy and for those who had already shown signs of cognitive decline at the start of the study. Many newer SERMs are on the verge of being marketed, each with its own special benefits.

What's more, neuroscientists are homing in on the precise molecular structure that gives estrogen its brain-saving powers. James Simpkins of the University of Florida suspects that the neuroprotective effect depends on the location of a *hydroxyl* group. He and others are working to synthesize "super"-SERMs that take advantage of this discovery. The bottom line is that we can legitimately expect within a few years the arrival of custom-built, safe, and effective brain-saving SERMs for both men and women.

Any hormonal manipulation is playing with fire. We are far from knowing the best way to optimize brain health with so-called sex hormones, yet the future holds tremendous promise. The evidence that these hormones have neuroprotective properties is so strong that I'm willing to climb out onto a futurist limb and make a prediction. Considering our 100,000-to-200,000-year tenure on earth, humans have only very recently lived long enough that the average person suffers the distressing effects of aging-related hormone withdrawal. Such withdrawal probably adds to the neuron-bashing burdens that rob us of our brains and selves. But this will be a passing problem in the history of humankind. We can already reduce the problem, and we should probably be a little bolder in taking advantage of the treatments we already have. We will soon put the problem behind us altogether, and live out our lives with much more hormonal comfort, safety, and mental fitness.

CHAPTER 8

Can Non-sex Hormones Keep You Smart?

It was 1987. The small, crowded room at Massachusetts General Hospital was pitch-dark but for the pale fluorescence of the X-ray view boxes arrayed against the wall like windows onto a grainy black-and-white world. Positron-emission tomography (PET) scans filled the array. The assembled doctors could all see the sliced images of Mrs. Bartholemew's brain; in a strangely appealing chiaroscuro pattern, the PET scans showed how much glucose was being used for energy in different parts of her brain. And we could all see that her brain looked unusual. Harvard's Robert Ackerman, a pioneer of PET scan research, asked us provocatively, "What's your diagnosis?"

The Cerebral Blood Flow fellows and I leaned forward, peering, squinting, trying to make clinical sense out of the array. Frontal lobe, temporal lobe, parietal lobe—everywhere we looked the brain appeared as dim as a worn-out firefly. We were used to seeing decreased glucose metabolism in one spot, maybe two. But this middle-aged woman's entire brain exhibited the dimming that indicated decreased glucose utilization, as if someone had simply turned down her cerebral lights. What could diminish the use of glucose in an entire brain?

"Diabetes of the brain?" suggested one wag.

We laughed. There was no such thing—or so we thought back in the mid-1980s. In fact, Mrs. Bartholemew did have diabetes, although that probably was not the major explanation for her very striking neuroimage; most diabetics do not show such big changes on brain PET scans. She was depressed, and major depression was the diagnosis Ackerman was looking for. But I never forgot the phrase *diabetes of the brain,* or the idea. Is it possible that diabetes—a condition that affects millions upon millions of men and women—alters cerebral function? Research has moved forward since then. We now suspect that "diabetes of the brain" may indeed be the most important hormonal cause of memory loss with aging.

A number of non-sex hormones influence the operation of the mind and the brain. We've already discussed one such group, the stress hormones. In this chapter we'll talk about other influential non-sex hormones, among which the most important, by far, is *insulin*. You usually hear about insulin when doctors are talking about diabetes, and diabetes absolutely deserves more attention by brain scientists. Yet, as you're about to see, the links between brain function and insulin even go beyond diabetes.

Diabetes is an awful disorder. Like a cruel hormonal octopus, it reaches out in many directions to harm organs throughout the body—wrecking blood vessels and eyes and kidneys and the nerves in the legs, causing depression and increased sensitivity to pain and heart attacks and ghastly infections, suggesting how much of our survival depends on the well-regulated metabolism of glucose. Diabetes is mainly caused by a failure of the hormone *insulin*, produced by the pancreas, to help move glucose into cells. This failure leaves cells starved for fuel, barely putt-putting along like cars running out of gas.

There are basically two types of diabetes. Type 1 usually occurs in children and is called *juvenile diabetes*; the main problem in type 1 is that the pancreas fails to make enough insulin. Type 2 usually occurs in adults and is therefore known as *adult-onset diabetes*. In type 2 the main problem is that cells throughout the body (and the brain) lose the ability to *respond* to the insulin and don't allow it to bring in the glucose; this is called *insulin resistance*.

This simple account of the difference between types 1 and 2 doesn't tell the full story, because type 2 is no simple beast. Early on, as their cells are resisting insulin's earnest efforts to move glucose inside them, people with type 2 have high insulin levels in their blood. This is because the pancreas cranks out extra insulin, like a fuel pump that's been opened wide to try to push fuel into cells. But later the pancreas begins to fail, like a pump finally running out of fuel, and insulin levels drop. At this point, cells face a double problem: insulin resistance plus too little insulin. The result is a devastating cut-off of glucose delivery to the insides of cells—and all the medical agonies of diabetes.

Both genes and lifestyle factors affect the risk of type 2 diabetes. But there's no escaping the fact: while some people with a strong genetic predisposition will get type 2 regardless of whether they gain excess weight, the real villain in this story is obesity. Even those who have *no* genetic risk factors are likely to get hammered by type 2 if they become obese. For decades, scientists have been baffled about why overweight people develop this dread disease. They now know that fat cells release a newly discovered hormone called *resistin* that makes the cells insulin-resistant. Contrary to popular myth, it doesn't matter how a person becomes obese, by eating sweets, or fats, or proteins; the result is the same. Gain too much weight, and the cells in many organs in the body lose their ability to bring in glucose, and they starve in the midst of plenty.

America is in the middle of an obesity pandemic. Because diabetes is closely linked to obesity, we are experiencing an unprecedented upsurge in this disease throughout the nation. What's especially astonishing is that we previously saw type 2 diabetes primarily among those older than age fifty, but with the rise in obesity among inactive young Americans, we are now commonly seeing this disease in *teenagers*. Eleven million Americans are currently diagnosed with the disease, and an estimated 6 million more are undiagnosed, for a rough total of 17 million. But that 17 million figure itself may be a serious underestimate. Since doctors have come to appreciate that even minor problems with *glucose handling* (the ability of cells to bring in glucose) have dangerous consequences, endocrinologists have recently broadened the definition of diabetes to include many more people. Thousands are now hearing the shocking news at their annual check-ups: "You've got diabetes." Women are especially at risk, and African American women are experiencing a silent epidemic. And as the proportion of Americans of Hispanic heritage rises, so does the prevalence of diabetes, since Hispanics may have twice the rate of type 2 diabetes.

Even taking into account the new definition of diabetes and the expanded prevalence estimates, however, we may *still* be hugely underestimating the problem. Doctors usually diagnose diabetes based on elevated blood glucose levels, but the underlying problem is really insulin resistance. Insulin resistance is silently damaging the bodies and brains of many more people who don't fit the formal diagnosis of diabetes. This condition is sometimes called *pre-diabetes*—a condition of subtle decline in the ability to use glucose, usually with no obvious symptoms. In other words, many millions of American adults are walking around completely unaware that they have trouble handling glucose—and are completely untreated.

Since tens of millions of people have type 2, in addition to the millions of pre-diabetics, we have to ask: how much of a problem is this for the brain? The answer is alarming. Recent studies show that even minor problems with glucose handling are associated with cognitive impairment.

In one study, Swedish researchers in the noble old university town of Uppsala followed 999 men from age fifty to age seventy. They found that men who had diabetes at age fifty were definitely more likely to have cognitive impairment at age seventy. But those men who had biochemical signs only of insulin resistance—and did *not* have clinical diabetes at age fifty—also had an increased risk of cognitive problems twenty years later. Other large studies from England and the Netherlands report the same result: insulin resistance or trouble handling glucose is associated with worsened cognition. In one of the great cognitive surveys of all time, Mayo Clinic neurologist David Knopman tested cognition in 10,963 men and women; those with diabetes showed a decline in frontal lobe ability and speed of processing information—even when they were in their *fifties*.

What Does Diabetes Do to the Brain?

These studies opened the eyes of the medical community to the disconcerting possibility that diabetes—or even pre-diabetes—significantly increases a person's risk of dementia. But a big debate rages about exactly *how* diabetes hurts brains. On one side are the traditionalist neurologists who say, "Sure, diabetes wrecks blood vessels, so it will increase your risk of *vascular* dementia. But it doesn't increase your risk of Alzheimer's; in fact, being a diabetic may even *decrease* your risk of Alzheimer's." (Some diabetics do make more of a special enzyme that breaks down beta-amyloid, perhaps giving them a slight advantage in the fight against ARNAT.) On the other side are a growing number of neurologists who say, "Vascular disease is just half the problem. Diabetes and Alzheimer's are a pair of closely linked medical monsters; they often work together, and their combined effect on the brain is about the same as the effect of King Kong Meets Godzilla on Tokyo."

As we saw in Chapter 4, the misadventures of the aging brain come down to two big problems: misfolded proteins and energy deprivation. Up until recently, most doctors believed that diabetes hurt brains only by depriving them of fuels, both by preventing them from using glucose and by disrupting their blood supply via vascular disease. Now that theory is beginning to look simplistic. New evidence suggests that diabetes can also cause misfolded proteins, the basic problem of Alzheimer's. If this proves true, it gives us a whole new reason to push for an urgent international campaign to control diabetes.

In fairness, there are good reasons for the debate about the relationship between diabetes and Alzheimer's. In early studies, scientists took one approach: "Let's take a big group of old people and see how many of the diabetics have Alzheimer's." In some cases, such studies showed that older diabetics were *less* likely to have Alzheimer's than nondiabetics—a surprising result. Even though the studies were flawed in various ways, the reports left scientists scratching their heads.

Then epidemiologists tried a new approach. Three large studies—one in Japan, one in Europe, and one in the United States—followed thousands of nondemented people for several years; all three found that the diabetics were about *twice* as likely as nondiabetics to develop Alzheimer's. For example, the Rotterdam Study followed 6,370 elderly people of both sexes for up to six years. People with diabetes were 1.9 times as likely as nondiabetics to develop Alzheimer's.

These new studies shook neuroscientists up, providing compelling evidence that the earlier studies had missed something important and that diabetes is associated with an increased risk of dementia. But the new studies went even further. They showed that vascular brain damage is far from the whole story. They showed that *diabetes seems to boost the risk of the most common of all dementias—Alzheimer's disease.*

Three Ways Diabetes Will Hammer Your Brain

Neuroscientists now believe that diabetes—and maybe even pre-diabetes—can wreak havoc in the brain in at least three major ways. One is that diabetes can cause vascular disease, damaging blood vessels small and large, which increases the risk of heart disease and strokes. The second is through episodes of low blood sugar, which leave brain cells gasping for energy. And third is the eye-opening, paradigm-shifting, newly discovered link between diabetes and Alzheimer's. The overall result might well be called *diabetes of the brain.*

Let's begin with the problem of vascular disease.

DIABETES AND BLOOD VESSELS

Diabetes causes decreased blood flow through the tiniest vessels of our brains, especially in the deep parts of the brain, where billions of neuronal wires route information past our ventricles. When we look at the brains of diabetics with MRI scans, we often find striking bright signals in this region, called *periventricular white matter hyperintensities*. When these hyperintensities are mild, they seem to have a negligible impact on thinking. But as neuropsychologist Kyle Boone and neurologist Charles De-Carli independently discovered, there's a threshold effect. Beyond a certain amount, neurons become stripped of their precious insulation, effectively disconnecting parts of the brain from one another, like an old switchboard with ratty wires. The result is multiple cognitive impairments.

But why does diabetes lead to microvascular problems in the first place? It might be out of pure RAGE.

One of the basic features of aging is the ugly effect of *advanced glycation end-products* (AGEs). Glycation is the process that turns raw hamburger meat from fresh pink to gooey gray when we leave it out too long on the kitchen counter. Glycation seems to speed up many aging processes, inside and outside the brain, but people who have trouble handling glucose (like diabetics and pre-diabetics) have double the level of AGEs in their blood. In addition, they may have altered tissue *receptors* for AGEs, which are called (inevitably) RAGEs. AGEs and RAGEs tend to wreck the flexibility of small blood vessels, leaving them stiff, narrow, and unable to properly deliver blood. This is one way that AGEs, RAGEs, and diabetes may hurt the brain.

Diabetes also harms big blood vessels, making them stiffer and narrower, substantially increasing the chance that they will become clogged with cholesterol deposits, which can eventually lead to a stroke. What's more, people with diabetes are much more likely to develop heart disease. While strokes *directly* cause brain damage, heart disease *indirectly* causes brain damage and can impair thinking in several ways (as we'll see in Chapter 10).

LOW BLOOD SUGAR

If the harmful effects of diabetes on the brain were limited to these vascular disasters, that alone would justify an enhanced public health effort to fight this increasingly common disease. But several large studies have proven that diabetics have higher rates of dementia *even if we eliminate the vascular problems* from the equation. How can we explain these results?

For one thing, diabetics are prone to hypoglycemic episodes, or periods of low blood sugar, which are a neuron-stressing experience. When we try to bring diabetes under control with insulin or pills, we're shooting for that "just right" blood sugar level—roughly between 60 and 100 mg/dl. But if a medication dose is even a tad too high, it can cause the blood sugar to plummet below 60. This depletion robs the brain of its basic energy supply, forcing the neurons into a mad search for alternative fuels. Remarkably, the brain can recover from one such episode of plunging blood sugar. But many people with diabetes experience *multiple* episodes of this kind; it's those who have multiple episodes whose neurons gasp and die.

Diabetics also have a markedly increased risk of depression, which (as we saw in Chapter 5) may potentially lead to brain damage. Mrs. Bartholemew's PET scan was dimmed by her melancholy, but her major depressive episode may have been partly provoked by diabetes—and the combination of diabetes and depression may have additive effects on the risk of cognitive decline.

But it's the third brain-hammering process that has recently caused the biggest stir: the ways that diabetes overlaps with ARNAT and Alzheimer's.

The Secret Links Between Diabetes and Alzheimer's

Neuroscientist Siegfried Hoyer and his group at the University of Heidel-berg have recently discovered that people with early Alzheimer's tend to leave glucose outside their brain cells, like fuel sitting in a can beside a car with a locked gas cap. Alzheimer's brains also have more insulin receptors than usual, as if the brain had built a bunch of new fuel lines in a frantic attempt to pull more glucose in for its needy cells.

If a neuron can't have glucose, what does it eat? There are two possi-bilities. First, it can turn to the alternative fuels called *ketone bodies* and *lactic acid*. Feeding them to neurons would be like putting alcohol and paint-thinner in your gas tank out of desperation. It works, up to a point. But ketone bodies and lactic acid burn inefficiently, with the result that they release free radicals that can poison the very neurons they are trying to help. Diabetics already tend to run low on *glutathione*—one of the best built-in antioxidants—which means that these free radicals can do unin-hibited harm. The second way that a glucose-deprived cell may gain nour-ishment is to eat itself. That is, just as people who are starving end up metabolizing parts of their own body to save other parts, glucose-deprived brain cells may start digesting parts of themselves in a last-ditch effort to find energy. Since hippocampal memory cells are extremely energy-hungry, our memory may be the first thing to go if our brains don't handle glucose well. These discoveries have led Hoyer and others to the-orize that Alzheimer's may be, to a greatly underestimated degree, a dis-ease of fuel deprivation. In other words, those of us with impaired glucose handling—millions and millions of Americans—may have high-risk, self-cannibalizing brains.

Diabetes hurts brain cells in other ways as well. We now have evidence that *insulin* (like estrogen) acts as a nerve growth factor—a remarkable new identity for this molecule. This means that people who are low on in-sulin are low on growth food for their brain cells. Moreover (wouldn't you know it), hippocampal memory cells have more insulin receptors than almost any other part of the brain, which again means that diabetes may nail human memory. Finally, diabetics are more than *twice* as likely as nondiabetics to be depressed. Since depression can lead to a stress hor-mone overload, and stress hormones can pound the hippocampus, this is one more way that diabetics are tied to the tracks of the memory-loss train.

So far the story seems clear: if you become overweight, you get diabetes; if you get diabetes, your neurons suffer a nightmarish parade of problems, including ratty wiring, cut-off fuels, unfettered free radical attacks, loss of growth factors, and excess stress hormones. All these effects help explain how diabetes hurts brain cells, but they don't tell us how diabetes may specifically boost the risk of Alzheimer's. We're getting there.

As I noted above, diabetes wrecks tiny blood vessels by encouraging the production of AGEs and RAGEs. But RAGE receptors also exist *right on neurons themselves*. New evidence suggests that these RAGEs build up during Alzheimer's. Once they're in place, they can rev up the ghastly beta-amyloid cascade and speed up brain cell death. So one way diabetes boosts Alzheimer's is by making RAGEs, which gives us a strong nudge toward the edge of that particular neurodegenerative cliff.

But the most amazing part of the story, based on some hot-off-the-presses discoveries, is that *diabetes helps produce the exact two misfolded proteins that destroy the brain in ARNAT/Alzheimer's.*

In Chapter 4 we saw that the root cause of ARNAT/Alzheimer's is a pair of misfolded proteins: beta-amyloid and tau. The first leads to plaques, the second to tangles. These misfolded proteins can overwhelm the brain, either because you produce too much of them, or because you can't break them down fast enough. For a decade, neuroscientists have known that in order to break down the nasty, toxic beta-amyloid molecule, you need special enzymes. And they've finally discovered one of the key enzymes that does the job: it's *insulin-degrading enzyme* (IDE), the enzyme that breaks down insulin. In other words, *the very same enzyme that breaks down insulin*—IDE—is crucial for saving the brain from beta-amyloid. Some people with diabetes continue to make plenty of IDE, so they actually continue to break down beta-amyloid and protect themselves from ARNAT. But many people with diabetes stop making enough IDE. This cessation robs brain cells of their ability to rip apart beta-amyloid before it does its nasty work, which may leave them defenseless against the creeping assault of ARNAT.

There's still more to the connection between diabetes and Alzheimer's. Tangles, one of the major problems in Alzheimer's, happen when too much phosphorus gets attached to tau, producing *hyperphosphorylated tau*—turning a healthy neuron into a train wreck of a brain cell. To get really technical for a moment (bear with me; this is cool), scientists have now found the enzymes that stick too much phosphorus onto tau. One of the main ones is *GSK-3 beta* (glycogen synthase kinase-3 beta). As it turns out, insulin controls GSK-3 beta. That means that if your insulin level is low (a major problem in diabetes), GSK-3 beta goes wild, and tau gets hyperphosphorylated. This is yet another direct connection between diabetes and Alzheimer's.

At this point, I'll offer my best guess as to how the Alzheimer's-diabetes link will look once research has shown us the whole chain of evidence, probably in the next ten years. Several key enzymes either make or break down tau and amyloid. An imbalance in these key enzymes means you get too many misfolded proteins, leading to plaques and tangles. The secret link is that *diabetes causes the misfolding of the exact proteins that cause Alzheimer's.* You don't even have to have obvious symptoms of diabetes for this process to begin whittling away at your intelligence. A huge number of people are walking around unaware that they have pre-diabetes—strolling blind near the edge of a neurodegenerative cliff.

This does not mean that every diabetic is doomed to Alzheimer's. Diabetics vary greatly in the duration of their illness, in the treatment they've received, in their levels of insulin, IDE, and GSK-3 beta, and in a whole lot of biological co-conspirators that we're only just beginning to investigate. These variations will modify how badly diabetes hurts a person's brain. That's why having diabetes does not *guarantee* that you'll get Alzheimer's; it just doubles your risk.

For diabetics and nondiabetics alike, all of these discoveries add up to a single message: we should no longer take mild glucose-handling problems lightly. Impaired handling of glucose is beginning to look like the most dangerous hormone problem of them all for the human brain. If the emerging theory of impaired glucose handling and neurodegeneration proves true, it is potentially a major public health discovery—the recognition of a treatable menace that's sapping the brain power of the nation and the world. I cannot put this too strongly. Of all the lifestyle-related threats to the human brain, this is potentially one of the most easily reversible—*if only we can get people to heed the warnings.*

Time for Action

Our society should respond to this menace to the mind with an all-out, jumping-up-and-down public health, education, and research campaign to make prevention, early diagnosis, and good control of diabetes more of a national priority. As primary-care doctors apply the new guidelines for diagnosing diabetes, they will diagnose many more people. This alone will be a big step forward, because it will potentially alert millions of people to take prompt steps to better health, hopefully in time to protect their bodies and brains.

But we could do more. Much more.

The conventional way of detecting diabetes is to use a random test of blood sugar, a test of fasting blood sugar, or an oral glucose tolerance test (in which a doctor gives a patient a specified dose of glucose in the morning, then measures the glucose in their blood every half hour for two hours). According to the new guidelines, a fasting blood sugar of 126 mg/dl or more is diagnostic of diabetes. It would be great if *any* of these tests were done routinely, but they're not. Doctors tend to do them only for patients in whom they suspect diabetes, such as those complaining of thirst or frequent urination, or those with a family history of diabetes. The result is that a third of diabetics slip through the cracks undetected.

An even bigger problem is modern medicine's terrible inadequacy at detecting pre-diabetes.

Let's say Joe is a healthy-feeling forty-five-year-old who goes in for his annual physical. His doctor measures his blood glucose and finds it's perfectly normal. The doctor concludes that Joe does not have diabetes. But the test does not tell him whether Joe is actually in the long pre-diabetic stage, where blood glucose levels may in fact be normal. Thus, the doctor does not test for the core problem, insulin resistance. Even the most compulsive family doctor on earth is bound to miss most cases of pre-diabetes—people like Joe, whose bodies and minds may be silently deteriorating even as they hear from their doctors, "Lookin' good!" We need to make the detection of diabetes and pre-diabetes a routine part of primary health care. And we need better tests to do so.

One such test, readily available and cheap, is the *hemoglobin A1C* (HgbA1C). Rather than a one-shot measure of glucose, the HgbA1C test gives the doctor a picture of the average glucose level over the previous two to three months. Unfortunately, too few family doctors use this test, and even those who use it miss lots of people in trouble, because it detects only high glucose levels; but *glucose levels may be totally normal even while pre-diabetes is kicking up a storm.*

We obviously need a better way to routinely screen adults for the earliest, subtlest signs of the sneaky mayhem of insulin resistance. A number of promising possibilities have been proposed, taking advantage of our growing knowledge of chemical changes that reveal pre-diabetes (including measures of insulin, amylin, leptin, C-peptide, adiponectin, and other markers). But so far we have yet to figure out the best, most cost-effective way to find pre-diabetics. The result is that we have no way to warn this huge group in a timely way and rescue them from the myriad preventable health problems they may already be developing in their bodies and brains.

Then comes the problem of treatment.

Many people with type 2 diabetes will achieve control over their condition by diet alone (as described in Chapter 11). Combining diet with exercise in a double-barreled approach greatly increases the likelihood of success without the need for medications. It's actually quite amazing how magnificently exercise and weight loss can turn the tide; a 5 percent weight loss can control many cases—if only we could get people to take that life-saving, brain-defending step. We've become far too dependent on medications, turning to them cavalierly before making the lifestyle changes that could solve the problem. Nonetheless, many people will eventually need to add oral hypoglycemic medications or insulin to help their bodies use glucose. And the new medications for diabetes—from oral agents called TZDs, to a long-lasting insulin that permits once-a-day injections, to experimental insulin inhalers—have made it easier than ever to control this brain-bashing disorder.

Tight control, or keeping blood glucose levels as close as possible to the normal range, may well provide a much better defense against microvascular disease than letting them slide up to 150 or 200. But most family doctors in managed care settings simply don't have the time to help their patients achieve tight control. In addition, tight control is a double-edged sword; the closer we tiptoe toward perfect glucose levels, the greater our chance of overstepping the target and falling off the edge into low blood sugar. That's a compelling reason to push for new technology to help us achieve safe, precise control of diabetes. A tiny implantable pump that constantly monitors blood sugar and delivers the perfect dose of insulin has already been tested, and it may be widely available by about 2005, making tight control much easier to achieve. Oral medicines with built-in micro-microchips that can monitor your blood sugar, release the right dose, and report back to the doctor via the Internet are under discussion. The most exciting news is that in 2001 a team of scientists at the National Institute of Neurological Disorders and Stroke coaxed mouse stem cells into behaving just like young pancreatic cells that make insulin. This stem cell research might lead to a ready supply of *healthy new insulin-producing cells* that could be provided to the millions of people waiting to be rescued from this dread condition.

But the best approach is to avoid diabetes in the first place. Obesity is the number-one cause of adult-onset diabetes. The United States is the first nation in the history of the world where too much food is more of a problem than too little. As endocrinologist Sandra Foo puts it, "We're seeing a great deluge of masses of people becoming overweight. . . . If we don't do something about it, we're going to have an epidemic on our hands and a national health crisis." Look around—we already have it. Weight loss may be the best, most natural defense of all against impaired glucose handling. Activity—even that most sublimely natural of exercises, a daily walk—can be a huge help. A three-year study of 3,000 overweight, sedentary people showed that a prudent diet and a brisk walk five days a week prevented full-blown diabetes even better than the popular antidiabetes drug Glucophage. Now that we know what's at stake, defending ourselves from excess weight takes on a new urgency. Overcoming the extraordinary unnaturalness of an inactive life and resisting the daily inundation of limitless amounts of seductively delicious foods is *not* a merely cosmetic concern—it's a chance to save your brain.

Other Hormones, for Better and for Worse

I was on a plane to the Cayman Islands. The woman next to me was saying something to me about her trip.

"A what?" I couldn't have heard her right over the noise.

"A GH tour," she answered. "You know, growth hormone!"

"You're on a growth hormone tour?" I guess I failed to contain my surprise. I had assumed that the main attraction of the Caymans was scuba diving, or, for those curtained off in the leathery sanctum at the front of the plane, liberal banking laws. But the middle-aged couple beside me, tearing into their smoked almonds, enlightened me. Tour operators were organizing groups to fly to the Caribbean and to Central America for a course of subcutaneous growth hormone injections—a fountain of youth in a 3 cc syringe. This was in the early 1990s, before the FDA approved genetically engineered human growth hormone for use in the United States.

"Here, son," the man smiled and extended a flushed and sweaty palm, "shake my hand."

I did. He squeezed, and his flush moved up to his face.

"That's quite a grip you've got, all right." I watched the receding indentations on my hand. "Growth hormone?"

"Growth hormone!" they replied together.

American endocrinologists—hormone specialists—used to reserve growth hormone for children with severe GH deficiencies or for those with extremely short stature. It was incredibly hard to get—obtained by extraction from human cadavers via a special program run by the NIH and distributed like rare ambrosia. Recombinant human growth hormone (rhGH) became available around 1988. This safe and effective drug was a terrific advance for the children for whom it was developed. But since the synthetic hormone was available in essentially unlimited quantities, rhGH treatment became a tantalizing prospect for some people hoping to turn back the creeping hands of Father Time—

strongly encouraged by some less-than-completely-ethical boosters riding the quasi-scientific tailgate of the anti-aging bandwagon.

Today the marketing of growth hormone injections to adults is part of
a national trend. A so-called "anti-aging medicine" movement has grown
up, promoting various inadequately researched interventions meant to
halt the natural progression of life. Hormones are among the remedies
most eagerly touted and sought after, and some doctors gladly supply
non-FDA-approved prescriptions wrapped in glowing promises of physical and mental rejuvenation. They cast aside restraint. They call hormones superhormones. From the penthouses of Manhattan's Upper East
Side to the mansions of Beverly Hills, from models to movie stars to body
builders to graying rock musicians, people are flocking to these doctors
and paying tens of thousands of dollars a year for hope in the form of a
hormone shot. These days suppliers often claim that treatments will also
help your brain.

The problem is, they're sometimes right. The question is how to find
the needle of truth amid the haystack of hoopla.

Using hormones to save our brains involves three related goals: (1)
treating *atypical* hormone deficiencies (such as hypothyroidism); (2) attempting to make up for *typical* aging-related hormonal changes (such as
menopause); and (3) giving superdoses of hormones in an effort to outdo
nature. The first of these goals fits the classic medical model: diagnose a
disease and fix it. But attempting to undo the typical effects of aging, or
to outdo nature, is pushing the envelope. Nonetheless, just as with ERT,
we should be open-minded about a search for ways to provide the body
with gentle, finely tuned hormonal help to maintain brain function somewhat longer than was anticipated in the 100,000-to-200,000-year-old human plan—a plan that never took into account the possibility that we'd
be teaching ourselves Spanish at age forty-five, or learning to windsurf at
seventy.

With this goal in mind, let's look at four hormones that have been proposed as possible brain savers: growth hormone, DHEA, melatonin, and
thyroid hormone.

Growth Hormone

Growth hormone is also called *somatotropin*, which basically means a
"growing-up agent" (*tropin*) "for the body" (*soma*). That's really the key
function of growth hormone: doing all the things needed to stretch a
seventeen-inch baby into a five-foot-nine-inch teenager. The amount of
growth hormone in our growing bodies is critical. If we have too little, we

end up dwarfs; if we have too much, we become giants. This is another example of the Goldilocks principle of "just right" physiology: both dwarfs and giants have short life spans. (So contrary to the claims of some GH boosters, perhaps the way to live the longest is to maintain normal, age-appropriate levels of growth hormone.)

Growth hormone peaks in the early teen years, shooting up as high as 700 micrograms per liter (mcg/l) to spark the growth spurts of adolescence. It not only makes us grow taller, but it also decreases body fat, promotes lean body mass and muscle growth, and helps build strong bones, and it may increase our energy. These actions have added to its attraction. Growth hormone levels decline about 14 percent each decade after age twenty, bringing typical adult levels down to around 200 mcg/l.

For decades doctors have suspected that growth hormone also affects the mind. Children with short stature due to GH deficiency are often passive and withdrawn, get held back in school, and have increased rates of depression and suicide as they get older. This outcome has long been accounted for in purely psychological terms: "You'd be depressed too if you were four foot three." But there may be more to it. People treated with growth hormone in research studies sometimes report an enhanced mood and sense of well-being that placebo-treated subjects do not. If growth hormone can improve mood, might it also affect cognition? Since true GH deficiency is rare, what we really want to know is whether the mild decline in growth hormone typical of aging adults will affect our intellect, and whether GH treatment can help keep us smart.

One way to answer this question is to compare the mental status of people with typical aging-related growth hormone decline before and after GH treatment. Endocrinologist Maxine Papadakis and her colleagues at the University of California in San Francisco did just that. They treated a group of older men with growth hormone for six months. While the men's GH levels rose and their lean body mass increased, the men had no difference in grip strength or physical endurance (despite the confidence of my airline seatmates). In terms of intellect, the picture was mixed, showing a slight improvement on one test of attention but a slight *decline* in overall cognition. Furthermore, GH has some completely unacceptable side effects, including diabetes, loss of energy, breast swelling in males, joint pains, and carpal tunnel syndrome, as well as a possible increased risk of prostate and perhaps colon cancer.

What should we conclude? For normal people in midlife and beyond, bumping up growth hormone levels doesn't seem to do much for cognitive abilities and might even make them worse; I can't recommend it for saving the brain. However, a handful of adults have larger-than-normal deficiencies of growth hormone, which *possibly* contributes to memory loss; by failing to find and treat this subgroup of people, we may be missing a bet. Soon we'll have synthetic molecules—designer growth hormones—that can provide specific, targeted benefits and decrease the risks. For the time being, however, the message should be clear: don't mess around with growth hormone.

DHEA

DHEA (dehydroepiandrosterone) enters the stage wearing a cloak—it is the hormone of mystery. It's generally thought to be important for human health; but despite forty years of research, there is a striking lack of consensus about what exactly this plentiful steroid hormone is supposed to do. Furthermore, there's a Grand Canyon–size gap between the exciting news about DHEA coming from the labs and the oddly disappointing results in human clinical studies. Recently, boosters have claimed that DHEA is yet another hormonal fountain of youth: an immune system booster, a defender against heart disease, a preventer of cancer. The DHEA story is a perfect example of how a stampede of speculation can leave good science choking in the dust. Our job is to corral the stampede and find the truth, because there are a few fascinating hints that DHEA *sometimes* helps to boost the function of the human brain.

DHEA levels peak at about age twenty-five, then drop steadily until levels are negligible, in the eighties. This decline makes DHEA one of the best markers of human aging. Once scientists realized the parallel, they wondered whether DHEA might be not only a marker but also a cause of aging. Proposals followed quickly for DHEA "replacement" therapy. Doctors (and, more often, nondoctors) began extolling the benefits. Books were written. Internet sites blossomed, and sales of this nonprescription compound exploded.

What intrigues neurobehavioral researchers the most is that DHEA is made not only in the adrenal glands but also in glial cells, the brain cells that support the neurons. In the lab, this mystery hormone has been shown to enhance neuronal excitability, defend neurons from free radical attacks, and even improve neuronal plasticity (the ability of neurons to grow and adapt in response to experience). It may also regulate the receptors for two neurotransmitters, NMDA and GABA, that play vital roles in memory. In fact, several studies have shown that DHEA enhances memory in rodents.

These promising results are just the beginning. There's also evidence that DHEA can fight the underlying problems of Alzheimer's. For instance, DHEA helps control inflammation, and inflammation is definitely a part of Alzheimer's. Furthermore, it boosts the levels of insulinlike growth factor-1, which helps neurons resist the vicious assault of beta-amyloid—another way that DHEA might help save the brain from Alzheimer's. DHEA may even defend the MTL memory system against death-dealing free radicals. Putting these findings together, we have perfectly good reasons to think that DHEA might block Alzheimer's—in theory.

Stanford psychiatrist Jerry Tinklenberg studied DHEA levels in twenty-seven Alzheimer's patients and found—surprisingly—that those with higher DHEA levels actually had *lower* cognitive scores. A larger study was conducted at the famous Hôpital de la Salpetrière in Paris; 622 older people had their DHEA levels checked and were then followed for four years. The people with high DHEA levels were just as likely to develop Alzheimer's as the others. In a Japanese study, doctors studied the effects of DHEA on *serum amyloid P component* (SAP), which is found in both atherosclerotic lesions and tangles and hence may play a role in *both* of the two main brain killers, vascular disease and ARNAT. But DHEA replacement therapy actually *increased* SAP in postmenopausal women—an unsettling finding that conceivably means DHEA therapy actually promotes Alzheimer's.

Okay, so DHEA clearly plays roles in many healthful processes and offers impressive hints of brain benefits in lab animals. But that Grand Canyon between the lab evidence and the human studies still stretches, and we now have hints that DHEA might do our brains more harm than good. What's more, DHEA therapy theoretically may increase the risk of prostate cancer, uterine cancer, lung cancer, and possibly breast cancer; women taking DHEA may experience excess facial hair growth or acne. Even more troubling is the fact that people treated with high doses of DHEA may suffer potentially severe liver damage.

The bottom line is that, until clinical studies persuasively show that this powerful hormone is at least safe and possibly helpful to the *human* nervous system, DHEA is a poor bet for saving your brain.

Melatonin

In the early 1990s a frantic exchange of claims, counterclaims, and testimonials shot back and forth between the melatonin believers and the melatonin skeptics. The book *The Melatonin Miracle* by Walter Pierpaoli and William Regelson staked out the ground on one side in this battlefield; the scientific paper "Melatonin Madness," published in the distinguished journal *Cell,* staked out the other. We heard that melatonin can aid sleep, prevent cancer, control AIDS symptoms, and enhance sexual intercourse. We also heard that melatonin is a dangerous and medically useless chemical, foisted on an unsuspecting public by greedy supplement peddlers. We know that the panacea claims made by the slicker melatonin boosters are too good to be true; they remind us of the old Western drama that begins with a snake-oil salesman setting up his display wagon under the watchful eye of the marshal. At the same time, we always wonder if melatonin might have genuine benefits despite the inflated claims. As the saying goes, even a shiny used car might run.

Melatonin is the main product of the pineal gland, a bean-size organ that sits at just about the center of the brain. Hindu mystics thought it was like a third eye; they had it just about right. Like our eyes, the pineal gland responds to light. When light hits our eyes, a signal shoots into the brain, takes a detour through the *suprachiasmatic nucleus* (the biological clock in the brain), and ends up at the pineal gland to say, "Hey, it's daylight—turn off that melatonin!" The pineal promptly stops making melatonin. Once it was discovered that melatonin is linked to our biological clock, scientists began to suggest that it could be used to control sleep. To make a long story short (and no pun intended), there's less there than meets the eye.

As it turns out, despite the billions of melatonin pills sold, only a subgroup of people—more often the elderly, and mostly those rare folks with genuine deficiencies of this hormone—may sleep more restfully with small doses of melatonin. Others who also *possibly* benefit are those who need to adjust to a new time schedule because of jet lag or shift work. This possible benefit may take on new importance because of the eye-opening discovery (mentioned in Chapter 6) that young women flight attendants with chronic jet lag have shrunken temporal lobes. This may represent an entirely new lifestyle-related cause of premature brain aging, one that's completely preventable.

But the real excitement about melatonin has nothing to do with sleep.

Soon after melatonin achieved hormonal celebrity status, grant money became available and neuroscientists threw themselves into figuring out how it works. It quickly became clear that melatonin does more than regulate sleep. For one thing, melatonin receptors exist in many areas of the brain, not just in the circuits involved in biorhythms. That means melatonin must surely do something other than process light. It helps regulate sexual reproduction in animals; perhaps it does so in humans; we are still sorting this out. But recent lab studies suggest yet another possibility: that melatonin is a two-fisted brain-defending antioxidant.

Melatonin is one of the most potent scavengers of hydroxyl radicals ever discovered. It can keep nitric oxide in check, boost enzymes that fight free radicals, and rescue neurons from lipid peroxidation (the process in which a neuron's fatty membranes dissolve, leaving it naked and helpless). Melatonin also protects against calcium-induced brain injury (a major player in both Alzheimer's and strokes) and defends hippocampal memory cells from the devastating effects of excitatory injury (a potentially great way to protect the memory system). It may even have a specific anti-Alzheimer's effect. We know that beta-amyloid hurts neurons partly by ripping apart their mitochondrial DNA with free radicals; researchers at the University of South Alabama have shown that melatonin completely protects neurons from this type of injury.

Whenever we hear promising results from the lab, we always need to restrain our enthusiasm. "Interesting," we nod. "But you're not going to get my heart pounding unless you can show me some good *human* evidence." Unfortunately, the small amount of available human research tells an incomplete story.

Most of the melatonin-for-cognition research to date has looked at the benefits of a good night's sleep, figuring that better sleep may promote alertness the following day. In one military study, army aircrews rapidly deployed to the Middle East were given either melatonin or placebo to help them sleep. Upon awakening, the melatonin-treated aviators had fewer errors on a test of mental vigilance. And in a small study of ten elderly people with mild cognitive impairment, researchers at the University of California at San Diego found that ten days of melatonin treatment slightly improved memory—although we don't know for sure whether this was due to better sleep or to one of melatonin's other intriguing brain benefits.

Unfortunately, just as with DHEA, there are no really well-done studies showing whether melatonin supplements can improve cognition in a lasting way or—via its neuroprotective actions—slow the progression of memory loss. Which brings us to the bottom line: should you take melatonin to stay smart? No, not at this time.

First, we simply don't have evidence that humans get the brain-saving benefits achieved in the lab. Second, even if pure, pharmacy-grade, uncontaminated melatonin were proven to have a brain benefit, you and I should not expect to get that product when we buy a bottle of melatonin. "Consumer-grade" melatonin is of widely varying purity and strength. Independent laboratory tests show that it's common for the dose and contents specified on the *label* to be different from what's in the *bottle*, and contaminants are occasionally found in over-the-counter melatonin. Moreover, even the purest melatonin carries the risk of side effects. Many people experience excessive daytime drowsiness, a mental hangover that may increase the risk of accidents, and headaches are common. Melatonin may impair fertility, reduce sex drive in men, and possibly damage the retina. There are case reports of melatonin sparking psychotic episodes, causing seizures in children, and being associated with autoimmune hepatitis. Particularly worrisome are reports that melatonin treatment may worsen depression; if this news is confirmed, it makes melatonin look like an even worse bet for the brain.

So store-bought melatonin is not a good bet for saving your brain—or even for getting a good night's sleep. But at the very least, the recent explosion in melatonin research will probably yield important nuggets for neuroprotection.

Thyroid Hormone

I was an intern when a couple flew from Hawaii to consult my then-boss, Dr. Robert Daroff, a distinguished leader in American neurology. This couple wanted the best; and they wanted to know why Eleanor, the forty-six-year-old wife, was losing her memory. When I examined her, it was obvious that her mind was sluggish. She spoke in a slow, depressed-sounding voice, her gaze cast down at the floor. I told her my first name several times; she couldn't remember it thirty seconds later. I asked, "Do you have children?"

"I . . . I'm not sure."

Eleanor was somewhat heavily built, but she really didn't have the other classic signs of hypothyroidism (low thyroid hormone levels), such as brittle hair or delayed relaxation after her reflexes were tapped. Then I held her hands and asked her to stoop to the floor and recover to standing. She was left squatting until I pulled her up.

"Do you have trouble climbing stairs at home?" I asked.

"No," she said. "We don't have stairs."

I took her to the hospital stairwell. She was exhausted after three steps up.

Difficulty climbing stairs due to weakness in the hip and thigh muscles is a classic sign of hypothyroidism. It turned out that Eleanor's thyroid hormone level was so low as to be almost undetectable. I wondered why she had to fly in from Hawaii to find this out; dysfunction of the thyroid gland is one of the most infamous causes of memory loss and dementia—and one of the easiest to diagnose.

The thyroid gland is a small, butterfly-shaped badge of soft tissue located beneath the skin on the front of the neck. This gland, like all hormone factories in the body, is ultimately controlled by the brain. A hormone called *thyroid-stimulating hormone* (TSH) swims down from the pituitary gland to the thyroid and delivers the instruction, "Make some thyroid hormone." From fetal life to old age, TSH serves as a crucial regulator of metabolism.

But during aging, about 4 percent of middle-aged or older people develop either overactive or underactive thyroid glands—double the rate in younger people. The majority of those affected are women. The immune system also becomes slightly paranoid with age: it begins to act as if parts of our own bodies were alien invaders and attacks them in a misguided effort to protect us. This happens much more often in women than in men. As a result, 23 percent of older women develop antibodies to their own thyroid—an amazingly large number. This leads to the most common thyroid problem of middle age and beyond, Hashimoto's thyroiditis, the problem that Eleanor had. Hashimoto's usually causes thyroid levels that are too low, but it can sometimes cause levels that are too high. Either way, too low or too high, thyroid hormone levels outside the normal range hurt the mind.

Since the middle of the twentieth century, we've known that the thyroid gland is absolutely essential to normal thinking. People with *overactive* glands making too much thyroid hormone are often jumpy, agitated, and hyper to the point that they can't keep their thoughts straight; people with *underactive* glands, making too little hormone, often have memory loss, difficulty solving spatial problems, and cognitive delay that can make thinking as slow as swimming in molasses. Hypothyroid patients such as Eleanor speak in a sluggish, distracted way, as if they were trying to read street signs in a fog. In addition, hypothyroidism often causes depression, sometimes very severe cases. Knowing this, whenever people come to the clinic with a memory or mood problem, *one of the first things we test is thyroid function.* In Eleanor's case, not only was her T4 level almost too low to detect, but her TSH level was about twenty-five times normal, a sign that her brain was working extremely hard to prod her sick thyroid gland into doing its job.

We gave Eleanor synthetic thyroid. Within a week her thoughts began to speed back up toward normal. When we came in on Saturday rounds, she smiled and thanked two of us by name. It was one of those magical moments that a sleep-deprived intern never forgets.

Clinical hypothyroidism like Eleanor's is trouble enough, but roughly 4 to 14 percent of older people of both sexes develop *subclinical* hypothyroidism. It has no obvious symptoms, and the blood level of T4 may even be normal. Doctors can often diagnose subclinical hypothyroidism by looking at the TSH level; just as the gas needle creeps down before the fuel tank is empty, the TSH level creeps up before the thyroid gland gives out, since the body is making TSH like crazy, yelling at the thyroid gland,

"Hey, get to work already!" Unfortunately, doctors are unlikely to check T4 and TSH in subclinical cases. Worse yet, even a high TSH level may not reveal subtle, mind-slowing thyroid problems. Since insufficient research has been done in this area, frankly we don't know how many Americans are suffering from subclinical hypothyroidism, or how badly this condition affects the brain.

But there's no debate about *clinical* hypothyroidism. Apart from diabetes, it may be our nation's most common hormonal cause of memory loss. Furthermore, neuroscientists now suspect that *hypothyroidism increases the risk of Alzheimer's.*

The EURODEM study—a multinational study of dementia in Europe—found that people with hypothyroidism were almost two and a half times as likely to have Alzheimer's as people who did not have hypothyroidism. Several U.S. studies have also shown this connection. To be fair, one Mayo Clinic study did not show an association between thyroid disease and Alzheimer's; the reason for this discrepancy is unclear. And we're still not sure to what degree prompt treatment of hypothyroidism reverses the march toward ARNAT. But all of the evidence points in the same direction: thyroid hormone can probably help save the brain from Alzheimer's.

Perhaps even more alarming is the possibility that the millions of older Americans with *subclinical* hypothyroidism are also at higher risk for Alzheimer's. There are inklings that this may be so. For example, when doctors at Stockholm's Karolinska Institute carefully tested memory in subjects aged seventy-five to ninety-six, they found that all the subjects had "normal" thyroid levels, but those at the lower end of the normal scale had worse memories. When psychiatrists at the University of Washington examined forty-four healthy older men, they found that all the men had T4 levels within the normal range, but those with "high-normal" levels had better cognition. And when researchers at the University of Milan in Italy studied a group of women with subclinical hypothyroidism, they found that these patients had more difficulty recalling a short story than normal women. Most importantly, their memories improved after treatment with T4.

Findings such as these have led to proposals that we should be more aggressive about diagnosing and treating subclinical hypothyroidism. Diagnosing is surely a good idea; it has been suggested that all women over age fifty be screened for thyroid levels, and I agree.

The bigger question is whether gentle thyroid replacement therapy for middle-aged or older people with slight elevations of TSH would boost their brain power and perhaps even reduce their risk of Alzheimer's. The question has no certain answer, but (unlike the shaky evidence for GH, DHEA, and melatonin), the evidence that thyroid hormone benefits memory is unquestioned. What we need now is a good, big prospective clinical trial of thyroid replacement therapy to defend the brain in cases of subclinical hypothyroidism. Such a study might well reveal that treatment of these subtle declines in thyroid function is a great (and underutilized) bet for saving the human brain.

To call a hormone "Superhormone!" is like calling blood "Superblood!"— a howler. Hormones are agents of human health, but that does not mean that everyone should be pumped full to bursting with excessive doses. The goal, rather, is for every organ—the brain included—to receive the exact right amount at the exact right time. Too little or too much can be equally disastrous. Some boosters in the anti-aging movement and the supplement-industrial complex want to lead us down the garden path in regard to hormone therapy; we shouldn't let them put blindfolds on us at the garden gate. Weirdly, solid FDA regulations are in place to protect us from the serious side effects of one hormone, testosterone, but we let schoolchildren buy a closely related hormone, DHEA. We need to expand the public's protection against the dark side of hormonal treatment. In the meantime, people should be wary of unproven claims, impure products, and hucksterism masquerading as forward thinking.

On the other hand, a great deal of exciting neuroscience suggests that the right use of hormones may help save the brain. Scientists are crossing into brand-new territory, discovering things about hormones that are completely remolding our thinking. We already know some great ways to use hormones to save brains. But sad to say, we're leaving millions of people in the lurch by failing to screen them for these completely treatable problems.

As research progresses, how many more people will we discover who can be defended from memory loss if we gently optimize their hormonal functions?

It's time we found out.

CHAPTER 9

Dodging Aluminum May Save Your Brain

It was a potluck dinner. My medical school classmates had gathered to shake off a big exam. We each brought a contribution from our variably inventive kitchens: tofu casseroles, pineapple pizza, mystery loaf. Mostly, there was beer.

"What's that?" one fellow asked, pointing to a pot of vegetables.

"Vegetables," answered the young woman next to him.

"No, I mean *that*!" He was getting excited. The crowd around the card table looked in the direction indicated by his quivering finger. "It looks like aluminum!" He was pointing to the pot.

The young woman next to him didn't know him well. She was deciding that she didn't plan to. "I think you're right. It looks like an aluminum saucepan. Excuse me." She rolled her eyes to her girlfriend as she moved away. But everyone was now intrigued. Somebody asked the guy why he was so excited, and he erupted with an overwrought declaration that this was how we could all get Alzheimer's disease. The responses were mixed, from shrugs and smiles to alarm, and the debate that followed was memorable. It's a debate that has raged both before and since throughout the world's medical community.

Does aluminum exposure cause Alzheimer's disease? There's good reason to wonder. In the 1970s and 1980s, based on lab experiments and human research, the alarming idea that exposures to aluminum might increase our risk for dementia elbowed its way through the crowd of hypotheses to the front rank of Alzheimer's theories. The *aluminum hypothesis of Alzheimer's disease* was born—and the dangers of aluminum in drinking water, cooking pots, antacids, and antiperspirants became hot topics for conversation. *Are these common sources of aluminum quietly eating away at our brains?* people wondered. The effect of aluminum on the risk of dementia is still among the most controversial subjects in the scientific movement to save our brains. There's some scary evidence on one side of the issue, and some reassuring evidence on the other. Whom are we to believe? And more importantly, what are we to do?

A Hundred Years of Uncertainty

Aluminum is all around us. It's the third most common element in the earth's crust, after oxygen and silicon. Forty percent of the world's arable land contains aluminum, and when acid rain hits such land, it frees up some of the aluminum and the run-off kills trees and sends fish into paroxysms of death—so we are hardly the only species that aluminum might endanger. Since we are literally surrounded by it, a certain amount of aluminum in our blood is normal, usually less than 10 mcg/l.

Aluminum gets into our bodies in four main ways: drinking water, eating food, taking medicines, and inhaling dust. Most of the media attention has been directed to the dangers of aluminum in drinking water, though drinking water may be the source of only a tiny fraction of the aluminum that some people take in—partly because aluminum levels in water are usually modest, and partly because less than one percent of the aluminum we swallow typically makes it into our bloodstream. Small amounts may also be swallowed with tea, grains, processed foods, foods cooked in aluminum pots, toothpaste, or aluminum-containing antacids. (In the case of antacids, these "small amounts" may amount to a thousand times the dose we get from typical drinking water.) Aluminum can also get into us through our lungs or even be absorbed from antiperspirants applied to our skin. Kidney patients on hemodialysis occasionally receive massive doses straight into their bloodstream, and workplace exposure can be extraordinarily high, especially among aluminum miners, welders, and the smelters who inhale dust in gray-hazed "potrooms."

But the *amount* of aluminum we're exposed to is only one factor in what this metal does to our minds and brains. At least three other factors are involved: the *type* of aluminum; the amount of environmental aluminum that actually gets into your *body*; and the amount of aluminum that gets into your *brain*.

Aluminum comes in many types, called aluminum "species." They include all sorts of salts and minerals such as aluminum hydroxide, aluminum fluoride, and aluminum sulfate. Some aluminum species are big, and some are small; some are incredibly prone to react with molecules in our bodies, and others aren't; some are very *lipophylic*, or "fat-liking," able to sneak through the lipid membranes into our brain cells, while others aren't. Not surprisingly, given these differences, studies that ignore *which* aluminum species people were exposed to sometimes come up with opposite results. It's like asking, "Do mushrooms make you sick?" It all depends on the type.

Then there's the question of absorption. Elderly people are more likely to absorb aluminum from their gastrointestinal tracts, so even low-dose exposures from water or food may lead to high levels of aluminum in their bloodstream. And for mysterious reasons, people with Alzheimer's seem even *more* likely to absorb aluminum. In addition, when certain other compounds such as silicon or fluoride are mixed with the source of aluminum (as is pretty common in municipal water supplies), it will affect how much of the aluminum your body absorbs.

Then once it is in the bloodstream, the aluminum may or may not make it into the brain. The *blood-brain barrier*—the blood vessels' extremely finicky system for allowing only certain substances to cross into brain tissue—is usually great at keeping aluminum out; only about one fifty-thousandth of the aluminum in our blood ever gets into our brain, so even if we swallow a lot, it may not lead to much brain accumulation. Generally speaking, bigger aluminum "species" are less likely to get past this brain defense (another reason to pay attention to the type of aluminum rather than just the amount). Furthermore, certain conditions can weaken the blood-brain barrier; older people, for instance—especially those with dementia—have weakened blood-brain barriers. As a result, not only will they absorb more aluminum from their gastrointestinal tracts, but more of that aluminum may sneak into their brains, multiplying the risk of brain accumulation.

To get a good, scientific answer to the question, "Is aluminum hurting your memory?" then, we have to dig beyond the surface. But one point is clear: when aluminum *does* get into the brain, it can wreak neuronal havoc.

The World's Most Plentiful Brain Poison

Perhaps the earliest indication that aluminum is bad for the brain came from a well-known experiment in 1897: when aluminum was injected under the skin of animals, it led to paralysis, tremors, spasticity, and very weird cells in their spinal cords. Since that original discovery, hundreds of lab experiments have confirmed that aluminum is neurotoxic to animals, and tons of studies have shown that aluminum poisoning causes extreme changes in animal behavior, including memory loss.

We've also known for nearly a century that aluminum is noxious to the human brain. The first human case of aluminum brain poisoning was described in the British medical journal *Lancet* back in 1921. That patient developed terrible changes in his behavior, not to mention uncontrollable shakes. The basic facts are universally accepted: aluminum *can* damage the brain and change human behavior for the worse. What we need to know is exactly *how* it hurts brains, and whether the aluminum we're likely to encounter in everyday life (like the pot of vegetables at the end of my classmate's quivering finger) will truly boost our risk of memory loss or dementia.

The excitement about aluminum as a cause of Alzheimer's started about 1965, when researchers injected small amounts of this metal into the brains of New Zealand white rabbits. Not only did the rabbits develop serious behavior problems, but when their brains were examined through the microscope, about 10 percent of them showed changes that looked suspiciously like the notorious tangles of ARNAT. It looked like the smoking gun of the aluminum-Alzheimer's connection. But better imaging methods, like electron microscopy, showed a key difference: the tangles caused by aluminum are either straight or curved into infinitesimal S's or C's, while the tangles in Alzheimer's are twisted together in pairs (like the familiar double helix of DNA). Other studies showed that the funny-looking tangles caused by aluminum are mostly made up of *neurofilaments*—one part of the superstructure of neurons—while Alzheimer's tangles are mostly made of *microtubules,* another part. These discoveries suggested that aluminum poisons brain cells in its own special way.

Subsequent lab experiments have revealed many ways in which aluminum wreaks havoc in the brain: it decreases division in glial cells, the helpmates of neurons; it alters DNA synthesis in ways that might lead to bizarre changes in neuronal function; it damages the lipids that all nerve cells need to maintain healthy membranes; it has poisonous effects on synapses; and it has a unique ability to rev up the formation of neuron-killing free radicals in a dangerous collaboration with iron. The stack of lab studies showing the damaging effects of aluminum on the central nervous system is so thick that if it fell on your foot, you'd limp for a month. Based on the lab evidence, we might reasonably say that aluminum is the world's most plentiful neurotoxicant. But does it really give people *Alzheimer's?*

Doubts about the existence of a genuine aluminum-ARNAT link arose not only because the tangles look different but also because the clinical picture of aluminum poisoning differs from that of Alzheimer's. For instance, kidney patients on dialysis are at high risk for aluminum poisoning: when aluminum creeps through dialysis filters and into their blood, some of it gets into their brains, leading to quick jerks of the body, seizures, and confusion. When such patients come to the neurology clinic, their lightninglike jerks make the condition unforgettably different from

Alzheimer's. Since some of these patients develop an early and awful dementia, it's clear that aluminum can hurt the human brain in lasting ways, but their clinical and molecular trouble looks like a distorted picture—a fun-house-mirror version of Alzheimer's—rather than the real thing.

At this point in the story, in the late 1980s, scientists concluded that aluminum might cause something that's *similar* to Alzheimer's, or something that *overlaps* with Alzheimer's, but not Alzheimer's itself. If aluminum played a big role in Alzheimer's, the thinking went, we might expect to find more aluminum in Alzheimer's brains. A few early studies reported that brains from Alzheimer's patients contain very high aluminum levels, yet later studies using better methods showed no higher levels. How about Alzheimer's blood? Yes, increased aluminum was sometimes found in the blood of Alzheimer's patients, but this might be a nonspecific effect of aging or ill health rather than a cause-and-effect link between aluminum and Alzheimer's.

But then physiologist Donald R. Crapper McLachlan of the University of Toronto decided to go beyond the simple assumptions of the early studies. Rather than just looking at total aluminum levels in the brain, he speculated that a tiny amount of aluminum might insinuate itself into the core of a neuron, the nucleus. If so, whole-brain aluminum content might not increase, but the aluminum might be building up nonetheless just where it would do the worst possible damage: harming our DNA. In fact, examining the brains of Alzheimer's patients, McLachlan found a *ninefold* increase in aluminum in the very parts of the nucleus that are most needed for gene expression.

This study, among others, opened neuroscientists' eyes to the possibility that a genuine, deep biological link existed between aluminum and Alzheimer's. But without conclusive proof, your average neuroscientist is, for good reason, a skeptic. He or she would say, "Sure, aluminum is one heck of a brain poison, but I won't be convinced that it causes *Alzheimer's* unless it's somehow linked to classic plaques and tangles." New research findings are shining light into that previously shadowy corner: it appears that aluminum is indeed linked to these two classic changes in the Alzheimer's-afflicted brain, because, as we now realize, *aluminum is a protein misfolder.*

Aluminum has been discovered within tangles exactly where we find hyperphosphorylated tau, the abnormal version of tau that turns the railroad tracks of microtubules into twisted hulks that eventually kill brain cells (see Chapter 4). And evidence is growing that aluminum actually *causes* these tangles: several laboratories have now shown that aluminum boosts the hyperphosphorylation of tau, the underlying cause of tau misfolding. So, in addition to making its own funny-looking, atypical tangles, aluminum seems to misfold tau, which would boost the risk of the typical tangles of Alzheimer's.

Aluminum has also recently been linked to the other main lesion in ARNAT, amyloid plaques. New reports show that even minuscule amounts of aluminum can boost the production of beta-amyloid, that dangerous insoluble stuff that forms a core at the center of many of these plaques. In fact, one study shows that aluminum can corrupt the usually innocent and neuron-friendly "non-A beta" form of amyloid into the nasty, insoluble, plaque-forming, brain-killing beta form. There's also evidence that aluminum can inhibit the breakdown of beta-amyloid once it's made—another way that this metal could lead to an overload of misfolded amyloid in the brain. Furthermore, when plaques are formed, tiny mobile inflammatory cells called *microglia* start to attack them by releasing free radicals. When aluminum is in the vicinity, it seems to increase the severity of free radical attacks, helping microglia to chew up synapses and leaving the mind a shambles.

Based on the latest discoveries, I will offer a new theory to explain the complex relationship between aluminum and memory loss: sure, aluminum has its own special way of poisoning brain cells, and yes, heavy-duty aluminum exposure can produce an atypical brain disease that's different from Alzheimer's. But aluminum *also* speeds up the exact problems at the root of Alzheimer's: it misfolds amyloid to make plaques, and it misfolds tau to make tangles. It's probably time to toss out the old-fashioned viewpoint that aluminum causes either Alzheimer's or a different condition. It can cause both.

I will even propose a tentative theory about which condition a person is most likely to get. There's no question that massive contact—true aluminum poisoning—causes serious intellectual damage. Aluminum miners and dialysis patients occasionally suffer massive, eye-glazing levels of exposure that leave them with definite cognitive impairments. Such impairments probably involve the atypical brain poisoning we call *aluminum encephalopathy*. In contrast, low-dose, long-term environmental exposure may be less likely to do this—but it may increase your risk of Alzheimer's.

Aluminum is a *risk factor* for these various brain changes, not a guarantee that they will occur. When you ask "Will exposure to aluminum make me forgetful?" it's like asking "Will exposure to sunlight give me a serious burn?" Lots of variables are involved in the final risk. The type of aluminum, the route of exposure, the condition of the gastrointestinal tract, the condition of the blood-brain barrier, and a host of yet-to-be-discovered genetic factors may all contribute to your final risk.

Massive doses of aluminum are rare. Our real question is whether the smaller doses that you and I are most likely to absorb will truly hurt our brains. Do people with typical environmental exposures to aluminum get more dementia?

Drinking Water and the Brain

Studies of the impact of environmental aluminum have focused on water because, even though the dose may be low, drinking water is the most common source of aluminum exposure in the world, it's just about impossible to avoid, and the very thought that our water supply is contaminated with a substance that hurts the brain is deeply unsettling. The modern era's dread of aluminum was launched in 1955 when a Canadian study showed that people from regions with high aluminum levels in their drinking water died with dementia listed on their death certificates more often than people from other regions. No autopsies were done, so we have no way of knowing if even one of those people had Alzheimer's. But that provocative study dropped a rock in the kettle. Ever since, researchers around the world have scrambled to see whether their own water could cause Alzheimer's disease. The story is far from complete, but there are hints that brain troubles begin when the level of aluminum in drinking water starts to creep up toward about 200 mcg/l.

For instance, a second Canadian study showed that people living in areas with aluminum levels of above 200 mcg/l had a 46 percent increase in the risk of dementia. A Norwegian study showed that the rate of dying with dementia was about 50 percent higher among people who lived in the region with the highest aluminum concentration in the water supply: 200 mcg/l. And a famously worrisome 1989 British study found that the risk of early-onset dementia seemed to be about 50 percent higher in districts where the aluminum level was above 110 mcg/l than in those where the level was lower than 10 mcg/l.

But no one actually looked at the brains to make sure these demented patients had Alzheimer's disease. A better way to investigate the question would be to find a group of typical, autopsy-proven cases of Alzheimer's, then go back to check their water supplies. A study from Ontario, Canada—one of the best studies in the field—did just that. Donald McLachlan and his group found that people who had spent the last ten years of their lives in areas where the aluminum level was at least 100 mcg/l in the drinking water had more than 2.5 times the risk of Alzheimer's disease. What's more, the higher the aluminum level, the higher the risk of Alzheimer's: at a cut-off of 125 mcg/l the risk rose to 3.6 times; at 150 mcg/l it was 4.4 times; and at 175 mcg/l it rose to 7.6 *times* the risk of Alzheimer's found in people who lived in areas with lower aluminum levels.

To be fair, not all studies of drinking water have found a relationship between aluminum levels and Alzheimer's. The same English group that did that worrisome 1989 study published a follow-up study in 1997 that found no relationship at all between Alzheimer's and aluminum in the drinking water, up to concentrations of 200 mcg/l. Swiss researchers took a different tack; rather than looking at dead people's brains, they looked at live people's minds. They tested the memory of 800 people between the ages of eighty and eighty-five. Half had grown up exposed to drinking water with aluminum concentrations of just 4 mcg/l, and the other half with concentrations of 98 mcg/l, about twenty-five times as much aluminum as the first group. The researchers found no difference between the two groups in memory. That may be because the highest exposure levels in this study—98 mcg/l—were still below the threshold required to do measurable harm. Just to make things complicated, a 1996 study in Bordeaux, France, found the opposite: that aluminum in the drinking water *was* related to cognitive impairment, even when the aluminum level was as low as 3.5 mcg/l!

What are we to think about this mysterious combination of scary and reassuring results? Does aluminum in drinking water threaten our brains or not? There is no easy answer, but there are some good reasons for the widely variable results. First, even when the local water is chock-full of aluminum, the risk of aluminum exposure may not be higher, since the acidity, the fluoride content, and the silicon content of the water can make a big difference in how much of its aluminum people will absorb. In fact, fluoride and silicon compete with aluminum for gut absorption, so some scientists say that if you live in a place with high levels of these chemicals in your drinking water, you may be well protected against aluminum poisoning. Second, individual physiology makes a big difference: older people may absorb much more aluminum from the water than younger people, and people whose blood-brain barriers are weak—either from age or ill health—may be letting aluminum slip in like fish through a tattered net. Third, there are surely yet-to-be-discovered genetic differences in our brains' responses to aluminum; as with any toxin, some of us are bound to be much more resistant than others.

The bottom line? The evidence linking aluminum in drinking water and dementia is too plentiful to ignore. There may or may not be a fire, but there's a whole lot of smoke.

Antacids, Antiperspirants, Foods, and a Notorious Experiment

Aluminum-containing antacids, as we've seen, may give us hundreds or even thousands of times as much aluminum as we get from drinking water. If the modest amount of aluminum in most drinking water is enough to contribute a little to the risk of Alzheimer's, then the *enormous* doses of aluminum in antacids would theoretically contribute greatly. But studies of

Alzheimer's done in Australia, Canada, England, Italy, and the state of Washington found no increase among people with higher use of antacids. What's more, a study of ulcer patients who were thought to use very high doses of aluminum-containing antacids for years found no increased risk of Alzheimer's. One possibility is that, at the very moment when antacids deliver aluminum to the body, they're also reducing acidity. Since aluminum absorption depends on acidity, antacids may be simultaneously delivering a whopping dose of aluminum and preventing the absorption of that metal. Whatever the reason, antacids don't seem a likely suspect.

How about antiperspirants? Most modern antiperspirants use aluminum salts as a major ingredient (they work wonders for controlling underarm sweat), and we know that aluminum can penetrate the skin. Several studies have reported a connection between antiperspirant use and dementia, others have found no such connection, and we're left lacking a definitive conclusion.

What about food? Small amounts of aluminum end up in many of the grain-based foods we eat; the amount depends on the grain itself, where it's grown, and how it's processed. A study from the State University of New York at Syracuse found that newly diagnosed Alzheimer's patients were more likely to have eaten larger amounts of pancakes, waffles, biscuits, muffins, corn bread, or corn tortillas. Even grain-product desserts were a risk factor. (Imagine, brownie-induced dementia.) On the other hand, black tea—one of the world's most popular beverages—contains a fair amount of aluminum, but there's no evidence that Alzheimer's is more common in tea-drinking countries.

This is the dilemma we're faced with: we have some positive evidence, some negative evidence, and a hundred years of uncertainty about the role of aluminum in dementia. It's possible that failure to take into account the many variables we've talked about has covered the road to the truth. To really see whether aluminum contributes to ARNAT or Alzheimer's disease, we'd have to do some kind of prospective study. We'd have to recruit a big group of genetically identical volunteers, deliberately expose them to low or high does of a specific type of aluminum for fifty years or so, and see what happens. Obviously, we're not going to do that. And even if we used mice for that kind of chronic exposure experiment, we might not learn as much as we'd hope to, since mice are resistant to aluminum toxicity!

So What's a Body to Do?

Despite all the inconsistency—despite the flawed studies and emotional biases and unanswered questions—the evidence as a whole is fascinating and troubling. Good scientists have repeatedly found some connection between aluminum and dementia. Whether it plays any causative role in ARNAT or in the eventual appearance of Alzheimer's disease is currently suspected but unproven. Whether it is a significant factor in accelerating the epidemic of memory loss among aging Americans is uncertain. My guess is that it plays a small but genuine role. But the most important question is not "Does aluminum cause Alzheimer's disease?" It's "Is aluminum bad for the brain?" The answer is clearly yes. Aluminum is a dementing molecule. That's a reason for concern and probably, for action.

Can dodging aluminum save your brain? It would be easy to say yes if we were routinely exposed to massive doses of aluminum, the kinds that unequivocally hurt the brain. If you smelt aluminum for a living and the air-filtration system is inadequate, fix it or quit. But most of us are exposed to much smaller doses. How small? Look at your water.

The World Health Organization (WHO) recommends that aluminum levels in drinking water be less than 200 mcg/l. This is a very reasonable standard, considering that the most worrisome levels are above that limit. But the U.S. EPA requires *no* measurement of water aluminum levels. Aluminum concentration in drinking water isn't even on the list of potential toxins to be considered for regulation down the road; it's on the list "requiring further study." As it stands, the EPA *recommends* levels between 50 and 200 mcg/l, but this is what is called a "secondary maximum concentration level," primarily designed for aesthetic purposes, since too much aluminum can discolor water. The EPA conducts no enforcement whatsoever for secondary standards. As far as the federal government is concerned, we're on our own with regard to aluminum in our drinking water.

Does your state government protect you? Not likely. Every state has its own standards for water quality, but reporting aluminum levels is usually completely optional, barring a known violation of a state-imposed standard. Even then, enforcement is rare. So the only way to determine whether your drinking water exceeds the WHO limit is to call your local utility. That can be something of an adventure.

Consider Los Angeles, city of angels, the largest municipality in the United States. Depending on what part of the city you live in and the time of year, your water comes variously from the Colorado River, the Los Angeles aqueduct, local wells, or a mixture of all three. The aqueduct water usually has aluminum levels below 50 mcg/l; so does most of the well water. But Colorado River water is hard as a rock, brimming with minerals, and when this water leaves the Weymouth treatment plant and heads for the city, it contains from 140 to 310 mcg/l of aluminum. This means that people living in the harbor area of L.A.—the ones who get pure, unmixed Colorado River water fresh from the snowfields of the high Sierras—are most at risk for aluminum exposures over the WHO limit.

So what should you do? This is clearly a case for Pascal's Bet. If you choose correctly, you might save your brain. If you choose to defend your brain from excess aluminum exposure, and fifty years from now it turns out that the concern was not justified, little is lost. Even though the evidence of a causal link between environmental aluminum and Alzheimer's is still somewhat inconclusive, we need a prudent plan. I recommend the following:

1. Determine the aluminum concentration in your local drinking water by calling your local water utility. If the concentration exceeds 200 mcg/l, seriously consider switching your family to bottled or filtered water. Unfortunately, some water bottlers cannot be trusted to give you an accurate measure of mineral content; this may make water filters a better bet. Resin-based water filter systems are impractical because they need to be regenerated with a dangerous caustic acid. Carbon filters simply don't work. Reverse-osmosis or distillation units are the most effective devices and will eliminate 98 to 99 percent of the aluminum in drinking water.

2. In general, limit aluminum-containing antacids to short-term use. If you have a condition that requires long-term protection of your stomach from acid, consider substituting a histamine 2 receptor blocker (like Pepcid AC), or ask your doctor about alternatives.

3. Consider whether it's worth it to you personally to reap the cosmetic and social advantages of aluminum-containing antiperspirants or the lightweight cooking advantages of aluminum pots. These are areas where the research is so preliminary that it's hard to make a recommendation.

4. If you or someone close to you requires hemodialysis, make sure the medical facility you use is extremely vigilant about protecting its patients from aluminum overdoses.

5. Avoid the use of calcium supplements labeled "oyster shell" or "natural source," which often contain aluminum (and even lead). Many safer formulations are available.

Finally, stay tuned to the neurobehavior news. The aluminum-brain connection is a story that's not going away.

CHAPTER 10

Saving Your Brain's Blood Flow

Sarah's head CT scan had been done minutes before. Those of us who had rushed her down to the CT scanner, then back up to the ER, were left with an image of her brain imprinted in ours. Scanning up from the foramen magnum at the base of the skull, one 1.6 cm-thick section at a time, we had watched as each new slice of brain appeared, like a fresh page in a picture book.

She had awakened that morning in her family's old summer place on Martha's Vineyard. Something felt wrong. As she rolled to get up, her right arm stayed put, flaccid beneath her. "Earl," she said to her husband. But she didn't really say it. She thought it; she meant to say it; but nothing came out. Soon she was on a Coast Guard helicopter headed for Boston.

Everything in the CT scan looked normal until the axial brain images reached the top of the temporal lobes. As the next page appeared, we drew back from the computer screen. It was as obscene as pornography—a big gaping darkness where important parts of her left hemisphere should have been. The fluid-filled ventricles toward the center of the brain, usually as symmetrical as the wings of a butterfly, were being pushed from left to right as the pressure of swelling brain tissue formed a contorted, half-collapsed abstraction. "Wernicke's," said the senior resident, pointing at lost language areas one by one. "Broca's. The arcuate fasciculus. Shit, shit."

A stroke is never good. A stroke that eliminates the parts of the brain required for speech and understanding is a tragedy.

At the end of our shift we went home, each to his or her own contemplations, sensing that we'd witnessed a monumental loss. Sarah had turned fifty the previous Sunday. She would probably never speak again. Though she was a complete stranger to us, we couldn't help identifying with this tanned and vital-looking woman who smiled at us kindly through her terror. We imagined ourselves in her place, then shrugged the thought away, realizing, worst of all, that her stroke was probably preventable.

The word *stroke* emphasizes the sudden slam of mortality into the tissue of the mind. A stroke is the rapid death of brain cells following a marked reduction in the delivery of oxygenated blood. If enough brain cells die at once or over the course of several strokes, and those brain cells happen to be in the parts of the brain needed for thinking, a person may lose the ability to conduct the affairs of life—the hallmark of dementia. Thus, neurologists speak of "vascular dementia," dementia resulting from strokes.

But this simplistic concept of strokes and vascular dementia is in desperate need of revision. The idea that *strokes* are the main way that vascular disease hurts the brain is one of the great myths of modern medicine—one we must debunk. Yes, we need to defend our brains from strokes, and in this chapter you will learn how to do that. But a stroke is the end result, the worst case, the final outcome of an unchecked process that usually begins in childhood and that may undermine the brain for decades. In fact, strokes and vascular dementia are really just the tip of the iceberg. We need to defend ourselves not only against these obvious, superficial problems but also against the vast bulk of the problem lurking beneath the clinical surface. It's time for a paradigm shift. To save our brains, we must deal with the earliest, subtlest threats to brain blood flow. Long before a stroke, most brains suffer from *cerebrovascular compromise* (CVC).

CVC is anything that stands in the way of the steadfast delivery of oxygen-rich blood to every cell in the brain. It includes sudden blockages in blood flow (as in a typical stroke), but it also includes too little blood pressure, too much blood pressure, stiff, inflamed blood vessels, and any of a number of other insidious changes commonly lurking in our brains. CVC is a cruel and hydra-headed beast. Tens of thousands of Americans are diagnosed with so-called vascular dementia, and millions more have been diagnosed with strokes, but *tens* of millions have CVC. Most of them have no idea of the trouble they're in.

In trying to understand CVC, we will be looking at the process that *leads* to strokes. We will see that strokes and other less extreme forms of CVC involve a conspiracy of biological demons including hypertension, cholesterol, atherosclerosis, platelets, and emotional stress. Then we will hear the terrific news that fairly simple preventive measures greatly improve our odds of dodging CVC. In fact, doing the right things to defend yourself against the CVC monster is a remarkably easy way to save your brain.

What Is a Stroke?

Strokes are the number-three cause of death in the United States, after heart disease and cancer. Each year about 750,000 Americans suffer a stroke. Many survive and are discharged from hospitals with poststroke disabilities. Sarah's stroke was absolutely typical, since strokes are notorious for striking down people in their prime: the peak years for stroke are from forty-five to sixty-five. Her stroke was also almost certainly preventable; as we soon learned, she had high blood pressure that she had never taken seriously and had allowed to go untreated for seven years. But for every person whose stroke is diagnosed, there are many others suffering vascular brain damage that is *never* diagnosed. The Cardiovascular Health Study revealed that up to one-third of the elderly have strokelike lesions in their brains that they and their doctors were never aware of. So tens of millions of Americans are living, unaware, with holes in their brains. Since even a tiny silent stroke can affect one's thinking ability, this is quite a disturbing state of affairs.

The good news is that the incidence of strokes has declined dramatically as a result of effective treatments for high blood pressure. The bad news is that toward the end of the 1990s the rate of this decline began to taper off, and that in some parts of the United States, especially in the southeastern "stroke belt," the decrease never occurred. African Americans have a strikingly high rate of strokes—80 percent higher than for Caucasians—producing a calamitous but little-known epidemic in this part of our population.

Strokes come in two major types. The first is an *ischemic* stroke—*ischemia* meaning "too little delivery of blood." Ischemic strokes typically happen when a blood vessel suddenly becomes blocked, like a stream that's suddenly blocked when a beaver drops the final log onto its dam. The second kind is a *hemorrhagic* stroke, in which a blood vessel bursts inside the brain, like a stream's bank giving way after a torrential rain. Since the majority of strokes are of the ischemic type, we will focus on them in this chapter. In many cases, people have a warning before an ischemic stroke, a kind of "ministroke" called a *transient ischemic attack* (TIA), often just a fleeting minute or two of blurred vision, dizziness, numbness, or weakness. Sometimes they don't even see their doctor about it. Despite the evanescence of TIAs, we should never take them lightly. People who have had a TIA are ten times as likely to suffer a full-fledged stroke.

No matter which variety of stroke we're talking about, the same basic mechanisms apply: when blood flow falls below a critical minimum for more than a minute or two, some brain cells—deprived of oxygen beyond any hope of recovery—will die. This vascular catastrophe is usually the result of a conspiracy among five key troublemakers: cholesterol, hypertension, emotional stress, atherosclerosis, and platelets.

Now it's time to separate the myths from the science and reveal a fairly revolutionary idea. These conspirators don't have to go to all the trouble of causing a stroke to wreak havoc. Each of them *by itself*, in its own way, can make brain inhospitable to mind. In this chapter, we'll see what they are, how they hurt your brain, and exactly what to do about them.

Cholesterol: Beyond the Myths

Cholesterol is a fat. Fats, or *lipids,* are the body's major way to store energy. Contrary to common belief, cholesterol is not a bad thing in and of itself; it's extremely valuable to the body. It forms a critical part of neuronal membranes and the insulation around neurons, so cholesterol actually makes up a huge proportion of the brain's weight. People are also sometimes surprised to learn that most of our cholesterol does *not* come directly from the fat-filled foods we eat; instead, it's synthesized by our own livers. We could eat rice and carrot sticks all day, but our livers would still convert some of these foods into cholesterol and pour it into our blood. Also, people's cholesterol-processing systems vary greatly: some people can eat almost anything and still have a low cholesterol level; others need to dodge fatty foods to lower their cholesterol; and still others could eat the healthiest diet on earth and still their livers would crank out cholesterol like crazed butter churns, keeping their levels high. Finally, even though people who are obese are more likely to have high cholesterol levels, people who are fit and slender can have them too.

Cholesterol travels through the bloodstream, like a melon on a truck, in the cholesterol-carrying transports called *lipoproteins.* When your doctor checks your lipid profile, he's looking not only at your total cholesterol level but also at the different types of cholesterol-filled transports, especially low-density lipoprotein (LDL), often called "bad" cholesterol because it tends to deposit cholesterol on artery walls, and high-density lipoprotein (HDL), often called "good" cholesterol because it ferries cholesterol from the entire body back to the liver, thus helping to prevent cholesterol from building up in the arteries. The lipid profile (total cholesterol and levels of LDL and HDL) is so predictive of heart attacks that an entire generation is now anxiously watching numbers their parents never worried about. Up until the year 2001, the magic number was 200; the doctor would say, "If your total cholesterol level is less than 200, you're probably fine." As we'll see later in this chapter, there's a more accurate way to calculate your real risk.

Fully *half* of American adults have either borderline or high blood cholesterol levels, making this health problem amazingly common. For decades high levels have been known to increase the risk of heart attacks, but only recently have we discovered that high levels also increase the risk of strokes. At least, some strokes. Consider MR. FIT—the Multiple Risk Factor Intervention Trials. This study of nearly 13,000 American men found that high cholesterol levels were associated with *ischemic* strokes, while *lower*-than-usual cholesterol levels were associated with *hemorrhagic* strokes. Still, since the great majority of strokes are of the ischemic type, elevated cholesterol is now recognized as a major threat to the brain.

But the big news is that high cholesterol levels seem to impair cognition *even without producing a stroke*. Studies from Texas, Japan, and Italy have all found that higher cholesterol levels among older adults are associated with lower cognitive performance. This is more than a little disturbing: it means that potentially half the adult population of America may be at risk of operating with less-than-optimal brain function. All of this research supports the theory that high cholesterol is busily launching a sneak attack on our brain cells long before we have a stroke. This gives us one heck of an incentive to keep our cholesterol down.

How much good does it do to lower your cholesterol? Roughly speaking, for men or women, with or without heart disease, a 10 percent reduction in an elevated cholesterol level will result in a 30 to 40 percent reduction in heart attacks. That's a huge difference! The percent reduction in ischemic strokes is probably in the same ballpark, which is why it is so heartening to know that the type of cholesterol-lowering drugs called HMG-CoA reductase inhibitors, better known as *statins,* have proved effective at preventing strokes among people with high cholesterol levels. When doctors at the Bowman Gray School of Medicine analyzed more than 19,000 patients taking statins such as simvastatin (Zocor) and pravastatin (Pravachol), they found that these drugs produced an impressive 27 percent decrease in strokes. This news has to get out; statins are a much underutilized defense against CVC.

Yet high cholesterol does not usually act alone. In the overwhelming majority of cases, high blood pressure—*hypertension*—is a fully culpable co-conspirator.

What Is Hypertension?

The number-one cause of CVC is hypertension. And since CVC is one of the easiest-to-fix causes of memory loss, hypertension is one of the main targets of the new effort to protect the brain. Hypertension is simply an abnormal, and usually symptomless, elevation in the blood pressure in the arteries. The word *hypertension* is potentially confusing, because *ten-*

sion suggests psychological stress. Stress can indeed raise your blood pressure, but it is a separate problem: you can have the serenity of a Zen master and *still* have hypertension, because the pressure in your arteries is determined by lots of factors other than emotions. About 55 million Americans have hypertension; only about 35 million of them know it. The other 20 million are walking down an alley in the dark, unaware that this silent killer is wrecking their arteries. Of the 35 million who are aware they are hypertensive, only 28 million seek treatment, and only half of these succeed in getting their pressure down to normal, either because the doctor does not provide sufficiently aggressive intervention or because the patient is less than fully compliant with the program. The most inescapable risk factor for hypertension is age, which means that with the aging of the population, this silent source of brain injury is growing rapidly. Adding together the unknowing, the untreated, and the undertreated, roughly 41 million people in the United States have blood pressure that's out of control. That's a *huge* number of people representing a substantial proportion of the population, and every one of them has a brain at risk.

The mechanics of hypertension are straightforward. As the heart squeezes and relaxes, it pumps out blood. The big squeeze is called *systole,* which produces the *systolic blood pressure.* The heart's relaxation between beats is called *diastole,* which produces our *diastolic blood pressure.* "Optimal" blood pressure is considered to be less than about 120 systolic over 80 diastolic (written 120/80). "Normal" adult blood pressure is considered to be less than 140 over 90, written 140/90. "Hypertension" refers to any elevation above 140/90.

If you sense an arbitrariness in these numbers, you're right. The boundaries between "optimal," "normal," and "hypertensive" are based entirely on the fact that higher numbers roughly predict who is more likely to run into vascular trouble. Many cardiologists say we'd do better if doctors did not wait until people had pressures of 141/91 but instead treated them when their systolic rose into the border zone of 130 to 139, or when their diastolic rose into the border zone of 85 to 89. This approach might actually *prevent* some of the changes in blood vessels that cause the rise.

Why are some of us hypertensive and others not? We should probably abandon the old idea that hypertension is a specific "disease." Diabetes, elevated cholesterol, physical inactivity, race, obesity, smoking, stress, excessive alcohol, and excessive salt intake all may contribute to hypertension. Even though "high blood pressure" is the final common result, each of these factors may hammer on our blood vessels in its own special way.

Diabetes: Many hypertensives have trouble handling glucose—so-called insulin resistance. It's not surprising that *severe* diabetes leads to hypertension, since this kind of diabetes almost always pounds the kidneys, which are directly involved in the control of blood pressure. What's surprising is that *mild* insulin resistance is so strongly associated with hypertension. The common link may be body mass, because obesity can lead both to hypertension and to insulin resistance.

Obesity: Weight gain seems to trigger hypertension in some people—and *not* just because obesity is associated with fat deposits in arteries. One theory is that obesity somehow flips on a genetic "hypertension switch," but this interesting idea needs to be fleshed out by further research.

Cholesterol: People with high cholesterol levels are caught in the vicious cycle of blood vessel damage causing hypertension causing more blood vessel damage. Excess alcohol use and *any* amount of cigarette smoking do the same.

Race: Urban blacks in America have about twice the rate of hypertension as whites and almost four times as many resulting vascular problems. We don't know if this is primarily related to lifestyle (such as high-fat, high-salt diets) or to genetic factors, or to both. Interestingly, obesity seems to be more closely linked to hypertension among blacks than among Caucasians. Recent research suggests a completely new avenue for prevention: many African Americans lose their ability to metabolize lactose as they reach adulthood, and their low intake of calcium-rich dairy products is surprisingly well correlated with high blood pressure. With all the lactose-free products available these days, that calcium problem is largely fixable.

African Americans are also particularly vulnerable to hypertension related to salt consumption. Of all the risk factors for essential hypertension, salt is the most controversial. Through the 1980s and most of the 1990s, doctors strongly advised a low-salt diet for all hypertensive patients. This may be a big mistake: only about 60 percent of all hypertensives are actually "salt sensitive"—whites somewhat less so, African Americans more so—and only a minority of those who are will see a big drop in their blood pressure by strictly limiting their salt intake.

Hypertension and the Great Brain Robbery

Up to this point, we've discussed hypertension as a risk factor for heart attacks and strokes. But a recent and rather shocking finding is that, just as elevated cholesterol levels seem to be associated with lower cognitive performance, people with hypertension may also experience cognitive loss even if they *don't* have strokes. This idea is still a bit controversial and is fraught with the potential for causing alarm. After all, many millions of people have hypertension. The notion that their thinking may not quite be up to par might cause them justifiable dread—and conceivably cause employers to discriminate against them. Yet a number of studies all suggest that this is indeed the case.

Just a sampling: a French study of more than 2,000 people found that systolic hypertension was linked to lower cognitive scores. A Swedish study of 999 men found that those who had diastolic hypertension at age fifty were more likely to have impaired mental status when they reached seventy. Recently, British researcher Gary Ford published a detailed study of 107 men with moderately high blood pressure (an average of 164/89), comparing their memory and other functions with those of people with pressures averaging 120/80. "In nearly every aspect of cognitive function we studied," concluded Dr. Ford, "the people with high blood pressure performed worse than those with normal blood pressure." And another recent study revealed that shrinkage of the language centers of the brain is more common among adults who have high blood pressure.

These and many other findings confirm the key point that the brain functions best when its blood supply is delivered under normal pressure. Living with a high-pressure blood supply is like trying to drink from a fire hose. Since 55 million Americans have hypertension, *a quarter of all Americans* may potentially be at risk for brain impairments from this cause alone. It's a disconcerting and inescapable thought: the typically high-salt, high-fat, high-calorie diet consumed by Americans, combined with their typically sedentary lifestyle, is contributing to a great American brain robbery.

These findings would be merely academic if we could do nothing about them. But there's solid evidence that control of hypertension yields major brain benefits.

For example, researchers at the University of Auckland examined the results of seventeen trials of antihypertensive treatment and concluded that decreasing systolic pressure by 10 to 12 points or diastolic by 5 to 6 points reduces stroke risk by 38 percent! A recent study of people with both diabetes and hypertension found that lowering the blood pressure all the way to 135/80 reduced strokes by *44 percent*—an amazing improvement. In mid-2000, as a result, the National Heart, Lung, and Blood Institute issued an advisory urging doctors to shoot for this lower blood pressure target for diabetics, and some doctors say we'd prevent even *more* strokes if we pushed for a still lower target of 130/80.

Will wrestling your pressure down also save you from dementia? One intervention trial gives us encouraging news: the Systolic Hypertension in Europe Trial found that antihypertensive treatment of elderly men and women who had moderately elevated systolic blood pressure led to a *50 percent* decline in the rate of dementia. Multiply that result by the tens of millions of people at risk, and the worldwide cognitive benefits of treating hypertension are potentially astounding.

I won't be shy about stating the implications. Given the strong evidence that hypertension itself—even without producing a stroke—impairs thinking and increases the risk of Alzheimer's, maintaining normal blood pressure is one of the best bets of all for protecting brain cells. Sure, it's also going to save your heart. But we ought to shout it from the rooftops: *Fight hypertension and save your brain!*

The Claws of Stress

If hypertension is the number-one vascular enemy of the brain, then stress is the number-one psychological contributor to hypertension. As we saw in Chapter 5, our stress systems, designed to detect threats such as charging wildebeests, now must respond to demanding bosses, angry customers, or the looming due dates of career-critical projects. Under such conditions, the nervous system flips into its fight-or-flight mode, and blood pressure goes up. In ancient times, this response helped power us out of danger, gearing us up to leap into battle or sprint away. Nowadays the same response may kill us.

Monkeys that are under emotional stress experience spasms in their coronary arteries and double the rate of development of atherosclerotic changes in their coronary vessels. Humans under stress are prone to accelerated atherosclerosis, coronary artery spasm, left ventricular enlargement, and hypertension. A study of 901 Finnish men under age fifty-five, reported by psychologist Thomas Kamarck of the University of Pittsburgh, gave subjects a mildly stressful test of memory; those who showed the most extreme blood pressure responses were also the ones with the greatest narrowing of their carotid arteries. In America, blacks in particular seem prone to this link between stress and hypertension. And Susan Everson of the University of Michigan School of Public Health has shown that hostile men are twice as likely to have strokes as their calmer peers. In addition, depression often contributes to stress.

Taken together, the available research strongly suggests that stress, anger, and depression contribute to the deadly chain of sympathetic arousal and CVC as well as to chronic hypertension. As we saw in Chapter 5, stress can hurt the brain by poisoning the hippocampus with an overload of stress hormones, but it can also hurt the brain by raising blood pressure, and may do so more commonly. If you find yourself clutched in the awful claws of stress and depression, your brain may be in for double trouble. Managed care organizations need to accept the strange-but-true fact that definitive treatment for stress and depression is a powerful form of vascular medicine.

Cholesterol, hypertension, and stress all may put the brain at risk for cerebrovascular compromise, but they do not do so overnight. What makes the clean-as-a-whistle, flexible-as-a-balloon arteries in the brain of a child turn into the stiff-walled, clogged-up tubes in a middle-aged person? It's the process we call *atherosclerosis*.

Atherosclerosis—Scourge or Plague?

It's an awe-inspiring feeling to pull a brain out of a cadaver. You can't help but reflect: *this is it, heavy in my hands, the seat of the self.* The first time I did this was in medical school. As soon as I turned the brain over in my hands, my lab partner pointed toward the vessels at its base.

"What's this?" she asked.

We probed the tangle of red and yellow arteries with our gloved fingers. It was the circle of Willis, the main interchange of the four large arteries that supply the brain's circulation. My scalpel had severed the arteries, and we could see that they were almost completely filled up with tough yellow gunk.

"Big Macs," said the anatomy professor, coming over to help. "That's what you're seeing. And fifty years of french fries." He took his stainless-steel probe and tried to insert it into the lumen, the tubular cavity of one of the arteries. It wouldn't fit. That artery was largely blocked by atherosclerosis.

Atherosclerosis is really the result of multiple factors. How much and how fast it builds up in our arteries depends on diet, lipid profile (especially LDL), activity, stress, hypertension, smoking, diabetes, and a bunch of different genes. (By this point, you've probably memorized the list; it's incredible how the very same lifestyle factors affect so many aspects of brain health.) Genetic differences mean that a few people can get away with outrageously unhealthful lifestyles and still have free-flowing arteries, but most of us are building little yellow beaver dams inside our arteries with each inactive day and each oversize meal.

We actually begin depositing cholesterol on the walls of our arteries at about age ten. As we get older, especially if our LDL levels are high, cholesterol will more likely get stuck to our arteries. The result is a cholesterol-filled *plaque,* a sticky yellow outcropping of fat-laden tissue that damages the artery even as it partially blocks the flow of blood. As plaques build up, our arteries become stiffer. That damming and stiffness raises our blood pressure, which further damages the artery wall, which attracts more cholesterol. Atherosclerosis and hypertension then egg each other on like two boys causing mischief at the back of the classroom; atherosclerosis boosts blood pressure, which in turn accelerates atherosclerosis. Inflammation makes the whole thing worse until, as often happens, the cholesterol plaques finally rupture and spew their load of inflamed yellow junk into the artery, causing a catastrophic blockade.

Recently, a surprising new factor has come into the picture—*infection.* Researchers at Columbia University and elsewhere have found that people who've been infected with the bacteria *Chlamydia pneumoniae* are almost *five times* as likely to suffer a stroke. (I'm not referring to the sexually transmitted form of chlamydia but a different type that infects the lungs of many people at some point in their lives.) By turning on inflammation in blood vessels, this little bug—a stealthy bacterial plague that indirectly attacks both heart and brain—revs up the same vicious cycle.

Another newly discovered risk factor for atherosclerosis that's getting well-deserved media attention these days is the common amino acid *homocysteine.* Modest amounts of homocysteine are good for the body, so many doctors say your homocysteine level is "normal" if it's between 8 and 20 micromoles per liter. B vitamins usually keep our homocysteine levels down in this range, but in people who have an inadequate intake of B vitamins (including folate, B6, and B1) homocysteine starts to pile up in the body, and blood levels quickly creep above 20.

How worried should we be by elevated homocysteine? It's controversial because only *some* of the studies show that people with high levels are more likely to suffer a stroke. But one thing seems clear: people who have low B vitamin levels are more likely to have high homocysteine, and people with levels above 20 are more likely to get atherosclerosis at a young age. Furthermore, about 25 percent of people who've suffered strokes have elevated homocysteine levels. As a result, the growing medical consensus is that high levels of homocysteine represent a previously hidden but serious risk factor for strokes and heart attacks.

In fact, some experts have suggested that the 20 level is too high and may lull us into a false sense of safety. Your risk of strokes may actually go up if your level is greater than 9. Sound familiar? This debate is very similar to the evolving standards for desirable cholesterol levels, blood sugar levels, and blood pressure levels. While the optimum levels have yet to be clarified, all the available evidence leads to the same conclusion: like cholesterol levels, homocysteine levels may be an important way to predict risk for vascular disaster.

High homocysteine would be trouble enough if it just caused strokes, but recent studies suggest an even bigger worry: that high homocysteine *by itself* may be associated with cognitive impairment and even with Alzheimer's disease. Studies from Sweden, England, and Wales have all reported that adults with elevated homocysteine levels face an increased risk of mental decline. It's possible, then, that B vitamin deficiencies lead to too much homocysteine, which leads to plugged-up arteries and other metabolic problems, which leads to subtle cognitive impairment in people who otherwise seem healthy and also increases our vulnerability to ARNAT. Given all these discoveries, controlling your homocysteine levels through B vitamin supplements may be another incredibly easy way to reduce your risk of atherosclerosis, strokes—and perhaps Alzheimer's.

Come the Platelets, and More

By itself, atherosclerosis is not enough to cause a stroke; the real trouble starts when an aging plaque begins to rupture—which brings on the assault of the platelets.

Platelets are the tiniest type of blood cells. They circulate freely through the bloodstream, a sort of roving team of biological Band-Aids that protect us against hemorrhage by plugging holes in damaged blood vessels. But when they come across a rupturing cholesterol plaque, they mistake it for something that needs to be plugged up. They stick to the damaged wall and spread, attaching to everything in the area, attracting white cells to the growing mass. Finally they form a plug that blocks the flow of blood like the final log a beaver drops across the stream. This plug leaves the neurons downstream gasping silently for help, like fish in a dry stream bed. Starved of oxygen, choking on a buildup of toxins, attacked by free radicals, and fried in the pan of local inflammation, neurons go into metabolic meltdown. The result is a mass of dead and dying brain cells, a chaotic wreckage replacing the organized structure that took years to build, but only minutes to destroy. To emphasize the need for emergency treatment, doctors are increasingly calling a stroke a "brain attack."

The multidecade slide into vascular disaster is a vicious, self-reinforcing cycle that not only causes strokes but obliges billions of neurons to limp along with barely adequate brain blood flow for years—a thought to give you pause as you approach those ubiquitous Temples of the Golden

Arches. The main message should be clear: you cannot control *all* of these factors, but you have enormous power to control *most* of what happens to your arteries. The sooner you decide, "That's it! It's curtains for you, you greasy vascular risk factors!" the better for your brain cells, and for your ability to think.

Which brings us to one of the most hotly debated issues in the field of cerebrovascular disease: exactly how do strokes, or decreased blood flow, affect the mind? This is the riddle of vascular dementia.

What Is Vascular Dementia, and Are You Getting It?

In 1994 the National Institute of Neurological Disorders and Stroke (a component of the National Institutes of Health) and the European organization Association Internationale pour la Récherche et l'Enseignement en Neurosciences (AIREN) jointly sponsored as distinguished a gathering of vascular dementia experts as has probably ever taken place. But the meeting was difficult, even frustrating. Toward the end, Jeffrey Cummings, an internationally-known behavioral neurologist at UCLA, stood to address the gathering: "There are so many bright people in this room, I can't believe we can't come to some consensus!" That statement summarizes the level of scientific agreement on vascular dementia (VaD).

Many medical meetings have run aground on the shoals of defining VaD. Vascular damage in the brain has an infinite number of combinations of degrees, locations, and causes, which in turn may cause an extremely broad spectrum of mental changes. For example, many people seem perfectly healthy and have never had a stroke, but crucial areas of the brain receive less-than-optimum blood flow. Others feel great but have actually had one or more little strokes without knowing it. (One young woman colleague of mine volunteered for an MRI scan as a "normal control" in her own research study—only to discover that she had a marble-size hole in her brain.) Still others have suffered cherry, egg, or lemon-size strokes, whether we know it or not. But contrary to the conventional story, the magnitude of the stroke is *not* the major factor in determining what happens to the mind. A big stroke that takes place in one location may cause virtually undetectable mental changes, while a small stroke in another may leave a person mute and helpless. In other words, the effects of vascular disease on mental performance are about as predictable as the effects of randomly assaulting a computer with a cordless drill—you may end up with anything from a working computer to a useless box of shiny parts.

In an effort to bring order to this infinitude of possibilities, doctors have tried to organize the broad spectrum of vascular dementia into two large categories: *dementia due to strokes* and *dementia due to white-matter changes*. The first is exactly what it sounds like—dementia that follows one or more strokes. The second involves changes in the inner tissue of the brain where billions of fat-sheathed axons—the white matter—carry signals to and fro. The cases of Jim and Pete illustrate the difference.

Jim was a fifty-five-year-old slightly chunky but top-level tennis-playing engineer who awoke one morning unable to speak or control the right side of his body. His wife frantically half-dragged him into the back of the family station wagon and rushed him to the ER. A CT scan showed that he had had a stroke in his left hemisphere. Over the course of a month, he recovered about half of his lost functions—an enormous relief for his wife and two teenage sons—but twenty months later he had another stroke, after which he couldn't follow a simple conversation or recognize his family. His case is a perfect example of true vascular dementia: severe cognitive decline after a series of strokes, an infrequent but real disorder.

Pete had a different problem: white matter changes. A successful long-haul truck driver, Pete had worked his way up to owning a fleet of three big rigs that were in constant motion, piling up miles and profits that would someday send his two daughters to college. When he developed high blood pressure, his internist suggested he cut down on fatty foods and salt and smoking. Pete smiles, recalling the clinic visit: "I told him, 'Sure, doc,' but I figured, 'Hell, life's too short for that bullshit,' " and he continued with his accustomed lifestyle. He had his first transient ischemic attack at age forty-two, just a little passing dizziness. By age forty-six his MRI scan showed cloudy-bright signals—hyperintensities—throughout the white matter near his ventricles. It looked as if cotton balls had replaced half his brain. He could carry on a lively conversation, but neuropsychological testing showed ragged gaps in several facets of his mind.

MRI scanning has revealed for the first time how common it is for American adults to exhibit these hyperintensities, even those whose thought processes seem normal. As a rule of thumb, about 25 percent of people over age sixty-five and 50 percent over seventy-five have some of these hyperintensities. *White matter changes* (as they are often called) are usually due to *microvascular disease,* meaning problems with blood flow through the millions of tiny vessels that bring life to the depths of the brain. Hypertension, diabetes, and smoking are the usual suspects. Mild changes may produce no detectable change in thinking, but when the white matter changes reach a certain critical degree of severity, people develop slowed thinking, memory loss, inattention, and poor problem solving. Even though these cloudy-white patches do not appear in the hippocampus, people with lots of white matter changes may also suffer poor blood flow there. This "hippocampal blood starvation" may explain the somewhat baffling fact that people with white matter changes often have hippocampal-type memory loss.

Jim with his strokes and Pete with his white-matter changes exhibit classic versions of vascular dementia. But contrary to popular belief, severe dementia is a rare outcome of vascular disease. There are two explanations for this. First, many of us are currently experiencing an insidious erosion of our brains because of decreased blood flow due to the various contributors to vascular disease—undiagnosed hypertension, atherosclerosis, narrowing of the carotid arteries, borderline insulin resistance, and/or mildly sticky platelets. The new paradigm suggests that these subtle types of cerebrovascular compromise, quietly capsizing human thought, constitute the vast bulk of vascular dysfunction, while more obvious cases like Jim's and Pete's are much less common. Up to a point, the brain brilliantly compensates for the changes wrought by vascular disease. It often devises clever compensations to keep its most important parts working, like a twin-engine Beechcraft that stays aloft despite losing one engine. This lets many people carry on without realizing the danger in their heads.

But the second reason that "pure" vascular dementia is uncommon is due to a completely different new idea: in most cases "vascular dementia" and "Alzheimer's disease" act as coconspirators in the robbery of the mind.

The Secret Link Between ARNAT and CVC

"Hold it . . . there, right there."

Neuroscientist Chris Zarrow showed me the slide in more detail. Under the double-headed microscope, each sample of cortex looked like a patchwork of pinkish neuronal rockets scattered across a hazy blue myelin sky. "There's one, see it? And . . . there." She was pointing out the characteristic beta-amyloid plaques of Alzheimer's disease. I had known the man whose brain we were examining. He'd died of a massive stroke. What were these mean spheres of beta-amyloid doing in his brain?

About a third to a half of those diagnosed with vascular dementia actually turn out to have Alzheimer's-type changes in their brains as well. Realization is now growing that the conventional wisdom—a strict dichotomy between Alzheimer's and vascular dementia—is a huge oversimplification. Like the strict division between Alzheimer's disease and normal aging, it's a convenient way of taking the complexity of human reality and cramming it into neat and reassuring boxes. It's an often forgotten fact that Auguste D., Dr. Alzheimer's original patient, had a significant amount of *vascular* disease in her plaque-and-tangle-ridden brain. If we're going to launch a revolutionary campaign against the real threats to human intellect, we have to move beyond the old dichotomy and acknowledge the powerful connection between Alzheimer's and CVC. Here's some of the evidence:

First, up to 60 percent of patients with Alzheimer's also have white matter changes in their brains (similar to Pete's). We know that ARNAT causes microvascular damage in virtually everyone with Alzheimer's, but we also suspect the flip side of the coin—that *white matter changes* may accelerate *ARNAT*. These white matter changes are not innocent by-standers; they've been proven to increase the cognitive impairments of Alzheimer's patients.

Second, as I mentioned in Chapter 4, one of the most startling discoveries from the Nun Study was that when the doctors examined the brains of the deceased nuns and found signs of Alzheimer's, the chance that a nun had in fact been demented in life was more than *twenty times as great if she had also had a stroke.* This suggests that the final impact of ARNAT on our minds may depend in large part on whether we also have CVC.

Third, down at the level of the much-abused neuron, both CVC and ARNAT involve many of the very same processes—inflammation, free radical attacks, nitric oxide dysregulation, excitatory neurotoxicity, and decreased cholinergic function—all of which lead straight to the neuronal damnation of cellular suicide. There's even evidence that atherosclerosis and Alzheimer's alter the molecular structure of blood vessels in overlapping ways.

Fourth—and most important for making life choices to save your brain—the risk factors for strokes *may also be risk factors for Alzheimer's.* Several recent high-quality studies have shown that high blood pressure increases the risk for Alzheimer's disease itself. This astonishing idea is just beginning to gain ascendancy among neuroscientists. When neurologist David Knopman looked at the effects of hypertension on cognitive function in almost 16,000 men and women in the Atherosclerosis Risk in Communities Study, he found that hypertension definitely increased the risk of mental decline typical of early Alzheimer's. And in the Rotterdam Study atherosclerosis and hypertension were associated not only with vascular dementia but also with *Alzheimer's.*

Putting all these findings together, we realize that ARNAT and CVC are not neatly separable problems. Like the interlocking fingers of two clasped hands, they interact and overlap. It's extremely common for vascular changes to contribute to ARNAT and to accelerate the dread arrival of Alzheimer's. That's why one of the most vital public health goals of all is to protect the human brain from CVC.

How to Defend Your Brain from CVC

What we need is a straightforward plan to defend ourselves against these terrible, largely preventable cerebral threats. Strokes are just one part of CVC, but tapping the rich vein of knowledge we've already found to help us dodge strokes is a great place to start to develop our CVC defense plan.

The most definite modifiable risk factors for a first-ever stroke are hypertension, diabetes, and heart disease. Other important risk factors include atherosclerosis, elevated cholesterol, high levels of homocysteine, smoking, obesity, physical inactivity, illicit drug or excessive alcohol use, narrowed carotid arteries, sleep apnea, oral contraceptives, and emotional stress. Reading the list we can check them off in our minds: preventable, treatable, or reversible. As I remember Sarah, Jim, and Pete, it's sobering to realize that nearly all of the stroke patients I've cared for could have avoided or greatly delayed that cerebral catastrophe if only they had had the information and the will to save their brains in time. Neuroscientists can't supply the will, but they *can* supply the information. This list of modifiable factors means that people *who wish to* save their brains and are willing to take appropriate measures have remarkable power over their fate.

At this point, it's time to look at exactly what to do about specific risk factors for CVC. We covered stress in Chapter 5 and diabetes in Chapter 8. Now let's take on four more biological bullies: hypertension, atherosclerosis, platelets, and cholesterol.

We'll start with an easy way to save billions of brain cells: avoid hypertension.

Target One: Hypertension

Treating high blood pressure has seemed like the slam dunk of modern pharmacology, a triumph of science in the interests of human health. But in November 1997 the National Heart, Lung, and Blood Institute announced an alarming trend. For the first time in twenty-five years, fewer Americans were aware that they had hypertension, fewer were getting treatment, and more were dying. That meant that more brain cells were being washed away by the fire hose of hypertension. It's currently estimated that only 29 percent of Americans with high blood pressure have their pressure under control. There are lots of reasons for this: some physicians' offices test for it infrequently, so it is not detected; many primary care physicians don't use antihypertensives aggressively; and many patients simply don't take their medications. The last is perfectly understandable—who wants to take a pill when you're feeling fine? But the lack of symptoms is exactly what makes hypertension such a stealthy killer.

We must use what we know about hypertension as a call to arms. The sooner and more effectively we overcome apathy and ignorance in the face of this dire threat, the more brains will be saved.

In a pyramid drawing of the steps of antihypertensive measures, the great granite base would be prevention. Given the vicious cycle in which changes in blood vessels lead to worse hypertension, which leads to further changes in blood vessels, prevention is particularly crucial. In fact, the whole idea of *treating* hypertension is problematic, since some damage has already occurred before hypertension is measurable. This has led to a revolutionary new idea: "We're shifting away from the notion that it's all about blood pressure to the fact that there's a vascular disease out there for which high blood pressure is a marker," says Michael Alderman of Albert Einstein College of Medicine. In other words, never mind the pressure; let's save the *vessels*. Furthermore, hypertension has effects on the brain that, we now realize, even successful treatment cannot completely reverse. That's why I favor a whole new goal: keep the horse in the barn.

In other words, if you really want to save your heart and brain, you should not wait around until you have measurably high blood pressure before doing anything. You should act early. This means embracing a diet that's low in fat and rich in fruits and vegetables; avoiding smoking and obesity like the plague; religiously pursuing regular physical activity; and finding ways to modify stress. Furthermore, since vascular damage unquestionably begins in childhood, a lifestyle favorable to vascular health—including a sane diet and regular physical activity—should be strongly encouraged from the earliest years. And not with lectures, but by example: you can't expect your children to stay active if you yourself stay glued to the couch. They won't think, "Yum, salmon!" if you make a trip to the McDonald's stroke-arama seem like a treat. Healthful living should be presented not as self-denial and privation but as something easy and pleasurable.

The second step up our pyramid for treating hypertension involves making lifestyle changes similar to those that help prevent hypertension in the first place: weight loss, exercise, smoking cessation, salt restriction, and a diet rich in fruits and vegetables and low-fat dairy foods. (We'll talk more about the potential benefits of a brain-saving diet in Chapter 11.) In many cases, these changes will bring blood pressure under control without medication.

But if making these changes is not sufficient to lower your blood pressure, you must take the final step to the top of the pyramid: antihypertensive medication. The field of hypertension treatment is constantly evolving, with new drugs—and even entirely new drug classes—appearing regularly. The following are the current options from which doctors usually choose: *diuretics*, which flush excess fluid from the body; *beta-blockers*, which slow the heart and reduce the force of its contractions; *calcium channel blockers*, which relax the muscles in the heart and blood vessels; *ACE inhibitors* (meaning *angiotensin converting enzyme* inhibitors), which decrease the manufacture of a powerful constrictor of blood vessels called angiotensin II; and *angiotensin-II receptor blockers*, a new type of drug that relaxes blood vessels. This book is not intended to substitute for the advice of a good doctor, but a couple of ideas may help you become a better partner with your doctor in making the best choice.

First of all, the choice should be made on the basis of good science, not good marketing. As Yale cardiologist Marvin Moser points out, diuretics have been known to be safe and effective for hypertension since the early 1950s, but there's been a swing away from prescribing these excellent medicines toward newer, more expensive drugs, thanks to the sexy lures of advertising. Obviously, the best drug is the one that works, not necessarily the one we see on TV.

Second, although it is reasonable to ask "Which treatment is the most effective and has the fewest side effects?" answering that question is not so simple, because many factors go into making the best choice for each individual. Age, sex, ethnicity, the presence of diabetes, and the function of the kidneys are just some of the factors that your doctor takes into account. A sensible approach to the choice of treatments is provided by the 1997 *Sixth Report of the Joint National Committee on Prevention, Detection, Evaluation, and Treatment of High Blood Pressure (JNC-VI)*. Every doctor has access to this report. Although doctors always want to individualize treatment, they should probably base an initial treatment choice on this current bible for hypertension care.

Third, new research is overturning some cherished assumptions. A 1998 analysis of ten clinical trials involving more than 16,000 people reported the striking discovery that, in those age sixty and over, beta-blockers were no better than placebo in reducing mortality. That's one reason why *JNC-VI* suggested that people over sixty should *not* be given a beta-blocker to begin with. Instead, they should start treatment with a small dose of that old reliable standby, a diuretic. Scientists also suspect that different types of antihypertensives can have profoundly different consequences. For instance, in one recent study, people treated with calcium channel blockers were *five times* as likely to have heart attacks as people treated with ACE inhibitors; while this finding needs further investigation, it warns us that we'd better not consider all antihypertensives alike.

The bottom line: taking on hypertension is not as simple as "lower your pressure, save your brain." Scientists must continue to study the best ways to achieve the ideal results for every individual. But I want to be absolutely unequivocal about the main message: there is a crystal-clear relationship between control of hypertension and decreased strokes, and there is an extremely likely relationship between controlling hypertension and preserving memory. Keeping your blood pressure under control is a *magnificent* bet for saving your brain.

BRUSH YOUR ARTERIES EVERY DAY

The next biological bully we have to defend ourselves against is *atherosclerosis*. When atherosclerotic plaques cling to the arteries in the heart, they cause heart attacks, and when they cling to the walls of the carotid arteries, they cause strokes; either one can rob you of memory. Doctors have worked for decades to come up with safe, practical ways to block the buildup of atherosclerotic plaques. Step one in the defense plan is always diet and physical activity. Both should be as regular a part of your daily life as brushing your teeth. A modest change in diet and an escape from the self-imposed prison of inactivity can not only slow the buildup but to some extent actually brush clean the plaques that threaten our hearts and brains. I'll discuss both diet and activity further in Chapters 11 and 17. But it bears saying more than once: a sensible diet and an active day are our ancient birthright. They are natural, the lifestyle we evolved to live and the lifestyle our brains evolved to expect before we abandoned the life of the body in our somewhat misguided quest for a civilization free from physical hardship.

That said, some people need more help brushing their arteries clean than others. Somewhat to our surprise, scientists have recently discovered that four completely different types of medicine can slow the buildup of atherosclerosis inside carotid arteries and reduce your risk of stroke.

The first drug shown to do this was *lovastatin* (Mevacor), one of the cholesterol-fighting "statin" group of drugs. It makes sense that controlling cholesterol levels would prevent the buildup of carotid plaques, but this was not proven until 1994. By 2000 we had learned that an altogether different class of drug, a calcium channel blocker called *amlodipine* (Norvasc) could also keep the carotids clean. Then in 2001 Canadian scientists reported that a third type of drug, an ACE inhibitor called *ramipril* (Altace), could do the job. Later in the same year, we learned from Swedish researchers that a beta-blocker called *metoprolol* (Toprol) could also prevent the buildup of carotid artery plaques. These drugs all act in different ways, suggesting that many unsuspected aspects of biology are involved in carotid atherosclerosis. Such discoveries are humbling. They remind us that we are just beginning to understand the intricate logic of the body. But they are, at the same time, exciting because they suggest that we already have multiple ways to defend our brains from a carotid-based stroke.

Doctors cannot assume that every drug in each of these four classes is equally protective. And they cannot prescribe these drugs to all adults. Each of them has side effects, so in every case and for every person, physicians will have to carefully balance the potential risks and benefits. But *millions* of people are already candidates for treatment with one or more of these drugs—and medical researchers should work fast to get a handle on who else among us should use one or more of our expanding arsenal of artery-brushing agents.

DEALING WITH PLATELETS

Moment by moment, perhaps hundreds of times a day, somewhere in the sinuous ramifications of your vascular system, a gang of platelets will begin to clump. Antiplatelet therapy can minimize the chance that those clumping platelets will rapidly form a clot that dams the blood flow to the brain and leaves a million neurons gasping. The four antiplatelet agents currently in widespread use are aspirin, dipyramidole, ticlopidine (Ticlid), and clopidegrel (Plavix). But who should take an antiplatelet agent to save their brain? Which agent should they take, and how much?

In this respect (realizing that it's slightly simplistic), we can divide the world's adults into three groups: high-risk people, medium-risk people, and low-risk people. People at high risk for stroke are those with the heart-rhythm disturbance called atrial fibrillation, or those who've already had a heart attack, a transient ischemic attack (a "mini-stroke"), or a stroke. Medium-risk people are those over fifty who have not had one of these vascular events but who live with a vascular risk factor (meaning high cholesterol, hypertension, obesity, smoking, diabetes, physical inactivity, or a family history of heart disease). Low-risk people are everyone else.

Let's look first at the benefits of antiplatelet medication for high-risk people. Most of the research has been done with aspirin, and multiple studies have shown that high-risk people taking doses of 30 to 1,200 mg of aspirin a day are less likely to have another stroke or heart attack.

But choosing the best dose is tricky because aspirin has a double effect. At low doses, it prevents platelets from clumping, but at higher doses, paradoxically, it may *increase* clumping. At present, most doctors believe that "low-to-medium dose aspirin"—meaning 81 to 325 mg a day— probably gives most people all the neuroprotection they need, and the lower end of that spectrum reduces the risks of bleeding. Thus, the widely

available 81 mg dose—"baby aspirin"—is probably about right for most
high-risk people.

Still, the aspirin story has a couple of interesting nuances. For one,
there are probably big genetic variations in the way our bodies respond to
aspirin, so today's one-size-fits-all approach may someday be replaced
with a more personalized approach involving a blood test to measure aspirin's effects. For another, the second European Stroke Prevention Study
has given us some evidence that the combination of 25 mg of aspirin with
200 mg of dipyramidole works much better than treatment with either
drug alone, producing an impressive 36 percent reduction in the risk
of stroke. Because of these results, there is a trend among academic doctors to shift high-risk people from aspirin therapy alone to the new as-
pirin/dipyramidole combination.

Ticlopidine and clopidegrel are also good antiplatelet agents, although
the first has somewhat fallen out of favor because clopidigrel, a newer
drug, has fewer side effects. Both drugs can reduce the risk of stroke in
high-risk patients, and both may be a bit more effective than aspirin. But
the extremely high cost of these medications limits their use. In fact, the
aspirin/dipyramidole combination probably works as well as these high-
priced agents—or even better—at a much lower cost.

High-risk people, in sum, have some dynamite antiplatelet options.
What about medium-risk people? In 1998 the American College of Chest
Physicians, somewhat contrary to the conventional line, boldly recommended low-dose daily aspirin (50 to 100 mg) for medium-risk people.
Other major health organizations have balked at this advice, pointing out
the limited evidence of benefits and the small risk of side effects such as
bleeding. You can sense the spirit of Pascal's Bet hovering over this debate, as many doctors lean toward the philosophy "Do no harm," while
the chest physicians lean toward "No risk, no gain."

I tend to agree with the chest physicians. By restricting the use of antiplatelet agents to the highest risk group, doctors may be losing a chance
to help many more people. But my own position is somewhat more conservative than that of the chest physicians: we know that the people who
are most likely to bleed into their brains when they take aspirin are those
with hypertension, especially those over age sixty-five. Therefore, I propose
that low-dose aspirin therapy be expanded to include *only* the medium-risk
folks who are younger than sixty-five and who have well-controlled blood
pressure. I'll bet the benefits will extend beyond merely preventing heart attacks and strokes; it's possible that antiplatelet therapy might *directly* reduce the burden of memory loss in this enormous medium-risk group.

Finally, the toughest question of all: should normal, apparently healthy,
low-risk people take an antiplatelet agent to save their brains? This is the real

puzzler. Again, doctors are trying to balance aspirin's power to decrease the risk of ischemic strokes (the most common type) against a possible increase in the risk of bleeding, including bleeding into the brain. Some experts advise, "Absolutely—we should *all* take aspirin"; others say this would be too risky. Opinions differ because study results differ—and study results probably differ because researchers haven't become savvy enough yet about how much aspirin to take and which subgroup of folks is most likely to benefit.

Consider three big studies: the Physicians' Health Study involved 11,000 healthy American male doctors who took either 325 mg of aspirin or a placebo every other day. The results showed that aspirin protected the doctors from heart attacks but not from strokes. In fact, the aspirin-taking doctors had a slight *increase* in brain hemorrhages. (Would they have done better with baby aspirin? We'll always wonder, since the size of the dose may well be very important.) Furthermore, the older we are, the less likely we may be to benefit from aspirin, and the greater our risk. For instance, in the Cardiovascular Health Study (including 5,000 men and women over sixty-five), elderly women taking various doses of aspirin had an increase in *all* kinds of strokes. (Aspirin did not make a real difference either way for men.) More recently, the Nurses' Health Study—which followed almost 80,000 healthy young-to-middle-age nurses—found that those who took one to six 325 mg aspirins per week had a *decreased* risk of ischemic stroke, but those who took more than fifteen had an *increased* risk of brain hemorrhages. This suggests that young adults and middle-aged people—possibly both women and men—need to take that "just right" amount to keep their brains healthy.

Science marches on, so we'll learn more about this vital matter very soon: in the Women's Health Study, 40,000 healthy women health professionals agreed to be randomized to take low-dose aspirin, with or without vitamin E. Results of this superb study will start to become available around 2004.

In the meantime, for my money, aspirin is an underused brain defender. While the risks are too big to recommend aspirin for *everybody,* many more high- and medium-risk people should be taking low-dose aspirin. (The aspirin/dipyramidole combination might work even better, but it's possibly riskier.) Men and women between forty-five and sixty-five should go over the facts with their personal physician and seriously consider taking one baby aspirin each day.

CONTROLLING CHOLESTEROL: CAN STATINS SAVE YOU FROM ALZHEIMER'S?

While hypertension is the number-one culprit in CVC (and probably an unrecognized contributor to Alzheimer's), elevated cholesterol has recently been recognized as an extremely common and woefully under-treated vascular problem in the United States. Fully half of American adults have either borderline or high blood cholesterol levels; and curious new hints suggest that high cholesterol may quietly erode our minds and brains even *without* increasing atherosclerosis or causing strokes.

In 2001, acting to control this monster threat, the National Heart, Lung, and Blood Institute released its *Third Report of the Expert Panel on the Detection, Evaluation, and Treatment of High Blood Cholesterol in Adults (Adult Treatment Panel [ATP] III)*. With a title like that, you know their recommendations are going to be a little more interesting than "Keep it under 200." In fact, the new guidelines made national headlines because they suggested that *many* more people than had previously been thought should take cholesterol-lowering drugs such as statins.

The *ATP III* guidelines give us a plan for determining a person's risk category; they then offer stepwise treatment recommendations for each subgroup. Under these new guidelines, LDL rather than total cholesterol is the main target of therapy, so the first step is to classify a person's LDL level. Less than 100 is "optimal," 100 to 129 is "above optimal," 130 to 159 is "borderline high," 160 to 189 is "high," and levels beyond 189 are "very high." Next, we add up a person's other vascular risk factors. The big-time risk factors are type 2 diabetes, bypass surgery, or disease in the carotid arteries or other large blood vessels. Risk also goes up for those with hypertension, smokers, men older than forty-five, and women older than fifty-five.

But people with different risk factors need different treatment. A seventy-five-year-old who's had a stroke and a heart attack needs to keep his LDL level under tighter control than does a twenty-five-year-old triathlete. For this reason, *ATP III* is not a lockstep response to the LDL level but incorporates human differences into its recommendations. The first step in every treatment it offers is "TLC" —not "tender loving care" but "therapeutic lifestyle changes." TLC includes a low-fat diet, weight control, and regular physical activity. If TLC doesn't bring the person's LDL down far enough, the second step is to add drug therapy, usually a statin. For example, a person with only one risk factor need not take a cholesterol-lowering drug until his LDL is above 189; but a person with two or more risk factors may need to take a drug if his LDL is above 129.

Looking to the future, doctors may offer even more sophisticated lipid cure, for instance, by taking into account our levels of HDL-2—an excellent predictor of our resistance to strokes and heart attacks. In the meantime, *ATP III* is a clear step forward. The full explanation of the *ATP III* guidelines is available free from the National Heart, Lung, and Blood Institute.

We know that reducing cholesterol pays huge benefits, not just in terms of preventing heart attacks and strokes but probably in terms of a direct effect on memory. Doctors can now say, "Control your cholesterol; your neurons will pay you back." But scientists have recently gone a big step further, as revolutionary news has swept across the medical frontier: *taking a statin drug may specifically save your brain from Alzheimer's.*

The first hints came from the laboratory. Feed a rabbit a high-cholesterol diet and beta-amyloid will build up in its brain. But give that same rabbit a statin, and its brain will be protected from beta-amyloid, in spite of the high-cholesterol diet. We know that statins decrease the very sticky, toxic Abeta42 that's most likely to cause ARNAT and Alzheimer's. Do people who take statins to control their cholesterol have a lower rate of clinical Alzheimer's? A team at Loyola University examined the records of 56,790 adult patients age sixty or over living in the Chicago area. They found that the patients who were currently taking statins were *70 percent less likely* to have Alzheimer's than those who were not taking statins. Neurologist David Drachman led a similar project in which researchers looked at the medical records of 60,901 patients over age fifty in the United Kingdom. If a patient had *ever* taken a statin, he was *71 percent less likely* to have Alzheimer's. These remarkable results held up whether the statin-takers were compared with patients in the general medical population or with non–statin-taking patients who also had high cholesterol levels. To say that the news caused a shock of excitement is an understatement. It caused an earthquake.

Still, we've got to keep our feet on the ground. Epidemiological studies like these are just the first step toward proving that statins may prevent Alzheimer's. Moreover, different people respond differently to statins; some even experience slight memory *loss* when they start taking them. So until prospective studies are completed (true double-blind studies with a placebo-treated control group), neurologists must hold off on announcing, "Take a statin; save your brain." At the time of this writing, one such study is under way: the Prospective Study of Pravastatin in Elderly at Risk (PROSPER) has enrolled close to 6,000 European subjects between seventy-two and eighty to test whether pravastatin can protect people from memory loss. (Unfortunately, age seventy-two may be a little late to start this type of neuroprotection, so the PROSPER study may never tell us whether healthy forty-five-year-olds should take a low-dose statin to ward off Alzheimer's.)

It's premature to leap up and click our heels, but the statin discovery may be an incredibly important step toward finding a safe and potent Alzheimer's blocker, one that's already sitting in tens of millions of American medicine cabinets.

Preventing strokes is good, but preventing CVC is better. Certainly *overt* strokes kill and wound millions of people each year, but the bulk of the danger is *covert*. Tens of millions in America have suboptimal cerebral blood flow, and we can and must do something about it. In addition to being supervigilant about insulin resistance and reducing stress, we can save our brains from CVC by controlling blood pressure, lowering cholesterol, maintaining normal homocysteine, and using antiplatelet therapy. In Chapters 11 and 17 I'll describe two more ways you can protect your brain from CVC: the Brain-Saving Diet and physical activity, which has benefits that may surprise you.

You hold the power to choose. When you decide to order the colorful salad instead of the fat-weeping fries, to go for a good walk instead of sitting through another thirty minutes of TV, or to commit to taking an antihypertensive pill religiously, you make a life-celebrating choice. The knowledge available today gives you tremendous power to optimize the life of your 100 billion neurons. There may be no more vivid example of the phrase "Knowledge is power." We have much more to learn, and new discoveries pour in every day, but we must place our bets based on the best available facts.

Every so often, the potential of preventive medicine shines through, even in its present imperfect state: in 2000, results were announced from the continuing Nurses' Health Study. Women who exercised at least thirty minutes per day, drank half a glass of wine or beer a day, maintained a healthful diet, were not overweight, and were nonsmokers lowered their risk of heart attacks by *83 percent* and their risk of strokes by *75 percent*! This is a magnificent confirmation of the power of a combination of brain-saving approaches. The researchers said that there is every reason to believe that the results would also apply to men.

Preventing strokes and preventing CVC are not necessarily the same thing, but if we have to bet—and we do—then we must bet that CVC starts hurting our thinking abilities long before we feel the slightest hint of trouble. Standard medical care means playing catch-up, chasing a horse that's already well out of the barn. Yes, for most of us, some damage has already been done, but the new approach is to leap in and, from this moment forward, protect our brains from further CVC. It's never too late. Whether you're twenty-five, fifty-five, or seventy-five, start now to make the changes in your life that will protect your arteries. (And do the same for your children too.) Improve your diet, control your weight, control your blood sugar, control hypertension, jump off the couch and start moving. Just do it. Get whatever help you need. The sooner you act, the smaller the harm, and the better the brain.

CHAPTER 11

Food for Thought:
The Brain-Saving Diet

Anthropologist Katherine Milton strode purposefully through the jungle, dripping with sweat. Her eyes were fixed on the double canopy overhead and on the activity half-hidden by the screen of leaves. There were no other humans for miles around, but she wasn't alone.

A howler monkey fifty feet above her suddenly gave out a screech. It swung its lithe dark body onto a branch with effortless grace, snatched a dangling fruit, and took a bite. Milton quickly swung her high-powered binoculars up to her eyes. She watched as the monkey gobbled down most of the fruit, then tossed the core down toward the forest floor with perfect insouciance and brachiated on its way. Milton rushed to grab the leftover fruit from the ground, zipped it into a plastic bag, and ran back to her jungle camp. Within hours, the fruit was packed in dry ice and headed for her lab at Berkeley's Department of Environmental Science, Policy, and Management.

Dr. Milton has chased monkeys through the jungle of Barro Colorado—a lush island in the middle of Panama's huge Lake Gatun—for twenty-six years. "The monkeys get used to your mopping your brow and following them around," she says. "They probably think: 'Oh, here's a new mammal.' " She has also studied the diets of six indigenous peoples, including the fabled lost tribe of the Yanamamo. Milton's work on the evolution of the human diet may provide us with clues to optimizing our diets for the sake of our brains.

Whether we are stalking woolly mammoths, foraging for mulberries, or cruising for McDonald's, we eat in order to survive and reproduce. To a major degree, in fact, our enormous brains evolved to make us brilliant finders of food. Every brain, in turn, benefits by our brilliant food-finding instincts, without which we would never take in the brain-essential nutrients we need. So the brain helps us eat, and eating helps our brains—a healthy, normal feedback loop that provides our brains with vital nutrition, so that we can go on finding food, making love, and raising babies.

But despite our unprecedented modern access to a wonderful variety of foods, we may actually be eating a *less* nutritious diet than our ancestors ate—and a less nutritious diet than our brains really need. For instance, Dr. Milton discovered that the average fifteen-pound monkey, foraging in the wild, takes in 600 mg of vitamin C, 6,400 mg of potassium, and 4,571 mg of calcium—*much* higher than human recommended daily intakes. Of course monkeys and humans have rather different guts. But if our brains evolved to expect similar nutrient doses, we may be underserving them on an ongoing basis. So the bad news is that we may be eating way too much of the wrong stuff; many of us have strayed so far from the natural diet we were designed for that our hearts and brains are in serious jeopardy. But the good news is that, by looking at the foods our brains evolved to expect and need, we may have a great way to optimize human brain function.

To talk about food for thought—the relationship between diet and the brain—is to talk about a bunch of vital questions: What are the essentials—the "bare necessities"—that the brain needs in order to grow and operate? What happens to our minds if we shortchange our brains in regard to these essentials? Are there sneaky forms of inadequate nutrition among "healthy" normal people that rob the brain of its full potential? Which foods have special neuroprotective qualities? Does obesity actually increase the risk of memory loss? Can we devise a delicious, satisfying, brain-saving diet?

Nutritional neuroscience is in its infancy, and I must not overstate the certainty of its conclusions. But digging carefully uncovers a gold mine of data that suggest the best diet for the brain.

Food for Thought: The Essentials

When we say "food for thought," all we mean is that we are what we've eaten. Your brain, that exquisite instrument of cognition, emotion, and dreams, is in fact entirely made from the foods your mother brought to her lips during your prenatal development, and from the foods that have been delivered to your own lips since your birth. People are designed to thrive on a wide range of foods. Like our tree-swinging forebears, we are omnivores who can eat plants or insects or other animals (although strong evidence shows that we evolved to eat primarily fruits and vegetables, along with a small amount of meat from the extremely lean wild animals we were able to hunt or scavenge, a type of meat that is virtually unobtainable in modern supermarkets). Our bodies and brains are enormously forgiving. As long as we take in enough essential nutrients, we can convert those building blocks into all of the molecules we need for a well-functioning brain.

Nonetheless, our diet must include a minimum of certain irreplaceable, brain-nourishing compounds—the brain's "bare necessities." We need enough calories to supply the brain with glucose, the main energy food of neurons. We need to eat certain essential amino acids and essential fatty acids—*essential* meaning that these substances cannot be turned into one another by our clever internal chemistry labs but *must* be supplied from the diet. We also need to eat certain *ions*: sodium and potassium to give our neurons their electrical power; magnesium to guard the gates of our memory cells; and calcium to tell a neuron, "Hey, pay attention to this!" We need iron because every red blood cell needs this metal if it's going to carry oxygen up to the brain. We need zinc and selenium, both of which help stave off the deadly attacks of free radicals. We need vitamins, and not just the classic antioxidants A, C, and E, but also the Bs, including B12, folate, and thiamine, all of which play crucial roles in maintaining a healthy brain. And no doubt we need to eat all sorts of brain-friendly compounds that we haven't even discovered, probably including the plant-based *phytochemicals* that science is just beginning to appreciate.

Generally speaking, as long as our diets contain enough of these essential building blocks, our neurons will do fine. They'll learn and retain and recall the lessons of a lifetime. But we go astray when we take in *too little* of the brain's bare necessities or when we eat *too much* total food. Either mistake will hurt our brains. I'll begin by addressing the "too little" part of the equation; then I'll address the dangers of "too much." And finally, I'll show you the "just right" Brain-Saving Diet.

Less-Than-Adequate Nutrition, Less-Than-Optimum Brain

Worldwide, the most significant cause of diet-related dementia is malnutrition. Hundreds of clinical studies have shown that when humans are deprived of calories, protein, vitamins, and minerals, thinking abilities are ravaged. Uncounted millions of people in developing nations suffer from overt malnutrition and exhibit lifelong mental handicaps as a result. (We can only guess how much this contributes to the cycle of poor education, economic insecurity, political instability, and violence.) But even marginal malnutrition hurts brains: when the Nutrition Collaborative Research Support Program studied the effects of marginal malnutrition in Egypt,

Kenya, and Mexico, it discovered that nutrition-related cognitive impairment begins in infancy; some recovery is possible, but some effects on the brain are probably permanent.

Malnutrition, either full-scale or marginal, is not confined to the poorest countries on earth. Surprisingly, it's found in the richest as well, such as the United States. Between 1988 and 1994, when the third National Health and Nutrition Examination Survey (NHANES III) studied a representative sample of the U.S. population, it labeled individuals "food insufficient" if they "sometimes or often did not get enough food to eat." Using this standard, food insufficiency affected 4.1 percent of Americans, or about 10.5 million people. And Second Harvest, the largest chain of food banks in America, reportedly served 26 million people in 1997, nearly 10 percent of the U.S. population.

Who is affected by this? The poor, of course. Food insufficiency is highest among low-income Mexican Americans, a very rapidly growing part of the population. Older Americans—another fast-growing group— are also especially vulnerable to less-than-adequate nutrition. Paradoxically, nutritional insufficiency among older adults is not just a matter of poverty or hunger; rather, older adults often simply want to eat less. Appetites frequently decline with age not only because of illness but also because of true neurobiological changes, such as an increased sensitivity to food-satisfaction hormones. The result: a substantial proportion of the elderly in the United States may not be hungry but they still suffer from less-than-adequate nutrition—a problem that may be associated with subtle mental impairments, even in people with good incomes and comfortable lifestyles.

Remarkably, less-than-adequate nutrition often hurts people who might otherwise seem young, fit, and well fed. Heavily processed fast food grabbed on the go followed by a fall into the sofa in the evening with a bag of chips and a diet soda—this diet defines many daily lives. College-age women in the United States, a group that starts with fine cognition and plenty of money for food, usually eat diets that are low in fiber, fruits, vegetables, and dairy products, setting themselves up for completely preventable deficiencies of iron, folate, calcium, and phytochemicals. We should be looking long and hard at the potential mental consequences of such unnatural diets.

What Every Brain Needs

What becomes of the mind when the brain is deprived of its bare necessities?

Unfortunately, we don't know exactly how much of what nutrients the brain needs for truly optimum function. We *do,* however, know the effects that *severe* deprivation of specific nutrients has on the mind and brain. By looking at what happens to people when their brains are severely deprived, we can begin to get an idea of the nutrients that are essential for human brains—our minimum daily neuronal requirements. B vitamins, ions, and phytochemicals are all excellent examples.

Deficiencies of B vitamins are all too common, even among people regarded as perfectly healthy. The most important B vitamins are B12, folate (also called folic acid or B9), thiamine (B1), and pyridoxine (B6). The B vitamins are interdependent, so that an excess of one may lead to a relative deficiency of the others—a good reason to take them together. For the purposes of optimizing the function of mind and brain, we should focus on B12 and folate.

B12

I'll never forget the first man I met who had a severe, long-term vitamin B12 (cobalamin) deficiency. Mr. Baxter was a tall, broad-shouldered gentleman with a ruggedly handsome face as weather-beaten as an old hickory barn. He advanced toward me down the hospital hallway, leaning heavily on a mismatched pair of aluminum forearm crutches, concentrating on each step like a newborn fawn. Lacking vitamin B12, the rearmost part of his spinal cord had withered, so he could neither feel his own feet nor instruct them where to go. Mr. Baxter's tongue was as smooth and red as uncooked steak, a classic sign of severe B12 deficiency. "Are you the clinic?" he asked me. He could not think clearly (another classic sign), which left him, in his early fifties, baffled by the world and dependent upon the twenty-four-hour-a-day support of his wife.

A low B12 level can unquestionably lead to dementia, as in the case of Mr. Baxter. Frankly, however, we should probably not focus solely on the occasional case like Mr. Baxter's—the classic and obvious tragedy of severe B12 deficiency. By the time such patients see a doctor, it's often too late for B12 treatment to restore their thinking abilities. Instead, our focus should be on all the *other* people in the community, including young adults, whose brains may be at risk because of completely unsuspected B12 deficiencies. This is a group we could help in time if only we could find them. And the stakes have recently gone up: researchers in the Oxford Project to Investigate Memory and Aging (OPTIMA) found that adults over fifty-five with low B12 levels had more than *four times* the usual risk of Alzheimer's.

People at risk for B12 deficiency include strict vegetarians (B12 cannot be obtained from plants), those on junk-food diets, those who chronically use ulcer medications, and those with a history of stomach surgery. The aging of the stomach may be an even more common risk factor: older adults tend to lose their ability to bring B12 into the bloodstream. Once this happens, even a good oral B12 supplement becomes almost useless; the B12 that gets swallowed is never absorbed. The conventional wisdom states that a B12 deficiency won't cause mental changes until it causes anemia, but this is probably a mistake. Even marginally low levels of B12 in people with perfectly healthy red cells have shown memory loss. One study of 260 "healthy" men and women over sixty, for instance, found that those with marginally low B12 levels had impairments in both memory and abstract reasoning.

What's a normal B12 level? Most labs say that a "normal" B12 level in the blood is anything greater than 250 picograms/liter (pg/l); anything lower than this is considered a sign of B12 deficiency. But it's possible that the brain is at risk even if the blood level is up as high as 400. That means some people who get their B12 checked are being told, "You're fine," when perhaps they're not. Furthermore, among its many roles in the body, B12 keeps *methylmalonic acid* (MMA) under control, so a high MMA level may be an even better indicator of brain-threatening B12 deficiency than the B12 blood level itself.

Fortunately, most young adults and many older adults will achieve perfectly good B12 levels with a well-rounded diet. Healthful sources include fish, poultry, dairy foods, and yeast. Those who have trouble maintaining a healthy diet can benefit from B12 supplements *if* their stomachs can still absorb B12; if not, they will need to get their B12 via monthly injections. Beware: there's a notorious medical gray market in B12 injections, as a few unscrupulous practitioners poke and charge people who have absolutely no need for injections, since their stomachs do a perfectly good job of absorbing B12. For most of us, whatever our blood level, taking a daily oral supplement of about 0.4 mg is a safe and good bet for protecting the brain.

How do you know if you are at risk and whether you need pills or injections? The present public health strategy for identifying those with B12 deficiencies is no strategy at all. Essentially, doctors wait for people to develop anemia or dementia or staggering gait and then, when it's too late, do a blood test. We need a better plan. We need solid public health research to guide family doctors in regard to how and when to measure B12. Until this research is done (and until doctors start using a better measure such as MMA), it might be prudent for doctors to routinely test

B12 levels every five years in adults over forty and to provide supplements for those whose levels fall below 400 pg/l.

FOLATE

Over the last twenty years, *folate* has come to be appreciated for its immense importance to the mind and brain, yet folate deficiency continues to affect virtually all segments of society. From 4 to 35 percent of people are deficient, depending on age, race, and location. The problem became more urgent in the mid-1990s, when scientists discovered that a very high proportion of pregnant women do not get enough folate and that low levels during the first month of pregnancy greatly increase the risk of fetal spinal defects. As a result, in 1998 the U.S. government mandated folate fortification of flour and grains. The results have been significant: in a study of residents of Framingham, Massachusetts, after this change the average blood levels of folate *doubled;* and the bonus was a 7 percent drop in homocysteine levels—a help in preventing strokes.

One might think that getting enough folate would be easy, since it's in so many foods; dark green leafy vegetables, dried beans, seeds, soy, whole grains, and citrus fruits are all good sources. But in spite of this wide availability, typical American diets provide insufficient intake. One reason is that folate (which refers to all forms of this vitamin) is different from folic acid (the form found in supplements and fortified foods). The folate in foods is only half as available to the body as the folic acid in pills. In addition, folate is not stored for long in the body, meaning that constant replacement is necessary. So even a healthful diet may not provide an adequate daily supply, and supplements may be necessary.

What makes folate very interesting right now is new evidence that this vitamin plays a role in brain aging. The OPTIMA study, for example, found that adults with low folate measures had more than three times the usual risk of Alzheimer's. Perhaps even more intriguing are recent results from the Nun Study: David Snowdon and his colleagues at the University of Kentucky examined blood samples that had been collected from thirty nuns and found that the lower the folate level, the more cortical atrophy appeared in the nuns' brains. Now *that's* a piece of news; it conceivably means that the cheap and simple measure of taking a folate supplement may help to protect our brains from shrinkage with age.

Some nutrition experts are concerned that giving people folate as a supplement can obscure a co-existing B12 deficiency. The answer to that is simple. As researchers at the National Center for Environmental Health at the CDC said in 1996, "A good policy option is available; require that all folic acid vitamin supplements also contain 0.4 mg of vitamin B-12." This dose (0.4 mg) may actually be more than we need; 6 mcg a day will probably do the trick. Furthermore, we should not restrict supplementation to those with low blood levels of folate. A review of the Framingham cohort concluded, "Many elderly people with 'normal' serum vitamin concentrations are metabolically deficient in cobalamin [B12] or folate." This is an unacceptable risk to brain function. It is an easy thing for adults to take a folate supplement and a B12 supplement. Therefore, as much as I usually favor the whole-foods, healthy-diet approach, this is one case where supplements probably offer a bonus. Anyone whose diet and lifestyle does not permit regular intake of folate-rich foods, especially adults over fifty-five, is at risk for deficiency. Supplementing with 400 to 600 mcg of folate and 6 mcg of B12 a day is about right. Pascal's Bet is the guiding philosophy: It might help. It won't hurt. Just do it.

IRON WORKS

Iron is essential to make hemoglobin, the messenger in red blood cells that picks up oxygen and delivers it to tissues throughout the body. That alone makes iron an absolutely essential nutrient for our oxygen-dependent brains. But iron does more: it keeps our neurotransmitters working, especially the dopamine and the opiate systems, and does routine maintenance on the brain cells involved in learning and memory. Yet iron deficiency is the single most common nutritional deficiency in the world. This is *not* just a third-world problem; it is astoundingly common among women in the wealthiest, best-fed societies on earth. Iron deficiency affects as many as 10 percent of American women in their childbearing years, largely due to menstrual blood loss; the rate of deficiency among young Danish women is 9 to 15 percent; and the French found that 93 percent of menstruating women and 28 percent of postmenopausal women were not taking in enough iron. For three prosperous populations in advanced nations, this is a staggeringly high rate of an easily treatable deficiency.

Young children with iron-deficiency anemia have cognitive problems, from mental retardation to poor school performance, as we've known for decades. Treating these children once their anemia is discovered may be too late; some of the brain damage is irreversible. But two pieces of news have completely changed our point of view about iron and brains. First, it was recently discovered that iron deficiency begins to hurt brain function even *before* there's any detectable anemia, because iron in the brain decreases well before red-blood-cell manufacturing is affected.

The second piece of news is that young children are not the only victims of iron-deficiency-based cognitive problems; adolescent girls are victims as well.

Pediatrician Jill Halterman at the University of Rochester School of Medicine recently studied 5,398 boys and girls between the ages of six and sixteen. While iron deficiency was rare among the boys, it appeared in 2.1 percent of girls age six to eleven, and among *8.7 percent* of the adolescent girls, those age twelve to sixteen. In the overwhelming majority of these adolescent girls, their iron deficiency would never have been detected by their pediatricians because *they had no anemia.* Yet their iron deficiency was enough to affect their thinking abilities. Seventy-one percent of the iron-deficient girls overall scored below average in math, and the iron-deficient adolescent girls had significantly worse math ability than their peers without iron deficiency.

Dr. Halterman posed a provocative question: could the high rate of undetected iron deficiency in adolescent girls help explain the sex difference in mathematical ability that's so often found between young men and young women? She also pointed out that the standard guidelines that pediatricians and family practice doctors use to detect iron deficiency are sure to fail, since these guidelines recommend only anemia screening, a test that the largest group of iron-deficient adolescent girls would pass with flying colors. That means doctors often miss a chance to rescue young brains. Another recent study showed that treatment of iron deficiency in nonanemic but iron-deficient girls led to solid improvements in their thinking abilities. I would ask an equally provocative question: if we allow a young woman to go through junior high school, high school, and college with her brain short of iron, will it increase her vulnerability to later memory loss? Let's not wait to find out. Even if we don't yet know the long-term consequences, it seems like a heck of a bad bet to allow 8.7 percent of America's young women to go through an iron-deficient adolescence and young adulthood.

Clearly, Dr. Halterman's results are a call to action. Researchers need to do other studies to confirm the results, and we need to know more. Family doctors need to be more energetic and sophisticated in screening their patients for this brain-draining problem. (For instance, rather than measure the blood iron level or the hemoglobin level, a better option would be to measure the *ferritin* level or the *reticulocyte hemoglobin content* [RHC]. Either of these indicators might reveal iron supply problems that conventional methods completely miss.) Doctors should probably check patients' iron levels more frequently, perhaps every two years starting at age twelve.

At the same time, we need to be wary of this powerful metal: just as too little can affect the mind, too much—especially later in life—may increase the risk of heart disease, make strokes more severe, and possibly even play a role in ARNAT/Alzheimer's. As is so often the case in nature's fine balance, there seems to be a "just right" amount of iron that will help our brains continue to operate at their peak potential; perhaps a high iron level is brain-friendly during the first half of life, while a somewhat lower level is better later on. But the most urgent matter is to make sure that children and young adults get all the iron they need.

Iron is usually obtained from the diet. It is readily available from red meats and from spinach and other dark green leafy vegetables, whole grains, beets, and raisins. Still, even those with excellent dietary intake may not get enough iron, and supplements of about 325 mg a day may be a good idea for many adults. Iron supplements should be used with caution; too much is linked to cancer, heart disease, and increased severity of strokes. Since these dangers are to some extent hereditary, the final risk/benefit calculation for iron supplementation can be complicated. That's why a blanket recommendation is not a good idea. As simple as it may seem, the decision to take an iron supplement should be made with the help of your doctor.

NEW IDEAS ABOUT OLD IONS

In 1978 the Center for Science in the Public Interest called salt "the deadly white powder you already snort." Distinguished organizations such as the National Heart, Lung, and Blood Institute and the National High Blood Pressure Education Program have described high salt in our diets as a scourge, a major cause of hypertension and hence heart disease and hence death. As we discussed in Chapter 10, it has been a long-standing truism that avoiding hypertension means avoiding dietary salt. But the issue is not so simple: recent evidence suggests that the antisalt message has been blown way out of proportion.

There are many salts, but the most familiar is "table salt" or sodium chloride, a combination of the two ions sodium and chloride. The study of table salt and health contains some surprises. Studies that compare salt intake between groups (say, between Americans and Chinese) tend to find that people who take in more salt are indeed more likely to have high blood pressure. But studies of salt intake within a given group of people (say, within all Americans) offer little proof that those who consume more salt have higher blood pressure. To get to the bottom of the matter, a team of scientists launched a very large study called Intersalt that looked at fifty-two "within-population" studies from around the world. The result: in forty-eight of these studies, *there was no overall relationship between salt and blood pressure*. Furthermore, in 1998 the *Journal of the American Medical Association* published a massive review of 114 studies; the authors concluded that, overall, the benefits of salt reduction on blood pressure are probably negligible. Despite this evidence, however, many physicians remain steadfastly opposed to salt. To settle the issue, it would take a big, prospective experiment. Which brings us to the DASH diet.

The Dietary Approaches to Stop Hypertension (DASH) study was a bold National Heart, Lung, and Blood Institute trial conducted at four top academic centers. Instead of worrying about salt, the scientists tested the theory that a well-rounded diet can control hypertension. They compared three different diets: a typical fatty American diet; a diet rich in fruits and vegetables; and a "combination diet" rich in fruits, vegetables, and low-fat dairy foods and reduced in total fat—the DASH combination diet. After three weeks on the DASH diet, people with high blood pressure achieved a reduction of 11.0/5.5 mm Hg—better than the usual effect of medication and much better than the effects of salt reduction. The bigger surprise was that even people with *normal* blood pressure achieved a reduction of 5.5/3.0 mm Hg; such a reduction could help healthy people stave off the slow slide into later hypertension. The amount of salt was the same in all three diets, so salt wasn't a factor. Fruits, vegetables, and low-fat dairy products did the trick. To be sure, there are some "salt-sensitive" people who can lower their blood pressure by avoiding salt. But DASH was the first real-world experiment to show that most people's blood pressure can be controlled without focusing on salt reduction.

What is it about the DASH diet that's so effective? We don't know, but plant-rich diets typically contain lots of potassium, and dairy foods contain calcium. It's beginning to look as if the real blood-pressure-lowering, stroke-blocking factor in a DASH-type plant-rich diet may be *high potassium* intake rather than *low sodium* intake. In another ambitious study—the Health Professionals Follow-up Study, which followed almost 44,000 men for eight years—men who ate nine servings of fruits and vegetables a day had a 38 percent lower risk of stroke than those who ate four or fewer. Why did these men do so well? The best guess is that it was the high potassium levels in bananas, potatoes, oranges, tomatoes, and spinach. We should consider the possibility that it wasn't potassium that saved these men from strokes; perhaps the fruits and vegetables provided other benefits, such as antioxidant vitamins or brain-saving phytochemicals. But another study found that men taking potassium supplements along with their diuretics for blood pressure control had a *64 percent lower risk of strokes* than those who took diuretics alone. Based on this preliminary evidence, it's time to seriously consider the possibility that a good potassium intake may help to save your brain by reducing your risk of stroke.

Calcium is a whole other story.

CALCIUM

Calcium is absolutely vital for every communication between neurons—one reason to speculate about the role of calcium in brain aging. And calcium deficiency is surprisingly common. The National Academy of Sciences recommends that people age thirty-one through fifty should get 1,000 mg of calcium each day. After fifty-one the recommended dose rises to 1,200 mg. Postmenopausal women who are not taking estrogen may be a special case: the NIH advises such women to take in 1,500 mg per day. Yet more than half of Americans take in less than 450 mg a day— a massive gap between what we do and what we need. How does this insufficiency affect the body and mind?

Dr. David McCarron of Oregon Health Sciences University in Portland strongly believes that we've been underestimating the vascular health benefits of calcium. Looking carefully at people who have vascular problems such as high blood pressure, he found that those who do most poorly are actually the ones with low *calcium* intake (instead of those with high sodium intake). Low-fat dairy sources of calcium, suggests Dr. McCarron, may be more effective in controlling hypertension than a low-sodium diet.

The results of the DASH study lend strong support to Dr. McCarron's theory. So do results from a new study from the University of Southern California, which reported that calcium supplements by themselves were terrific at lowering blood pressure among African American teens. Perhaps low calcium, rather than high salt, is the real demon behind so-called "salt-sensitive" hypertension. And perhaps even people *without* salt-sensitivity and *without* hypertension would have happier blood vessels if they took in sufficient calcium. In 2000, Norwegian researchers reported that, in a study of more than 15,000 adults, those who consumed the most calcium-rich dairy products had the lowest blood pressure. So we may be missing a bet if we focus only on calcium's benefits to bones. From the point of view of blood vessels and brains, bones evolved as a convenient storage depot for calcium! The sense is growing that we should have a good calcium intake not only to help keep our bones strong and resilient but as a simple way to defend the brain against the mental ravages of CVC.

Nonfat dairy products are an excellent source of calcium and actually have higher calcium levels than dangerously fatty whole milk products. Fortunately for those who pale at the thought of drinking four glasses of skim milk every day—and for the many people, especially African Americans and Asians, who become lactose intolerant with age—there are many good alternatives, including calcium-fortified orange juice, soybeans, dark green leafy vegetables, and canned sardines (with bones). Calcium supplements are another possibility.

But concerning supplements, two cautions should be raised. First, as we noted earlier, oyster shell calcium is sometimes contaminated with lead, an element that's no friend to the brain. For optimum brain safety, pick one of the other calcium supplements, such as calcium carbonate or citrate, and take it with food to improve absorption. Second, the Honolulu Heart Program found that men who used dairy products to get their calcium reduced their risk of stroke, but men who used nondairy sources of calcium did *not* benefit. This is another impressive argument for the whole-foods philosophy; dairy foods may contain crucial substances that may boost our absorption of calcium, or help protect the brain in ways scientists have yet to discover, so it's probably best to use food sources instead of pills to bring calcium into your diet.

This raises a vital point about the search for a brain-saving diet: as much as we might wish to identify each and every compound that is required for optimum cerebral function, we can't right now. Until we can, the most practical approach is to choose a well-balanced diet rich in the plant-based nutrients that the brain probably evolved to expect. At this point, we can name two diets that fill the bill: the DASH diet, which we've just described, and the *Mediterranean diet*.

The *Mediterranean diet* gained popularity in the 1960s when researchers discovered that Greeks on the island of Crete ate relatively high-fat meals yet they were only *one-twentieth* as likely as Americans to die of heart attacks. While the Mediterranean diet is similar to the DASH diet, it differs in subtle yet important ways. Rather than simply reducing total fat, the Mediterranean diet focuses on reducing *animal* fat. It advises eating little or no red meat, although it includes plenty of fish, and it actually *encourages* fat intake in the form of olive oil. It suggests daily intake of fruits, vegetables, whole grains, beans, legumes including peanuts, and nuts including walnuts and almonds—and it encourages regular physical activity and optional modest wine drinking.

Ever since the rather astonishing discovery of the heart-saving benefits of this diet, researchers have been searching for the "Mediterranean secret," the special feature of the diet that explains its great benefits. Is it the wine? The veggies? The fiber? The fish? The answer is probably "All of the above." Each component of this diet may have its own benefits, leading to a serendipitous synergism due to the combination of all rather than to any one element. To take just one example out of many: a handful of peanuts, a popular component of this diet, has been shown to provide 2.5 hours of appetite suppression, making this an excellent snack that could *reduce* food cravings. More important, peanuts and even peanut butter can actually lower the level of LDL (the "bad" cholesterol). And in the huge Nurses' Health Study, women who routinely ate more than five servings of peanuts per week had about a one-third lower risk of heart disease. But if there's any one overall "secret" of the Mediterranean diet, it's probably that Greeks and Italians tend to get their fat from fish, olive oil, and other vegetable fats, all of which tend to increase HDL (the "good" cholesterol)—a great way to prevent heart attacks and strokes.

Both the Mediterranean diet and the DASH diet give us the calcium, the potassium, and the fat control that will help to save our brains from CVC. And they both also offer the newly appreciated benefits of *phytochemicals*.

PHYTOCHEMICALS

Researchers have been humbled to realize how many compounds in whole foods may be crucial to health. It's as if they thought they'd come to the end of the foods-for-health story when they discovered vitamins, and now they've discovered a whole new book. For example, more than 80 percent of all studies of diet and cancer prevention show that people who eat more fruits and vegetables are less likely to develop certain cancers. Many researchers initially guessed that these benefits could be explained by the healthful antioxidant vitamins A, C, and E, which in the test tube have lots of cancer-fighting properties. But few studies confirm that vitamins by themselves do the trick. If vitamins can't fully explain the benefits of plant-rich diets, then something else must be going on. That something else is probably phytochemicals.

Phyto- comes from the Greek word for "plant," and *phytochemicals* refers to a rapidly expanding pharmacopoeia of biologically potent

compounds found in various fruits and vegetables. More than 170 phytochemicals, for instance, have been found so far in oranges, and it's fair
to assume that thousands more lurk undiscovered. The discovery of the
phytochemicals is quietly revolutionizing the sophistication of dietary
recommendations in preventive medicine. Roughly speaking, the phytochemicals can be divided into *flavonoids, carotenoids, indoles, phenolic
acids, phytoestrogens,* and *allylic sulfides,* several of which may be particularly helpful to the brain.

At least four thousand *flavonoids* have already been found; they're especially common in vegetables, fruits, red wine, ginkgo biloba, and tea.
Not only are they powerful antioxidants and not only do they somewhat
inhibit the growth of certain tumors, they have multiple beneficial effects
on blood vessels. Flavonoids decrease the oxidation of LDL, saving blood
vessels from fatty deposits; they decrease the clumping of platelets, which
may make them reduce the risk of strokes and heart attacks; and they help
control inflammation, which may not only help decrease the risk of
strokes but may also conceivably inhibit the inflammatory component of
Alzheimer's. (It would be easy to test this theory in transgenic mice;
maybe we ought to get on it.) In the Zutphen Elderly Study, men who ate
diets containing the most flavonoids had a *50 percent* reduction in heart
attack deaths and a whopping *73 percent* reduction in the risk of strokes
compared with men who ate diets with the fewest flavonoids—an amazing brain-saving finding, if this study is replicated. The foods in this study
most associated with the benefit were tea, apples, and onions.

There are probably more than five hundred *carotenoids,* a family of
chemicals that provide the distinctive colors to carrots, sweet potatoes,
tomatoes, and watermelon. Dark green leafy vegetables such as kale and
spinach are also rich in carotenoids. Although the most famous carotenoid is beta-carotene—our primary source of vitamin A—the body
actually converts about 10 percent of *all* carotenoids into vitamin A.
(We'll discuss vitamin A further in Chapter 12.) Recently, attention has
been drawn to a completely different carotenoid called *lycopene,* which is
abundant in cooked tomato products (even ketchup). Some evidence suggests that lycopene may reduce the risk of heart attacks in men, so foods
rich in lycopene may be another vascular health-promoting, CVC-
preventing part of a brain-saving diet. A related plant pigment is *lutein,*
the yellow pigment that colors egg yolks that's also actually most common in dark green leafy vegetables. James H. Dwyer at USC's Keck
School of Medicine has recently studied 480 men and women between age
forty and sixty, finding that those with the highest blood levels of lutein
had the least thickening of the carotid artery walls—a specific way that
lutein-rich vegetables may protect the brain from strokes.

Phenolic acids are found in strawberries, raspberries, tomatoes, and nuts. These compounds probably inhibit DNA damage to some extent. But until scientists do further research, I can only speculate that these compounds somewhat help neurons defend themselves from the DNA-busting effects of aging.

Phytoestrogens, such as coumestans, lignans, and isoflavones, are converted to estrogenlike compounds by interacting with bacteria in the gut. They are particularly high in soy foods such as tofu. Their main beneficial effect is to lower cholesterol, which would reduce the risk of CVC, and their estrogenlike activity may possibly defend postmenopausal women against cognitive decline. But anything strong enough to stimulate an estrogen receptor potentially has cancer-promoting side effects. So although occasional soy use is perfectly fine, it's way too soon to recommend deliberate self-dosing with these agents.

Allylic sulfides, found in onions and garlic, have been claimed to lower cholesterol, a possible aid in fighting CVC. But the take-garlic-to-control-cholesterol story has been plagued by inconsistent research results. With so many other well-proven ways to fight cholesterol, for now you should just enjoy garlic for its savory appeal and not count on it to save you from vascular disaster.

Basics of the Brain-Saving Diet

Typical American diets are sadly lacking in phytochemicals. And it's possible—although it has yet to be proven—that the aging-related cognitive decline that is essentially universal in Western society may be somewhat connected to our plant-poor diets. However, we can say this much with confidence: a fruit- and vegetable-rich diet is great for vascular health, and vascular health is great for the brain. Katherine Milton, whose jungle research inspires us to consider optimum human diets, puts it like this: "It seems prudent for modern-day humans to remember their long evolutionary heritage as anthropoid primates and heed current recommendations to increase the number and variety of fresh fruits and vegetables in their diets rather than to increase their intakes of domesticated animal fat and protein." Put simply, we should eat what we were built to eat.

Evidence is growing that a fruit- and vegetable-rich diet does even more. By keeping brain blood vessels open, blocking free radical attacks, protecting DNA, and reducing inflammation, such a diet directly opposes many of the demonic molecular forces that underlie Alzheimer's itself. I can't put this strongly enough: though much more research is needed and the size of the benefit may not be determined for years to come, a fresh fruit- and vegetable-rich diet is a sensible and remarkably safe bet to keep your brain in top working order.

At this point, we can already summarize the basics of the Brain-Saving Diet. It would include lots of fresh fruits and vegetables, low-fat dairy products for protein and calcium, good sources of iron, potassium, folate, and other B vitamins, and a limited amount of meat. In other words, it would look a lot like the Mediterranean diet—a diet that many nutrition authorities—including the European office of the World Health Organization and the Harvard School of Public Health—consider superior to the standard U.S. Department of Agriculture food pyramid.

Might such a diet keep you alive longer? Nutritionists at the City University of New York followed 42,254 women (average age sixty-one) for more than five years. Those who had the highest intake of desirable Mediterranean-style foods had a 30 percent lower rate of death. Might such a diet keep you *smarter* longer? That's what we really want to know. In a recent study of 260 men and women in Spain, those who had a higher intake of fruit, carbohydrates, thiamine, folate, and vitamin C, and a lower intake of monounsaturated fatty acids, saturated fatty acids, and cholesterol did indeed have better cognitive function than those with poorer diets. I don't want to carve this conclusion in granite, but this is the first real-world evidence that you can in fact devise a Brain-Saving Diet from readily available and pleasing foods.

The Search for a Brain Food

Some scientists have suggested that we can go further. Multiple studies have examined the mental effects of specific foods, hoping to find a true "brain food." The results are mixed, with some hits and some misses. But all we need is one hit—the discovery of a food that may legitimately be expected to boost the strength of the brain.

PRECURSOR LOADING

Even in the final stages of dementia, Mr. Freeman had dignity. His hair formed a resilient white halo about his ancient head. He smiled whenever anyone approached his bed and searched their eyes with his. As if immune to fatigue and gravity, he kept his torso bent at the waist, lifting his trunk off the hospital bed and reaching out with his hands for hours at a time. He was a wealthy man. He, and his very large company, made soup.

The patient's employees, as I heard it, loved him. That bulky, gentle, dignified man had built up a community and treated his employees like family. So when he began to lose his mind to Alzheimer's disease, his chemists consulted the world's literature and concocted a special chicken soup for him, filled with lecithin. It didn't work.

Now we know why.

Certain chemicals form the building blocks of neurotransmitters. When the brain manufactures these transmitters, it needs ample supplies of these precursors on hand. It needs tryptophan to make serotonin, tyrosine to make dopamine and norepinephrine, and lecithin and choline to make acetylcholine (the transmitter that's most badly depleted in Alzheimer's disease). Foods vary greatly in their content of these neurotransmitter precursors, so it would seem reasonable to hope that, by varying our diets to load up on precursors, we might increase the production of the neurotransmitters. But dozens of studies have failed to show any benefit from precursor loading.

One reason precursor loading doesn't work is that the precursors have a heck of a time making it up to the brain; not only is their absorption from the gut erratic, but these big molecules have trouble crossing the blood-brain barrier. That's why the brain does not actually depend on diet for its supply of precursors. Instead, it makes it own fresh precursors from the amino acids that readily cross into the brain, and it can make all of the ones it needs by converting the building blocks from other compounds in the brain. Furthermore, low levels of precursors are not usually the cause of low levels of neurotransmitters. Rather, in conditions such as Alzheimer's and Parkinson's, transmitter levels are low because the cells that assemble the transmitters are dead and gone. That means a "precursor loading diet" is like trucking bricks to a construction site where the masons are out sick; the extra bricks pile up, and nothing gets built. For all of these reasons, the dignified CEO could not benefit from his lecithin-laced chicken soup, and in the years since, neurochemical diets have fallen out of favor as a way to save the brain.

But some foods do contain significant amounts of neurochemicals with possible brain-saving effects. Consider chocolate.

CHOCOLATE, LOVE, AND BRAINS

Chocolate and love are related. Condemned in Renaissance Europe as an erotic indulgence, celebrated as an accessory to wooing, a common self-medication for the lovelorn, chocolate is the most common object of nondrug craving in North America, inspiring midnight supermarket runs and furtive bites in private places. Chocolate has recently been appreciated for its manifold impact on the neurochemistry of emotion.

It might be helpful to begin by defining *chocolate*. Chocolate comes in many grades depending on its cocoa content. High-grade chocolate is more than 60 percent cocoa. It is invariably dark, often bittersweet, and as smooth as silk. It is completely different from typical American "milk chocolate," a pale impostor that rarely contains more than a few percent cocoa. The cocoa content is crucial, so most of what follows applies only to good-quality dark chocolate.

Chocolate contains caffeine. A good bittersweet bar has about one-third the caffeine of a cup of coffee. (Milk chocolate has barely 10 percent as much.) Chocolate also contains another stimulant, *theobromine*, and a box of dark chocolate may contain enough to send a dog into fatal epileptic fits. Both stimulants may produce mild arousal and a feeling of well-being in humans. But arousal in itself is not necessarily health enhancing; other chemicals in chocolate may be even more important to the body and mind.

One is phenylethylamine (PEA), a naturally occurring amphetamine-like compound. PEA is also found in the human limbic system. A surprising number of people who suffer depression after the breakup of a romantic relationship turn to chocolate for relief, and although the reasons are controversial, some psychiatrists have suggested that lovelorn people seek chocolate because its PEA content has a unique mood-elevating impact—an effect similar to the giddy feeling of new love. Yet such mood effects for chocolate-derived PEA have never been demonstrated in a good placebo-controlled study, so I have to withhold any advice on this mood-enhancing benefit.

Chocolate also contains three other compounds that seem likely to affect the function of the brain. First, it contains chemicals that may boost the levels of *anandamide,* a naturally occurring brain compound that binds to our built-in cannabinoid receptors. Thus, good chocolate may literally mimic the effects of marijuana. (This helps explain how brownies-with-marijuana could trigger a synergistic stimulation of our central cannabinoid receptors, transiently heightening sensation and pleasure.) Considering these effects, we might wonder whether regular intake of chocolate could slightly help the brain by somewhat relieving depression, stress, and even chronic pain.

Chocolate also contains 1MeTIQ, a chemical suspected of inhibiting the development of Parkinson's disease. Could sufficient chocolate intake have a modest anti-Parkinson's effect? And chocolate contains antioxidants similar to those found in red wine; we'll soon see how such antioxidants may help to save the brain.

But the big news about chocolate is the discovery that it contains *procyanidins*. These intriguing molecules tend to link to one another, forming chains of double, triple, or quadruple length. At a special seminar of the American Association for the Advancement of Science in 2000, researchers announced that the longer versions of procyanidins (quadruple or more) act as both antioxidants and anti-inflammatories. They can block nitric acid, relax smooth muscles, and decrease blood clotting—all effects that could reduce the risk of strokes and heart attacks. These promising discoveries have prompted the Mars candy company to fund research to produce new kinds of chocolate that are high in long-chain procyanidins—potentially the most delicious form of health food ever created!

At this point, it's too soon to say that regular chocolate intake enhances vascular health and helps protect the brain from strokes. Unfortunately, the very deliciousness of chocolate may undermine its benefits: if it prompts people to eat more than they should, any vascular benefit could go down the fat-filled atherosclerotic tubes. Therefore I am not advocating high-dose dark chocolate as a brain-saver. Still, the hints of a multifaceted impact on the nervous system are more than enough to justify further research. The benefits will be most concentrated in high-grade chocolate, or chocolate with more than 60 percent cocoa (such as French Valrhona or Belgian Callebaut). And even though chocolate contains saturated fat, most of it is in the form of stearic acid, which does not raise cholesterol. All things considered, one could hardly name a more pleasant strategy to soothe the central nervous system and—just possibly—protect the brain.

Nor is chocolate the only stimulating food with potential brain-saving properties.

TEA: A WAKE-UP FOR THE BRAIN?

In 1641 Dutch physician Nicolaes Tulp wrote in his *Observationes Medicae* that tea drinkers are "exempt from all maladies and reach an extreme old age." Tulp may have been on to something. But more than 350 years later, despite reams of data and hot debates, we still don't know for sure whether tea contributes to longevity, prevents diseases, or protects the brain. What's certain is that tea is a fascinating beverage.

Leaves from the subtropical evergreen *Camellia sinensis* are the source of more than three thousand varieties of tea consumed around the world. To make green tea, the leaves are processed gently by steaming; they are processed more vigorously by drying to make oolong tea; and to make "black" tea, they are crushed, exposed to air, and *really* processed, fermenting dark brown. Green tea is generally favored in Asia, while Westerners overwhelmingly favor black tea; only 4 percent of the tea we drink in the United States is green. (Note that herbal "tea" is another beverage altogether and usually contains no *C. sinensis* at all.)

Health claims for tea abound, especially for green tea. It has been claimed to prevent gastrointestinal cancer, skin cancer, heart attacks, strokes, bone loss, infection, constipation, and bad breath. The cancer claims are somewhat controversial, because different large studies have come up with contradictory results. For instance, among 35,369 post-menopausal women followed in Iowa, those who drank two or more cups of tea a day (mostly black tea) had about 30 percent lower rates of gastrointestinal and urinary tract cancers. And a smaller Chinese study specifically found that green tea lowered the risk of stomach cancer. But among 26,000 men and women followed in Japan between 1984 and 1992, green tea drinking did not appear to protect against gastric cancer. Let's just say the anticancer properties of tea remain uncertain.

Much more pertinent to our goal of neuroprotection, both green and black teas seem to protect against vascular problems, including heart attacks and strokes. A Dutch study compared the risk of vascular problems in 500 middle-age men; heavy tea drinkers had not only a 68 percent reduced risk of death from heart attacks but also a 73 *percent reduced risk of strokes.* In a larger Dutch study that included 3,454 men and women, those who drank one or two cups of tea daily lowered their risk of vascular disease by 46 percent, while those who drank four cups a day lowered their risk by 69 percent. For unknown reasons, women in this study seemed to get more of a benefit than men. And in Japan 5,910 nonsmoking, nondrinking women in two villages were only half as likely to suffer a stroke if they drank five or more cups of green tea per day.

So both black and green tea may have some pretty amazing antistroke and anti–heart attack properties. How come?

The simplest explanation is that tea protects cells from oxidation. All three teas—green, oolong, and black—contain flavonoids, which have powerful antioxidant properties. Multiple studies have confirmed that tea's flavonoids can block oxidative DNA damage (which may play a role in the aging process) and can also block the oxidation of lipids in the bloodstream (a great way to fight atherosclerosis). The tea antioxidant that gets the most attention is called *epigallocatechin-3-gallate* (EGCg). Lester Mitscher of the University of Kansas reported in 1997 that green tea contains much higher levels of EGCg than black tea. EGCg is twice as powerful an antioxidant as resveratol (the antioxidant found in red wine) and may be more effective than the antioxidant vitamins C and E in protecting some cells from damage. EGCg may also inhibit the growth of cancers of the oral and digestive tracts. Reports such as this have led to the popular theory that green tea is more healthful than black tea because it contains more of this powerful antioxidant.

But EGCg is just one of many *catechins,* a group of related chemicals found in both green and black tea. In fact, black tea beats green tea in the content of some catechins, as well as in other compounds called *theaflavins* with health-promoting powers, so it may be an oversimplification to say that green tea is better than black tea. Moreover, tea's apparent antistroke and anti–heart disease powers may not be entirely due to its antioxidants; tea may have other benefits, such as an ability to keep our platelets from clumping, lower our cholesterol levels, and possibly even dissolve blood clots. A Swiss study even suggests that tea helps the body preferentially burn fat, which could explain why tea drinkers tend to be more slender—and slenderness, as we discussed in the last chapter, may be helpful to the brain.

Overall, lots of evidence indicates that tea drinking has possible health benefits. We might hypothesize that the vascular benefits translate into a reduction in the risk of dementia, including both CVC and Alzheimer's. Yet several caveats in the tea-for-the-brain story are worth considering.

First, despite all the exciting press, most studies find no link one way or the other between tea and dementia. In fact, two studies—the Canadian Study of Health and Aging and one Australian study—found trends toward an *increased* rate of Alzheimer's among tea drinkers (although these findings did not reach statistical significance). We cannot ignore this discouraging data. One possible explanation is that tea contains aluminum. Since aluminum is suspected of boosting the risk of ARNAT, the impact of aluminum exposure might wipe out any brain-saving benefit of tea. But this is unlikely, because only a small amount of aluminum is found in tea, only a small proportion of tea's aluminum is available for absorption from the gut, and only a tiny amount absorbed from the gut will ever make it into the brain. Some scientists have speculated that tea's chemicals might be antioxidants at low doses but pro-oxidants at higher doses; this could lead to a Goldilocks Effect in which modest tea intake is helpful but heavy tea drinking—the five-cups-a-day habit—is hurtful. But my own best guess has to do with the milk connection: milk interferes with absorption of the antioxidants in tea. Since Western black tea drinkers are highly prone to add milk, they may be regularly defeating tea's health advantages—which would explain why Western studies fail to show a dementia-prevention benefit.

Just to add another level of intrigue to the legal stimulant story, some evidence suggests that *coffee* drinking is associated with a reduced risk of Parkinson's disease. In a thirty-year follow-up of 8,000 Japanese American men in the Honolulu Heart Program, non–coffee drinkers had five times the risk of developing Parkinson's over those who drank twenty-eight ounces or more of coffee per day (enough to float a small boat). But we have to be careful: just because parkinsonians drink less coffee than people without Parkinson's does not necessarily mean that coffee *protects* against Parkinson's. An equally likely possibility is that people developing Parkinson's have a blunted response to the pleasant brain-stimulant effects of coffee because they have low dopamine levels, so they simply have less reason to drink it.

The bottom line regarding coffee, tea, and the brain: there is little evidence that coffee saves brains. But both lab and epidemiological evidence indicates that tea drinking reduces the risk of strokes and heart attacks. The provocatively simple possibility that tea drinking could help save the brain from aging-related degeneration has not been adequately studied, so we must consider it only a long-odds bet and push for better research to resolve this important question. (An Asian study of tea intake and dementia would be a sensible step, since it would largely bypass the milk issue.) In the meantime, you have little reason to avoid tea—and some tantalizing hints that your brain would benefit if you were to drink it in modest amounts.

DRINKING AND THINKING

> One of the two things that men who have lasted for a hundred years always say: either that they have drunk whisky and smoked all their lives, or that neither tobacco nor spirits ever made the faintest appeal to them.
>
> EDWARD VERALL LUCAS

Ever since the first discovery, in some gentle farce lost in the mists of time, that drinking the juices of a pile of fruit left warming in the sun sometimes produces a unique state of mind, humans have been enjoying alcoholic beverages. And they have probably been arguing about the risks and benefits of alcohol for just as long. Hippocrates recommended the moderate use of wine as a medicine but cautioned that "undiluted wine drunk in large quantities renders a man feeble; and everybody seeing this knows that this is the power of wine." This is the essence of the consensus of physicians from ancient to modern: heavy drinking is obviously bad for health, but light drinking may possibly be good. What is the evidence, and how might alcohol help protect the human brain?

Drinking alcohol, first of all, seems to have an impact on longevity. In 1982, in the largest study of its type ever done, researchers from the American Cancer Society gave questionnaires to 490,000 men and women and asked them to record how many drinks they had each day. (A "drink" is defined as 10 to 12 grams of pure alcohol—roughly 4 ounces of wine, 12 ounces of beer, or 1.25 ounces of hard liquor.) After ten years, the study population was divided into three groups: "nondrinkers" who essentially abstained, "moderate drinkers" who had about one drink a day, and "heavy drinkers" who had five or more drinks a day. The moderate drinkers were actually 20 percent *less* likely to die than the nondrinkers; most of this life-saving benefit was due to a reduction in heart disease. At the same time, the heavy drinkers were 20 percent *more* likely to die than the moderate drinkers. This looks like a perfect example of the Goldilocks Effect. Humans seem to live longest if they take the middle path, neither teetotaling nor drinking too much.

But the devil is in the details. First, young people at low risk for heart disease got only a slight advantage by moderate drinking; it was people over age sixty with high risk of heart disease who were most likely to benefit. What's more, women who reported having at least one drink a day had a slightly increased risk of dying of breast cancer.

What are we to conclude? One major finding has held up in study after study: one drink a day seems to substantially reduce the risk of cardiac disease, the number-one killer in developed countries. That brings us to the famous French Paradox. In the 1970s doctors noticed that French people tended to eat high-fat diets but were nonetheless miraculously immune to heart disease, with rates less than half those of similar-age people in the United States. The explanation seems to be that the adult French person's dutiful consumption of wine (averaging 15.85 gallons a year, compared to 1.92 gallons in America) offers a true heart-saving benefit.

As to the risk of breast cancer, in a combined study of 300,000 American women, those who drank one or fewer drinks a day had a breast cancer rate of twelve out of 10,000, while those who abstained had a rate of *eleven* out of 10,000. We should pay heed to this small difference, but since heart disease kills more than five times as many women every year as breast cancer does, the net effect is that light drinking is very likely to promote women's longevity.

Recently, the apparent cardiac benefit has been found to extend to the brain. While *heavy* drinking increases the risk of brain hemorrhages, *light* drinking seems to help prevent the much more common ischemic type of strokes. Based on a study of 22,000 male physicians, Harvard epidemiologist Julie Buring has reported that consuming between one drink a week and one drink a day reduces men's stroke risk by 20 percent. Interestingly, drinking *more* than one drink a week had no real advantage; the benefits were the same for daily and weekly indulgers. This finding fits perfectly with the Nurses' Health Study, which showed that women who drank an average of half an alcoholic beverage a day had a reduced stroke risk. Since strokes are a major tragic cause of mental disability in the Western world, light drinking may well have a truly positive impact on cognition.

How does drinking affect the mind? Clearly, in the short run, alcohol intoxication makes us dumb. Sixty percent of men and 30 percent of women have experienced some regrettable outcome from an episode of drinking (driving while intoxicated, missing school because of a hangover, and so on), usually in the teen years or early twenties. And heavy, persistent alcohol intake can be devastating to the intellect. Chronic heavy drinking puts a big strain on the body's use of thiamine, which can produce a ghastly deficiency state, killing brain cells in exact parts of the limbic circuitry that are most crucial for memory, to produce the nasty condition known as Korsakoff's psychosis. And alcoholic liver disease is a horrific thing to see—I visualize the orange-skinned, bloated patients staggering down the hall of the liver service, pajamas in disarray and minds elsewhere.

But *light* drinking may have a completely different effect on the mind. In one Swedish study, for example, regular alcohol use was associated with higher cognitive test scores. In a study from Rush-Presbyterian-St. Luke's Medical Center in Chicago, older people who drank a small amount of alcohol did better than nondrinkers on a test of short-term memory.

Does drinking per se save a brain from strokes and possibly benefit cognition, or is it simply that educated people with other good health habits tend to be light drinkers? Some evidence suggests that it's the latter: perhaps contrary to conventional lore, Americans in the upper educational and socioeconomic brackets are more likely to drink. And one large American survey found that moderate drinkers were more likely than either nondrinkers or heavy drinkers to exercise, watch their diets, and get a good night's sleep. Furthermore, a Danish study of almost 50,000 men and women found that wine drinkers in particular were likely to eat more salads, more fish, more vegetables, and more fruit. So despite the strong evidence of vascular benefits for light drinking, other medicosocial factors could explain at least part of the healthy hearts and mental sharpness of light drinkers.

Another way to get at the long-term impact of alcohol on the mind is to compare the rates of Alzheimer's among drinkers and nondrinkers. Among eight large U.S. and European studies, only one showed that alcohol increased the risk of Alzheimer's—and that one specifically referred to the impact of heavy alcohol consumption. The other studies found no difference one way or the other. Unfortunately, these studies do nothing to help us figure out whether light drinking is beneficial, because they lumped together all drinkers, from the lightest to the heaviest. A fascinating recent report (from France, of course) gets closer to the heart of our question: researchers at the University of Bordeaux followed 3,777 local residents over sixty-five for three years. Light drinkers—those who drank up to two glasses of wine a day—were *45 percent less likely to develop*

Alzheimer's disease than nondrinkers. This single study would be no basis to start a backyard vineyard, but the results have recently been confirmed by an even bigger study: early in 2002, Dutch researchers announced that, among 5,395 people age fifty-five and older, those who consumed one to three drinks per day had a 42 percent lower risk of dementia than did nondrinkers, and those who drank less—but more than one drink a week—had a 25 percent lower risk. These wonderfully intriguing findings strongly suggest that light drinking does good things for the aging brain well beyond its antistroke effect.

Do the cognitive benefits of light drinking depend on what you drink? Red wine has received special attention as the form of alcohol most likely to prevent vascular disease, partly because the French Paradox has been reported among red wine drinkers in France, Italy, and Greece. If red wine indeed has a special vascular-health benefit, it may be due to the flavonoid *resveratrol.* Resveratrol is also present in red grape juice (which means that people who do not wish to place their bets on regular alcohol intake may conceivably get a partial brain benefit from nonalcoholic grape juice). But in a study of nearly 130,000 adults enrolled in the Kaiser-Permanente health plan, red wine, white wine, and beer had equal vascular protective effects (all somewhat more protective than hard liquor).

So why does alcohol itself seem to protect us from heart attacks and strokes (and possibly Alzheimer's)? Three theories offer good answers. One: alcohol lowers our total cholesterol, increases our HDL or "good" cholesterol, and somewhat protects us from blood clotting; the boost in HDL alone could do wonders to keep our arteries free of fatty deposits. Two: Swiss scientists have shown that alcohol reduces the growth of excess muscle cells in arteries that typically occurs after a high-fat meal; this would allow our arteries to tolerate a fattier diet with less regret. And the third theory is a beautiful demonstration of pharmacogenomics, the understanding of how people with different genes get different effects from the same agents: Harvard researchers reported in 2001 that the gene for the enzyme that breaks down alcohol (alcohol dehydrogenase) has two forms. Moderate drinkers who have the "slower" form of the gene are more likely to keep their HDL levels high and are less likely to suffer heart attacks. So rather than saying "Everyone will benefit from light drinking," it's probably more accurate for doctors to say "People in one big genetically determined subgroup will get a big benefit from light drinking; people in another subgroup will get less of a benefit." This is the kind of discovery that will make twenty-first-century medicine exciting, letting us customize a health prescription for a person's genes.

How are individuals to make the decision about drinking? As Twain warned us, everyone is different. Alcohol is potent stuff that creates a risk of terrible harm to some, perhaps offers a modest benefit to others, and an even bigger benefit to still others.

For some people, drinking clearly offers more risk than benefit, including pregnant women, those with liver disease, those with a particular weakening of the heart muscles called *cardiomyopathy*, those taking medications that interact with alcohol, and perhaps those with a personal or family history of breast cancer. Another group that must be wary are those with a family history of alcoholism. Moreover, young people with few cardiac risk factors are unlikely to get much of a vascular benefit from drinking. The biggest group that should refrain from light drinking by far is those who have developed alcohol dependence or abuse in the past. (*Dependence* means a compulsive pattern of use; *abuse* means that the person continues to use alcohol despite serious negative consequences for family or career or health.) About 10 percent of women and 20 percent of men in America will develop alcohol dependence or abuse at some point in their lives—usually early in life and, in some cases, transiently. For this unfortunate minority, drinking is not a blessing; it's a curse, and no potential brain-saving benefits justify the risk of regular drinking.

But the other 60 to 75 percent of American adults, especially those who are middle-age and older, may get a true heart- and brain-saving benefit from "neuroprotective alcohol therapy"—which may occur with as little as one drink a week.

This brings us right back into the snapping jaws of controversy. If several glasses of wine or beer per week can help to save the heart and brain, should people who drink less begin to drink more? The American Heart Association (AHA) says, "No!" pointing out that the risks of uncontrolled drinking are terrible, and that the vascular benefit of light drinking is no better than what we can achieve with diet plus exercise. So the AHA insists that doctors should recommend these other measures and *never* recommend drinking.

This smacks of antimedical puritanism. There are surely many people who have never had a problem with drinking but have given up the habit, or who drink only on special occasions, all of whom have no tendency to substance abuse and no medical contraindications—and all of whom might protect their hearts and brains by drinking several glasses of wine or beer each week. If they've had no trouble with alcohol by age thirty, these folks are extremely unlikely to be turned into alcoholics by such a dietary change. Rather than issuing a fierce and paternalistic "No!" doctors should identify such people, especially those with risk factors for vascular disease, and candidly give them the best current knowledge about alcohol's apparent benefits and risks. In fact, the benefits of the Mediterranean diet may well come from its unique *combination* of food and wine;

tossing out the wine because of an excessive fear of alcohol is unscientific, since the best for cerebral health may actually be this whole-diet approach. America definitely needs fewer heavy drinkers, but—putting it boldly—*America may also need more light drinkers*. Therefore I offer the possibly shocking proposal that we return to the most ancient medical wisdom of all: a little alcohol, sensibly consumed, may be a first-rate tonic for the nation's cognitive health.

Fats and Brains

Like our arboreal ancestors, human beings were designed to take in large amounts of fruits and vegetables, ripe with carbohydrates, amino acids, vitamins, and other phytochemicals. But fairly early in primate evolution another component became a regular part of our feast: fats. How do fats figure in the Brain-Saving Diet?

Different types of fat appear to have different effects on health. A *saturated* fat is one whose carbon atoms are hooked up to one another by single bonds; if it has just one double bond, it's called *monounsaturated*; if it has two or more double bonds, it's *polyunsaturated*. *Trans-fatty acids* have a chemical bond that sticks up in the opposite direction from another bond, like an opposable thumb. Trans-fatty acids naturally occur in lamb, beef, and dairy products, but they are also manufactured when we *hydrogenate* vegetable oils—the process that produces stick margarine and solid shortening. Meat, cheese, whole and 2 percent milk, ice cream, pizza, and most pastries include saturated fats; french fries, fried chicken, and doughnuts are often especially high in trans-fats. Americans typically eat a fairly fatty diet, getting an average of 34 percent of their calories from one or another of these types of fat.

Nutrition experts have told us for thirty years that saturated fats—the kind found in butter—will invariably hurt our hearts and shorten our lives and that cutting them from our diets will both lower our "bad" LDL cholesterol levels and prolong our lives. But three sophisticated computer analyses suggest that these claims are, to a shocking degree, sheer mythology. For instance, if people with serious vascular risk factors greatly decrease their intake of saturated fats, they'll probably gain about a year of life; but to almost everyone's surprise, if *healthy nonsmokers* make the same dietary switch, they'll probably get just a few extra *weeks* of life. Hey, that's a lot of trouble to go to for such a small gain!

It's about time to dispel the mythology of fat and to clarify what we know.

First, eating fat doesn't make you fat, and avoiding fat doesn't make you thin. Research shows that whenever people reduce their fat intake, they make up for it with other foods—often overdosing on simple carbo-hydrates, sugary grenades of fat-free pastries that actually *explode* the rate of obesity.

Second, high levels of LDL cholesterol are truly associated with vascular disease, and taking cholesterol-lowering medicines will truly improve the cholesterol profile and help prevent heart attacks. But strangely enough, *there's weak evidence that avoiding saturated fats in the diet really lowers cholesterol levels.* Yes, a *subgroup* of folks can lower their cholesterol levels by following a strict low-fat diet; these are the people with *diet-responsive high blood cholesterol.* Genes seem to make a big difference in whether a person is a member of this lucky group. But since 90 percent of cholesterol comes from the liver, diet has little to do with the problem in many cases, and surprisingly, for many people, following a strict low-fat diet is more likely to produce burger dreams than low cholesterol levels. For instance, in the recent Lyon Heart Study, 605 heart attack survivors were randomized to eat either a "Western" diet that included much more sat-urated fat or a Mediterranean diet that included much less saturated fat. These extremely different diets led to virtually no difference in the pa-tients' cholesterol profiles—a result that amazed traditional nutritionists. Nonetheless, 44 of the Western-diet patients had another heart attack, while only 14 of the Mediterranean-diet patients did. This suggests that a Mediterranean diet can indeed save the heart—*but not because it lowers cholesterol.* The Mediterranean diet works in more interesting ways.

Third, the vilest villain in the heart part of the story is not saturated fats, it's *trans-fatty acids.* Trans-fats, which make up just 4 to 7 percent of typical American diets, seem to be uniquely dangerous; they prompt HDL levels to plummet and make blood vessels too stiff to respond properly to stress. Interestingly, when Americans were scared away from saturated fats in the 1970s and 1980s, they often turned to the stick margarines that were usually trans-fat-laced heart killers.

Finally, we need every kind of fat to some degree, and the Mediter-ranean diet is a step forward, with its emphasis on monounsaturated fats, but polyunsaturated fatty acids (PUFAs) with lots of double bonds may be the ones we should especially seek out. PUFAs are the exact kind of fat that makes up the membranes of every single neuron; pound for pound, *about two-thirds of our brain is PUFAs.*

The search for the best fats perhaps comes closest to the search for a true brain food. Knowing what we do about different fats, can we choose the ones that are healthiest for the brain? The answer is a qualified yes.

In both animal experiments and human epidemiology, PUFAs do more for brains than do competing dietary fats. For instance, when rats are fed a diet high in saturated fats, their memory is impaired; but rats fed either a low-fat diet or a high-fat diet containing PUFAs do better on memory tests. Babies whose formula is supplemented with PUFAs appear to do better at problem solving. And even within the PUFA group, some PUFAs may be better for the brain than others—which brings us to a fish tale.

PUFAs fall into either of two groups: the omega-6s and the omega-3s. American diets tend to be heavy in the less healthful omega-6s, found, for instance, in corn oil. Omega-3s, on the other hand, are found in flaxseed oil, canola oil, soy and walnut oils, and especially certain fish. The fish richest in omega-3s are fatty, cold-water fish such as sardines, salmon, mackerel, tuna, trout, and herring. Without these omega-3s, our bodies are obliged to build all their cell membranes from saturated fats; but if we take in enough omega-3s, it can use them to build cell membranes, providing us with more elastic ones. In the heart, this seems to make electrical transmission work more reliably, decreasing the chance of fatal arrhythmias. And in the brain, omega-3s may promote better neurotransmission. Indeed, eating fish with omega-3s seems to have all sorts of practical health benefits. It may ease arthritis, improve irritable bowel syndrome, reduce inflammation, and most important for overall public health, save the heart. For example, a thirty-year study of almost 2,000 people in Chicago found that those who ate small amounts of fish had a 42 percent reduction in deaths from heart disease. And a recent Italian study of 11,324 patients found that those who took 850 mg per day of supplemental omega-3s had a 45 percent decline in sudden cardiac deaths.

This stuff is *really* good for the heart. How about the brain? Several impressive studies have shown a specific benefit of omega-3-rich fish for cognition. In the Zutphen Elderly Study, Dutch epidemiologist Sandra Kalmijn showed that elderly men who ate fish had a 55 percent lower risk of cognitive decline than men who ate no fish. She also showed—among almost 5,500 women and men followed in the Rotterdam Study—that high intakes of overall fat, saturated fat, or cholesterol led to a doubling of the risk of dementia. In contrast, *fish* consumption led to a 60 percent *reduction* in the risk of dementia in general and a *70 percent reduction in the risk of Alzheimer's disease.*

Omega-3s may even be able to prevent or treat depression. A 1998 study of eleven countries found that the rate of depression was inversely proportional to fish consumption. And at least one controlled experiment, a collaboration between researchers at Harvard and Baylor, showed that omega-3s do a great job of controlling bipolar mood disorders. A larger study is under way at the NIH to further test this theory. It's too soon to say "Eat salmon for depression"; but we should keep an eye out for further proof of this brain-friendly effect.

One nuance to the fish story may be important. In the Zutphen Elderly

Body Mass Index Chart

Height (Feet and Inches)

Weight (Pounds)	5'0"	5'1"	5'2"	5'3"	5'4"	5'5"	5'6"	5'7"	5'8"	5'9"	5'10"	5'11"	6'0"	6'1"	6'2"	6'3"	6'4"
100	20	19	18	18	17	17	16	16	15	15	14	14	14	13	13	12	12
105	21	20	19	19	18	17	17	16	16	16	15	15	14	14	13	13	13
110	21	21	20	19	19	18	18	17	17	16	16	15	15	15	14	14	13
115	22	22	21	20	20	19	19	18	17	17	17	16	16	15	15	14	14
120	23	23	22	21	21	20	19	19	18	18	17	17	16	16	15	15	15
125	24	24	23	22	21	21	20	20	19	18	18	17	17	16	16	16	15
130	25	25	24	23	22	22	21	20	20	19	19	18	18	17	17	16	16
135	26	26	25	24	23	22	22	21	21	20	19	19	18	18	17	17	16
140	27	26	26	25	24	23	23	22	21	21	20	20	19	18	18	17	17
145	28	27	27	26	25	24	23	23	22	21	21	20	20	19	19	18	18
150	29	28	27	27	26	25	24	23	23	22	22	21	20	20	19	19	18
155	30	29	28	27	27	26	25	24	24	23	22	22	21	20	20	19	19
160	31	30	29	28	27	27	26	25	24	24	23	22	22	21	21	20	19
165	32	31	30	29	28	27	27	26	25	24	24	23	22	22	21	21	20
170	33	32	31	30	29	28	27	27	26	25	24	24	23	22	22	21	21
175	34	33	32	31	30	29	28	27	27	26	25	24	24	23	22	22	21
180	35	34	33	32	31	30	29	28	27	27	26	25	24	24	23	22	22
185	36	35	34	33	32	31	30	29	28	27	27	26	25	24	24	23	23
190	37	36	35	34	33	32	31	30	29	28	27	26	26	25	24	24	23
195	38	37	36	35	33	32	31	31	30	29	28	27	26	26	25	24	24
200	39	38	37	35	34	33	32	31	30	30	29	28	27	26	26	25	24
205	40	39	37	36	35	34	33	32	31	30	29	29	28	27	26	26	25
210	41	40	38	37	36	35	34	33	32	31	30	29	28	28	27	26	26
215	42	41	39	38	37	36	35	34	33	32	31	30	29	28	28	27	26
220	43	42	40	39	38	37	36	34	33	32	32	31	30	29	28	27	27
225	44	43	41	40	39	37	36	35	34	33	32	31	31	30	29	28	27
230	45	43	42	41	39	38	37	36	35	34	33	32	31	30	30	29	28
235	46	44	43	42	40	39	38	37	36	35	34	33	32	31	30	29	29
240	47	45	44	43	41	40	39	38	36	35	34	33	33	32	31	30	29
245	48	46	45	43	42	41	40	38	37	36	35	34	33	32	31	31	30
250	49	47	46	44	43	42	40	39	38	37	36	35	34	33	32	31	30

☐ Underweight ☐ Weight Appropriate ☐ Overweight ☐ Obese

Study, Kalmijn and her colleagues separated the effect of omega-3s from that of fish; the *fish itself* seemed to produce the superior cognitive impact, which possibly means that substances in fish other than omega-3s are also good for the brain—another argument for the whole-foods approach. For instance, fish is an excellent source of selenium, another one of the brain's bare necessities. Therefore, instead of specifically championing omega-3s, we should probably simply eat fish and revel in the health benefits until some future time when we better understand why it's so good for us. Fatty fish is probably the closest thing on earth to a genuine brain food.

Does Obesity Affect Thinking Abilities?

At the first national nutrition summit in 1969, the focus was on saving Americans from hunger. At the fifth national summit, held in 2000, the focus swung dramatically; the main concern was on saving Americans from fat. How might obesity affect the brain?

I was on a ferry on a fjord in frightful weather. Even the hardiest of tourists, not to mention the local Norwegians, had retreated inside from driving rain and bitter cold. We rubbed portholes in the condensation of the windows to see the green and gray towers of mountains that seemed to press about us, mounting sheerly from the charcoal water to disappear in mist. It was beautiful.

A Norwegian girl nearby was returning home after a year in New York as an au pair. She had thrown herself down across from me—a bundle of freckled limbs and travel fatigue and hypervigilance as homecoming approached. She propped herself up on her backpack, took out bread and a Swiss Army knife and a hunk of cheese, and offered me a generous piece. I asked her about her year in America. The first thing she said was, "Americans are so . . . large!"

She meant fat. Visitors from almost every other country disembark at almost any American airport or port of call and marvel at the bellies and buttocks and thighs that waddle past, the hulking shoulders, the padded arms. And it's true—too many Americans are fat. Doctors determine who is *overweight* or *obese* based upon the body mass index (BMI, the relationship between a person's height and weight; see the graph). Based on BMI, 55 percent of Americans are currently overweight or obese. Compare this figure with a 14.5 percent obesity rate in 1980. Charles Hennekens, chief of preventive medicine at Harvard's Brigham and Women's Hospital, has summarized it simply: "The U.S. is probably the heaviest society in the history of the world." It is a national tragedy: an obesity epidemic—the irony of plenty. Nor is obesity confined to America. The single most salient fact about food intake in developed countries is that it is excessive.

Why is it so extraordinarily hard for Americans and others to control their food intake and avoid obesity? As I mentioned in Chapter 1, our brains evolved to make us brilliant finders of food. Since our wild-living ancestors could not count on a reliable supply, our brains motivated us to take in excess calories when food was plentiful, and to store the extra energy in the form of fat in case times get tough. Thus today, whenever we encounter desirable food, we feel a ferocious impetus to eat far more than we need to satisfy our appetites. Technological advances have now supplied those of us in developed countries with much more delicious food than we could ever take in. There's trouble lurking in that horn of plenty. Excess intake of energy-dense foods—foods that are very rare in nature, foods that were rarely found on earth during the 50-million-year march of primate evolution to Homo sapiens, the very foods that we have learned to provide for ourselves via the lightning-fast cultural advances of the last 10,000 years following the birth of agriculture—can lead to diseases that were virtually unknown among our hunter-gatherer ancestors. They are diseases of civilization. Obesity. Type 2 diabetes. Heart disease. All of them may affect the brain.

The modern food industry exploits our bio-heritage by offering us two types of food that we were designed to yearn for but practically never found in nature: trans-fat-filled pieces of domesticated animals, and energy-dense, nutrient-poor sweets. People are irresistibly attracted to these amazingly energy-dense, nutrient-poor foods; they respond to them with a burst of subjective pleasure and a rush of brain dopamine; more craving and more intake follow, and the end result is the exact opposite from what many of us are looking for: weight gain. In addition, rather than filling up gradually (the usual effect of foraging), we can put away a 1,500-calorie meal in a matter of minutes, which makes it impossible for our satiety systems to kick in. So we tend to find ourselves surprised at feeling "stuffed"—more than satisfied—half an hour after a meal, when the brain finally gets the appetite-control message, "Enough already!" In essence, our cultural evolution has pulled the rug out from under our biological evolution. We've made such incredible quantities of food so quickly and readily available to ourselves that we eat more than we naturally want to eat, and the excess may actually *reduce* our survival.

It may also harm our brains.

At this point, I'll propose a theory, a testable hypothesis that will live or die by the findings of the research community. I propose that obesity increases the risk of aging-related memory loss.

My reasoning is as follows. Obesity—in most cases a direct result of modifiable behavior—initiates a dangerous cascade that puts our neurons in jeopardy. It retards our metabolism, upsets our hormonal balance, and slows us down physically, which subverts the health benefits of activity. Obesity is a risk factor for hypertension, atherosclerosis, insulin resistance, heart disease, and, indirectly, strokes. Fat in our blood vessels causes oxidative stress, which begins a vicious cycle that spreads vascular disease throughout the body and up to the brain. It increases the chance that the big carotid arteries serving the brain will become narrowed, that the tiny arterioles in the brain will become tortuous, and that the medium-size vessels will develop clots or receive them when emboli are unleashed from the heart—all variations on the theme of CVC. Obesity greatly increases the risk of overt diabetes, but even more commonly, it causes the silent siege of undiagnosed insulin resistance. This adds stress to the most basic operations of neurons and stokes the fires of oxidation and glycation (the sugary transformation of cells that accelerates aging). And, since CVC teams up with ARNAT, America's obesity epidemic may actually boost the rate of the most common dementia of all—Alzheimer's.

I should be clear that epidemiological studies have *not* shown obesity to be a risk factor for Alzheimer's (although this may simply be because obese people die of heart attacks before they're old enough to show the signs of Alzheimer's). But growing evidence indicates that obese people do indeed perform less well on some tests of mental performance. In Uppsala, Sweden, for example, when 504 men age sixty-nine to seventy-four years underwent neuropsychological testing, obese men had lower cognitive test scores regardless of their socioeconomic status. Even when strokes were excluded, the obese men were *still* the ones who were cognitively challenged. To look at the question from a slightly different point of view, researchers at Loma Linda University examined 99 Seventh-Day Adventists who were over age seventy-five. Those who had eaten more calories in 1976 had lower mental status scores in 1991. The authors concluded, "This raises the possibility that higher consumption of calories in middle age may accelerate the decline in cognitive function seen with aging, as apparently occurs in some animals." Exactly.

Obesity is not an obscure risk factor. If it is a risk factor for memory loss, even a minor one, it could—at least theoretically—affect half of the U.S. population.

Now that's food for thought.

The Brain-Saving Diet

A wealth of new discoveries at the frontiers of nutritional neuroscience give us strong evidence that diet can lower our risk of CVC and ARNAT. What we need is a general approach that takes advantage of this science and gives us a satisfying, enjoyable way to reap the rewards of everything

Brain-Saving Diet Pyramid

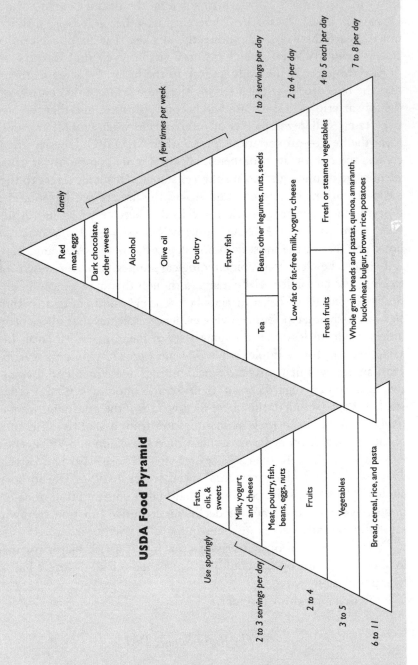

Rarely — Red meat, eggs

A few times per week — Dark chocolate, other sweets; Alcohol; Olive oil; Poultry; Fatty fish

1 to 2 servings per day — Tea; Beans, other legumes, nuts, seeds

2 to 4 per day — Low-fat or fat-free milk, yogurt, cheese

4 to 5 each per day — Fresh fruits; Fresh or steamed vegetables

7 to 8 per day — Whole grain breads and pastas, quinoa, amaranth, buckwheat, bulgur, brown rice, potatoes

USDA Food Pyramid

Use sparingly — Fats, oils, & sweets

2 to 3 servings per day — Milk, yogurt, and cheese; Meat, poultry, fish, beans, eggs, nuts

2 to 4 — Fruits

3 to 5 — Vegetables

6 to 11 — Bread, cereal, rice, and pasta

we've learned so far about food and the brain. Such a diet should also help us control our intake and idealize our weight. This is the basis of the Brain-Saving Diet.

Although the Mediterranean diet is a wonderful starting point, superior in many ways to both the USDA food pyramid and even the DASH diet, we need to modify it for optimum neuroprotective effect. This modified diet includes a sensible balance of carbohydrates, proteins, and fats; a typical ratio would be 55 percent of calories from carbohydrates, 15 percent from proteins, and 30 percent from fats (with 40 percent of those fats being PUFAs, especially omega-3s). Rather than worrying too much about saturated fats, it's probably more important to avoid *trans*-fats, which will soon become easier as food producers are required to list trans-fat content on their labels. Rather than worrying excessively about salt, we should make sure we take in enough potassium and calcium. And rather than considering all carbohydrates to be created equal, we need to watch their *glycemic index*. The glycemic index tells us how fast a carbohydrate breaks down into glucose; the slower, the better. For example, soybeans have a glycemic index of 20, apples have an index of 52, oatmeal has an index of 78, and a baked potato has a surprisingly high glycemic index of 116, which is even higher than white bread at 100. People who eat foods with a high glycemic index are more prone to heart disease, so we want to make a revision in the white-pasta-heavy Mediterranean diet—and get most of our carbs from low-glycemic sources.

A daily diet that fits beautifully with this overall plan is shown in the illustration, which compares the Brain-Saving Diet with the USDA food pyramid. Our new diet will include seven to eight servings of whole grains and grain products; four to five servings of vegetables; four to five servings of fresh fruits; two to four of low-fat or nonfat dairy products; five to seven weekly servings of nuts, seeds, and legumes; and limited concentrated sweets. (Note that the size of a "serving" can vary a lot. I mean a half-cup of grains, nuts, and legumes; a piece of fruit or three-quarters of a cup of juice; a cup of raw vegetables or a half-cup of cooked vegetables; a cup of milk or yogurt; and four ounces of fatty fish or three ounces of lean poultry.) Particular fruits and vegetables that perhaps offer special benefits to the brain include apples and onions for their flavonoids; dark green leafy vegetables such as kale and spinach as well as carrots and sweet potatoes for their carotenoids and lutein; cooked tomatoes for their lycopenes; strawberries, raspberries, tomatoes, and nuts for their ellagic acid and ferulic acid; some soy products for their coumestans, lignans, and isoflavones; and some peanuts for their cholesterol-lowering and appetite-suppressing power. Blueberries are a great source of antioxidants, though you'll probably get all the antioxidants you need from those eight to ten daily servings of just about *any* fruits and vegetables (with the exception of iceberg lettuce, a product with about the nutritional value of pale green paper). Grains such as quinoa, amaranth, and buckwheat are especially rich in nutrients.

You have virtually no reason to eat red meat, although frankly a burger a month (with ketchup for lycopenes!) will not do much harm. An occasional egg is also fine. Better nutrition would come from one to two weekly servings of white-meat poultry. But if you had to choose just one animal food to add to your diet for the sake of your brain, the best would be three or more four-ounce servings of fatty fish each week. Fish such as sardines, herring, and salmon lead the omega-3 pack with 2 to 4 grams of omega-3s per serving, but even canned tuna, with 1 gram, can help.

Adults who have none of the alcohol risk factors listed earlier should exercise their personal judgment and seriously consider joining the millions of healthy Western Europeans who enjoy one to six glasses of wine each week. Use tea (black or green) instead of coffee, and perhaps indulge in a small amount of good dark chocolate.

Whole foods are the best source of nutrients, but realistically, some people will need to take supplements. I recommend a multivitamin, but be sure it includes 0.4 mg of B12 and 400 to 600 mcg of folate a day. Ask your doctor about iron supplements.

This is the essence of the Brain-Saving Diet. It may be among the most healthful, palate-pleasing, and reliable bets for neuroprotection, a bet that will increase your chances of optimum human brain function and help preserve your brain from the many demons of aging. As a bonus, it will probably help many people lose weight, by providing them with more long-lasting satisfaction-per-calorie. Your goal is not a frantic pursuit of anorexic "perfection" but a life-embracing approach to a healthy body mass index. Still, to avoid obesity, you must gain control over the ravenous beast of unrestrained appetite.

In this regard, two modern discoveries are worth solid gold. First, we would truly eat less and be equally satisfied if we simply *ate more slowly*. The fast-food lifestyle subverts all our built-in neurosatiety mechanisms. Joining the slow-food movement—returning to the concept of a leisurely meal, preferably shared with family or friends—recruits the wonderful physiology that helps us know when enough is enough. Second, numerous studies have confirmed that the best intentions to control appetite are subverted by *inactivity*. Physical activity has a nearly magical influence on appetite. All you need is a little regular physical activity to activate your brain/body self-regulating system to better adapt your appetite to your caloric expenditures. It's not necessary to work out like a galley slave to control your appetite. If you are *somewhat* physically active, if you activate yourself above that critical minimum—for instance, by thirty minutes of brisk walking a day—you will flick the neurological switch that turns on a natural signaling system that can painlessly and powerfully bring your appetite into line with your true needs.

An honest diet book would be four words long: *Eat less. Exercise more.* I offer a more realistic revision: *Eat right, exercise some.* Break free of the chains of obesity, return to the virtues of our ancient dietary heritage, take the time to enjoy a good meal, and the time to enjoy the active life that that meal makes possible. These are some of the most powerful things you can do to unleash the amazing potential of your brain.

CHAPTER 12

Good News:
Antioxidants Save Your Brain

We were up in Seattle for the American Academy of Neurology's 1995 annual meeting. Web "Wild Child" Ross, my friend and neurobehavioral co-conspirator, had flown in from Hawaii with his colleagues from the Honolulu Heart Program, where he runs the brain research component. Elbow deep in a bargain seafood smorgasbord slathered in saturated fat, we were catching up. "Fish," said Web thoughtfully, as he dipped the Alaskan king crab's red leg into hot, lemon-scented butter, then pulled it out to wave at us for emphasis. We watched as it slipped through his fingers to land in his beer just as he finished his thought, "Brain food." When we stopped laughing, we began to talk about whether there's really any such thing as brain food. The idea that the right diet could help save the brain was just beginning to get attention. Fish had its champions, but all of us, we admitted to one another, were hedging our bets by taking vitamin E.

Later at the meeting we heard the results of a study of older Japanese Americans in Washington State. The research subjects had been graded according to their performance on a battery of neuropsychological tests. One environmental exposure factor stood out: those with the highest cognitive status were those who had regularly taken vitamin E.

When someone asks, "How can I protect myself from Alzheimer's disease?" I know that a quick answer is never complete; that's the reason for this book. But forced to offer a brain-saving plan in two seconds, I'd go straight to the bottom line of an exciting collection of research studies and simply say, "Take vitamin E."

The reasons are straightforward. First, entirely apart from Alzheimer's, aging itself weakens the antioxidant defense systems of the brain. Second, Alzheimer's and other forms of neurodegeneration definitely involve excess oxidation, with *free radicals* (extremely dangerous molecules that are produced as a natural by-product of brain metabolism) burning up our neurons like high-speed rust; in effect, we spend our whole lives using our built-in antioxidants to keep free radicals from eating us alive. Third, there is exciting evidence that antioxidants in general are neuroprotective, and that antioxidants that occur in foods and herbs, as well as certain synthetic antioxidants, may protect the brain from free radicals. Fourth, of all the inexpensive, low-risk, and readily available antioxidants, vitamin E is the one that seems most likely to protect the brain. Reviewing this evidence, one would need a heart of stone not to get excited. True, the size of the protective effect may be modest; true, *some* antioxidant supplements may make things worse for human health rather than better; and true, individuals differ in the extent to which our brains will benefit from an antioxidant boost. But the benefit of antioxidants may turn out to be one of the most important discoveries in the history of human neuroprotection.

In this chapter, I will focus on three antioxidants: vitamin E, vitamin C, and beta-carotene, the major source of vitamin A. I'll briefly look at the basics: how the brain is doomed to some damage because it burns oxygen for fuel, and how aging makes this oxidation process more dangerous. Then I'll discuss the encouraging evidence that human brains can benefit from the salvation of certain antioxidants.

Oxygen and Brains: The Good and the Bad

Every brain cell gets its energy from glucose and oxygen. It burns these fuels in its tiny powerhouses, the fiery furnaces we call mitochondria, just as a car burns fuel in its engine. But in one of the great ironies of biology, just as a car spews out potentially toxic exhaust fumes, mitochondria also spew out an extremely toxic by-product: free radicals. The less efficient our mitochondria, the more free radicals they make. Aging guarantees that we will have more and more mutations in our mitochondrial DNA; these mutations act like wrenches tossed into the engine of the cell, making it less efficient; so aging means an inescapable increase in free radicals.

Free radicals are not all bad: acting as Jekyll-and-Hyde compounds in the brain, they serve us well when they help kill invading bacteria or fight the growth of cancers. But free radicals are also responsible for potentially deadly neuronal stress. Like bloody-minded soldiers, crazed with energy and deaf to reason, they can crash through the defensive lines of our neuronal membranes, proteins, mitochondria, and DNA, oxidizing everything in their path, and causing the untimely death of brain cells.

Neurons are very prone to free radical injury for three reasons: they burn lots of oxygen, so they make a lot of free radicals; they tend to have weaker antioxidant defenses than other cells in the body; and their membranes are made up of fatty acids or *membrane lipids*. Membrane lipids are incredibly likely to react with free radicals, which often leads to an interesting chain reaction. One free radical rips a hydrogen right off a fat in a membrane; in response, the membrane says, "Oh yeah?" and makes another free radical, leading to a self-propagating assault that tears into the membrane like a chain saw into a watermelon. This process is called *lipid peroxidation*, which means that the fatty parts of membranes are so badly oxidized that the neuron may literally rupture.

Many neuroscientists believe that free-radical-induced lipid peroxidation is one of the keys to memory loss. The reason is that our hippocampal memory cells are very "heavy breathers": that is, they have a superhigh rate of oxidative metabolism, so they are especially likely to make too many free radicals, which hurt the very cells that made them—which in turn may help to explain why our memories invariably deteriorate with age. Considering that stress, illness, and aging itself make mitochondria less efficient and boost the production of free radicals, we begin to see why the aging brain is so vulnerable to rampaging oxidation.

Aging boosts the dangers of oxidation in other ways too. Older brains suffer because oxygen reacts with *proteins* inside our brain cells; this leads to the creation of bizarre versions of the proteins (called *carbonyl derivatives*) that can ruin signaling between neurons. And aging means that free radicals have been quietly oxidizing and corrupting the DNA *in the nucleus itself*—a process akin to scribbling on the blueprint of life. In effect, free radicals are the bully-boys of neurophysiology. At this point, neuroscientists have moved beyond wondering whether free radical oxidation is involved in neurodegeneration to wondering whether it is the very essence of brain aging.

Fortunately, our brains come equipped with lots of natural antioxidants, including such familiar molecules as estrogen, melatonin, and vitamin C. But several other built-in antioxidant defenders may be even more important. Our front-line antioxidant defensive team includes the four enzymes *glutathione peroxidase, superoxide dismutase, nitric oxide synthase,* and *catalase*. Each of these defenders acts like a three-hundred-pound linebacker, poised to block any free radicals that dare to cause trouble. In fact, rather than acting on their own, the real role of antioxidant vitamins may be to assist these heavy-duty brain-defenders. It's hard to overstate the power these defenders have over our biological destinies. For instance, in 1999 scientists showed that, by making a simple change in the catalase gene in roundworms, they could create a superworm that lived up to *six times* the normal life span. This announcement inspired a burst of international news, since it suggested that simple gene therapies to boost antioxidant defenses could conceivably prolong human life.

What emerges is a picture of oxidation and antioxidants fighting over the life of our neurons in a pitched battle to maintain the health of the cells that make us ourselves. This battle is important to the human mind because there's a direct link between antioxidants and memory. For instance, if a researcher blocks the natural antioxidant defenses in a rat, that rodent's hippocampus will malfunction; he'll have poor memory and get lost in a maze. But if the researcher gives him vitamin E, his hippocampal memory cells will resist the stress of oxidation. And in one of the nicest demonstrations of the neuroprotective value of antioxidant-rich foods, researchers at Tufts University in Boston fed aging rats either strawberry extracts, spinach, or vitamin E. Spinach did the best job of all of protecting their memories (one reason I emphasize fruits and vegetables rather than a cabinet full of supplements), but vitamin E was also effective.

But the most important thing of all is the recent discovery that beta-amyloid does its dirty work, in part, by recruiting free radicals; it uses these free radicals as weapons to destroy our neurons. In other words, *ARNAT and Alzheimer's involve a free radical rampage.* What's more, new mouse experiments show that antioxidants can block this assault—exciting evidence that free radical fighters may be able to defend our brains from the number-one cause of aging-related memory loss. In addition, dozens of animal experiments suggest that antioxidants can defend the body against vascular disease. That means antioxidants potentially save the brain from *both* processes that contribute the most to memory loss: ARN, including Alzheimer's, and CVC, including strokes.

The next step is to look at antioxidants in people. Even though ARN and CVC interact and overlap, it will simplify our trip through the forest of research to consider them separately as we try to answer three key questions: (1) Can antioxidants help prevent strokes? (2) Can antioxidants protect or even enhance human cognition? and (3) Can antioxidants help save the brain from various forms of ARN? The answers are probably yes, yes, and yes.

Antioxidants May Save Your Brain from Strokes

In the Zutphen Elderly Study, a Dutch project, 552 middle-age men participated in a dietary survey. As I mentioned in Chapter 11, intake of flavonoid-rich fruits and vegetables was associated with an amazing 73 percent reduction in stroke risk in these men; but beta-carotene by itself was associated with a 46 percent reduction—a pretty impressive effect. In 1971, in a study conducted in the gorgeous Swiss city of Basel, 442 older people gave blood samples measuring their levels of vitamins E, C, or beta-carotene. Twenty-two years later, in 1993, the researchers found that the people who had started with good antioxidant vitamin levels ended up having fewer strokes and heart attacks. In the U.S. Second National Health and Nutrition Examination Survey, which looked at more than 6,000 men and women, those with the highest levels of vitamin C had 26 percent fewer strokes than those with the lowest levels. And in the most exciting discovery to date, in the year 2000 Japanese researchers reported the results of a study of 880 men and 1,241 women who were followed for twenty years; those with the highest blood levels of vitamin C had a *70 percent* lower risk of strokes!

Still, for every positive finding, there's one to give us pause. For instance, in the U.S. Physicians' Health Study, 22,071 male physicians were randomly assigned to take beta-carotene or not. After thirteen years, it appeared that this particular antioxidant produced no difference in the rate of strokes.

Is your head spinning yet? It would be great if all these studies led to the same conclusion, but the truth is elusive. One possible explanation for the difference in results is that not all vitamins are created equal. For instance, for some reason vitamin C seems to work better than beta-carotene. Another reason may be that studies often lump together two very different types of strokes—the common ischemic type and the uncommon hemorrhagic (bleeding) type. While the Physicians' Health Study reported no difference in strokes *overall,* it actually found that ischemic strokes *were* significantly reduced, while brain hemorrhages were *not.* Findings such as this have led to the theory that antioxidants probably decrease the risk of the common ischemic strokes, while they may have no benefit (or may slightly increase the risk) for the less common hemorrhagic strokes.

Now perhaps we're on to something. If antioxidants specifically protect the brain from ischemic strokes, how would they do so? One good answer comes from the big French study called the Étude sur le Vieillissement Artériel (Study of Arterial Aging). Researchers looked at antioxidants and carotid artery narrowing in nearly 1,200 men and women. They found that people with higher vitamin E levels had significantly more free-flowing carotid arteries, suggesting that one way antioxidants help prevent strokes is by decreasing atherosclerosis in the big arteries leading to the brain. Other research suggests that antioxidants also defend against the buildup of atherosclerosis in the vessels within the brain itself. Still other research suggests a third benefit: after a stroke, there's always a burst of neuron-killing free radicals; antioxidants seem to rescue neurons from this deadly burst of oxidation.

Unfortunately, not all the news about antioxidants and vascular disease is so pleasing. Nutrition experts have long assumed that vitamins A, C, and E might help manage heart disease, but this may not be true. Despite decades of research, for instance, there's no proof that vitamin C supplements are good for the heart. It seems odd that antioxidants would help prevent strokes but not heart disease, yet that's what the available research seems to suggest. And an interesting recent experiment at the University of Washington suggests that antioxidants may actually *undercut* the benefit of cholesterol-lowering medications: patients who take such drugs usually get both a decline in "bad" LDL and an increase in "good" HDL, but, strangely, those who combined antioxidants with their anticholesterol drugs failed to get that desirable HDL boost.

Taking antioxidants on a regular basis, therefore, may reduce the risk of *having* a stroke and may even reduce the *impact* of a stroke, should one ever happen. But these agents are not panaceas; you cannot assume that your heart will also benefit from this strategy to aid the brain.

Antioxidants May Help Preserve (or Even Enhance) Cognition

If antioxidants help to maintain good blood flow in the brain, it's logical to guess that they would also protect us from vascular dementia. Here's where the research done by my friend Web Ross comes in. Web, along with Karen Masaki and other colleagues in the Honolulu-Asia Aging Study, looked at self-reported vitamin use and mental status in 3,385 older Japanese men. Men who reported using both vitamin E and vitamin C in 1988 had a significantly lower risk of vascular dementia three to five years later. Unfortunately, we don't know the exact doses that people were taking; some may have been taking just a little, others taking megadoses. But this result is one of the first hints that vitamin E and C supplements save the brain not only from strokes but also from cognitive decline.

Karen and Web's study tells us much more as well. Among the 2,999 healthy men *without* dementia, *those who had been using either vitamin E or C also had significantly better cognitive performance.* Now *that's* the kind of news we're looking for. Antioxidant vitamins may be able to keep us thinking for longer with our usual and customary level of cognition, and they may even *improve* our thinking abilities—an obviously attractive benefit.

The Honolulu-Asia study is just one of a number of population studies showing that antioxidant vitamins are good for cognition. The Rotterdam Study also showed that beta-carotene had a cognition-preserving effect; a study of 260 older people in Spain found that those with better intakes of vitamin C and beta-carotene had better mental status; a study of 117 retired Australians found that those who took vitamin C supplements were less likely to have severe cognitive impairment; and in the Basel study, those who had higher beta-carotene and vitamin C blood levels scored better on tests of memory twenty-two years later.

These results might send you hightailing straight to the supplement store, but other results are less persuasive. Some scientists have even pointed out a potential confounding factor: "Well, of course, people who take vitamins do better; they tend to be college-educated!" Is it possible that all these studies found good results among vitamin users just because college-educated people are better at resisting dementia and, *by coincidence,* tend to take vitamins? Fortunately, new evidence helps answer that provocative question: the Austrian Stroke Prevention Study found in 1998 that higher blood levels of vitamin E were associated with better cognitive function even after controlling for years of education. That means the benefits are *not* due solely to higher education; anyone might benefit.

But the Austrian study went even further. It revealed that, even after all the stroke risk factors are removed from the equation, vitamin E *still* helps cognition. This is where things get interesting. Since the people in this study got a cognitive benefit regardless of whether they had vascular problems, it suggests that vitamin E must save brains from problems *other* than strokes. What might those problems be? Scientists strongly suspect that vitamin E fights most kinds of neurodegeneration and slows the development of ARNAT and Alzheimer's.

Antioxidants May Protect the Brain Against Alzheimer's, Parkinson's, and Other Forms of ARN

Strong evidence suggests that oxidation plays a key role in two main forms of ARN, Alzheimer's and Parkinson's. In the forest of research findings, this evidence is as broad and solid as an oak. Neuropathologist William R. Markesbury at the University of Kentucky, for instance, has shown that lipid peroxidation is revved up in Alzheimer's brains, especially in the places where degeneration is the worst. Beta-amyloid (the main neuronal assassin of Alzheimer's) uses free radicals to rip apart neurons, leaving us with rusty brain cells filled with poisonous oxidized fats and proteins. But (Twain's Maxim again), people are different. *Some* people who get Alzheimer's have the genetic allele for *APOE*-ε4, while others don't. One extremely interesting discovery is that your *APOE* gene status may control how badly you need antioxidants. This might turn out to be a good reason to do genetic testing in young adults, so we know who needs the strongest antioxidant defense.

The studies that get us most excited are the ones showing that antioxidants can rescue neurons from a rusty death. Several labs have shown, for example, that giving vitamin C or E to mice will block beta-amyloid's marauding impact on their brains. In a Japanese study, when beta-amyloid was injected into rats' brains, their learning and memory were impaired; but when they were treated with vitamin E, it prevented these memory problems. It's incredibly hard to study this phenomenon in humans, but when Stanford researchers examined the brain of one Alzheimer's patient who had taken vitamin E supplements for four years, they discovered that his temporal lobes were unusually resistant to oxidation. He probably started taking vitamin E far too late to save his brain, but he may have been on the right track.

This swelling tide of evidence persuades many neuroscientists that antioxidants can probably help defend our brains from ARNAT and Alzheimer's. As Dr. Markesbury puts it, "Long-term treatment of subjects at risk for AD [Alzheimer's], using more efficacious antioxidant therapeutic agents, could potentially slow neuron degeneration and delay or prevent the onset of the disease." Amen.

Antioxidants are possibly also protective against Parkinson's disease. Strong evidence to that effect came from the Rotterdam Study: among more than 5,000 healthy, nondemented people, those who took the surprisingly low dose of just 15 IU a day of vitamin E were 50 percent less likely to develop Parkinson's disease, and those who took in 1 mg (33 IU) a day of beta-carotene were 40 percent less likely to develop Parkinson's. But when Web Ross and his colleagues examined the dietary histories of more than 8,000 men of Japanese ancestry living in Hawaii, they found that, although eating legumes was associated with a reduced risk of Parkinson's (another hint at the value of whole foods), vitamin E intake wasn't. At this point, the scale is pretty evenly balanced, with several research groups confirming Web's negative finding for vitamin E and several confirming the positive Rotterdam results.

It seems clear that antioxidants are crucial defenders of the brain. The evidence seems strong for Alzheimer's and weaker for Parkinson's. But mixed results demand more proof. The next step? Clinical trials of antioxidants to rescue people from various forms of neurodegeneration.

Antioxidant Trials for Parkinson's

Elvis had rakish sideburns, an errant strand of hair grazing one eye, a trademark half-smile, and a honey drawl. He was doing great until the drugs got to him—the drugs I gave him to keep him moving.

"Doc," he asked me, "am I ever gonna get off this stuff?"

Elvis was a policeman. Named for his mother's musical hero, he had assumed some endearing features of his namesake's persona. But at the age of thirty-three, startlingly early, Parkinson's had crept up on him, appearing first as a tendency to rub his right thumb rhythmically across his index finger in the squad car—which he camouflaged by rubbing his St. Christopher's medal—and soon after by a subtle catch in his long-legged stride. By age thirty-eight, his anti-Parkinson's medicines were beginning to plague him with the "on-off" syndrome, swinging him unmercifully between the near paralysis of undertreatment and the writhing dance of overtreatment. I had brought him into the hospital for a tune-up. We talked about the plans for the admission and how he could help us find the optimum treatment with a half-hourly diary of his movements. Elvis shook his head (an awkward neck twist at the peak of his dose). "Truth now. Will the medicines keep me from getting worse?"

No, I admitted. The medicines could only treat his symptoms. They didn't protect his brain cells from the relentless march of neurodegeneration. I drew a picture that showed his brainstem and his substantia nigra (the brainstem's main factory for dopamine), and I explained that Parkinson's disease destroys dopamine neurons, in part because of the artillery assault of free radicals.

He frowned at the idea of free radicals running around his brain with artillery. "Hell, shoot me up with some Kevlar!" he suggested.

Elvis had the right idea—Kevlar for vulnerable neurons. A year later the results of the DATATOP study came out, the first really large-scale intervention trial to use antioxidants as if they were Kevlar—body armor for neurons in the Parkinson's brain.

DATATOP stands for Deprenyl and Alpha-Tocopherol Antioxidative Therapy of Parkinsonism. In the DATATOP study, patients at twenty-eight academic medical centers were randomly assigned to receive one of four treatments: Deprenyl (generic name selegiline, a drug that helps block oxidation of dopamine), vitamin E (dl-alpha-tocopherol), both treatments, or a placebo. The results: after more than a decade of study, Deprenyl did in fact seem to somewhat slow the progression of Parkinson's, but vitamin E provided no convincing additional benefit.

I can guess at several possible explanations for the DATATOP results. First, the experimenters gave their subjects a man-made form of vitamin E, the *dl* form of alpha-tocopherol, which may be much less potent than the natural *d*-alpha-tocopherol. Second, before people begin to show Parkinson's symptoms they have to lose about 90 percent of their dopamine neurons. That means that the patients had lost almost all their dopamine cells even before they entered the DATATOP study; we may need to take vitamin E much earlier in life—before the battle is lost—if we want to rescue the brain. Third, 90 percent of the time Parkinson's disease probably involves some kind of environmental factor, perhaps a toxin (such as a pesticide) or a virus. So the patients in this study may have been exposed to a brain-cell-killing toxin many years before they got their molecular Kevlar, and we could not expect it to have much of a protective benefit so long after the damage had begun. Finally, the people who are most likely to get hammered by Parkinson's seem to be those who have both the environmental exposure *and* a problem in the genes in their mitochondria. So—going back to the twenty-first-century idea of pharmacogenomics, in which treatments should really be personalized for our particular genome—it's likely that only *some* people will benefit from an antioxidant boost.

My bet is that multiple factors are involved: the type of vitamin E, the dose, the other protective foods in the person's diet, the antioxidant needs of the particular brain cells that get steamrollered by Parkinson's, and the person's genes. All of this fancy figuring comes down to a tentative conclusion: Deprenyl may help people who already have Parkinson's, but vitamin E is probably too little, too late.

Still, for many of us, the real question is whether vitamin E can help *protect* humans from ARNAT and Alzheimer's.

Antioxidant Trials for ARNAT

Despite the mixed results of DATATOP, back in 1995 the neuroscience community remained excited about vitamin E's brain-saving potential. Indeed, their collective instinct that vitamin E really works was so strong that it created an ethical quandary: *Yes, we cannot prove that vitamin E saves the brain, but what if it turns out to work and we didn't tell anyone?* The pressure was building for a formal clinical trial of vitamin E for Alzheimer's disease.

Mary Sano at Columbia University, with the help of the twenty-three-center Alzheimer's Disease Cooperative Study Group, recruited 341 patients with Alzheimer's disease. The patients were given Deprenyl, vitamin E (again, the unnatural *dl* form), both, or a placebo for two years. The dose of vitamin E was a gigantic 2,000 IU a day. (The government's Reference Daily Intake for adults is 22 IU a day, so these patients were receiving 91 times the recommended dose.) Dr. Sano looked at the impact of these treatments from several points of view: Did they keep the patient functioning longer? Did they keep the patient out of a nursing home? Did they slow cognitive loss?

Dr. Sano published her result in 1997, and to speak candidly, it left neurologists scratching our heads. On the one hand, she found that *all* of the treatments helped keep people out of nursing homes to some degree, and that vitamin E helped the most. In fact, vitamin E decreased the chance of a patient needing to be admitted to a nursing home by 58 percent—a terrific result. But when she looked at cognitive test scores, she found that *none* of the treatments really helped slow down cognitive decline.

If vitamin E had a good overall outcome on daily life but no measurable cognitive benefit, then what exactly were these antioxidants doing? My interpretation is that antioxidants cannot magically arrest neurodegeneration in people whose brains are already so far gone. Even if Dr. Sano had used natural *d*-alpha-tocopherol, I would expect only a slight behavioral benefit, if that. The problem is that the very idea of *treating* Alzheimer's with antioxidants is probably off track. The major benefit of antioxidants is probably as a *prevention,* so they must be taken much sooner to have a real brain-saving effect. Still, the Columbia University study's impact has been so big that these days it's hard to find a "vitamin E virgin"—an Alzheimer's patient *not* taking vitamin E—since so many doctors prescribe it for every patient. (Deprenyl has not caught on to the same degree because it has some troubling side effects, such as a risk of blood pressure changes.)

If vitamin E can't *treat* Alzheimer's disease, can it *prevent* ARNAT and Alzheimer's in people who don't already have cognitive changes? Even as I write this, a five-year NIH study of several thousand people is under way to try to resolve that question. But unfortunately the conclusion will be quite limited, because this study involves giving vitamin E to middle-age people who *already* have mild cognitive impairment. It will not answer the question that really keeps us up at night: can antioxidant supplements protect the brains of normal, healthy, clear-thinking people? The mix of exciting promise and uncertainty has befuddled us to the point that doctors at the University of London published a paper in 1997 titled "Will the 'Good Fairies' Please Prove to Us That Vitamin E Lessens Human Degenerative Disease?"

Frankly, it would take a project of immense proportions and many years' duration to really answer this best-of-all questions. A true primary prevention study to test the brain-saving effects of vitamin E would have to begin in adolescence, involve 10,000 to 100,000 people, and last more than fifty years. What's more, vitamin E may be just one of a number of food-based antioxidants involved in long-term neuroprotection, all of which probably interact with each other in complex ways. Evolution designed our brains to flourish when we take in a *combination* of antioxidants by eating a variety of fruits and vegetables, not just a single supplement. Perhaps the brain-saving benefit of vitamin E depends, for example, on a person maintaining adequate levels of vitamin C, plus regularly eating enough of some phytochemical (plant-based nutrient) that we haven't even discovered. In addition, scientists really don't know the ideal dose of vitamin E; there's probably a threshold at, say, 100 or 300 or 600 IU a day, where the benefits kick in. Furthermore, genetic differences between people—such as *APOE* status—may determine individual needs for antioxidant supplements. For all of these reasons, I am somewhat doubtful that we can get much out of a five-year study of a few thousand people who already have cognitive loss. Put delicately, the current NIH study may not tell us what we need to know.

This is where we're obliged to put aside all the books and articles, all the graphs and statistics, close our eyes, and do a calculation that draws on the available facts, intuitive judgment, and, one would hope, a pinch of wisdom. The "good fairies" are otherwise engaged. This is where we place our bets.

I would bet that antioxidant-rich foods can produce a decrease in oxidative stress on the brain cells that are most critical for thought and memory. I'd also bet that taking supplemental vitamin E—in addition to following the Brain-Saving Diet rich in fruits and vegetables, grains and legumes, and fish, and assuring adequate intake of iron, B12, folate, potassium, and calcium—will meaningfully slow the average rate of ARN. I'd bet my life on it.

What's the best dose of vitamin E? There's the rub. The studies that have asked people "Do you take vitamin E?" don't help us pinpoint the best dose; intake varies too much. The lab rat studies can't answer the question since their subjects aren't humans. Mary Sano's research project doesn't help much; it used a massive dose—2,000 IU—that doctors cannot recommend to healthy adults because it creates some risk of bleeding. It's a poor trade-off to have a decreased risk of Alzheimer's at age eighty but suffer a cerebral hemorrhage at age fifty. So I'd definitely suggest a lower dose for most people. On the other hand, the current U.S. recommended daily allowance of 22 IU may be way too low to get the available benefit.

Someday research will reveal the dose that's best for most of us. Better yet, someday doctors may check the actual vitamin E levels in their patients, just as they check thyroid hormone and B12 levels, and *personalize* the dose. In the meantime, I propose that 400 to 600 IU a day of natural vegetable oil–based *d*-alpha-tocopherol is a good bet to help save the brain and possibly even improve cognition. It seems like a reasonable dose for almost everyone—probably low enough to avoid side effects and high enough to offer a real benefit.

Vitamin C, Beta-Carotene, and Other Antioxidant Options

I've focused on vitamin E because it's an especially promising agent. But there is evidence (albeit mixed) that vitamin C, beta-carotene, and other antioxidants may also help to save our brains.

Today 50 million Americans take vitamin C on a regular basis, spending

$500 million a year on this supplement alone. What are they getting for their money? Lab experiments show that vitamin C can be a brawny defender against free radical attacks on neurons. Human studies look promising as well, but as always, we have to hike through a forest of research in search of the truth. A Swiss study suggests a cognitive benefit from both beta-carotene and vitamin C; British and Australian studies both suggest cognitive benefits for those taking vitamin C; the Rotterdam Study suggests a benefit from beta-carotene but *not* from vitamin C; and the Monongahela Valley and Zutphen studies both suggest that *neither* of these vitamins helps cognition. But all of these were population studies—studies that simply looked at what vitamins people chose to take and how well their thinking worked. We have no idea what doses these folks took, or for how long, or starting at what age. A true clinical trial, like those for vitamin E, would be far better, but to date no large experiments have been done exploring whether beta-carotene or vitamin C supplements can help Alzheimer's patients or, more important, protect healthy people from memory loss.

Once again, we could wander until dawn through this forest of data and never find our way out. So the decision to recommend vitamin C or beta-carotene really comes down to a judicious balancing of possible risks versus possible benefits.

And there are indeed some potential risks. In April 2000, for the first time in history, the Institute of Medicine of the National Academy of Sciences made formal recommendations for upper limits of vitamin intake. It recommended daily limits of 1,000 IU for vitamin E and 2,000 mg for vitamin C. (The institute did not believe that enough evidence existed to recommend *either* a lower or an upper limit for beta-carotene.) One reason for these limits is a concern about side effects at high doses, such as hemorrhages with vitamin E and diarrhea with vitamin C. But another worry is that recent work has shown that cancer cells are more likely than healthy ones to hoard antioxidants. This has made scientists very wary of blanket recommendations for antioxidant supplementation.

Not all antioxidants are created equal. Vitamin E has preserved its reputation for good benefits and very low risks, but beta-carotene and vitamin C have not fared so well. The massive Finnish Alpha-Tocopherol, Beta-Carotene Cancer Prevention Study found that beta-carotene actually *increased* the rate of lung cancer among male smokers—a shocking finding that made headlines around the world. Soon afterward another U.S. trial involving more than 18,000 men and women smokers found the same thing. And further studies showed that beta-carotene may also increase the risk of fatal heart attacks among people who have previously had a heart attack. So beta-carotene is a vitamin sporting two black eyes.

As for vitamin C, a small British study suggested in 1998 that modest doses can actually act as *pro-oxidants* and increase the damage to people's DNA. This study provoked disbelief—until an even stronger study was done at the University of Pennsylvania and published in the journal *Science* in 2001. This second study showed that vitamin C indeed promotes the formation of *genotoxins*—agents that damage DNA. Both studies were done in the test tube, so we can't be certain how they will apply to people. But a recent study from the University of Southern California suggests that vitamin C may indeed produce harmful effects in humans: over an eighteen-month period, 573 men and women taking daily doses of at least 500 mg developed an inner artery wall layer that was two and a half times as thick as that of people not taking supplements; smokers taking vitamin C developed walls *five* times the thickness of those who didn't— a setup for a stroke. So what happened to Linus Pauling's famous theory that we need megadoses of vitamin C for good health? That notion has simply not stood the test of science and time.

The new discoveries of the potential risks of vitamin C should be put into perspective. First, lots of evidence indicates that vitamin C is safe, although safety diminishes at higher doses and in smokers. And some people are truly at risk for deficiencies, including those who eat vitamin C–deficient diets (lacking in food sources such as citrus fruits, tomatoes, broccoli, and green peppers) and those taking aspirin or the antibiotic tetracycline, as well as women taking oral contraceptives. For this special group, 200 mg of vitamin C may be a safe and healthful bet: it gives about the maximum "bioavailability," or maximum rate of absorption. At 500 mg a day, we tend to excrete the extra vitamin that we can't absorb; at 1,000 mg a day, urinary levels of oxalate and urate increase, which can cause crystal formation and raise the risk of kidney stones; and at 4,000 mg a day, diarrhea and the significant risk of kidney stones make vitamin C a bad bet. Second, *everyone is different*. Antioxidant supplements may protect one person from disease and harm another, perhaps because of genetic differences that we have yet to uncover. (If I had to guess, I'd say that antioxidants do the most good for people at high risk for vascular problems, and the most harm to people at high risk for cancer.) Third, smokers seem to get in the most trouble with both beta-carotene and vitamin C, so they may have to be especially cautious in their vitamin intake. Given the uncertainty about the size of the brain-saving benefits from beta-carotene and vitamin C supplements, and given the new worries about side effects, I feel it's too soon to recommend their widespread use. Let's give it another look in a few years.

To summarize: the grand and winding paths of scientific discovery lead

us through the forest of data to the point where I would rank the antioxidant vitamins in terms of their neuroprotective potential in this order: E,
C, beta-carotene. Since most studies of human populations show that the
highest cognitive function is maintained by people who keep their beta-
carotene and vitamin C levels in the range obtained from eating a healthful diet, most people have little reason to take supplements of these two
antioxidants. Moreover, the benefits we associate with various vitamins
may actually come from the *combination* of vitamins with phytochemicals, so people eating a plant-rich diet may get benefits that beat the pants
off a shelf of supplements. Perhaps the only people who should take supplemental vitamin C are those at risk for deficiencies. Vitamin E, on the
other hand, seems to be a special case. Achieving brain-optimum levels of
vitamin E from diet alone may be hard. So if I were to pick just one antioxidant supplement for the optimum brain benefit, I'd pick vitamin E.

Other Popular Antioxidant Options

The list of antioxidants that might save the brain hardly ends with the vitamins: literally hundreds of other antioxidants may have neuroprotective
powers. Many are naturally occurring, and we will look at these in Chapter 13. Others are synthetic, and pharmaceutical companies are racing to
synthesize a "star" antioxidant. The best of these experimental agents will
likely be tested in mouse models of aging and Alzheimer's disease in the
near future. But for now let's take a look at three readily available and
well-championed options: zinc, selenium, and coenzyme Q-10.

ZINC

Zinc tablets sell like hotcakes in the virus-friendly winter months because, in recent years, the lore has spread that zinc can shorten the duration of the common cold. This idea is based partly on a 1996 study by
Michael Macknin of the Cleveland Clinic reporting that zinc lozenges
taken within twenty-four hours of the start of a cold can reduce the mis-
ery by about two days. Unfortunately, subsequent studies have not confirmed this encouraging claim. At present the zinc-lozenges-for-the-cold
question remains unresolved; so we'll look instead at zinc for the brain.

Zinc plays many valuable roles in the nervous system. It's an essential
micronutrient necessary to fulfill the most basic of all life functions, syn-
thesizing DNA. It's also a key ingredient of a powerful enzyme that detox-
ifies neuron-attacking free radicals, copper/zinc superoxide dismutase
(SOD). In fact, deficiencies of copper/zinc SOD contribute directly to one
of the world's most unforgiving neurological diseases, amyotrophic lateral

sclerosis (ALS). Though ALS is often referred to as Lou Gehrig's disease, after the famed Yankee first baseman, it is perhaps equally well known for its impact on Stephen Hawking, the astrophysicist whose astonishing accomplishments in the face of ALS leave us in awe. The fact that Dr. Hawking, one of the recognized geniuses of modern history, could reinvent the human understanding of the birth of the universe while probably deficient in this zinc-based enzyme is strong evidence that we may not need much zinc/copper SOD for high-quality cognition. But zinc by itself *does* seem to have some effect on thought.

Numerous studies have linked zinc deficiency to dementia or cognitive impairments. Young zinc-deficient rats have learning problems. Adolescent female monkeys modestly deprived of zinc are inactive and inattentive. Marginally zinc-deficient children in Mexico exhibit growth retardation as well as cognitive impairments. But true zinc deficiency is probably infrequent among well-fed human adults—about 1 percent—and there is little evidence that it plays much of a role in adult cognitive decline in our society.

Actually, the recent concern has been just the opposite: researchers are looking very carefully at the possibility that an *excess* of zinc can hurt the brain and even contribute to Alzheimer's disease. Several studies have found *increased zinc levels* in the brains of people who have died of Alzheimer's. One speculation is that zinc contributes to the clumping of beta-amyloid (the neurotoxic substance most frequently associated with ARNAT). Zinc may also help to chop up the amyloid precursor protein, possibly making fragments that go on to become beta-amyloid. In addition to these direct links with Alzheimer's disease, zinc may be considered a general dealer of neuronal death—whipping up both excitatory neurotoxicity and cellular suicide.

Not all the evidence points this way. Among twelve of the sisters in the Nun Study (that wonderful long-term study of aging and the brain), the ones with normal zinc levels had fewer senile plaques in their brains, while those who had lower-than-normal zinc levels in their blood had *more* Alzheimer's-type plaques. This makes it appear that maintaining at least a normal zinc level is better than a lower level. One possible reason may be that zinc is part of the brain's injury-response system. If so, we'd expect to find more zinc in Alzheimer's-afflicted brains not because it's a troublemaker but because it has actually been recruited to help control plaque development. Whatever zinc's relationship to Alzheimer's disease, the Nun Study hints that maintaining a normal zinc level may be a good idea. So should you take zinc supplements?

Zinc has a notoriously narrow "therapeutic window," meaning there's a small difference between the dose that helps and the dose that hurts.

SAVING YOUR BRAIN

Doses of as little as 90 mg per day—popular among some supplement users—can impair immunity, lower HDL ("good" cholesterol), and cause anemia. Zinc supplements also interfere with the gut absorption of copper and iron. More is not better. Until we get a better handle on what zinc has to do with Alzheimer's disease, it seems most prudent *not* to use zinc supplements in the hope of protecting the brain. A better bet is to simply eat natural sources of zinc such as seafood, poultry, soybeans, and milk as part of a well-balanced diet.

SELENIUM

Selenium is not a metal, although its bright gray metallic appearance inspired its name, from *selēnē* the Greek word for "moon." We absorb tiny amounts of selenium in various foods such as fish, and a certain level of selenium is completely normal in the body. Maintaining adequate selenium levels seems to be important in defending us against vascular diseases, which makes selenium an honorable soldier in the fight against strokes and CVC. Selenium is also essential for muscles. For instance, in the wild and beautiful Wind River mountains of Wyoming, wildlife biologists noticed that the lambs of bighorn sheep were stumbling and staggering. Brilliant detective work revealed that pollutants were wafting on the winds from hundreds of miles away, changing the soil chemistry, causing the selenium levels to drop alarmingly in the plants these sheep depend on—and producing a form of muscular dystrophy. But selenium may do even more for the brain.

In particular, selenium deficiency alters mouse behavior in a variety of ways. Females lose their exploratory drive and get lost in a maze, evidence that mammalian brains need selenium for normal cognition. Selenium deficiency is also bad for human brains. If our intake drops below about 40 mcg a day, we cannot make enough Se-Gpx, a brain antioxidant that serves as a hefty shield against the artillery assault of free radicals.

In terms of human research, in the French Étude sur le Vieillissement Artériel study, low selenium levels were associated with age-related narrowing of the carotid arteries; that means selenium could possibly help save us from strokes. And in one human behavioral study, eleven men volunteered to be confined to a psychiatric research unit and try high or low selenium diets. The moods of those men who started with lower selenium levels went downhill on a low-selenium diet.

It's clear, therefore, that our brains want selenium. So we must be worried about the recent discovery that as we age, selenium deficiency becomes very common. In fact, a recent study of outpatients at a U.S. Veterans Administration hospital found that a low blood level of selenium was the most common nutritional deficiency. The Nove Study may reveal what happens to selenium levels over time: 53 healthy women and 52 healthy men were studied in Nove, a village near Vicenza, Italy. In this healthy group, selenium levels definitely declined with age, suggesting the possibility that aging drives up our body's demand for selenium.

The problem with selenium—its Mr. Hyde face—is that like zinc, it has a narrow "therapeutic window"; it can become quite toxic at levels that are just twice those needed for optimum health, giving us little room for error between too little and too much. And too much selenium probably hurts the nervous system. A study of 5,182 residents of Reggio Emilia, Italy, found that those who were exposed to *higher*-than-usual selenium levels in their water supply had a frighteningly high rate of ALS—the paralytic nightmare of Lou Gehrig's disease.

Some people in the United States may also be overexposed to selenium because this element occurs naturally in spring and well waters. The EPA recommends an upper limit of 50 mcg/l, but levels as high as 400 to 9,000 have been reported in some U.S. water supplies. Oil refinery wastes and irrigation of selenium-rich soil can move selenium into lakes and streams. Even a slight increase in water's selenium concentration can deform fish embryos; we have to wonder what it does, in the long term, to humans. Selenium is also used in photocopy machine drums, a potential source of on-the-job toxic exposure. But the fact is that, in the United States, *the most common cause of selenium toxicity is probably the taking of selenium supplements.*

We should probably conclude that 400 mcg a day pushes the limit of safety. The government's recommended daily intake is 55 mcg per day. Anywhere from 50 to 200 mcg per day is likely to be more than adequate for optimum health, without getting too close to the danger zone. Since almost everyone can get this amount from a normal diet (particularly good sources include broccoli, bran, chicken, milk, and tuna), supplements seem to offer more of a risk than a benefit to the brain.

COENZYME Q-10 AND HEAVY BREATHERS

Coenzyme Q-10 is one of a number of chemicals involved in keeping our mitochondrial engines running smoothly, and it has recently acquired some modest fame because it's quite good at sucking up excess free radicals, taking them out of circulation before they can do harm to neurons in the area. For this reason, Q-10 is regarded as a promising antioxidant that might protect the brain against Parkinson's, Huntington's, ALS, and even aging itself.

In an impressive laboratory demonstration of these effects, neurologist Flint Beal at Massachusetts General Hospital fed rats some Q-10. Not only did Q-10 protect neurons in their brainstems from a toxin—suggesting that it may help save the brain from Parkinson's disease—but it also *increased the life span* of mice with genes like those in ALS. When Dr. Beal gave Q-10 to humans with Huntington's chorea, he found that it helped to decrease signs of oxidative stress in their brains.

Dr. Beal is not alone in demonstrating the potency of Q-10 in fighting neurological disease. Researchers at Columbia University recently showed that Q-10 can decrease seizures and improve strength in people who stagger because of a neurological disease called *familial ataxia*. Heroin users who wreck the white matter in their brains by inhaling heated heroin vapors have also shown neurological improvement with oral Q-10. Cardiologists are excited because of evidence that Q-10 can protect blood vessels from atherosclerosis. But Q-10 may not be for everyone. It may be that only people with a specific problem in their mitochondria will benefit. And a recent study showed that people with Parkinson's have *normal* Q-10 levels, suggesting that this antioxidant is not a big factor in Parkinson's disease.

The big question, of course, is whether Q-10 might save us from ARNAT and Alzheimer's. Good evidence indicates that ARNAT involves a roadside breakdown in our mitochondrial engines. Vitamins A, C, and E are not the best repairmen for broken mitochondria; coenzyme Q-10 is better at this job. So in theory you'd want to add Q-10 to your antioxidant cocktail for optimum neuroprotection. One intriguing finding is that Alzheimer's brains show *increased* levels of Q-10. Like the increased zinc levels found in Alzheimer's brains, this may just be a sign that the brain is working harder to fight off free radicals. If that's the case, then Q-10 supplements may help protect the neurons that are among the most metabolically active in the nervous system—the hippocampal memory cells, the brain's heavy breathers. If so, they might be good for memory. I'm eager to see some solid research in this area; in particular, it would be great to test Q-10 on mice that have been genetically engineered to mimic Alzheimer's. For the time being, it's a bit premature to take Q-10 in the hopes of saving your brain.

Evolution made us clever omnivores; we can eat just about anything, plant or animal, and survive. But the body and mind probably work *best* when we take in enough of the right kind of food, including antioxidants. Paradoxically, when people figured out how to farm about 10,000 years ago, it gave us a *stable* food supply but not necessarily a *better* one. So as we've detoured from the forest to the supermarket, we've drifted away from our evolutionarily optimum diets. Based on her sweaty jungle adventures, Katherine Milton speculates that early humans "probably did take in more vitamins and minerals than the average modern American." If so, the rise of agriculture (and fast-food joints) may have led humans to deviate from the intake of antioxidants for which the brain was optimized.

For most of my professional life, I've been dubious about the wisdom of prescribing supplemental vitamins for healthy people. The scientific evidence seemed shaky, the purported benefits seemed exaggerated, the risks seemed unexplored, some proposals smacked of unethical hucksterism, and some of the fiercest proponents seemed, well, loopy. In general, a natural diet of fruits and vegetables, grains and beans has always seemed better, in order to provide not just the vitamins but the innumerable whole-foods benefits of phytochemicals, potassium, calcium, trace elements, and fiber that may help to save the brain. Moreover, encouraging the use of supplements might lull people into the false assumption that they are doing the best they can for their bodies. They're not. For instance, beta-carotene is just one of about seventy-five carotenoids in a carrot, any one of which might someday be proven to be "the good one." Whole foods are almost *always* sufficient and superior sources of the antioxidants that the brain needs for optimum functioning.

But two thoughts have made me reconsider my whole-foods stance. First is the possibility that our brains evolved to expect more vitamins than we typically give them. Second is my growing understanding of the magnitude of the lifestyle change that doctors ask of their patients when they recommend the Brain-Saving Diet and regular physical activity. Some people are just not going to eat the recommended seven to ten servings of fresh fruits and vegetables a day and jog a few miles around the neighborhood before or after work. Therefore, to assure the greatest number of people a benefit, and to be more realistic about the malleability of human habits, I find myself recommending supplements.

We live at a moment in history when the benefits of antioxidant supplements are becoming tantalizingly exciting, but as always the devil is in the details, and we have yet to work out those details. As a result of all these unresolved mysteries, very good scientists differ in their opinion about what to recommend. Some researchers are *extremely* enthusiastic about supplement antioxidants to protect the brain from Alzheimer's. University of Colorado scientist Kedar Prasad, for example, has recommended a multiantioxidant cocktail of vitamins A, C, E, selenium, chromium, zinc, and N-acetylcysteine! There are indeed theoretical reasons for every ingredient in this cocktail, but researchers have never tested any two of them together in any animal model of Alzheimer's—let alone in humans—and I would not recommend taking this approach until medical facts have caught up a little more with science theory. But I believe we already know enough for a more conservative approach.

To summarize the supplement story, taking 400 to 600 IU of natural *d*-alpha-tocopherol each day is probably a good, safe bet for the brain, regardless of your success in the grander arena of diet and exercise. As we noted in Chapter 11, especially for people over fifty-five and those whose intake of fish, poultry, and dark green leafy vegetables is limited, an additional 400 to 600 mcg of folate and 0.4 mg of B12 may also be a safe and healthful bet. I recommend vitamin C supplements only for people who are at risk for vitamin C deficiency; such people may benefit from 200 mg each day. I would not recommend supplemental beta-carotene. And, as always, even such a simple step as starting antioxidants is something to discuss with your doctor. Every day scientists learn more about how to use these surprisingly powerful compounds. For example, in 2001 a report suggested that antioxidants may defeat the effectiveness of statins for controlling cholesterol—a baffling and important interaction between two good treatments. Since medical science is always advancing, please allow your doctor to help you weigh the benefits and risks.

Hopefully, you will be inspired to pursue the most natural and joyful life you can—to embrace the Brain-Saving Diet and regular physical activity, root out sources of emotional stress, seek intellectual challenge, and protect your heart and your head. Hopefully as well, ongoing research will clarify the benefits of the many available antioxidants. In the meantime, of all the steps you might take, taking vitamin E may be one of the simplest and best bets to save your brain.

CHAPTER 13

Botanicals for the Brain:
The Growing Promise of Natural
Neuroprotection

I had just sat down at a bar in Ayacucho, Peru, and asked for a cold beer when I met a ginkgo farmer. Actually she was a nurse, but she planned to become a ginkgo farmer. Kristine was working with the Nobel prize-winning French organization Médecins Sans Frontières (Doctors Without Borders), as I learned when she and her rowdy colleagues invited me over to share their three-legged table and tormented me by insisting that I try to speak my awful French. Kristine mentioned that she was about to finish her tour of duty and return home to Burgundy. She'd decided to take a break from nursing and go into agriculture.

"Wine?" I asked.

Kristine smiled and shook her head. The future, she assured me, was in ginkgo.

"*L'arbre le plus ancien*—the oldest tree in the world," she explained. Like some living fossil, the ginkgo has flourished unchanged for longer than any other tree now living on earth. She described the tree's beauty, its medicinal properties, its market potential. "You'll see," she said, beaming confidence, and leaned forward conspiratorially. "Already it is *très populaire* in Europe. Someday America, *exactement la même chose*—the very same thing!"

Kristine was right. Ginkgo biloba's sales in the United States are now rivaled only by those of echinacea, garlic, goldenseal, and ginseng. (St. John's wort, valerian, and kava are moving up the botanical top-ten chart with a bullet.) U.S. sales of medicinal herbs—more accurately called botanicals—topped $4 billion in 1998, up from just $839 million in 1991. About one-third of Americans used herbal remedies in 1998, whereas fewer than one in twenty did so a generation earlier, a dramatic swing in national health habits. A survey of visitors to health food stores found that about 84 percent take herbs to *prevent* a malady rather than to treat one. Although it's heartening that people are taking more interest in preventive medicine, how much genuine health benefit they've derived from this botanical frenzy is debatable. My job, therefore, is to sift through the mountain of claims and counterclaims to figure out whether any botanicals might be a true boon to the brain.

Three Barriers

But before I examine specific plants, it's important to warn you that three barriers are blocking our road to the truth. One is the shortage of good research. Another is the uncertainty about which is better, whole botanicals or ingredients found in botanicals. And the third problem is the quality of the products themselves.

A SHORTAGE OF GOOD RESEARCH

If examining the evidence for and against antioxidants was enough to make our heads spin, at least our vertigo came from looking at a flurry of good science. In the case of botanicals, however, I must come up with solid recommendations for people's lives based on what is, in many cases, a shocking shortage of science. There is an astonishing gap between the widespread human use of botanicals and the limited evidence of their benefits. The list of botanicals promoted to retard aging or enhance brain function is long, and you might well wonder how many have been proven to have brain-saving powers. The answer is shown in Table 3.

What's shocking is not that so many substances are touted without proof by supplement promoters but that researchers have done so little either to prove or disprove these tantalizing claims. Here we are embarking on the twenty-first century, the moon a day trip, the scientific method available for centuries, with literally hundreds of genuinely promising possibilities for health enhancement arrayed before us waiting to be properly evaluated—just as they have waited for five thousand years.

OYSTERS VERSUS PEARLS: WHOLE BOTANICALS, EXTRACTS, AND INGREDIENTS

The second barrier is the problem of figuring out what *part* of a plant is most likely to help. Some herbalists encourage the use of *whole botanicals*—crushed leaves, stems, seeds, or roots, such as ginseng powder. Some support the use of *extracts*—separated and standardized formulations such as the ginkgo preparation called EGb 761 or the ginseng preparation called G 115. And some support the use of *biologically active ingredients* that have been isolated and purified, such as the ginkgo

Table 3

Botanicals for the Brain

A PARTIAL LIST OF BOTANICALS PROPOSED TO HAVE ANTI-AGING OR BRAIN-AIDING POWERS	A COMPLETE LIST OF BOTANICALS PROVEN TO HAVE THOSE POWERS
Acidophilus	
Aconitum alkaloids (Chinese)	
Aloe	
Alpiniae fructus (Asian)	
Astragalus	
Beta-eudesmol (Chinese)	
Catechins	
Celastrus paniculatus	
Club moss (Chinese; source of huperzine)	
Cnidium rhizome (Asian)	
Codyceps	
Coriaria lactone (Chinese)	
Dan Shen (radix *Salviae miltiorrhizae*) (Chinese)	
Deer antler velvet	
Dihydroergocristine	
Dong quai (Chinese)	
DX-9386 (Chinese formulation)	
Ehmannia root (Asian)	
Evening primrose (*Oenothera biennis*)	
Foti	
Galanthamine	
Garlic	
Genistein	
Ginkgo biloba	
Ginseng	
Green tea	
Guarana (*Paulinia cupana*)	
Hachimijiogan (Asian formulation)	
Hoasca (ayahuasca) (Amazonian)	
Huperzine A and B (from club moss)	
Japanese angelica root	
Kamikihi-To (Chinese)	
Kava (*Piper methysticum*) (Polynesian)	
Lignans	
Ligusticum chuanxiong (Chinese)	
Ligusticum wallichii (Chinese)	
Lycopene	
Maharishi Amrit Kalash (Indian/Ayurvedic)	
Mentat (BR-16A) (Indian/Ayurvedic)	
Myricetin (in ginkgo)	
Nao Li Shen (Chinese formulation)	
Peony root (paeoniflorin and tetramethylpyrazine)	
Phytic acid	
Propolis	
Psyllium	
Quercetin (in ginkgo)	
Qingyangshen (Chinese)	
Raubasine	
Rutin	
S-adenosylmethionine (SAMe)	
Schizandra	
Shilajit (Indian/Ayurvedic)	
Shimotsu-to (Chinese formulation)	
Sho-saiko-to-go-keishi-ka-shakuyaku-to (TJ-960) (Japanese formulation)	
Soybeans	
St. John's wort	
Sulforaphane	
Toosendanin (Chinese)	
Trasina (Indian/Ayurvedic)	
Turmeric	
Wine	
Yizhiling granule (Chinese)	

flavonoid called ginkgolide A, or the ginseng ingredient called ginsenoside Rb1. Which is likely to prove more healthful—the whole plant, the extract, or the ingredient?

Plants used for nutrition and plants used for medicine are crucially different. In general, I favor the whole-foods approach, because a blueberry may contain a dozen antioxidants, so it's better to eat the whole blueberry rather than a pill containing just one antioxidant. But using plants as *medicines* is completely different. Anything potent enough to be a *medicine* at the right dose must be potent enough to be a *poison* at the wrong dose. So doctors have learned to prescribe the isolated, purified *ingredients* from plants to produce reliable results. Thus, while many botanicals are still sold as whole plants or extracts—and extracts tend to be more potent than whole plants—the ultimate goal is really to find the specific biologically active ingredient—the pearl in the oyster.

The rewards of identifying the active ingredient of a botanical can be extraordinary. For example, once purified quinine was isolated from cinchona bark, we had a life-saving antimalarial drug rather than a plant that produced famously ballistic digestive toxicities. Similarly, foxglove was used in western Europe as a folk remedy for about five hundred years before its active ingredient, digitalis, was isolated; only then did it become possible to use this ingredient in a way that helped save hearts rather than stop them. Or consider American wild yams, which were used with erratic results for menstrual disorders for about two hundred years before researchers discovered that they contain the hormone progesterone. Once that was known, women could use purified progesterone and get benefits they could count on, rather than eating a bucket of yams that had a very unpredictable effect.

Therefore, if we want to use botanicals as medicine, we should be wary of claims about whole plants and extracts, which are invariably complex mixtures of half-studied compounds. Increasingly, science will help us find the pure, active ingredient—the diamond in the lump of coal.

THE QUALITY OF THE PRODUCTS

The third barrier on the road to the truth about botanicals is the wildly inconsistent quality of the botanicals available in America. The main reason for this inconsistency is a law that has denied American consumers quality control in botanicals for almost a decade: in 1994, the Dietary Supplement Health and Education Act was passed to protect the interests of the supplement industry. Under this law, medicinal herbs are considered "food supplements," a label that allows their makers to dodge any requirement to prove that they are either safe or effective. This law makes botanicals immune from oversight by the FDA unless and until—like tainted hamburger meat—they cause serious trouble reported by multiple people. In 2001 the spokesman for the Herbal Products Association dismissed the idea that supplement-makers should report the injuries and illnesses caused by botanicals, saying there is "no public need." Even when a tragedy strikes, the onus lies on the FDA to prove that the product is unsafe, rather than on the seller to prove that it's safe. "We are 100 percent sure that our product is safe," said a California herbalist to a *Los Angeles Times* reporter in 1997, even as teenagers lay in comas after accepting free samples of his Chinese herb.

As a result of this law, herbal preparations may contain almost anything. Scientists at Sweden's Karolinska Institute analyzed the content of fifty popular ginseng preparations sold in Europe and the United States. When ginsenosides (the active ingredients in ginseng) were present at all, their content varied greatly, from 1.9 to 9.0 percent. Six of the products sold in the United States contained no ginsenoside whatsoever (though to be fair, several of these were so-called "Siberian ginseng," an unrelated plant with a marketable name). *Consumer Reports,* similarly, tested the contents of ten popular U.S. ginseng preparations in 1995, and again the ginsenoside content varied enormously among different brands.

Contaminants or undeclared additional drugs are common. Case in point: a young Swedish athlete was found in a doping test to be using the banned drug ephedrine. He protested his innocence, claiming he'd taken nothing but ginseng. When the ginseng preparation he took was analyzed, it was shown to contain no ginseng whatsoever but large amounts of ephedrine. Some bottles labeled as ginseng actually contain mandrake (which causes memory loss) or snakeroot (which can cause depression), and many contain high levels of lead, cadmium, or pesticides. Some manufacturers deliberately add adulterants, including steroids, stimulants, and antibiotics.

Thus, hundreds of thousands of Americans are paying good money for spectacularly useless, inaccurately labeled, and sometimes dangerous herbal preparations, while hundreds of thousands of others are buying botanicals that could potentially offer real health benefits—and we don't know who's getting what. The only restraint on this galloping gray market of poorly tested substances is the Federal Trade Commission (FTC), which requires advertisements to be "truthful and verifiable." But the FTC has no way to verify the truthfulness of supplement industry claims; *it is not a scientific body.* Quality assurance is left to the manufacturers. The fox, by law, is guarding the henhouse. As a result, Americans who wish to use botanicals get no guarantee of purity, no testing for safety, and no proof that what's in the bottle is good for human health.

Despite these three roadblocks on the way to the truth, scientists are increasingly doing good research on botanicals for the brain. The question we most want answered is: if you take a certain botanical every day for ten or twenty or thirty years, will it make you significantly more resistant to memory loss? At this point, no one can state with certainty that any botanical will or will not give you this benefit. But I can help you make some well-informed bets.

Let's look at the botanicals that have been most highly touted as beneficial to the brain.

Ginkgo Biloba Might Possibly Help Save Your Brain

Emperor Shen Nung, who reputedly lived about twenty-eight centuries before Christ, is believed to have been China's first great herbalist. In his botanical health guide, the *Pen T'sao Ching*, he sings the praises of ginkgo for memory. Remarkably enough, in all the years since the publication of that masterwork, no one has done a satisfactory study to see whether ginkgo can actually prevent memory loss. But even without proof, millions of people today are taking ginkgo in the hope of boosting their brain power.

Just as Kristine told me, leaves, seeds, and other parts of the decorative and sometimes immense ginkgo biloba tree are among the most ancient of all natural remedies. Ginkgo is sold in Asia mostly as dried crushed plant parts, while in the United States and in Europe it is sold mostly as extracts—a batch of ingredients that are considered to have the best medicinal properties. In the wild and woolly American herbal market, more than twenty-five ginkgo extracts of varying potency and quality are being sold. But in western Europe, where physicians routinely prescribe ginkgo, there are several pharmaceutical-grade ginkgo extracts, of which the two best known are EGb 761 and Tanakan. Most of what I will discuss here is based on research into EGb 761 (the most-studied compound) and may or may not apply to other ginkgo products.

EGb 761 has two main components, *flavonoids* and *terpenes*. Pharmacy-grade gingko preparations like EGb 761 are typically formulated to contain 24 percent flavonoids and 6 percent terpenes. Let's start by looking at the remarkable potential of those flavonoids.

The flavonoids in ginkgo include *quercetin, myricetin, kaempferol,* and *isorhamnetin,* most of which are powerful antioxidants. They seem to do a great job of fighting oxidation in the brain: they protect neurons from oxidative stress, preserve the mitochondria's ability to make energy, and (most important) block lipid peroxidation, which can rip through a neuronal membrane like a pin through a balloon. They also block apoptosis (cellular suicide). Some evidence suggests that they even rescue hippocampal memory cells from oxidation. In addition, they seem to boost neurotransmitter function in several ways: by increasing uptake of dopamine and serotonin, which may enhance signaling; by boosting choline uptake, which could enhance the manufacture of the memory-critical transmitter acetylcholine; by helping to resist the aging-related decline in serotonin receptor function, which would be good for mood; and by acting as monoamine oxidase (MAO) inhibitors, which may not only have an antidepressant quality but may also dampen the fires of oxidative stress.

As if nature did not want to quit there, ginkgo is also packed with the remarkable terpenes. Three percent of EGb 761 is the terpene *bilobalide,* which can defend hippocampal memory cells when they are stressed by low oxygen supplies, as might happen in a stroke or a heart attack. The two terpenes *ginkgolide A and B* may help to fight emotional-stress-induced brain injury. Perhaps most valuable of all, ginkgolide B apparently inhibits *platelet-activating factor* (PAF), which encourages platelets to clump and turns on inflammation. Since platelet clumping is involved in cerebrovascular compromise and inflammation is involved in Alzheimer's, *ginkgolide B could theoretically provide a double defense against the two main threats to the aging brain.* Moreover, PAF is involved in long-term potentiation, the electrical marker of learning. By controlling PAF, it's possible that ginkgolide B may help support learning and memory.

As if these free-radical-busting, membrane-saving, PAF-blocking skills weren't enough, ginkgo has one more extremely interesting effect. As we get older, the mossy fibers that reach up to the hippocampal neurons, bringing in the signals that form new memories, thin somewhat. Ginkgo may keep these mossy fibers as bushy as the brow of youth, acting as a kind of nerve growth factor. Think of it as Rogaine for the brain.

Our knowledge of all these exciting benefits has come from test-tube or animal experiments. But we really want to know whether ginkgo helps *people.* Here we come up against that first barrier on the road to botanical truth: lots of clinical research has been done with ginkgo, but most of it was done so badly that it does not give us trustworthy information. As I've noted before, the only way to assure that a substance offers a genuine benefit is to do a double-blind placebo-controlled study. A 1992 review of forty ginkgo studies, mostly done in Europe, found that *none* of them involved double-blinding and placebo controls. The weakness of most of the European research in no way diminishes the possibility that ginkgo might work; it just compels scientists to dig in and do better studies. So there was a sense of reaching a milestone when the results from the first North American EGb trial were finally released in 1997.

Pierre Le Bars of the New York Institute for Medical Research and the North American EGb Study Group have conducted the only double-blind placebo-controlled U.S. study of ginkgo for dementia published to date. Seventy-eight people treated with EGb 761 (120 mg a day), and 59 people in the placebo group completed the full year of the study. The EGb-treated group showed no cognitive change, while the placebo group declined by 1.5 points on a cognitive scale—a treatment advantage of only a few percentage points but enough to be statistically significant. Clinicians following these patients noticed no difference with treatment, but caregivers for the patients noticed a slight improvement in the treated group. The results were much the same whether the researchers looked at the entire group of demented patients or at the subgroup with Alzheimer's disease. Thirty percent of the EGb-treated patients experienced one or more side effects, compared with 31 percent in the placebo-treated group, suggesting that side effects with this medicine are minimal. This study, the best of its kind, is fairly solid evidence that a typical dementia patient taking pharmaceutical-grade ginkgo may experience a slight benefit.

Neurologist Barry S. Oken and colleagues at Oregon Health Sciences University have attempted to tease out the impact of ginkgo specifically on Alzheimer's disease. Out of the fifty studies they reviewed, only four were good placebo-controlled studies that actually measured cognitive impact. The results: of 212 patients included in these four studies, those treated with ginkgo had a 3 percent advantage on a standard cognitive test.

Three percent is not quite what we were hoping for. While better results may come from isolating the most active constituent of ginkgo—a possibility that's definitely worth exploring—at present we have no evidence of anything beyond that 3 percent benefit.

We have to consider the side effects as well. Allergic skin responses occur with ginkgo; headaches are common. More worrisome, several people using ginkgo have bled into their brains (although it's not certain that ginkgo alone caused the bleeding). The terpenes are probably responsible for this bleeding tendency. Commercially sold ginkgos do not mention this risk of bleeding, and actually, for people taking ginkgo in a mix that includes just 6 percent terpenes, the risk of cerebral hemorrhage at 120 mg a day is probably quite low. But ginkgo should be avoided by those with peptic ulcers or other conditions causing a tendency to bleed, and by *everyone* in the week before any surgery.

What shall we conclude about gingko for the brain? Given the limited evidence of benefits, it is premature for physicians to prescribe ginkgo for demented patients outside controlled clinical trials. Ethically, doctors cannot promote compounds based on such modest testing. But the tantalizing evidence for ginkgo's beneficial activities is already inspiring better research, giving us reason to hope that ginkgo may soon yield up an active ingredient that can help people with Alzheimer's.

What about ginkgo as a brain-saver for healthy people who wish to *prevent* cognitive problems? We can be cautiously excited that the flavonoids in ginkgo may conceivably help prevent both ARNAT and CVC. The terpene components—in a purified and precisely dosed form—might help reduce the risk of CVC. Much further work is needed, particularly on the interactions of ginkgo with the antiplatelet agents (such as aspirin) that many people may take to prevent stroke, with other antioxidants, and with sedating drugs. The bottom line is that no scientific study has ever shown that ginkgo can preserve the brain from the insidious loss of mental abilities as we age. Forty-eight hundred years of uncertainty have yet to be overcome.

That uncertainty may change soon. At the time of this writing, the National Center for Complementary and Alternative Medicine (a new division of the NIH) is giving ginkgo to 3,000 healthy older people in a placebo-controlled trial. The researchers will follow the subjects for three years to see if ginkgo truly prevents dementia. Despite the fact that this study is far too brief, and regardless of the outcome, this research is a thrilling advance; it's the first time in history that a large controlled study has been done to test a botanical in healthy people for prevention of memory loss.

While we await the results of further research, here are my recommendations: if you or someone you love already has dementia, there are better treatments than ginkgo. If you are beginning to experience troublesome memory loss, *please* get a medical evaluation before embarking on a course that may simply delay the diagnosis of a treatable condition. If your memory is okay, as of today we have no clinical evidence that ginkgo will prevent cognitive decline. But I *would* venture to bet that, very soon, we will have solid evidence about the brain-saving benefits of gingko extracts or purified ingredients, one way or the other. Since ginkgo is not risk-free, let's wait for more persuasive results before committing ourselves to daily ginkgo for the brain.

Ginseng Saves Rat Brains; How About Humans?

Trespassers creep between strands of barbed wire armed with shovels and trowels; fields are trampled and turned; farmers sleep between rows of green shoots with spotlights and shotguns; it's only a matter of time before someone gets shot. Hidden marijuana plantations? Secret coca fields? No, it's Wisconsin's thirteen hundred ginseng farmers guarding their crops from poachers like shepherds from wolves. Wisconsin ginseng is hot.

Although ginseng was popular in Asia thousands of years before it became popular in the United States, faith in the superiority of American ginseng is widespread. The soil, the climate, and a special genetic strain make Wisconsin's crop the champagne of ginseng. Ninety-seven percent of Wisconsin ginseng is exported to Asia, where it is sold—like Wisconsin cheese—with a special seal of authenticity. This is not an overnight phenomenon. Ever since the eighteenth century, American ginseng has been favored in China, where it is regarded as a nearly magical aphrodisiac. But the Western fascination with Eastern medicine has shifted the distribution dynamic somewhat. Now even Americans buy American ginseng. (Or at least they think they do. As we noted before, many bottles labeled "ginseng" are short on ginseng and long on contaminants.)

Ginseng is derived from any one of the twelve plants of the genus *Panax,* including *Panax ginseng* or *Panax notoginseng* from China and *Panax quinquefolius* or *trifolius* from eastern North America. ("Siberian ginseng," "Brazilian ginseng," and "Indian ginseng" carry the ginseng name only because the roots look somewhat ginsenglike; they're actually all derived from other plants, and none contain the active ingredients I'll be discussing.) Extracts of ginseng plants contain many biologically active steroids called *ginsenosides.* The prospect of ginseng-related manslaughter in Wisconsin derives from the fact that American ginsengs may be the very best in terms of ginsenoside content. After all, if this botanical really does what it has traditionally been known for—enhancing physical (including sexual) stamina—or what it has more recently been promoted for—improving mental sharpness—it is one very valuable crop.

How might ginseng serve the brain? Ginsenosides seem to rescue neurons whenever blood flow to the brain is reduced. Researchers at Kyoto University showed that if rats are fed ginseng for a week, and then the arteries to their brains are temporarily pinched off, brain function will be much better preserved. Ginsenoside Rb1 in particular has been shown to rescue the hippocampal memory cells. Ginsenosides are beneficial because they are strong antioxidants, scavenging the free radicals that show up to kill neurons when blood flow is compromised. This benefit may be especially good for protecting people from memory loss related to CVC, such as those at risk for strokes or heart attacks, or those with chronic hypertension or diabetes. Like aspirin, ginsenosides also inhibit the clumping of platelets, which could also help save the brain from strokes. Ginsenosides may boost the memory-aiding transmitter acetylcholine, which may partly explain ginseng's memory-enhancing impact in animals. And they may even rev up the production of nerve growth factor, another way ginseng may help the brain recover from injury.

But for all of these benefits, the hottest ginseng research involves a completely different effect of ginsenosides: these compounds may play a role in regulating *nitric oxide,* a gas that is deeply involved in biological signaling. The nitric oxide effect of ginsenosides may explain ginseng's weak Viagra-like action, dilating the penis's corpus cavernosum and enhancing erections. Of more relevance to brain function, the nitric oxide link could explain ginseng's claimed ability to soothe emotional stress, since nitric oxide may temper the release of stress hormones. There's also evidence that ginsenosides may regulate long-term potentiation (LTP), the presumed electrical basis of learning, which may depend on nitric oxide signaling.

Ginseng's many brain benefits in the lab translate into proven cognitive benefits in animal experiments. For example, if aged rats take ginseng regularly, they are better at finding their way out of a maze. When rats are given scopolamine (a drug that mimics the chemistry of Alzheimer's), ginsenoside Rb1 improves their memory. Ginseng has been shown to improve learning in brain-damaged rats. To be fair, all of these memory-boosting benefits are not really neuroprotective; their effect on thinking may be temporary, like that produced by a cup of coffee. But ginseng may actually *save* brains from some types of aging-related damage: new evidence indicates that ginseng helps preserve memory in rats challenged by lack of blood flow in the brain, making this botanical a potential shield against strokes.

As for ginseng's effect on humans—here you may feel as if you've awakened on Christmas morning to find a gift certificate to a hardware store on Guam. For all of the extraordinary potential that ginseng and its various ingredients show in lab animals, the human studies have been quite disappointing. For example, a British study was conducted on sixty-four "healthy" volunteers. (I put healthy in quotes because all participants qualified for the diagnosis of *neurasthenia,* which essentially comes down to listlessness.) Ninety days of combined treatment with ginseng and ginkgo produced a brief stimulantlike benefit, similar to the effects of caffeine, but no sign of a lasting cognitive effect. Even more discouraging, when 60 geriatric patients in a rehabilitation hospital in Norway received a ginseng/vitamin preparation for eight weeks, they showed *less* improvement on a learning test than the placebo-treated patients! In fact, a recent review of all the double-blind placebo-controlled studies with ginseng found no evidence of any benefit to patients with Alzheimer's, any benefit to cognition, or any slowing of mental decline in aging.

Still, if I had to bet, I'd say that the gaping chasm between the lab results and the human results comes from the fact that most human studies use the *whole crushed ginseng root* instead of the pure, biologically active ingredient, perhaps ginsenoside Rb1 or Rb2 or another ingredient we have yet to discover. What's more, giving crushed ginseng to humans can be both an inexact science and a risky business. There's no telling what you'll actually get in a bottle labeled "ginseng." And if it *does* contain ginseng, it may interact with other drugs in your body, such as estrogens, steroids, MAO inhibitors, and blood thinners.

Therefore, until studies are done that identify the safe and beneficial ingredient of ginseng and show that at least some people get a meaningful brain-saving benefit from it, to take the products currently being sold as "ginseng" is to take a leap of faith off a cliff of uncertainty. Give it a few years. So many promising experiments are under way that I bet scientists will find the real brain-beneficial ingredients. Then all we'll have to do is force Congress to pass a law that assures we get safe and genuine supplies of this ancient and intriguing herb.

St. John's Wort Might Help Alleviate Depression

David came to the clinic with his diagnosis under his arm and unfurled it with a flourish. "I thought I was doing pretty good for an old fart, but then I saw this." An accordion-paged computer printout unfolded to the floor. David pointed to a line. I followed his finger. The line of type was an indecipherable jumble of letters and symbols. I was at a loss.

The gruff and stocky computer scientist grabbed the cascading printout. "Here it is. An error." He tapped the page and grinned. "I'm a programmer of the old school. I don't make coding errors. I've got Alzheimer's."

He was right. It was hard to believe at first, and it took another year before he made a single error on the Mini–Mental State Examination, the brief standard screening test for dementia. Yet this brilliant fifty-two-year-old man, a leader of his local Mensa chapter, had correctly detected his own decline in cognition at the first squeak of trouble.

That discovery had plunged him into a dark and painful depression. He had been trying to shake off his unbearable mood by taking St. John's wort, he said, then set the bottle on top of the printout and folded his arms defiantly. "I know you may not go for this alternative medicine fad, but I think it's been a help." Ten minutes later, grief overcame bravado; his voice choked and he fought back tears as he told me about his nightly battle with thoughts of suicide.

St. John's wort (*Hypericum perforatum*) was so named because this plant produces its yellow flower on or about the feast day of St. John the Baptist, June 24. *Wort* is just Old English for "root" or "herb"; herbalists generally refer to this wort by its scientific name, hypericum. Hypericum was popular for centuries as a folk remedy for snakebites. More recently, and with an astounding growth curve of sales and use, it has been embraced as a treatment for mild to moderate depression. American sales of St. John's wort exploded from $20 to $200 million between 1995 and 1997 alone. While hypericum is not considered to have direct brain-saving activity, it may conceivably dampen the harmful effects of depression and stress, which could produce an indirect but important neuron-sparing benefit.

Many promoters of St. John's wort theorize that it works just like Prozac and similar antidepressants of the type called selective serotonin-reuptake inhibitors (SSRIs). Others disagree, pointing to the evidence that extracts of St. John's wort are more likely to work like MAO inhibitors, a different type of antidepressant. Still others point to evidence that extracts of this wort interact with receptors for glutamate, GABA, and benzodiazepines (antianxiety drugs like Valium), meaning that St. John's wort has been accused of consorting with half the neurotransmitters in the brain. The problem is that none of these chemical effects have been convincingly linked to the herb's clinical impact in humans, so we remain in the dark about how precisely St. John's wort works—if indeed it does.

Which of St. John's wort's various constituents is most likely to produce the antidepressant effect? Extracts from St. John's wort contain at least three ingredients that might be active, including *hypericin, pseudo-hypericin,* and *hyperforin.* Many herbalists claim that hypericin is the most active ingredient, but new evidence suggests that the antidepressant effect is related not to hypericin but to hyperforin. Unfortunately, hyperforin content is not even listed on most labels.

Despite these uncertainties, it would be a mistake to underestimate this herb. St. John's wort is an extremely promising natural psychiatric agent that stands out impressively in the garden of botanicals, with strong hints from research that it's at least somewhat uplifting for low mood:

When Klaus Linde at Ludwig Maximilians University in Munich pooled the results of twenty-seven studies involving 2,291 outpatients who had mild to moderately severe depression, he found the response rate was 56 percent for hypericum versus 25 percent for placebos. Still, the benefits seem to be confined to people with mild depression; in three out of four studies of *major* depression, hypericum was less effective than standard antidepressants. A more encouraging meta-analysis was done by researchers at the University of Hawaii. Unlike Dr. Linde's analysis, the Hawaiian team restricted their analysis to only the most carefully done studies. They found that hypericum was 50 percent more likely than placebo to treat depression successfully, making it about as helpful as the old tricyclic antidepressants. And in 2000, Barak Gaster at the University of Washington looked at 388 articles on this subject. Only two of the studies, he found, were truly first-quality research; in those two, St. John's wort proved more effective than placebo but 6 to 18 percent *less* effective than tricyclic antidepressants. But comparison with the obsolete tricyclic is off the mark; what we really want to know is how St. John's wort stacks up against *modern* antidepressants—the selective serotonin-reuptake inhibitors such Prozac, Zoloft, and Paxil. At the time of this writing, only one study has compared St. John's wort head-to-head with Prozac. In this German study of 240 patients, the two treatments seemed equally good for reducing depression.

This bouquet of promising results has wilted somewhat under criticisms that virtually all of these studies were flawed. But the hints of a possible mood benefit were so strong that the NIH finally agreed to fund a rigorous study of St. John's wort for depression. The results, published in the *Journal of the American Medical Association* in 2001, showed that the botanical worked no better than a placebo.

Overall, the data convincingly suggest that St. John's wort may help people with milder depressions, but it does *not* seem effective in treating major depression. What's more, although it is generally safe, the wort is not entirely free of its own side effects—the most common of which are stomachaches, dizziness, fatigue, and photosensitivity (rapid sunburning for fair-skinned people). The wort can also reduce the effectiveness of dozens of other medications, from oral contraceptives to anti-AIDS and cancer drugs. And you should not combine this herb with prescription antidepressants because of the risk of toxic interactions. Unfortunately, with the appearance of St. John's wort in every supermarket in America, such reservations have been trampled in a stampede of popularity. We know it's promising; we know little else.

Should you take it?

For severe, major clinical depression, the answer is easy. Depression is a heartrending, life-threatening disease. A severely depressed person taking St. John's wort is akin to a person with heart failure pulling foxglove from the backyard and eating it. The mood-improving ingredients may or may not be present in the extracts currently marketed, and even if they were, they would probably be too weak to help. If you or someone you love gets depressed, please see a doctor. These days the combination of modern medicines and compassionate therapy can safely and effectively rescue a depressed patient from unbearable mental agony.

For mild depression, the answer is harder. Those with a slightly down mood, the winter blues, or a temporary setback in love may possibly achieve some mental relief from this wort. Frankly, taking a medicinal agent known to affect multiple neurotransmitter systems without medical supervision seems like the ultimate metamorphosis of the go-ask-Alice spirit of the 1960s into twenty-first-century do-it-yourself health care. Nonetheless, since there's evidence of a slightly beneficial effect for mildly low mood, for people taking no other medications and with no other medical problems, a short-term trial of St. John's wort is a fairly low-risk bet. I do not recommend long-term use.

Personally, I have high hopes that research on this fascinating plant will soon lead to the isolation of powerful ingredients that can reduce the corrosive effect of emotional pain on the brain. But I would advise waiting until this botanical yields its genuinely active ingredient, rather than taking the currently available extracts of unknown contents and purity in the hopes of defeating the dragon of depression.

Can Garlic Help Save the Brain?

In 1997 Americans spent $71 million on medicinal garlic (*Allium sativum*), thanks in part to several scientific studies suggesting that it can lower cholesterol, and in part to an encouraging marketing campaign for new garlic pills that supposedly do not cause breath strong enough to peel paint. The main theory has been that allicin, a phytochemical in garlic, can decrease blood cholesterol by 10 points if used daily for several months. Some very good science stands behind this theory. The multiple constituents of garlic, in lab experiments, have significant antioxidant and anticoagulant properties. Garlic may lower blood pressure, inhibit clot formation, reduce blood lipids, and prolong the life of spontaneously hypertensive rats—all effects that may help save the brain from CVC. It has also been linked to improved memory in one breed of rapidly aging mice. The question, as always, is whether these promising lab findings translate into human benefits. The answer is—perhaps.

Stephen Warshafsky of New York Medical College in Valhalla combined findings from five controlled studies of garlic for high blood cholesterol levels and found that patients taking garlic preparations achieved a 9 percent decrease in those levels. Findings such as these have fed the public's hope. But garlic has recently slipped from favor, in part because of a study published in the *Journal of the American Medical Association* in 1998 showing that the purported cholesterol-busting properties may not be real: when 25 people with moderately high cholesterol took a commercial garlic pill for six months, they showed no reduction at all in their cholesterol levels. The study's principal author, pharmacologist Heiner Berthold, wrote, "We were surprised that the overall effect of the garlic drug on cholesterol was zero." Garlic supplement sellers retorted, "But that was a garlic *oil* formulation; surely a *dried* garlic pill would do better." But separate studies, at the Christ Hospital Cardiovascular Research Center in Cincinnati and at Oxford University, that *did* use dried garlic found no cholesterol-lowering benefit.

The garlic story is far from resolved. Entirely apart from the inconsistent findings of a cholesterol-lowering effect, garlic may help to prevent platelet clumping and may slightly lower blood pressure, both of which are good for protecting the brain from CVC. It even has some antibacterial properties. Ever since the recent discovery that bacteria may be the secret agent behind many heart attacks and strokes, the idea of eating foods with naturally antibiotic properties has taken on new meaning—garlicky spaghetti sauce for the health of your brain!

Perhaps more exciting for brain-saving purposes are reports from the University of Tokyo that garlic contains compounds that promote the survival of hippocampal memory cells. One of these compounds, called allyl-L-cysteine, was even shown to promote the outgrowth and branching of axons—a nerve growth factor–like effect—quite an intriguing finding regarding this common and delightful flavoring. Although it's too soon to claim that garlic will lower your cholesterol, fight off stroke-causing bacteria, and spruce up your hippocampus, you may want to include garlic in a healthy Brain-Saving Diet on the assumption that it is an excellent, low-risk bet that may contribute to protecting your health and your memory.

Marijuana Might Help Save the Brain

Lab rat 1: Did you hear the good news? Marijuana-related compounds are neuroprotective!

Lab rat 2: What have you been smoking?

The psychoactive properties of the fragrant herb *Cannabis sativa* have been known for perhaps five thousand years, and its medicinal properties were documented in a fifteenth-century B.C. Chinese medical text. But two trends are quite recent: a worldwide expansion in the herb's recreational use, and the serious scientific investigation of its pharmacologically active compounds. Very roughly speaking, 300 million people around the world are users of marijuana in its various forms and potencies, including bhang, charas, ganja, and hashish (this last named for the founder of the Persian cult of Assassins). Use in the United States is remarkably common, especially by middle-school and older adolescents, and 90 percent of illicit drug use at present is marijuana use. In other words, the two most popular herbal supplements used by Americans are not those sold in health food stores; they are instead tobacco, our favorite addictive botanical, and marijuana, our favorite illegal botanical. We cannot consider tobacco a potential brain-saver; though nicotine has some valuable neuroactive properties, it would be a bad bet to risk one's life with tobacco in the hopes of a neuroprotective effect. Marijuana, on the other hand, is a very promising herb. Visions of rainbow-painted school buses, movable feasts of brownie-fueled rebellion, and counterculture couture aside, what have users been smoking?

The resin obtained from the leaves, stems, and flowering tops of the female hemp plant contains more than sixty substances with pharmacological potency, of which the best known three are delta-9-tetrahydrocannabinol (THC), cannabinol, and cannabidiol. Taken together, these substances are called *cannabinoids*. Cannabinoids stimulate our nervous system because our brains evolved built-in receptors for marijuanalike compounds. So far scientists have identified two such cannabinoid receptors in the brain, called CB1 and CB2. Both of these receptors play a role in our emotional response to the *exogenous* cannabinoids, meaning the cannabinoids found outside the body.

Our society has known about these exogenous cannabinoids for many years—the sweet-smelling green-brown botanical sold in plastic bags in high school hallways and parking lots. But the discovery of the CB1 and CB2 receptors in the brain naturally led to the question, what are cannabinoid receptors doing in the human body? Scientists have finally identified the *endogenous* cannabinoids, the body's own natural cannabinoids for which these receptors were designed. Two have been discovered so far. (They are called *anandamide* (ANA) and *sn-2 arachidonoylglycerol* (2-AG).) In fact, 2-AG may be the more important marijuanalike molecule for regulating human brain functions.

Given the experience of millions of marijuana users, it's no surprise to learn that built-in cannabinoids play a role in regulating mood, perception, and appetite. In animal experiments, cannabinoids also produce pain relief, decreased body temperature, and sometimes catalepsy (a rigid, withdrawn state). Possibly cannabinoids function somewhat like endorphins, to rescue us from painful stresses. In fact, the potential for using our cannabinoid system as a new approach to pain relief is quite exciting. Cannabinoids may actually turn on neurons in the brainstem to send pain-dampening signals down the spinal cord.

But there's more to human cannabinoids than pain or stress relief. In addition to binding to their own CB receptors, cannabinoids also bind to NMDA receptors—the exact receptors that control our hippocampal memory cells. The bad news about binding to NMDA receptors is that this can impair memory: animals given high doses of marijuana or THC have definite trouble with short-term memory. Typical human recreational exposures produce little cognitive impact, but severe intoxication with marijuana can temporarily hurt attention, reaction time, and short-term memory. The good news about binding to NMDA receptors—and the most exciting discovery about cannabinoids—is that this is a great way to save neurons from excitotoxic cell death (death due to excess stimulation that can occur in strokes, head trauma, and Alzheimer's). In fact, as reported by the National Institute of Mental Health in 1998, naturally occurring cannabinoids indeed protect neurons against NMDA-based excitotoxicity. The same study also showed that cannabinoids are potent antioxidants; a nonpsychoactive type of cannabinoid called *cannabidiol* was even better at defending brain cells from free radical attacks than either vitamin C or vitamin E. In one test tube experiment, cannabidiol prevented *more than half* of the neuronal death of the type expected during a stroke. Based on these encouraging findings, neuroscientists see a huge potential for cannabinoids as treatments for brain disorders, and they've begun human trials.

The cannabinoid called *dexanabinol* is considered a good candidate for medicinal use because it has no psychoactive side effects. In one trial, Israeli neurosurgeon Nachshon Knoller gave dexanabinol to 30 head injury patients within six hours of their injuries; the cannabinoid doubled the proportion of those who could resume daily activities three months later. Which leads to the *really* provocative question: if cannabinoids are neuroprotective, might regular use defend the brain from strokes and Alzheimer's?

One study has attempted to explore the long-term impact of marijuana smoking on the risk of cognitive decline. Constantine Lyketsos at Johns Hopkins University looked at mental performance among 1,318 adults under age sixty-five. Of these men and women, 511 admitted to some use of marijuana, including 366 light users and 145 heavy users. Over thirteen years, cognition subtly declined among the entire group, just as we'd expect with aging. But there was no difference in the decline seen in nonusers, light users, and heavy users. This study has been widely interpreted as proving that long-term marijuana smoking has no effect on cognition one way or the other.

However (darn it), this study actually tells us very little about whether cannabinoids can save the brain. First, the people in this study were not taking a measured dose of a pharmaceutical-grade medication; they were taking whatever they got from their dealers, which probably varied enormously in cannabinoid content. The quality of street marijuana is extremely variable, and sellers often combine marijuana with an alarming spectrum of other substances. (For instance, in Texas, fat marijuana cigarettes called "blunts" are dipped in embalming fluid laced with PCP.) Second, the subjects were simply too young to develop dementia, and the study was stopped too soon to determine whether marijuana smokers were protected from Alzheimer's. Third, marijuana cigarettes contain toxic tars. Since marijuana smokers inhale deeply and hold the smoke in their lungs, chronic users have many of the same respiratory problems as tobacco smokers in terms of coughing, wheezing, and signs of early chronic obstructive pulmonary disease (COPD). Lung damage from smoking the weed could potentially compromise cerebral function in a way that negates any benefits to the brain.

In the final analysis, smoking crude marijuana will always be problematic. In addition to the risk of lung damage, there remains the sticky problem of psychoactive effects. Even marijuana dealers with the noblest intentions, who grow exclusively for medicinal use, cannot control the cannabinoid content of their products. For all these reasons, I predict that the concept of "medical marijuana" will fall out of favor, just as "medical foxglove" became a pharmaceutical embarrassment once digitalis was available. Yes, millions of people will smoke marijuana as long as the world goes around, but medical marijuana should be replaced by safer delivery systems and by specific discovery of the most beneficial constituents—the herbal "essence"—that's best for brain cells.

In summary, I absolutely do not recommend smoking marijuana in search of a cerebral benefit. But there's legitimate reason to be excited that, in the near future, doctors will be using pure cannabinoids to help save the brain.

Other Botanicals for the Brain

The list of botanicals with neuroprotective potential is long and troubling. Long, because the search for medicinal botanicals may predate the dawn of humanity; Homo erectus probably did trial-and-error experiments with plants to salve his wounds. Troubling, because we have so little to show for this 100,000-plus-year search. I've focused on ginkgo, ginseng, garlic, and St. John's wort because they are among the best studied, but a number of other botanicals may have neuroprotective properties.

For example, *kava* is a mild sedative, widely used as a social lubricant in the South Pacific. My first encounter with kava was one sultry night in Fiji; the guys from the village gathered in a clearing around a wooden bowl the size of a washtub, squatting to stir the soupy juice, downing cup after cup, and singing with progressive mellowness as the night wore on. Kava extract, from the Polynesian plant *Piper methysticum,* includes at least five biologically active constituents. They have calming and muscle-relaxant effects, though kava's most intriguing effect in brain research is that it seems to act as an antiepileptic drug. Since kava can protect lab animals against decreased blood flow to the brain, it may contain some substance that could conceivably help protect us from cerebrovascular compromise. But this research is very preliminary, and kava may produce unpredictable interactions with other sedatives, from alcohol to prescription drugs. As a clinician, I would love to be able to offer an antianxiety treatment with lower addictive potential and less chance of making someone drive off the road than the most commonly prescribed medicines for anxiety, the benzodiazepines (drugs like Valium and Xanax). Conceivably, a purified kava flavone will do the trick. But kava is unlikely to save your brain; there are much better ways to dodge CVC.

The Chinese club moss (*Huperzia serrata*) contains the potent anticholinesterase *huperzine A*. In other words, it contains a member of the exact same family of drugs that we use in prescription Alzheimer's treatments such as Aricept, a compound that can boost cholinergic function to help support memory. Some evidence suggests that huperzine A is even more powerful than its prescription counterparts, probably explaining why it came to be valued for memory loss in China hundreds of years before we even had a name for Alzheimer's disease. Pharmacy-grade huperzine A may someday offer a fine alternative to the current Alzheimer's treatments. More important, preliminary evidence indicates that boosting cholinergic function may do more than just slightly slow the pace of Alzheimer's; it may *prevent* neuron death to some degree in healthy brains. Don't take it yet, but stay tuned for further research into the brain-saving benefits of this ancient herb.

Mentat, also known as BR-16A, is an Ayurvedic formulation popular in India. A few studies with lab rats suggest that it has a beneficial impact on learning, but the available human research is very weak.

Peony root extract includes gallotannin and paeoniflorin. Several animal studies suggest that gallotannin can protect hippocampal neurons under certain stressful conditions and that paeoniflorin can help rats find their way through mazes. Again, supportive human data is missing.

As we know from Table 3, the list of potentially neuroactive botanicals goes on and on. At a certain point, we have to set aside the dazzling array of options and answer a practical question: should you take a botanical to protect your brain?

This is where the risk-averse investors step aside: botanicals are the junk bonds of health care. There's no way to be sure that they are safe or effective, because of incomplete research and inadequate regulation. So three things should help us decide whether to use botanicals in the new millennium. The first is NIH-funded research. Pharmaceutical companies will not risk a huge research investment in a nonpatentable product, so the NIH's National Center for Complementary and Alternative Medicine should be funded to expand its support for serious research into herbal remedies. Second, industry regulation is not just an option, it's a must. It is obviously more profitable to sell lead as gold if the consumer cannot tell which is which. Until there is scientific oversight and assurance that we get what we pay for when we buy a botanical, we are gambling on the goodwill of a freewheeling business to voluntarily cut its profit margins to fulfill its promises. American consumers, like consumers the world over, deserve pure products and basic legal protections.

Third, we bet. As best as I'm able to, I have laid out the facts. People armed with the facts can decide for themselves. I would summarize the wager as follows.

At present, only two botanicals show impressive scientific evidence of neuroprotective effects: ginkgo biloba and ginseng. Of the two, the evidence is stronger for ginkgo. Part of the proposed ginkgo benefit is an antioxidant effect. But if you are already taking vitamin E and are enjoying a fruit- and vegetable-rich diet, it's unclear that ginkgo's antioxidants will add anything. Another benefit might be an antiplatelet effect, similar to that obtained from aspirin. But if you are already taking aspirin, adding ginkgo could possibly increase your risk of bleeding. Ginkgo may provide additional neuroprotective benefits that a plant-rich-diet-antioxidant-vitamins-aspirin regimen cannot, but no studies directly compare the benefits of these two regimens in any animal, let alone a long-term study in humans.

So it becomes a highly personal decision. If you are impatient to do more—fully aware of the shortage of credible evidence of a long-term benefit—you may wish to try a standardized ginkgo extract, sold by a reputable firm, at a dose of 40 mg three times a day. You may in fact reap a benefit that the rest of us will lose. It will be many years before we know.

CHAPTER 14

Smart Drugs:
Utopian Dream or
Fast-Approaching Reality?

I saw the best minds of my generation destroyed by madness,
    starving, hysterical, naked,
dragging themselves through the negro streets at dawn look-
    ing for an angry fix,
angelheaded hipsters burning for the ancient heavenly con-
    nection to the starry dynamo in the machinery of night.
                    ALLEN GINSBERG, *HOWL* (1956)

Hulking warehouses, grimy cinderblock walls, dumpsters grandly graffi-
toed with hip-hop runes were barely visible in the sulfurous midnight
glow deep in the industrial underbelly of Los Angeles. A wasp-waisted
dog, feral and leprous, padded silently by. X marked the spot on the flyer,
where an intersection on the Thomas Brothers' mapbook had been labeled with a code word for the drug Ecstasy. This was the place. I might
have known from half a mile away, the music was that loud. An enormous bouncer lounged like a grandee on a stool by a battered steel door.
He offered no sign of welcome or indeed of life as I extended the paper
flyer for his inspection, so I tugged the thick door and went in.

   Imagine a mosh pit videoed by Brueghel the Elder, a fast-forward trip-
tych of writhing bodies slipping in liquid din. I had never been to a rave.
A musician friend had urged me to go, describing it as an enlightening experience. An education to be sure, I thought as I surveyed the sociable
melee. A sign over a folding table caught my eye; it read "BBs," which, I
was informed by a helpful young lady twinkling with body piercing, stood
for Brain Boosters. It seemed like a timely service to offer. I shouldered
my way through the crowd to the table and shouted, "What you got?"
A shaved-headed boy of perhaps thirteen smiled with disconcerting

innocence as he passed me a glass tube filled with blue liquid, and a pill. I didn't recognize the liquid—perhaps it was "blue nitro," a popular drug of abuse in the late 1990s and reliable precipitant of rave-related hospital visits. But I knew the pill. It was Hydergine.

Hydergine (generic name ergoloid mesylate) is a prescription drug that may enhance some aspects of cerebral function. It was the first drug to be approved by the FDA for the treatment of dementia. To find it in that setting, marketed that way, seemed high-test irony.

Does the urge for chemically inspired oblivion insidiously morph into the wish for chemically enhanced performance? Are these seemingly opposite goals truly separate or actually of a piece? Is the medicine of one generation the recreation of another? If sixty-three-year-olds in carpeted clinics and thirteen-year-olds in basement bacchanals are taking the same pills for roughly the same reasons, what does it say about the human urge for cerebral enhancement? Reviewing the milestones of twentieth-century America, historians will wonder at the whirls and eddies of social tolerance, the prescription of some drugs, the proscription of others, and the shifting attitudes that have swung like a pendulum in a tornado, often doing damage at both extremes. One chapter of that history will be devoted to smart drugs, positioned precariously between the counterculture and the mainstream, between the ironic and the earnest applications of the philosophy of "better living through chemistry." And one chapter of this book will explore the truth about these drugs. Most are not ready for routine medical use, but a few are available *today* and are very close to being prescribed by your family doctor to save—or even boost—the function of your brain.

What Is a Smart Drug?

The phrase *smart drug* is usually reserved for a special group of agents that enhance cognition overall. A smart drug is different from a botanical, because it's man-made instead of natural, and it's different from a stimulant such as cocaine, nicotine, or caffeine because it may have intellect-boosting powers beyond merely pricking alertness. I will focus here on the most promising drugs in this truly special category.

But before we look at the leading smart drugs, we might consider the question that bedevils every researcher: how do we know if a smart drug works?

One way to test a smart drug is to see if it boosts blood flow in the brain; promoters of smart drugs often point to increased cerebral blood flow as evidence of a compound's mental benefits. But revving up blood flow will not necessarily enhance thought. Cocaine, for

example, impressively increases cerebral blood flow, but it does not improve mental function (regardless of how insightful a fellow in the midst of
a cocaine high may imagine himself to be). Another test for a smart drug
might be to see whether it helps protect the brain against a *drop* in blood
flow, as occurs in strokes. Researchers will give a smart drug to a rat, tie
off an artery to its brain, and see whether the drug saves neurons. While
this test may be highly revealing about the value of a drug for emergency
rat brain rescue, it may not tell us much about the effects it would have on
humans who took it for years; short-term benefits in rats rarely translate
into long-term benefits in people. A third test to prove that a smart drug
works is to show that it boosts the brain levels of a particular neurotransmitter. But the nervous system is as finely tuned as an elegant computer program, and a drug that simply boosts a neurotransmitter might be about as
helpful to your brain as a big jolt of electricity would be to your computer.

A better way to test the powers of a smart drug would be to test its effect on "smartness"—that is, on memory and other mental functions. The
simplest way to do this is to just give the drug to subjects—mice or humans—and see whether it improves their scores on cognitive tasks. But
many garden-variety stimulants, from nicotine to caffeine to ampheta-
mines, will pass this test, yet they don't give us a lasting brain benefit. In
fact, the pharmacological definition of a *stimulant* is "a drug that can
cause seizures"; when the nervous system gets wired by excess stimulation
for too long, it tends to collapse. A more popular lab test has been to give
subjects scopolamine, a drug that mimics one of the main problems in
Alzheimer's—the loss of the crucial transmitter acetylcholine. The idea is
that any drug that helps us overcome scopolamine may also help us fight
Alzheimer's. But overcoming drug-induced confusion is not really the
same as boosting day-to-day thinking ability. A final way to test the
power of a potential smart drug is to give it to demented patients and see
if it helps. First with tacrine (Cognex), then with donepezil (Aricept), and
currently with a dozen similar drugs at various phases of clinical development, doctors have seen significant gratifying effects with these drugs,
mostly in the form of slowing the relentless march of cognitive decline.

But *none* of these prescription drugs has been shown to improve the
healthy brain. Not one. Not ever. So even though researchers are achingly
close to identifying synthetic drugs that do good things for the mind, what
follows here will be a story about first steps—the tentative efforts of a science that is just leaving its rat-lab home for a foray into the outside world
of human medicine. Like the research on botanicals, the research on smart
drugs has been highly variable in quality. Many studies have been done in
Europe by ad hoc teams of family doctors recruited as "researchers," using hopelessly dated methods for diagnosing dementia. Now, a great deal

of wonderful scientific work is done in Europe, but most of the work on smart drugs just doesn't make the cut.

These caveats notwithstanding, some exciting discoveries are beginning to revolutionize the field, giving us good reason to believe that genuine memory-enhancing drugs will become available in the next several years, and you're likely to hear more and more promising news about them. So let's look at the best bets.

We can divide these drugs into four big groups: nootropics; nerve growth factors; drugs that boost a neurotransmitter; and amyloid blockers (by far the hottest group).

Nootropics

Noo comes from νουσ (pronounced "noose"), Greek for "mind." *Tropic* comes from τροπος (pronounced "tropos"), meaning "growth." So a nootropic should be a mind-growing agent. Italian pharmacologist C. Giurgea introduced the term *nootropic* in 1972, proposing that certain drugs improve mental function by boosting brain metabolism. The main effect of most nootropics is *vasodilation,* or dilation of the arteries in the brain. While vasodilation does move more blood through the brain, this in itself does not seem to make people smarter. When we are thinking hard, our brains don't have a wall-to-wall increase in blood flow; they have a precise increase in blood flow to just a few small areas. Taking a drug that increases blood flow everywhere in the brain is like flooding a town to water one garden. And artificially boosting blood flow may not be such a great idea: it would also rev up free radical production, which could actually speed up brain cell death.

Yet it would be a mistake to dismiss nootropics out of hand. The best of them might even do what they are supposed to do.

PIRACETAM

Piracetam is the original nootropic. It's been used by European doctors since the 1970s and is still one of the most prescribed antidementia drugs in the world. It has gradually been joined by other members of the same drug family, its rhyming kin: aniracetam, nefiracetam, oxiracetam, pramiracetam, and levetiracetam. The various "iracetams" truly do many things in the brain that *might* support cognition, but after thirty years of use, we still don't know how they work. Following the piracetam story is like walking through a boxwood maze; the stroll is very interesting, but we're not sure it's leading us where we want to go.

Mazes are exactly how researchers test drugs on rodents—and there's evidence that this drug can improve maze learning in aging rodents. In one study, for example, piracetam improved the maze navigation of ten-month-old mice (pretty old, in mouse years) to the level of youthful two-month-old mice. Piracetam also helps rats overcome the confusing effects of scopolamine, which, as mentioned, mimics Alzheimer's. Similarly, piracetam-treated rabbits are better at learning the eyeblink reflex (a type of learning that is impaired in people with Alzheimer's), so this drug possibly improves some types of learning in Alzheimer's.

For all of the impressive data on mouse, rat, and rabbit memory, however, the studies with humans have been inconclusive at best. True, piracetam helps people resist the memory-scrambling effects of scopolamine, but if we simply test cognition in *healthy* people, without drugging them into befuddlement, piracetam does nothing for cognition. Some researchers optimistically interpret this to mean "Okay, piracetam may not boost memory in your average Joe, but it *will* help the millions of people who have low levels of acetylcholine in their brains, as in ARNAT and Alzheimer's." But no persuasive study has ever shown that piracetam helps Alzheimer's patients.

Inflated "memory-boosting" claims aside, however, piracetam has a completely different effect that may make it a genuine brain-saver: it *does* seem to rescue people who are having a stroke.

The scene is repeated thousands of times nightly all over the world. A middle-age couple lies sleeping together in bed. His arm goes numb, his mouth goes slack, and then half his body shudders toward paralysis—classic symptoms of a stroke. His wife awakens, sensing his distress. If this were the mid-1990s and she rushed her husband to the emergency room of one of fifty-five hospitals in ten European countries, he could have been enrolled in one of the first major tests of a smart drug as a treatment for acute stroke. Three months later, he may, in fact, have done better than nature usually permits—about 19 percent better—if he was treated with piracetam. That's a big enough benefit to make the difference between living at home with assistance or requiring institutional care. This was the conclusion of the massive Piracetam in Acute Stroke Study, led by Belgian neurologist Peter Paul De Deyn.

Piracetam's stroke-rescue benefit may be due to its ability to make red blood cells more "bendable," helping them squeeze through tight spots in arteries after a stroke. This might be just the ticket to save neurons that are struggling to survive on borderline blood supplies. In addition, piracetam may improve the energy efficiency of neurons that are struggling along on limited supplies of oxygen; this would be like increasing the gas mileage of your car just when you're sixty miles from the next station and running on fumes. These healthful effects may not only rescue your brain after a stroke but may even conceivably improve mental function in the tens of millions of people who have chronically limited brain blood flow due to atherosclerosis, diabetes, or high blood pressure.

So should you take piracetam in the hopes of cognitive enhancement? Although this drug has many potential brain benefits, at this point it's still a shaky bet. We really need a good NIH-quality study—the sooner, the better—to figure out how to use this promising smart drug to save the brain.

HYDERGINE

The word *ergot* has an interesting origin. *Ergot de coq* is French for "spur of a cock," the fierce little dewclaw that turns a cockfight into such a bloody affair. The rye grass fungus looks a lot like a cock's spur; hence the name ergot, as this fungus has been known for centuries. In the Middle Ages, epidemics of ergotism spread throughout Europe when people ate loaves of ergot-contaminated rye bread. It made tens of thousands of people's fingers and toes turn purple and black and fall off from gangrene, caused convulsions, and produced the most florid insanity. Hydergine is the brand name for a combination of four ergot derivatives that is widely prescribed as a drug to enhance cognition. Hmm.

Let's suspend our disbelief and give Hydergine a chance. Like most agents that are powerful enough to help, it's also powerful enough to hurt. Ergot is actually one of the Western world's oldest botanically derived medicines. Several ergot-based medicines remain in active use in modern medicine: ergonovine, which is used to contract the uterus in obstetrics; ergotamine, a treatment for migraine; bromocryptine, an anti-Parkinson's drug; and Hydergine—the same "brain-boosting" drug that I was offered at that chaotic Los Angeles rave. There are several good reasons to suspect that Hydergine may benefit the mind: it has antioxidant powers, it may improve brain cell efficiency, and it actually seems to regulate the signals involved in memory. Rats given Hydergine may do better in mazes. One human PET scan study suggested that Hydergine even improves the brain's ability to burn glucose for energy. Hydergine also seems to prevent platelets from clumping in the carotid artery—an effect that may help protect us against having a stroke.

But is Hydergine good for human thinking? In one novel human experiment, healthy volunteers inhaled gas that was low in oxygen (a treatment that's somewhat similar to the oxygen deprivation of a stroke). Those who had been given Hydergine in advance of this treatment had better mental performance. But far and away the most famous Hydergine study appeared in the *New England Journal of Medicine* in 1990, in which researchers studied 80 patients with Alzheimer's who used the usual Hydergine dose of 3 mg a day. Unfortunately, they showed no benefit at all after six months of treatment. In fact, patients treated with Hydergine exhibited *worse* performance on a standard test of mental speed. From that point on, Hydergine began to slip from favor in the United States (although it remains hugely popular in Europe).

More recently, a grand effort was made to review all the human evidence about Hydergine, when neuropsychologist Jason Olin and psychiatrist Lon Schneider at the University of Southern California looked at 151 trials. Based on a careful review of the best evidence, they arrived at three important conclusions. One, somewhat to our surprise, Hydergine indeed assists mental function slightly better than a placebo. Two, the drug was more likely to help people with vascular dementia than those with Alzheimer's. (Interestingly, physicians in Germany are more likely to use Hydergine for Alzheimer's than for vascular dementia, exactly opposite to what the research seems to support.) Three, the benefits were seen more often with high doses, especially doses *above 4 mg a day* (the standard dose is only 3 mg a day). A truly effective dose of Hydergine, Olin and Schneider proposed, might be *much* higher than the standard dose, and really helping people might take doses up to 9 mg a day—*three times* the standard. This finding makes us wonder whether researchers have been getting inconsistent results with Hydergine because they've been using the wrong dose.

Can Hydergine prevent memory loss in healthy people? In a rare model of clinical research stamina, someone tried to find out. The project was begun in Basel, Switzerland, in 1976. Almost 150 elderly volunteers were recruited; all agreed to take either Hydergine or a placebo on a daily basis. Five years later those taking Hydergine actually performed better on some parts of an IQ test, though the difference was so small that it could have been due simply to chance. This is the sort of result that drives neurologists crazy. Here's one of the only prospective studies of neuroprotection in the history of medicine, and the results are inconclusive! If the research group had included 1,000 people rather than 150, we all might be taking Hydergine today. It didn't. We don't.

Given all the promising evidence, I'd bet that *some* people would be better off if they took Hydergine. Folks with atherosclerosis or narrow carotid arteries would seem most likely to benefit. But as more and more people take aspirin or other antiplatelet drugs on a regular basis (not to mention ginkgo), the addition of Hydergine becomes riskier since it might increase the risk of bleeding. The bottom line: thirty years of prescribing have gone by, and we still cannot recommend this drug in good conscience because no one has done an adequate study and found an effective dose. Until such a study is done (come on, you Hydergine researchers!), taking Hydergine to prevent CVC and ARN is a shaky bet.

Piracetam and Hydergine are just two of the nootropic smart drugs. I've given them special attention because they are widely used in many places in the world, and because they are representative of the whole smart drug dilemma, a tale of half-finished research and tantalizing conclusions. But they're hardly alone. Dozens of synthetic compounds are vying for the front position in the smart drug race. Here are the other top competitors.

OTHER PROMISING "SMART" NOOTROPICS

One of the most interesting new agents—a compound that perhaps falls somewhere between a nootropic and a neuroprotective agent—is *phosphatidylserine.* We all need phosphatidylserine for thinking; it's one of the lipids that make up the membranes of every brain cell. In multiple experiments, doses of phosphatidylserine have helped defend old rats against memory loss. These experiments are so persuasive that thirty-five clinical trials with phosphatidylserine have already been done. The best study was conducted by psychologist Tom Crook, who enrolled 149 older men and women who had mild memory loss. After three months, the oldest folks in this group were better at recognizing faces, recalling stories, and remembering telephone numbers—all useful, real-life benefits.

But there's a fly in the ointment. These studies used a type of phosphatidylserine that was derived from cows; at this point, doctors can't give it to anyone because of the concern that it might infect people with mad cow disease (bovine spongiform encephalopathy). While a new soy-based form of phosphatidylserine is available, no one knows if it will offer the same benefits. The bottom line: large-scale research with humans using the new formulation is needed before I can recommend taking this very promising drug.

Vinpocetine is another nootropic that's been used by European doctors for decades. In the lab, it truly has brain-beneficial effects, such as improving cerebral blood flow, helping neurons recover from strokes, and blocking the calcium overflow that can kill neurons in a matter of seconds. But human trials have yet to show that vinpocetine offers a mind-enhancing benefit. *Pyritinol* is yet another nootropic, most popular in Germany. A few studies suggest that it helps animals overcome injuries to the exact part of the frontal lobe that produces acetylcholine, a problem similar to Alzheimer's. But again, the human research is weak.

My conclusion: *all* of these drugs show great promise in the lab, but *none* of them has been conclusively proven to boost thinking abilities in humans. At this point, the nootropics are bunched like racehorses on the far turn of the track; there's no telling which one will break out of the pack and be the first to win the title of "safe and effective for saving the brain."

Personally, I would set aside the whole notion of using nootropics to boost brain function beyond normal. The focus on this highfalutin goal, I believe, has distracted researchers from investigating a much more realistic possibility: that these drugs *help protect us from cognitive decline.* Considering what's at stake—the fast-growing epidemic of memory loss—it's time for some serious NIH-sponsored research into nootropics.

Growth Factors

When I first heard the term *nerve growth factor* in neurobiology class, like all my classmates, I felt a momentary thrill; it sounded like manna for the mind. "Don't be misled by the name," the professor shook his head, reading our very thoughts. "Unfortunately, you can't take nerve growth factor to bulk up your brain." As it turns out, my professor may have spoken too soon.

Nerve growth factor (NGF) is a classic *neurotrophin*. Neurotrophins are small proteins that promote the growth and survival of neurons. One of their main jobs is to guide neurons toward one another during fetal development, a sort of "come hither" signal that attracts growing neurons as the sun attracts vines. But the name *nerve growth factor* is somewhat misleading, because NGF can also work as a neurotransmitter, promote the survival of white blood cells, and even help to control inflammation. In fact, neuroscientists are starting to think of NGF in a new way—not just as a promoter of neuronal growth but as a jack-of-all-trades protein that plays many roles throughout the body and brain.

Could NGF work as a smart drug? After all, NGF levels decline as we age, and so does cognition, so it seems reasonable to speculate that supplemental NGF might help restore the youthful function of aging brains. This still looks like a good bet, although neurobiologist Eliot Mufson has found evidence that Alzheimer's is more a matter of inadequate *receptors* for NGF. If memory loss is indeed due to the decline in NGF *receptors,* then treating older people with NGF would be akin to shouting at the deaf: we would be increasing the signal but ignoring the real problem of a weakened receiver. Nonetheless, the evidence that nerve growth factor provides lab animals with a cognitive boost is so plentiful that neuroscientists continue to investigate how to give supplemental NGF to humans.

For a clinical trial, what would be the right dose of NGF? Experimenting in the rodent lab with different doses, Mayo Clinic neuroscientist Anna Conti found that a low dose actually produced the best neuron growth, while higher doses actually *inhibited* growth. Some human experiments may be failing because of excessive dosing, she cautioned. This may be another example of the Goldilocks Effect: too much or too little NGF hurts the brain; we need the "just right" dose to help neurons grow—and we have to be very careful to avoid overdoing it when we give NGF supplements to people.

NGF may be a boon for the aging mind, but delivering this huge, ungainly molecule into the human brain can be a problem. NGF is a *really* big protein. Normally if we swallow a big protein in a pill, it gets broken down in the stomach; if we inject it, it's usually stymied from entering the brain by the blood-brain barrier. Furthermore, a short course of neurotrophins won't do the job. We need some way to deliver NGF constantly—perhaps for many years—to keep neurons in peak condition through late adulthood. Still, the promise of NGF supplementation is so enticing that scientists are currently testing multiple ways to get this molecule into the brain.

One option is to use an infusion pump: drill a hole in the head, insert a plastic catheter, and hook it up to an NGF pump like the ones used for intravenous lines. But infusion pumps are awkward. They need periodic refilling and pose the risk of infection. The second alternative is to use cell transplanation. Researchers at the University of Rochester School of Medicine have already taken discarded human fetal cells and engineered them to produce mouse NGF. These hybrid cells could potentially be transplanted into the brain in the same way that fetal dopamine–making cells are already transplanted into the brains of Parkinson's patients. A third option is to put NGF in plastic capsules and insert them into the brain. Neuroscientist Jeffrey Kordower was among the first to try rescuing the neurons in this way: he genetically modified cells from baby hamsters so that they would make human NGF, then encapsulated the cells in plastic—essentially creating tiny NGF factories. Next, he inserted these plastic capsules into the brains of six monkeys that had previously had brain surgery that left them with memory loss. Amazingly, *nearly normal brain function was restored.* Encapsulated NGF can also cause normal cells to grow bigger than normal. My old professor may have to eat his words: NGF supplements may in fact be able to bulk up the human brain.

Still, all of these options for getting NGF into the brain are far too invasive to be recommended for healthy people. In my opinion, they would be justifiable only for very severe brain disease or toward the end of life. NGF supplements would become much more attractive if we could get them into the brain without opening the head.

Several clever solutions to this problem have already been developed. First, neurobiologist Cristina Backman has figured out a way to allow NGF to ride along with iron, like a hitchhiker, and sneak into the brain. This trick successfully delivered NGF into the brains of rats, restoring damaged neurons to completely normal function—an impressive feat. Japanese researchers use a different approach: they've discovered that the two drugs idebenone and propentofylline act as "NGF synthesis boosters"; feeding these agents to rats turns on the brain's own NGF production and restores mental performance after a brain injury. And perhaps the best news comes from the Alzheimer's Disease Cooperative Study group, which has been working with an experimental smart drug with the code name AIT-082. This drug is especially interesting because it not only protects animal brains from degeneration but *restores* working memory in old mice. Apparently, AIT-082 works by boosting the brain's production of NGF and other growth factors, leading to luxuriant sprouting of new neuronal connections. When the study group tried this drug in healthy elderly people in 1998, it seemed to *improve both their memories and their speed of information processing*—one of the most promising smart-drug experiments ever done. This NGF-stimulation approach may turn out to be the best bet for humans over the next decade.

By whatever means, getting NGF into the brain is a genuinely thrilling new avenue for protecting and enhancing brain function. It has already been used in clinical trials for patients with Alzheimer's. If the noninvasive approach proves successful, some people may soon be taking a mild drug that will turn on their brain's own powers of growth and healing.

A number of other neurotrophins might also work as smart drugs, including BDNF (brain-derived neurotrophic factor), CNTF (ciliary neurotrophic factor), and TGF-beta 1 (transforming growth factor-beta 1). TGF-beta 1 is especially promising because it seems to fight the effects of beta-amyloid. But, apart from NGF, the growth factor that's causing the most excitement these days is ILGF-1 (insulinlike growth factor-1).

ILGF-1 levels decline with age, which some scientists propose may contribute to the aging-related decline in our mental powers; boosting our ILGF-1 levels accordingly, might make us smarter. And in fact, some studies have shown that this growth factor has a positive impact on cognition. For instance, when scientists at Johns Hopkins University implanted pumps in the brains of both young and old rats to deliver ILGF-1, not only did it improve memory, it reversed some aging-related changes in emotional responses, making us wonder whether ILGF-1 might help older people to resist depression. Indeed, the fact that ILGF-1 boosted memory in *young healthy animals* is one of the first discoveries of its kind.

While growth factor therapy for the human brain is not quite ready for prime time, the research is moving very fast. Initially, it will be used to treat brain degeneration. But neurotrophins may soon offer adults a safe and easy way to improve their capacity for thought, a genuine—and rather unsettling—possibility.

Drugs That Boost a Neurotransmitter

"Doctor," she began tentatively, "I have a question."

Susan is the daughter of one of my Alzheimer's patients. She is also one of the people who got me thinking about writing this book, since she posed such compelling questions about how she might avoid her mother's fate. "I guess I should have asked you first, but, you know"—she laughed—"I just thought it might perk up my brain a bit. So . . . well, I sort of took some of my mother's tacrine."

Neurologists too have considered the possibility of using drugs like tacrine to "perk up the brain": not as Susan had done, borrowing a prescription drug from a demented relative, but as a perfectly legitimate choice to enhance human memory. This possibility fell out naturally from the important discovery in the 1970s that *cholinergic function* (the actions of the neurotransmitter acetylcholine) is extremely low in people with Alzheimer's. Suddenly the conclusion was "Aha! Alzheimer's is caused by a lack of acetylcholine!" and the search was on for a cholinergic treatment. But some doctors have also been murmuring quietly about a more daring possibility: using cholinergic drugs to enhance thinking abilities.

We can't take acetylcholine itself; if we swallowed it, it would be dissolved in the stomach, and if we injected it, it would never make it past the blood-brain barrier. But we do have three promising methods of cholinergic treatment: give the building blocks of acetylcholine; give drugs that mimic acetylcholine; and boost acetylcholine levels with drugs that block the natural breakdown of this neurotransmitter (the method that has already become standard therapy for Alzheimer's).

BETTER BRAINS THROUGH BOOSTING BUILDING BLOCKS

As we saw in Chapter 11, we make acetylcholine in our brains from choline and lecithin. Taking choline or lecithin has failed again and again to help cognition, but researchers have had more success with a new agent called *citicoline.*

Citicoline is one of the ingredients in *phosphatidylcholine,* our main dietary source of choline. In a large number of animal experiments, citicoline has been shown to boost the production of acetylcholine, to help build cell membranes, and to improve neuronal signaling. To test whether humans might reap practical benefits, neuroscientist Richard Wurtman at the Massachusetts Institute of Technology conducted a placebo-controlled trial with 95 older men and women. For the volunteers who started out with below-average memory, citicoline indeed improved their ability to remember a short story. One study is not enough, but if several large-scale studies confirm this result, we could soon be using this cholinergic building block to save people who are on the edge of dementia.

BETTER BRAINS THROUGH MIMICKING ACETYLCHOLINE

When acetylcholine is released by a "sending" neuron, it floats across the synapse and binds to its receptors on the "receiving" neuron like a key in a lock. Many scientists have suggested, "Hey, let's boost memory by giving people a drug that mimics acetylcholine by binding to cholinergic receptors!" That's a great idea in theory, but it's a little tricky in practice.

There are basically two types of acetylcholine receptors, nicotinic and muscarinic. We call the first one a *nicotinic* receptor because nicotine turns out to be the perfect stimulant for this receptor. Nicotine actually boosts some aspects of cognition temporarily, and some evidence indicates that nicotine may slightly delay brain aging. We can't use nicotine as a smart drug because it's extremely addictive, but new *non*nicotine drugs that act on the same receptors look very promising in preliminary experiments. Still, most of the research on mimicking acetylcholine has focused on drugs that bind to the other type of receptor, the *muscarinic* receptor, especially the subtype called the *M1 receptor.* Some of the drugs that bind to M1 receptors are a hundred times as powerful as the current treatments for Alzheimer's. Several of these new M1 drugs are already in human clinical trials.

By 2004 one or more of these new muscarinic or nicotinic drugs may be proven safe and effective for Alzheimer's. Once that occurs, there could be increasing pressure to try these molecular mimics to enhance cognitive function in normal healthy people. My own bet is that they *will* work, but only for people who are already sliding toward the edge of the Alzheimer's cliff—people who've lost thousands of their cholinergic neurons and are beginning to become forgetful.

BETTER BRAINS THROUGH BLOCKING THE BREAKDOWN
OF ACETYLCHOLINE

Neurology professors used to give lectures, flashing 35 mm slides that divided dementias into "treatable" on one side and Alzheimer's on the other. Then in the 1990s came a very happy inconvenience for us: the FDA approved several revolutionary new medications. We all had to remake our lecture slides; Alzheimer's is now a treatable disease.

The reason for this wonderful progress is the arrival of *acetylcholinesterase inhibitors* (AchEIs). It's easy to see why AchEIs might help: when a neuron sprays acetylcholine into the synaptic cleft, it has only a short time to make it across to the "receiving" neuron. Any acetylcholine left floating in the cleft is quickly broken down by a chemical called acetylcholinesterase. AchEIs inhibit acetylcholinesterase, allowing acetylcholine to survive longer and promote memory better. In more than two hundred studies, AchEIs have proven their worth as safe and effective treatments for Alzheimer's.

The currently approved AchEIs include tacrine (Cognex), donepezil (Aricept), rivastigmine (Exelon), and galantamine (Reminyl). All of them do a great job of inhibiting acetylcholinesterase, and galantamine has the extra benefit of helping to regulate nicotinic signaling. On *average,* these medications don't really boost brain function; they merely slow down the decline enough that patients remain independent for an extra eight months or so. But from the first experiments with AchEIs, it was clear that different people can have very different results: some get no benefit at all, while others actually get a *boost* in memory. Could this be a real "smart drug" effect, in the sense of boosting brain power? That's doubtful, because it seems to work only for people who are running low on acetylcholine. Healthy young adults do not have this problem—which is one reason I advised Susan not to take her mother's tacrine.

But there's a new twist in the plot: in addition to providing temporary relief of dementia, we're beginning to suspect that these drugs actually *protect* the brain from ARNAT and Alzheimer's.

Marty Farlow, a professor of neurology, is tree-tall, Santa-bearded, and about as deeply involved in clinical Alzheimer's research as any living neurologist. He and his colleagues at the University of Indiana asked a question that seemed to come out of left field: could AChEIs save neurons from beta-amyloid? In other words, put aside for a second all this concern about revving up cholinergic function; look instead at whether these drugs can alter the underlying process of ARNAT. The answer turned out to be, tentatively, yes. In Dr. Farlow's experiments, cholinergic treatments truly defended neurons against the attack of amyloid. The question from out of left field has started a whole new ballgame. The finding that these drugs may have neuroprotective effects opens up the possibility that *healthy adults could take AchEIs to prevent brain aging*.

It's too soon for doctors to recommend AChEIs for healthy young adults, but it's not too soon for Susan and me—and perhaps several million other people—to push for research to investigate this exciting possibility. The recent discovery that cholinergic drugs may save the brain from beta-amyloid completely changes our expectations. All of a sudden we're not just looking at treating dementia, we're looking at arming the brain against aging and *preventing the long and natural decline in memory*. That's not a theory you can test with the typical six-week drug trial; six years is more like it.

Increasingly, researchers will need brave, healthy volunteers to participate in well-designed studies of *preventive* brain-saving treatments. We will probably offer these treatments first to people who are more likely to develop Alzheimer's, such as those who carry the *APOE-ε4* gene or those who have many close relatives with Alzheimer's. Susan fits that profile; in addition to her mother, she has two aunts and an uncle in nursing homes, their minds ravaged and lost to dementia. Toward the end of our conversation, Susan made it very clear to me: when NIH begins to fund studies of cholinergic medications for healthy young adults, she'll volunteer in a minute.

AMPAKINES

When you hear Gary Lynch lecture, with his encyclopedic knowledge of the brain and his laser intensity, you know the cure for memory loss is right around the corner. In his lab at the University of California at Irvine, Dr. Lynch has spent decades figuring out the chemistry of memory. But rather than working on acetylcholine, he's focused on a different neurotransmitter that's equally important to memory: glutamate. Recall that glutamate is the transmitter that carries new information to the hippocampal memory cells. Every time you commit something to memory, from the name of your congressman to the location of your glasses, you depend on glutamate to bind to its receptors. Lynch has proposed that *ampakines*—newly created drugs that bind to the AMPA type of glutamate receptor—might boost human memory.

He's got some proof to back up his theory: research in multiple labs has shown that ampakines improve cognition in several species. For instance, neurologist Kelvin Yamada has found that ampakines boost cognition in both rats and monkeys. Based on this preliminary work, in a series of experiments collaborating with doctors at the Karolinska Institute in Sweden, Dr. Lynch gave ampakines to human volunteers. He showed that ampakines enhance four kinds of memory: visual memories, recognition of odors, maze learning, and remembering the location and identity of playing cards. This work has sent a shiver of excitement through the usually cautious neuroscience community.

But all is not roses. Dr. Yamada and other scientists warn that under some conditions ampakines *increase neuronal death*. This seems to be the damned-if-you-do, damned-if-you-don't type of drug: you can boost AMPA function and improve memory, but you risk killing the very neurons you need for memory. That's why the currently available ampakines are a poor bet. A new generation of these drugs is on the way; these may allow us to tread the treacherous path to safe and lasting cognitive benefits.

THE PROZAC SURPRISE

When it comes right down to it, almost every neurotransmitter plays a role in memory, and experimental drugs that work on those transmitters have been shown to boost memory in the lab. You may hear about drugs called *benzodiazepine inverse agonists,* which work with the GABA system. You may also soon hear about smart drugs called *5 HT3 receptor-blockers,* which work with serotonin. You can't get a prescription for any of these drugs today; it may be a decade before the FDA approves them for human use. But astonishingly, a serotonin drug *is* now available in every neighborhood pharmacy, one that might permanently enhance the powers of the brain: Prozac.

Princeton psychologist Barry Jacobs is sometimes known as "Mr. Serotonin" because he's studied the serotonin system in cats and other animals for many years. By coincidence, his office neighbor is professor of neurobiology Elizabeth Gould, who is famous as one of the first to show that adult animals create new neurons in their old brains (neurogenesis). Dr. Jacobs got to talking with Dr. Gould, and they were both curious to know what effect serotonin-boosting drugs such as Prozac might have on neurogenesis. To their mutual surprise, when they gave Prozac to rats and measured the impact on neurogenesis, they found that the Prozac-treated rats made *70 percent more neurons*! And surprising news about Prozac just keeps popping up. In 2001, a University of Pennsylvania study of

3,600 smokers showed that those taking Prozac, Zoloft, or other serotonin-reuptake-inhibiting antidepressants had a 65 percent reduction in heart attack risk.

We have to proceed cautiously when we hear such remarkable news. We don't want three generations rushing to buy Prozac on the Internet in the hopes of saving their hearts and building up their brains. But if these findings are confirmed, it will force us to seriously debate who among us should be taking Prozac and similar antidepressants as genuinely mind-expanding drugs.

Amyloid Blockers: The Smartest Drugs of All?

As we saw in Chapter 3, ARNAT and Alzheimer's result when the big amyloid precursor protein (APP) is sliced like a cookie roll in the wrong place, producing a toxic piece called beta-amyloid; the "knives" that slice off the amyloid chunk are enzymes called secretases. While the exact identity of these two molecular knives was unknown, they were given the names *beta-* and *gamma-secretase*. Neuroscientists thought, "All we have to do is identify the beta and gamma cleavage enzymes and stop them from slicing up APP, and we can prevent Alzheimer's." But a major obstacle stood in the way: they couldn't find either one.

Then in 1999, in a momentous convergence of efforts, four different drug companies independently found the actual chemical structure of beta-secretase. Scientists now call this enzyme *BACE*, short for *beta-site amyloid cleavage enzyme*. The discovery of BACE gives us, for the first time in history, an extremely promising target for the development of drugs to fight Alzheimer's. Neuroscientists are also fast narrowing the search for the second knife that cleaves APP, the *GACE* or *gamma-site amyloid cleavage enzyme*. A tire-burning race is now under way between the big pharmaceutical companies to find good, safe inhibitors of BACE and GACE. Such a drug could potentially block the manufacture of beta-amyloid and save us all from Alzheimer's.

At this writing, BACE inhibitors are already being manufactured. Within several years, they will be tested on humans. We have to cross our fingers; we don't know whether these new drugs will work, and we don't know that BACE and GACE inhibitors won't produce bizarre and undesirable side effects. But it's hard to overstate the promise of this advance.

Then in 2000 an even more astonishing advance was made: the world had its first glimpse of an Alzheimer's vaccine. My car radio was tuned too low for me to hear clearly, but the phrase "vaccine for Alzheimer's disease" came through loud and clear. I waved pleasantly to the tanned fellow whose BMW I had nearly rear-ended, then turned up the volume.

Dale Schenk of Elan Pharmaceuticals and his colleagues had done an experiment so simple but so clearly hopeless that no one had bothered to try it before. They got some mice that had been genetically engineered to develop the amyloid plaques of Alzheimer's disease, then injected them with beta-amyloid. This provoked the mice to make *antibodies* against beta-amyloid. On July 8, 1999, Schenk announced the results: the majority of mice had virtually no plaques in their brains. If the mice were young when they got the treatment, plaques never formed. And if the mice were old—their brains peppered with plaques—*the treatment took the plaques away*! Alzheimer's researchers were thunderstruck. "This is wild and amazing," said Sangram Sisodia. "Conceivably," said Marcelle Morrison-Bogorad of the National Institute on Aging, "you could immunize people against Alzheimer's disease." Phase I trials for safety in normal volunteers went well; at least, no one got sick. By 2001, Alzheimer's patients were getting the vaccine on an experimental basis. But by 2002, it became clear that something was going very wrong: a half-dozen of the patients developed a terrifying condition called "encephalitis," or brain inflammation.

What went wrong? One possibility is that an Alzheimer's vaccine is a pipe dream. Alzheimer's is not a classic immune invasion or infection, so the very idea of a vaccine may be off base. Yet neuroscientists are fervently hoping we can go back to the drawing board, fix the problem, and make a vaccine that can help people as much as it helps mice—potentially the smartest drug of all.

We are pushing the envelope, on the verge of a breakthrough in the use of smart drugs to assist human brain function. Neuroscientists must learn more before doctors routinely prescribe these very promising drugs, and everyone involved must proceed with caution to assure safety and efficacy. And obviously, we must seriously consider the ethical and philosophical question: what will it mean to society to have truly effective prescriptions to boost brain power? Your family doctor is not quite ready to give you a cocktail of ginkgo, Hydergine, Aricept, and Prozac based on the rapidly growing evidence of brain-saving, mind-enhancing effects. But don't blink; we're getting there fast.

The Alzheimer's vaccine is a few years off, but our amazing immune systems can help to save our brains from aging-related changes in simpler ways even now. You don't need to turn to botanicals or newly discovered smart drugs. You can already do the job with medications that have been available for more than a hundred years: anti-inflammatories.

CHAPTER 15

More Good News: Anti-inflammatories Help Save Your Brain

Annabelle, a fourth-year medical student, was confident. She'd spent nearly a year on the wards and had seen a lot. She wanted to see the new clinic patient on her own, then present the case to me. How could I argue? Freedom is the best professor.

Clinic visits are typically about twenty minutes long. Annabelle came back to the conference room more than an hour later, her confidence waning. She seemed not to know where to begin. "Ah . . ." she said slowly, "I think there are a couple things going on." Not for her the sterile clinical bullet "This is an eighty-six-year-old Caucasian female with a history of rheumatoid arthritis since age forty-five . . ." *A couple things.* Her candid confusion was in fact exactly right, for no simple accounting could do justice to the dazzling complexity of Mrs. Molnar.

Mrs. Molnar had arthritis. Her nerves were tunneling through such fiercely contorted masses of overgrown bone, from her spine to the tips of her toes, that it had become almost impossible to say where they were most compressed, and which compression most desperately needed intervention so that maybe she could dress herself for another year or two. Mrs. Molnar had done her best to help Annabelle. She had asked the student for a pen; then, barely controlling it with the gnarled thing that was her hand, she had drawn little diagrams on her own arm. "This is the C6 dermatome," she'd explained, "and this area here is where the external cutaneous nerve goes." So Mrs. Molnar had offered the student a couple of surprises. One, patients rarely give doctors neuroanatomy lessons, but Mrs. Molnar had been a nursing instructor. Two, we often expect eighty-six-year-old people to be somewhat cognitively impaired, but Mrs. Molnar was crystal clear. Her mind—trapped in her crippled, twisted, arthritis-shackled body—was a diamond.

Mrs. Molnar is not alone. Controlling for age, education, and a host of other factors, older people with arthritis are *on average* more likely than those without arthritis to be mentally sharp. And this has given us a vital clue about how to keep other minds sharp too.

One way scientists study cognitive loss is to look at large groups of people who have been taking certain medicines over many years and compare their thinking abilities with those who have not. People with arthritis often take anti-inflammatories. Anti-inflammatories include *steroids* and *nonsteroidal anti-inflammatories* (known by the popular abbreviation NSAIDs). NSAIDs include over-the-counter drugs such as aspirin and low-dose ibuprofen, as well as a large number of prescription drugs such as Motrin (prescription-strength ibuprofen), Indocin (indomethacin), and Naprosyn (naproxen). Multiple studies have found that older people with arthritis are less likely to suffer from dementia than people of the same age who do not have arthritis. This discovery, first noted in the early 1990s, led to the logical question: does arthritis somehow protect the brain, or does the *medication* most arthritics take—anti-inflammatories—protect the brain? If it's the medication, could *anyone* take anti-inflammatories and get some protection from the creeping ravages of aging-related memory loss? The answer—as neurologists have been excited to discover—is a highly probable yes.

Twins

At the tail end of the 1980s, epidemiologist Joe Rogers reviewed the medical records of more than 4,000 veterans in the Puget Sound Veterans Administration system. He made a startling finding: among veterans with rheumatoid arthritis, the incidence of Alzheimer's was roughly five times lower than the incidence among nonarthritic veterans. It was he who first speculated that the difference might be due to the fact that people with arthritis regularly use anti-inflammatory medications.

Other scientists initially greeted his important insight with skepticism. At that time, it was almost unheard of to discuss Alzheimer's as an inflammatory disease. As one renowned authority remarked, "You think Alzheimer's is like arthritis of the brain? Nothing will come of this." Other doctors also raised the important point that perhaps the anti-inflammatories were not responsible for the difference in the rate of dementia; perhaps the difference came about because those with rheumatoid arthritis had some serendipitous lowering in genetic vulnerability to Alzheimer's. A more convincing study was needed, one that could figure out whether brain preservation among people with arthritis was due to drugs or genes. The best study would compare genetically identical people—ideally, twins. This leads us to the historic contribution of John Breitner.

I first met John at a conference by the sea. Round-faced, dark-haired, and built like a drum, John is one of the world's leading experts on twins and Alzheimer's. We were at a twins symposium at a hotel overlooking the sunny harbor of Redondo Beach, California. He was reporting a simple study: he had found 50 elderly twin pairs—genetically identical twins—in which one twin had Alzheimer's and the other didn't. After exploring all the factors that might explain why one twin developed this problem while the other was spared, he could find only one significant difference: the spared twin had arthritis, used an anti-inflammatory drug, or both. Was it the anti-inflammatory medication or some effect of the arthritis itself that was protecting the brain? He controlled for the presence of arthritis—and the association between better cognition and anti-inflammatories was still there. From that point on, the neurological community has been getting excited about the revolutionary idea that inflammation plays an important part in Alzheimer's—so anti-inflammatories may help protect our aging brains.

Dr. Breitner's study was published in 1994. It was the first of many. Twenty-three retrospective studies from nine countries have all reached the same conclusion: people who have used anti-inflammatories tend to show a lower prevalence of memory loss. One of the best: Walter Stewart, looking at almost 1,700 adults enrolled in the Baltimore Longitudinal Study of Aging, found not only that people taking NSAIDs had a lower risk of Alzheimer's but that the longer they took them, the lower their risk: those who used NSAIDs for less than two years had a 35 percent risk reduction, while those who used them for two or more years at any point in their lives had an impressive *60 percent* risk reduction. The other potentially important finding of Dr. Stewart's project was that ibuprofen and similar NSAIDs seemed more potent than aspirin as a defense against Alzheimer's.

To be fair, studies in Boston, Australia, and France found no cognitive advantage among those taking anti-inflammatories. At the very least, the conflicting results from all these studies must give us pause about the whole business of retrospective research. Here we are, bunching together observations on people of various ages, sexes, races, and medical conditions, with or without vascular disease, with or without various genetic risk factors for ARN, who have taken any of more than a dozen different anti-inflammatories at low, medium, or high doses for anywhere between a week and perhaps fifty years—and trying to conclude something about the power of these medicines to stave off dementia. It's remarkable that anything at all washes out from panning for gold in such a muddy stream. Still, the overwhelming preponderance of such research (fourteen out of fifteen studies in one review) tells us that taking anti-inflammatories lowers the risk of dementia for both women and men.

Even more encouraging was a British study by Martin Prince at London's Institute of Psychiatry. Rather than looking at the incidence of Alzheimer's disease—which is, after all, just an extreme part of the spectrum of ARNAT—he looked at more subtle decline in memory, the type of decline that inevitably affects us all. Among more than 2,600 people age sixty-five or older, those who were taking NSAIDs over a two-and-a-half-year period of observation showed less decline. The youngest people in the group—those studied at age sixty-five—showed the biggest benefit. This does not necessarily mean that NSAIDs don't help older people. But since both the Rotterdam Study and the Prince Study showed that younger folks seemed to get more of a benefit, we may need to take anti-inflammatories before brain damage has gotten too far along if we want to use them to help save our brains. This might be called the "early bird" hypothesis of anti-inflammatory brain protection. And this seems to be borne out by perhaps the most promising proof of all: Bas in't Veld and colleagues in the Rotterdam Study group did an impressive seven-year-long study of almost 7,000 healthy people over age fifty-five. In 2001, they reported in the *New England Journal of Medicine* that the protective effect of anti-inflammatories seems tightly tied to how long the medications are used. People who used NSAIDs for one to twenty-three months had a 17 percent lower risk of Alzheimer's, *but people who used these drugs for more than two years had an 80 percent lower risk.* What's more, almost all the benefit seemed to go to those who took their NSAIDs more than two years before the onset of memory loss. This strongly supports the early bird hypothesis—that you need to take these brain-saving medications well before ARNAT turns into Alzheimer's if you want to protect your mind.

But what does inflammation have to do with aging-related brain deterioration? Naysayers notwithstanding, during twenty years of intensive study it has become clear that inflammation is a major factor in the slow and silent brain assault of ARNAT.

Professional Killers Roaming Your Brain

Your body has superb defenses against any potential offending agent. One is the immune system, which can generate either a *specific* reaction to an

alien protein (the so-called antigen/antibody reaction) or a *nonspecific* reaction to any substance that looks as if it might cause trouble. Either way,
whenever the body launches an assault with its arsenal of immune defensive
weapons, the result is a local firefight. That firefight is called inflammation.

Inflammation typically involves pain, heat, redness, swelling, and increased movement of fluid across the walls of blood vessels. Special cells
swarm to the site of inflammation to swallow up invaders, and dozens of
chemicals assist, known as *inflammatory mediators*. Perhaps the most familiar of these mediators are the *histamines,* which make our noses run
when the pollen count is high. While histamines are not currently thought
to play a major role in dementia, four other inflammatory mediators
probably do play a role; we call them the Four Musketeers of Inflammation: the *inflammatory cytokines,* the *arachidonic acid metabolites,* the
acute phase reactants, and the *complement system.*

Cytokines ferry messages to help the immune response, and the *inflammatory cytokines* in particular seem to boost inflammation in
ARNAT. The *arachidonic acid metabolites* are probably the main targets
of our most popular anti-inflammatory drugs; evidence suggests that they
are probably involved in Alzheimer's. The *acute phase reactants* are chemicals that flit through the bloodstream to the site of the inflammatory firefight, where they help destroy the invader; they too seem to feed the fire
of ARNAT. But the real firebrand among the Four Musketeers is the *complement system.* The complement system fights offending agents using a
special weapon called the *membrane attack complex* (MAC)—a biological flame-thrower that essentially burns a hole in the cell membrane, exposing the delicate interior and allowing calcium to flood in to poison the
cell. The complement system also plays a second and equally important
role; it marks foreign invaders for attack by professional killer cells
known as *microglia.*

Microglia are tiny but potent cells that roam the brain looking for
trouble. When they spot a target, such as a plaque, a tangle, or a damaged
neuron, they attack it using a machine-gun spray of nitric oxide (which
produces some really nasty free radicals), or they surround it with gluey
arms and eat it by sucking it into an enzymatic chamber of death. Think
of microglia as mercenaries recruited by the Four Musketeers to help battle invaders.

The details of the inflammatory response sound devilish, but the big picture of inflammation is straightforward: chemicals boost the inflammatory
process, and killer cells leap into the area to wipe out offending agents and
clear debris.

But inflammation is not always in the body's best interest. For one thing, many people's bodies have an unfortunate tendency to mistake parts of themselves for invaders and to launch self-destructive attacks; this is what happens in the self-immune or *autoimmune* diseases such as rheumatoid arthritis. For another thing, *inflammation* is a truly evocative name for the scorching nature of the immune attack. Like a flame-thrower swung wildly in battle, the fire of inflammation may inadvertently singe or kill surrounding healthy tissue. And that's where we may find the connection to aging-related memory loss. Early in life the Four Musketeers and their mercenary microglia partners—the rough knights of inflammation—mostly protect us, wielding that flame-thrower with care. But as we get older, they begin to do us more harm than good. Out-of-control inflammation and microglia are in fact important to producing ARNAT and Alzheimer's.

Imagine that you are on a tour of your aging brain. Many of your neurons look perfectly healthy. Others are beginning to show the wear and tear of decades of use, with compromised blood flow, too many free radicals to handle, accumulating DNA damage, a tendency to get overexcited by neurotransmitters, and two special changes that are considered hallmarks of ARNAT: misfolded beta-amyloid, leading to plaques, and misfolded tau, leading to tangles. Sensitive scientific methods have now revealed that both plaques and tangles contain many markers of inflammation. Plaques, in particular, are just brimming with them: cytokines, prostaglandins, acute phase reactants, the deadly MAC flame-thrower—all of these features of inflammation and others have been identified in the pink amyloid plaques that bloom like bomb-strikes around damaged neurons. Beta-amyloid may even use the biological flame-thrower of the complement system as its weapon of choice to hurt brain cells. Most important of all, microglia—the brain's roaming professional killers—are prominent in Alzheimer's-type plaques. It's now thought that microglia play the key role in attacking neurons near plaques. Once these killer cells have been attracted into the area, they release a withering and sometimes deadly barrage of neurotoxins.

I'm not talking here about a classic autoimmune disease like rheumatoid arthritis or lupus. In those conditions, the attack on normal tissue is carried out by immunoglobulins. Immunoglobulins are not involved in the brain-barbecue of ARNAT, so Alzheimer's is not exactly "arthritis of the brain." A slightly different type of chronic, self-destructive inflammation simmers in our aging brains—a local attack on ourselves that gets out of hand. The Four Musketeers mean well. They see a plaque or a tangle, and they say, "Zounds—here's an invader! Call out the microglia!" But their fiery response goes awry, and neurons in the vicinity get badly burned as part of the collateral damage. We can't feel it; the brain has no pain-sensitive neurons. So unlike arthritis, the attack goes undetected—until dementia has us in its iron grip.

Not every brain will suffer such inflammation to the same degree. Whether you will get a small, adaptive inflammatory response or a big, fiery, maladaptive response depends on many individual factors. Among people with hypertension, diabetes, head trauma, poor diet, or even emotional stress, the risks of the inflammatory firefight may go up; they may go down among those taking estrogen, which is known to fight this exact type of inflammation. And the risks probably depend on several *inflammatory risk factor genes*: although most of us carry the benign *APOE-ε3* allele, about 17 percent carry *APOE-ε4*, the allele that markedly increases the risk of Alzheimer's. It's possible that the *APOE-ε3* protein can block inflammation, while the ε4 protein cannot. ε4's failure to save our brains from inflammation may be one reason that people with ε4 alleles are at higher risk for memory loss. New research suggests that many *other* inflammatory genes can influence our risk of Alzheimer's—and even our risk of strokes—which helps to explain why some of us will go for many years without showing memory loss and others burn out large swaths of neurons and become forgetful earlier in adulthood.

The evidence for the role of inflammation in Alzheimer's is now overwhelming. If we inject beta-amyloid into a rat's brain, it attracts and activates microglia. Microglia that have been activated in this way release inflammatory cytokines and free radicals, killing neighboring neurons—a clear link between Alzheimer's-type beta-amyloid, inflammation, and brain cell death. And a classic marker of inflammation called *alpha-1-antichymotrypsin* is elevated in the blood of many Alzheimer's patients, a sign that they are chronically battling inflammation. When I mentioned this discovery to Annabelle in the clinic, she astutely asked, "Could we test a person's blood for that chemical to see whether they have Alzheimer's?"

"Excellent question," I replied. "Unfortunately, lots of other things could make this test positive, so it wouldn't really be a good test for Alzheimer's." But Annabelle's quick question raises an intriguing possibility: maybe we could use a blood test of this kind to identify people who have a *tendency* to produce an excessive inflammatory response. In fact, researchers at Leiden University in the Netherlands recently found evidence that older people whose blood shows signs of an oversize inflammatory response are *thirteen times* as likely to have Alzheimer's. That doesn't necessarily mean that everyone with Alzheimer's is inflammation-prone. But it does mean that we may have a simple way to find inflammation-prone people. These folks could get the biggest brain-saving benefit from anti-inflammatories—and they might be among the first to whom we would offer anti-inflammatory treatment specifically to prevent memory loss.

Finally (and this is the lab research that makes neurologists think that we may have found a terrific avenue leading to effective human therapy), multiple experiments have shown that treating rodents with NSAIDs greatly reduces the signs of brain inflammation. But can anti-inflammatory drugs truly prevent Alzheimer's-type changes in rodents' brains? The answer is a resounding yes: in mice that have been genetically engineered to mimic Alzheimer's, treatment with NSAIDs neatly and consistently undermines the ability of beta-amyloid to fire up inflammation and cause neuronal death. We even have an idea about how NSAIDs accomplish this wonderful brain-saving trick: according to the best-accepted theory, NSAIDs work their anti-Alzheimer's magic by inhibiting the enzyme known as *cyclooxygenase* (COX). Interfering with the action of COX helps to contain the fires of brain inflammation. Put simply, this means that certain NSAIDs might help to prevent Alzheimer's. Which brings us to the heart of the matter: the attempt to save the human brain.

The Acid Test: Prospective Trials

Joe Rogers of the University of Washington was one of the first to give NSAIDs to people with Alzheimer's. In the early 1990s he recruited 28 such patients and treated half of them with indomethacin (Indocin), a popular prescription NSAID, for six months; he gave the other half a placebo. The placebo-treated group declined with time, but the group treated with the NSAID showed a 2 percent improvement. This study was too short and too small to get really excited about, but it certainly made neurologists think: are we missing an opportunity to curb Alzheimer's?

Then the Italians jumped in with another early clinical trial. A group in Padua, while testing the effects of the NSAID etodolac (Lodine) in more than 300 people with arthritis over age sixty, also looked at cognition; a subset of the younger patients in this group showed some cognitive improvement. This may be more evidence of the "early bird" hypothesis that the sooner we begin to fight brain inflammation, the better.

The next step came with an American multicenter trial of anti-inflammatories for Alzheimer's—a study conducted by the huge Alzheimer's Disease Cooperative Study group. The researchers recruited 138 patients and gave half of them placebos and the others low-dose prednisone, a steroid. Unfortunately, this study told us very little about the brain-saving potential of anti-inflammatories, for several reasons. First, despite the fact that prednisone indeed has anti-inflammatory effects, almost *none* of the prior studies suggested that this steroid had ever helped protect the memory of arthritis patients; the vast majority of the exciting results have come instead from studying patients who had taken *non*steroidal anti-inflammatories. Two, prednisone is a powerful glucocorticoid, a hormone with side effects ranging from chemical diabetes to potentially severe mood swings. These side effects make it impossible to prescribe anything beyond absolutely minimal doses of prednisone on a long-term basis to millions of people in the hope of saving the brain. Third, as we've seen in Chapter 5, excess glucocorticoids can poison our hippocampal memory cells—the exact opposite of the effect we want. Fourth, the subjects in this study were demented Alzheimer's patients, not normal healthy adults, so even if the results had been promising, the study could not tell us whether you and I should take this medicine to prevent cognitive loss. As it turned out, the results were far from encouraging: after a year, the prednisone-treated group showed more memory loss and more psychiatric problems such as agitation than the placebo-treated group.

If NSAIDs look more promising than steroids for brain protection, why was this steroid trial even attempted? Frankly, it seems a shame that, at the critical moment when we finally had an inkling of how to save the brain with anti-inflammatories, so much effort was diverted into this steroid cul-de-sac. But this detour was inspired by very real concerns: researchers in the mid-1990s were terrified of the side effects of NSAIDs.

NSAIDs Cause Gastrointestinal Bleeds

Linda sat up in bed, pale as snow, goose bumps dotting her arms, and discreetly pulled the white cotton blanket up to her shoulders and tucked it behind her back. She smiled and started talking about her husband. He was a pilot, on duty that night somewhere over the Atlantic in the cockpit of a Boeing 747. She was a schoolteacher, happy about summer vacation and about seeing her parents who were visiting from Minnesota. Midway through laughing at herself for the nuisance it would cause everyone that she was in the hospital, she vomited a liter of blood. "Oh," she said, looking at the blanket. "Sorry."

When her primary care doctor had prescribed Motrin for her menstrual cramps, he had been trying to help her. She'd been taking the medicine for six months now. Every so often she'd noted some slight stomach discomfort, but it had quickly subsided after an antacid tablet. She had never felt any real abdominal pain or nausea, or noted any change in her bowel movements. Then after tonight's Sunday dinner, she'd suddenly felt sick and brought up a cup of blood. Her sister had rushed her to the emergency room. Linda, like untold thousands of others across the country, was experiencing the most common side effect of NSAIDs: an acute gastrointestinal (GI) bleed.

She almost died that night. I was an intern and sort of knew what to do, although I'd never done it. Her hematocrit, the measure of red cells remaining in her bloodstream, should have been forty; it was eighteen. I got her IV running like mad to support her fluid volume, typed and crossed her for four units of packed red cells, and inserted a large-bore tube into her stomach to lavage (wash) it and to monitor further blood loss, during all of which, in the most astounding mix of denial, sunny temperament, and imperturbability, she never stopped giggling. The surgeons were paged immediately. Endoscopy was done quickly and showed a massive bleeding ulcer in her stomach. In the morning after surgery she was comatose, partly from blood loss and partly from medications. Two days later she awoke and apologized for all the trouble. Her husband appeared at the bedside, a big man with silver at his temples, still in his navy-blue uniform with gleaming brass buttons. He held her hand and cried like a child. She stroked his head tenderly, reassuring him.

That's the problem with NSAIDs.

We don't know how many Americans die from NSAID-related GI bleeds every year; estimates range from 3,500 to 25,000. We'll probably never know, because there is no good way to compile the reports from all the emergency rooms, clinics, and nursing homes where patients appear vomiting blood or are noted to be silently, painlessly bleeding through their lower intestines. But we do know that an enormous number of people take these medications, that a shockingly high proportion of them develop bleeding ulcers—and that most never know it themselves. For example, back when all NSAIDs still required a prescription, about 13 million Americans used them intermittently every year, and about 3 million took them daily; they were the most prescribed medicine for people over age sixty. Since the FDA has permitted over-the-counter sales of NSAIDs such as Advil, Nuprin, and Alleve, self-prescribing has exploded, often without any consultation with a doctor. We don't even know exactly how many people take these drugs. But we do know that Americans now spend $8 billion on NSAIDs every year, and worldwide roughly 30 to 60 million people take one or more of these drugs each day.

The dirty secret of NSAIDs (that even many doctors don't know) is that if you use an endoscope to randomly examine the upper GI tracts of people taking these drugs, 15 to 30 percent of them will have ulcers. And as many as 4 percent of people who take these drugs, like Linda, will hemorrhage. That adds up to an *amazing* number of life-threatening GI bleeds. The medication's packaging cautions people that they might experience stomach discomfort and doctors and pharmacists caution patients to be wary if their stomach bothers them, but there is a deadly mismatch between such warning symptoms and the occurrence of bleeding ulcers. Forty percent of those with ulcers, like Linda, will have virtually no pain and no warning until they have a major bleed. As a result, this class of drugs is the nation's number-one cause of serious medication-related side effects, especially among the elderly. Certain factors definitely increase the risk of GI bleeding: age over sixty, the first three months of use, combined use of several NSAIDs (or an NSAID combined with a steroid), and the use of high doses. But there's really no telling who is going to get into serious trouble. Men or women, young or old, high dose or low, these drugs can strip the gut of its natural protections, leaving it naked to the attack of its own powerful acids.

It only takes one Linda to teach a young doctor to respect the potent danger of NSAIDs. Still, the excitement about their potential as a defense against Alzheimer's has inspired some mildly ostrich-headed perspectives. At one meeting I spoke with a talented Ph.D. bench scientist who'd taken part in the research demonstrating that NSAIDs have neuroprotective properties. He announced, blushing modestly, that his discovery could save millions of lives if only everyone would take these medications. "If I were a clinician, I'd put all my patients on them," he declared.

"Wouldn't you be concerned about the risk of GI bleeds?" I asked.

"Naw, that's a rarity."

"Um, I think five thousand American deaths a year seems like a concern."

"Five thousand!" he guffawed. "I don't believe it. If NSAIDs caused that many deaths, they never would have been allowed on the market!"

In fact, five thousand annual deaths may be a serious underestimate—the correct figure could be a lot higher. If the bench scientist followed his plan, he would find himself with a hundred hospitals full of Lindas.

NSAIDs are uniquely hard on the GI tract for the same reason that they are uniquely good at fighting inflammation: they inhibit the COX enzyme. In the mid 1990s researchers discovered that there are at least two forms of COX—COX-1 and COX-2. COX-1 increases the production of "stomach saving" prostaglandins. These chemicals protect our stomachs from digestive acids and thereby keep us from burning holes in our stomachs every time we eat a meal. COX-2, on the other hand, increases the production of inflammatory prostaglandins, the chemicals that boost inflammation to help us fight injuries and offending agents. The problem is that most NSAIDs inhibit *both* COX-1 and COX-2: at the same time that they dampen inflammation by turning off COX-2, they create the risk of a devastating GI bleed by turning off COX-1.

Annabelle, the medical student, grasped the implications instantly. "So, if we could invent a drug that inhibits COX-2 without inhibiting COX-1 . . ."

Exactly. A medicine that would selectively inhibit COX-2 would theoretically provide all the anti-inflammatory benefits we need without any of the GI side effects.

That conversation took place in 1996. Since then, such medicines have been created; they are the newly available *selective COX-2 inhibitors*. With a multimillion-dollar investment, a huge advertising budget, and a memorable Wall Street flourish, the first COX-2 inhibitor was approved by the FDA in December 1998 and brought to market in early 1999. Celecoxib (brand name Celebrex) hit the pharmacies running. Pent-up demand by patients and doctors for exactly this type of drug sent first-month sales soaring. Two and a half million prescriptions were written in the first six months of 1999. By 2000 a second COX-2 inhibitor had come to market: rofecoxib (brand name Vioxx). Because of their immense appeal and their powerful effects, Celebrex and Vioxx were soon touted as the world's new "superaspirins." Many similar drugs are presently at various stages of investigation and are on their way to approval.

The safety record of these drugs has been encouraging. While they *can* cause gastrointestinal bleeding and even death, they do so at a much lower rate than the nonselective NSAIDs they are meant to replace. Roughly speaking, selective COX-2 inhibitors cause only about one-third as many ulcers (visible through an endoscope) as the older drugs, and about one-fifth to one-tenth as many clinical hemorrhages. However, they may also pose inescapable risks to the kidneys and liver, since the new COX-2 drugs may be just as hard on those organs as the older anti-inflammatories. Those likely to be particularly vulnerable to such risks are people over age sixty, smokers, patients with a history of ulcers or kidney disease, and people using aspirin or other NSAIDs at the same time. All of these considerations need to be taken into account in deciding who should be taking these medications.

Should You Knock Your COX Off?

Should you be taking a COX-2 inhibitor (or any other anti-inflammatory) to save your brain?

Before I discuss who—if anyone—might consider long-term use of these medicines for neuroprotection, I need to be candid about the limits of our current knowledge. Not to throw cold water on a hot hypothesis, but we have a lot to learn about the role of inflammation in memory loss, and about the biology of NSAIDs.

For instance, the amount of COX-2 in Alzheimer's brains varies tremendously, so perhaps only some of us suffer from this particular type of brain inflammation—meaning that only some of us might benefit from taking NSAIDs. This is where a good blood test to measure your personal tendency to inflammation would help. (Twain's Maxim reminds us of our individual medical destinies.) In addition, evidence suggests that COX-1 is also elevated in Alzheimer's brains, so it's possible that using selective COX-2 inhibitors would not fully solve the brain-barbecue problem. Furthermore, the doses of anti-inflammatories necessary to save the brain might be completely different from the doses that ease an aching shoulder after a Saturday softball game.

Most important, the best way to save the brain from the inflammatory fires of ARNAT may not be to fight COX, but to quench the fires lit by a completely different batch of inflammatory mediators—such as the *lipooxygenases,* or the *leukotrienes,* or *TNFalpha,* or *nitric oxide,* or *PPARgama—all* of which are suspected of aiding and abetting the cerebral arson of Alzheimer's, and any one of which could be the key to prolonging the life of the mind. Since each of these operates separately from COX-2—and since new drugs are rapidly being created that can fight these alternative targets—it's way too soon to say that you'll get the best neuroprotective effect by blocking your COX.

All of this means neuroscientists should be really cautious about predicting that taking COX-2 inhibitors will save the brain. Taking them for a long period of time may also mean tinkering with an essential part of the immune system. Dampening this part of the inflammatory response may be great for protecting the brain against some problems (such as Alzheimer's), but it may wreck the brain's defenses against other problems. Or it may be good for the aging brain but harmful for the body as a whole. Sure, doctors can block your COX, but we really want to know more about the consequences before we recommend it for nearly universal use, as we do vitamin E.

Indeed, by 2001 the caution flags were up: the *Journal of the American Medical Association* reported that people taking Celebrex or Vioxx had about twice the risk of heart attacks and strokes as people taking naproxen, an older NSAID. Worried patients deluged their doctors with questions. Sales of COX-2 inhibitors dropped off. This particular dark cloud may turn out to be a tempest in a teapot: the reason for the difference in the rate of strokes may be that naproxen actually *lowers* stroke risk, rather than that COX-2 inhibitors *raise* the risk. But we can't dismiss the risk completely, and other clouds are looming on the horizon as well. In one long-term animal experiment, mice were genetically engineered to have no COX-2 (which makes it roughly similar to a person whose COX-2 has been chronically blocked); superficially, the mice seemed to function normally, but those little transgenic mice invariably developed kidney trouble and had a shortened life span. Putting it bluntly, a short life span is not the best way to avoid aging-related memory loss.

A multicenter study called the Alzheimer's Disease Anti-inflammatory Prevention Trial is currently under way, testing both an older NSAID and a COX-2 inhibitor to see whether either can slow the progression of Alzheimer's. Unfortunately, like the vast bulk of today's Alzheimer's research, it focuses on people who *already* have severely damaged brains. Such studies cannot answer the big questions that could have a huge impact on public health and private suffering: who among us should take NSAIDs to prevent Alzheimer's, and when should we begin?

In Search of the Bottom Line

Should you take an anti-inflammatory to save your brain? Unfortunately, it's a little too soon for me to answer this bold question. For all our optimistic guesswork, as of the dawn of the twenty-first century, physicians are still unsure of whether to prescribe these medications for neuroprotection, and if so, who to prescribe them to. Even if doctors could fairly judge who had the best profile for taking these drugs, they would need to know at what age people should begin taking them: twenty-five? forty-five? sixty-five? For how long? At what dose? And should we take them in combination with aspirin (which many people take to stave off vascular problems) or not?

Let's consider that crucial aspirin question.

Aspirin is better than a COX-2 inhibitor at preventing heart attacks and strokes, but the COX-2s are probably better than aspirin at preventing Alzheimer's. We may need *both* substances to keep our brains operating at peak efficiency. The aspirin should overcome any possibility of an increased risk of strokes posed by COX-2 inhibitors, so combining them is theoretically the most sensible fire-fighting approach of all. But the devil is in the details: if you combine a COX-2 inhibitor with a baby aspirin, it may reduce the aspirin's power to save your brain from CVC. There is also a small risk of an increased bleeding tendency when these two are combined, but with the 81 mg dose of coated aspirin, that risk is probably minimal. In fact, many arthritis specialists already give their patients both aspirin and a COX-2. Although it's extremely hard to measure the benefits or risks, perhaps more of us should be making this bet for the good of our brains.

COX-2 inhibitors may soon be available without a prescription, and some people will be tempted to use them to make up their own anti-inflammatory cocktail. But all sorts of different medical factors need to be considered in such a choice. I strongly propose that the decision to combine two anti-inflammatories (like all of those just outlined) demands a close partnership between doctor and patient, not a flip of the coin at the drugstore.

Another consideration is that human research on anti-inflammatories and memory loss is desperately needed. Although short-term studies are under way, a much better (but extremely difficult) approach would be to study the benefits in a long-term, prospective trial to prevent memory loss in cognitively healthy young adults. And since it's almost certain that individuals will differ greatly in how they are affected by this treatment, research is also needed to identify the subgroup of adults most likely to benefit from the anti-inflammatory approach to saving the brain. For example, within a few years, you will carry your genome to your family doctor on a little plastic card, and he or she will be able to check you for "pro-inflammatory genes." If you have them, your doctor will pay special attention to helping you avoid a neuronal barbecue.

A Promising Alternative: Propentofylline and its Kin

Mrs. Molnar smiled. Her rheumatologist had already switched her to a COX-2 inhibitor. It seemed to help her arthritis, and now she had some reason to believe that it might even help keep her sharp. Back in the scruffy little doctors' room in the county hospital, Annabelle and I filled out the requisitions for an MRI and a nerve conduction test to sort out what to do about her progressive hand weakness. Yet Annabelle looked perturbed. Finally she said, "For those of us who don't have arthritis or *APOE*-ε4, well, I mean, might there be an alternative to the COX-2 drugs?" She was really asking the perfectly valid question, *What about me?*

Physicians would like to save everyone's brain from inflammation, but the aspirin/COX-2 combo may not be the best brain-saving plan for everyone. Are there other ways to fight the inflammatory fires of ARNAT? One alternative approach seems to deserve the excitement it has been generating in the neuroscience community—a drug we already mentioned briefly in Chapter 14: *propentofylline.*

Propentofylline is a very promising medication. It's about as close as a drug can get to being an essential part of the backbone of life. As you may know, DNA is built from four nucleotide bases, abbreviated C, A, T, and G. *A* stands for adenine; adenine breaks down to become xanthine; and propentofylline is one of a family of man-made versions of xanthine. Since its biological forebears are essential to tens of thousands of life-enhancing functions, you might predict that propentofylline and its kin could possibly play many beneficial roles in the body. Neuroscientists first got excited about propentofylline because it helps protect the brain in animal models of strokes and trauma. But what's really intriguing is that it blocks the attack of microglia.

Microglia, as we've seen, are roaming mercenaries that attack neurons with all manner of inflammatory weapons. A drug that controlled microglia could potentially help block the chain reaction that leads to neurodegeneration. Propentofylline seems to do that and more. It is something of a Swiss Army knife of a drug: it can block the clumping of platelets and help protect the brain from strokes, and it may defend neurons from a half dozen other demons of brain aging as well, including energy deprivation, excess excitement, and free radicals. Overall, you might think of this drug as a brakeman that keeps our neuronal physiology from jumping off the tracks.

Even this does not exhaust its repertoire of beneficial effects.

In experiments with mice and rats, propentofylline powerfully stimulates glial cells to produce nerve growth factor (NGF) along with multiple other growth factors. In other words, drugs in the propentofylline family may be stimulators of brain growth. Boosting NGF may be the way this synthetic drug mimics the brain-healing effects of the natural compounds from which it's derived. And it may even grant this drug a certain anti-aging potential: propentofylline also protects rats' hippocampal memory cells from many kinds of stress. Most important for the purpose of preventing Alzheimer's, if we put propentofylline in rat chow, the rats become resistant to the memory loss produced by beta-amyloid. With all this going for it, we naturally want to know if this medication can help a slightly larger animal.

Five double-blind, placebo-controlled clinical trials (conducted under the auspices of the European/Canadian Propentofylline Study Group) have suggested that propentofylline can help save human brains too. In both Alzheimer's disease and vascular dementia, patients treated with propentofylline showed a slower decline in mental status than did placebo-treated patients. The side effects were quite limited. What's really intriguing is what happened when patients were taken off the drug: although their mental status deteriorated somewhat, it didn't plunge back down to the previous level but stayed at a higher level. This means that propentofylline perhaps does more than just give people a temporary mental boost; unlike the cholinergic treatments for Alzheimer's that are currently on the market, *propentofylline may actually help block the underlying process of neurodegeneration.*

With any new drug, its efficacy, its safety, and—more and more in this strange new world of managed health care—its cost-effectiveness are always debated. A Swedish study estimated that propentofylline might cut the cost of dementia care by about 4 percent. As the Swedish research put it: "The drug acquisition costs are more than offset by the savings achieved in the cost of care." Not much, but it adds up.

If propentofylline and drugs in its family can frustrate the deadly attack of beta-amyloid on neurons, could they prevent Alzheimer's if they were taken by healthy people on a regular basis? The answer is a definite maybe. It's never been tried. One way to test this idea might be to give propentofylline to mice that have been genetically altered to develop Alzheimer's-type brain changes, then see if it protects their brains and memories if it's given from an early age. If such an experiment were successful (and if no evidence of serious side effects shows up), it would definitely justify a clinical trial in healthy volunteers.

In the clinic, I mentioned this possibility to Annabelle. She smiled. "Sign me up."

It's easy to see why neuroscientists are working in a quiet frenzy: many people have neurons that are currently toasting in the fiery furnace of inflammation. We are right on the verge of practical ways to douse the embers of this inflammatory fire, but we haven't yet passed over the threshold onto firm ground. It all comes back to Twain's Maxim: individual differences determine who is most likely to need these medicines and who is most likely to bleed from them. Pending new discoveries, once again, it's time to place educated bets.

My own wager would be that, for NSAID treatment, the benefits are likely to outweigh the risks in the following groups: people with established Alzheimer's; people with an increased risk of ARNAT, such as those with the *APOE-ε4* genotype, those with a strong family history of Alzheimer's, postmenopausal women who are not taking estrogen, and those who've had a head trauma followed by a day or more of subtle confusion, and people who have other compelling reasons for regular use of NSAIDs besides neuroprotection, such as those with rheumatoid arthritis. I would further bet that the risk of combination therapy with aspirin is justified in these cases, so long as that therapy is monitored by the family doctor. Simple precautions (such as periodic blood tests and checking the stool for microscopic amounts of blood) might yield terrific safety dividends.

At this point, I would hesitate to recommend long-term anti-inflammatory use of any kind as a *universal* protection against aging-related brain changes. Unless you're in one of the above groups, hold off just a bit—probably at least a couple of years. And pound your congressional representatives into supporting the necessary medical research. Let's get the answers quickly—and boost our chances of saving our brains.

CHAPTER 16

Saving Your Brain by Saving Your Skull

How many apples fell on Newton's head before he took the hint! Nature is always hinting at us. It hints over and over again. And suddenly we take the hint.

ROBERT FROST

It was a classic Boston summer day—hot, sunny, and perfect for summer sports. People were Rollerblading on the Commons, sailing on the Charles, shouting and sweating through pick-up games of soccer. And as sometimes happens on such a fine day, the emergency room was seeing its share of patients with sports-related head traumas. Bill was there because of a Little League game. He was eleven. Two hours earlier, he'd been beaned.

As I came in, the intern was just finishing his exam: "How many fingers?"

"Ten," the boy answered. "But you're only sticking out two of them."

"What's five plus seven?"

The boy rolled his eyes and sighed. "A math problem?"

I began to get the picture. As the neurology resident on call, I'd been asked to help sort things out. The intern thought Bill seemed fine, but his parents, both standing there anxiously in the little curtained cubicle, had insisted on a neurological consultation. They knew their child. Something was wrong.

I asked Bill if I could ask him a couple of questions, apologizing that they might be pretty easy for him. He made a face at his mom, who nodded encouragingly. Then he said, "Knock yourself out." I didn't comment on the irony.

"So, who won the series last year?"

This was 1987. He groaned. "The Mets. Beat us in the seventh."

"And who won the Cy Young Award?"

"Clemens"—he brightened, meaning the rocket-armed Red Sox pitcher—"with an ERA of 2.48." His dad suppressed a grin and shifted to perch on the gurney. If Bill was going to start quoting Major League earned run averages, he wanted to be comfortable.

Bill and I got along okay. He bet me that Roger Clemens would win the American League Cy Young Award again in '87. We put a nickel on it with his mom acting as banker. (He won.) He told me how to calculate batting averages and ERAs. He described the baseball game he had been playing that hot afternoon, his favorite bat, and the skinny opposing pitcher. But he couldn't remember what the count had been when his head intercepted the rising curve that went high and inside. He wasn't sure who had been ahead in the game. Or the score.

"And what was the first question I asked you?"

"Uh"—this time his smooth brow furrowed as his eyes went straight up—"what's twelve times five?"

His parents were right. Bill was still a bit dazed and confused, though he had been knocked out for less than a minute. His long-term memory and reasoning worked fine, but his short-term memory—his cerebral tape recorder—was a mess, a pattern curiously similar to early dementia.

I ordered a CT scan. Two hours later the scan was done, and it showed no apparent abnormality. I gave the family that news; then I retested Bill, asking him to memorize four simple words. Several minutes later he could only recall two of them.

"Batting .500," his dad said with a smile. "Not too shoddy."

His very-relieved parents listened politely as I described the warning signs of undetected problems or delayed worsening; but the normal CT seemed to have made their anxiety vanish. As the family walked out through the sliding-glass doors of the ER, Bill waved back. I knew at the time that CT scans very often miss brain damage due to head trauma. What I didn't know was that Bill's head injury might boost his risk of Alzheimer's.

Why would a head injury in childhood or young adulthood increase your risk of dementia fifty or sixty years later? That's the mystery we will try to solve in this chapter.

Head Trauma, the Silent Epidemic

Two million head injuries occur in America every year. This is a very rough estimate, based on educated guesswork by the NIH Interagency Head Injury Task Force, which faced the impossible task of looking at the small proportion of head injuries that are reported and making a guess about the huge number that really happen. How many of your own lifetime head injuries did you report? The point is, most people who suffer mild head injuries never see a doctor. For the subgroup of patients who do go to the ER, doctors sometimes dismiss the head trauma as a nonevent unless the patient has a fractured skull. Even if the victim goes to the hospital and the doctor takes it seriously, only 10 to 20 percent of people with head injuries will be admitted, and only one-third of those will have their primary diagnosis coded as a head trauma. With no national reporting system for ER diagnoses, all of this makes any effort to count the total number of head injuries in the United States about as reliable as counting catfish in the Mississippi with a hand net. Since many of us have had some kind of head injury during our lives, it's possible that that two million figure is actually a monstrous underestimate. That's one reason why head injury is called the silent epidemic.

From the time we begin to toddle unsteadily, through our years of tipping over our high chairs, running into the corners of tables, jumping off our parents' beds, tripping on the playground, colliding on the playing field, and having our teeth rattled in fist fights—and in "disciplinary" encounters with open or closed hands—opportunities for a blow to the head are so numerous that *every* human has probably experienced head injury of some degree before they start dating. But what degree of head injury is worrisome? At what point in the spectrum between a quick bump into an open kitchen cabinet door and a terrible blow to the head followed by prolonged coma should we be concerned that the brain has suffered lasting harm? Frankly, neurologists don't yet know for sure. But evidence is accumulating that even so-called "mild" injuries may have long-term effects on our ability to think.

Although both men and women suffer head injuries, the rate among men is two to three times the rate among women, especially under age thirty. Motor vehicle accidents, on-the-job accidents, falls, assaults, and sports injuries are the major causes of adult head trauma. Of these, auto accidents are by far the biggest threat, but about 800 head injury deaths in bicycle accidents and 2,100 deaths in motorcycle accidents occur each year—and these figures barely begin to suggest the number of brain-disabling bicycle and motorcycle head injuries *short* of death. The table shows, in very rough order of frequency, the most common ways that adults suffer head injury.

These head injuries have terrible consequences. The total cost of head injuries in the United States is estimated at a jaw-dropping $40 billion per year. Half of that is the cost of fatal injuries, and the other half is the cost of caring for the 80,000 survivors who are most seriously disabled.

But the statistics are silent about the cost of mild, unreported injuries,

The Most Common Causes of Head Injury

1. VEHICULAR ACCIDENTS
Automobile

Motorcycle

Bicycle

Snowmobile

Motor boat/personal watercraft

2. NONVEHICULAR INCIDENTS
Trip-and-falls and other domestic accidents

Domestic assaults and abuse

Fights

Gunshot wounds

3. SPORTS AND RECREATIONAL ACTIVITIES
Football

Baseball

Skiing

Skateboarding

Roller skates or in-line skates

Soccer

Hockey

Rugby

Boxing

Sailing

Equestrian sports

Bull riding

because doctors have only begun to realize that these can have long-term repercussions. Young Bill went home looking good, the crisis apparently over. That may or may not have been the case. Every single head trauma, mild or severe, has the potential to undercut the brain's neuronal resilience—and to come back to haunt us much later in life.

I'll explain this chain reaction in a moment. But first let's look at the basics.

What Is a Head Injury?

"Your honor," the attorney began as he stepped toward the bench. He turned to point accusingly at my unfortunate patient, Wendell. "This man did not even have a skull fracture. Yet counsel for the plaintiff would have us believe he suffered a 'major' head injury. The only thing major here is the size of his claim."

The judge tipped his head toward me, where I sat on the stand. I asked the attorney if he could please rephrase his statement as a question. He did: how could I call my patient's head injury "major" if there was no skull fracture? Wendell was sitting in his wheelchair, paying attention as best he could when his incomplete mind didn't wander off. Two years before, when the driver of his wheelchair van neglected to strap in his wheelchair, the chair had gone flying on a sharp turn. Wendell was knocked out for only a minute or two, yet the blow had badly shaken his left temporal lobe—adding confusion, memory loss, and epilepsy to his previous problem of paraplegia. The attorney's question about a skull fracture sounded reasonable, at least to anyone who hadn't had to explain to a mother or father or spouse why their loved one was lying in a hospital bed in a coma, despite a perfectly intact skull. I thought of an analogy, grim but vivid. A head in a skull is not like an egg in a shell; it's more like a cat in a can. You can shake that can, drop it to the floor, even pitch it out the window. The can may not change much. But the cat will. The answer to the attorney: yes, we can suffer a major brain trauma without fracturing the skull. It's common.

Perhaps the attorney's question was a reflection of what we learn about head trauma as we grow up. During your most daring childhood pranks, your parents may have warned you that if you didn't stop what you were doing right then, "you're going to break your skull!" It's a popular misconception that a fractured skull is the worst-case scenario; as a result, this is the type of head injury many people fear, while more dangerous types of head injuries are rarely discussed. In fact, skulls can function like energy-absorbing steering columns to absorb the brunt of an impact; a fractured skull may save your brain.

Hollywood is the prime source of another popular misconception about head injury—that a "knockout," a period of unconsciousness after a blow to the head, is basically harmless. A thousand movies dramatize the same reassuring fiction: John Wayne gets shanghaied and pistol-whipped into unconsciousness by the bad guys and wakes up a minute later—his forehead being dabbed with a cool gingham cloth by the town's feisty widow—to drawl with a half-smile, "If I'd a known you were coming, ma'am, I woulda' got a shave." This apparently benign sequence of events, in which a knockout is followed by a rapid recovery, is best left to movie fantasy. Our hero would be just as likely to awaken slowly, slur his speech, stagger, and vomit. Or he might wake up, run to his horse, mount up, and chase the bad guys a mile down the trail—only to tumble off his horse during a post-traumatic seizure. Or after spending a week in a coma, he might sluggishly awaken to spend the rest of his life in a permanent state of vegetation. What happens all depends on what part of the brain gets hurt, how much it bleeds, and how many neurons get ripped or poisoned by secondary biological events.

We talk about "head injury" because that's what we see first—the head, with its bleeding scalp, its egg-size lump, or even its indented skull. But the head itself is just packaging. Recently, a few prominent cases of the "shaken baby syndrome" have raised public awareness about the fact that the brain can be irreparably harmed even when the head looks fine. In fact, *head injury* becomes a concern to human behavior only insofar as it results in *brain injury*. Thus, we should be wary about talk of "head injury," since *traumatic brain injury* (TBI) is our real concern.

TBI is almost always incurred indirectly. By this I mean that the brain itself practically never comes in contact with the steering wheel, the fist, the hardwood floor, or the ceramic coffee mug lying innocently in the backseat of the car that suddenly becomes a killer projectile in a sudden stop. Yes, there are many injuries in which the brain is penetrated, for example, by an ice pick or a bullet. But most brain injuries involve *closed* head trauma, in which the skull remains intact, though the brain may nonetheless suffer grievously as it swings and slams into its own bony container.

Consider a thirty-five-mile-per-hour frontal car crash. Your head moves forward at thirty-five miles per hour until your skull meets the steering wheel, at which point your head's speed of travel decreases abruptly to almost zero. But for a fraction of a second, your *brain* keeps traveling at thirty-five miles per hour. This soft, nearly gelatinous mass, run through with miles of axons, surrounded by a wafer-thin cushion of spinal fluid, takes a quick and dangerous trip inside your head until it collides into your skull's internal walls: your frontal lobes slam into your frontal bones, and your temporal lobes collide with a spiky-sharp ridge of temporal bone that rises up from the inner base of your skull. The fragile veins that bridge the gap from brain to skull get torn, like mooring cables ripped from a tanker in a storm. The axons stretch like bungee cords, and some get sheared like wheat by a tornado. Similar things occur whether the head is suddenly decelerated in a fall, suddenly accelerated by a punch, or even when there is no actual impact to the head at all, as in the flailing head movements of a whiplash injury or a shaken baby.

The bottom line in closed head trauma is that no matter what the *head* hits, the *brain* hits the skull. Furthermore, no matter what *part of the head* absorbs the initial blow, the frontal and temporal lobes reliably take the brutal brunt of the collision. The reason is simple: because of the internal landscape of the skull, these two parts of the brain routinely collide with the roughest bones. The wing of the temporal bone, in particular, rises up in front of the temporal lobe like a tall, sharp speed bump that trips and rakes the structures essential for new learning. That's why young Bill could not remember his baseball game's score. That's why Wendell was now a confused epileptic. The judge took the point.

What Is a Concussion?

Although Bill's injury was milder than Wendell's, both were knocked out for a minute or two, so both suffered a *concussion*—a temporary loss of awareness or consciousness related to a TBI. But why did they lose consciousness in the first place? One theory (originally suggested by Alexander and Ayub Ommaya at the NIH) says that the deeper the shock wave penetrates into the brain, the more likely we are to lose consciousness. Recall from Chapter 1 our simplified neuroanatomy: the brain as Tootsie Roll Pop, with an outer candy shell of cortex and an inner chocolate core of limbic system, perched atop the slender stick of the brainstem. According to the NIH theory, we are most likely to be knocked unconscious if the shock wave rolls down through the outer layers of tissue to reach the uppermost part of the brainstem—a part of the brain that's absolutely vital for awakeness and awareness. Some injuries are more likely than others to stamp on the burning fuse of consciousness.

The reason some people develop more memory loss than others after a TBI is that TBIs vary greatly. Some are mild, some are moderate, and some are severe. But scientists disagree, to a surprising extent, about exactly how to tell the difference.

A few doctors rate the severity of a head trauma based entirely on the duration of loss of consciousness. According to this system, if the victim wakes up within half an hour, it's a "mild" TBI, while if it takes him longer to wake up, the TBI is considered more severe. Since both Bill and Wendell were unconscious for less than five minutes, using this measure, we'd have to conclude that both had "mild" traumas. But if we pay attention only to how long it takes a person to wake up, we may not get a full picture of what has happened to the thinking parts of his brain. Consider an analogy: if your computer screen goes blank for ten minutes, then "wakes up"—you might say that it experienced a mild problem. But what if, bright screen notwithstanding, it garbles every word you type for the next six months? We'd hardly say that the ten minutes the screen was blank gives us a complete measure of the severity of the problem! The same is true of the brain. Measuring how long it takes a person to wake up is a quick and easy way to rate the severity of an injury, but unfortunately, it's a very crude way to determine how badly a human brain is damaged.

Another way to measure severity is based on the victim's recovery of memory. Using this system, if a victim regains day-to-day memory within twenty-four hours, his trauma was "mild," but if it takes him more than twenty-four hours, his trauma was more severe. "Day-to-day memory" means the ability to keep track of time and passing events and the details of conversations. For instance, Bill's difficulty recalling all four words for me in the ER several hours after his injury hinted that his brain was still having some trouble fully supporting day-to-day memory. Wendell's brain was clearly unable to support this kind of memory two years after his fall. This measure is called the *duration of post-traumatic amnesia* (PTA). Though the PTA takes a little training to measure, it is potentially a much better predictor of the persisting effects of a head trauma on thinking than duration of unconsciousness. That's because, though the duration of unconsciousness is a good measure of what happened to his *brainstem,* the time needed to recover day-to-day memory is a better measure of what happened to the MTL memory recorder.

This is just one way that TBIs differ. And the more doctors understand about what trauma does to the human brain, the clearer it becomes that two head injuries that superficially seem to be the same may actually be as different as a penguin and a rhinoceros. These biological differences help us predict whether a head injury will have trivial effects on our future, or put us onto a one-way track to Alzheimer's.

How a Blow to the Head Can Affect the Whole Brain

Whether you slip on the ice, get felled by a baseball, or strike the steering wheel with your forehead, some of the energy will be focused on one local area of the brain (producing *focal damage*) and some will spread through the brain (producing *diffuse damage*). The main concern about focal damage is that it can produce bleeding in the head. This means you can get "blood on the brain," be it on top of the brain's dural wrapping, underneath the dura, or deep in the brain itself. Any form of bleeding inside the skull can cause trouble, because it puts pressure on a brain that has nowhere else to go. Sometimes a neurosurgeon must literally drill a hole in the head to relieve this pressure.

But for all the attention neurologists give to such focal forces and blood on the brain, these bloody local injuries may ultimately do us less long-term harm than the diffuse damage caused by the shock wave as it races through the skull—a deadly kind of spreading havoc that hits the axons themselves.

In 1956 pioneering neuropathologist Susan Strich noticed something odd about the brains of patients who developed dementia after head injury. Even if the brain looked intact superficially, a more careful inspection revealed microscopic hemorrhages and a curious-looking injury to the long axons of the neurons; they appeared as if they'd been wrenched halfway to breaking. Dr. Strich hypothesized that two things happen during a head injury. First, the long axons can be twisted or even sheared, like spaghetti breaking when a grocery bag falls. Second, the big bundles of axons that connect the heaviest parts of the brain (such as the axons of the corpus callosum, which connects the left and right hemispheres) take the brunt of this swinging motion, just as the stem of an apple on a tree is stressed in a high wind. It took years for neuroscientists to realize that the changes Dr. Strich saw account for the most terrible outcomes to cognition, personality, and life itself. We now call this nasty combination of brain changes *diffuse axonal injury* (DAI).

DAI explains about 35 percent of deaths following head trauma, and neuroscientists used to think that it happens only in severe head trauma. Now we know better: even a mild injury such as Bill's can produce DAI in some cases, which helps to explain why some people who experience a minor bump are plagued by mysterious, long-lasting cognitive complaints and others aren't. But DAI is hugely underdiagnosed because it's all but invisible to conventional CT scanners. Recent advances in MRI scanning somewhat increase the odds of seeing DAI-type brain damage, and some academic medical centers even use functional scanners—PET, SPECT, or fMRI—in an effort to look for DAI. In the meantime, neurologists have finally come to appreciate that there's a lot more to TBI than the big focal bleeds that used to grab our attention. Now we're painting a picture of the trauma that's invisible to the naked eye, down to the level of individual neurons.

For example, when the curveball hit Bill, it initially struck his batting helmet, driving the padded interior into his left temple. This caused his skull to bow inward for an instant. (We usually think of the skull as rigid, but it will actually bend a good deal before it breaks.) The inner table of his skull, in turn, collided with his brain's dural sac; the cushion of spinal fluid squished aside, and the dura slammed into Bill's brain. A shock wave rocketed through the soft substance of neurons and glia and blood vessels, possibly producing some degree of DAI. That shock wave turned on dozens of molecular cascades. It's hard to say how many of these cascades became activated in Bill's case, or how far along the sequence he went—hopefully, not far—but in such cases we might not know right away.

The new understanding of head trauma tells us that the real damage may not be immediate. Just as melting snow at the mountaintop eventually causes a spring flood down in the valley, the molecular cascades of TBI and DAI evolve gradually and may take a week or two to fully develop. During the minutes, hours, days, and weeks after a head injury, a team of molecular demons is unleashed, including many of the same evildoers we met on our tour of aging-related neurodegeneration: excitatory neurotransmitters, excess calcium, and free radicals.

The initial force of a TBI literally rips pores, or holes, in the membrane of our brain cells. Dangerous amounts of calcium pour into the cell through those pores. Like a pin in the flank of a horse, this injection of excess calcium pricks dangerous calcium-dependent enzymes into wild misbehavior. These enzymes break down the neuron's internal scaffolding, begin the explosive disgorging of the brain cell's contents into the surrounding area, and even turn on cellular suicide. A witches' brew of inflammatory chemicals also spills onto the damaged neuron; this in turn recruits mercenary microglia into the area, which eat the wounded neuron like hungry piranhas. It's something like Alzheimer's disease playing out in fast-forward.

Of course, the brain doesn't receive this pummeling without putting up a fight. For every blow, the neuron mounts a defense, as natural antioxidants and "anti-suicide" proteins and growth factors rush to the rescue. The point is that the moment the baseball hit Bill's helmet, a dozen processes were set into motion that might kill his neurons, and a dozen others responded in ferocious defense—a brain at war with itself. Again, even if the initial blow hits the top or the back of the head, the spreading shock wave tends to take its battle to the *frontal lobes*, the home of identity; to the *temporal lobes*, the home of memory; and to the bundles of *axons*, which allow different parts of the brain to talk to each other. In essence, the shock wave threatens the most precious contents of the head.

This molecular story helps to explain two very different consequences of head trauma. First, the victim can have trouble with his memory—a mild and hopefully temporary problem like Bill's, or a persistent problem like Wendell's. Second, even if the victim seems to completely recover—even if his memory tests out just fine and he goes on to run a business, or get a Ph.D., or conduct an orchestra—the ghostly residual harm of a head trauma may well haunt him forever.

TBI Increases the Risk of Dementia and Alzheimer's

Studies from the United States, Canada, Australia, Europe, and Japan have all found a high rate of past head trauma among Alzheimer's patients. In a review of eleven big European studies, a history of head trauma with loss of consciousness was 80 percent more common among Alzheimer's patients than among normal elderly people. The rate of past head trauma among Alzheimer's patients has been reported to be as high as 43.5 percent—ten times the rate among the normal elderly. Furthermore, head trauma may increase the risk not only for Alzheimer's, the most common type of dementia, but for dementia in general, including *vascular* dementia. This is important because it suggests that a battered brain remains at risk for a wide spectrum of biological problems later in life. Still, we should be wary of saying, "He got hit in the head, so he'll get demented." Head traumas vary tremendously, and victims of head traumas vary tremendously. *Some* traumas are like getting pecked by a penguin, and others are like getting rammed by a rhinoceros.

What makes the difference? One factor is severity. When Duke University researchers collected the past service records of 1,776 World War II Navy and Marine veterans, they found that 548 had had head trauma as young soldiers. The young men who had *moderate* head traumas had twice the risk of developing memory loss later in life, and those who had *severe* head trauma had four times the risk of developing dementia. And a study from Columbia University found that the link between head trauma and Alzheimer's is strongest for people who were unconscious for at least five minutes. Even though duration of unconsciousness is a very crude measure of severity, this study is another hint that the more severe a TBI, the more it boosts the risk of Alzheimer's.

Another factor is age. The brain usually recovers better in young people than in old people, and indeed, there is evidence that people with early-life head injuries may be less likely to get Alzheimer's than those with late-life head injuries. But even very young soldiers with TBIs will go on to have an increased risk of dementia, so people who had head injuries in their teens and twenties are by no means off the hook.

Third, different traumas may produce their greatest impact on different parts of the brain. As we saw with Bill and Wendell, two people can be knocked out for the same period of time, but one of them will have a much longer duration of post-traumatic amnesia. Again, this is because *different parts of the brain are involved in "awakeness" and in memory.* Since the PTA tells us much more about how badly the *hippocampus* got pounded, it's possibly a much better predictor of the risk of subsequent

Alzheimer's. Few doctors and fewer coaches are aware of the importance of the PTA, but it's very valuable, and should probably be taught to every medical student.

A fourth big factor is the victim's genome. Differences in brain aging, as we've seen again and again, come down to the interaction of genes with environment. Such a genes-environment interaction has been discovered by neurologist Richard Mayeux. Tall, silver haired, and possessed of seemingly boundless energy, Dr. Mayeux runs the busy Alzheimer's program at Columbia University. When he and his colleagues studied 236 older people living in the nearby community, he was not surprised to find that those who carried the *APOE-ε4* allele had twice the usual risk of Alzheimer's. But he was astonished to find that people who had *both* a head trauma *and* an *APOE-ε4* allele had *ten times* the risk of developing Alzheimer's. This suggests that the environmental event of head trauma combined with the ε4 genotype may multiply our late-life risk of Alzheimer's.

The Missing Link

We know that head trauma is incredibly common, especially among young adults. We know that dementia is incredibly common, mostly among older adults. But why should a head injury in youth have such a profound effect fifty or sixty years later? A recent discovery may explain exactly why a bump on the head may boost our lifetime risk of dementia.

In 1990 Glasgow neuropathologist Gareth W. Roberts studied the brains of a small group of former boxers. He found that their brains were peppered with beta-amyloid, the toxic stuff found in Alzheimer's plaques. Roberts went on to gather the brains of more than 152 people who had died within two and a half years after a blow to the head. Fully 30 percent of these people had beta-amyloid deposits in the cortex. The older the victim, as we might expect, the higher the likelihood of beta-amyloid deposits, but even young people develop this problem: one of the head trauma victims with beta-amyloid on the brain was *a ten-year-old child*. This discovery was quite a revelation, and it's led neuroscientists to appreciate a vital new fact: no matter how old we are when we receive a blow to the head, in many cases new proteins are released: the big amyloid precursor protein (APP) and its small-but-potentially-deadly conspirator beta-amyloid. This fact appears to be the missing link between head trauma and Alzheimer's.

Since Roberts's discovery, a veritable flood of evidence has confirmed the link. TBI boosts beta-amyloid levels in people's spinal fluid. TBI can turn on the presenilin-1 gene, one of the mutant genes that produces familial Alzheimer's. Rats that have experienced mild blows to the head will develop twisted microtubules interlaced with misfolded tau, a wreckage akin to tangles. And, in humans, spinal fluid tau levels go up more than a thousand times after head injury. The streams of evidence are converging into a river. Even though the symptoms of severe memory loss may not appear for decades, microscopic signs of Alzheimer's-type change may show up in our brains just days or weeks after a head trauma! This seems to suggest that APP, beta-amyloid, and even misfolded tau are a common part of the brain's response to injury.

Nature always has a plan. Perhaps, in some ways, these injury responses are good for the battered brain. Perhaps the APP/beta-amyloid injury-response system evolved early in primate history partly to limit the damage done by head trauma, an incredibly common event in the natural world. This response system might protect some neurons, assist the repair of others, use its synapse-building skill to help rebuild damaged circuits, and terminate the truly irreparable cells. In other words, this might be a perfect example of an evolutionary trade-off: the APP/beta-amyloid–nerve growth factor–injury-response system provides us with brain first-aid immediately after a trauma; the trade-off is an increased risk of memory loss many years later. Until humans started living for seventy or more years (a very recent historical occurrence), virtually no one had to pay this price. Now many of us do.

Putting together everything we know about head injury and dementia, I would propose the following theory. First, that the risk of developing dementia many years after a TBI depends on the type of trauma; if the MTL memory recorder was slammed hard, or if there's some degree of DAI, or both, the mind will pay a bigger price down the road. So all other factors being equal, I'd predict that Wendell would be more likely than Bill to develop dementia fifty years later, because his memory recorder surely took the harder hit. Second, genetic differences strongly influence the long-term risk; some TBI victims have genes that help them efficiently fight off the effects of trauma, while others' genes turn their fight with trauma into a bar-wrecking donnybrook that harms the very brain it's trying to save. And if a person is so unlucky as to have a hippocampus-harming head trauma *and* an injury-worsening genome— no matter how modest the trauma seemed at the time—it will come back to haunt him in the most devastating ways. Given what we now know about the link between TBI and Alzheimer's, it's obvious that *you should do everything in your power to limit your exposure to head trauma during your entire life.*

Head trauma is not inevitable. We can make simple choices that will significantly reduce our lifetime exposure to TBI and the subsequent risk of a broken brain. Now that we know what's at stake, it's time to talk about how to protect your head at work, at play, and on the road.

Brains at Work

On-the-job accidents are a common and hugely reducible cause of TBI. Head injuries are the injuries that workers are least likely to recover from, are the most common cause of workers' compensation claims, and lead to 25 percent of deaths on the job. To get an idea of the amount of brain damage we're talking about, approximately 75,000 disabling occupational face and head injuries occur in America every year, and many more take place that are not considered "disabling," partly because no one checks for hidden effects on the brain. As one might expect, construction workers suffer a disproportionately high rate of injuries. Falling objects are just one notorious threat; the Occupational Safety and Health Administration (OSHA) lists such brain-battering missiles as rivets, hammers, and even an oven! But construction workers are hardly alone. Many jobs put the head at risk; the table lists jobs in which the brain is especially likely to be traumatized.

Occupations with High Frequencies of Head Injury

Construction workers, especially heavy or highway

Loggers and sawyers

Miners

Carpenters

Electricians, including linemen

Mechanics and repairers

Plumbers and pipe fitters

Assemblers

Packers, wrappers

Welders

Laborers

Freight and stock handlers, warehouse laborers

Military personnel

The federal government has naturally tried to limit the toll of on-the-job brain trauma. OSHA requires employers to think about what workplace hazards may result in a head injury and to train their employees to keep their heads safe. OSHA also requires hard hats "when working in areas where there is a potential for injury to the head from falling objects." This sounds very reasonable, but the outrageous fact is that America has a terrible track record for protecting workers' brains.

One problem is that employers, who are rarely trained in the matter, are expected to figure out for themselves whether workers need head protection. In addition, if the employer says, "You'd better wear a hard hat every day," this is subject to labor/management negotiations, and workers may complain that head protection is uncomfortable or inconvenient. As a result, during the vast majority of on-the-job brain injuries, the victim is not wearing a helmet. Another perhaps even more disturbing fact lies buried in the depths of a 1994 government document explaining the rules for head protection: experts pointed out that most head injuries occur due to blows to the front, back, or sides of the head, while the approved hard hats are designed to protect heads only from blows from *above*.

The result is an erratic safety net that fails to catch too many potentially brain-battering situations. Our society needs to establish a system in which expert safety advisers visit big construction sites and issue firm guidelines for head protection. Employers and employees should be given better education about the hazards of their jobs; employees who operate dangerous machinery (or drive buses) should be screened with more care; hard hats should be individually fitted, worn religiously, and required to meet a reasonable safety standard for front, back, and side impacts; and workers at heights should be required to demonstrate the basic rope-handling skills of teenagers in a rock-climbing camp. A little effort might produce a big reduction in the terrible toll of occupational brain injury and early mental deterioration.

Yet none of these safeguards would do much to eliminate another major cause of workplace injuries: assaults. Assaults accounted, in one study, for an amazing 29 percent of on-the-job brain injuries. Generally, assaults at work involve men beating on other men (although, in the military, head-injuring fights between women soldiers are also frequent). Assaults to the head, on the job or off, are a devastating source of brain injuries. In my opinion, modern law should do more to discourage such attacks, ranking deliberate assaults on human heads as a half-step shy of attempted murder.

Of course, creating momentum for such a humane modernization of the legal system in a society in which men get paid millions of dollars to publicly target one another's brains—for sport—may be difficult.

Giving Our Brains a Fighting Chance

Boxing makes me mad. In fact, whenever I see a boxing match, I get so enraged at the insupportable cruelty of it, the shameful inhumanity of it, the basic brutality of it, that I want to shout "No!" My muscles begin to bunch and my tendons tauten like bowstrings as my body unconsciously prepares itself to leap into the ring to stop the fight by beating the participants into a high-speed retreat! But then, perhaps boxing is popular precisely because it evokes such primitive instincts.

The goal of boxers is to knock each other out. This probably produces permanent brain damage—a ghoulish goal for a modern sport. I enjoyed watching boxing when I was younger, but after caring for a number of former boxers, I can no longer watch two human beings pounding each other's heads with sixteen-ounce gloves without thinking of the grim and potentially life-changing cerebral consequences.

When I first saw Muhammad Ali (then named Cassius Clay) practicing that sweet science, I was more dazzled than dismayed. Ali was glib, graceful, outrageous, and determined. I followed his career, impressed by the man's physical courage and indomitable spirit, and later—after sixty-one professional bouts and a decline into the near stasis of parkinsonism—by his dignity during his public battle with neurodegeneration. Ali's "ropa-dopa" strategy of absorbing blows to wear out his opponent may have contributed to the fact that he almost certainly lost most of the dopamine-based brain system that once gave him his grace. He probably also has more plaques and tangles than he ought to at his age. As I mentioned earlier, the discovery of the beta-amyloid link between head trauma and Alzheimer's disease came first from a study of boxers' brains. Now that we know its effects, boxing, like gladiatorial combat, should probably be retired to the colorful realm of sports history.

Many athletic contests do not overtly make knockouts their raison d'être, but they nonetheless have that effect. The Brain Injury Association reports that more than 750,000 Americans experience sports-related injuries each year, of which 82,000 involve a brain injury requires medical attention. These numbers actually greatly underestimate the problem, since most concussions go unreported. In 1999 research published in the *Journal of the American Medical Association* estimated 63,000 annual concussions among high school students alone. Football is notorious for head trauma; 20 percent of high school players and 33 percent of college players suffer concussions, and at least one out of every 3.5 professional games (a likely underestimate) involves knockouts, for a total of about 100,000 concussions from football alone each year. When the TV announcers gaily refer to this event with the euphemistic word *ding*, they are actually describing a brain injury with potentially lifelong consequences. And once a football player sustains his first concussion in a game, he is six times as likely to sustain another, probably because of slowed reaction time and mild confusion.

Even some supposedly noncontact sports take a toll on the head. Consider soccer.

When her team was declared the winner of the historic 1999 World Cup, Brandi Chastain ripped off her shirt in an unforgettable display of sheer athletic exuberance, watched on TV by millions. She was later quoted as explaining, "I lost my mind for a second." After all, her team had just beaten a superb Chinese team by a hair. But an hour earlier we all had watched and worried as her teammate Michelle Akers lay facedown near the goal, got up slowly, and left the game with a concussion. About 5 percent of soccer players sustain a known TBI, not counting the vastly greater number who may be subtly affected by "heading" the soccer ball (using their heads to redirect a ball in play). I hope Chastain was correct, that she just lost her mind for a second. But the impact of the game on her and her teammates' minds may perhaps persist somewhat longer than that: heading soccer balls has recently been shown to be correlated with brain damage, and soccer players score lower than other athletes on scores of memory and planning.

Brain injury also ranks as the most common type of injury among children and adolescents participating in winter recreations such as ice hockey, skiing, snowboarding, and sledding. Baseball, Rollerblades, skateboards and scooters, golf and gymnastics, wrestling and martial arts, equestrian polo and water polo, sailing and hang gliding—all of these appear in the long and diverse list of sports associated with recreational TBIs. New evidence shows that two or more significant blows to the head while playing sports can harm a teenager's thinking abilities for years. We need a sensible approach to weighing the great good of sports against the great bad of TBI.

Toward that end, the American Academy of Neurology has come up with guidelines for the management of concussion in sports. The guidelines tell coaches and players how to rate the severity of a concussion, how to judge what type of evaluation is needed, and how soon it's safe to return to play. These guidelines are an excellent start. They reflect both our concern and our growing knowledge about the long-term effects of TBIs. Still, a couple of revisions are in order.

First, the guidelines permit the coach to send a player back into a game after a "mild" concussion. That may not be a great idea; even the slightest residual confusion or mental slowing could set the athlete up for another injury—and two-in-a-row is known to be very bad for the brain. A better rule of thumb would be that a player who experiences *any* confusion after a head injury should sit down and save his brain. Second, the guidelines are not clear about who should evaluate the player if he or she is concussed. I would propose a no-ifs-ands-or-buts brain-saving rule: if a player is confused for more than fifteen minutes after a head injury, he *must* be assessed by a neurologist. Third, the guidelines say that if the athlete has a headache or other symptoms for more than a week, he should get a CT scan or MRI, and if the scan shows an abnormality, the athlete is out for the season. I'm not sure that we should count on the results of these conventional brain-images to make such an important decision; CTs and MRIs are remarkably weak tools for detecting DAI. The best detector of subtle signs of brain injury is still a physician with expert knowledge of head trauma, someone who can uncover any incoordination, subtle emotional changes, or slowing of mental speed. Child or adult, professional or weekend warrior, anyone who suffers a knockout on the field of play should be seen by a brain-injury specialist for this kind of assessment. Finally, the guidelines say that an athlete who is knocked out but has no complaints after one or two weeks can return to play with no medical follow-up. But many postconcussive symptoms take longer to appear. I'd suggest that anyone who is truly knocked out deserves at least one follow-up medical exam two or three months after the injury.

My goal is not to pull people away from the games they love. We don't need neurologists to prowl the sidelines with stretchers and MRI scanners. But we do need sensible guidelines to limit the long-term consequences of head injuries as much as we can—to save our brains while we revel in the vital joy of sports.

And for certain favored human activities—football and hockey, bicycling and motorcycle riding—we need helmets.

Woodpeckers, Helmets, and the Human Brain

The woodpecker slams its beak into the tree trunk at a speed of twelve to fifteen miles an hour, thousands of times a day. Amazingly, woodpeckers apparently do not suffer brain damage (although it might be hard to tell). Naturalist E. O. Wilson speculates that two things save woodpecker brains: one, these birds have such tight-fitting skulls that, when the beak hits the tree, the brain doesn't slosh forward to slam into the bony skull; and two, they keep their heads and bodies in a stiff line as they hammer, which prevents dangerous rotational movement of the brain.

People are not built like woodpeckers; nor do we have the thick skulls of moose or goats or other species that use head-butting for ritual contests of sexual rivalry. So our brains are going to slosh forward in a collision, and our skulls may break. To mitigate this risk, humans have worn helmets for thousands of years.

Helmets can help in several ways. They absorb the kinetic energy of a blow; they disperse the energy so that the impact gets spread out over a larger surface area (a feature called load spreading); they decrease the abruptness of brain deceleration inside the skull; and—with some designs such as the integrated helmet-and-Quasimodo-like neck pad you see on some football players—helmets can mimic the woodpecker's stiff posture by preventing the head from snapping back relative to the neck and shoulders.

Five large studies have shown that helmets reduce the risk of brain injury for bicyclists by an average of 88 percent. And if a bicyclist wearing a helmet does sustain an injury, it is often limited to a concussion rather than the type of catastrophic, coma-producing injury we often see in helmetless riders. Helmets are also incredibly effective for motorcycle riders; in 1993, two years after California implemented its helmet law, there was an annual savings of $35 million in medical costs for those involved in motorcycle accidents, and 73 percent of the decline in the costs of hospitalization was attributed to decreased need for treatment of brain injuries. The conclusion is obvious: if every rider of a bicycle or motorcycle wore a helmet, the toll taken by TBI in both money and brains could be drastically reduced.

That's a big if, because despite all the evidence about the protective value of helmets, not every rider wears one. For example, in a 1990s study conducted over a five-year period in British Columbia, more than 70 percent of injured bicyclists reported no helmet use. What inspires people to use or not use helmets? It seems to depend on many factors, including age, education, economic status, and a temperamental desire for risk seeking. Sex is another big factor; males are less likely to wear helmets and are more likely to have accidents. And money is definitely an object: in a discount price program in Grand Junction, Colorado, when helmets were sold at $5 to $15 over two years, community helmet use increased from 10 to 37 percent. Helmet wearing was rare when most baby boomers were growing up, and as a result, few adult riders today have caught the wave. But the risk of serious brain injury shoots up if the rider is over age thirty-nine. School-based educational programs increase youth helmet use, so even though adults may be more resistant to change, helmet education programs sponsored by employers, municipalities, and health insurers would probably make a big difference in reducing the number of brains at risk.

The savings would go up further with better helmet design. This is one of the hidden barriers to good brain protection: practically all of the engineering to prevent TBIs is focused on protecting the *skull* instead of protecting the *brain*.

People who test helmets fit them onto dummies, cadavers, or monkeys. Then they drop them or smash them and test them primarily to see whether the skull within will fracture. They do little or no testing for side impact resistance. They don't account for rotation of the head. They don't consider the fact that the head is attached to the neck with a spinal cord that we also need to take care of. But when people are admitted to hospitals after accidents, there is a greater loss of consciousness, longer comas, and more serious outcomes by far when there is bleeding in the brain, diffuse axonal injury, or spinal cord damage than when the skull is fractured. To put it bluntly, who cares if you fracture your skull? We're interested in saving brains, not bones! What we need is *biofidelity*—helmet engineering that has something to do with real life. Current testing procedures have minimal biofidelity, and the result is that—even in this era of astonishing medical knowledge and materials science—we are giving people suboptimal helmets.

Some of the solutions are obvious. A meeting of the minds between neuroscientists and engineers could result in improved designs for hard hats, bicycle helmets, and motorcycle helmets. In the meantime, even the current designs are a huge improvement over bare-naked heads, and we should all wear the best helmets we can get. Advocates should encourage expanded safety programs in schools and identify opportunities for education of adult riders. Helmet sellers should be expected to complete a minimal training course in fit and function. Helmet laws for adults are politically touchy, but the remarkable difference they make in preventing indescribable suffering and reducing the enormous public costs of medical care mandates that legislators in the twenty-some states without such laws should fight to secure this public health good.

And then we'll only have to worry about the main cause of head injuries: automobile accidents.

Head Injury for Dummies

The National Highway Traffic Safety Administration (NHTSA) is charged with studying America's most dangerous daily activity, the use of the automobile. Since 1979, NHTSA's New Car Assessment Program (NCAP) has used crash-test dummies in accident simulations. These dummies have evolved from the crude mannequins of old into highly sophisticated instruments that mimic the human body's response in a crash—call them "smart dummies." The component of the "dummy-response" that's used to predict the effects of a crash on a human head is called the head injury criterion (HIC).

HICs are numerical estimates of the damage your head would suffer in a frontal collision. For example, an HIC of 1,000 is claimed to predict about an 8.5 percent risk of death from head injury—the risk that the government regards as acceptable for passenger cars. HICs lower than 1,000 mean a reduced risk, and HICs greater than 1,000 mean an increased risk. The good news is that the average HIC has dropped significantly in recent years, thanks to the evolution of modern safety features. Safety glass, energy-absorbing steering columns, padded dashboards, seatbelts, and front air bags have all improved the head injury numbers for crash-test dummies. As a result, passenger cars tested in the NCAP program have exhibited a striking decline from an average HIC of about 1,300 in 1980 to about 600 in 1998.

The bad news is that an HIC tells us less than meets the eye. We need to know what happens to the brain in auto accidents, but it's extremely hard to do a good brain-injury experiment to find out. We cannot use live people. We cannot use our closest ape relatives, chimpanzees; a chimp would be a poor substitute for a five-foot-nine human with a very different shape of skull and brain, and besides, it's a gruesome idea. So the early brain-injury research used human cadavers.

Starting in the 1950s, engineers measured the force it takes to fracture the skull of a cadaver. But as we've already seen, a skull fracture is not very useful for telling us what a TBI does to the brain. So in the hopes of better biofidelity, scientists pumped dye into the blood vessels of 41 cadavers' brains, then rated the severity of injury based on the amount of dye that leaked out of the vessels, attempting to estimate the likelihood of bleeding in the brain. The weakness of this experiment is obvious: after death, no heartbeat pumps up the blood vessels, no nerve activity tenses the muscular walls of arteries, no platelets plug leaks, no molecular pumps protect the blood-brain barrier, and no free radicals or excitatory transmitters are poised to explode cells. Most importantly, these tests give us absolutely no information about DAI, the really deadly problem in head trauma.

Based on these primitive cadaver tests, NHTSA went on to build its crash-test dummies. The current model is called the Hybrid III. When the government does crash tests, it measures the forces that impact the Hybrid III's head, but these tests are based entirely on *whether the same forces would cause a fracture in a cadaver skull or a dye leak in a cadaver brain*. In other words, all the data we get about brain safety in automobiles come from studying plastic folks designed to mimic cadavers, not people. As a result, we're really not at all sure how well the HIC predicts brain damage in auto accidents.

The HIC is better than nothing. We should definitely consider it when we choose a car. But we *must* develop better measures if we want to build twenty-first-century cars that will save the brain.

The Brain-Toll of Rollovers

America's recent love affair with sport utility vehicles (SUVs) has brought the dangers of vehicle rollovers screaming into the headlines. In 1999 an estimated 47,000 people were injured in rollover crashes on U.S. roads, the highest number in history. And between 1991 and 1999, 1,142 people died in rollover crashes of Ford Explorers alone. What this data does not reveal is that, should you survive, *rollover crashes are extremely likely to leave you brain-damaged.*

You don't have to tell Stephen Terraszas of Vacaville, California, who cares for his wife, Elizabeth. On August 22, 2000, on a trip home from a Lake Tahoe vacation, their Ford Explorer rolled over. He turned around to see his wife dangling upside down, suspended by her seatbelt, blood dripping down her head. She's suffered permanent brain damage. He still hasn't told her that their three-year-old son, Nicholas, died in the accident. If vehicle manufacturers insist on making cars that roll over, they could at least improve the roof-crush problem.

NHTSA long ago proposed to inform consumers about the rollover tendency of various cars, but auto manufacturers (with the help of certain lawmakers) fought for twenty-seven years to prevent the release of this information. The times are a-changin'. Late in 2000, over the objections of the auto industry, Congress finally passed a law that permits NHTSA to report rollover risk. On the NHTSA website, we can now look up a vehicle's static stability factor (SSF). The SSF is found by dividing the height of the car's center of gravity into half of the distance between the tires; this tells us how "tippy" the car will be. An SSF of 1.45 or more indicates a rollover risk of less than 10 percent, while an SSF of 1.04 or less indicates a rollover risk of 40 percent or greater. We clearly want the highest SSF we can get. The problem is that, while passenger cars are built with their center of gravity about 20 inches off the road, most SUVs' center of gravity is 6 or 7 inches higher, with serious consequences for stability. For example, the 2001 Honda Accord has an SSF of 1.45—quite good. By comparison, the 2001 Ford Explorer has an SSF of 1.06—very bad.

In fairness, the SSF is *not* a perfect way to predict real-life rollovers. A dozen factors from springs and shocks to electronic stability controls to driver aggressiveness all play a role in rollover risk. Auto manufacturers will not tell you how strong their roofs are, a factor that may make all the difference in preventing your head from being crushed. But the SSF, like the HIC, is currently the best information we have.

The Double-Edged Sword

The weight of a car affects road safety, and two simple laws predict how. Law 1: the lighter the vehicle, the less risk to other road users. Law 2: the heavier the vehicle, the less risk to its occupants. This is putting it mildly. In fact, a hundred-pound difference in the weight of two colliding cars makes a major difference in the risk of death. Let's add the effects of age and sex. A fifty-year-old woman driving a 2,500-pound car will have 10.8 times the risk of death, in a head-on collision, of a twenty-year-old man driving a 3,000-pound car. Our personal-interest incentive to get a heavy vehicle goes up rapidly if we are older, or female, or surrounded by drivers in heavy cars. Although these calculations are based on the risk of death, it's a fair bet that the same laws apply to some extent to the risk of brain injury.

Unfortunately, most weighty passenger vehicles are high-riding SUVs or full-sized pickup trucks—vehicles that tend to have mediocre crash-test performance, middling head protection, and a nasty tendency to roll over. You have a stark choice: your head is better protected in a heavier car; but if you drive such a car, you put everyone in lighter cars at increased risk of harm. Could we ask for a more elegant conundrum for the social contract, balancing the good of the one versus the good of the many? Ideally, all of us would agree to buy 3,000-pound sedans with bumpers fixed eighteen inches up from the ground. This will never happen; personal expression is at stake. So those who buy themselves an extra hundred pounds of metal start a bloody competition in which consumers leapfrog one another to get ahead. The arms race of progressively bigger family vehicles (mostly tippy SUVs) not only clogs the pavement with ungainly street-oxen but drains what's left of the world's fossil fuel reserves at an ungodly rate. At a certain point, increasing public awareness of SUV rollover tendencies may begin to act as a disincentive.

The Ideal Car for Saving Your Brain

"If you wanted her to have the world's best protection against head injury, what car would you want your wife to drive?" I asked.

"Sorry," the engineer replied, "I'm not at liberty to say."

Stan Backaitis, senior crash-test engineer at NHTSA, may have seemed exceedingly diplomatic in his answer, but he deserves credit for his principled stance against seeming to promote one particular car over another. And he is a scientist, which gives him the appreciation that there's no simple answer. We understand it's complex. We understand Stan's reluctance to offer an opinion.

We still want an answer.

"Well, would you at least say that she's safer in a Hummer than a Hyundai?"

Dr. Backaitis laughed. "You might be surprised. Look," he said, trying to make his position clearer, "a car is like a knife. You can stab someone, or you can use it for some utility. It all depends what you do with it."

He's right, of course. Cars with perfectly good safety features can have absurdly bad safety records. A Chevy Camaro has fairly good crash-test performance, but its typical driver is a young single man who drives too fast, and high-speed single-vehicle crashes push the death rate for those driving Camaros up to three times the national average. So the HIC crash-test measurement and the SSF rollover measure are just two elements of the grand equation that lets us calculate whether a particular car will boost the odds for our brains. Surprisingly, the addition of the new side air bags and side head bags does *not* give cars a better HIC. (This may be because the government does not test head impact in side collisions.)

Pushed to offer some guidelines, however, I might say this much: all other factors being equal, in two cars of the same weight, *the lower the HIC and the higher the SSF, the better.* The table on page 339 lists some popular motor vehicles, along with their HICs and SSFs, based on the most current information available at the time of this writing.

Data such as these give us only a rough guide to real-world performance. But motor vehicle accidents are clearly the major cause of head trauma for adults, and they may well be a significant contributor to the terrible and accelerating toll of aging-related cognitive decline. Your car is a mobile helmet, so you want the best. This is one clear opportunity to make a lifestyle choice that may save your brain. These are my suggestions:

First, drive safely. That does not mean simply the conservative defensive driving that is always healthful. It means getting your vision tested as part of your annual physical and getting your hearing checked every few years as well. If you are older than seventy, you might bravely step forward and volunteer to retake your driver's test every few years. If your skills have eroded, it's far better to find out about it before you are upside down in a ditch having a tête-à-tête with the jaws of life. Males under age twenty-five must be persuaded—by strict enforcement and serious penalties—to find a less deadly way to express their natural competitive urge than by aggressive driving.

Second, buckle up. This song is much sung, yet a substantial number of people still drive without seatbelts and fail to ensure that all their passengers are safely buckled in. That's like a pilot saying, "Hey folks, there's usually enough fuel; no reason to check the gauge before takeoff." Wearing your seatbelt and shoulder harness at all times vastly reduces the risk of head injury and injuries of every kind.

Table 4
Head Injury Criterion (HIC) and Static Stability Factor (SSF) of Several Popular Motor Vehicles

MAKE	MODEL/YEAR*	WEIGHT (LBS.)	HIC DRIVER	HIC PAS-SENGER	SSF**
Acura	2001 3.2 TL 4-door with standard side air bag	3,493	547	541	
Audi	2001 A8 with standard side head and air bags	3,751	384	384	
Chevrolet	2001 Silverado Ext. cab 4x4 pickup	4,423	825	704	1.19
Chevrolet	2001 Suburban 4-door 4x4 with standard side air bag	5,699	659	467	1.08
Chrysler	2001 PT Cruiser, 4-door with optional side head and air bags	3,203	1080	467	1.26
Ford	Crown Victoria, 4-door	3,922	361	289	1.51
Ford	2001 Explorer with or without optional side head and air bags	4,258	567	558	1.06
Ford	2001 F-150 4x4 4-door pickup truck	4,650	439	571	1.12
Ford	2001 Taurus with or without optional side head bag	3,393	345	370	1.43
Ford	2001 Windstar with or without optional side head and air bags	4,231	256	516	1.26
Honda	2001 Accord 4 door with optional side air bag	3,078	258	414	1.45
Honda	2001 Odyssey minivan	4,244	309	379	1.32
Jeep	2001 Grand Cherokee 4-door 4x4	3,968	998	773	1.09
Lexus	2001 IS 300 4-door with standard side air bag	3,302	547	614	
Lexus	RX-300 4x4				1.21
Mercedes	1998 c230 4-door with side air bag	3,190	647	654	

continued on next page

MAKE	MODEL/YEAR*	WEIGHT (LBS.)	HIC DRIVER	HIC PAS-SENGER	SSF**
Mercedes	2000 ML-320 with side air bag	4,396	510	227	1.13
Nissan	2001 Altima 4-door	3,054	585	429	
Toyota	2001 Corolla 4-door with or without optional side air bag	2,498	722	566	1.42
Toyota	2001 Camry 4-door with or without optional side air bag	3,175	525	428	1.45
Toyota	2001 Sienna minivan	3,973	468	395	1.25
Volvo	2000 S70 4-door with standard side air bag	3,126	259	294	
Volvo	2001 S80 4-door with standard side head and air bags	3,556	401	282	

*   Unless otherwise noted, the vehicle was tested without side head or side air bags.

** SSF data available as of October 2001. New data are regularly added to the NHTSA website.

Third, adjust your headrest so that it is behind your head, not behind your neck; this makes all the difference in avoiding whiplash.

Fourth, drive a vehicle that has front- and side-impact air bags and, if possible, head bags as well; as they become available, head bags should be pursued like diamonds. Even though these inflatable bags or curtains have not been absolutely proven to help, all the preliminary evidence says they do. As of 2001, side head bags are already available in some Fords, Mercedes, BMWs, and SAABs. Look for cars that incorporate an inexpensive and simple improvement recommended by the National Crash Analysis Center: adding an inch of padding to all the hard surfaces near the driver's head. This could make a *big* difference in brain injuries on the American road.

Fifth, even though the HIC gives us less information than we want, until the government improves its methods we should choose a car with the lowest possible HIC—under 350 is good; under 200 is probably within reach. (If you don't find what you're looking for in the table, it's easy to look up these numbers on NHTSA's website.)

Sixth, buy a car that stays on all four wheels, with an SSF of 1.45 or more.

Seventh, choose a fuel-efficient two-ton car, then drive all the more safely, knowing that every pound on your side increases the risk for your fellow citizens.

Perhaps the ideal car for brain safety would be an agile tiger weighing more than 4,000 pounds, with daytime running lights, a bumper tall enough to engage the nose of a pickup truck, side head bags, extra interior padding, a very strong roof, an SSF greater than 1.45, and an HIC less than 300. There's no such beast. But the Ford Windstar, Honda Odyssey, and Toyota Sienna minivans all come pretty close (soccer moms rule), the Ford Crown Victoria is a clever bet (as police long ago discovered), and the Volvo S80 or XC90 might make the cut on further testing. Please understand: I list these models with no intention of promoting any vehicle or manufacturer, but the various cars on the road differ remarkably in their safety, and much is at stake. It is absolutely in your interest to know the differences and to reward the engineers who have been striving—with real success—to design transportation that may save the human brain.

Finally, if you are sufficiently outraged by the poverty of information that guides auto safety in the United States, and you happen to be a member of Congress, please introduce a bill to fund NHTSA to research *brain injury* (not dummy injury) in motor vehicles. If you're not a congressperson, write to one. There's a lot riding on it.

Dollars for Sense

As we have seen, conservatively speaking, head trauma affects about two million people in the United States every year—an astonishingly large number of victims. The annual cost of head trauma is about $40 billion a year, of which $20 billion is associated with the care, rehabilitation, and lost wages of survivors. But no one (to the best of my knowledge) has added up the additional monstrous cost of an increased rate of dementia.

Let's do it right now. For the sake of argument, I'll assume that only half of the annual head injuries—one million—will be severe enough to boost the risk of dementia, and that people who have had a head injury also have about twice the usual risk of dementia. At this point only a health economist (or a bookie) would wish to calculate the odds, but as a first approximation, without head trauma about 15 percent of us would normally develop dementia during our lifetimes, live an average of eight years thereafter, and need an average of $250,000 in care. But among the one million of us per year who have had a TBI, twice as many will develop dementia. That eventually means an excess of 150,000 new dementia cases each year. The cost for the nation is an additional $37.5 billion per year. Add to this the imponderable extra cost of behavioral changes after minor head trauma—all the painful distress of post-traumatic memory loss, depression, anxiety, and aggression that affects productivity and the quality of life—and you have a much greater expense. Therefore, if our nation spent an additional $30 billion per year on head trauma prevention *purely to reduce the added cost of dementia,* it might represent a terrific bargain.

Any such number is an estimate; I yield to those experts who are better able to do the math. I offer this calculation mainly to encourage our society to seriously discuss this looming dilemma: as baby boomers age, the burden of national memory loss is due to become immense, and the number of cases of Alzheimer's disease will balloon due to head trauma. This is a brain drain we can ill afford. We should do something about it.

Focused investment at every level of society could save brains from trauma. Families, schools, employers, corporations that make consumer products, and sports organizations could all help to protect brains. Putting neuroscience to work in brain-saving engineering could greatly reduce the long-term burden of aging-related memory loss.

Historically, it was doctors and government that pushed for safety glass, seatbelts, collapsing steering columns, and energy-absorbing dashboards. But more recently consumers themselves have begun to exercise their power to influence the industry toward building safer cars, by pushing for the introduction of air bags and antilock brakes. These features were first perceived as luxuries, then as desirable accessories, then as necessities. The same sequence is likely to occur with innovations to help save our brains. Vote for safety when you buy a car. It's a potent way to inspire automakers to take advantage of terrific advances in neuroscience and bioengineering, and a good bet for you.

Then all you'll need is the inspiration to get out of your car and walk. Because, as you're about to see, exercise saves the brain.

CHAPTER 17

Brain Fitness I: Using Your Body to Build Your Brain

The Tengpoche Monastery sat on its rocky base, stacked high in tiers of sugar-white walls, trimmed with chocolate-brown beams, perched on the mountain in Nepal like a vision of Lhasa—or a giant wedding cake on a lofty plateau.

"Go . . . now ain't that a sight!!" The accent sounded more East End than East Asia. A trim balding man with a wisp of white fringe peeking from beneath a sweat-stained blue bandana had just topped the rise. He stood there, erect under the weight of his backpack, one hand atop the branch he'd found for a walking stick, grinning.

"Not quite 'ampstead, is it!" his wife agreed in a Cockney dropped H as she came up beside him. Expertly shrugging off her backpack, she plopped down onto the moss. The man did the same. They sat together, silent a moment, taking in the scene—the towering snow-capped peaks, the slate gray rock and evergreen moss of the plateau, and the monastery, primal and regal, rising toward the utter blue of the nearby sky—a nice reward for their tough, uphill, high-altitude trek. Although they appeared to be in their late seventies, they were barely winded.

"Has Sir 'illary come?" the man asked me.

I was sitting nearby on a rock, drinking water from a plastic bottle. "Not yet." I smiled back. "They say he's coming by helicopter."

"Helicopter? Gor, and 'im the climber." To his amusement, Sir Edmund Hillary, the first Westerner atop Mount Everest, would be flying up to the monastery rather than walking like the rest of us.

Today was a special day: a tiny hydroelectric project was bringing electricity to the famed monastery for the first time. Hillary was due for the ceremony. Climbers and trekkers who happened to be in the region had gathered on the plateau for a glimpse of history.

"I'm Edward." The man smiled at me.

"Gracie," the woman introduced herself.

And while we waited to meet Sir Hillary, they told me the story of how they'd come to be here, the life changes that had brought them all the way from Cheapside to Nepal. A decade before this trek to Mount Everest Base Camp, Edward had been an overweight pipe fitter en route to his first heart attack.

"Doc told me, 'Cut it out, or you'll be pushin' daisies inside a year.' My belly was out to 'ere." He put his hand in the air six inches from his waist. "Six pints a night."

"When d'you stop a' six?" his wife chided gently.

"I didn't mind 'em. Then—boom—like a 'orse sit on me chest." He described his heart attack, his recovery, and the physical therapist who had encouraged him to walk, then to start jogging. A ten-kilo weight loss followed, then a decision to give up the pipes for something more interesting. A course in computer repair, and now a thriving new business.

"Mark me down for it: you'll be usin' the computer to buy knickers and jam before I'm gone." He winked like a conspirator. "It's made me a new man! If you were smart, you'd go 'nto computers as well."

Unquestionably Edward had been smart to get into computers; it sounded like an exhilarating lifestyle change. The question—though a decade passed before I even thought to ask it—was whether his smartness was in any way the result of his new-found fitness. Some new evidence says it might well have been.

Exercise is good for the heart; this commonplace of preventive medicine is now familiar to schoolchildren and their grandparents alike. Now new discoveries have shown us the secret biological links between a sound body and a sound mind, leading to a revelation: exercise is *great* for the brain. In this chapter, we'll start with the basics—how physical activity can prolong your life and defend your heart. Then we'll move on to the good stuff—how fitness seems to do everything from blocking strokes to adding new neurons to your brain.

Just Do It, and Live

The basic point about physical activity and physical fitness is that they lengthen life. Multiple studies of human longevity, sorting through dozens of factors from genes and sex and race to alcohol use and personality, have shown over and over that people who are fit or active or both live longer.

Note that *activity* and *fitness* are two different things. *Activity* means just what it sounds like—moving about, doing physical activities. We measure activity in terms of the amount of energy burned to do a particular task; for example, it takes about 100 kcal of energy to walk a mile.

Doctors can get a rough idea of a person's activity level by adding up all the things the person says he's done that week, from watching TV to working in the garden to walking up a couple flights of stairs. But the problem with measuring activity levels is that measurements are typically based on whatever people tell us, and some people are understandably tempted to exaggerate ("Uh, sure, Doc, I jog five miles every day, rain or shine").

Fitness, on the other hand, is a person's actual ability to do things—and that's something doctors can measure with much more precision. What's more, we are able to separately measure two major types of fitness: *aerobic fitness,* or endurance, and *anaerobic fitness,* or strength. As we shall see, both types enhance our lives, but only the first type seems to build our brains.

Aerobic fitness is the type of fitness you get when you engage your big muscle groups in continuous motion, such as jogging, swimming, dancing, or bicycling—anything that gets your heart rate up, but not to the point that you are forced to stop due to shortness of breath or exhaustion. (When New Zealand led the world in training their long-distance runners back in the 1960s, they used a rule for keeping the exercise aerobic: if you can't carry on a conversation, you're running too fast.) Still, at some point, no matter how hard you're working or how fast you're running, you can't further increase how fast you're burning oxygen to make energy. That point is your maximal velocity of oxygen use, known as your VO_2MAX.

The VO_2MAX is a great measure of aerobic fitness, so exercise physiologists have developed a reliable way to measure it in the lab. You stand on a treadmill, and they gently clip your nose shut and ask you to breathe through a clear plastic tube that's hooked up to a computer. You start walking, then jogging, then running; the treadmill gradually tips up and goes faster and faster; finally you reach the point where the computer says, "That's it; you've reached your maximum velocity of burning oxygen." That's your VO_2MAX. A typical middle-age man or woman who gets infrequent exercise might have a VO_2MAX of 25 to 30; frequent joggers may have a VO_2MAX of more than 45; a good marathon runner might have a terrific VO_2MAX of 70; and the highest VO_2MAX our technicians have measured in the lab at my hospital was 94, in a wild, inveterate cross-country skier. But you don't have to be a wild man to get aerobically fit. Continuous moderate-intensity activity of almost any kind will build up and maintain your VO_2MAX.

Anaerobic exercise is the other side of the coin; it is also called *strength training*—high-intensity exertion done in quick bursts, like running a hundred-yard dash or weight lifting. It's called anaerobic because it involves the type of work beyond our capacity to burn oxygen for energy, at which point the body starts making lactic acid, the chemical that makes our muscles burn like fire when we overdo it. Anaerobic strength training definitely belongs in the mix for older adults who want to maintain lean muscle mass. It offers all kinds of functional benefits, from pushing your way through heavy doors to arm-wrestling your twelve-year-old to catching yourself when you're about to fall.

The main point: whether it is activity, aerobic fitness, or anaerobic fitness, higher levels lengthen your life.

One of the best examples of this benefit was shown by the Harvard Alumni Health study, which followed 10,269 men who started college between 1916 and 1950. When these men were an average of forty-six years old, they were questioned about how many flights of stairs they typically climbed, how many city blocks they walked, and how often they pursued various types of recreation. Ten years later, when they were an average of 57.5 years old, they were interviewed a second time, to see whether they had become more or less active. They were then followed for nine *more* years to see who would survive. The results: the men who were living a vigorous life back when they were age forty-six were 13 percent less likely to die during the next nineteen years. Better yet, the men who took up a moderate sports activity during their forties or fifties had a *23 percent lower death rate*—impressive evidence that you'll live longer if you increase your activity level in middle age. And men don't have to go to Harvard to get these benefits: similar results come from studies of men from all walks of life—railroad workers, longshoremen, Seventh-Day Adventist men, middle-aged Finnish men. In every group studied, those with more active lifestyles or higher levels of fitness had lower mortality rates. Those who combine physical activity with other healthy habits enjoy even more dramatic results: based on their studies, researchers at the Royal Free Hospital have estimated that a fifty-year-old man who is obese, inactive, and a smoker has only a 42 percent chance of surviving the next fifteen years; but if that man is not obese, never smoked, and is moderately active, his chance of survival jumps to *89 percent*.

Fit women also live longer. The Cooper Institute for Aerobics Research in Dallas gave treadmill tests to 3,120 women, ranking them as low, moderate, or high in fitness. After eight years, the researchers calculated their death rate (expressed in terms of *person-years*). Low-fitness women had a death rate of 40 per 10,000 person-years; moderate-fitness women had a much lower death rate of 16, and high-fitness women had a much *much* lower death rate of 7—stunning proof that fit women live longer.

It's not just a matter of longer life—it's a matter of higher *quality* of life. People who exercise regularly have lower rates of heart attacks, strokes, and colon cancer, not to mention, if the preliminary evidence is confirmed, a lower risk of breast and prostate cancer. Why does exercise lengthen life? The answer is easy: it defends us from most of the major causes of death. And the number-one cause of death in the United States and in many other developed countries is heart disease.

Activity and the Human Heart

Edward almost died in the course of his heart attack. Thanks to a fast trip to the hospital and quick medical action, he lived to whisper to his distraught wife twelve hours later, "Don't fret, love." But many who experience their first heart attack don't survive. So the simple explanation for why exercise prolongs life largely comes down to the fact that exercise prevents that first heart attack.

Nearly a dozen American studies have shown that people in more active occupations, on average, face just half the risk of a heart attack that people in sedentary occupations face. The European Seven Countries Study pooled data on retired men in Finland, Italy, and the Netherlands and found that active men had much reduced cardiac risk factors. And after years of relative neglect, medical epidemiologists have finally turned their attention to women's hearts: the 1998 Canada Fitness Survey showed that women in the top 25 percent in terms of weekly activity had just half the risk of fatal heart attacks that women in the least-active group had. When we look at official fitness measures such as VO_2MAX, the evidence is even stronger: a study of Finnish men found that those with the highest VO_2MAX had just a *quarter* of the risk of dying from a heart attack than those with the lowest fitness measures had.

Thus, mountains of evidence show that fitness saves the hearts and lives of men and women. But to play the devils' advocate, one might ask, "So what?" The main reason for the incredible increase in the number of cases of memory loss is that we are living so much longer. So if exercise prolongs life, won't it simply boost our chances of living to the age when we can't remember why we're exercising? In fact, the opposite is true; most evidence suggests that people who are fit also spend more years with sharp wits. There are several reasons for this, but the main explanation is the most obvious one: fitness keeps blood flowing freely through the brain, so *exercisers dodge cerebrovascular compromise.*

Fitness Saves Your Brain from CVC

A decade before I met him on the mountainside, Edward had been religiously indulging in classic pub delights of fish and chips, bangers and mash, washed down with hefty quaffs of amber ale. Long before the fateful, life-changing day when the blood flow to his heart muscle dropped too low and he suffered his heart attack, the blood flow to his brain was almost surely dropping off as well. His heart was beating less efficiently; his blood pressure was inching into the danger zone; the stiff, clogged arteries in his neck were offering unnatural resistance to the vital pulses of oxygen-rich red cells; and the half-blocked arterial rivers in his brain were starting to pinch off blood flow to the tenuous little tributaries that fed the depths of his white matter. What's more, every time he loosened his belt a notch, Edward's bulging middle provoked the nasty metabolic changes of obesity. His spare tire boosted his risk for the form of insulin resistance I called "diabetes of the brain," when neurons become less able to burn glucose for thought. These unhappy processes probably began their insidious erosion of Edward's higher faculties when he was thirty or thirty-five. He probably never noticed it; only sensitive neuropsychological testing would have revealed what was really happening—the subtle slowing of information processing along thousands of miles of internal connections due to the gradual buildup of CVC, acting like mud that clogs the machinery of thought.

As we know from Chapter 10, there are two versions of CVC: stroke, and all the problems that limit delivery of blood to the brain short of a stroke, from a weak heart to high blood pressure to narrowed arteries to insulin resistance. Exercise seems to prevent *both* versions of CVC.

In the Physicians' Health Study, for instance, more than 21,000 doctors were followed for more than eleven years; the doctors reported, among other things, how often they exercised vigorously enough to "work up a sweat." Those who did so at least once a week had a 20 percent lower stroke risk than those who exercised less. The recent Northern Manhattan Stroke Study found not only that greater activity led to fewer strokes, but that it had a clear "dose-response" effect (meaning better results with more activity): people involved in light or moderate activity had a 60 percent reduction, while those involved in heavy activity had a *77 percent reduction in the risk of stroke*. This protective effect was seen in young people and older people, men and women, whites, blacks, and Hispanics, whether they had hypertension or diabetes, smoked or didn't, were slender or obese. The list of studies yielding similar results reads like a who's who of public health research, and powerfully supports the conclusion that fitness saves brains from strokes. All these results have led to the first-ever national consensus guideline: the Prevention Advisory Board of the National Stroke Association stated in May 1999 that taking "a brisk walk for as little as 30 minutes a day" can help prevent stroke.

Now, not everyone will have a stroke, but just about *everyone* has some degree of CVC by age forty. That's why it is perhaps even more important that fitness protects the human brain from CVC *short* of strokes. This more subtle benefit is harder to measure, since we are often completely unaware that CVC is chewing away at our brains until we are rushed to the ER half-paralyzed and speechless. But physical activity counteracts most of the biological factors that, long before a stroke, harm blood vessels and insidiously weaken the fabric of cognition: it helps control hypertension; it makes the heart beat more efficiently; it improves the ability of blood vessels to dilate; it lowers "bad" LDL cholesterol levels and raises "good" HDL (which helps prevent arteries in the brain from getting narrow and stiff); it boosts the body's sensitivity to glucose, which decreases the risk of diabetes; and it even lowers fibrinogen levels. (Fibrinogen is a component of blood that makes it more likely to clot; hence it is a big factor in the risk of stroke.) Furthermore, as measured using an ultrasound machine, those who are fitter have more blood flowing toward their brains. And exercise has a near-magical ability to reduce obesity, that major co-conspirator with vascular problems.

But the CVC-fighting benefits of exercise go still further.

Some of the most exciting new research on this subject comes from biopsychologist William Greenough and his colleagues at the University of Illinois: they've shown that exercise and learning encourage the growth of new capillaries—those tiniest of blood vessels—in the brains of old lab rats. Exercise also helps larger vessels resist the effects of aging: a study at the University of Pisa shows that the blood vessels of vigorous older people work just as well as those of athletes half their age. Blood vessels' use of nitrous oxide (to protect against clogging and keep themselves dilated) generally declines with aging, but the Pisa study showed that, for aerobically fit people at an average age of sixty-three, this system continued to work as well as it did *in typical twenty-seven-year-olds*. Another dynamite piece of evidence comes from legendary cerebrovascular researcher John Sterling Meyers. He divided a group of normal volunteers approaching age sixty-five into three groups: those who continued to work, those who retired but kept up regular physical activities, and those who retired but did not participate in regular physical activities. Over a four-year period, cerebral blood flow declined in retirees who became inactive but remained good both in those who kept working and in those who retired but kept physically active. The bottom line: in many important ways, an active life helps save your brain from CVC.

More Brain Benefits

And fitness does much more for the brain. Recent lab studies have let us see the molecular miracle of fitness in action.

Rats love to run. Whether out of sheer instinct for movement, or perhaps for stress relief, a rat given a smooth-spinning exercise wheel may run up to a mile and a half a night. A recent study showed that if we give an exercise wheel to an out-of-shape older rat, as he gets fitter, he will start making more mitochondria inside his neurons, essentially giving himself a more efficient brain. Endurance training has also been shown to regulate the rodent immune system, including those nasty inflammatory cytokines. Such cytokines are believed to be directly involved in ARNAT and Alzheimer's, so this may actually be a specific way that exercise helps our brains fight off Alzheimer's.

However, what's really interesting is the possibility that physical activity actually *boosts neuronal growth*. Consider a recent experiment done at the University of California at Irvine: the researchers gave rats different amounts of access to running wheels, from zero to seven nights a week, then checked the rats' brain chemistry. The more nights a rat ran, and the farther it ran each night, the greater the expression of brain-derived neurotrophic factor (BDNF), a key protein for growing and nurturing brain cells in the hippocampus. This experiment amounts to perhaps the first demonstration in history that *exercise may encourage the growth of hippocampal memory cells!* We know that a high-fat diet can reduce BDNF levels in the brain; neuroscientists at UCLA's Brain Research Institute are now testing the possibility that exercise may actually *reverse* the decline in BDNF seen in older rats who've grown up on a high-fat diet. It's easy to imagine how such discoveries might apply to helping people overcome the first world's obesity-induced brain drain.

What's the cognitive payoff? After all, it's one thing to say that fitness is associated with fewer strokes, better cerebral blood flow, billions more oxygen-rich red blood cells rushing every day through freer-flowing vessels in the pulsing depths of our brains, better burning of glucose, better control of inflammation, and a better broth of neuronal growth factors. It's another thing to say it helps the mind. Indeed it does.

Fitness and Cognition

Study after study has shown that, on average, adults with higher levels of fitness have higher levels of cognitive functioning. For instance, in multiple research projects conducted during the 1980s and 1990s—including studies from Ohio State University, Scripps College, the University of Texas, Maastricht University in the Netherlands, and the Australian National University—older men and women who were more physically active had higher average cognitive scores.

Of course, these are just average findings; there are always exceptions, and we all may know someone as sedentary as a house cat who is nonetheless brilliant, or someone else who is as strong as a tree—and just as bright. Exercise alone does not predict intelligence; fitness is just one of many factors that benefit the mind. Genes and early education will always limit the brain-benefits of exercise, so a fellow who spends the spring getting into shape to run his first 10K may push his IQ up a point or two, but he won't see a quick and dramatic boost in his memory. Moreover, exercise doesn't boost *every* type of thinking; new research shows that fitness improves particular mental abilities.

Specifically, fit people show their advantage in *fluid* intelligence rather than in *crystallized* intelligence. This makes intuitive sense; as I mentioned in Chapter 3, crystallized intelligence (often-used information that we gain early in life) is quite resistant to loss with aging and tends to stay with us whether or not we are physically fit. Fluid intelligence on the other hand (the ability to learn new information) is more sensitive to aging-related decline. As it turns out, this is also the exact sort of intelligence we are most likely to retain if we are active and fit.

Other features of cognition that tend to slip with aging—and tend to be protected by fitness—include *frontal lobe functions,* which cover a wide range of skills, such as the ability to make a good plan or ignore distractions while solving a problem, and *speed of information processing.* The latter is the ability to make lightning-fast decisions, such as when to slam on the brakes in traffic, how much to tip at a Paris restaurant, or how to drive a rental car from Heathrow airport to a London hotel at rush hour, staying left, reading the street signs as they flash by, and surviving all the last-minute turns. Such rapid-fire decision making requires cognitive speed, and the Maastricht Aging Study showed that aerobically fit people at every age from twenty-four to seventy-six had higher cognitive speed. Such brain-taxing abilities are sometimes measured with tests of *complex reaction time,* and University of Texas researchers indeed found that older women who had better aerobic fitness had faster complex reaction times. What's more, among 6,979 British men and women aged eighteen to ninety-four, those who walked more had faster complex reaction times.

As always, we have to wonder whether these benefits are all just a matter of good genes. Someone might speculate, "Maybe the folks who have genes for intelligence just happen to have genes for living an active life." That's why a study of 222 Swedish twin pairs is so important: despite having identical genes, *the fitter member of each twin pair was more likely to have the higher cognitive scores.*

Thus, we have super evidence that fitness leads to better mental performance in key areas. Among young people, all other things being equal, those who are fitter have the advantage; and among older people, those who *stay* fit are more likely to *keep* their youthful mental abilities. In other words, *fitness almost certainly helps prevent aging-related cognitive loss.*

That leads naturally to the next question: if you get fit, will you get bright? Multiple studies have been done to test this idea. Some say yes.

Use Your Muscles and Protect Your Brain from ARNAT

In a classic study, physiologist R. E. Dustman divided 45 older men into three groups. Fifteen men began doing aerobic exercise, 15 began strength training, and 15 remained inactive. After four months, the men in the aerobic exercise group had a 27 percent improvement in VO_2MAX. *Both* groups of exercisers showed cognitive gains, but the men who did aerobic exercise had bigger gains than the strength trainers. Women get cognitive benefits from exercise as well: psychologists at the Prince of Wales Medical Research Institute in Australia enrolled more than 90 healthy older women in a long-term exercise program; twelve months later the exercising women had not only better muscle strength but longer memory spans and faster reaction times as well. Similar results have come from at least five other exercise-for-intellect experiments involving both men and women.

As exciting as that may sound, not every study of exercise-for-cognition produces positive results. It's asking a lot to expect fitness programs to *boost* braininess; their main effect, instead, is to help us *keep the braininess we already have.* Look at it this way: neurodegeneration and CVC typically chip away at our brains over the course of thirty to sixty years. Every year of inactivity potentially means a further decline in thinking. People who've stayed fit over those years have resisted these processes, meaning that they now show the results *of decades* of brain self-protection. But fitness experiments typically last only from one month to one year. We really can't expect exercisers to show a big cognitive advantage over nonexercisers in such a short time period. Multiyear studies at both the University of Washington and at California State University at

Fullerton found that fitness training did little to *improve* the cognition of previously sedentary older adults. But at the end of these studies, the exercisers definitely had higher scores than nonexercisers, because they *maintained* their intellects.

So, to fit our conclusion within the larger story of human aging, we might say that exercise does about the same thing for brains that it does for bones: it has a minor effect on boosting bone density, but it has a major effect on preventing the loss of bone density, thus preventing osteoporosis. In the same way, increasing your activity level may make you only a *little* brainier, but its more important effect is to fight off the demons of CVC and neurodegeneration, year in and year out, keeping your neurons plastic and your mind agile—ready to learn, eager for new challenges, able to advise.

Of course, what we would *really* like is unequivocal proof that exercise prevents Alzheimer's disease. Scientists are just about there.

For instance, in the famed Framingham Heart Study, recent data from more than 4,000 people showed that active men and women definitely had a lower risk of dementia. Smaller studies done in Denver and in the Japanese town of Hisayama showed the same thing. To be fair, not every study has shown that exercise beats back the demons of Alzheimer's. But a study released in 2000 by neurologist Arthur L. Smith and his colleagues at Case Western Reserve University confirms the typical findings: based on participation in sports between ages twenty and fifty-nine, people who had been active were 3.5 times less likely to have Alzheimer's than those who had been inactive. The neurologists suggested that exercise actually shifts brain chemistry away from the production of neuron-killing beta-amyloid. As if this weren't enough, in 2001 a gorgeous report came out from the Canadian Study of Health and Aging: 4,615 randomly selected men and women aged sixty-five years or older were questioned about their physical activities and were followed for five years. A "high level of activity" was considered exercise three or more times per week at an intensity greater than walking. In the most impressive news yet about the mental benefits of physical activity, highly active people had a 42 percent lower rate of cognitive impairment and a *50 percent lower rate of Alzheimer's.*

Such studies do not prove a cause-and-effect relationship; nor should we expect a fitness program to reverse the memory loss of existing Alzheimer's, or to save everyone's brain. One of my Alzheimer's patients was a tall, blue-eyed, gentle-spirited pulmonologist who had taken up long-distance running with his athletic wife. He nonetheless developed all the mind-mangling features of Alzheimer's at the incredibly early age of forty-eight. Clearly, there's a limit to how much fitness can do to save the brain, and for an unlucky few, genes will overwhelm the preventive effects of a healthful lifestyle. But for the majority of us, the news is terrific. Active people have a lower risk of dementia in general and Alzheimer's in particular.

This research might be considered the model of intervention for twenty-first-century medicine: new discoveries guiding us to behaviors that promote the whole spectrum of physical, emotional, and cognitive health. Seen in this light, exercise ranks right up there with nutrition and sanitation as one of the most amazing forms of preventive medicine in human history. We want to shout this promising news from the housetops: "Go for it!"

There's More: Exercise and Emotional Resilience

When you look at all of the good that exercise does for hearts and lungs, muscles and brains, you might want to immediately bookmark your place here and go out for a jog. Bear with me, because there's more: exercise also builds resistance to psychological stress.

Untangling the relationship between exercise, stress, and mood is actually rather tricky. People in good sprits are naturally more likely to feel energized, so they're more likely to be active, while people with depression are more likely to feel glued to the couch by an unshakable torpor. So it's no big surprise when—for example, in the Harvard Alumni Study—researchers find that the more active people were less depressed. The real question is whether there's a cause-and-effect relationship: can regular physical activity boost human mood?

The answer is yes. Nearly a score of well-designed intervention programs have shown that both aerobic and anaerobic fitness programs enhance the sense of well-being. This is not just a "runner's high," that brief euphoria that may result from the release of endorphins and that enables athletes to float blissfully through the fifth mile of their daily run. This sense of well-being is a much more continuous and lasting experience, making us less prone to irritability, anxiety, and depression over all the months or years we get regular exercise. It seems to work for all ages and both sexes. In a study of Korean women between sixty and seventy-five years old, for instance, a simple walking program both boosted their VO$_2$MAX and reduced their anger levels. And in the big British "Prince of Wales" study, not only did exercising women gain in strength and memory scores, but they also experienced reductions in anxiety and depression.

Exercise also helps to control the more serious symptoms of clinical depression. Involvement in an aerobic exercise program improves mood scores in major depression, "atypical depression," and seasonal affective disorder, according to several research projects. And in one much-quoted study conducted at Duke University, psychiatrists found that a modest exercise program treated major depression just as well as Zoloft (sertraline), a potent and proven serotonin-reuptake inhibitor.

I do not recommend physical activity in itself as an adequate prescription to rescue someone from the living hell of major depression; that life-threatening condition requires prompt medical attention. But as an adjunct to more definitive treatments, exercise may be terrific medicine.

When I first met Celine, a thirty-eight-year-old mother of three who was still stricken with grief eighteen months after the sudden death of her father, she could barely drag herself to her appointments. Her face was a somber mask; she sat bent in her chair as if pulled down by the weight of her heart. After two months with regular psychological support and antidepressants, her face became more animated; her posture began to unbend. She also began to talk about the things she used to love doing—family bicycle rides, hikes in the local mountains. Once that energy began to flow back into her body, I strongly urged her to restart her favorite activities, beginning slowly with an early morning walk. Another month passed; she came in looking, for the first time, like a person with hopes for the future. "We hiked up Mount Wilson on Sunday. Mark and the kids had fun." She smiled a brief and glorious smile.

The exact reason for the antidepressant benefit of exercise remains unknown. Some neuropsychiatrists speculate that exercise restores normal brain endorphin levels; others that activity improves the function of serotonin-producing neurons. But a very interesting recent discovery suggests a completely different mechanism: neurobiologists at the University of California at Irvine took rats and exposed some of them to an antidepressant, and others to both an antidepressant and a running wheel. After twenty days, those who got both exercise and the antidepressant had a *much* bigger increase in neuron-growing BDNF levels in the hippocampus than those who had only taken antidepressants. Whatever the mechanism, regular activity seems to help lift the leaden load of depression, accelerating the recovery of hope and health. Furthermore, roughly speaking, 20 percent of all people are predisposed to chronic sadness or *dysthymia*. It's a good bet that regular exercise could help prevent such people from lapsing into true clinical depression. The potential benefit to the brain is obvious: since emotional stress, anger, and severe or chronic depression can worsen the aging-related changes in the hippocampal memory cells, exercise may actually cushion the brain from the hammer of aging.

Another benefit of exercise is improved sleep. Unfit people sleep poorly after a physically taxing day. Fit people, on the other hand, sleep better. As long as they finish their brisk half-hour-around-the-neighborhood walk at least four hours before bedtime, they'll fall asleep more quickly, sleep more soundly, and feel better-rested the next day. Exercise also reduces the risk of sleep apnea—periods of interrupted breathing that can leave middle-age men, in particular, exhausted, cognitively slowed, and at higher risk for strokes and heart attacks. The conclusion is clear: stay fit, sleep well, think better.

We can go a step further: exercise may also reduce the risk of strokes precipitated by anger. How? Anger switches on the fight-or-flight system, leading to an outpouring of the stress hormones. In the natural world of an earlier era, when nearly everyone was fit, this revved up the pumping action of the heart and prepared us for wrestling tigers. But in our strange modern world where so many of us are unfit, stress hormones sometimes produce a deadly sequence: the tone in our blood vessels responds to stress abnormally, constricting too much. So the heart fruitlessly tries to push out blood, like a fire hydrant trying to push out water when the fire hose is squished under a truck. As a result, at the very moment when you are fuming mad, you may experience a transient but deadly drop in blood flow to your major organs, including your brain—a set-up for an anger-induced stroke. Exercise improves the way your arteries respond to stress, helping get blood up to your brain at stressful times. This benefit, combined with the sleep-enhancing, antidepressive, antiglucocorticoid, and hippocampal-neuron-saving benefits, makes fitness a remarkable, and hugely underestimated, way to fortify the brain against the poisonous influence of emotional distress.

Exercise Builds a Better Brain

A recent discovery in the field of neuroscience adds an astonishing new dimension to the link between fitness and the brain.

As I mentioned in Chapter 3, one of the most encouraging findings ever in brain science is the realization that the adult hippocampus produces brand-new neurons—adult *neurogenesis*. This happens when stem cells are recruited from our "stem cell piggy-bank" (the repository of extra stem cells located next to the brain's ventricles) and are turned into working brain cells. Neurobiologist Henriette van Praag at the Salk Institute in La Jolla, California, asked the provocative question: might exercise boost neurogenesis?

She gave running wheels to one group of mice but not to others. The rodents with wheels ran on them night after night. Later, when she examined the mouse brains, she found that the running mice grew *twice* as many new adult neurons in their hippocampi as did sedentary mice. Somehow, running signaled the central nervous system to convert more stem cells into working neurons. Running builds brains—at least in mice. "This is terribly exciting," says cognitive neuroscientist Neal J. Cohen, "given that we know the hippocampus plays a role in the memory of new facts and new events."

Why would evolution come up with this astonishing system to build new neurons in response to running? It may simply be a matter of better health. But another speculation is that running usually means rapid exposure to new territory, or hunting, or being hunted. In any of these situations, the animal is obliged to learn fast. Covering new ground, being able to navigate home, or figuring out survival strategies in the predator-versus-prey food-chain means absorbing a lot of new information. It's too soon to say for sure that humans get the same brain-building benefit as mice, but the implications of this work are potentially astonishing: active adults may prepare their brains for new situations by making new neurons.

All this was discovered a decade after I met Edward and Gracie on that high Himalayan plateau. It never occurred to me at the time that these adventurous Londoners might be manufacturing more neurons since they took up hiking. It would be unscientific for me to conclude that Edward's newfound enthusiasm for life—his embrace of new learning, his career change to the challenging world of computers, perhaps even his lust for travel—were due to better cellular signaling, enhanced cerebral blood flow, and new neurons produced by his improved physical fitness. But it's worth considering. For many years, doctors gave seniors the standard advice: "Stay active, stay sharp." That used to sound like a jolly aphorism. We now have reason to believe that it's an apt description of the way the human brain works, rebuilding itself to face new challenges every day.

How Much? What Type?

It's easy to see the big picture: humans evolved for action; inaction leads to less-than-optimum cerebral health and exposure to fewer new cognitive challenges; thinking suffers. The question is how we can use this knowledge to benefit our brains. How much should you exercise? And what kind of exercise should you do?

To some people, exercise means the calisthenics they hopped through in school. To others, it means an hour in the weight room, or even chasing a toddler down the cookie aisle at the local supermarket. It's true that increased activity, regardless of the type, seems to lower the risk of stroke and dementia, but almost all of the available evidence suggests that the type of physical activity that best prolongs life, prevents heart attacks, prevents strokes, and preserves the brain is aerobic exercise.

For example, as we saw in Dustman's classic study from 1984, aerobic training was better than strength training for boosting cognition among older men. In a more recent study, University of Illinois cognitive neuroscientist Arthur Kramer recruited 124 sedentary men and women between sixty and seventy-five years old. Half of the volunteers were enrolled in a program of stretching and toning, while the other half were enrolled in a program of aerobic walking. The walkers gradually increased their walks to forty-five or sixty minutes, three times a week. After six months, the "toners" showed no improvement in cognitive speed, while the "walkers" exhibited better aerobic fitness—and a 25 percent improvement in cognitive speed.

How much aerobic exercise is necessary to get such a benefit? For decades, fitness experts have recited the same mantra: calculate your maximal heart rate by subtracting your age from 220, then work out vigorously enough to keep your heart rate at 85 percent of that maximum, and do this for twenty consecutive minutes four times a week. But if a sedentary person leaped into his sneakers to follow this advice, he might end up panting on the side of the track after ten minutes. Rapid efforts to reverse years of inactivity are not a good idea. Men in particular tend to overdo it in the first days of a fitness program; they get exhausted, achy, or injured, then abandon the program. That's why, rather than the old aerobic formula, the Centers for Disease Control offers more flexible advice: every adult should engage in *moderate* intensity activity for at least thirty minutes, five or more times per week, or *vigorous* activity for at least twenty minutes three or more times per week.

We all have an instinctive sense for what "moderate" or vigorous" means, but a much more accurate way to measure activity is in terms of metabolic equivalents, or METs. One MET is the volume of oxygen we burn in a minute while sitting quietly—about two and a half quarts. For instance, a 155-pound man burns one MET while sitting and watching TV (this measure must be adjusted upward if he's watching a play-off game with money on the line). The table on page 359 lists typical MET levels for different activities, and states whether or not they are aerobic. To figure out which of these constitutes vigorous activity for your age and sex, use the following formula: for men, multiply your age by 0.55, subtract that number from 60, and multiply that result by 0.17. For women, multiply your age by 0.37, subtract that number from 48, and multiply that result by 0.17. A forty-five-year-old woman, according to the math, would be doing vigorous activity at 5.3 METs or more. So she'd get in her recommended activity by gardening five times or swimming three times a week.

Surprising though it may sound, moderate exercise provides almost all of the health benefits of higher-intensity exercise. The Harvard Alumni Study, for example, showed that both moderate and intense exercisers had a lower risk of stroke, but intense exercisers did not really get more of a health benefit than moderate exercisers. This finding suggests that we must cross a threshold activity level to get a benefit, but once we get over that threshold, we may gain only a little from additional activity. A similar outcome came from the Royal Free Hospital study I mentioned before, where researchers followed more than 7,000 men: up to a point, the higher the level of the men's activity, the lower their risk of strokes, heart attacks, diabetes, and death. But beyond the moderate level of activity, *there was no further measurable benefit.* In fact, excessive activity carries its own set of risks: overtrained athletes can suffer immune dysfunction, increased oxidative stress, and hormone abnormalities such as an interruption in normal growth and menstrual periods. (Look at those dazzling but undergrown female Olympic gymnasts.)

In other words, very high levels of activity will indeed increase your *fitness,* but they may offer little *health* advantage over moderate levels. Once again, Goldilocks rules. Underactivity is dangerous. Overactivity is dangerous. There is a broad and happy medium of activity that suits the human body to a T. And there is perhaps no better moderate aerobic activity than a good, brisk walk.

Activities and Metabolic Equivalents

ACTIVITY	METs	AEROBIC?
Sitting	1.0	No
Painting	3.0	No
Weeding	3.5	No
Walking	3.5	Yes
Brisk walking	4.5	Yes
Raking leaves	4.3	Yes
Golf	4.5	No
Calisthenics*	5.5 to 8.0	Yes
Snow shoveling	6.0	Yes
Weight lifting*	6.0 to 10.0	No
Tennis	5.5	Yes
Swimming laps**	6.0 to 12.0	Yes
Jogging**	6.0 to 10.0	Yes
Stair climbing	8.0	Yes
Running	13.0	Yes

*   Calisthenics can be anaerobic if the heart rate is permitted to fall; weight lifting can be aerobic if the heart rate is kept elevated. The MET value of both varies with the particular exercise.

** The MET value of swimming and jogging both vary with speed and body mass index; the MET value of jogging also depends on terrain.

Walking Your Way to a Better Brain

Think of it this way: we evolved to flourish by using a variety of physical skills, from running full stride to catch prey or escape predators, to loping proudly back to the communal fire with fresh-killed game, to leaping and dodging in the hide-and-seek of courtship in the forest. But above all, we evolved to walk—walking a few hours to gather berries, or walking hundreds of miles in the winter to follow a migrating reindeer herd. All it took was a million years of evolution for us to become expert walkers, as our pelvis rotated to put our legs in line with our spine, our skull rotated so that we could look forward, and our stride advanced from the bow-legged waddle of our chimplike precursors to the graceful ground-eating gait of bipedalism. Calorie for calorie and pound for pound, straight-legged walking is about the most energy-efficient way for a land animal to get from point A to point B. Dolphins may be the lords of the sea, eagles may be the kings of the sky, cheetahs and gazelles may be faster at the sprint, but humans are the princes of the promenade. We evolved to expect a certain type of activity, and optimum health seems to be linked to seeking that same type of activity in our daily lives. Thus, if I had to name a single form of activity that could re-create our evolutionary heritage, it would be walking.

Consider the Nurses' Health Study. In 1986, 72,488 healthy female nurses age forty to sixty-five began completing a series of detailed questionnaires about their activities. Researchers followed these women for the next eight years, documenting what happened to their activity levels and to their health. The results were published in the *New England Journal of Medicine* in 1999: those who reported at the beginning of the study that they typically walked at a brisk pace for three or more hours each week went on to have a 35 percent lower risk of coronary events than women who walked infrequently. What's more, if women who were sedentary took up activity in middle age, they had fewer heart attacks—more support for the doctrine "It's never too late." Speed counts; those who walked more than three miles per hour had better coronary results than those who walked less than two miles per hour. Better yet, the same study showed that a brisk walk for an hour a day would also cut a woman's risk of type 2 diabetes *nearly in half.* That means that walking saves women from two of the major factors that can accelerate brain aging.

Men get similar benefits from walking. In the Honolulu Heart Program and the Harvard Alumni Study, regular walkers had lower rates of heart attacks, or strokes, or both.

Walkers may also become better thinkers. We've already seen that walkers gained a 25 percent improvement in cognitive speed in the

University of Illinois exercise project. Similar results came from a study done at the University of Stockholm: 20 men and 20 women, averaging sixty-six years old, were randomly assigned to do mental exercises or to walk three times a week. The walkers—but not the mental exercisers—showed improved complex cognitive abilities. But the best news came from the Canadian Study of Health and Aging. Recall that "vigorous activity" produced an impressive 50 percent decrease in the risk of Alzheimer's. But more moderate activity—at the level of walking—produced a very respectable 33 percent decrease in the risk of Alzheimer's.

Neuroscientists are torn between excitement and caution. Could such an incredibly modest fitness program really enhance cerebral blood flow, improve neuronal oxygen delivery, boost the efficiency of glucose consumption, diminish stress- and depression-related hippocampal jeopardy, and perhaps even activate neurotrophins and favor the manufacture of new neurons? Could walking save your brain? Wow. It's definitely too soon to make an absolute statement. I don't want to exaggerate the level of scientific certainty we've reached. But it looks like we've found an excellent bet: walk, and save your brain.

The Return of the Body

Most of us are much less active than were our vigorous, muscular forebears. In a modern world that has robbed us of the natural demand for physical activity, we grow slow and jumbo-sized and, finally, forgetful. But a parade of evidence shows that a sound body truly leads to a sound mind. It seems clear that reviving our natural instinct for activity could have profound consequences for the health of our brains.

What are we going to do about it?

The Surgeon General's 1996 Report on Physical Activity stressed regular moderate activity. As Surgeon General David Satcher revealed to the *Los Angeles Times,* "We used 'physical activity' because we don't want to imply that it's a regimen like an exercise program." Quite right—the ultimate goal is not to make a nation of Spartan warriors or even nightly gym attendees and morning joggers. The goal is to restore natural activity to modern life.

Following this simple advice could almost certainly lead to wonderful brain benefits that public health officials never even considered. But how do we get there from here? Slogans such as "Just do it" are probably as effective for producing fitness as "Just say no" is for resolving the nation's massive drug problem. If it were so easy to change our lifestyles, we'd be a nation of slender Olympians. Instead, only 20 percent of Americans meet the government's recommended activity level. Even with the best of intentions, only one-quarter of those who take up exercise—like Edward and Gracie—will lastingly break the chains of inactivity; up to three-quarters will drop out and return to dangerous, brain-draining inactivity.

Reviving our natural life of the body takes three things: motive, means, and opportunity. If we tie up a woman with chores and child care and work, she may have all the motivation in the world but lack the opportunity. If a man buys a treadmill, an exercise bicycle, and a health club membership, he may have the means but lack the motive. Heart attacks do it for some, like Edward. In fact, tens of thousands of people every year take their first adult exercise as part of post–heart attack rehabilitation. That's a heck of a way to get motivated. It would obviously be better to inspire people *before* that attack, not after.

What does it take to inspire a mass jailbreak from the prison of modern passivity? Ideally, fitness should be woven into the very fabric of daily life, not patched on awkwardly at the end of the day. Of course, we cannot expect to go back to hunting and gathering, or replace desk chairs with exercise bikes in every office. But if we really want to put the surgeon general's advice into action, we'll start reevaluating school programs, work schedules, and city designs to see whether they are structured to give people the motive, means, and opportunity for safe, natural activity. We don't need the George Jetson future of moving sidewalks and floating martinis. We need just the opposite. Let's also enlist the medical profession in this cause. Some doctors may think that nothing they say will actually help, but this isn't true. In a 2001 report from the Activity Counseling Trial, when sedentary adults age thirty-five to seventy-five were given a slight nudge by their family doctors—just a few minutes of counseling a few times a year—within two years 20 percent more of the patients were meeting the government's recommended full activity level.

Here are some strategies that anyone can use to sit less and move more. Routinely wear soft-soled, low-heeled walking shoes (rather than those strange, stiff devices that are standard business and social wear), so that you're ready to stride out at every legal opportunity. Join a class to learn a team sport you never picked up as a child. Walk to lunch. Shun elevators as the muscle robbers that they are if you are going up less than five flights. Buy a treadmill (proven to be the best aerobic fitness device), and position it in front of the TV so that the one with the best view is the weight-shedding walker. Strap the baby into a Snuggli backpack while you burn up the road for half an hour on your exercycle. Rescue a dog from the pound and walk him a mile each morning and night. Set a goal, and have a friend quiz you on your progress. Make a romantic commitment to walk after dinner with your spouse every night, rain or shine. Take that golden thirty minutes a day as your human birthright, precious and nonnegotiable. Save yourself from the culture of inactivity. Start to-day. Know that every day you take those minutes, you've helped set back the clock of aging and made a vital contribution to your mind.

Finally, let's turn our attention to the other proven way to grow new brain cells: thinking.

CHAPTER 18

Brain Fitness II:
Using Your Mind to Build Your Brain

Another objection to age is that this weakens the memory. Certainly, if you fail to give it exercise, or if you are not particularly intelligent.

CICERO, CATO THE ELDER ON OLD AGE (44 B.C.)

"My synapses."

"I beg your pardon?" I asked.

"My synapses," repeated Julie, the physical therapist. "You asked what I was working on." She smiled, looking up from the book she was bent over in the corner of the clinic, studying between patients. "I'm working out my brain. I figure if I learn something new every day, I'll get great synapses."

Like triceps, or something. She may have a point.

When Julie's mother developed Alzheimer's disease, Julie rapidly plunged from the heights of delight, with a happy marriage blessed with a new baby, to the depths of distress brought on by unsought membership in the "sandwich club": young adults in a middle generation who find themselves simultaneously taking care of their growing children and their ailing parents. After several years of mutual denial, she and her mother had both accepted that her mother's memory loss made it unsafe for her to remain in her own home, so she moved in with Julie, her husband, and her baby. It was scary. Keys got lost, water was left boiling until the kettle burned, and then one day Julie's mom returned from the grocery store without the baby—an oversight. Julie was absolutely determined that her young daughter, Marianne, not find herself saddled in her own adulthood on that particular horse from hell. So Julie was using a free moment to sit in the corner of the clinic, reading about dinosaurs to exercise her synapses, hoping thus to avoid Alzheimer's disease.

How many Julies are doing the same? How many *should* be?

We don't know. At least since the second century B.C., philosophers such as Cicero have extolled the virtues of mental exercise as a way to hold off the memory loss of aging. But for all the advice of classical philosophers, the pronouncements of modern pop psychologists, the urgings of talk-show pundits, and the trend for perfectly good adult-education classes to promote themselves with seductive but unproven claims that they will "boost your brainpower," we don't know to what extent mental activity defends the aging mind and brain. The reason we don't know is that, as with many mysteries of nature versus nurture, the experiments that would *really* answer the question are impossible to perform.

In fact, the only way to tell whether a lifetime of vigorous mental activity truly helps save the brain from memory loss would be to take two comparable groups of people and randomly assign one group to live a mentally challenging life and the other a mentally stultifying life. Imagine the dean addressing your graduating college class: "Okay, folks, we have a great opportunity to contribute to science. Starting today, half of you will join group A. The other half will join group B. Group A will be asked not to read books, take a challenging job, teach their children, do cross-word puzzles, play musical instruments, or watch the Discovery Channel for the rest of their lives. Group B will not only do all of these things but will also be expected to learn Greek, write a four-movement symphony every other year, and teach college physics. Then we'll give you all a brief memory test at age eighty-five—and that will be that! Volunteers, please raise your hands. Not all at once, now."

Given the impossibility of absolute proof, we will instead look carefully at some fascinating evidence from neurobiology, epidemiology, and psychology about the possible role of mental exercise in boosting brain power, deterring memory loss, and preventing Alzheimer's disease. Our goal is similar to that of the archeologist who tripped over a big piece of the Rosetta Stone half-buried in the sand: to uncover the real story, based on the tantalizing fragments before us.

The news is good. There is an ancient truth and secret biological wisdom behind that short poem, "Use it or lose it." The latest findings speak directly to the age-old question of whether our potential for brain enhancement is a lifelong capacity, and whether exercising our brains will save them. The answer, within certain intriguing limits, is yes.

Kicking Up Tantalizing Fragments

We have known for decades that more education is associated with better health. Educated people simply live longer, for a variety of reasons, including better access to health care, better nutrition, less exposure to industrial and outdoor pollution, better compliance with medications for their high blood pressure or diabetes, and better avoidance of health-risky behaviors such as smoking and obesity. As gerontologist Paolo Timiras of the University of California at Berkeley has put it, "A higher level of education has also emerged as a factor in prolonging life and reducing disability and disease in old age." But education does not just make life longer; it makes life better. More education, especially high-school graduation, seems to be associated with a lower risk of memory loss and Alzheimer's. That's one heck of an association. Furthermore, as we saw in Chapter 6, people who pursue cognitively demanding occupations are less likely to experience mental decline. Putting these two discoveries together, we could say that *cognitive challenge*—in either youth or adulthood— seems to do wonders for the human brain. Let's look at the most interesting evidence.

In one well-known study, Harvard researchers interviewed 3,037 people over age sixty-five living in the working-class Italian community of East Boston; over a three-year period, those who had had more formal education definitely showed less mental decline. This result is an example of the late-life benefits of early-life education. A longer study of 1,488 people in Baltimore (followed for an average of 11.5 years) also found that more education in early life led to less mental decline. Early-life education also seems to specifically protect the brain from Alzheimer's: when researchers from the University of California at San Diego examined more than 5,000 elderly Chinese living in the Shanghai area, they found that those over seventy-five with little or no education were *three times* as likely to be demented as those who had attended middle school. Similar studies from Finland, Israel, Italy, France, Taiwan, Sweden, and the Netherlands have come to the same conclusion: those with more education are simply much more likely to escape the curse of Alzheimer's. To be fair, one study conducted by the Mayo Clinic failed to show that education protects against Alzheimer's, but the people in the Mayo Clinic study were so uniform in ethnic, economic, and educational background that any education-related difference may have been hard to perceive. Studies from Iowa and New Haven have shown that people who have *already* been diagnosed with Alzheimer's tend to decline more slowly if they have at least finished high school. So early-life education does seem to help protect us from aging-related decline, from getting Alzheimer's, and from going downhill quickly if we get it. This conclusion seems to support a genuine neurobiological basis for the Talmudic observation, "The unlearned lose the power of clear thinking as they grow old, but scholars gain in it as their years advance."

How much education do we need to protect the brain? Several studies have shown that literacy reduces the risk of Alzheimer's, which suggests that even the modest educational achievement of learning to read—a skill usually acquired by age ten—may help save the brain. The Shanghai study showed that middle school helped prevent Alzheimer's, and the Baltimore study showed that people with less than eight years of school were more likely to decline later in life, but that schooling *after* nine years added little to this protective effect. That might suggest that if you want to get the brain-saving effect of education, you'd better boost your brain function with cognitive stimulation by your teen years. That might sound a little disheartening if you're reading this after age twenty and wish to do more for your brain. But in the Nun Study, the Catholic sisters who had been to college were at least twice as likely to be functionally independent at age seventy-five. Taken together, these studies strongly suggest that elementary school, middle school, high school, and college all produce brain-saving effects.

You might be concerned that you're stuck with the brain you developed by the end of college—your early twenties—and that subsequent cognitive stimulation may do little to protect it later in life. But that's probably not the case. As we saw in Chapter 6, pursuing a cognitively demanding occupation through adulthood seems to protect against memory loss: a Swedish study showed that manual labor was associated with five times the risk of Alzheimer's when compared with more mentally stimulating jobs, and a French study showed that residents of Bordeaux who worked as laborers were two to three times as likely to become demented as those who worked as professionals. You might think, "Aha! But professionals get this benefit because they already had great educations, not because they led intellectually challenging adult lives." But there's good evidence that a mentally challenging occupation may even help protect the brains of people who did *not* get a terrific education; a Columbia University study showed that people with a *modest* education who nonetheless got into a high-level job had a reduced risk of Alzheimer's. It's great to know that a good, neuron-stimulating job later in life may indeed overcome the dastardly effects of a limited, neuron-numbing education earlier in life.

The brain-protecting effect doesn't necessarily require a neuron-rousing job; even mentally stimulating leisure activities may do the trick. The Victoria Longitudinal Study from British Columbia (a study of 250 middle-aged and older adults) revealed that just about any kind of "intellectually engaging activities serve to buffer individuals against decline." But the best proof comes from a very recent study done by neurologist Robert Friedland of Case Western Reserve University: he collected lifestyle histories from 193 Alzheimer's patients—recording their participation in various mental activites between the ages of forty and sixty—and compared them with older people without Alzheimer's. Those who had done more *active* mental activities, such as working crossword puzzles, reading, or playing a musical instrument, were much less likely to develop Alzheimer's. In fact, the Alzheimer's patients were more than *four times* as likely to have fallen below the average in such active mental leisure activities. The Alzheimer's patients did, however, beat the normal subjects in one activity: watching TV.

It's no surprise that people with more education or with high-level jobs or with mentally active lifestyles score better on tests of intellect. Of course they do; they've been regularly giving their brain a workout. But biologically speaking, why would a higher level of mental activity through the life span be associated with less aging-related decline in intellect, a lower risk of Alzheimer's, and a slower decline if Alzheimer's occurs?

The Volvo Effect

In life it is training rather than birth which counts.
IHARA SAIKAKU (1642–1693)

Training is everything. The peach was once a bitter almond; cauliflower is nothing but cabbage with a college education.
MARK TWAIN, *PUDD'NHEAD WILSON* (1894)

The first thing we need to sort out is whether mental activity protects the brain or some other factor is responsible for this apparent protective effect. That is, those of us with higher levels of education or cognitively challenging jobs are less likely to get Alzheimer's, but does education *itself* block the hammers of aging from squashing our neurons, or do the people who stay in school also happen to have been born with brains that are intrinsically more resistant to aging? It basically comes down to two possibilities: either mental stimulation (at school or on the job) truly changes the brain in ways that protect us from memory loss, or people who pursue more schooling and higher-level jobs happen to have built-in ARNAT-resistant neurons. In essence, it's a question of nature versus nurture: which one saves the brain?

Some research studies support the idea that nature is in charge. For instance, psychiatrist Brenda Plassman and her colleagues at Johns Hopkins gave cognitive tests to 930 elderly veterans; she then compared their scores in late life with the scores they received when they took the army's entrance intelligence test fifty years before. It turned out that their scores as young recruits were the biggest single factor in predicting their cognitive status fifty years later. This finding suggests that, no matter what education or jobs these men may have subsequently held, their native intelligence was the best predictor of their brain function in late life. Similar findings come from the Nun Study. As part of their preparation to enter the religious life, an average of sixty years ago, the sisters wrote autobiographies. Researchers analyzed the linguistic ability exhibited by those youthful novices and compared this evidence with their brains, examined after death many years later. In fourteen nuns who had died, all of those who had poor linguistic skills as young adults had Alzheimer's, but none of those with high-level linguistic skills had Alzheimer's. This is impressive evidence that if you start low, you tend to stay low and you have a big risk of Alzheimer's—a sort of Calvinist theory of brain predetermination.

But there is also evidence for the opposite point of view—that the nurturing effects of a good education and a challenging occupation can reconfigure the fate of the brain. When neurologist Linda Hershey went to the Central Population Registry of Finland, she found 17,357 pairs of same-sex adult twins. She looked at their education and at whether they were identical (sharing all their genes) or fraternal (sharing half their genes). She found that twins with higher education had a lower risk of Alzheimer's—no big surprise. But the main advantage of a twin study is that it allows us to look at the relative contribution of *genes* and *environment*. If the main reason that people with more education escape Alzheimer's is that they have great genes, we would expect that—no matter how much education they got—identical twins would be more alike in terms of the risk of Alzheimer's than fraternal twins. But, impressively, Dr. Hershey found that it *didn't matter* whether the twins were identical or fraternal; education had the same brain-saving effect. While I don't want to jump to conclusions, this is pretty good evidence that the fate of the brain is not solely a matter of genes. No matter what genome we happen to have, nurturing factors such as a good education may help protect the brain from decline.

So we have some evidence that nature (native intelligence) saves brains, and other evidence that nurture (a stimulating environment in youth and adulthood) saves brains, but the *real* story probably involves the interplay of genes with environment. (It's like asking why people who drive Volvos are less likely to die in car accidents: does the car itself protect them, or do people who buy Volvos tend to drive more carefully? *Both* factors almost certainly contribute to the final result.) Biology is *always* a blend of nature and nurture. Cicero was prescient when he said that aging is more likely to steal our memory "if you fail to give it exercise [nurture], or if you are not particularly intelligent [nature]." Strong brains are both born and made, and strong brains resist memory loss.

Will a mentally stimulating life genuinely prevent ARNAT and Alzheimer's? Suppose an educated person gets Alzheimer's-type brain changes at age sixty or seventy; would education give her such a deep reserve of mental power that the impact is hidden under the cloak of competence? (In other words, does the Volvo truly help you *avoid* the fender-bender, or does the car still drive so well after the crash that you hardly know it happened?) This brings us to the *reserve hypothesis of Alzheimer's disease*. According to this theory, a well-educated person can have serious brain damage from early Alzheimer's, yet—due to his powerful mental reserve—perform just as well as a less-well-educated person whose brain is in better shape.

Columbia University neurologist Yaakov Stern did a neat experiment to test this theory: he recruited 58 Alzheimer's patients and scanned their brains with a xenon-based scanner. Ordinarily, Alzheimer's causes diminished blood flow in the temporal and parietal lobes, but Stern found that the higher the patient's education, the *worse* their blood was flowing. Now that might sound bad, but it's not. It means that highly educated people can have ARNAT cooking in their brains for a longer time—slamming into their neurons in a series of cortical fender-benders—before the change becomes apparent and they are diagnosed with Alzheimer's. So just as we would predict from the reserve hypothesis, better-educated people can do just as well as less educated people, even when their brains sustain more damage! In other words, education saves the brain partly by giving us a wonderful *reserve* capacity, a capacity to tolerate ARNAT for years before we get impaired (just as a tough car may keep rolling down the highway despite an accident or two). The reserve hypothesis was first proposed more than a decade ago by two pioneers of Alzheimer's research, Robert Katzman and Robert Terry.

Terry, a neuropathologist, and Katzman, a neurologist, have contributed (as used to be said of some Chicago voters) early and often to the neuropathological hypothesis of Alzheimer's disease—the idea that Alzheimer's is a disease of plaques and tangles. But in 1988 they encountered a rather baffling fact. Some of the brains they had collected from elderly people were peppered with Alzheimer's-type plaques, but some of those brains were from the "control" group—*the people with normal thinking abilities*. How could these individuals have been able to think, recall, and conduct the affairs of their lives totally normally to all appearances while the tissue in their heads was quietly being devoured by the lesions of neurodegeneration? How had they, and not others, resisted the mind-bashing impact of Alzheimer's disease? Katzman and Terry pondered their finding, then looked at the relationship between the total weights of those still-working brains and the weights of the demented people's brains. They found that people with lots of plaques in their brains who were still able to think had bigger brains. *Ah,* they thoughtfully concluded, *some of us must have more of a "brain reserve" than others. Some of us just aren't as bothered by the slow attack of ARNAT.* The changes are happening in our brains, the battle is fought, and the scars are accumulating, but our wonderful brain reserve confers a resistance—almost like an immunity—to these cerebral fender-benders. We shrug like old soldiers, lifting our shirts to show off the scar: "Yeah, they nearly got me with that one." But they didn't get us. Or at least, we hardly feel it yet. Our brains are simply too robust to show memory loss. The reserve hypothesis was born.

A lot more evidence supports it as well. When scientists at the National Institute on Aging repeated Yaakov Stern's brain-scanning experiment, using the more sophisticated technology of the PET scan, they too found evidence that well-educated people can continue to function in spite of the assault of ARNAT. Neuropsychiatrist C. E. Coffey performed a similar experiment, but rather than looking at Alzheimer's patients, he looked only at elderly people who had few or no cognitive problems. He did MRI scans on 320 such healthy people. His results may sound wild at first: for every year of education a person had, their brains showed about a teaspoon *more* shrinkage. One might think, "Arg! Education shrinks the brain!" But remember that the group of old people who were scanned all had similar levels of cognition—so *the educated people were managing to keep up using smaller remaining brains.*

The reserve hypothesis is one good reason that living a cognitively stimulating life may save your brain. But there's more to it. From the first twinklings of neurotransmission in the fetal brain, a cognitively stimulating environment works magic on our synapses. And the result is not just a brain that resists memory loss (like a car that keeps driving despite three bashed-in fenders); it's a brain that resists the dings and dents of aging—like a tank on the freeway of life.

The Mozart Effect

We are born sensitive and from our birth onwards we are affected in various ways by our environment. As soon as we become conscious of our sensations we tend to seek or shun the things that cause them, at first because they are pleasant or unpleasant, then because they suit us or not, and at last

because of judgments formed by means of the ideas of happiness and goodness which reason gives us.
JEAN-JACQUES ROUSSEAU, *EMILE* (TRANS. B. FOXLEY) (1762)

Cats and monkeys, monkeys and cats—all human life is
there.
HENRY JAMES

As we saw in Chapter 3, while the human fetus develops, youthful neurons
promenade through the nervous system, looking for their places, moving
to the fixed positions they will occupy for the rest of their lives. Then these
youthful neurons ambitiously stretch out, literally networking, sending
their axons reaching for contact and communication with other neurons.
The axons from one neuron meet dendrites from another neuron, and they
form new connections, points of electrical intercourse, synapses. For
decades, scientists assumed that this early stage of brain development is a
largely self-running program. Give an embryo energy and nutrition, and it
will dance this dance. But new evidence indicates that even before we are
born, our *neurons need stimulation* to make the proper connections. For
instance, how does the fetal visual cortex learn to see when it's so dark in
there? Harvard researchers have recently discovered that the retina of the
eye sends spontaneous sparkling specks of stimulation back through the
brain that "teach" the occipital cortex how to see. This prepares the baby
for the bright lights of the delivery room, and—more importantly—for eye
contact with Mom within days of birth. The point is that very early in life,
everything is a lesson. The brain is built into a useful organ by these millions and billions of lessons. This idea is hardly new.

"We are born sensitive and from our birth onwards we are affected in
various ways by our environment," wrote Swiss-born French-living
philosopher Jean-Jacques Rousseau in his wonderful essay *Emile*, published almost thirty years before the French Revolution. Rousseau imag-
ines the education of an imaginary orphan named Emile, offering a
practical, employable guide filled with loving observations of childhood
that ring true even today. He advises, "The newborn child requires to stir
and stretch his limbs to free them from the stiffness of being curled up so
long." And more,

In the dawn of life, when memory and imagination have not begun to function, the child attends to what affects its senses. . . .
He wants to touch and handle everything; do not check these
movements which teach him invaluable lessons. Thus he learns to
perceive the heat, cold, hardness, softness, weight, or lightness of

bodies, to judge their size and shape and all their physical properties. . . . It is only by movement that we learn the difference between self and not self; it is only by our own movements that we gain the idea of space. The child has not this idea, so he stretches out his hand to seize the object within his reach or a hundred paces from him. . . . Be careful therefore to take him about, to move him from place to place and to let him perceive the change in his surroundings, so as to teach him to judge of distances.

Thus did Rousseau elegantly describe the *pas de deux* of education, the part of the dance of brain development that cannot be done alone but depends hugely on the partnering of outside influences—the modification of synapses by parent-aided experience that constitutes the birth of identity. Here he more than anticipated present-day biopsychology, with its emphasis on the role of independent exploratory activity in molding the plastic infant brain. He was also throwing down a scientific gauntlet at the feet of the royalty, for few ideas are more democratic than the idea that human potential is actualized not by heredity but by learning. (After *Emile*'s publication in 1762, Rousseau fled France to avoid arrest.) And children's learning, Rousseau hastened to point out, is effortless. Building the brain in infancy and childhood happens with near-magical reliability. At the earliest stages, every sensation must be dealt with as a new one, every cause and effect—as simple as closing and opening our eyes, willing it to happen and watching our world grow dark, then light—is an experiment the results of which will be granted a place in the castle within us where we build an intricate, working, intelligible, and utterly interactive model of the world.

Rousseau knew little about the brain, but his ideas about education have been confirmed by two hundred years of progress in neuroscience. One gigantic milestone on this road was the work of Harvard neurobiologists David Hubel and Torsten Weisel.

In a classic experiment, Hubel and Weisel covered the eyes of newborn kittens and monkeys on just one side. As a result, no sensory experience of the outside world was available to encourage the development of certain parts of the occipital cortex—the primary visual area of the brain. Even if their eyes were uncovered later, these animals were never able to see with them, despite the fact that the eyes themselves were fine. In decades of similar experiments, two things became clear: we need experience to literally build our brains, and the effects of experience on brain development depend very much on the timing of the experience. That is, there is a *critical period* when we must experience certain things, or our brains forever after work at less than their full potential. A third finding, reported in 1972, was that amino acids get assembled into working proteins in the part of the cortex that experiences vision but *not* in a visually deprived cortex. This was the first solid proof that life experience itself turns on DNA to physically sculpt the brain—a perfect illustration of what neuroscientists call *experience-dependent plasticity* (EDP).

EDP simply means that the brain is assembled, maintained, and improved by life experiences. The *quality* of those experiences definitely influences the quality of the brain. Sure, 50 percent of IQ is determined by genes, but the *other* 50 percent is due to environment. This gives us a great motivation to optimize our environment for the sake of our brains. Recall the wonderful experiments of neurobiologist Mark Rosenzweig, who reared some rats in isolation and others in the enriched environment of a social cage. As his experiments were elaborated, enrichment became more and more interesting for the rats, with multiple-level cages, chutes and ladders, and treadmills and levers to operate. As Dr. Rosenzweig and others have shown, rearing in an enriched environment does many things to improve the brain, increasing the size of synapses, lengthening dendrites, increasing the number of dendritic spines, increasing the thickness of the cortex and the weight of the brain. These changes prove the *plasticity* of the brain in response to experience. Good environment in youth is good for brains. So two hundred years apart, the Swiss philosopher Rousseau and these modern biologists confirmed what every parent knows by instinct: children need experience to grow up.

The next question, of course, is how long EDP works. Hubel and Weisel's cats and monkeys showed that there are critical periods during which the brain is primed to learn. Does the human capacity for EDP drop off in adulthood? It's one thing to talk about providing a rich social milieu for infants—it has been dramatically proven that early interaction is essential for normal cognitive development—but for how long do new life experiences continue to enrich the human nervous system? What's the longevity of plasticity? We know that the rate of protein synthesis declines in rat brains after weaning. We know that metabolic activity in rat brains peaks during the earliest life stages, when synapses are growing like California wildfires, and it falls thereafter. We know that nerve growth factor declines with age, potentially frustrating later attempts to build up the brain. Do we therefore irrevocably lose the chance to build up our brains after childhood?

To some extent, we do. Any brain-saving plan must realistically accept the normal constraints of development. We grow in height fastest from age ten to fourteen; but if we maintained that rate of growth indefinitely, a lot of ceilings would have to be adjusted. The same is true of the growth of the brain; a drop-off in the pace of growth in adulthood is absolutely essential. Still, thirty years of research give us good reason to expect that the brain has a lifelong potential for synaptic plasticity. In other words, the whole brain does not grow forever, but it *changes* forever.

First, investigators find that dendrites *increase* in the parahippocampal gyrus (right next to the hippocampus) at the same time as they *decrease* in the middle frontal gyrus. So it seems that some neurons are shrinking while others are actually growing with age, expanding their branches and reaching out to connect with more neuron neighbors—or even that individual neurons may undergo *both* losses and gains of dendrites in the lifelong process of EDP.

Rousseau observes, "Living and feeling creatures are always learning." Modern neurobiology confirms that, throughout life, the brain continues to have and use the carpentry tools for framing the superstructure of new ideas. Further evidence of EDP in the aging brain comes from animal studies of two fascinating processes: axon sprouting and reactive synaptogenesis. *Axon sprouting* refers to the fact that when nerve fibers are damaged or lost, fibers from undamaged neurons often sprout, like new buds in a rosebush, to form new connections. *Reactive synaptogenesis* is the process by which synapses are replaced by new synapses. Although the overall process of reinnervation slows down in older animals, both axon sprouting and reactive synaptogenesis just keep rolling along in the aged rodent brain. Learning never stops. Synapses get formed at every age.

Experiments on the brain impact of environmental enrichment encourage us to have faith in our everlasting capacity for EDP. Dr. Susumu Ando's lab at the Tokyo Metropolitan Institute of Gerontology, for example, recently found that rats reared in isolation had a big aging-related loss of *synaptophysin* (the protein of synapse building), but elderly rats reared in enrichment actually had *higher* synaptophysin levels in certain brain areas than young rats. That's an impressive piece of evidence that a cognitively challenging environment might in some ways keep an old brain younger than a young one. In another series of experiments, Rosenzweig's group showed that nearly all of the benefits that come from social rearing occur in the brains of rats *no matter when* they were assigned to enriched environments—at 25 days old, or 105 days, or 285 days (ancient in rat-years). In yet another experiment that directly tests how learning a new skill benefits the brain, young (three months) and old (eighteen months) rats were trained to do a task; sophisticated measurements showed that the old rats showed every bit as much increase in hippocampal excitability as the young ones.

Observations of wild animals confirm these lab findings. For instance, ornithologists recently made an extremely interesting discovery: birds that forage for food have bigger hippocampi than nonforaging birds; that's probably because the hippocampus is crucial for spatial navigation—the brain's built-in global positioning system. The exciting thing is that the hippocampus grows *larger* during the foraging season and *smaller* during the other seasons, *even in quite old birds*. This extraordinary example of a lasting capacity for real brain change in response to changing cognitive demands suggests a very exciting conclusion: throughout the animal kingdom, and throughout the life span, exposure to cognitive challenges builds up the brain.

And what of humans? Can intellectual challenges in later life increase the size or connectivity of our brains? Several studies hint provocatively that they can. As we saw in Chapter 6, a study of the brains of London cabbies showed that the longer these drivers spent on the job, the bigger became the spatial navigation region of their brains. Another terrific study comes from neurobiologists Arnie Scheibel and Bob Jacobs. Working at UCLA's Brain Research Institute, Scheibel and Jacobs examined the brains of twenty people who had died free of dementia. Dr. Scheibel described the results this way:

The 20 brains lumped themselves into three groups: the first group had a sort of average dendritic length, the second group had a step-up to a considerably greater dendritic length, and the third group was one more step up in length. We searched and searched and we couldn't for the life of us figure out why these brains sorted themselves into three groups. Then we went back and looked at their educational background. Those in the first group had elementary school educations only, the second group were high school graduates, and the third group had college or more, in some cases graduate school. We were so stupid not to have thought of this before! Now these brains were [examined] thirty years after the subjects had finished their education, so the education must have had a lasting effect. We decided that the kind of life your education prepares you for—whether it was as a truck driver or a laborer (not that there's anything wrong with those lives, but it's just a different kind of cerebral challenge), or some more cognitively demanding life—was responsible for this difference. This rather remarkable correlation between dendritic length and education fits with everything we know about the growth of dendrites in relation to life experience, since dendrites increase or decrease in length throughout life depending on activity.

The fact is that human brains have an astonishing capacity for experience-dependent plasticity, and that they maintain a good deal of this wonderful capacity right through adult life. This discovery may indirectly provide the answer to the crucial question we asked before: does learning merely give us a brain that keeps going despite some ARNAT (the reserve hypothesis), or does learning actually give us a brain that resists damage in the first place? Learning does both—and even more.

Fred Gage and his colleagues at the famed Salk Institute for Biological Studies have been pounding away at the question of brain development for decades. In 1997 they reported an incredible finding that violated received dogma: they showed that mice reared in an enriched environment not only had *more* neurons in their hippocampus, they had *new* neurons. And not just a few: they found 40,000 more neurons in one tiny section of the brains of the cognitively challenged mice. This was the first proof that an intellectually challenging environment *can literally build new neurons into an adult brain!*

This startling finding has two possible explanations: either learning just promotes longer survival of stem cells that are turning into neurons anyway, or learning literally turns on the *production* of brand-new neurons from stem cells in the adult brain. At first Gage and his colleagues settled on the first explanation; it seemed a little too much to completely break through the conceptual door that protected the long-standing no-new-neurons dogma. But more recent research has blown the hinges off that final door. Princeton biologist Elizabeth Gould took some adult rats and trained them in a water maze, a spatial navigation task in which they have to learn where a platform is hidden in a big pool of milky water. In 1999 she reported that this training *doubled* the number of completely new adult-generated neurons. It is reasonable to guess that the same thing happens in adult human brains. This finding adds a thrilling new dimension to the idea of EDP. "It is very likely that if you lead a very mentally active life you are engaging the hippocampus," says Gould. Conversely, "a lack of learning opportunities may have a negative structural impact on the brain." So when Julie the physical therapist used a spare moment to read about dinosaurs in the clinic, she was certainly building her synapses, but she may have been doing more. It's possible that she was actually helping to turn her supply of stem cells into a fresh batch of neurons.

Imagine what's happening to your brain at this very moment. Aging is proceeding. Whether you have lucky ARNAT-resistant genes or unlucky

ARNAT-sensitive genes, lots of things are hammering on your neurons. DNA mutations are accumulating. Excitatory neurotransmitters are stressing-out your glutamate receptors. Calcium is leaking into places where it doesn't belong. Kinases are probably mucking up your neurofilaments on the way to forming tangles; and troublesome secretases are probably slicing up your amyloid precursor proteins on the way to forming plaques. Free radicals are having their way with your cell membranes. As a result, some of your synapses are withering away. At the very same time, as you are reading this book—hopefully immersed in some exciting new ideas—new synapses are forming. And just possibly you are adding new brain cells to your hippocampus! That's the story of adulthood, a constant ebb and flow, give and take, with some processes tearing down synapses and others building them up. Obviously, we cannot completely control the myriad aging-related processes that hammer on our neurons. Until scientists find the key to immortality, we can never claim that we have won this battle. But we can fight. You can do your best to counter synaptic losses with synaptic gains. You may even be able to make new neurons simply by leading a cognitively challenging life. So (to different degrees in different people with different genes), you can use your new-found knowledge of your brain's remarkable lifelong capacity for EDP to hold back the marauding molecular hordes, to build up your personal mental mountains even as natural forces are working to erode them in the inevitable cycle of life, and to make your brain better, and stronger, and maybe even wiser.

The question then becomes, if you want to optimize your brain-building potential, what should you do?

This brings us to the Mozart Effect.

The Mozart Effect for Adults

Much has been written in recent years about the importance of infant (and even fetal) experience in brain development. One popular claim is that babies who are exposed to classical music become mentally sharper. And there's actually a whiff of science behind this claim. As Rousseau suggested, at the very earliest stages of human development, living itself is full of life lessons. When a baby hears the thrilling "Kyrie" from Mozart's Requiem in D minor, the sounds themselves are filled with provocative, and evocative, meaning. As the baby listens, we can well imagine new synapses being formed, reinforcing her sensitivity to tempos and rhythms, to octaves and scales, to the subliminal logic of chord progressions, and even to the instinctive emotional link between major keys and gladness and minor keys and sadness.

HOWEVER (and this is a giant-size however), once we've heard a bunch of symphonies, we've learned those lessons. The brain will wrap itself around rhythm and harmony without getting tied in a mental knot. The Mozart Effect is a great way to describe how the infant brain can make hay (actually, synapses) out of just about any life experience. But listening to a Mozart symphony at age forty has a completely different effect.

The music washes over us in all its classical luxuriance. The sprightly variation in time-signatures is familiar. The harmonies make sense. But the brain-stimulating effect of passive listening at this stage in life is mostly a matter of sheer delight. Frankly, once your brain has drawn what lessons it can from early passive listening, your tickets to the Thursday-night concert series are not going to do much for you in the way of brain building.

And here's where we come to the crucial point about mental stimulation and the brain: *passive* experience does little for the adult brain. To keep the brain learning and growing, we need to generate *active responses to cognitive challenges*. Is there a Mozart Effect for adults? Yes. But consider two cognitive challenges: Number one, listen to Mozart's grand opera, *Don Giovanni*. Number two, write an aria in the same style. Guess which one will build up your brain?

A wealth of new scientific evidence shows us the difference between the effects of passive and active experience on the brain. Active response to cognitive challenges is unquestionably what turns on our adult neurons. Here is a simple experiment to demonstrate this point: read the following ten words—sea, sandwich, Saturday, shirt, sun, sit, same, simple, soup, silly. Now, quick as you can, make up a list of ten other words beginning with the letter *s*, excluding proper names: _____, _____, _____, _____, _____, _____, _____, _____, _____, _____. The first task is nearly effortless, but you can almost *feel* your brain working on the second task. In fact, experiments using PET scans show us the remarkable difference: passively reading words indeed perks up the brain; it makes cerebral blood flow and metabolism increase a tiny bit in several areas of the cortex. But actively generating a list of words that begin with a certain letter causes a *big* increase in brain activity, especially in the left prefrontal lobe. In another experiment, as chess masters and chess amateurs played against a computer, their brains were scanned with a special magnetic imaging device. Both groups showed *gamma bursts*—signs of increased brain activity. But the masters, who already *knew* thousands of patterns of chess moves, merely activated the *remembering* part of the brain; the amateurs, who were seeing and learning patterns of moves for the first time, revved up the *learning* parts of the brain—the medial temporal lobes. For all of the chess masters' undeniable brilliance, it was the amateurs who were more likely to be growing their brains.

Experiments such as this reveal that different types of life experiences stimulate brain activity in hugely different ways. For the sake of simplicity, let's divide mental tasks into five types: knowing, recognizing, learning, generating, and teaching. Each of these activities is associated with very different degrees and types of cortical activity. They also produce very different, somewhat predictable effects on the growth of the synapses. "Understanding is a lot like sex," said physicist Frank Oppenheimer. "It has a practical purpose, but that's not why people do it normally." Understanding something—*knowing* something—helps us survive. But *learning* something helps the brain survive.

For example, you *know* what a dog is. That knowledge requires a certain amount of brain activity; it requires that a pattern of connectivity between certain brain cells be maintained, year in and year out, by the idling of cortical neurons. It requires very little brain energy, used mostly for this minimal "housekeeping" of synapses you already have; but knowing does not require you to *build* any new synapses. Then suppose you might *read* the word *dog* or hear a dog bark or even listen to the movingly sappy canine chorus in Disney's *The Lady and the Tramp*. The sensory experience makes sense because, using the clever decoding system toward the back of your brain, you can take in and recognize the word or the sounds. This too requires some brain activity, but it probably does little to provoke the growth of synapses. Then let's say you *learn* (and I was surprised by this) that poodles may be the most intelligent dogs. Now you're cookin'. To make new information stick in your brain, you absolutely have to turn on the hippocampus, transcribe DNA, make new proteins, modify existing synapses, and maybe even make a new neuron or two. Now let's say you're on television, with a chance to win a million dollars, and the exceedingly well groomed moderator says: "For your final question, in the next ten seconds, list the names of six breeds of dogs that begin with the letter *p*." That's the kind of cognitive challenge that really revs up the brain. "Poodle," you say, "Pomeranian, um, Pekingese . . ." *Generating* a new word list—a list you have probably never consciously generated before—calls upon a host of cerebral resources. It turns on synapses you've formed in the past and sends signals between them like bolts of lightning; it strengthens them because the context of the experience is a challenge attached to a big reward; and it forces you to pull together previously weakly connected data into a freshly minted pattern, a process with enormous power to reconfigure the brain. By the time you get to Pug and Great Pyrenees and Portuguese

Water Dog, you've probably sent a few synapses roaring into overdrive. Finally, you *teach* a child how to tell those six breeds apart. While knowing how to tell dogs apart requires a little brain activity, teaching what you know requires lots. It requires you to think about the distinguishing features of the breeds, how to put those features into words, how to monitor whether your student is getting the message, and how to modify the lesson to maximize the result. Again, the brain is launched on a high-energy adventure, and synaptic connections will definitely be formed that were never there before.

Okay, so here's the hierarchy of cognitive stimulation: knowing and recognizing do little to build the brain, but learning and generating and teaching do much more. Insofar as they involve synaptic modification by experience, these brain activities may do what past education cannot: alter the very course of aging. To some degree (a degree we badly wish to know but don't), this force exactly opposes the synaptic corruption of ARNAT and Alzheimer's.

You can already guess how awareness of this hierarchy will help us save the brain. *Knowing* is the end result of education, and education gives us a reserve to face the knocks of brain aging (the Volvo effect). But knowing is static. *Learning, generating,* and *teaching* are dynamic. Knowing is like idling at a stop sign. Recognizing is like a dull commute to work. But learning is like navigating on a grand cross-country trip; generating is like entering a drag race to fresh understanding; and teaching is like—well, there's nothing quite like teaching. Just imagine the activity of your brain as you help your son understand fractions, or give your daughter her first behind-the-wheel driving lesson. Learning, generating, and teaching are the hallmarks of the cognitively challenging life. So long as we face cognitive challenges—from our final trimester as a fetus to our final days on earth—we will keep right on building our brains.

This news is terrific. The lifelong capacity of the brain to refresh itself in response to cognitive challenges is a wonderful system. Embracing a life of cognitive challenges at any age is reasonably certain to build a rampart against the insidious erosion of aging-dependent neural jeopardy.

So why do we have this system, and what exactly should we do to take full advantage of it?

The Evolution of Saving Your Brain

> Socrates: Again, the healthy condition of the body is
> undermined by inactivity and indolence, and to a great
> extent preserved by energy and motion, isn't it?

Theaetetus: Yes.

Socrates: And so with the condition of the soul. The soul
    acquires knowledge and is kept going and improved by
    learning and practice, which are of the nature of move-
    ments. By inactivity, dullness, and neglect of exercise, it
    learns nothing and forgets what it has learned.

Theaetetus: True.

Socrates: So, of the two, motion is a good thing for both
    soul and body, and immobility is bad.

PLATO, *THEAETETUS* (153 B.C.)

There is a reason for everything we've discussed to this point, a deep and
ancient biological wisdom that has emerged from evolution. It may be
worth a moment to reflect on why certain types of cognitive challenge are
especially likely to refresh the adult human brain. Indeed, if we figure out
the evolutionary reason for our lifelong capacity for EDP, it may actually
give us the best, most practical, most natural ways to protect our brains
against aging.

Consider, again, the early modern humans—bursting with mental vigor
to face the hard challenges of life as they explored their way out of Africa.
Death came early. Only a few survived to age forty, fewer to fifty and beyond. With so few mature adults around, there was not much selective
pressure to create great genes for long-lasting brains. But what pressure
there was would favor genes that made brains that could help perpetuate
the mature person's DNA. How? By giving that mature person the ability
to provide for and to *teach* their offspring.

As I said in Chapter 4, the main evolutionary purpose of our lifelong
capacity to build and maintain synapses is not just learning but teaching.
There is a unique wisdom that only comes with age. When we keep our
minds vigorous into later years, we can impart this wisdom to our offspring to maximize their chances of reproductive fitness and hence our
own. We cannot expect—nor necessarily want—our full powers of EDP
to persist. Nonetheless, a thick rope of deduction supports the idea that
new learning in adulthood increases synaptic connectivity. This is the real
evolutionary meaning of "use it or lose it." Neurodegeneration, simply
put, is *relatively greater brain injury than brain maintenance and repair*.
The brain evolved a great strategy to help resist this corrosive effect, but
only because it has value to our survival and that of our offspring. Those
who continue to face cognitive challenges will help maintain their brains
by building synaptic connectivity. And teaching is one heck of a cognitive
challenge.

Of course, adults have lots of other challenges—finding food and finding the way back home, helping with cooperative hunting over long distances, inventing and making tools, navigating the wilds of social and sexual relations, all sorts of mentally stimulating experiences that involve the brain-building mental activities of learning and generating. But teaching and looking out for our offspring are perhaps the most important reasons for mature adults to keep their brains working for the long haul, since the impact of these activities on our children and grandchildren so magnificently serves the most profound imperative of life—to produce and protect the next generation.

What, precisely, should you do to use this knowledge to help save your brain? Memorize the list of presidents? Read the encyclopedia? Will formal "mental exercises" or courses in mnemonics help? Certainly not as much as their advocates might claim. Contrary to popular belief—and contrary to the well-meant but neuroscientifically naive advice of some anti-aging gurus—research consistently shows little lasting brain enhancement from memory-training programs, with the exception of therapies for those recovering from strokes or head trauma. As Professor Timiras puts it, "I think it is useless to be doing exercises with the brain, memorizing things again and again. That's just a bauble for the poor people who are desperate for help." In the same category is a New Age treatment called brain-wave biofeedback, in which the client is hooked up to an EEG machine and taught to influence his own brain waves. This kind of biofeedback may be somewhat useful for temporary pain relief, but it contains none of the essential ingredients of a real-life brain-building mental challenge.

Do not be taken in by seductive marketing. Formal cognitive training programs or brain-wave boosters are not the answer.

The real answer is to live life to its fullest—not merely watch television and wait for cataracts to blur the image, and not merely exist and occupy space and pass time and await the moment when the wristwatch is taken from the wrist. Leap with both feet into the future. "Old men ought to be explorers," says T. S. Eliot. He was right, because exploratory activity—encountering and embracing novelty, diving into new seas of neural natation—is the key to enhancing lifelong synaptic plasticity. Any kind of active, deliberate learning seems to challenge the nervous system in uniquely fruitful ways—but it will have this effect only if it is exciting enough, and pleasing enough, to keep us motivated and engaged on an ongoing basis. As Confucius admonished, "Study as if you were never to master it; as if in fear of losing it." He would not be surprised to learn that the best neurobiological evidence of real synapse-building comes from studies of the benefits of *active, energetic learning,* responding to the flung-down gauntlet of a cognitive challenge. Care about what you learn passionately, and *apply* it daily in a newly challenging lifestyle, and the brain will thrive. This is the type of life activity most likely to grow the brain.

Never stop. Never be caught saying to your children, "Oh, I don't keep up with those things." Never retire your mind. Go back to school. Learn a game that you haven't mastered yet, such as chess or bridge. Change your career at age fifty. Create a website, learn to speak Spanish, take up that musical instrument you've always wanted to play, volunteer in a fresh environment, write that book you've always meant to, polish the poems and paintings that hint at your wit and your passion. As Abraham Joshua Heschel writes in *The Insecurity of Freedom,* "It is wrong to define education as preparation for life. Learning is life, a supreme experience of living, a climax of existence." It is *activity*—taking possession of new knowledge, manipulating it and finding new connections, and, more than any other brain activity, generating new ideas and teaching them—that seems most likely to rev up synaptic synthesis. Travel. Compose. Invent. Or better yet, *teach,* for that may be what our ever-developing brains exactly evolved to do in later life. Teaching is not a toil or a duty—it is a joy on earth. This joy has a difficult-to-pinpoint beginning, but it should have no end, not in maturity, not in retirement, not in old age. Exploring with our minds delights our brains. Helping others explore with theirs can also be our sheer delight and pleasure right up until the final breath and sigh. *That's* the natural way to save your brain.

CONCLUSION

What the Future Holds for the Human Brain

We should all be concerned about the future because we will
have to spend the rest of our lives there.
CHARLES FRANKLIN KETTERING (1949)

We are blessed and cursed to live in interesting times, favored and tested
by history as the first to understand genes. What's ahead for the human
brain? As difficult as it may be to predict the future, the trajectory
of modern discovery points in one direction: we will have new capacities on every front of biology and medicine to control the DNA, proteins, chemicals, tissues, organs, and organisms that live on earth. Yes,
we will prevent and control many diseases, sparing humanity immense
grief. But our newly won talents will also present us with awful choices.
I will do my best to describe some of the inventions that are currently being developed to benefit the brain. At the same time, I will try
to provide some sense of the ethical challenges that are about to test our
souls.

First, *ARNAT and Alzheimer's will be controlled.* I have emphasized
prevention in this book—that's the best bet for brain protection today. At
the same time, researchers are attacking the problem of aging-related neurodegeneration on a dozen fronts, and breakthroughs that seemed too
good to hope for just a decade ago will soon enhance prevention, reduce
symptoms, or even repair the damage done by ARNAT/Alzheimer's,
Parkinson's, frontotemporal lobe dementia, and a long list of other
threats to the integrity of mind and brain. BACE- and GACE-inhibitors
(see Chapter 14) will soon come on the market—drugs that will block the
molecular butter knives that slice off the most dangerous fragments of the
big amyloid precursor protein. We will also have a new class of drugs that

can help break down beta-amyloid. And an Alzheimer's vaccine may successfully limit the brain damage caused by beta-amyloid (although it may have unintended consequences for the APP/amyloid injury-response system that could limit its use). The *APOE*-ε4 problem will be eliminated; even before gene therapy becomes routine, family doctors will be giving the 25 percent of us who carry ε4 alleles special preventive drug therapy, probably starting by age thirty.

What's more, science will soon successfully tackle the terrible problem of misfolded proteins. IBM is building a $100 million supercomputer called Blue Gene, whose job will be to study how proteins twist and coil and fold themselves into useful three-dimensional shapes—and how they misfold. That job is staggering. At a quadrillion calculations per second, it will take Blue Gene a year to decipher the folding of a single protein. But this knowledge will give us incredible new insights into the major threat to the aging brain. On another front, scientists have recently discovered that every cell has a triage system that determines whether a protein is good, badly folded but reparable, or misfolded so badly that it can never be fixed. A molecule called *CHIP* decides the fate of misfolded proteins, and a molecular trash-compactor called the *UP (ubiquitin-proteasome) system* rids the brain of the proteins that CHIP decides are misfolded beyond repair. Both CHIP and the UP system seem to malfunction in Alzheimer's, Parkinson's, Huntington's, ALS, and aging itself. We will soon have *broad-spectrum antimisfolding agents* to keep our CHIP-UP system running smooth, drugs that—somewhat like the brave little tailor of the fairy tale "Seven with One Blow"—will defeat many brain diseases at the same time.

We will have *new ways to use magnets to diagnose and treat brain disorders*. Magnetic resonance imaging will take seconds, not minutes. Better computerized interpretation of these magnetic images will show us not just what things look like but exactly what they are made of, whether they are good or bad, and what drugs they will respond to. Security agencies are already looking into ways to scan people as they walk by, or even from a distance. The same technology will make its way into medicine—and we may soon stroll through a machine (like today's metal detectors) that will know immediately whether any of our organs are in trouble. This will allow for painless, accurate, instantaneous diagnosis of brain tumors, multiple sclerosis, ARNAT, and preclinical Parkinson's—early enough for new treatments to have maximum benefit.

Magnets will be used to treat us as well: neurologist Alvaro Pascual-Leone, director of Harvard's new Laboratory for Magnetic Brain Stimulation, and other researchers have discovered that externally applied magnetic impulses—a technology called *repetitive transcranial magnetic stimulation* (rTMS)—can be used to treat disorders of the mind and brain. Multiple experiments suggest that rTMS can improve movement in people with Parkinson's and effectively treat depression. Canada's Health Ministry has already approved rTMS for the treatment of depression, and our FDA is considering a similar move. Magnetic stimulation may come to be a standard therapy for human disorders of movement and mood.

Inflammation will be controlled. The more we learn about the inflammatory response, the more we will appreciate its unexpectedly central role in problems such as ARNAT/Alzheimer's, and the better we will design drugs to selectively target the Four Musketeers of inflammation and the mercenary microglia (described in Chapter 15). Rheumatoid arthritis will vanish into history. Multiple sclerosis will be vanquished. And much of the harm of Alzheimer's will be averted with a pill that will have fewer side effects than Motrin, Nuprin, or Alleve.

Smart Drugs will get smart enough to use. We will easily be able to enhance brain function by improving the delivery of energy to cells, by assuring the ready activity of nerve growth factors, and by revving up the operation of our MTL memory recorders with once-a-day pills that will boost the efficiency of our AMPA receptors.

Botanicals-for-the-brain will finally deliver on their five-thousand-year-old promise. By isolating and purifying the brain-friendly components of ginkgo biloba, ginseng, and a host of other remarkable plants, we will be able to provide gentle and truly effective herbal enhancement of mental health and cerebral function.

You will know your every gene. The map of "the human genome" is an accomplishment, but as I mentioned earlier, it is also a fiction. There is no human genome; there are billions of them. Only a small number of the countless variations between people's genomes makes a notable difference, such as variations in eye color, highest-genetically-possible running speed, or risk for memory loss. To find the clinically important differences, scientists are rushing to map *single nucleotide polymorphisms* (SNPs), the tiniest snippets of difference between our genomes. Scientists are also rapidly identifying *quantitative trait loci* (QTLs)—places in the genome that are important for determining who among us is at special risk for Alzheimer's, Parkinson's, strokes, heart disease, or diabetes. And doctors will soon be able to perform *genome-wide profiling of gene-transcription* (GWPGT). If knowing your genome is like knowing the names of the members of your basketball team, GWPGT is like knowing who's up and playing on the court; that is, it tells you not only which disease-prone genes you happen to carry but which of your 40,000 genes are currently active or inactive—a whole new way to understand health, disease, and optimum body operation. You already know your lifestyle. When you know your genome, what those genes do, and how they interact with your lifestyle, you will have remarkable power to control your health destiny.

This is not an altogether happy notion. Eventually, we will have treatments for an immense number of genetically based health problems; but first we will go through an awkward transition phase during which we can predict your health future in detail but can do somewhat less about it than anyone would wish. The goal is to reduce human suffering, not compound it with anxiety. As a result, the need for wise and sensitive genetic counseling will explode. A tiny group of subspecialists will no longer be able to handle the demand; medical schools will have to educate *every* doctor as a genetic counselor.

Replacement parts for broken brains will be routinely inserted. We currently grow human embryonic stem cells into dopamine-producing brain cells, carefully drill holes in the heads of people with Parkinson's disease, and implant the cells in their brains. The earlier we do this, the better: the benefit of stem cell implants seems to depend on getting the cells in while patients are still young enough to respond to them. While this method is still being perfected, it has already been shown to give transplant recipients five to ten years of significantly freer movement. Similar stem cell implants will take hold to treat Alzheimer's: in 2001 neurologist Mark Tuszynski and his team at the University of California at San Diego took some skin cells from a sixty-year-old woman with early Alzheimer's and genetically modified the cells, turning them into tiny factories to manufacture nerve growth factor; then they inserted them deep within the patient's brain. The hope is that these NGF factories will boost the function of the acetylcholine-producing cells in her brain and give her back her memory. Results are pending at the time of this writing. Every brain condition that depends on having enough of the right kind of cells could be treated with this new technique.

The treatment of strokes will be revolutionized. We have made the first strides toward recognizing a stroke as a brain attack—a matter as urgent and treatable as a heart attack. And we already have several drugs, such as *tissue plasminogen activator* (tPA), that can be used in the emergency room to rescue brains in the three hours after a stroke. But because the time from stroke onset to treatment is so short and so critical for success, we will want to do more in the window of opportunity between the first symptoms and the initiation of therapy. We may, for instance, develop clot-busting drugs that are safe enough for EMTs to use in the ambulance. We may begin to use a completely different class of stroke-fighting drugs, both in the acute treatment and the chronic prevention of strokes—such as the new *glycoprotein IIa, IIIb inhibitors*—drugs that bind to receptors on the surface of blood platelets to keep them from clumping into clots. Even newer neuroprotective drugs are on the way: PP1 helps control the dangerous early brain swelling and compression of blood vessels that accompanies a stroke; in mice, it has been shown to reduce the size of strokes by 70 percent. Agents such as PP1 will soon be available to humans.

If you are still paralyzed when you get to the ER, clot-busting drugs may not be injected in your vein, which sends them all over the body, but instead delivered straight to the clot, using catheters threaded gently into the brain. In experiments at Baptist Memorial Hospital in Memphis, this technique has already shown promise as a way to open up the crucial window of time from the first twinge of symptoms to effective brain-saving treatment. Should you nonetheless have lasting brain damage from a stroke, doctors will offer to replace the damaged brain regions using implanted embryonic stem cells.

Probably more important, we will become better and better at preventing strokes. Family doctors will begin to use new tools to predict who is most at risk, checking not only your homocysteine and fibrinogen levels at your annual physical but also using more sophisticated measures such as *C-reactive protein* and *proinsulin levels*. This, along with the stroke-prevention medicines chosen to work best with your individual genome, will vastly reduce your risk of ever needing those EMTs, ERs, or neurosurgeons.

Sex hormone replacement will become safe, effective, and nearly universal. Men and women alike will be able to escape the aging-related changes in our bodies and minds that are caused by sex hormone withdrawal. Super-selective estrogen receptor modulators will come of age. Androgen replacement therapy will be perfected. These will provide adults of both sexes with a new experience of middle and later adulthood—free from many of the undesirable physical and mental effects of the "change of life."

Pharmacogenomics will play a major role in medicine. Each of us carries hundreds of genes that control the way drugs affect us. Clinically important gene variations have already been identified that make some people respond to medications differently from others. Indeed, it's likely that no two humans on earth share the identical combination of these

drug-sensitive genes (not even identical twins, who differ in their mitochondrial DNA). The current system of one-medicine-one-dose for
everyone with a certain disorder will soon seem quaint and rather dangerous. Instead, we will all carry credit-card-size copies of our genome.
Our doctors will insert them into scanners and instantly see on their
computer screens which drugs, at what doses, are best for us as individuals.

None of these advances are free from risk; every one has some downside.
For example, the pressure to find a smart drug is immense. It has become, at the outset of the twenty-first century, as inflamed an exercise as
the medieval search for the philosopher's stone, which reputedly turned
lead into gold. Yet the very idea of a smart drug is problematic. Billions
of years of evolution got us to this point, carefully selecting the best compromise between too little and too much neuronal excitement, with carefully timed changes that usually suit us for each stage of life. Tipping the
balance may have unintended consequences. This is not to say that we
will never find safe and effective prescriptions for memory enhancement.
We will. Still, this may be a case of the old saying, be careful what you
wish for . . .

What will it mean for us to boost our brain function, not temporarily, but permanently? Smart drugs may make us different people.
Perhaps we would be better, in some sense. But any drug that can make
us "better" will make us other than we were. How far can we go in
"enhancing" the mind before we threaten to lose the self or alter
the timing in the natural changes in ourselves that suit us for our voyage of life? When a drug appears that simply makes you brighter, leaving your personality and identity largely intact, how will that affect
your family? Your community? Your nation and its relationship to other
nations of the world? These questions demand a high level of intro-
spection, as well as a hot and urgent dialogue across all disciplines and
borders.

Still and all, this ethical debate pales beside the one that's already con-
fronting us: what to do with our genes. Three major aspects of the genetic
revolution have created immediate challenges to society; all relate, in
some way, to the future of the brain. These are cloning, stem cells, and
gene therapy.

Cloning Einstein's Brain

The day the world learned that Scottish embryologist Ian Wilmut had successfully raised a cloned sheep named Dolly, a medical student caught me

in the hallway. "Great!" he said. "Start the countdown to cloning Einstein's brain!"

This science fiction scenario, spun out in novels and movies ever since the 1962 release of James D. Watson's book, *The Double Helix*—with different DNA donors chosen as the presumptive source material, from Einstein to Hitler—has now become a nearly practical idea. At the time of this writing, members of a space-alien-oriented religious organization, the Raelians, claim to have recruited a large group of women who've volunteered their wombs; they may be making progress toward cloning a chosen child. Three separate groups of scientists, all with the credentials that make their promises credible, have publicly announced their intention to clone humans, ostensibly to help infertile couples create children. And in 2001 a Massachusetts biotech company announced the first cloning of human embryos.

True, a law has been passed against human cloning in the United States. The penalties include fines of up to $5 million. But in 2000 a private citizen paid the Russians $20 million for a quick trip to the international space station. How much more would a wealthy person pay for a clone of himself or of some favorite personage? The human ambition for the gratification of personal expression is boundless and implacable. Add the hope of a form of immortality, and the stakes go up. There are tens of thousands of millionaires in the world, and thousands of scientists with the skill required. Who can doubt that, here or elsewhere, sooner or later, law or no law, clones will be born?

The ethics of cloning are no challenge at all. It should not be done, period. Using current technology, the effort is guaranteed to result in a ghastly series of miscarriages, stillbirths, and deformed, nonviable, or early-to-die babies. When a viable clone is born (which I predict will occur before 2010), it will indeed eventually develop a brain that in many ways resembles that of its DNA donor. It will have most of its donor's genes, but not all, since bits of mitochondrial DNA will remain in the egg that gets fertilized to make the clone. Yes, it will have some behavioral traits in common with its donor—but far less than one might imagine. It will have even less behavioral resemblance to the original model than a twin reared apart in a foreign land, since it will not even share the uterine environment of its common-gene relative.

Clone Einstein's brain? It will never happen. We could easily grab some Einsteinian DNA and potentially cook up a boy with an aptitude for mathematics, abstract ideas, and music. A product of his own unique nurture, this boy's brain would be, in a billion ways, different from Einstein's. He might become a brilliant violinist—or a tax accountant for a bioengineering company.

The ethics of cloning are both straightforward and trivial compared with the ethics of another technology. Our government is currently facing the incredibly important challenge of choosing a wise path in the matter of stem cell research.

Stem Cells

In the embryo, all cells are created equal, each with the potential to become knee or liver or brain or any of the two hundred or so cell types in the body, until special signals send them down the path of differentiation. These cells are called stem cells. In 1998 James Thompson of the University of Wisconsin became the first person to nurture a "line" of such embryonic stem cells, meaning that he isolated a stem cell and encouraged it to indefinitely make copies of itself. Research on embryonic stem cells will allow doctors to provide ailing patients with any tissue or organ that their body may need to restore healthy function. These cells could be used to treat Alzheimer's, Parkinson's, strokes, spinal cord injury, diabetes, heart disease, muscle disease, bone disease, leukemia—the list is long and the promise is incredible. In 2000, Sylvia Elam of Scottsdale, Arizona, age sixty-six, became one of the first stroke victims in the world to benefit from stem cells implanted in her brain. Her husband, Ira, summarized the results: "It was absolutely beyond our wildest dreams."

There are actually many ways to obtain stem cells. In addition to embryonic cell clusters, scientists could get them from bone marrow, placentas, fetuses, umbilical cord blood, living adult human brains, cadaver brains, pigs, or cancer cells. Unfortunately, every option other than embryonic stem cells has problems, from the lack of resilience and premature aging problem of adult cells, to the risk of transfer of animal virsues or cancers. This is why scientists are so excited and hopeful about the chance to revolutionize medicine with embryonic stem cell research.

This brings us to the ethical question. At present tens of thousands of frozen embryonic cell clusters are sitting in the freezers of fertility clinics, doomed either to indefinite cold storage or to be discarded. These cell clusters could be used for this stem cell research. It is a matter for philosophers and theologians to declare the boundaries of science that they think are right. It is a matter for politicians to decide what research the NIH is permitted to support. But it is a matter for all citizens to judge the wisest, most just course for our nation.

Fortunately, new technology may rescue us from this ethical

dilemma: stem cells have recently been created by *parthenogenesis*—turning an unfertilized egg into a pseudo-embryo. Advances such as this may allow all of us to cheer for wonderful new treatments that may save the lives of millions of living human beings throughout the nation and the world.

Gene Therapy and Germ-Line Engineering

Yet cloning and stem cell research are both ethically trivial beside the final challenge that faces us right now: should we make brighter, longer-living humans? We can. There isn't a shred of doubt. Whatever *some* humans decide in this matter, not *all* humans will abide by that decision. Gene therapy is already happening, and somewhere, someday soon, someone will attempt human germ-line engineering.

Gene therapy means two different things. *Somatic gene therapy* means doing our best to fix genes—or improve them—in the cells that make up a single human body. *Germ-line engineering* is completely different: it means fixing or improving the genes in the sperm and eggs, so that the changes will be carried on indefinitely, from generation to generation. French scientists have successfully used somatic gene therapy to rescue a girl with a rare immune disease; in the near future, somatic gene therapy will be perfected to treat hundreds of diseases. But the greatest ethical challenge in the history of the world may be the decision about germ-line engineering. Buckle your seatbelts and hold on to your hats. We are entering the era of synthetic evolution.

Consider the following: fruit fly scientist Seymour Benzer—one of the great minds of biology—has found a gene that allows fruit flies to live one-third longer than ever before. He calls it the *Methuselah gene*. Neurologist Stephan Helfand has found another fruit fly gene he calls *INDY* (for "I'm not dead yet"); a simple change in the INDY gene allows flies to live 90 percent longer than usual. Small changes in other genes called *InR* and *chico* allow flies to keep buzzing long after their nonaltered peers have stopped. *SIR-2.1*, a gene that controls the life span of yeast, has been manipulated to make a worm with a life span that's increased by 50 percent. And the activation of a gene called *daf-16* in worms can quadruple its life span. As biologist Cynthia Kenyon says about the genetics of aging, "It's all coming together." Recent findings strongly suggest that the genes that control aging in fruit flies, worms, and yeast are likely to control a biological master aging clock, a clock that involves the "insulinlike signaling pathway," a clock that these species seem to share with all animals, including humans—a clock that can be reset by genetic manipulation. The implications for using this knowledge to help humans live to age 125, 150, or longer are startling.

Next, consider that in 1999 a Princeton University team led by Joe Tsien announced the creation of the "Doogie Mouse" by genetic engineering, a mouse with a change in its glutamate receptors—and an astonishingly good memory. It was tricky. It took several years. But it changed, in a stroke, 3.8 billion years of brain evolution. In other mouse-behavior-changing experiments, scientists have inserted a gene from the prairie vole, a very sociable fellow, into the house mouse, a loner, and created a sociable house mouse. At this point, inserting genes for desirable behavioral characteristics into animals is completely practical.

Next, consider advances in human behavioral genetics, a field that rose from pure speculation to reality in a decade and a half. An X-linked gene has been found that helps determine human aggression. A gene on chromosome 17 boosts physical stamina. In 1998 a gene was found on chromosome 6 (again, related to the insulinlike signaling pathway) that seems to confer higher intelligence in children. In 2000 a gene for depression was identified at the New York State Psychiatric Institute. In 2001 Anthony Monaco of Oxford University reported the discovery of a gene on chromosome 7 that seems to give humans the gift of language.

We already have virtually all the technology needed to alter such genes to maximize or minimize their effects. We know how to insert such "edited" genes into the human genome. We know how to grow a baby from this edited DNA. What will become of the world, when scientists—perhaps working secretly like the team that made Dolly—start to make a cadre of strong, happy, sociable, long-living geniuses? Caleb Finch at the University of Southern California, another modern genius of biology, has pointed out that human DNA differs from that of chimpanzees by 1 percent. He has initiated a project to map the chimpanzee genome, compare it with the human genome, and find the 1 percent of genes that turn an ape into a man. What will become of humankind when we advance the genome by *another* 1 percent?

We are in the midst of a bioscience revolution the dimensions of which stretch the bounds of human imagination, and the weight of which shakes the foundations of human identity. This revolution will compel the utmost of us as we face seductive possibilities—bioethical dilemmas impossible to consider in another age. Aldous Huxley's Brave New World is absolutely in our grasp. But grasping this extraordinary science is not comfortable; there has never been a hotter potato. We need to find a balance between scientific progress and ethics that will yield a net human and humane benefit—the greatest good we have the wisdom to do. We must decide as a society with shared aspirations for health and happiness how to make these decisions. The fact is undeniable: we are today in a position to redesign humanity. The consequences could be wonderful or terrible. Could a slight change in the human genome lead to world peace? A century ago, before such things were practical, poet Charlotte Perkins Gilman wrote: "Before such things can come, You idiotic child, You must alter human nature!" Yes, human germ-line engineering could lead to world peace; nothing other than a change in human nature will do so. But who should write the code for Humankind version 2.0? Do humans have the collective wisdom to decide how and whether to make humans more wise? That is the ethical question that our generation faces today. This decision, perhaps more than any other, will test our souls.

Ten Ways to Save Your Brain

We have visited the wide world of the human brain, past, present, and perhaps future. At this point, it might be useful to summarize what we can conclude about the best ways to preserve, optimize, and enhance the brain function we have. These ten methods are not mutually exclusive; they overlap, since the things we can do for ourselves may work to our brain's benefit in more than one way.

1. *Do everything you can to assure that adequate blood gets delivered to every cell in your brain.* Block cerebrovascular compromise at every turn. This means following the Brain-Saving Diet outlined in Chapter 11. It means willfully escaping from the near-paralytic inactivity of modern life and resuming something closer to the natural life of the body, as recommended in Chapter 17. It means controlling stress, as described in Chapter 6, dodging insulin resistance and the curse of diabetes, as described in Chapter 8, and of course controlling blood pressure, atherosclerosis, platelets, and cholesterol, using the astonishing new spectrum of methods described in Chapter 10.

2. *Control stress and depression,* even if this means finding a new job, choosing a new avocation, or reassessing a relationship. It means using the specific methods of stress assessment and stress relief outlined in Chapter 5. It also means dealing with job

stress as discussed in Chapter 6, and taking full advantage of the remarkable stress-busting effects of exercise as shown in Chapter 17. "Believe that life is worth living," as William James advised, "and your belief will help create the fact." Controlling stress and depression means making a heartfelt effort—at times requiring the expert help of a trusted family doctor, a pastor, rabbi, psychologist, or psychiatrist—to learn to savor life and love.

3. *Return to a more natural diet,* as outlined in Chapter 11. Follow the Brain-Saving Diet, and you may gradually become aware of the change in your energy and alertness—not to mention sheer gustatory delight. Take advantage of the selective use of supplementary vitamins and minerals as outlined in Chapters 11 and 12. Switch from coffee to tea. Discuss the benefits of wine with your doctor. Dine, as much as you can, in good company, with slow and simple grace.

4. *Stay physically active.* Build the life of the body, for which we are so beautifully adapted, back into the habits and pleasures of daily existence, as explained in Chapter 17. This is essential. I know that it's sometimes hard to get going. But as Epictetus taught, "Lead the good life, and habit will make it pleasant."

5. *Get a good job,* one that feeds the spirit as well as the mind, for all the reasons explained in Chapter 6—and retire only when retirement beckons with positive attractions.

6. *Avoid neurotoxicants.* This includes not only taking the prudent approach to aluminum outlined in Chapter 9 but also avoiding the on-the-job exposures described in Chapter 6.

7. *Avoid head trauma* like the bubonic plague, using the methods outlined in Chapter 16.

8. *Pursue forever the pleasures of the learning-nourished mind,* not with dull "mental exercise," but with the naturally stimulating methods described in Chapter 18.

9. *Stay alert to evolving news about the links between the mind, the brain, and your health.* We are on the verge of rapid change. We

must not rush in blindly. But we should get ready to take advantage of the safe and effective bets among hormone replacement therapies (Chapter 7), botanicals (Chapter 13), smart drugs (Chapter 14), and anti-inflammatories (Chapter 15).

10. *Finally, form a partnership with your doctor to save your brain.* Discovering the most promising path to good brain health is as easy as reading this book. But *achieving* a lasting change in health habits is a job more easily read about than done. For the most strongly motivated, information is enough, and a book will do the job. For others, like the pipe fitter Edward, a life-changing event—such as a heart attack or the birth of a grandchild—will flick the switch of motivation. But for many of us, the most reliable way to guarantee a life-saving, brain-saving, long-term change in health behaviors is to work with a *trusted* physician. Work with your doctor in every respect. Form a brain-protection (and heart-protection) team. If your current doctor is unable or unwilling to join you in this project, find another. The world is full of good doctors who truly want to help (if only the insurance companies would let them). Get a complete physical every year. Keep track of the blood levels that help you prolong the active life of your mind— cholesterol, B12, folate, thyroid functions, homocysteine, and iron—as well as the other simple laboratory tests I've recommended in this book. Then sit down with your doctor and decide on the lifestyle changes that are necessary to optimize the health of your brain.

Successful change in health behaviors involves four steps. First, the patient and doctor must agree on the goals. Second, they should set priorities and agree on how a change in behavior can lead to their highest-priority goals. Third, they should work together to develop a practical, *personalized* plan. And fourth, they should agree on a system of ongoing support for the plan, which may include peer groups, support organizations, follow-up phone calls, and nurse-practitioner home visits— but *must* include follow-up clinic visits at least three to four times a year. Most of all, this partnership requires the restoration of the one thing that managed care has most carelessly discarded from the doctor-patient relationship: *time to talk!*

The massive explosion of neuroscience knowledge is finally putting the power of brain protection in our hands. We are finally coming to see the deep roots of brain change and the realistic possibility of preventing and delaying cognitive loss. Yet for all our PET scans, blood tests, and smart drugs, the single best thing we can do for the future of our brains may be to live the fullest, healthiest, happiest life possible. "Live all you can; it's a mistake not to," as Henry James advised. This is in our power. Your power. The time to start is now.

Selected References

A note to the reader: more than 14,000 scientific articles were reviewed over the course of five years in researching *Saving Your Brain*. This literature represents an immense (and often underappreciated) effort by thousands of people working in the scientific community around the world. One can't help but feel grateful for this extraordinary body of work and thought, and cheered by these efforts to understand aging-related brain change and to find the methods that are most likely to optimize human brain function.

Below, I offer a very brief selection of some of the best references that address the content of each chapter. References are listed in topical groups so that readers can more easily find articles on a particular subject. Within the groups, the listing is alphabetical, based on the last name of the first author. Truly outstanding works—especially key contributions or gorgeously written summaries—are indicated with a star.*

Abbreviations for Some Common Journal Titles:
(Other Abbreviations Are Those of the National Library of Medicine)

Alzheimer Dis Assoc Disord=	*Alzheimer Disease and Associated Disorders*
Ann NY Acad Sci=	*Annals of the New York Academy of Sciences*
Ann Neurol=	*Annals of Neurology*
Arch Intern Med=	*Archives of Internal Medicine*
Arch Neurol=	*Archives of Neurology*
BMJ=	*British Medical Journal*
JAGS=	*Journal of the American Geriatrics Society*
JAMA=	*Journal of the American Medical Association*
NEJM=	*New England Journal of Medicine*
Proc Natl Acad Sci USA=	*Proceedings of the National Academy of Sciences of the United States of America*

Selected References for the Introduction to Part I: Why Brains Change

Butler, Robert N. Living longer, contributing longer. JAMA 1997;
    278:1372–1373.
* Dychtwald, Ken. *Age Wave: The Challenges and Opportunities of an Aging
    America*. New York: Bantam, 1990.
* Evans DA, Funkenstein HH, Albert MS, et al. Prevalence of Alzheimer's disease in
    a community population of older persons. Higher than previously reported.
    JAMA 1989; 262:2551–2556.
Fratiglioni L, De Ronchi D, Aguero-Torres H. Worldwide prevalence and incidence
    of dementia. Drugs Aging 1999; 15:365–375.
McCann JJ, Hebert LE, Bennett DA, Skul VV, Evans DA. Why Alzheimer's disease
    is a women's health issue. J Am Med Women Assoc 1997; 52:132–137.
Schumock GT. Economic considerations in the treatment and management of
    Alzheimer's disease. Am J Health Syst Pharm 1998; 55(21 Suppl):17S–21S.
van Reekum R, Simard M, Cohen T. The prediction and prevention of Alzheimer's
    disease—towards a research agenda. J Psychiatry Neurosci 1999; 24:413–430.
Wetle T. Living longer, aging better. JAMA 1997; 278:1376–1377.

Selected References for Chapter 1: Adam's and Eve's Brains

THE EVOLUTION OF THE HUMAN BRAIN

Eccles, John C. *Evolution of the Brain: Creation of the Self*. London: Routledge, 1989.
* Mithen, Steven. *The Prehistory of the Mind: The Cognitive Origins of Art, Reli-
    gion and Science*. London: Thames and Hudson, 1996.
Scheibel, Arnold B and Schopf, J William, eds. *The Origin and Evolution of Intelli-
    gence*. Sudbury: Jones and Bartlett Publishers, 1997.
Tattersal I. *Becoming Human: Evolution and Human Uniqueness*. New York: Har-
    court Brace & Company, 1998.
Victoroff J. The evolution of aging-related brain change. Neurobiolol Aging 1999;
    20:431–438.

THE STRUCTURE AND FUNCTION OF THE HUMAN BRAIN

Afifi AK, Bergman RA. *Functional Neuroanatomy: Text and Atlas*. New York: Mc-
    Graw-Hill Professional Publishing, 1997.
Feinberg TE, Farah MJ. *Behavioral Neurology and Neuropsychology*. New York:
    McGraw-Hill, 1997.
Gazzaniga MS, Ivry RB, Mangun GR. *Cognitive Neuroscience: The Biology of the
    Mind*. New York: W.W. Norton & Company, 1998.
Kandel ER, Schwartz JH, Jessell TM, eds. *Principles of Neural Sciences*. New York:
    McGraw-Hill, 2000.
Mesulam MM. *Principles of Behavioral and Cognitive Neurology*. Oxford: Oxford
    University Press, 2000.
Nieuwenhuys R, Ten Donkelaar HJ, Nicholson C. *The Central Nervous System of
    Vertebrates*. Springer Verlag, 1998.
* Pinker S. *How the Mind Works*. New York: W.W. Norton & Company, 1997.

Selected References for Chapter 2: What and Where Is Memory?

MEMORY—THE GENERAL IDEA

Bear MF. How do memories leave their mark? Nature 1997; 385:481–482.
Eichenbaum H. How does the brain organize memories? Science 1997; 277:330–2.
Fuster JM. Distributed memory for both short and long term. Neurobiol Learn
    Mem 1998; 70:268–74.
Gabrieli JDE. Cognitive neuroscience of human memory. Ann Rev Psychol 1998;
    49:87–115.
* Rosenzweig MR. Aspects of the search for neural mechanisms of memory. Ann
    Rev Psychol 1996; 47:1–32.
* Squire, Larry R, Kandel, Eric R. Memory, From Mind to Molecules. New York:
    Scientific American Library, 1999.
Thompson RF, Kim JJ. Memory systems in the brain and localization of a memory.
    Proc Natl Acad Sci USA 1996; 93:13438–13444.

THE ROLE OF THE HIPPOCAMPUS

Hampson RE, Simeral JD, Deadwyler SA. Distribution of spatial and nonspatial in-
    formation in dorsal hippocampus. Nature 1999; 402:610–4.
Teng E, Squire LR. Memory for places learned long ago is intact after hippocampal
    damage. Nature 1999; 400:675–7.

WORKING MEMORY

* Courtney SM, Petit L, Maisog JM, Ungerleider LG, Haxby JV. An area specialized for
    spatial working memory in human frontal cortex. Science 1998; 279:1347–51.

THE AMYGDALA AND EMOTIONAL MEMORY

Cahill L, McGaugh JL. Mechanisms of emotional arousal and lasting declarative
    memory. Trends Neurosci 1998; 21:294–9.

THE ROLE OF THE BASAL GANGLIA

Menon V, Anagnoson RT, Glover GH, Pfefferbaum A. Basal ganglia involvement in
    memory-guided movement sequencing. Neuroreport 2000; 11:3641–5.

THE ROLE OF THE CEREBELLUM

Thompson RF, Thompson JK, Kim JJ, Krupa DJ, Shinkman PG. The nature of rein-
    forcement in cerebellar learning. Neurobiol Learn Mem 1998; 70:150–76.

Selected References for Chapter 3: The Brain's Voyage of Life

THE BIOLOGY OF AGING

Arking, Robert. Biology of Aging: Observations and Principles, Second Edition.
    Sunderland, MA: Sinauer Associates, Inc., Publishers, 1998.

* Finch, Caleb E. *Longevity, Senescence, and the Genome*. Chicago: The University of Chicago Press, 1990.
Finch CE, Tanzi RE. Genetics of aging. Science 1997; 278(5337):407–11.
Kirkwood TB, Austad SN. Why do we age? Nature 2000; 408(6809):233–8.
Partridge L. Evolutionary theories of ageing applied to long-lived organisms. Exp Gerontol 2001; 36:641–50.
* Wachter KW, Finch CE, eds. *Between Zeus and the Salmon: The Biodemography of Longevity*. Washington, D.C.: National Academy Press, 1997.

NEURODEVELOPMENT

Black JE. How a child builds its brain: some lessons from animal studies of neural plasticity. Prev Med 1998; 27:168–71.
de Vries MW. Babies, brains and culture: optimizing neurodevelopment on the savanna. Acta Paediatr Suppl 1999; 88:43–8.
Nowakowski RS, Hayes NL. CNS development: an overview. Dev Psychopathol 1999; 11:395–417.

TYPICAL COGNITIVE CHANGES WITH AGING

Happe FG, Winner E, Brownell H. The getting of wisdom: theory of mind of old age. Dev Psychol. 34(2): 358–62, 1998.
Luszcz MA, Bryan J. Toward understanding age-related memory loss in late adulthood. Gerontology. 45(1): 2–9, 1999.
* Powell, Douglas H. *Profiles in Cognitive Aging*. Cambridge, MA: Harvard University Press, 1994.
Small SA, Stern Y, Tang M, Mayeux R. Selective decline in memory function among healthy elderly. Neurology 1999; 52:1392–1396.
Ylikoski R, Ylikoski A, Keskivaara P, et al. Heterogeneity of cognitive profiles in aging: successful aging, normal aging, and individuals at risk for cognitive decline. Eur J Neurol 1999; 6:645–52.
Zelinski EM, Burnight KP. Sixteen-year longitudinal and time lag changes in memory and cognition in older adults. Psychol Aging 1997; 12:503–513.

HOW BRAINS CHANGE WITH AGE

Delacourte A, David JP, Sergeant N, et al. The biochemical pathway of neurofibrillary degeneration in aging and Alzheimer's disease. Neurology 1999; 52:1158–1165.
Dickson DW. The pathogenesis of senile plaques. J Neuropath Exp Neurol 1997; 56:321–339.
Drachman DA. Aging and the brain: a new frontier. Ann Neurol 1997; 42:819–828.
Morrison JH, Hof PR. Life and death of neurons in the aging brain. Science 1997; 278:412–419.
Sandbrink R, Monning U, Masters CL, Beyreuther K. Expression of the APP gene family in brain cells, brain development and aging. Gerontology 1997; 43:119–31.
Victoroff J. Central nervous system changes with normal aging. In: Sadock BJ, Sadock

VA, eds. *Kaplan and Sadock's Comprehensive Textbook of Psychiatry, VIIth Edition*. Philadelphia: Lippincott Williams and Wilkins, 2000, pp. 3010–3020.

Wickelgren I. For the cortex, neuron loss may be less than thought. Science 1996; 273:48–50.

Selected References for Chapter 4: What Is "Alzheimer's," and Are You Getting It?

DEFINITION OF AD

* Anonymous. Consensus recommendations for the postmortem diagnosis of Alzheimer's disease. The National Institute on Aging, and Reagan Institute Working Group on Diagnostic Criteria for the Neuropathological Assessment of Alzheimer's Disease. Neurobiol Aging 1997; 18(4 Suppl):S1–S2.

Ball MJ, Murdoch GH. Neuropathological criteria for the diagnosis of Alzheimer's disease: are we really ready yet? Neurobiol Aging 1997; 18(4 Suppl): S3–S12.

Cookson WO. Disease taxonomy—polygenic. Br Med Bull 1999; 55:358–65.

Khachaturian ZS. Diagnosis of Alzheimer's disease. Arch Neurol 1985; 42:1097–1105.

McKhann G, Drachman D, Folstein M, et al. Clinical diagnosis of Alzheimer's disease: report of the NINCDS-ADRDA work group under the auspices of Department of Health and Human Services Task Force on Alzheimer's Disease. Neurology 1984; 34:939–944.

SYMPTOMS, DIAGNOSIS, AND TESTING FOR ALZHEIMER'S

* Corey-Bloom J, Thal LJ, Galasko D, et al. Diagnosis and evaluation of dementia. Neurology 1995; 45:211–218.

Small GW, Rabins PV, Barry PP, et al. Diagnosis and treatment of Alzheimer's disease and related disorders. Consensus statement of the American Association for Geriatric Psychiatry, the Alzheimer's Association, and the American Geriatrics Society. JAMA 1997; 278:1363–1371.

Victoroff J. The neurological evaluation in geriatric psychiatry. In: Grossberg, George, ed. *Comprehensive Review of Geriatric Psychiatry, Third Edition*. Washington, D.C., American Psychiatric Press, Inc.: 2002.

Victoroff J, Mack WJ, Lyness SA, Chui HC. Multicenter clinicopathological correlation in dementia. Am J Psychiatry 1995; 152:1476–1484.

"MILD COGNITIVE IMPAIRMENT"

Almkvist O, Basun H, Backman L, et al. Mild cognitive impairment—an early stage of Alzheimer's disease? J Neural Transm 1998; 54(Suppl):21–29.

Celsis P. Age-related cognitive decline, mild cognitive impairment or preclinical Alzheimer's disease? Ann Med 2000; 32:6–14.

Elias MF, Beiser A, Wolf PA, et al. The preclinical phase of Alzheimer disease: a 22-year prospective study of the Framingham cohort. Arch Neurol 2000; 57:808–813.

THE BIOLOGICAL BASIS OF ALZHEIMER'S

Braak H, Braak E. Evolution of the neuropathology of Alzheimer's disease. Acta
    Neurol Scand Suppl 1996; 93(Suppl 165):3–12.
Gerober E, Dickson D, Sliwinski MJ, et al. Memory and mental status correlates of
    Braak staging. Neurobiol Aging 1999; 20:573–579.
Mattson MP, Furukawa K. Short precursor shortens memory. Nature 1997;
    387:457–458.
Terry RD, Masliah E, Salmon DP, et al. Physical basis of cognitive alterations in
    Alzheimer's disease: synapse loss is the major correlate of cognitive impair-
    ment. Ann Neurol 1991; 30:572–580.
Yanker BA. New clues to Alzheimer's disease: unraveling the roles of amyloid and
    tau. Nat Med 1996; 2:850–852.

THE GENETICS OF ALZHEIMER'S

Myers AJ, Goate AM. The genetics of late-onset Alzheimer's disease. Curr Opin
    Neurol 2001; 14:433–440.
Plassman BL, Breitner JC. Recent advances in the genetics of Alzheimer's disease
    and vascular dementia with an emphasis on gene-environment interactions.
    JAGS 1996; 44:1242–1250.

APOLIPOPROTEIN E AND ALZHEIMER'S

* Corder E, Saunders A, Strittmatter W, et al. Gene dose of apolipoprotein E type 4
    allele and the risk of Alzheimer's disease in late onset families. Science 1993;
    261:921–923.
Evans DA, Beckett LA, Field TS, et al. Apolipoprotein E epsilon4 and incidence of
    Alzheimer disease in a community population of older persons. JAMA 1997;
    277:822–824.
* Mayeux R, Saunders AM, Shea S, et al. Utility of the apolipoprotein E genotype in
    the diagnosis of Alzheimer's disease. Alzheimer's Disease Centers Consortium
    on Apolipoprotein E and Alzheimer's Disease. NEJM 1998; 338:506–511.
Smith JD. Apolipoprotein E4; an allele associated with many diseases. Ann Med
    2000; 32:118–127.

The Spectrum of Neurodegenerative Disorders

OVERVIEW

Caselli RJ. Topography, histology, and seminology in dementia. Arch Neurol 2000;
    57:899–900.
Hardy J, Gwinn-Hardy K. Genetic classification of primary neurodegenerative dis-
    ease. Science 1998; 282:1075–9.
Perl DP, Olanow CW, Calne D. Alzheimer's disease and Parkinson's disease: distinct
    entities or extremes of a spectrum of neurodegeneration? Ann Neurol 1998;
    44(3 Suppl 1):S19–31.

PARKINSON'S DISEASE

Aarsland D, Tandberg E, Larsen JP, Cummings JL. Frequency of dementia in Parkinson disease. Arch Neurol 1996; 53:538–542.

Kosel S, Hofhaus G, Maassen A, Vieregge P, Graeber MB. Role of mitochondria in Parkinson disease. Biol Chem 1999; 380:865–70.

Marsden CD, Olanow CW. The causes of Parkinson's disease are being unraveled and rational neuroprotective therapy is close to reality. Ann Neurol 1998; 44(3 Suppl 1):S189–96.

Spacey SD, Wood NW. The genetics of Parkinson's disease. Curr Opin Neurol 1999; 12:427–32.

DEMENTIA WITH LEWY BODIES

* McKeith IG, Galasko D, Kosaka K, et al. Consensus guidelines for the clinical and pathologic diagnosis of dementia with Lewy bodies (DLB): report of the consortium on DLB international workshop. Neurology 1996; 47:1113–24.

FRONTOTEMPORAL LOBAR DEMENTIA

Johnson JK, Head E, Kim R, Starr A, Cotman CW. Clinical and pathological evidence for a frontal variant of Alzheimer disease. Arch Neurol 1999; 56:1233–1239.

Neary D. Overview of frontotemporal dementias and the consensus applied. Dement Geriatr Cogn Disord 1999; 10(Suppl 1):6–9.

THE EPIDEMIOLOGY OF ALZHEIMER'S AND RELATED DISORDERS

Hebert LE, Scherr PA, Beckett LA, et al. Age-specific incidence of Alzheimer's disease in a community population. JAMA 1995; 273:1354–9.

Ott A, Breteler MMB, van Harslcamp F, et al. Prevalence of Alzheimer's disease and vascular dementia. BMJ 1995; 310:970–2.

"ALZHEIMER'S" VERSUS "NORMAL AGING"

Almkvist O. Functional brain imaging as a looking-glass into the degraded brain: reviewing evidence from Alzheimer disease in relation to normal aging. Acta Psychol 2000; 105:255–77.

Brayne C, Calloway P. Normal ageing, impaired cognitive function and senile dementia of the Alzheimer's type: a continuum? Lancet 1988; i:1265–7.

Davis DG, Schmitt FA, Wekstein DR, Markesbery WR. Alzheimer neuropathologic alternations in aged cognitively normal subjects. J Neuropathol Exp Neurol 1999; 58:376–88.

Hulette CM, Welsh-Bohmer KA, Murray MG, et al. Neuropathological and neuropsychological changes in "normal" aging: evidence for preclinical Alzheimer disease in cognitively normal individuals. J Neuropathol Exp Neurol 1998; 57:1168–74.

"ALZHEIMER'S" VERSUS "VASCULAR DEMENTIA"

Aguero-Torres H, Winblad B. Alzheimer's disease and vascular dementia. Some points of confluence. Ann NY Acad Sci 2000; 903:547–52.

De Jong GI, De Vos RA, Steur EN, Luiten PG. Cerebrovascular hypoperfusion: a risk factor for Alzheimer's disease? Animal model and postmortem human studies. Ann NY Acad Sci 1997; 826:56–74.

Kalaria RN. Cerebrovascular degeneration is related to amyloid-beta protein deposition in Alzheimer's disease. Ann NY Acad Sci 1997; 826:263–71.

Shi J, Perry G, Smith MA, Friedland RP. Vascular abnormalities: the insidious pathogenesis of Alzheimer's disease. Neurobiol Aging 2000; 21:357–61.

Skoog I. Vascular aspects in Alzheimer's disease. J Neural Transm Suppl 2000; 59:37–43.

* Snowdon DA, Greiner LH, Mortimer JA, et al. Brain infarction and the clinical expression of Alzheimer disease. The Nun Study. JAMA 1997; 277:813–7.

* Thomas T, Thomas G, McLendon C, Sutton T, Mullan M. [beta]-amyloid-mediated vasoactivity and vascular endothelial damage. Nature 1996; 380:168–171.

Selected References for the Introduction to Part II: Twain's Maxim and Pascal's Bet

OVERVIEW

Aisen PS, Davis KL. The search for disease-modifying treatment for Alzheimer's disease. Neurology 1997; 48(5 Suppl 6):S35–41.

Fratiglioni L. Epidemiology of Alzheimer's disease and current possibilities for prevention. Acta Neurol Scand Suppl 1996; 165:33–40.

* Kondo K, Niino M, Shido K. A case-control study of Alzheimer's disease in Japan—significance of lifestyles. Dementia 1994; 5:314–26.

Mattson MP. Existing data suggest that Alzheimer's disease is preventable. Ann NY Acad Sci 2000; 924:153–9.

PASCAL'S BET

Leshno M. On using the standard gamble to determine utilities for uncertain health states. Med Decision Making 2001; 21:82–3.

TWAIN'S MAXIM

Arbuckle TY, Maag U, Pushkar D, Chaikelson JS. Individual differences in trajectory of intellectual development over 45 years of adulthood. Psychol Aging 1998; 13:663–75.

Maimone D, Dominici R, Grimaldi LM. Pharmacogenomics of neurodegenerative diseases. Eur J Pharmacol 2001; 413:11–29.

Wilson RS, Gilley DW, Bennett DA, Beckett LA, Evans DA. Person-specific paths of cognitive decline in Alzheimer's disease and their relation to age. Psychol Aging 2000; 15:18–28.

Zeliniski EM, Gilweski MJ, Shaie KW. Individual differences in cross-sectional and

3-year longitudinal performance across the adult life span. Psychol Aging 1993; 8:176–186.

Selected References for Chapter 5: Is Stress Destroying Your Brain?

OVERVIEW OF STRESS AND DEPRESSION

Blake LM. Aging, stress, and affective disorders. Semin Clin Neuropsychiatry 2001; 6:27–31.

Doris A, Ebmeier K, Shajahan P. Depressive illness. Lancet 1999; 354:1369–75.

Miller TW, ed. *Stressful Life Events*. Madison: International Universities Press, Inc., 1989.

Steffens DC, Skoog I, Norton MC, et al. Prevalence of depression and its treatment in an elderly population: the Cache County study. Arch Gen Psychiatry 2000; 57:601–7.

STRESS AND HORMONES

* Bremner JD, Licinio J, Darnell A, et al. Elevated CSF corticotropin-releasing factor concentrations in posttraumatic stress disorder. Am J Psychiatry 1997; 154:624–9.

Korte SM. Corticosteroids in relation to fear, anxiety and psychopathology. Neurosci Biobehav Rev 2001; 25:117–42.

Negrao AB, Deuster PA, Gold PW, Singh A, Chrousos GP. Individual reactivity and physiology of the stress response. Biomed Pharmacother 2000; 54:122–8.

* O'Connor TM, O'Halloran DJ, Shanahan F. The stress response and the hypothalamic-pituitary-adrenal axis: from molecule to melancholia. QJM 2000; 93:323–33.

Yehuda R. Biology of posttraumatic stress disorder. J Clin Psychiatry 2001; 62 (Suppl 17):41–6.

CARDIOVASCULAR FUNCTION AND STRESS

Nyklicek I, Vingerhoets JJ, Van Heck GL. Hypertension and objective and self-reported stressor exposure: a review. J Psychosom Res 1996; 40:585–601.

Patel C. Stress management & hypertension. Acta Physiol Scand Suppl 1997; 640:155–7.

STRESS AND COGNITION

* de Quervain DJ, Roozendaal B, McGaugh JL. Stress and glucocorticoids impair retrieval of long-term spatial memory. Nature 1998; 394:787–90.

Dufouil C, Fuhrer R, Dartigues JF, Alperovitch A. Longitudinal analysis of the association between depressive symptomatology and cognitive deterioration. Am J Epidemiol 1996; 144:634–41.

McCauley J, Kern DE, Kolodner K, et al. Clinical characteristics of women with a history of childhood abuse: unhealed wounds. JAMA 1997; 277:1362–8.

* McEwen BS, Sapolsky RM. Stress and cognitive function. Curr Opin Neurobiol 1995; 5:205–16.

Speck CE, Kukull WA, Brenner DE, et al. History of depression as a risk factor for Alzheimer's disease. Epidemiology 1995; 6:366–9.

Yaffe K, Blackwell T, Gore R, et al. Depressive symptoms and cognitive decline in nondemented elderly women: a prospective study. Arch Gen Psychiatry 1999; 56:425–430.

BRAIN CHANGES WITH STRESS

Bremner JD, Narayan M, Anderson ER, et al. Hippocampal volume reduction in major depression. Am J Psychiatry 2000; 157:115–8.

* Gould E, Tanapat P, McEwen BS, Flugge G, Fuchs E. Proliferation of granule cell precursors in the dentate gyrus of adult monkeys is diminished by stress. Proc Natl Acad Sci USA 1998; 95:3168–71.

Markowitsch HJ, Kessler J, Van Der Ven C, et al. Psychic trauma causing grossly reduced brain metabolism and cognitive deterioration. Neuropsychologia 1998; 36:77–82.

McEwen BS. Stress and the aging hippocampus. Front Neuroendocrinol 1999; 20:49–70.

Nelson CA, Carver LJ. The effects of stress and trauma on brain and memory: a view from developmental cognitive neuroscience. Dev Psychopathol 1998; 10:793–809.

* Sapolsky RM. Why stress is bad for your brain. Science 1996; 273:749–50.

Sato R, Bryan RN, Fried LP. Neuroanatomic and functional correlates of depressed mood: the Cardiovascular Health Study. Am J Epidemiol 1999; 150:919–929.

Starkman MN, Giordani B, Gebarski SS, et al. Decrease in cortisol reverses human hippocampal atrophy following treatment of Cushing's disease. Biol Psychiatry 1999; 46:1595–602.

Vogel G. New brain cells prompt new theory of depression. Science 2000; 290:258–9.

STRESS AND DEPRESSION: APPROACHES TO TREATMENT

Astin JA. Stress reduction through mindfulness meditation. Effects on psychological symptomatology, sense of control, and spiritual experiences. Psychother Psychosom 1997; 66:97–106.

Echols JC, Naidoo U, Salzman C. SAMe (S-adenosylmethionine). Harvard Review of Psychiatry 2000; 8:84–90.

* Kent JM. SNaRIs, NaSSAs, and NaRIs: new agents for the treatment of depression. Lancet 2000; 355:911–8.

Kim H, Streltzer J, Goebert D. St. John's wort for depression: a meta-analysis of well-defined clinical trials. J Nerv Ment Dis 1999; 187:532–538.

Linde K, Mulrow CD. St John's wort for depression. Cochrane Database of Systematic Reviews [computer file] 2000; 2:CD000448.

* Pearlstein T. Antidepressant treatment of posttraumatic stress disorder. J Clin Psychiatry 2000; 61(Suppl 7):40–43.

Schulberg HC, Katon W, Simon GE, Rush AJ. Treating major depression in pri-

mary care practice: an update of the Agency for Health Care Policy
and Research Practice Guidelines. Arch Gen Psychiatry 1998;
55:1121-7.
* Williams JW Jr, Mulrow CD, Chiquette E, et al. A systematic review of newer
pharmacotherapies for depression in adults: evidence report summary. Ann
Intern Med 2000; 132:743-56.

Selected References for Chapter 6: Is Your Job Eating Your Brain?

OVERVIEW OF OCCUPATION AND DEMENTIA

Gun RT, Korten AE, Jorm AF, et al. Occupational risk factors for Alzheimer
disease: a case-control study. Alzheimer Dis Assoc Disord 1997; 11:21-7.
Munoz DG, Ganapathy GR, Eliasziw M, Hachinski V. Educational attainment and
socioeconomic status of patients with autopsy-confirmed Alzheimer disease.
Arch Neurol 2000; 57:85-9.
Schulte PA, Burnett CA, Boeniger MF, Johnson J. Neurodegenerative diseases: occupational occurrence and potential risk factors, 1982 through 1991. Am J
Pub Health 1996; 86:1281-8.
Stern Y, Alexander GE, Prohovnik I, et al. Relationship between lifetime occupa-
tion and parietal flow: implications for a reserve against Alzheimer's disease
pathology. Neurology 1995; 45:55-60.

ALZHEIMER'S AND SOLVENTS

Daniell WE, Claypoole KH, Checkoway H, et al. Neuropsychological function in
retired workers with previous long term occupational exposure to solvents.
Occup Environ Med 1999; 56:93-105.
Morton WE. Solvent toxicity and cognition impairment. Arch Neurol 2000;
57:282.
Palmer K, Inskip H, Martyn C, Coggon D. Dementia and occupational exposure to
organic solvents. Occup Environ Med 1998; 55:712-715.

PARKINSON'S AND PESTICIDES

Gorell JM, Johnson CC, Rybicki BA, Peterson EL, Richardson RJ. The risk of
Parkinson's disease with exposure to pesticides, farming, well water, and rural
living. Neurology 1998; 50:1346-1350.
* Hubble JP, Kurth JH, Glatt SL, Koller WC, et al. Gene-toxin interaction as a puta-
tive risk factor for Parkinson's disease with dementia. Neuroepidemiology
1998; 17:96-104.
Le Couteur DG, McLean AJ, Taylor MC, Woodham BL, Board PG. Pesticides and
Parkinson's disease. Biomed Pharmacother 1999; 53:122-30.

METALS AND BRAIN DAMAGE

Cuajungco MP, Lees GJ. Zinc and Alzheimer's disease: is there a direct link? Brain
Res Rev 1997; 23:219-36.

Gorell JM, Johnson CC, Rybicki BA, et al. Occupational exposures to metals as risk factors for Parkinson's disease. Neurology 1997; 48:650–658.

Gorell JM, Johnson CC, Rybicki BA, et al. Occupational exposure to manganese, copper, lead, iron, mercury and zinc and the risk of Parkinson's disease. Neurotoxicology 1999; 20:239–47.

OVERVIEW OF JOB STRESS

Arnetz BB, Wiholm C. Technological stress: psychophysiological symptoms in modern offices. J Psychosom Res 1997; 43:35–42.

Hellerstedt WL, Jeffery RW. The association of job strain and health behaviours in men and women. Int J Epidemiol 1997; 26:575–83.

JOB STRESS AND STRESS HORMONES

Sluiter JK, van der Beek AJ, Frings-Dresen MHW. Work stress and recovery measured by urinary catecholamines and cortisol excretion in long distance coach drivers. Occup Environ Med 1998; 55:407–413.

JOB STRESS AND THE VASCULAR SYSTEM

Johnson JV. Decision latitude, job strain, and myocardial infarction: a study of working men in Stockholm. The SHEP Study Group. Stockholm Heart Epidemiology Program. Am J Pub Health 1998; 88:382–8.

Pickering T. The effects of occupational stress on blood pressure in men and women. Acta Physiol Scand Suppl 1997; 640:125–8.

Steenland K, Johnson J, Nowlin S. A follow-up study of job strain and heart disease among males in the NHANES1 population. Am J Ind Med 1997; 31:256–60.

* Theorell T, Alfredsson L, Westerholm P, Falck B. Coping with unfair treatment at work—what is the relationship between coping and hypertension in middle-aged men and women? An epidemiological study of working men and women in Stockholm (the WOLF study). Psychother Psychosom 2000; 69:86–94.

WOMEN, WORK, AND STRESS

Frank E, Dingle AD. Self-reported depression and suicide attempts among U.S. women physicians. Am J Psychiatry 1999; 156:1887–94.

Goldstein IB, Shapiro D, Chicz-DeMet A, Guthrie D. Ambulatory blood pressure, heart rate, and neuroendocrine responses in women nurses during work and off work days. Psychosom Med 1999; 61:387–96.

Luecken LJ, Suarez EC, Kuhn CM, et al. Stress in employed women: impact of marital status and children at home on neurohormone output and home strain. Psychosom Med 1997; 59:352–9.

Richman JA, Rospenda KM, Nawyn SJ, et al. Sexual harassment and generalized workplace abuse among university employees: prevalence and mental health correlates. Am J Pub Health 1999; 89:358–63.

* Williams RB, Barefoot JC, Blumenthal JA, et al. Psychosocial correlates of job strain in a sample of working women. Arch Gen Psychiatry 1997; 54:543–8.

Selected References for Chapter 7: Can Sex Hormones Keep You Smart?

OVERVIEW OF SEX HORMONES, THE MIND, AND THE BRAIN

Birge SJ. Is there a role for estrogen replacement therapy in the prevention and treatment of dementia? JAGS 1996; 44:865–70.

Burkman RT, Collins, JA, Greene RA. Current perspectives on benefits and risks of hormone replacement therapy. Am J Obstet Gynecol 2001; 185(2 Suppl):S13–23.

Green PS, Simpkins JW. Estrogens and estrogen-like non-feminizing compounds. Their role in the prevention and treatment of Alzheimer's disease. Ann NY Acad Sci 2000; 924:93–8.

Henderson VW. Estrogen, cognition, and a woman's risk of Alzheimer's disease. Am J Med 1997; 103(3A)Supplement:11S–18S.

McEwen BS, Alves SE, Bulloch K, Weiland NG. Ovarian steroids and the brain: implications for cognition and aging. Neurology 1997; 48(5 Suppl 7):S8–15.

Sherwin BB. Estrogen and cognitive functioning in women. Proc Soc Exp Biol Med 1998; 217:17–22.

THE BIOLOGICAL BASIS OF ESTROGEN'S NEUROPROTECTIVE EFFECTS

Inestrosa NC, Marzolo MP, Bonnefont AB. Cellular and molecular basis of estrogen's neuroprotection. Potential relevance for Alzheimer's disease. Mol Neurobiol 1998; 17:73–86.

* Yaffe K, Lui L, Grady D, et al. Cognitive decline in women in relation to non-protein-bound oestradiol concentrations. Lancet 2000; 356:708–712.

ESTROGEN AND COGNITION: EPIDEMIOLOGICAL STUDIES

Grodstein F, Chen J, Pollen DA, et al. Postmenopausal hormone therapy and cognitive function in healthy older women. JAGS 2000; 48:746–52.

Kawas C, Resnick S, Morrison A, et al. A prospective study of estrogen replacement therapy and the risk of developing Alzheimer's disease: the Baltimore Longitudinal Study of Aging. Neurology 1997; 48:1517–1521.

* Paganini-Hill A, Henderson V. Estrogen deficiency and risk of Alzheimer's disease in women. Am J Epidemiol 1994; 140:256–261.

Rice MM, Graves AB, McCurry SM, et al. Postmenopausal estrogen and estrogen-progestin use and 2-year rate of cognitive change in a cohort of older Japanese American women: the Kame Project. Arch Intern Med 2000; 160:1641–9.

Yaffe K, Sawaya G, Lieberburg I, Grady D. Estrogen therapy in postmenopausal women: effects on cognitive function and dementia. JAMA 1998; 279:688–695.

ESTROGEN AND STROKE

de Valk-de Roo GW, Stehouwer CD, Meijer P, et al. Both raloxifene and estrogen reduce major cardiovascular risk factors in healthy postmenopausal women: a

2-year, placebo-controlled study. Arterioscler Thromb Vasc Biol 1999; 19:2993–3000.

Hurn PD, Macrae IM. Estrogen as a neuroprotectant in stroke. J Cereb Blood Flow Metab 2000; 20:631–52.

THERAPEUTIC TRIALS OF ESTROGEN FOR COGNITION

Shumaker SA, Reboussin BA, Espeland MA, et al. The Women's Health Initiative Memory Study (WHIMS): a trial of the effect of estrogen therapy in preventing and slowing the progression of dementia. Control Clin Trials 1998; 19:604–21.

Steffens DC, Norton MC, Plassman BL, et al. Enhanced cognitive performance with estrogen use in nondemented community-dwelling older women. JAGS 1999; 47:1171–5.

SELECTIVE ESTROGEN RECEPTOR MODULATORS = SERMS

McDonnell DP. Selective estrogen receptor modulators (SERMs): a first step in the development of perfect hormone replacement therapy regimen. J Soc Gynecol Investig 2000; 7(1 Suppl):S10–5.

SEX DIFFERENCES IN THE HUMAN MIND AND BRAIN

Barrett-Connor E, Kritz-Silverstein D. Gender differences in cognitive function with age: the Rancho Bernardo study. JAGS 1999; 47:159–64.

Coffey CE, Lucke JF, Saxton JA, et al. Sex differences in brain aging: a quantitative magnetic resonance imaging study. Arch Neurol 1998; 55:169–79.

Rabinowicz T, Dean DE, Petetot JM, de Courten-Myers GM. Gender differences in the human cerebral cortex: more neurons in males; more processes in females. J Child Neurol 1999; 14:98–107.

ADAM, TESTOSTERONE, AND COGNITION

Alexander GM, Swerdloff RS, Wang C, et al. Androgen-behavior correlations in hypogonadal men and eugonadal men. II. Cognitive abilities. Horm Behav 1998; 33:85–94.

Barrett-Connor E, Goodman-Gruen D, Patay B. Endogenous sex hormones and cognitive function in older men. J Clin Endocrinol Metab 1999; 84:3681–5.

Morales A, Heaton JP, Carson CC 3rd. Andropause: a misnomer for a true clinical entity. J Urol 2000; 163:705–12.

Papasozomenos SC. The heat shock-induced hyperphosphorylation of tau is estrogen-independent and prevented by androgens: implications for Alzheimer disease. Proc Natl Acad Sci USA 1997; 94:6612–7.

Sih R, Morley JE, Kaiser FE, Perry HM 3rd, Patrick P, Ross C. Testosterone replacement in older hypogonadal men: a 12-month randomized controlled trial. J Clin Endocrinol Metab 1997; 82:1661–7.

Selected References for Chapter 8: Can Non-sex Hormones Keep You Smart?

OVERVIEW

Rosenberg LL, Timiras PS. Ageing and the endocrine system. In: Pathy M S, ed. *Principles and Practice of Geriatric Medicine, 3rd Edition.* New York: John Wiley & Sons Ltd., 1997, pp. 1–7.

GLUCOSE, DIABETES, AND MEMORY LOSS

Elias PK, Elias MF, D'Agostino RB, et al. NIDDM and blood pressure as risk factors for poor cognitive performance. The Framingham Study. Diabetes Care 1997; 20:1388–95.

Fontbonne A, Berr C, Ducimetiere P, Alperovitch A. Changes in cognitive abilities over a 4-year period are unfavorably affected in elderly diabetic subjects: results of the Epidemiology of Vascular Aging Study. Diabetes Care 2001; 24:366–70.

Gregg EW, Yaffe K, Cauley JA, et al. for the Study of Osteoporotic Fractures Research Group. Is diabetes associated with cognitive impairment and cognitive decline among older women? Arch Intern Med 2000; 160:174–180.

Lovestone S. Diabetes and dementia: is the brain another site of end-organ damage? Neurology 1999; 53:1907.

Messier C, Gagnon M. Glucose regulation and cognitive functions: relation to Alzheimer's disease and diabetes. Behav Brain Res 1996; 75:1–11.

Ott A, Stolk RP, van Harskamp F, et al. Diabetes mellitus and the risk of dementia: the Rotterdam Study. Neurology 1999; 53:1937–42.

* Vanhanen M, Soininen H. Glucose intolerance, cognitive impairment and Alzheimer's disease. Curr Opin Neurol 1998; 11:673–7.

Vekrellis K, Ye Z, Qiu WQ, et al. Neurons regulate extracellular levels of amyloid beta-protein via proteolysis by insulin-degrading enzyme. J Neurosci 2000; 20:1657–65.

GROWTH HORMONE AND ADULT COGNITION

Bartke A, Coschigano K, Kopchick J, et al. Genes that prolong life: relationships of growth hormone and growth to aging and life span. J Gerontol A Biol Sci Med Sci 2001; 56:B340–9.

Baum HB, Katznelson L, Sherman JC, et al. Effects of physiological growth hormone (GH) therapy on cognition and quality of life in patients with adult-onset GH deficiency. J Clin Endocrinol Metab 1998; 83:3184–9.

Deijen JB, de Boer H, van der Veen EA. Cognitive changes during growth hormone replacement in adult men. Psychoneuroendocrinology 1998; 23:45–55.

* Rollero A, Murialdo G, Fonzi S, et al. Relationship between cognitive function, growth hormone and insulin-like growth factor I plasma levels in aged subjects. Neuropsychobiology 1998; 38:73–9.

MELATONIN AND THE BRAIN

Chyan YJ, Poeggeler B, Omar RA, et al. Potent neuroprotective properties against the Alzheimer beta-amyloid by an endogenous melatonin-related indole structure, indole-3-propionic acid. J Biol Chem 1999; 274:21937–42.

Huether G. Melatonin as an antiaging drug: between facts and fantasy. Gerontology 1996; 42:87–96.

Reiter RJ, Cabrera J, Sainz RM, et al. Melatonin as a pharmacological agent against neuronal loss in experimental models of Huntington's disease, Alzheimer's disease and parkinsonism. Ann NY Acad Sci 1999; 890:471–85.

Slotten HA, Krekling S. Does melatonin have an effect on cognitive performance? Psychoneuroendocrinology 1996; 21:673–80.

DHEA AND THE BRAIN

Berr C, Lafont S, Debuire B, Dartigues JF, Baulieu EE. Relationships of dehydroepiandrosterone sulfate in the elderly with functional, psychological, and mental status, and short-term mortality: a French community-based study. Proc Natl Acad Sci USA 1996; 93:13410–5.

Buffington CK. DHEA: elixir of youth or mirror of age? JAGS 1998; 46:391–2.

Hillen T, Lun A, Reischies FM, et al. DHEA-S plasma levels and incidence of Alzheimer's disease. Biol Psychiatry 2000; 47:161–3.

THYROID HORMONE AND COGNITION

Baldini IM, Vita A, Mauri MC, et al. Psychopathological and cognitive features in subclinical hypothyroidism. Prog Neuropsychopharmacol Biol Psychiatry 1997; 21:925–35.

Dugbartey AT. Neurocognitive aspects of hypothyroidism. Arch Intern Med 1998; 158:1413–8.

Prinz PN, Scanlan JM, Vitaliano PP, et al. Thyroid hormones: positive relationships with cognition in healthy, euthyroid older men. J Gerontol A Biol Sci Med Sci 1999; 54:M111–6.

Selected References for Chapter 9: Dodging Aluminum May Save Your Brain

ALUMINUM: FACTS AND POLICIES

Savory J, Exley C, Forbes WF, et al. Can the controversy of the role of aluminum in Alzheimer's disease be resolved? What are the suggested approaches to this controversy and methodological issues to be considered? J Toxicol Environ Health 1996; 48:615–35.

Yokel RA. The toxicology of aluminum in the brain: a review. Neurotoxicology 2000; 21:813–28.

ALUMINUM, MEMORY LOSS, AND ALZHEIMER'S—EPIDEMIOLOGICAL STUDIES

* Forbes WF, Hill GB. Is exposure to aluminum a risk factor for the development of Alzheimer disease?—Yes. Arch Neurol 1998; 55:740–1.

Gauthier E, Fortier I, Courchesne F, et al. Aluminum forms in drinking water and risk of Alzheimer's disease. Environ Res 2000; 84:234–46.

Martyn CN, Coggon DN, Inskip H, Lacey RF, Young WF. Aluminum concentrations in drinking water and risk of Alzheimer's disease. Epidemiology 1997; 8:281–6.

Munoz DG. Is exposure to aluminum a risk factor for the development of
    Alzheimer disease?—No. Arch Neurol 1998; 55:737–9.
Rondeau V, Commenges D, Jacqmin-Gadda H, Dartigues JF. Relation between alu-
    minum concentrations in drinking water and Alzheimer's disease: an 8-year
    follow-up study. Am J Epidemiol 2000; 152:59–66.

ALUMINUM: LABORATORY STUDIES

Armstrong RA, Winsper SJ, Blair JA. Aluminium and Alzheimer's disease: review of
    possible pathogenic mechanisms. Dementia 1996; 7:1–9.
Bondy SC, Truong A. Potentiation of beta-folding of beta-amyloid peptide 25-35
    by aluminum salts. Neurosci Lett 1999; 267:25–8.
Campbell A, Bondy SC. Aluminum induced oxidative events and its relation to in-
    flammation: a role for the metal in Alzheimer's disease. Cell Mol Biol (Noisy-
    le-grand) 2000; 46:721–30.
Makjanic J, McDonald B, Li-Hsian Chen CP, Watt F. Absence of aluminium in neu-
    rofibrillary tangles in Alzheimer's disease. Neurosci Lett 1998; 240:123–6.
* Shin RW. Interaction of aluminum with paired helical filament tau is involved in
    neurofibrillary pathology of Alzheimer's disease. Gerontology 1997; 43(Suppl
    1):16–23.

Selected References for Chapter 10: Saving Your Brain's Blood Flow

CHOLESTEROL AND COGNITION

Moroney JT, Tang MX, Berglund L, et al. Low-density lipoprotein cholesterol and
    the risk of dementia with stroke. JAMA 1999; 282:254–260.
Muldoon MF, Barger SD, Ryan CM, et al. Effects of lovastatin on cognitive func-
    tion and psychological well-being. Am J Med 2000; 108:538–546.

HYPERTENSION AND COGNITION

Elias MF, Robbins MA, Elias PK, Streeten DH. A longitudinal study of blood pres-
    sure in relation to performance on the Wechsler Adult Intelligence Scale.
    Health Psychol 1998; 17:486–93.
* Kilander L, Nyman H, Boberg M, Hansson L, Lithell H. Hypertension is related
    to cognitive impairment: a 20-year follow-up of 999 men. Hypertension
    1998; 31:780–6.
Launer LJ, Masaki K, Petrovitch H, Foley D, Havlik RJ. The association between
    midlife blood pressure levels and late-life cognitive function. JAMA 1995;
    274:1846–1851.

ATRIAL FIBRILLATION AND COGNITION

Kilander L, Andren B, Nyman H, et al. Atrial fibrillation is an independent determi-
    nant of low cognitive function: a cross-sectional study in elderly men. Stroke
    1998; 29:1816–20.

ATHEROSCLEROSIS, CAROTID ARTERY NARROWING, AND COGNITION

Cerhan JR, Folsom AR, Mortimer JA, et al. Correlates of cognitive function in middle-aged adults. Atherosclerosis Risk in Communities (ARIC) Study Investigators. Gerontology 1998; 44:95–105.

HOMOCYSTEINE AND COGNITION

Kalmijn S, Launer LJ, Lindemans J, et al. Total homocysteine and cognitive decline in a community-based sample of elderly subjects: the Rotterdam Study. Am J Epidemiol 1999; 150:283–9.

Miller JW. Homocysteine and Alzheimer's disease. Nutri Rev 1999; 57:126–9.

"VASCULAR DEMENTIA"

Breteler MM. Vascular involvement in cognitive decline and dementia. Epidemiologic evidence from the Rotterdam Study and the Rotterdam Scan Study. Ann NY Acad Sci 2000; 903:457–65.

Chui HC, Victoroff JI, Margolin D, et al. Criteria for the diagnosis of ischemic vascular dementia proposed by the State of California Alzheimer's Disease Diagnostic and Treatment Centers. Neurology 1992; 42:473–80.

Di Carlo A, Baldereschi M, Amaducci L, et al. for the Italian Longitudinal Study on Aging Working Group. Cognitive impairment without dementia in older people: prevalence, vascular risk factors, impact on disability. The Italian Longitudinal Study on Aging. JAGS 2000; 48:775–782.

Garde E, Mortensen EL, Krabbe K, Rostrup E, Larsson HB. Relation between age-related decline in intelligence and cerebral white-matter hyperintensities in healthy octogenarians: a longitudinal study. Lancet 2000: 356:628–34.

* Roman GC, Tatemichi TK, Erkinjuntti T, Cummings JL, Masdeu JC, Garcia JH, Amaducci L, Orgogozo JM, Brun A, Hofman A, et al. Vascular dementia: diagnostic criteria for research studies. Report of the NINDS-AIREN International Workshop. Neurology 1993; 43:250–60.

Victoroff J, Mack WJ, Grafton ST, Schreiber SS, Chui HC. A method to improve interrater reliability of visual inspection of brain MRI scans in dementia. Neurology 1994; 44:2267–2276.

THE LINKS BETWEEN CEREBROVASCULAR COMPROMISE AND ARNAT/ALZHEIMER'S

Kalaria RN. The role of cerebral ischemia in Alzheimer's disease. Neurobiol Aging 2000; 21:321–30.

Kojro E, Gimpl G, Lammich S, Marz W, Fahrenholz F. Low cholesterol stimulates the nonamyloidogenic pathway by its effect on the alpha-secretase ADAM 10. Proc Natl Acad Sci USA 2001; 98:5815–20.

Kudo T, Imaizumi K, Tanimukai H, et al. Are cerebrovascular factors involved in Alzheimer's disease? Neurobiol Aging 2000; 21:215–24.

Sparks DL, Martin TA, Gross DR, Hunsaker JC 3rd. Link between heart disease, cholesterol, and Alzheimer's disease: a review. Microse Res Tech 2000; 50:287–90.

TREATING HYPERTENSION

* Forette F, Seux M-L, Staessen JA, et al. Prevention of dementia in randomised double-blind placebo-controlled Systolic Hypertension in Europe (Syst-Eur) trial. Lancet 1998; 352:1347–1351.

Joint National Committee on Prevention, Detection, Evaluation, and Treatment of High Blood Pressure and the National High Blood Pressure Education Program Coordinating Committee. The Sixth Report of the Joint National Committee on Prevention, Detection, Evaluation, and Treatment of High Blood Pressure. Arch Intern Med 1997; 157:2413–2446.

Moser M. Why are physicians not prescribing diuretics more frequently in the management of hypertension? JAMA 1998; 279:1813–6.

AVOIDING ATHEROSCLEROSIS AND STROKES

Burke GL, Arnold AM, Bild DE, et al. (CHS Collaborative Research Group). Factors associated with healthy aging: the Cardiovascular Health Study. JAGS 2001; 49:254–62.

Gorelick PB, Sacco, RL, Smith DB, et al. Prevention of a first stroke: a review of guidelines and a multidisciplinary consensus statement from the National Stroke Association. JAMA 1999; 281:1112–1120.

FIGHTING PLATELETS

Anonymous. Proceedings of the American College of Chest Physicians 5th Consensus on Antithrombotic Therapy. Chest 1998; 114(Suppl):439S–769S.

Antiplatelet Trialists' Collaboration. Collaborative overview of randomised trials of antiplatelet therapy, I: prevention of death, myocardial infarction, and stroke by prolonged antiplatelet therapy in various categories of patients. BMJ 1994; 308:81–106.

Sacco RL, Elkind MS. Update on antiplatelet therapy for stroke prevention. Arch Intern Med 2000; 160:1579–1582.

CONTROLLING CHOLESTEROL TO PREVENT BOTH STROKES AND
ARNAT/ALZHEIMER'S

* Bollen EL, Gaw A, Buckley BM. Statin therapy and the prevention of dementia. Arch Neurol 2001; 58:1023–1024.

* Jick H, Zornberg GL, Jick SS, Seshadri S, Drachman DA. Statins and the risk of dementia. Lancet 2000; 356:1627–31.

Moawad MA. Possible relationship between statin use and decreased incidence of dementia: are we ready for a new indication for these drugs? Arch Intern Med 2001; 161:1909–10.

National Cholesterol Eduction Program; ATP III Guidelines at-a-glance. Quick Desk Reference. U.S. Department of Health and Human Services. NIH Publication 01-3305, 2001.

Wolozin B, Kellman W, Ruosseau P, Celesia GG, Siegel G. Decreased prevalence of

Alzheimer disease associated with 3-hydroxy-3-methyglutaryl coenzyme A reductase inhibitors. Arch Neurol 2000; 57:1439–43.

Selected References for Chapter 11: Food for Thought: The Brain-Saving Diet

OVERVIEW OF DIET, HEALTH, AND THE BRAIN

Algeri S. Potential strategies against age-related brain deterioration. Dietary and pharmacological approaches. Ann NY Acad Sci 1992; 663:376–83.

Bellisle F, Blundell JE, Dye L, et al. Functional food science and behaviour and psychological functions. Br J Nutr 1998; 80 (Suppl 1):S173–93.

Deschamps V, Barberger-Gateau P, Peuchant E, Orgogozo JM. Nutritional factors in cerebral aging and dementia: epidemiological arguments for a role of oxidative stress. Neuroepidemiology 2001; 20:7–15.

Grand A, Pous J, Vellas B, Albarede JL. Alzheimer disease: protective factors. Am J Clin Nutr 2000; 71:643S–649S.

Newman PE. Could diet be used to reduce the risk of developing Alzheimer's disease? Med Hypotheses 1998; 50:335–7.

Riedel WJ, Jorissen BL. Nutrients, age and cognitive function. Curr Opin Clin Nutr Metab Care 1998; 1:579–85.

UNDERNUTRITION AND HEALTH

Alaimo K, Briefel RR, Frongillo EA, Olson CM. Food insufficiency exists in the United States: results from the Third National Health and Nutrition Examination Survey (NHANES III). Am J Pub Health 1998; 88:419–426.

Allen LH. The nutrition CRSP: what is marginal malnutrition, and does it affect human function? Nutr Rev 1993; 51:255–67.

CALORIC RESTRICTION AND AGING

Bruce-Keller AJ, Umberger G, McFall R, Mattson MP. Food restriction reduces brain damage and improves behavioral outcome following excitotoxic and metabolic insults. Ann Neurol 1999; 45:8–15.

Masoro EJ, Austad SN. The evolution of the antiaging action of dietary restriction: a hypothesis. J Gerontol A Bio Sci Med Sci 1996; 51:B387–91.

IRON AND THE BRAIN

Bruner AB, Joffe A, Duggan AK, Casella JF, Brandt J. Randomized study of cognitive effects of iron supplementation in non-anaemic iron-deficient girls. Lancet 1996; 348:992–996.

* Halterman JS, Kaczorowski JM, Aligne CA, Auinger P, Szilagyi PG. Iron deficiency and cognitive achievement among school-aged children and adolescents in the United States. Pediatrics 2001; 107:1381–6.

VITAMINS AND MEMORY LOSS

Crystal HA, Ortof E, Frishman WH, et al. Serum vitamin B12 levels and incidence
    of dementia in a healthy elderly population: a report from the Bronx Longitu-
    dinal Aging Study. JAGS 1994; 42:933–6.
McCaddon A, Davies G, Hudson P. Nutritionally independent B12 deficiency and
    Alzheimer disease. Arch Neurol 2000; 57:607–608.
Ortega RM, Manas LR, Andres P, et al. Functional and psychic deterioration in
    elderly people may be aggravated by folate deficiency. J Nutr 1996;
    126:1992–9.
Regland B, Blennow K, Germgard T, Koch-Schmidt AC, Gottfries CG. The role of
    the polymorphic genes apolipoprotein E and methylene-tetrahydrofolate re-
    ductase in the development of dementia of the Alzheimer type. Dement Geriatr
    Cogn Disord 1999; 10:245–51.
* Selhub J, Bagley LC, Miller J, Rosenberg IH. B vitamins, homocysteine, and neu-
    rocognitive function in the elderly. Am J Clin Nutr 2000; 71:614S–620S.

OBESITY, HEALTH, AND THE BRAIN

Grabowski DC, Ellis JE. High body mass index does not predict mortality in older
    people: Analysis of the Longitudinal Study of Aging. JAGS 2001; 49:968–979.
Hill JO, Peters JC. Environmental contributions to the obesity epidemic. Science
    1998; 280:1371–4.
Levin BE. The obesity epidemic: metabolic imprinting on genetically susceptible
    neural circuits. Obesity Res 2000; 8:342–7, 2000.
* Shaper AG, Wannamethee SG, Walker M. Body weight: implications for the pre-
    vention of coronary heart disease, stroke, and diabetes mellitus in a cohort
    study of middle aged men. BMJ 1997; 314:1311–7.
Weinsier RL, Hunter GR, Heini AF, Goran MI, Sell SM. The etiology of obesity:
    relative contribution of metabolic factors, diet, and physical activity. Am J
    Med 1998; 105:145–50.

DIET AND THE VASCULAR SYSTEM

Ascherio A, Rimm EB, Giovannucci EL, et al. Dietary fat and risk of coronary
    heart disease in men: cohort follow up study in the United States. BMJ 1996;
    313:84–90.
Gariballa SE. Nutritional factors in stroke. Br J Nutr 2000; 84:5–17.
Pietinen P, Ascherio A, Korhonen P, et al. Intake of fatty acids and risk of coronary
    heart disease in a cohort of Finnish men. The Alpha-Tocopherol, Beta-
    Carotene Cancer Prevention Study. Am J Epidemiol 1997; 145:876–87.

ALCOHOL AND THE BRAIN

Elias PK, Elias MF, D'Agostino RB, Silbershatz H, Wolf PA. Alcohol consumption
    and cognitive performance in the Framingham Heart Study. Am J Epidemiol
    1999; 150:580–9.
Galanis DJ, Joseph C, Masaki KH, et al. A longitudinal study of drinking and

cognitive performance in elderly Japanese American men: the Honolulu-Asia
    Aging Study. Am J Pub Health 2000; 90:1254–9.
Goldberg DM, Soleas GJ, Levesque M. Moderate alcohol consumption: the gentle
    face of Janus. Clin Biochem 1999; 32:505–18.
* Orgogozo JM, Dartigues JF, Lafont S, et al. Wine consumption and dementia in
    the elderly: a prospective community study in the Bordeaux area. Rev Neurol
    (Paris) 1997; 153:185–92.

FISH, THE HEART, AND THE BRAIN

Albert CM, Hennekens CH, O'Donnell CJ, et al. Fish consumption and risk of sud-
    den cardiac death. JAMA 1998; 279:65–6.
* Iso H, Rexrode KM, Stampfer MJ, et al. Intake of fish and omega-3 fatty acids
    and risk of stroke in women. JAMA 2001; 285:304–12.
Wainwright P. Nutrition and behaviour: the role of n-3 fatty acids in cognitive func-
    tion. Br J Nutr 2000; 83:337–9.

CHOCOLATE, THE MIND, AND THE BRAIN

di Tomaso E, Beltramo M, Piomelli D. Brain cannabinoids in chocolate. Nature
    1996; 382:677–8.
Small DM, Zatorre RJ, Dagher A, Evans AC, Jones-Gotman M. Changes in brain
    activity related to eating chocolate: from pleasure to aversion. Brain 2001;
    124(Pt 9):1720–33.
Yamagishi M, Osakab N, Takizawa T, Osawa T. Cacao liquor polyphenols reduce
    oxidative stress without maintaining alpha-tocopherol levels in rats fed a vita-
    min E-deficient diet. Lipids 2001; 36:67–71.

TEA, HEALTH, AND THE BRAIN

Geleijnse JM, Launer LJ, Hofman A, Pols HA, Witteman JC. Tea flavonoids may
    protect against atherosclerosis: the Rotterdam Study. Arch Intern Med 1999;
    159:2170–4.
Mukhtar H, Ahmad N. Tea polyphenols: prevention of cancer and optimizing
    health. Am J Clin Nutr 2000; 71(6 Suppl):1698S–702S.
* Youdim KA, Joseph JA. A possible emerging role of phytochemicals in improv-
    ing age-related neurological dysfunctions: a multiplicity of effects. Free Radic
    Biol Med 2001; 30:583–94.

Selected References for Chapter 12: Good News: Antioxidants Save Your Brain

OXIDATION AND THE AGING BRAIN

de Benedictis G, Carrieri G, Varcasia O, Bonafe M, Franceschi C. Inherited vari-
    ability of the mitochondrial genome and successful aging in humans. Ann NY
    Acad Sci 2000; 908:208–218.
Cottrell DA, Blakely EL, Johnson MA, et al. Mitochondrial DNA mutations in dis-

ease and ageing. Novartis Foundation Symposium 2001; 235:234–43; discussion 243–6.

ANTIOXIDANTS AND STROKES

Daviglus ML, Orencia AJ, Dyer AR, et al. Dietary vitamin C, beta-carotene and 30-year risk of stroke: results from the Western Electric Study. Neuroepidemiology 1997; 16:69–77.

Keli SO, Hertog MG, Feskens EJ, Kromhout D. Dietary flavonoids, antioxidant vitamins, and incidence of stroke: the Zutphen study. Arch Intern Med 1996; 156:637–642.

Schmidt R, Hayn M, Reinhart B, et al. Plasma antioxidants and cognitive performance in middle-aged and older adults: results of the Austrian Stroke Prevention Study. JAGS 1998; 46:1407–1410.

ANTIOXIDANTS AND COGNITION

Berr C, Richard MJ, Roussel AM, Bonithon-Kopp C. Systemic oxidative stress and cognitive performance in the population-based EVA study. Étude sur le Vieillissement Artériel. Free Radic Biol Med 1998; 24:1202–1208.

Jama JW, Launer LJ, Witteman JC, et al. Dietary antioxidants and cognitive function in a population-based sample of older persons. The Rotterdam Study. Am J Epidemiol 1996; 144:275–280.

* Launer LJ, Kalmijn S. Anti-oxidants and cognitive function: a review of clinical and epidemiologic studies. J Neural Transm Suppl 1998; 53:1–8.

Masaki KH, Losonczy KG, Izmirlian G, et al. Association of vitamin E and C supplement use with cognitive function and dementia in elderly men. Neurology 2000; 54:1265–1272.

Perrig WJ, Perrig P, Stahelin HB. The relation between antioxidants and memory performance in the old and very old. JAGS 1997; 45:718–724.

OXIDATION AND THE POTENTIAL PROTECTIVE ROLE OF ANTIOXIDANTS IN ARNAT, PARKINSON'S, AND OTHER FORMS OF ARN

Behl C, Davis J, Cole GM, et al. Vitamin E protects nerve cells from amyloid beta protein toxicity. Biochem Biophysics Res Commun 1992; 186:944–950.

Butterfield DA, Howard B, Yatin S, et al. Elevated oxidative stress in models of normal brain aging and Alzheimer's disease. Life Sci 1999; 65:1883–1892.

Christen Y. Oxidative stress and Alzheimer disease. Am J Clin Nutr 2000; 71:621S–629S.

de Rijk MC, Breteler MM, den Breeijen JH, et al. Dietary antioxidants and Parkinson disease. The Rotterdam Study. Arch Neurol 1997; 54:762–765.

Floyd RA. Antioxidants, Oxidative Stress, and Degenerative Neurological Disorders. Proc Soc Exp Biol Med 1999; 222:236–245.

* Markesbury WR. The role of oxidative stress in Alzheimer disease. Arch Neurol 1999; 56:1449–1451.

Morris MC, Beckett LA, Scherr PA, et al. Vitamin E and vitamin C supplement use and risk of incident Alzheimer disease. Alzheimer Dis Assoc Disord 1998; 12:121–126.

ANTIOXIDANT TREATMENT AND PARKINSON'S

Shoulson I. DATATOP: a decade of neuroprotective inquiry. Parkinson Study Group. Deprenyl and tocopherol antioxidative therapy of parkinsonism. Ann Neurol 1998; 44(3 Suppl 1):S160–S166.
The Parkinson Study Group. Effects of tocopherol and deprenyl on the progression of disability in early Parkinson's disease. NEJM 1993; 328:176–83.

ANTIOXIDANT TREATMENT AND ARNAT/ALZHEIMER'S

Pitchumoni SS, Doraiswamy PM. Current status of antioxidant therapy for Alzheimer's disease. JAGS 1998; 46:1566–1572.
Prasad KN, Hovland AR, Cole WC, et al. Multiple antioxidants in the prevention and treatment of Alzheimer disease: analysis of biologic rationale. Clin Neuropharmacol 2000; 23:2–13.
Sano M, Ernesto C, Thomas RG, et al. A controlled trial of selegiline, alpha-tocopherol, or both as treatment for Alzheimer's disease: the Alzheimer's Disease Cooperative Study. NEJM 1997; 336:1216–1222.

ZINC

Koh JY, Suh SW, Gwag BJ, et al. The role of zinc in selective neuronal death after transient global cerebral ischemia. Science 1996; 272:1013–1016.

SELENIUM

Foster LH, Sumar S. Selenium in health and disease: a review. Crit Rev Food Sci Nutr 1997; 37:211–228.
Sher L. Selenium and human health. Lancet 2000; 356:943.
Vinceti M, Guidetti D, Pinotti M, et al. Amyotrophic lateral sclerosis after long-term exposure to drinking water with high selenium content. Epidemiol 1996; 7:529–532.

COENZYME Q10

Matthews RT, Yang L, Browne S, Baik M, Beal MF. Coenzyme Q10 administration increases brain mitochondrial concentrations and exerts neuroprotective effects. Proc Natl Acad Sci USA 1998; 95:8892–8897.

Selected References for Chapter 13: Botanicals for the Brain: The Growing Promise of Natural Neuroprotection

OVERVIEW

Foster DF, Phillips RS, Hamel MB, Eisenberg DM. Alternative medicine use in older Americans. JAGS 2000; 48:1560–65.

Klepser TB, Klepser ME. Unsafe and potentially safe herbal therapies. Am J Health Syst Pharm 1999; 56:125–138.

Winslow LC, Kroll DJ. Herbs as medicines. Arch Intern Med 1998; 158:2192–99.

Wong AHC, Smith M, Boon HS. Herbal remedies in psychiatric practice. Arch Gen Psychiatry 1998; 55:1033–1044.

GINKGO BILOBA

Cohen-Salmon C, Venault P, Martin B, et al. Effects of ginkgo biloba extract (EGb 761) on learning and possible actions on aging. J Physiol Paris 1997; 91:291–300.

* Le Bars PL, Katz MM, Berman N, et al. A placebo-controlled, double-blind, randomized trial of an extract of ginkgo biloba for dementia. North American EGb Study Group. JAMA 1997; 278:1327–1332.

Oken BS, Storzbach DM, Kaye JA. The efficacy of Ginkgo biloba on cognitive function in Alzheimer disease. Arch Neurol 1998; 55:1409–15.

GINSENG

Lim JH, Wen TC, Matsuda S, et al. Protection of ischemic hippocampal neurons by ginsenoside Rb1, a main ingredient of ginseng root. Neurosci Res 1997; 28:191–200.

Wesnes KA, Faleni RA, Hefting NR, et al. The cognitive, subjective, and physical effects of a ginkgo biloba/panax ginseng combination in healthy volunteers with neurasthenic complaints. Psychopharmacol Bull 1997; 33:677–683.

ST. JOHN'S WORT

Cott JM, Fugh-Berman A. Is St. John's wort (Hypericum perforatum) an effective antidepressant? J Nerv Ment Dis 1998; 186:500–501.

Kim HL, Streltzer J, Goebert D. St. John's wort for depression: a meta-analysis of well-defined clinical trials. J Nerv Ment Dis 1999; 187:532–538.

Linde K, Mulrow CD. St John's wort for depression. Cochrane Database of Systematic Reviews [Computer File] 2000; (2):CD000448.

GARLIC

Berthold HK, Sudhop T, von Bergmann K. Effect of a garlic oil preparation on serum lipoproteins and cholesterol metabolism: a randomized controlled trial. JAMA 1998; 279:1900–1902.

Isaacsohn JL, Moser M, Stein EA, et al. Garlic powder and plasma lipids and lipoproteins: a multicenter, randomized, placebo-controlled trial. Arch Intern Med 1998; 158:1189–1194.

CANNABINOIDS

Anonymous. Dronabinol in Alzheimer's disease. Harvard Mental Health Letter 1998; 15:7.

Lyketsos CG, Garrett E, Liang KY, Anthony JC. Cannabis use and cognitive decline in persons under 65 years of age. Am J Epidemiol 1999; 149:794–800.

Nahas G, Sutin K, Bennett WM. Review of marihuana and medicine. NEJM 2000; 343:514–515.

Pertwee RG. Medical uses of cannabinoids: the way forward. Addiction 1999; 94:317–320.

Pope HG Jr, Yurgelun-Todd D. The residual cognitive effects of heavy marijuana use in college students. JAMA 1996; 275:521–527.

KAVA

Volz HP, Kieser M. Kava-kava extract WS 1490 versus placebo in anxiety disorders: a randomized placebo-controlled 25-week outpatient trial. Pharmacopsychiatry 1997; 30:1–5.

HUPERZINE A

Cheng DH, Tang XC. Comparative studies of huperzine A, E2020, and tacrine on behavior and cholinesterase activities. Pharmacol Biochemi Behav 1998; 60:377–386.

Selected References for Chapter 14: Smart Drugs: Utopian Dream or Fast-Approaching Reality?

WHAT IS A SMART DRUG?

Riedel WJ, Jolles J. Cognition enhancers in age-related cognitive decline. Drugs Aging 1996; 8:245–274.

Whitehouse PJ, Juengst E, Mehlman M, Murray TH. Enhancing cognition in the intellectually intact. Hastings Center Report 1997; 27:14–22.

PIRACETAM AND ITS KIN

Bartolini L, Casamenti F, Pepeu G. Aniracetam restores object recognition impaired by age, scopolamine, and nucleus basalis lesions. Pharmacol Biochem Behav 1996; 53:277–283.

De Deyn PP, Reuck JD, Deberdt W, Vlietinck R, Orgogozo JM. Treatment of acute ischemic stroke with piracetam. Members of the Piracetam in Acute Stroke Study (PASS) Group. Stroke 1997; 28:2347–2352.

HYDERGINE

Schneider LS, Olin JT. Overview of clinical trials of hydergine in dementia. Arch Neurol 1994; 51:787–798.

PHOSPHATIDYLSERINE

Pepeu G, Pepeu IM, Amaducci L. A review of phosphatidylserine pharmacological and clinical effects. Is phosphatidylserine a drug for the ageing brain? Pharmacol Res 1996; 33:73–80.

Pepping J. Phosphatidylserine. Am J Health Syst Pharm 1999; 56:2038, 2043–2044.

VINPOCETINE

Miyazaki M. The effect of a cerebral vasodilator, vinpocetine, on cerebral vascular resistance evaluated by the Doppler ultrasonic technique in patients with cerebrovascular diseases. Angiology 1995; 46:53–58.

PYRITINOL

Herrmann WM, Stephan K, Gaede K, Apececche M. A multicenter randomized double-blind study on the efficacy and safety of nicergoline in patients with multi-infarct dementia. Dement Geriatr Cogn Disord 1997; 8:9–17.

GROWTH FACTOR THERAPY

* Rollero A, Murialdo G, Fonzi S, et al. Relationship between cognitive function, growth hormone and insulin-like growth factor I plasma levels in aged subjects. Neuropsychobiol 1998; 38:73–79.
Skaper SD, Walsh FS. Neurotrophic molecules: strategies for designing effective therapeutic molecules in neurodegeneration. Mol Cell Neurosci 1998; 12:179–193.
Yamada K, Nitta A, Hasegawa T, et al. Orally active NGF synthesis stimulators: potential therapeutic agents in Alzheimer's disease. Behav Brain Res 1997; 83:117–122.

MIMICKING ACETYLCHOLINE

Furey ML, Pietrini P, Haxby JV, et al. Cholinergic stimulation alters performance and task-specific regional cerebral blood flow during working memory. Proc Natl Acad Sci USA 1997; 94:6512–6516.
Robbins TW, McAlonan G, Muir JL, Everitt BJ. Cognitive enhancers in theory and practice: studies of the cholinergic hypothesis of cognitive deficits in Alzheimer's disease. Behav Brain Res 1997; 83:15–23.

BLOCKING THE BREAKDOWN OF ACETYLCHOLINE

Lahiri DK, Farlow MR, Nurnberger JI Jr, Greig NH. Effects of cholinesterase inhibitors on the secretion of beta-amyloid precursor protein in cell cultures. Ann NY Acad Sci 1997; 826:416–421.

AMPAKINES

Ingvar M, Ambros-Ingerson J, Davis M, et al. Enhancement by an ampakine of memory encoding in humans. Exp Neurol 1997; 146:553–559.
Lynch G, Granger R, Ambros-Ingerson J, et al. Evidence that a positive modulator

of AMPA-type glutamate receptors improves delayed recall in aged humans. Exp Neurol 1997; 145:89–92.

AMYLOID BLOCKERS

* Sinha S, Anderson JP, Barbour R, et al. Purification and cloning of amyloid precursor protein beta-secretase from human brain. Nature 1999; 402:537–540.
Steinhilb ML, Turner RS, Gaut JR. The protease inhibitor, MG132, blocks maturation of the amyloid precursor protein Swedish mutant preventing cleavage by beta-secretase. J Biol Chem 2001; 276:4476–4484.

Selected References for Chapter 15: More Good News: Anti-inflammatories Help Save Your Brain

ANTI-INFLAMMATORIES: EPIDEMIOLOGICAL EVIDENCE

Broe GA, Grayson DA, Creasey HM, et al. Anti-inflammatory drugs protect against Alzheimer disease at low doses. Arch Neurol 2000; 57:1586–1591.
in 't Veld BA, Ruitenberg A, Hofman A, et al. Nonsteroidal antiinflammatory drugs and the risk of Alzheimer's disease. NEJM 2001; 345:1515–21.
McGeer PL, Schulzer M, McGeer EG. Arthritis and anti-inflammatory agents as possible protective factors for Alzheimer's disease: a review of 17 epidemiologic studies. Neurology 1996; 47:425–432.
Stewart WF, Kawas C, Corrada M, Metter EJ. Risk of Alzheimer's disease and duration of NSAID use. Neurology 1997; 48:626–632.

THE ROLE OF INFLAMMATION IN ALZHEIMER'S

Akiyama H, Barger S, Barnum S, et al. Inflammation and Alzheimer's disease. Neurobiology of Aging 2000; 21:383–421.
Eikelenboom P, Rozemuller AJ, Hoozemans JJ, Veerhuis R, Gool WA. Neuroinflammation and Alzheimer disease: clinical and therapeutic implications. Alzheimer Dis Assoc Disord 2000; 14(Suppl 1):S54–61.
Lim GP, Yang F, Chu T, et al. Ibuprofen suppresses plaque pathology and inflammation in a mouse model for Alzheimer's disease. J Neurosci 2000; 20:5709–5714.
Lukiw WJ, Bazan NG. Neuroinflammatory signaling upregulation in Alzheimer's disease. Neurochem Res 2000; 25:1173–1184.
* McCusker SM, Curran MD, Dynan KB, et al. Association between polymorphism in regulatory region of gene encoding tumour necrosis factor alpha and risk of Alzheimer's disease and vascular dementia: a case-control study. Lancet 2001; 357:436–439.
McGeer PL, McGeer EG. Autotoxicity and Alzheimer disease. Arch Neurol 2000; 57:789–790.

PROSPECTIVE TRIALS OF ANTI-INFLAMMATORIES

Aisen PS. A multicenter trial of rofecoxib and naproxen in Alzheimer's disease. Alzheimer's Disease Cooperative Study Web Site 2001.

Aisen PS. Anti-inflammatory therapy for Alzheimer's disease: implications of the prednisone trial. Acta Neurol Scand 2000; 176(Suppl):85–9.

Todesco S, Del-Ross T, Marigliano V, Ariani A. Efficacy and tolerability of etodolac in aged patients affected by degenerative joint disease (osteoarthritis) in its active phase. Int J Clin Pharmacol Res 1994; 14:11–26.

RISKS OF NSAIDS: CONVENTIONAL VS. SELECTIVE

Langman MJ, Jensen DM, Watson DJ, et al. Adverse upper gastrointestinal effects of rofecoxib compared with NSAIDs. JAMA 1999; 282:1929–1933.

COX-2 INHIBITORS

* Blain H, Jouzeau JY, Blain A, et al. Non-steroidal anti-inflammatory drugs with selectivity for cyclooxygenase-2 in Alzheimer's disease. Rationale and perspectives. Presse Med 2000; 29:267–273.

PROPENTOFYLLINE AND ITS KIN

Bachynsky J, McCracken P, Lier D, Alloul K, Jacobs P. Propentofylline treatment for Alzheimer disease and vascular dementia: an economic evaluation based on functional abilities. Alzheimer Dis Assoc Disord 2000; 14:102–111.

Kittner B. Clinical trials of propentofylline in vascular dementia. European/ Canadian Propentofylline Study Group. Alzheimer Dis Assoc Disord 1999; 13(Suppl 3):S166–S171.

Selected References for Chapter 16: Saving Your Brain by Saving Your Skull

HEAD TRAUMA, THE SILENT EPIDEMIC

Jennett B. Epidemiology of head injury. Arch Dis Child 1998; 78:403–406.

Max W, MacKenzie EJ, Rice DP. Head injuries: costs and consequences. J Head Trauma Rehabil 1991; 6:76.

WHAT IS A HEAD INJURY?

Andrews, Brian T. Catastrophic brain injury. Neurosurgery 1997; 40:416.

Eames P. Traumatic brain injury. Curr Opin Psychiatry 1997; 10:49–52.

Evans, Randolp W. Neurology and Trauma. Philadelphia: W.B. Saunders Company, 1996.

Gennarelli TA, Graham DI. Neuropathology of head injuries. Semin Clin Neuropsychiatry 1998; 3:160–175.

WHAT IS A CONCUSSION?

* Alexander MP. Mild traumatic brain injury: Pathophysiology, natural history, and clinical management. Neurology 1995; 15:1253–1260.

Bohnen N, Jolles J. Neurobehavioral aspects of postconcussive symptoms after mild head injury. J Nerv Ment Dis 1999; 180:683–92.

HOW A BLOW TO THE HEAD AFFECTS BRAIN AND BEHAVIOR

Deb S, Lyons I, Koutzoukis C, et al. Rate of psychiatric illness 1 year after traumatic brain injury. Am J Psychiatry 1999; 156:374–378.
Landy PJ. Neurological sequelae of minor head and neck injuries. Injury 1998; 29:199–206.
Parker RS, Rosenblum A. IQ loss and emotional dysfunctions after mild head injury incurred in a motor vehicle accident. J Clin Psychol 1996; 52:32–43.

TBI AND THE RISK OF DEMENTIA, ALZHEIMER'S, AND PARKINSON'S

Lye TC, Shores EA. Traumatic brain injury as a risk factor for Alzheimer's disease: a review. Neuropsychol Rev 2000; 10:115–29.
* Mayeux R, Ottman R, Maestre G, et al. Synergistic effects of traumatic head injury and apolipoprotein-Є4 in patients with Alzheimer's disease. Neurology 1995; 45:555–557.
Schofield PW, Tang M, Marder K, et al. Alzheimer's disease after remote head injury: an incidence study. J Neurol Neurosurg Psychiatry 1997; 62:119–124.
Seidler A, Hellenbrand W, Robra BP, et al. Possible environmental, occupational, and other etiologic factors for Parkinson's disease: a case-control study in Germany. Neurology 1996; 46:1275–84.

THE MISSING LINK

Gentleman SM, Greenberg BD, Savage MJ, et al. A[beta]42 is the predominant form of amyloid [beta]-protein in the brains of short-term survivors of head injury. Neuroreport 1997; 8:1519–1522.
Raby CA, Morganti-Kossmann MC, Kossmann T, et al. Traumatic brain injury increases [beta]-amyloid peptide 1-42 in cerebrospinal fluid. J Neurochem 1998; 71:2505–2509.
Roberts GW, Gentleman SM, Lynch A, Graham DI. [beta]A4 amyloid protein deposition in brain after head trauma. Lancet 1991; 338:1422–1423.

BRAINS AT WORK

Daughton S. Head injury in the workplace. AAOHN Journal 1990; 38:497–501.
Janicak CA. An examination of occupational fatalities involving impact-related head injuries in the construction industry. J Occup Environ Med 1998; 40:347–350.

SPORTS AND THE BRAIN

Collins MW, Grindel SH, Lovell MR, et al. Relationship between concussion and neuropsychological performance in college football players. JAMA 1999; 282:964–970.

Drachman DA, Newell KL. Weekly clinicopathological exercises: case 12–1999: a 67-year-old man with three years of dementia. NEJM 1999; 340:1269–1276.

* Jordan BD, Relkin NR, Ravdin LD, et al. Apolipoprotein E epsilon4 associated with chronic traumatic brain injury in boxing. JAMA 1997; 278:136–40.

Matser EJT, Kessels AG, Lezak MD, et al. Neuropsychological impairment in amateur soccer players. JAMA 1999; 282: 971–973.

HELMETS AND THE HUMAN BRAIN

Max W, Stark B, Root S. Putting a lid on injury costs: the economic impact of the California motorcycle helmet law. J Trauma 1998; 45:550–6.

OSHA standards 29 CFR 1926.100 for construction and 29 CFR 1910.132 and 1910.135 for general industry (copies enclosed) outline the requirements for head protection. OSHA 04/06/1994 • Federal Register # 59:16334–16364.

Patton E. Head protection for industrial and construction applicants. Occup Health Saf 1996; 65:68–9.

Rivara FP, Thompson DC, Patterson MQ, Thompson RS. Prevention of bicycle-related injuries: helmets, education, and legislation. Ann Rev Pub Health 1998; 19:293–318.

MOTOR VEHICLES AND THE BRAIN

Code of Federal Regulations—Transportation: "Standard No. 201: Occupant protection in interior impact," 49 CFRg571.201, 08.04.1997 1719.

Digges K. The prevention of head and neck injuries in motor vehicle crashes. GWU/NCAC, 1998.

Kahane CJ, Hackney JR, Berkowitz AM. Correlation of NCAP performance with fatality risk in actual head on collisions. Report # DOT HS 808 061; Wash. DC: NHTSA 1994.

Krafft M, Kullgren A, Lie A, Tingvall C. The risk of skull/brain injuries in modern cars. Swedish National Road Administration Paper number 98–S6–O–14 [1998].

* Margulies SS, Thibault LE. A proposed tolerance criterion for diffuse axonal injury in man. J Biomech 1992; 25(8):917–23.

Mellander H. HIC—the head injury criterion. Practical significance for the automotive industry. Acta Neurochir 1986; 36(Suppl):18–20.

Selected References for Chapter 17: Brain Fitness I: Using Your Body to Build Your Brain

OVERVIEW OF FITNESS, ACTIVITY, HEALTH, AND LONGEVITY

Ferrucci L, Izmirlian G, Leveille S, et al. Smoking, physical activity, and active life expectancy. Am J Epidemiol 1999; 149(7):645–653.

Lee I, Hsieh C, Paffenbarger RS Jr. Exercise intensity and longevity in men: the Harvard Alumni Health Study. JAMA 1995; 273:1179–1184.

US Department of Health and Human Services. *Physical Activity and Health: A Report of the Surgeon General.* Atlanta, GA: US Department of Health and Human Services, Centers for Disease Control and Prevention, National Center for Chronic Disease Prevention and Health Promotion 1996; 1–8,85–172,175–207.

FITNESS AND CVC

Blumenthal JA, Sherwood A, Gullette EC, et al. Exercise and weight loss reduce blood pressure in men and women with mild hypertension: effects on cardiovascular, metabolic, and hemodynamic functioning. Arch Intern Med 2000; 160:1947–58.

Hu FB, Stampfer MJ, Colditz GA, et al. Physical activity and risk of stroke in women. JAMA 2000; 283:2961–2967.

Lee IM, Paffenbarger RS Jr. Physical activity and stroke incidence: the Harvard Alumni Health Study. Stroke 1998; 29:2049–54.

* Rogers RL, Meyer JS, Mortel KF. After reaching retirement age physical activity sustains cerebral perfusion and cognition. JAGS 1990; 38:123–128.

Sacco RL, Gan R, Boden-Albala B, et al. Leisure-time physical activity and ischemic stroke risk: the Northern Manhattan Stroke Study. Stroke 1998; 29:380–387.

FITNESS AND COGNITION

Christensen H, Mackinnon A. The association between mental, social and physical activity and cognitive performance in young and old subjects. Age Ageing 1993; 22:175–82.

Emery CF, Huppert FA, Schein RL. Relationships among age, exercise, health, and cognitive function in a British sample. Gerontologist 1995; 35:378–85.

Hill RD, Storandt M, Malley M. The impact of long-term exercise training on psychological function in older adults. J Gerontol 1993; 48:P12–7.

* Kramer AF, Hahn S, Cohen NJ, et al. Ageing, fitness and neurocognitive function. Nature 1999; 400:418–419.

Steinberg H, Sykes EA, Moss T, et al. Exercise enhances creativity independently of mood. Br J Sports Med 1997; 31:240–5.

ACTIVITY AND PROTECTION FROM AGING AND ALZHEIMER'S

Anonymous. Keeping active can prevent Alzheimer's disease. J Psychosoc Nurs Ment Health Serv 2000; 38:7.

Broe GA, Creasey H, Jorm AF, et al. Health habits and risk of cognitive impairment and dementia in old age: a prospective study on the effects of exercise, smoking and alcohol consumption. Aust N Z J Public Health 1998; 22:621–623.

Fabrigoule C, Letenneur L, Dartigues JF, et al. Social and leisure activities and risk of dementia: a prospective longitudinal study. JAGS 1995; 43:485–90.

* Laurin D, Verreault R, Lindsay J, MacPherson K, Rockwood K. Physical activity and risk of cognitive impairment and dementia in elderly persons. Arch Neurol 2001; 58:498–504.

Okumiya K, Matsubayashi K, Wada T, et al. Effects of exercise on neurobehavioral function in community-dwelling older people more than 75 years of age. JAGS 1996; 44:569–72.

THE BIOLOGICAL BASIS OF THE BRAIN-SAVING EFFECT OF PHYSICAL ACTIVITY

Carro E, Nunez A, Busiguina S, Torres-Aleman I. Circulating insulin-like growth factor I mediates effects of exercise on the brain. J Neurosci 2000;20:2926–33.

Gomez-Pinilla F, So V, Kesslak JP. Spatial learning and physical activity contribute to the induction of fibroblast growth factor: neural substrates for increased cognition associated with exercise. Neuroscience 1998; 85:53–61.

Mattson MP. Neuroprotective signaling and the aging brain: take away my food and let me run. Brain Res 2000; 886:47–53.

Neeper SA, Gomez-Pinilla F, Choi J, Cotman C. Exercise and brain neurotrophins. Nature 1995; 373:109.

Russo-Neustadt A, Beard RC, Cotman CW. Exercise, antidepressant medications, and enhanced brain derived neurotrophic factor expression. Neuropsychopharmacology 1999; 21:679–82.

* van Praag H, Kempermann G, Gage FH. Running increases cell proliferation and neurogenesis in the adult mouse dentate gyrus. Nat Neurosci 1999; 2:266–70.

EXERCISE AND EMOTIONAL RESILIENCE

Blumenthal JA, Babyak MA, Moore KA, et al. Effects of exercise training on older patients with major depression. Arch Intern Med 1999; 159:2349–56.

* Salmon P. Effects of physical exercise on anxiety, depression, and sensitivity to stress: a unifying theory. Clin Psychol Rev 2001; 21:33–61.

Scully D, Kremer J, Meade MM, Graham R, Dudgeon K. Physical exercise and psychological well being: a critical review. Br J Sports Med 1998; 32:111–20.

Slaven L, Lee C. Mood and symptom reporting among middle-aged women: the relationship between menopausal status, hormone replacement therapy, and exercise participation. Health Psychol 1997; 16:203–8.

EXERCISE BUILDS BETTER BRAINS: HOW MUCH? WHAT TYPE?

DiLorenzo TM, Bargman EP, Stucky-Ropp R, et al. Long-term effects of aerobic exercise on psychological outcomes. Prev Med 1999; 28:75–85.

McMurray RG, Ainsworth BE, Harrell JS, Griggs TR, Williams OD. Is physical activity or aerobic power more influential on reducing cardiovascular disease risk factors? Med Sci Sports Exerc 1998; 30:1521–9.

Pate RR, Pratt M, Blair SH, et al. Physical activity and public health: a recommendation from the Centers for Disease Control and Prevention and the American College of Sports Medicine. JAMA 1995; 273:402–407.

Shephard RJ. What is the optimal type of physical activity to enhance health? Br J Sports Med 1997; 31:277–84.

WALKING YOUR WAY TO A BETTER BRAIN

Hakim AA, Petrovitch H, Burchfiel CM, et al. Effects of walking on mortality among nonsmoking retired men. NEJM 1998; 338:94–9.

Shin Y. The effects of a walking exercise program on physical function and
    emotional state of elderly Korean women. Pub Health Nurs 1999;
    16:146–54.

Selected References for Chapter 18: Brain Fitness II: Using Your Mind to Build Your Brain

EDUCATION PROTECTS US FROM COGNITIVE DECLINE:
EPIDEMIOLOGICAL EVIDENCE

Cobb JL, Wolf PA, Au R, White R, D'Agostino RB. The effect of education on the
    incidence of dementia and Alzheimer's disease in the Framingham Study. Neu-
    rology 1995; 45:1707–12.
Evans DA, Hebert LE, Beckett LA, et al. Education and other measures of socioeco-
    nomic status and risk of incidence of Alzheimer disease in a defined population
    of older persons. Arch Neurol 1997; 54:1399–405.
Graves AB, Rajaram L, Bowen JD, et al. Cognitive decline and Japanese culture in
    a cohort of older Japanese Americans in King County, WA: the Kame Project. J
    Gerontol B Psychol Sci Soc Sci 1999; 54:S154–61.
Hall KS, Gao S, Unverzagt FW, Hendrie HC. Low education and childhood rural
    residence: risk for Alzheimer's disease in African Americans. Neurology 2000;
    54:95–9.
Orrell M, Sahakian B. Education and dementia. BMJ 1995; 310:951–952.
Stern Y, Gurland B, Tatemichi TK, Tang MX, Wilder D, Mayeux R. Influence of
    education and occupation on the incidence of Alzheimer's disease. JAMA
    1994; 271:1004–1010.

EDUCATED BRAINS RESIST COGNITIVE DECLINE

Coffey CE, Saxton JA, Ratcliff G, et al. Relation of education to brain size in nor-
    mal aging: implications for the reserve hypothesis. Neurology 1999;
    53:189–196.
Hershey LA. Environmental differences in twin pairs discordant for Alzheimer's
    disease. JAGS 1999; 47:768.
Plassman BL, Welsh KA, Helms M, et al. Intelligence and education as predictors of
    cognitive state in late life: a 50-year follow-up. Neurology 1995;
    45:1446–1450.
Snowdon DA, Kemper SJ, Mortimer JA, et al. Linguistic ability in early life and
    cognitive function and Alzheimer's disease in late life: findings from the Nun
    Study. JAMA 1996; 275:528–532.
Stern Y, Albert S, Tang MX, Tsai WY. Rate of memory decline in AD is
    related to education and occupation: cognitive reserve? Neurology 1999;
    53:1942–1947.
Wilson RS, Bennett DA, Gilley DW, et al. Premorbid reading activity and
    patterns of cognitive decline in Alzheimer disease. Arch Neurol 2000;
    57:1718–23.

COGNITIVE CHALLENGE BUILDS A COGNITIVE-DECLINE-RESISTANT BRAIN

Eriksson PS, Perfilieva E, Bjork-Eriksson T, et al. Neurogenesis in the adult human
   hippocampus. Nat Medicine 1998; 4:1313–7
* Gould E, Beylin A, Tanapat P, Reeves A, Shors TJ. Learning enhances adult neurogenesis in the hippocampal formation. Nat Neurosci 1999; 2:260–5.
Nilsson M, Perfilieva E, Johansson U, Orwar O, Eriksson PS. Enriched environment increases neurogenesis in the adult rat dentate gyrus and improves spatial
   memory. J Neurobiol 1999; 39:569–78.
Rosenzweig MR, Bennett EL. Psychobiology of plasticity: effects of
   training and experience on brain and behavior. Behav Brain Res 1996;
   78:57–65.
Rousseau, Jean-Jacques. Emile. Translated by Foxley, B. London: Everyman,
   1993.
van Praag H, Kempermann G, Gage FH. Neural consequences of environmental
   enrichment. Nat Rev Neurosci 2000; 1:191–8.

CONCLUSION

Carlson MC, Seeman T, Fried LP. Importance of generativity for healthy aging in
   older women. Aging (Milano) 2000; 12:132–40.
* Hultsch DF, Hertzog C, Small BJ, Dixon RA. Use it or lose it: engaged lifestyle
   as a buffer of cognitive decline in aging? Psychol Aging 1999; 14:245–63.

Selected References for Conclusion: What the Future Holds for the Human Brain

* Blank, Robert H. Brain Policy: How the New Neuroscience Will Change Our
   Lives and Our Politics. Washington, D.C.: Georgetown University Press, 1999.
Ehrenstein D. Immortality gene discovered. Science 1998; 279:177.
Flax JD, Aurora S, Yang C, et al. Engraftable human neural stem cells respond to
   developmental cues, replace neurons, and express foreign genes. Nat Biotech
   1998; 16:1033–9.
Hashimoto Y, Niikura T, Tajima H, et al. A rescue factor abolishing neuronal cell
   death by a wide spectrum of familial Alzheimer's disease genes and Abeta. Proc
   Natl Acad Sci USA 2001; 98:6336–41.
Ho DY, Sapolsky RM. Gene therapy for the nervous system. Sci Am 1997;
   276:116–20.
Kirkwood TB. Genetics and the future of human longevity. J Royal Coll Physicians
   London 1997; 31:669–73.
Marshall E. Ethicists back stem cell research, White House treads cautiously. Sci-
   ence 1999; 285:502.
Mattson MP. Emerging neuroprotective strategies for Alzheimer's disease: dietary
   restriction, telomerase activation, and stem cell therapy. Exp Gerontol 2000;
   35:489–502.
Montgomery HE, Marshall R, Hemingway H, et al. Human gene for physical performance. Nature 1998; 393:221–222.
Prochazka A, Mushahwar VK, McCreery DB. Neural prostheses. J Physiol 2001;
   533(Pt 1):99–109.

* Steel, MD, Knight. Research on aging: an agenda for all nations individually and
    collectively. JAMA 1997; 278:1374–1375.
Yandava BD, Billinghurst LL, Snyder EY. "Global" cell replacement is feasible via
    neural stem cell transplantation: evidence from the dysmyelinated shiverer
    mouse brain. Proc Natl Acad Sci USA 1999; 96:7039–34.

Index